Behavioral Finance and Decision-Making Models

Tripti Tripathi
Jiwaji University, India

Manoj Kumar Dash
Khallikote University, India

Gaurav Agrawal
Indian Institute of Information Technology and Management Gwalior, India

A volume in the Advances in Finance, Accounting, and Economics (AFAE) Book Series

IGI Global
DISSEMINATOR OF KNOWLEDGE

Published in the United States of America by
IGI Global
Business Science Reference (an imprint of IGI Global)
701 E. Chocolate Avenue
Hershey PA, USA 17033
Tel: 717-533-8845
Fax: 717-533-8661
E-mail: cust@igi-global.com
Web site: http://www.igi-global.com

Library of Congress Cataloging-in-Publication Data

Names: Tripathi, Tripti, 1982- editor. | Dash, Manoj Kumar, editor. | Agrawal, Gaurav, 1977- editor.
Title: Behavioral finance and decision-making models / Tripti Tripathi, Manoj Kumar Dash, and Gaurav Agrawal, editors.
Description: Hershey, PA : Business Science Reference, [2019]
Identifiers: LCCN 2018026761| ISBN 9781522573999 (hardcover) | ISBN 9781522574002 (ebook)
Subjects: LCSH: Investments--Decision making. | Finance--Decision making.
Classification: LCC HG4515 .B44 2019 | DDC 332.601/9--dc23 LC record available at https://lccn.loc.gov/2018026761

This book is published in the IGI Global book series Advances in Finance, Accounting, and Economics (AFAE) (ISSN: 2327-5677; eISSN: 2327-5685)

British Cataloguing in Publication Data
A Cataloguing in Publication record for this book is available from the British Library.

For electronic access to this publication, please contact: eresources@igi-global.com.

Advances in Finance, Accounting, and Economics (AFAE) Book Series

Ahmed Driouchi
Al Akhawayn University, Morocco

ISSN:2327-5677
EISSN:2327-5685

Mission

In our changing economic and business environment, it is important to consider the financial changes occurring internationally as well as within individual organizations and business environments. Understanding these changes as well as the factors that influence them is crucial in preparing for our financial future and ensuring economic sustainability and growth.

The **Advances in Finance, Accounting, and Economics (AFAE)** book series aims to publish comprehensive and informative titles in all areas of economics and economic theory, finance, and accounting to assist in advancing the available knowledge and providing for further research development in these dynamic fields.

Coverage

- Theoretical Issues in Economics, Finance, and Accounting
- Economics Geography
- Ethics in Accounting and Finance
- Corporate Finance
- Wages and Employment
- Behavioral Economics
- Risk Analysis and Management
- Applied Accounting
- Borrowing and Lending
- Evidence-Based Studies

IGI Global is currently accepting manuscripts for publication within this series. To submit a proposal for a volume in this series, please contact our Acquisition Editors at Acquisitions@igi-global.com or visit: http://www.igi-global.com/publish/.

The Advances in Finance, Accounting, and Economics (AFAE) Book Series (ISSN 2327-5677) is published by IGI Global, 701 E. Chocolate Avenue, Hershey, PA 17033-1240, USA, www.igi-global.com. This series is composed of titles available for purchase individually; each title is edited to be contextually exclusive from any other title within the series. For pricing and ordering information please visit http://www.igi-global.com/book-series/advances-finance-accounting-economics/73685. Postmaster: Send all address changes to above address.

Titles in this Series

For a list of additional titles in this series, please visit: www.igi-global.com/book-series

FinTech as a Disruptive Technology for Financial Institutions
Abdul Rafay (University of Management and Technology, Pakistan)
Business Science Reference • copyright 2019 • 302pp • H/C (ISBN: 9781522578055) • US $195.00 (our price)

The Circular Economy and Its Implications on Sustainability and the Green Supply Chain
Ulas Akkucuk (Bogazici University, Turkey)
Business Science Reference • copyright 2019 • 327pp • H/C (ISBN: 9781522581093) • US $215.00 (our price)

Planning and Analyzing Foreign Direct Investment Projects Emerging Research and Opportunities
Halil Sarıaslan (Başkent University, Turkey)
Business Science Reference • copyright 2019 • 338pp • H/C (ISBN: 9781522576969) • US $215.00 (our price)

Maintaining Financial Stability in Times of Risk and Uncertainty
Abhishek Behl (Indian Institute of Technology Bombay, India) and Sushma Nayak (Symbiosis International University (Deemed), India)
Business Science Reference • copyright 2019 • 377pp • H/C (ISBN: 9781522572084) • US $265.00 (our price)

Global Trends of Modernization in Budgeting and Finance
Denis Ushakov (Suan Sunandha Rajabhat University, Thailand)
Business Science Reference • copyright 2019 • 354pp • H/C (ISBN: 9781522577607) • US $215.00 (our price)

Corporate Insolvency Law and Bankruptcy Reforms in the Global Economy
Amit Kashyap (Nirma University, India)
Business Science Reference • copyright 2019 • 261pp • H/C (ISBN: 9781522555414) • US $185.00 (our price)

Time Bank as a Complementary Economic System Emerging Research and Opportunities
Lukas Valek (University of Hradec Kralove, Czech Republic) and Vladimir Bures (University of Hradec Kralove, Czech Republic)
Business Science Reference • copyright 2019 • 208pp • H/C (ISBN: 9781522569749) • US $175.00 (our price)

Economic Dynamics of Global Energy Geopolitics
Ahmet Salih Ikiz (Muğla Sıtkı Koçman University, Turkey)
Engineering Science Reference • copyright 2019 • 305pp • H/C (ISBN: 9781522542032) • US $195.00 (our price)

IGI Global
DISSEMINATOR OF KNOWLEDGE

701 East Chocolate Avenue, Hershey, PA 17033, USA
Tel: 717-533-8845 x100 • Fax: 717-533-8661
E-Mail: cust@igi-global.com • www.igi-global.com

Editorial Advisory Board

Table of Contents

Section 4
Behavioral Corporate Finance

Detailed Table of Contents

In Turkey, the first step of the individual pension system was based on volunteerism, but the voluntary system resulted in limited participation. Thus, the second step of the system has started to be implemented mandatorily since 2017, and participants were allowed to opt-out the system within two months. More than half of participants in the system preferred to leave the system. Therefore, this study aims to examine individual factors affecting their decision of staying in this system. A survey study was conducted with 374 people selected using the random sampling method. As a result of the study, a positive relationship was found only between the dependent variable and gender, but a significant relationship was determined only between the dependent variable and education level. Based on the results of this study, it is suggested that if the system will need to be improved, the low-performing fund management of the new individual pension system should be re-audited, and the confidence in the system should be increased in this way.

The chapter deals with the study of customers' expectations as well as their perceptions for service quality in banking sector. Again, the study focuses on the influence of major demographic variables such as age, income, education, and occupation on customers' expectations and perceptions for service quality. Moreover, this research work has been carried out with the help of primary data collected through a survey of 300 retail banking customers (i.e., 150 ICICI Bank customers and 150 SBI customers of Agra region). In India, retail banking is one of the fastest growing industries. The present study has endeavored to examine the service quality aspects of the two leading banks in Agra region and will also help the other private and public sector banks and financial institutions to have a better understanding of customer needs and the booming opportunities in retail banking in India.

Over the past decades, Cloninger et al. have developed a biosocial model of personality based on four temperaments and three characteristics. This multidimensional psychobiological model of personality presents in the temperament and character inventory – revised (TCI-R) form. Temperament subscales are novelty seeking (NS), harm avoidance (HA), reward dependence (RD), and persistence (P), and character subscales are self-directedness (SD), cooperativeness (CO), and self-transcendence (ST). The study has been used in different disciplines of science, especially in psychology. Behavioral finance is one of these disciplines of science. TCI is frequently used, especially for investor biases. In this chapter, TCI is used to examine the relationship between investor biases and personality. The first three chapters are about personality. Personality, personality approaches, and personality measurement methods examined in these sections. In the fourth part, emotional biases in financial investment decisions searched. In the fifth part, literature studies showing the relationship between personality and financial decisions included. Finally, a field survey is conducted, and findings are revealed.

Section 3
Behavioral Approach to Financial Issues and Investment

The purpose of this chapter is to study the determinants of market capitalization and to investigate the impact of determinants of market capitalization. This chapter uses secondary data from 2003-2016 relating to market capitalization, income per capita, stock market liquidity, etc. The study employed descriptive test and normality test to describe the basic features of data and their distribution. The multicollinearity test has also been used to check the interdependence among independent variables. Multiple regression statistics has been used to determine the impact of independent variables on dependent variable. The results show that there is a positive impact of determinants on development of stock market except political risk and inflation. The findings will help stock market authority, individuals, and companies to understand the factors that affect share prices.

The objective of this chapter is to examine the long-run and the short-run relationship between India, China, and Japanese stock markets and key macroeconomic variables such as exchange rates and inflation (proxied by consumer price index) of ASIAN 3 economies (India, China, and Japan). Monthly time series data spanning the period from 2008 January to November 2016 has been used. The unit root test, the cointegration test, Granger causality test, and pooled mean group estimator have been applied to derive the long-run and short-run statistical dynamics. The findings of pooled estimated results of ASIAN 3 countries show that exchange rate has a positive and significant long-run effect on stock markets while the inflation has a negative and insignificant long-run effect. In the short run, there is no statistically significant relationship between macroeconomic variables and stock markets. This study emphasizes the impact of macroeconomic variables on the stock market performance of a developing economy (India and China) and developed economy (Japan).

Financial inclusion is a multidimensional approach. With technology intervention in financial inclusion, electronic banking activity in rural India leads to increased use of financial services and better living standards. In the rising market, many people using mobile phones still are not able to access banking

Credit rating evaluates credit worthiness of corporate and securities issued by government. It provides investors with unbiased reviews and opinion about the credit risk of various securities. The main aim of the chapter is to identify the relationship between the financial ratios and rating symbols. The sample of 158 firms is taken into consideration that discriminates best ratings given by credit rating firms. In order to examine the variability in ratings issued by various rating agencies, the time period of eight years starting from April 2009 to March 2017 has been selected. The study employed the multinomial logistic regression model to explain the relationship among the variables. The analysis suggests that variables such as debt to equity ratio, profit after tax, returns on capital employed, and return on net worth are those having the highest impact on ratings and thus there is also discriminating power among Indian rating agencies.

This chapter focuses on the need, requirements, implementation, challenges, and impact of the goods and services tax on the Indian economic scenario. The major stakeholders in the process are the Government of India (GOI), the individual states, the industry, the businesses, and the biggest tax reform since independence of India in 1947. Often considered as overdue, it seeks to remove the various shortcomings and the loopholes in the existing system of indirect taxation in the country. The GST bill saw more than a decade of political and economic upheaval in the country. Subsequently, it became an act on 8th September 2016. The various strategic analysis approach (SAA) of the GST mechanism (e.g., SWOT analysis, value chain analysis, PEST analysis, and SAP-LAP analysis) give an in-depth account of the various issues and potential challenges in the implementation of the GST.

In a self-resilient economy, banking system assumes importance in imparting momentum to economic growth and prosperity through mobilization of financial assets. Performance of banks, irrespective of their nature and function, is germane to their asset creation and maintenance capacity. In a neo-liberal regime, radical policy changes have crept into loan mechanism, thereby subjecting the banks to efficiently recover the loans, which is a vital asset for any banking firm. In this context, the authors through intensive review of literature identified micro and macro banking factors responsible for productive NPA management.

The macro banking factors refer to the economic environment whereas the micro banking factors refer to the bank and branch-specific factors. The authors identified the critical role of organizational structure, involvement of employees, and organizational efficiency in driving prudent NPA management. The authors have found that the efficiency in managing NPAs differ in public and private banks, which is attributed to involvement of employees.

Foreword

In today's competitive environment, where businesses are on constant pressure to perform or perish; what makes a business sustainable is Behavioral Finance. The editors present a brief outline of the origins of behavioural finance; including the role that experimental and survey methods play in the study of financial behaviour; summarize the contributions made by the papers in the issue and consider their implications; and assess why research in behavioural finance is important for finance researchers and practitioners. Behavioral decision-making studies the basic psychology of decision-making, while behavioral economics and behavioral finance study the role of irrational thinking in economic and financial decision-making, respectively. Global financial markets are influenced by many factors: the economic processes which take place in the country and the world, institutional and political constraints, information dissemination and accessibility, and so on. However, one of the most important factors is the people's reaction and perception. For each investor, regardless of financial instruments, business is a constant decision-making process. The book aims to analyse the research of non-professional investors' financial behaviour in a historical-theoretical perspective. This book reveals the aims of recognition and emotional factors on market movements focusing on a limited number of investor rationality and explains the psychological effects of investing activities. The methods of analysis and synthesis, description and comparison were also included in this book.

This book compiles various research chapters which are contributed by eminent researchers globally. The book has range a chapter on topics from concept, revises, methodology, effects of emotional on investment, behavioral finance models, critical thinking. It also touches upon soft issues like emotion, happiness, service innovation and psychological influence factors. This type of project will open new windows of research and applications. I sincerely think that these issues are of paramount importance and have been pretty well researched and commented in the form of research chapters in the book.

It is my pleasure to write a short and a simple "Foreword" to this edited book volume titled: *Behavioral Finance and Decision-Making Models*, published by IGI Global-USA, under the able editorship of Dr. Tripti Tripathi, Dr Manoj Kumar Dash and Dr Gaurav Agrawal. I congratulate the editors and the contributors who had put in a lot of effort and time in bringing out this book.

S. G. Deshmukh
Indian Institute of Information Technology and Management Gwalior, India

Preface

INTRODUCTION

Since the mid-1950s, the field of finance has been dominated by the traditional finance model developed by the economist of the University of Chicago. The Central assumption of the traditional finance model is that people are rational. Standard Finance theories are based on the premises that investor behaves rationally and stock and bond markets are efficient. As the financial economist were assuming that people(investors) behaved rationally when making financial decisions, psychologists have found that economic decision are made in an irrational manner, so they challenge this assumption of standard finance. Cognitive error and extreme emotional bias can cause investors to make bad investment decisions, thereby meaning that they act in irrational manner. Over the past decade, field of behavioural finance has evolved to consider how personal and social psychology influence financial decisions and behaviour of investors in general. The finance field was reluctant to accept the view of psychologists who had proposed the behavioural finance model. This was the time when financial economist started to believe that the investor behaves irrationally. Human brains process information using shortcuts and emotional filters even in investment decisions. It is an attempt to explain how the psychological dimensions influence investment decisions of individual investor, how perception influences the mutual funds market as a whole. It is worth exploring whether field of psychology helps investor to make more reasonable investment decisions.

Traditionally, economics and finance have focused on models that assume rationality. The behavioural insights have emerged from the application in finance and economics of insights from experimental psychology. Behavioural finance is relatively a new field which seeks to provide explanation for people's economic decisions. It is a combination of behavioural and cognitive psychological theory with conventional economics and finance. Inability to maximise the expected utility (EU) of rational investors leads to growth of behavioural finance research within the efficient market framework. Behavioural finance research is an attempt to resolve inconsistency of Traditional Expected Utility Maximization of rational investors within efficient markets through explanation based on human behaviour. For instance, Behavioural finance explains why and how markets might be inefficient.

An underlying assumption of behavioural finance is that, the information structure and characteristics of market participants systematically influence the individual's investment decisions as well as market outcomes. Investor, as a human being, processes information using shortcuts and emotional filters. This process influences financial decision makers such that they act seemingly in irrational manner, and make suboptimal decision, violate traditional finance claim of rationality. The impact of this suboptimal financial decision has ramification for the efficiency of capital markets, personal wealth, and the performance of corporations. Irrational decision could be either due to processing of wrong information or interpretation with inconsistent decisions. Behaviour finance focuses upon how investors interpret and act on information to make informed investment decisions. Investors do not always behave in a rational, predictable and an unbiased manner indicated by the quantitative models. Behavioural Finance places an emphasis upon investor behaviour leading to various market anomalies.

The emergence of behavioral finance has presented a new realm for analyzing the ways in which investors make decisions that includes psychological factors as well as providing new grounds upon which it question conventional methods of modeling investor behavior. The challenge that behavioural finance assembles is aimed particularly in the direction of the efficient market hypothesis (EMH), which is the model that Statman refers to standard finance Model. Behavioural finance challenge hypothesis that standard finance model of on'how investor decision is inaccurate', as it fails to include psychological and value expressive preferences in calculations.

Thus behavioural finance can be described in the following ways:

1. Behavioural finance is the integration of classical economics and finance with psychology and the decision-making sciences
2. Behavioural finance is an attempt to explain what causes some of the anomalies that have been observed and reported in the finance literature.
3. Behavioural finance is the study of how investors systematically make errors in judgment or 'mental mistakes'.

According to behavioural finance, investor's behaviour in market depends on psychological principles of decision making, which explains why people buy and sell investments. It focuses on how investors interpret information and act on information to implement their financial investment decisions. In short psychological process and biases influences investors decision making and influence the market outcomes

RATIONALE AND GOALS OF THE BOOK

Although behavioral finance had been gaining support in recent years, it is not without its critics. Some supporter of Efficient Market Hypothesis (EMH) and standard finance theory criticize the behavioural finance approach. Behavioural Finance is a new approach to financial market that has emerged, at least in part, in response to difficulties faced by the traditional paradigm. In broad terms it argues that some financial phenomena can be better understood by models in which some agents are not fully rational. Because of the many flaws of accepted economic theory, behavioural finance serves as a good complement. The assumptions of perfectly rational individuals and perfect information seem to work in some situations. Behavioural finance then gives explanations as to why the market behaves as it does. Most of people know that emotions affect investment decisions. People in the world of investments commonly talk about the role that greed and fear play in driving stock markets. Behavioural finance extends this analysis to the role of biases in decision making, such as the use of simple rules of thumb for making complex investment decisions. In short Behavioural finance uses psychology to explain this behavioural decision making. Behavioural finance takes a different approach, through recognising the cognitive errors and emotions, human being is prone to while making financial decisions. It is an attempt to describe human behaviour positively, to understand how people behave in financial settings. This helps to understand, psychological influences market. behaviour when investor perception influence markets and how the market action influence investors perception. Thus, behavioural finance can be presented as the field which combines behavioural and cognitive psychological theory with conventional economics and finance to provide explanation for why people/investors make irrational choices or irrational financial decisions. Behavioural finance could be most interesting in the academic world for the time being.

This book addresses the gap in the behavioral finance and modeling literature by providing a thematically collections of chapters seeking to link theoretical models with practical studies of business. The theme and chapter sof the book addresses behavioral model from holistic view point and adopt an evidence based approach to investigate the important behavioral finance and models. The purpose of this peer reviewed edited books is to focus on current and future behavioral finance issues, practices and models. The main goal of this edited book includes:

1. To provide all encompassing holistic discussions of behavioral finance and modeling
2. Give reader's innovations on empirical models, management research and case studies
3. Strengthen the current behavioral research management body of knowledge and closed the gap in the literature on Behvioural finance research
4. Expand the understanding of behavioral fiancé and investment approach from various social and economic perspectives.

Our target audience was primarily behavioral finance researchers and management practitioner. We anticipated scholars, researchers, policy makers, investors, decision makers, bankers etc would be interested in this book.

SUMMARY OF THE BOOK THEMES AND CHAPTERS

'Behavioral Finance vs. Traditional Finance' by Sinem Derindere Koseoglu: This chapter explored the evolution of modern behavioural finance theories from the traditional finance theories in detail. Over the past sixty years traditional finance theory has assumed that investors have very little difficulty making financial decisions and are well-informed, careful and consistent. The traditional finance theory holds that investors are not confused by how information is presented to them and not swayed by their emotions. However, reality clearly does not match these assumptions.

'Linking Personal Values to Investment Decisions among Individual Shareholders in a Developing Economy' by Dr. Otuo Serebour Agyemang: This chapter examines the link between personal values and investment decisions among individual shareholders in a developing economy. It contributes to our knowledge of behavioral finance and decision sciences that individual shareholders' personal values have influence on their investment decisions and the choice of companies they invest in. It employs a grounded theory approach. The chapter highlights that individual shareholders hold value priorities and that honesty, a comfortable life and family security play a significant role in their lives and their investment decisions and the kind of companies they make an investment in. In addition, to the individual shareholders, there is a clear distinction between a comfortable life and a prosperous life in the sense that they are not incentivized more by the latter but the former in their investment decisions.

'Chicken-Egg Dilemma for the Relationship Between Price and Volume in Borsa, Istanbul' by Prof. SadullahÇelik, AybenKoy: This chapter empirically examines the relationship between stock prices and stock volumes for Borsa Istanbul, the only stock exchange in Turkey. The price-volume debate has been a common focus in the literature as the chicken-egg dilemma probably since the financial markets started to operate in a competitive manner. This chapter employs Borsa Istanbul and also considers the sector indices of the market. We employ frequency domain causality analysis and wavelet coherence analysis with comparisons of the results for each sector. The findings showed that (1) it is hard to argue for the existence of a distinct pattern in an emerging stock market like Borsa Istanbul, (2) there are several periods that propose challenges like the increasing foreign share, foreign shocks transmitted to the domestic market and local effects, and (3) speculation is an inherit part of stock markets and it is not possible to get rid of but rather act timely to minimize the adverse consequences and to deter market-wide repercussions.

'Does Parasocial Breakup Affect the Stock Market Returns? Evidence From an Emerging Market' by Dr. Ibrahim Bozkurt, Dr. MercanHatipoglu: This chapter analyzes the impact of parasocial breakup on the stock returns in Borsa Istanbul as an emerging stock market. In this study, 129 Turkish TV series finales, broadcasted between 2005 and 2015, are employed as a negative mood proxy. In line with the purpose of this chapter, GARCH-M model is used to obtain a more efficient parameter and alternative mood proxy dummies and other macroeconomic variables are incorporated into the analyses to examine the robustness of the effect of parasocial breakup on stock market returns. The analysis presents robust evidence that the negative mood increases the stock market returns. It is also found that the effect of parasocial breakup on returns depends on the types of TV series and the channels they are broadcasted on.

'Emotional Finance Plays an Important Role in Investment Decision' by Sarika Keswani: Most of the investors focus on human emotions not expressing openly while making investment decisions. Emotions have a powerful position in making investment decisions. It drives human behavior that is consistent with economic predictions while making investments. Emotions play a significant role while making decisions on investments just like any other business decisions. Behavioral finance tries to combine behavioral and cognitive psychological theory with conventional economics and finance, to provide justifications for why people make irrational financial decisions. The aim of this chapter is to understand whether emotional phases affect investors' decisions in different investment situations basing on levels of uncertainty. Positive emotions like self-confidence, challenge, and hope increase the decision-makers tendency to exaggerate the commitment and negative emotions namely embarrassment and strain do not.

'Individual Factors Affecting the Participation of Turkish People in the New Individual Pension System' by Emine Ebru Aksoy: In Turkey, the first step of the individual pension system was based on volunteerism, but the voluntary system resulted in limited participation. Thus, the second step of the system has started to be implemented mandatorily since 2017, and participants were allowed to opt-out the system within 2 months. More than half of participants in the system preferred to leave the system. Therefore, this study aims to examine individual factors affecting their decision of staying in this system. A survey study was conducted with 374 people selected using the random sampling method. As a result of the study, a positive relationship was found only between the dependent variable and gender, but a significant relationship was determined only between the dependent variable and education level. Based on the results of this study, it is suggested that if the system will to be improved, the low-performing fund management of the new individual pension system should be re-audited, and the confidence in the system should be increased in this way.

'Comparative Analysis of Service Quality Perception Between Public Sector and Private Sector Banks of India' by Dr. Deepika Singh Tomar,Dr. Rohit Singh Tomar: This work deals with the study of customers' expectations as well as their perceptions for service quality in banking sector. Again, the study focuses on the influence of major demographic variables such as age, income, education and occupation on customers' expectations and perceptions for service quality. Moreover, this research work has been carried out with the help of primary data collected through a survey of 300 retail banking customers (i.e. 150 ICICI Bank customers and 150 SBI customers of Agra region). In India, retail banking is one of the fastest growing industries. The present study has endeavored to examine the service quality aspects of the two leading banks in Agra region and will also help the other private and public sector banks and financial institutions to have a better understanding of customer needs and the booming opportunities in retail banking in India.

'Personality and Emotional Biases' by Dr. SezenGüngör, Dr. EnginDemirel Mrs. Nihan Tomris Küçün: Cloninger has developed a biosocial model of personality. This multidimensional Psychobiological Model of Personality presents in the Temperament and Character Inventory. Temperament subscales are novelty seeking, harm avoidance, reward dependence and persistence and character subscales are self-directedness, cooperativeness, and self-transcendence. The study has been used in different disciplines of science, especially in psychology and behavioral finance. TCI is frequently used, especially for investor biases. In this chapter, TCI is used to examine the relationship between investor biases and personality. Initial chapters are about personality. Personality, its approaches and measurement methods are examined in these sections. Then emotional biases in investment decisions are searched. In the fifth chapter, literature studies showing the relationship between personality and financial decisions are included. Finally, a field survey is conducted, and findings are revealed.

'Determinants of Market Capitalization in India and Its Impact' by Mr. Chandrika Prasad Das and Dr. Rabindra Kumar Swain: The purpose of this research paper is to study the determinants of market capitalization and to investigate the impact of determinants of market capitalization. This research paper uses secondary data from 2003 – 2016 relating to Market capitalization, income per capita, stock market liquidity etc. The study employed Descriptive test and Normality test to describe the basic features of data and their distribution. The Multicollinearity test has also been used to check the interdependence among independent variables. Multiple regression statistics has been used to determine the impact of independent variables on dependent variable. The results show that there is a positive impact of determinants on development of stock market except political risk and inflation. The findings will help stock market authority, individuals and companies to understand the factors which affect share prices.

'Macroeconomics and Its Impact on Stock Markets of India, China, and Japan' by Dr. Amith Vikram Megaravalli: The study examine the long-run and the short-run relationship between India, China and Japanese stock markets and key macroeconomic variables such as exchange rates and inflation (proxied by consumer price index) of ASIAN 3 economies (India, China and Japan). Monthly time series data spanning the period from 2008 January to November 2016 has been used. The unit root test, the cointegration test, Granger causality test and pooled mean group estimator have been applied to derive the long-run and short-run statistical dynamics. The findings of pooled estimated results of ASIAN 3 countries show that exchange rate has a positive and significant long-run effect on stock markets while the inflation has a negative and insignificant long-run effect. In the short run, there is no statistically significant relationship between macroeconomic variables and stock markets. This study emphasises on the impact of macroeconomic variables on the stock market performance of a developing economy (India and China) and developed economy (Japan).

'Digital Financial Inclusion in India: A Review' by Dr. Gaurav Agrawal, Mrs. Pooja Jain: Financial inclusion is a multidimensional approach. With technology intervention in financial inclusion, electronic banking activity in rural India leads to increased using financial services and better living standards. In the rising market maximum number of people using mobile phone but still they are not access to banking products and financial services. This indicate that a huge untouched market for commercial banks. In India, mobile banking services are still in the early stages of development. Thus, the main objective of our study to understand the factors that would act as drivers towards the adoption of mobile financial services and understand people's intention to adopt and use of mobile banking services which lead to increases accessibility towards financial products among rural people as well improve standard of living and overall development of the nation. The study focus on utilizing secondary source which is related to financial inclusion to understand the new banking technology and identified people's behavior towards adoption and uses of banking services.

'Employees Perception Regarding CSR Initiatives of the Companies in India' by Mr. Vikrant Vikram Vikram Singh, Dr. Manoj Pandey, Prof. (Dr.) Anil Vashith: This study is an attempt to understand the impact of CSR on a very important stakeholder of the company i.e. an employee of the company. Employees are integral part of the company and at the same time they can be the costumer of the company if using the product or services offered by the company. This thing makes him a powerful tool to analyze the impact of various initiatives of the organization which will have long lasting impact on the company as well as on the society as a whole. This study is conducted through a survey by preparing questionnaire for obtaining information from the employees of different organizations regarding their perception w.r.t. CSR activities. The result of the report shows that CSR engagement of the company has positive impact on the employee. But, the report also suggests that companies are lacking in terms of their CSR initiatives from last few years. It further suggests that inputs and methods of the CSR activities by the organizations should improve in order to increase the productivity and belongingness of the employees.

'The Impact of Tax Policies on Behaviour of Albanian Taxpayers' by Ms. Dorina Plaku, Prof. Eglantina Hysa: The Albanian state has experienced many changes of this system over the years due to the policies and different regimes that have followed but there has always been a tendency for improvement. The tax system and the informality are the mirror of the economy of the country, especially the favorable tax/fiscal policies that have been adapted to the economy, which bring economical development and integration of all the gaps to a proper economic environment. The study aims to find out the effects of tax changes on the taxpayers. Furthermore the study focuses on how the business performance has been indicated from the tax control. The data is collected from a survey which was focused in small and big businesses that operates in the capital city of Albania, in Tirana. The questionnaire is realized during April 2018. The main finds of the study are the different perception of businesses for the tax control and the impact of the fiscal changes on these businesses. All this fiscal changes that the businesses faced were more in disfavor of the small businesses.

'Credit Rating and Its Interaction With Financial Ratios: A Study of BSE 500 Companies' by Dr. Shraddha Mishra, Dr. Reenu Bansal: Credit rating evaluates credit worthiness of corporate and securities issued by government. It provides investors with unbiased reviews and opinion about the credit risk of various securities. The main aim of the study is to identify the relationship between the financial ratios and rating symbols. Methodology - The sample of one hundred and fifty eight firms is taken into consideration that discriminates best ratings given by credit rating firms. In order to examine the variability in ratings issued by various rating agencies; the time period of eight years starting from April, 2009 to March, 2017 has been selected. The study employed the multinomial logistic regression model to explain the relationship among the variables. Findings- The analysis suggests that variables such as debt to equity ratio, profit after tax; returns on capital employed and return on Net worth are those having the highest impact on ratings and thus there is also discriminating power among Indian rating agencies.

'An Impact Assessment of Goods and Services Tax in India Through Strategic Analysis Approach (SAA)' by Dr. Tripti Tripathi, Dr. Manoj Kumar Dash: This work focuses on the need, requirements, implementation, challenges and impact of the goods and services Tax on the Indian economic scenario. The major stakeholders in the process are the Government of India (GOI), the individual States, the industry, the businesses, and biggest tax reform since independence of India in 1947. Often considered as long due, it seeks to remove the various shortcomings and the loopholes in the existing system of indirect taxation in the country. The GST bill saw more than a decade of political and economic upheaval in the country. Subsequently, it became an ACT on 8th September, 2016, the various strategic analysis approach(SAA) of the GST mechanism, viz. SWOT Analysis, Value Chain Analysis, PEST Analysis and SAP-LAP Analysis give an in-depth account of the various issues and potential challenges in the implementation of the GST.

'A Review on Role of Macro and Micro Banking Environment on Non-Performing Assets Management' by Dr. Biswajit Prasad Chhatoi, Mr. Sharada Prasad Sahoo: In a self-resilient economy, banking system assumes importance in imparting momentum to economic growth and prosperity through mobilisation of financial assets. Performance of banks, irrespective of their nature and function is germane to their asset creation and maintenance capacity. In a neo-liberal regime, radical policy changes have crept into loan mechanism, thereby subjecting the banks to efficiently recover the loans, which is a vital asset for any banking firm. In this context, the authors through intensive review of literature identified Micro and Macro banking factors responsible for productive NPA management. The macro banking factors refer to the economic environment whereas the micro banking factors refer to the bank and branch-specific factors. The authors identified the critical role of Organisational Structure, Involvement of Employees and Organisational efficiency in driving prudent NPA management. The authors have found that, the efficiency in managing NPAs differ in public and private banks, which is attributed to involvement of employees.

Acknowledgment

The editors would like to acknowledge the help of all the people involved in this project and, more specifically, to the authors and reviewers that took part in the review process. Without their support, this book would not have become a reality.

We would like to thank each one of the authors for their contributions. The editors wish to acknowledge the valuable contributions of the reviewers regarding the improvement of quality, coherence, and content presentation of chapters. Most of the authors also served as referees; we highly appreciate their double task.

We are grateful to the series editor, the editors would like to thank Rachel Ginder, Jan Travers, Kayla Wolfe, Lindsay Johnston, Vasilia (Lia) Kambouroglos and all members of IGI publishing house for their assistance and timely motivation in producing this volume.

We would like to express sincere gratitude to Prof. S. G. Deshmukh (Director, ABV-Indian Institute of Information Technology and Management, Gwalior) for his constant motivation, encouragement, the academic support facilities and wonderful research environment provided to carry out the research work at the Institute. We convey our heartfelt thanks soaked with reverence to Prof. Deshmukh for his valuable tips and learned suggestions.

We hope the readers will share our excitement with this important scientific contribution on the body of knowledge about Behavioural Finance.

Tripti Tripathi
Jiwaji University, India

Manoj Kumar Dash
Khallikote University, India

Gaurav Agrawal
Indian Institute of Information Technology and Management Gwalior, India

Section 1

Behavioral Finance Theory

Chapter 1
Behavioral Finance vs. Traditional Finance

Sinem Derindere Koseoglu
Independent Researcher, Turkey

ABSTRACT

This chapter explored the development of behavioral finance theories from the traditional finance theories in detail. Traditional financial theory has assumed that investors are perfectly well-informed in making financial decisions for many years. However, the reality shows that these assumptions are not valid, especially over the last two decades. It is observed that investors exhibit irrational behaviors by acting with emotions even if they are well-informed. Because of the awareness of the importance human psychology in investment decisions, behavioral researchers have advanced their research in this direction. Thus, behavioral finance theories have been developed with this in mind.

INTRODUCTION

This chapter investigated the development of behavioral finance theories starting the traditional theories framework. Traditional financial theories have supposed that individuals are well-informed in making financial decisions, cautious and consistent for many years. It argues that investors are not surprised that they are presented with information because it accepted that all information is known, and they do not behave by their emotions. According to the traditional finance theory, the aim of the investors is maximum utility, and always acts without prejudice and rational manner for this purpose. Today, this aspect of finance has changed dramatically. Nevertheless, the real financial markets do not match to these assumptions. Especially over the past two-three decades this aspect of traditional finance has changed dramatically.

The interest of the behavioral finance field has been increasing during the last two-three decades due to the empirical evidence that individuals rarely behave by the assumptions of traditional finance theories and formation the perception that the theory of finance should take into account the observed individual behavior. Investigations in behavioral finance area have indicated that human psychology is very vital role in making financial decisions. Therefore, behavioral researchers generally conduct research from psychology to better understanding of financial decision-making process.

DOI: 10.4018/978-1-5225-7399-9.ch001

The crises, panics, downfall, enthusiasm and bubbles that happen in the financial markets are the most important indicators that humans are not always rational. This area, which examines psychology, sociology, anthropology and finance together, is called behavioral finance. According to this behavioral finance theory, investors often show irrational behavior, unlike the traditional definition, and often prejudge investment decisions. "Why do investors make irrational decisions?" is the main field of study of behavioral finance. Cognitive errors and prejudices that investors often make are identified in studies conducted.

Today, strong psychology as well as financial literacy and market experience are among the basic requirements for being a leading investor. Learning the basic concepts of behavioral finance will enable the investor to become aware of the prejudices and cognitive errors of his / her feelings and thoughts.

In this chapter these two finance fields have been focused with general principles and reflect the requirements of a comprehensive view on the subject. It has been also aimed to analyze how finance theory evolved over time from Efficient Market Hypothesis to Behavioral Finance and put forward the results for investors, corporate finance decision makers, market regulators and policy makers by examining pros and cons of EMH which had gained both theoretical and empirical success since it's first appearance in 1960's till the beginning of 1980's. As a result, the aim of the chapter is to provide a better understanding of the different perspectives of traditional and behavioral finance disciplines as a whole.

TRADITIONAL FINANCE THEORY AND DECISION MODELS

This part of the chapter examines what traditional theories and their models are and includes all details about these.

The beginning of the classical economics is in the middle of the 18th century. Mill (1844), presented the notion of "rational economic man", whose aim to maximize his utility by taking into account the constraints he faced. According to the aim of maximizing utility, the traditional finance theories have four foundation blocks:

1. Perfectly rational investors;
2. Efficient markets;
3. Constructing portfolios depending on the rules of traditional Mean-Variance model,
4. Risk-return trade off. Expected returns on investments are explained by differences in risk.

Modern portfolio theory dates back to 1950s. In 1952, Markowitz (1952) determined initial form of mean-variance portfolio theory. Sharpe (1964) adopted this theory as a definition of investor behavior and presented the Capital Asset Pricing Theory (CAPM). According to the CAPM, differences in expected returns are only determined by differences in risk. Fama (1965) also described efficient markets concept.

A summary table is provided for the theories to be explained in this part below. In Table 1 the traditional finance theories have been summarized that will be compared with behavioral finance. Summarizing theories such as traditional theory of investor preference, the expected utility theory, Markowitz Mean-Variance portfolio theory, Capital Asset Pricing Model (CAPM), arbitrage asset pricing theories (APT), and Fama-French three factor model,

Table 1. Traditional finance theories

Theory/Finding	Author	Year	Model
Homo Economicus	John Stuart Mill	1844	*Expected Utility*
Expected Utility Theory	Daniel Bernouille	1738, 1954	*Expected Utility=f(weighted average of all possible levels of utility)*
Theory of Games and Economic Behavior	John von Neuman and Oscar Morgenstein	1944	
Subjective Utility Theory	L. Savage	1964	*Expected Utility=f(weighted average of all subjective probability of utility)*
Markowitz Portfolio Theory	Harry Markowitz	1952	*Expected return = f (weighted average of all possible expected return)*
Capital Asset Pricing Model	Treynor	1962	*Expected return = f (beta and market factor)*
	William Sharpe	1964	*Beta, systematic risk factor*
	John Linter	1695	*Beta, systematic risk factor*
	Jan Mossin	1966	*Beta, systematic risk factor*
Efficient Market Hypothesis	E. Fama	1965, 1970	*Expected return=f(historical, public and all private information)*
Arbitrage Pricing Theory	Stephen Ross	1976	*Expected return = f (macroeconomic or company-specific factors)*
Three Factor Model	Fama & French	1992	*Expected return = f (market risk, market capitalization, book-to-market)*

Expected Utility Theory and Subjective Utility Theory

Investment decisions such as portfolio preference, fund preference, investment of individual securities are all decisions of under uncertainty and based on maximizing expected utility. Expected Utility Theory (Bernouille; 1738, 1954) claims that investors choose their investments under uncertainty according to expected utility values of opportunity set. Namely, Bernouille's Theory tries to explain investor behavior under uncertainty. Bernouille assumes that investors are rational when trying to explain this question under uncertainty. Investors are rational, and they select the highest expected utility alternative. Utility is the sum of the products of probability and utility for all possible securities and investors choose to the alternative which gives the highest utility. This decision also depends on the investor's risk attitude towards risk. According to the investors risk attitude, decision makers is classified as risk averse, risk neutral and risk loving investor.

According to the Theory, the expected utility for each opportunity (Li) defined by all possible consequences (C_1, C_2,…, C_n), namely shows the utility of obtaining these results, and the probability of occurrence of consequences *(P_1, P_2,…,P_i, with $\sum P_i=1$).*

$$EU(Li) = U(C_1)*P_1 + U(C_2)*P_2 + \ldots + U(Cn)*Pi \qquad (1)$$

$$EU\left(L\right) = \sum_{r=i}^{n} U(C_i) * P_i$$

The term expected utility was first introduced by Bernoulli and he used it to clarify the St. Petersburg paradox[1], as the expected value was insufficient for its solution.

Later, this theory has been improved and embodied by Neuman and Morgenstern (1944). They used the theory to explain the rational decision-making behavior. In their book called "Theory of Games and Economic Behavior", which is accepted the cornerstone of expected utility theory, built a mathematical formulation for Bernoulli's solution of the paradox. They improved a set of axioms for the preferred relations in order to guarantee that the utility function is well-behaved.

The expected utility theory, which has a vital role in finance literature, has been criticized due to the rational investors assumption which is the basic assumption of the theory. Also, it is often not possible in real life to determine the likelihood of the consequences of these decisions before the investor has made certain decisions. To overcome this problem, the *Subjective Utility Theory*, developed by Savage (1964), defines preferences as a utility function multiplied by subject's subjective probability assessment. However, the theory has also started to be criticized intensively as well as expected utility theory because of the rational investors assumption.

Markowitz Portfolio Theory

Markowitz (1952) first described mean-variance portfolio theory, he then improved and introduced full form of it in 1959. The Markowitz Mean-Variance portfolio theory is an investment theory based on the thought that risk-averse investors create portfolios to aim of maximizing expected return depending on a certain market risk level. The relationship between risk and return is parallel, thus the higher risk deserves higher reward. Constructing optimal portfolio is a process of selecting from many risky and risk-free securities. Markowitz portfolio indicates that as you insert securities into a portfolio the total risk of the portfolio (standard deviation/variance) decreases, however the expected return of the portfolio is the sum of weighted average of the expected returns of each security. By investing in portfolios rather than in individual securities, investors can have chance to decrease the total risk of investing without sacrificing return. Markowitz, while setting up this Mean-Variance Portfolio model, accepts efficient financial markets and rational investors. However, many deviations from the efficiency are observed in real financial markets.

Capital Asset Pricing Model (CAPM)

The CAPM introduced with the development of Markowitz Portfolio model, defines the relations between systematic risk measure (beta) and expected return for securities. The basis of the CAPM was established by Treynor (1961), Sharpe (1964), Lintner (1965) and Mossin (1966) while aiming to develop Markowitz portfolio theory. The base of the model depends on risk-return trade of in stock market. While developing their theories they assumed that it can be risk-free borrowing and lending as well as rational decision-making.

According to the CAPM, expected returns are function of risk, and beta is the measure of systematic risk. In theory, the model combined risk-free securities with a tangency portfolio consisting of risky securities to form mean-variance efficient portfolios that would provide the investor the optimal investment decision.

Assumptions of CAPM are as below;

- Infinitely divisible investment alternatives,
- Rational investors,
- Risk averse investors,
- Efficient markets,
- Nobody can distort prevailing market values,
- Borrowing and lending at the risk-free rate without any restriction,
- No transaction costs,
- No tax
- Perfectly competitive market

The CAPM is expressed as an equation as below;

$$E(r_i) = r_f + \beta_i * [E(r_m) - r_f] \tag{2}$$

where r_f is the risk-free rate of return, βi is the systematic risk of a security or a portfolio, $E(r_m)$ is the expected market returns, and E(ri) is the theoretical expected return under the perfect market assumption. New theories have been developed as the theories fail to describe expected returns of securities.

The CAPM has been used in practice for many years, however, it is subject to various criticisms due to its assumptions and some results in practice. Therefore, new asset pricing models have been developed which take into account other factors as well as beta.

Arbitrage Pricing Theory (APT)

The APT has very fewer assumptions compare to CAPM. However, its implementation can be harder than CAPM, because of the many other factors as well as market factor that are embodied in the Arbitrage Pricing Model to explain expected rate of return for securities. Ross (1976) introduced the APT depending on that the returns of securities are impacted by many factors. These factors are classified as macroeconomic and firm-specific or microeconomic factors.

The APT does not identify the risk factors of the model. Instead, it includes the risk premium of many macroeconomic factors in its formula. In the APT model, the returns of a security is explained by many factors not only market factor. Expected return can be explained as follow based on APT.

$$E(r_i) = r_f + \beta_{i1} * F_1 + \beta_{i2} * F_2 + \ldots + \beta_{kn} * F_n + \varepsilon_i, \tag{3}$$

$$E\left(r_i\right) = r_f + \sum_{r=i}^{n} (B_{in} * F_{in}) + \varepsilon_i$$

where r_f is the risk-free rate; F_i is factors affects expected return, such as macroeconomic or firm-specific factor; β is factors coefficients shows the sensitivity of the security return in relation to the certain factor; and ε_i is the error term.

Fama-French Three Factor Model

Fama & French (1992) claim that systematic risk criteria (beta) as an explanatory variable of the risk and return relationship does not fully capture all of the risk factors. Therefore, they add another two factors in their model to explain stock returns. They show that the risk premium depends on three main factors; the market factor (stated by the CAPM), the size of the company factor and the book/market equity ratio factor. In their article, the empirical results show that these factors are able to explain the American stock returns, and positive returns from small size as well as value firms. According to the some empirical studies, the relations between firm size and return is negative, and the relations between book/market equity ratio and return is positive. In other words, stock return is negatively affected by company size and positively affected by book/market equity ratio.

The mathematical representation of the Fama & French three factor model is:

$$E(r_i) = r_f + \beta_1*(r_m-r_f) +\beta_2*(SMB)+ \beta_2*(HML)+ \varepsilon_i, \tag{4}$$

Where; $E(r_i)$ is expected rate of return of an asset , r_f is the risk-free rate; β; factor's coefficient which represents sensitivity of the asset in relation to related factors, (r_m-r_f) is the market risk premium, SMB (Small Minus Big:Company Size Factor) shows excess returns of small market value companies over large market value companies, HML (High Minus Low) shows excess returns of values stocks over growth stocks, ε_i is the error term.

An unexplained part of the expected return with CAPM is explained by adding two more factors. However, there are still unexplained elements of the expected return.

Efficient Market Hypothesis (EMH)

Fama (1965) first presented the concept of "efficient market" in his article. Fama described the efficient market in which all firms aimed to maximize profits, all of whom wanted to estimate future market prices and where all information was open to market participants. The central assumption and paradigm of Traditional Finance Theories is the Efficient Market Hypothesis (EMH), which claims that financial markets are efficient because prices fully reflect all available and important information.

In the famous article of Fama (1970), appears in the Journal of Finance, the detailed formalization of the efficient market provided. Fama claims that it would be impossible to have excess returns in the market economy since markets are open to all information. The EMH became very famous during 1970s and many researches have been done to test the hypothesis validity.

Fama's EMH based on three main assumption and argument;

1. Rational investors,
2. Even if some investors are sometimes irrational, their trades are not consistent and eliminate each other so their investment behavior do not affect prices in the long term, in the long term prices will be arrive trade of level.
3. Even if some irrational investors, there are many arbitrageurs in the market and they cancel the effect of those investment act.

The empirical results from the 1970s indicated that any fresh news about an asset should be reflected in its price immediately and fully and asset prices should not act as act unless there is new information about the company, because it should be exactly equal to value of the asset

Fama (1998) described three types of information, and thus distinguished three different hypothesis of market efficiency: *weak form, semi-strong form* and *strong form efficiency.* In the *weak form efficient market,* the price of a stock considers all available past information. Therefore, It is assumed that it is impossible to obtain a gain/return greater than the market based with a trading strategy using past information. In the *semi-strong form efficient markets,* the price of a stock reflects all available past information, plus all available public information. Thus, the use of past and published information does not allow to obtain an extraordinary gain. In the *Strong form efficient markets,* the price pf a stock reflects the information contained in the time series of prices, publicly available information, and lastly all considered private information. So, in the strong form efficient market, it is assumed that it is impossible to implement any strategy that will obtain a gain higher than the market based. If the EMH is valid, it means that active portfolio management does not work in the efficient markets. In other words, it is not possible to beat the market (obtaining a gain greater than the market equilibrium return).

If we assume the existence of irrational investors, this would not change the idea these markets are efficient. It is claimed that trade of irrational investors has not systematic effect, in other words has random effect of cancelling each other out, thus this does not effect on prices. The situation does not change where investment strategies are interrelated. For instance, when an irrational investor leads to fall below the underlying value of a stock, an arbitrageur buys it in that market and sells it in another market. So, this operation brings the stock value to the level of its core value. Those actions enable the efficiency of markets. In the late 70s, empirical results showed that EPH valid both theoretically and empirically. The EMH states that financial markets are characterized by sufficiently wide number of transactions, and with no entry or exit barriers. Therefore, the market price of securities reflects in all available information, this make guarantee of the best estimate of the value of the security; not provide any arbitrage opportunities, given that the prices remain in stable market equilibrium.

Even if the EMH is the main paradigm of and the most powerful assumption behind the traditional finance theories, these are also probably the main object to be most criticized hypothesis by researchers. Therefore, especially after introducing Efficient market concept, this will be ideal starting point for the understanding of Behavioural Finance.

The Markowitz Mean-Variance Portfolio Theory, Capital Asset Pricing Model (CAPM) and Arbitrage Pricing Theory (APT), Fama & French three factor model are all the quantitative models. And the most important assumptions under these theories are rational expectations and efficient markets. However, many research showed that the invalidity of these assumptions. Especially, the inefficiency of the markets are supported with a number of anamolies found with a certain redundancy over the last two decades.

Some empirical evidence confirms almost all the assumptions of traditional financial theory. For instance; Jensen (1978) indicates that validation of the EMH. Shiller (2002) also showed empirical evidence to validity of CAPM, EMH, and many other traditional financial theories. Nevertheles, in the late 70s, it began to be published the first empirical work questioning the validity of the traditional finance theories, especially for the EMH. These studies indicate some events that cannot be explained by the traditional financial theories. Researchers have been found many anomalies which leads to the birth of Behavioral Finance research area.

Rozeff and Kinney (1976) showed a higher return in January, compared to the other months. It is the first study to indicate an abnormal market returns at certain times of the year. In their study, it has been used stock returns for New York Stock Exchange (NYSE) for the period from 1904 to 1974. According to their experiment result the average return in January higher than the average returns of the other months in NYSE. This higher returns in January compared to the other months of the year also seen in subsequent years in NYSE and also in the equity markets of other countries. This phenomenon was called "January effect". When daily stock returns have been analyzed, results also showed another financial market anomaly where stock returns on Mondays have been in general lower than preceding Friday, called "weekend effect" (Cross, 1973). All these anomalies in stock returns are called "calendar effect" in the literature. In time, empirical results also showed fundamental anomalies, technical anomalies, as well as calendar anomalies.

Moreover, the situations of speculative bubbles, crises, panic and sudden downfall in financial markets for recent years indicate that overall security prices move not foreseen by the EMH. Speculative bubbles, crises, panics, downfall, enthusiasm as well as anomalies that occur in the financial markets are events that the traditional finance theories play a very limited role in answering those financial markets situations. Traditional finance theories alone are very weak to explain issues such as (i) why do investors are irrational? (ii) Why do stock returns fluctuate for reasons other than risk? Therefore, the researchers have recognized the importance of incorporating behavioral factors into the traditional theories to get a more realistic insight into the functioning of stock markets. Especially researchers in psychology have found that financial decisions are often made in an irrational manner.

BEHAVIORAL FINANCE THEORY AND DECISION MODELS

Behavioral finance examines how the behavior of individuals in the financial markets affected by psychological factors and the resulting impact on investment decisions, thus affecting the returns.

In this section, behavioral finance theories and their models will be explained. Table 2 provides summary of behavioral finance theories and their researchers, significant contributions that have been taken place in this chapter. Traditional finance theories are insufficient to explain the behavior of financial markets alone. Today, researchers recognize the importance of adding behavioral factors in to the traditional finance theories as become a more practical model.

Unlike traditional finance theories four foundation blocks, Behavioral finance theories provides alternatives foundation blocks for the foundation blocks of standard finance. It expresses investors as "normal" not rational, although the financial markets are difficult to bear, they are not perfectly efficient, investors do not always conduct their portfolio on Markowitz mean-variance model, and the expected returns are related by not only risk also many other factors. According to behavioral finance:

1. Normal Investors, (instead of rational)
2. Although it is difficult to beat, the financial Markets are inefficient, (instead of efficient markets)
3. Conduct portfolios by the rules of behavioral portfolio theory (instead of Markowitz Mean-Variance Model)
4. Expected returns are modeled by behavioral asset pricing theory, expected returns are related by more than risk factors, (instead of CAPM and systematic risk factor beta),

Table 2. Behavioral finance theories

Theory/Model	Author	Year
Theory of Moral Sentiments	A.Smith	1759
Wealth of Nations	A. Smith	1776
Psychological features of utility function	J.Bentham	1789
Extraordinary Popular Delusions and the Madness of Crowds	C. Mackay	1841
Psychology of the Stock Market	G.C. Selden	1912
Psychological decision theory	F. H. Knight	1921
Models of bounden rationality	H. A. Simon	1955
Rational Choice Behavioral Model	H. A. Simon	1956
Cognitive dissonance theory	L. Festinger, H. W. Riecken and S. Schachter	1956
Utility functions, risk aversion and also risks considered as a proportion of total assets.	J. Pratt	1964
Introducing some heuristic biases	A.Tversky and D.Kahneman	1973, 1974
The Prospect Theory	D. Kahneman and A. Tversky	1979
Introducing Framing Bias	A.Tversky and D.Kahneman	1981
Volatility of the equity markets.	R. Shiller	1981
Introducing mental accounting bias	R. Thaler	1985
Overreaction Theory	De Bondt and Thaler	1985
Dual Theory	Menahem E. Yaari	1987
The bounded rationality	H. A. Simon	1991
Decision Making Under Risk	A.Tversky and D.Kahneman	1992
Underreaction and overreaction model (representative bias, conservative bias)	Barberis, Shleifer and Vishny	1998
Behavioral asset pricing and behavioral portfolio theories	M. Statman	1999
Behavioral Finance and Efficient Market Hypothesis relations	A. Shleifer	2000
A Calibration Theorem.	Matthew Rabin	2000
Incorporation of prospect theory in asset prices	Barberis Huanf and Santos	2001
Behavioral factors and trading behavior relations.	Grinblatt and Keloharju	2001

Behavioral finance theories have emerged as a branch of social psychology that captures the human side of decision making process. The first studies about behavioral finance actually date back to as far as 18th century. "*Theory of Moral Sentiments*" (1759) and "*Wealth of Nations*" (1776) by Adam Smith are the first significant studies in this finance branch. Those of A.Smith's studies suggest the existence of an "invisible hand" which guides them in making decision such as social, economic or financial decisions. The books try to explain the influence of emotional and mental factors on economic decisions and focus on role of feelings like pride, shame, insecurity and egotism etc. Like A. Smith, Jeremy Bentham (1789) also emphasizes the psychological aspects of utility function. J. Bentham argues that human concern for happiness makes it impossible for them to make a decision that is entirely devoid of emotions, happiness is the ultimate human concern.

In 19th Charles Mackay (1841) published his influential book called *"Extraordinary Popular Delusions and the Madness of Crowds"*. The book states the phenomena of "madness of crowds" especially during speculative bubbles. C. MacKay in his book explained the market manner for flower tulip in Holland (a speculative bubble in tulip flower market) with crowd psychology. In other words, the book explained the human, social, and economic psychology of financial bubbles. The study shows that the investors are irrational and behave with imperfect information, so the markets are inefficient.

G.C. Selden (1912) also wrote the book "*Psychology of the Stock Market*". Even though the origins of investors' behavior date back to 18th century, the author also is famous with being the first researcher about investors' psychological behavior. His book depends on "upon the belief that the movements of prices are dependent on the mental attitude of the investing and trading public." The author in his influential book describes; how financial markets are affected by sentiments like fear, shame, insecurity, greed, and panic. Investment psychology guides affects the general market and individual securities movement. A very important first step for the introduction of research in a new field such as behavioral finance, as by the time it was believed that prices followed the EMH and that investors were rational. For G.C. Selden it is important to keep in mind that human emotions have an important influence in the 'game' of the stock market. Also important to note is the clear distinction Selden makes between investors and speculators. Investors caring about an adequate return on their investments while speculators do not care about fundamental analysis, just on being able to 'buy low' and 'sell high'. Nonetheless mentions that "sales of investors are small compared with the speculative business". Besides the psychology behind the speculative cycle, the author writes about other topics that make this book a must read for an introduction in the metacognitive aspect in the stock market dynamics, such as "the panic and the boom", "mental attitude of the individual", "confusing personal with the general" among others.

Frank H. Knight (1921), in his book called *"Risk, Uncertainty and Profit"*, dealt with the definition of the distinction between decisions under "risk" (known chance or measurable probability) and decisions under "uncertainty" (unmeasurable probability or indeterminable chance). However, a deep reading of F.H. Knight (1921) reveals several psychological factors beyond this risk-uncertainty concepts, many of which foreshadow very important development in psychological decision making. For instance, he was the first to write on ambiguity aversion in literature. He concluded that investors dislike uncertainty (ambiguity) more than they dislike risk. Knight's description of economic decision making shared with Herbert A. Simon's (1955, 1956) concept of *"bounded rationality"*, whereby choice behavior is regulated by cognitive and environmental constraints. The phenomenon of bounded rationality shows the weaknesses of investors. This phenomenon assumes that investors buy the securities which promise optimal satisfaction. These securities are not taken for granted. This hypothesis underlines that the choices of individuals are rational however, subject to the limited information and cognitive capacity. Knight explained characteristics of risky choice that were to become basic components of *"prospect theory"* (D. Kahneman and A. Tversky, 1979): *"the reference dependent valuation of outcomes, and the non-linear weighting of probabilities. Knight also discussed several biases in human decision making and pointed to two systems of reasoning: one quick, intuitive but error prone, and a slower, more deliberate, rule-based system. A discussion of Knight's potential contribution to psychological decision theory emphasizes the importance of a historical perspective on theory development, and the potential value of sourcing ideas from other disciplines or from earlier periods of time."*

Psychologists Festinger, Riecken and Schachter (1956) developed a new concept in social psychology: "the *theory of cognitive dissonance*". This concept is one of the most influential theories in the social psychology history. According to the concept, individuals determine their behavior and cognitive according to their past experiences and values. Therefore, if one recalls an experience as worse than it actually is, he is motivated to avoid similar experiences, and alternatively, if one remember an experience better than it actually is, he will make a lot of effort to experience similar experiences. In other words, investors tend to ignore or minimize any information that contradicts their beliefs. When two concurrently held cognitions are inconsistent, this will produce a state of cognitive dissonance. Therefore, cognitive dissonance results in investors avoiding discordant beliefs, considering beliefs that support the preferred belief.

J. Pratt (1964) also *"considers utility functions, risk aversion and also risks considered as a proportion of total assets."*

Informal origins of Behavioral finance theories date back to 18th and century; such as the studies of A. Smith's 1759 and 1776 *"Theory of Moral Sentiments"* and *"Wealth of Nations", S. Mackay's 1841 "Extraordinary Popular Delusions and the Madness of Crowds"* are those very important ones. In addition, especially, G.C. Selden's 1912 "Psychology of the Stock Market" study as well as Festinger's 1956 "the theory of cognitive dissonance" and Pratt's 1964 discussion on "risk aversion and the utility function" are those of crucial studies from 19th century. These have been briefly summarized above. Nevertheless, the real official onset of behavioral finance is starting with D. Kahneman and A. Tversky's serial influential articles. The first study, they published together in 1971, *"Belief in the Law of Small Numbers"*, in which they conclude that *"People have erroneous intuitions about the laws of chance. In particular, they regard a sample randomly drawn from a population as highly representative"*. The initial step was to adapt psychological experiments in decision theory to real-world scenarios. They have tried to answer how investors make financial decisions in real financial markets, especially by examining the psychology factors of financial decisions. The psychologically aspects are more accurate description of decision making, compared to the expected utility theory's rational investor. A. Tversky's mathematical study on the normative theory and D. Kahneman's 'psychophysical emphasis on the difference between objective stimulus and subjective sensation' blended perfectly to serve the answering of decision-making problem.

In D. Kahneman and A. Tversky's 1972 article titled *"Subjective probability: A judgment of Representativeness"*, was examined the "Representativeness bias". They later explained this concept in more detail in their 1973 article titled *"On the psychology of prediction"*. They state that representativeness plays a vital key role in intuitive predictions made by investors.

Another influential study published in 1974, titled *"Judgment under Uncertainty: Heuristics and Biases"*, was about on "Representativeness, Availability and Anchoring" heuristics. They stated that *"a better understanding of these heuristics and of the biases to which they lead could improve judgment and decisions in situations of uncertainty"*.

Even if they published the articles in 1973 and one in 1974, their 1979 study has been revolutionized. The study will enable D. Kahneman to receive Nobel Prize in Economics in 2002. Behavioral finance theories and empirical studies of it have rapidly risen since mid-1980s, after this official start. As of this date, D. Kahneman and A. Tversky have conducted a number of serial academic studies on the decision-making of investors. In 1979, D. Kahneman and A. Tversky's study called *"Prospect Theory; A Study of Decision Making Under Risk"* was released. The study was about *"a critique of expected utility theory as a descriptive model of decision making under risk"*. So, another model was evolved was called "Prospect Theory" in place of expected utility theory. *"Prospect Theory"* tries to explain the way of individuals selecting between probabilistic alternatives which involves risk, and the probabilities of outcomes are known. The theory is a descriptive theory of decisions under risk and gives great importance to the way individuals interpret decision problems. They showed that, rather than calculating the universe of potential outcomes and selecting the optimal one, investors calculate outcomes against a subjective reference point, such as the purchase price of a stock.

Moreover, the value maximization function in the Prospect Theory differs from that in Markowitz Mean Variance Model. In the classical mean-variance model, the wealth maximization is based on the ultimate wealth position while the prospect theory takes into account gains and losses. According to Prospect Theory investors are *loss averse,* which means they are willing to take on risk in the face of losses whereas stay away from risk to protect their gains. Investors's attitudes against gains and loss differ. This is the fact that investors make different choices even if the identical ultimate wealth levels. Investors can take more risks for not to lose, but they want to ensure their potential gains. In a negative situation, the investor wants to do more and move to a positive balance. Therefore 1979 study was about on "frame dependence". *"An important aspect of the framing process is that investors tend to perceive outcomes as gains and losses, rather than as ultimate states of wealth Gains and losses are defined relative to some neutral reference point and changes are measured against it in relative terms, rather than in absolute terms."* According to the theory, investors are not fully rational, and they pay attention losses more than the same amount of profit, they show loss aversion behavior.

They in 1979 also indicated the existence of certain phenomena that contradict the Expected Utility theory: "the certainty-effect", "the reflection-effect" and "the insulation effect".

Prospect theory has been more successful in finance, because it takes into account behavioral factors that the expected utility model does not. The descriptive success of prospect theory depends on some important psychological insights into how investors behave against the potential gains or losses. The theory was also improved in 1992 by authors.

The economist M. Allais (1953) has made an important criticism of the Expected Utility theory. He showed that investors overestimate the results regarding reliable and underestimate the results regarding probable. His inference about investors decision making contradicts with the Expected Utility theory. Because, the utility of each case is completely the linear combination of the probability of each outcome according to Expected Utility Theory.

Menahem E. Yaari (1987) states a change into expected utility theory and called this "dual theory of choice under risk". The dual theory of choice under risk has been presented to resolve specific theoretical problems that expected utility could not answer. *"One of the most important features of the latter is that risk aversion is equivalent to diminishing marginal utility. Yaari argued that risk aversion and diminishing marginal utility are different features and proposing a theory which allowed for linear risk averse utilities. The linearity property makes modelling behavior of risk-averse agents much simpler."*

In another important paper A. Tversky and D. Kahneman (1981) also introduced the effect famous as *Framing*. Framing is an important cognitive bias in behavioral finance. Framing refers to how the same problem is expressed in several different ways and went through to decision makers. Therefore, framing can affect the decisions completely different from the traditional finance rational investors.

They indicated that the choice is systematically reversed, when the same problem is presented in different ways. Investors' preferences are influenced by this '*Framing effect*'. Traditional Finance theories suggest that all of our investments consist of a basic portfolio and while conducting the basic portfolio, investors should take into account that the risk of one asset should be eliminated by the risk of the another. Traditional financial theory concentrates on the total wealth extensively instead of individual assets. Nevertheless, human psychology tends to focus on the behavior of individual assets rather than a portfolio. Hence, investors tend to fret over the poor performance of a specific asset when reviewing portfolios. These "narrow frames" make the investors more sensitive to loss. On the other hand, while evaluating investments at the aggregate level in the "wide frame" effect, investors tend to approve short-term losses and their impacts. This result is also an assumption of Prospect Theory in 1979.

There are different types of framing effects have been stated in the literature. In A. Tversky and D. Kahneman (1981) study the framing effect classification is risky choice. The "risky preference framing effect" related to how investors make decisions according to negatively or positively framing. Investors tend to be risk averse when uncertain outcomes are framed positively but they tend to be risk seeking when uncertain outcomes framed negatively. According to prospect theory investors first frame the uncertain outcomes according to their beliefs, then make decisions by final phase of evaluation. In the study, it is indicated that how people manage risk and uncertainty. Substantially, human behavior is very irregular while evaluating risk under uncertainty. Human behavior is not risk-averse all the time (different from traditional finance theory); rather they are risk-averse against gains but risk-seeking against losses. Investors tent to focus on the outcomes that are thought more certain than that are considered more probable, the concept called *"certainty effect"*.

R. Shiller (1981) study on the volatility of the equity markets is also an important in behavioral fiancé literature. He conduct a number of empirical studies and these studies show many results inconsistent with traditional finance theories, and all these empirical results are described as anomalies in Financial markets. He explained the fact that equity return volatility is far too high to against the new information about dividends payouts in the future.

In 1985 Richard Thaler also introduced the concept of "Mental accounting" in the behavioral finance literature. According to Mental Accounting feature, investors tend to divide complex information into manageable categories. They separate their securities into different categories depending on the purpose each category fulfills. It is argued that individuals classify personal funds differently and therefore tend to make irrational decision in spending and investment.

Individuals psychological self thinks about fund and risk through "mental accounts" lead to separate their wealth into different pools. In general, human make this depending on goals or time horizon. This can also change according to risk tolerance, investing some fund in risky assets for high gains while the rest of it is investing more conservatively. Mental Accounting is related to cognitive operations used by each one to carry out of all financial activities during daily life. This make humans separate their fund into different buckets based on different purposes. Individuals often assign different functions to each security pool, which can cause irrational behavior on their investment decisions. Mental Accounting is like codes of investors use while assessing an investment decision.

According to Thaler, people think about relative value rather than absolute terms. They not only enjoy the value of the object, but also enjoy the quality of the deal - the transaction utility. Also, people often do not fully consider opportunity costs and are susceptible to the sunk cost fallacy. Investors often does not consider the relations between each investment held in each mental buckets as traditional theory does. Creating mental accounts also leads investors to concentrate on the individual accounts rather than entire wealth position. This concept of mental accounting is called "narrow framing",

Other features of mental accounting related to that investors vary in their attitudes towards risk between their different mental accounts. Investors might be risk adverse for an account, while risk seeking for another depending on how the speculative of each account. Framing and dividing wealth into separate mental buckets has the drawbacks noted by Markowitz, covariance between securities and buckets are ignored, therefore it can confront with the investors an investment portfolio lie below the efficient frontier.

Another important concept for Behavioral Finance is *Overreaction Effect.* This effect has been argued by DeBondt and Thaler (1985) that there existed a strong tendency for both low and high performing securities in one period to experience reversal in following years. They published a study titled "Does the stock market overreact?" in the The Journal of Finance. *Overreaction* indicates that *"extreme movements in stock prices will be followed by subsequent price movements in the opposite direction".* De Bondt and Thaler (1985) remark that investors reactions can be change overtime, their investment strategies can be sometimes too conservative and other times can be too reactive. Therefore, this issue could not be solved by the assumptions of traditional finance and became one of the gray areas in finance. This refers that securities which have experienced important downfall in relation to the market over a period will surpass the market over the equivalent period of time. De Bondt and Thaler (1985) also stated the concept of long-run overreaction. They indicated that investors systematically overreacting to unexpected news events, which shows invalidation of weak-form efficiency in the equity market.

De Bondt and Thaler (1987) show additional evidence of the overreaction behavior of the financial markets. They anticipate that the security prices would remove temporary swings from their original core values due to the market confidence and pessimism. Their results indicated that losers/winners, measured and classified by their performance relative to the aggregate stock market over the past 3 to 5 year period, consistently surpassed or underperformed the market in the following 3 to 5 year period. Shefrin and Statman (1985) also observed that investors tend to sell the rising stocks very early and hold downward securities for too long.

In the literature, some explanations have been suggested for the overreaction behavior of the financial markets. Financial markets can be overreacting due to the "size effect"; firms perform better than large firms and the portfolio of losers tends to be smaller. Another reason for overreaction is that the reversal in the stock returns reflects changes in equilibrium required returns. That is the significant movements in the leverage will lead to high changes in a firms' CAPM beta values. Hence, betas of the extreme losers go beyond the betas of the top gainers. These differences in the betas obviously clarify huge differences in stock returns.

Overreaction or underreaction features of the financial markets are important evidence of that investors are limited rationale. Traditional financial theories based on the assumption of rational investors cannot explain for these features of the financial markets. Especially the significant autocorrelation of security returns in the financial markets shows the biased reaction of investors to new information, such as overreaction and underreaction.

Barberis, Shleifer & Vishny (1998) stated that individuals have some mental biases during the decision making process. First, it is *representative bias,* in which investors make inferences and judgments according to a small sample and ignore the whole population. Another is the *conservative bias*, in which investors cannot update their expectations on time depending on new information. Overreaction and Underreaction behavior of financial markets can also explain by these biases. The representative and conservative biases overreaction and underreaction to new information respectively.

Daniel, Hirshleifer & Subrahmanyam (1998) also try to give answer to overreaction and underreaction behavior of financial markets from another perspective. They classified investors as informed investors and uninformed investors. While uninformed investors do not have mental biases, informed investors do. These mental biases include *overconfidence* and *self-attribution*. Overconfident, *"informed investors focus on private information and underestimate the value of public information. Such investors likewise overestimate their ability to forecast and underestimate their forecasting error. Overconfidence can lead to mispricing of securities. Overconfidence is also encouraged by another mental bias, namely, self-*

attribution, which is when investors attribute their success to their own abilities and attribute failure to external noise."

In 1990s and 2000s *the Behavioral Asset Pricing Model (BAPM)* was introduced instead of CAPM, and *Behavioral Portfolio Theory (BPT)* was introduced instead of Markowitz portfolio theory. Statman (1999) states that CAPM try to determine the equilibrium security return at a given point of time, whereas do not explain stock market bubbles during a period of time. The *BAPM* developed by Shefrin and Statman (1994). This model tries to explain the market interaction according to different traders, such as "informational traders" and "noise traders". Information traders invest in according to CAPM thus they are rational whereas noise traders commit cognitive errors and they do not follow the CAPM. Therefore, in the case of noise traders, the expected return of securities is related to behavioral betas.

Behavioral Portfolio Theory (BPT) of Shefrin and Statman (2000), asset preference in a portfolio depending on the risk tolerance, investing some fund in risky assets like a gamble, while the rest of it is investing more conservative assets like an insurance. Behavioral economist authors used this mental account feature of human in their behavioral portfolio theory. According to author individual's behavioral portfolios are formed like a layered pyramid, and each layer shows a separate mental account. Behavioral investors conduct their portfolios as the pyramids of securities. Each layer in the pyramid is related to its certain purpose and risk attitude. The BPT tries to identify investor behavior with its different attitude towards risk. While the classical Markowitz model the portfolio is evaluated as a whole, and the risk attitude of the investors is accepted as consistent, the BPT model evaluates the different layers of all wealth and the risk attitude differs for different layers.

The first layers represent asset buckets consist of conservative assets which aimed to avoid loss and provide 'protection from poverty'. Later layers represent asset buckets consist of risky assets which aimed to provide of high returns and 'hopes for riches'. This idea explains why an individual investor shows risk-averse and risk-tolerant behavior, according to mental account considering. The BPT model is able to answer the question about investors contradictive buying attitude like buying 'insurance' and 'lottery tickets' at the same time. According the BPT theory investors do not deal with relations between different layers for different mental accounts. They all isolated each other. However, according the Markowitz mean variance model the relations between each security in the whole portfolio is the most important factor in diversification process aiming to decrease risk at a certain return level.

Figure 1. Layers represent assets designed
Source: Adapted from Statman (1999)

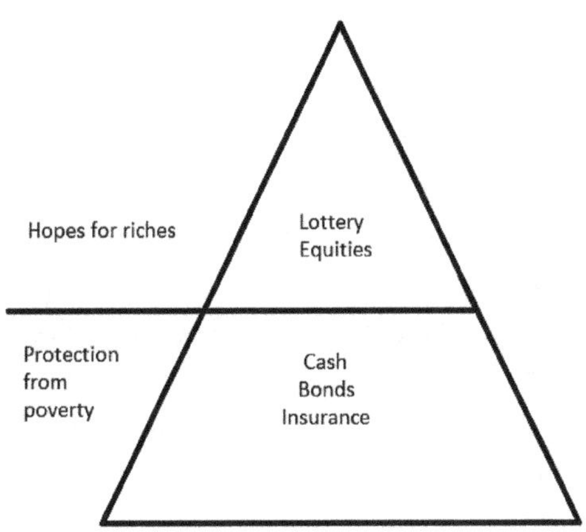

The BPT is a theory depending on different goals and purposes. According to theory, individuals divide their fund into several mental accounts/buckets. The layers of pyramid shaping depending on the goals such as insurance, retirement period, university education, or being rich at the top of the pyramid.

A basic feature of (BPT) is that it does not consider the whole portfolio as viewed in the traditional Markowitz mean variance model. Different mental accounts have been created by dividing the entire portfolio in line with specific objectives, and each of these account/layer shapes the pyramid. Each mental account layers are associated with specific objectives and attitudes toward risk differs across layers. A mental account layer can be a "downside protection" layer, designed to protect investors from being poor. Another may be an "upside potential" layer, designed to give investors a chance to become rich. Investors may hate risk in the downside protection layer, while they may love risk in the upside layers. These are normal investors.

The behavioral finance researches have been increased dramatically especially in 2000s.

Shleifer's (2000) study of *"Inefficient Markets: An Introduction to Behavioral Finance"*, considers descriptive theories of preference under risk. This is an alternative study for financial markets from behavioral perspective. The author acknowledges the fact the in real financial markets, irrational investors trade against arbitrageurs whose resources are limited by risk aversion, short horizons, and agency problems. He provides behavioral models that try to identify many market anomalies such as the over-performance of stocks, the closing price puzzles, price bubbles, crises in financial markets and collapse of hedge funds.

Shefrin (2000) published an influential book titled *"Beyond Greed and Fear"* which was about behavioral finance and the psychology of financial decision making. The same year R. J. Shiller (2000) also published another book *"Irrational Exuberance" which* was about a convincing case that the US equity market was overvalued due to the structural, cultural and psychological factors. Rabin (2000) also presents a theory indicating that expected utility theory is completely inappropriate explanation for perceivable risk aversion when it is concert modest stakes. Lee and Swaminathan (2000) indicated that past trading volume provides a vital link between 'momentum' and 'value' strategies, investors can use this information to beat the market, and these results shows the inconsistency of EPH.

Informal origins of Behavioral finance theories date back to 18th and century; such as the studies of A. Smith's 1759 and 1776 *"Theory of Moral Sentiments"* and *"Wealth of Nations", S. Mackay's 1841 "Extraordinary Popular Delusions and the Madness of Crowds"* are those very important ones. In addition, especially, G.C. Selden's 1912 "Psychology of the Stock Market" study as well as Festinger's 1956 "the theory of cognitive dissonance" and Pratt's 1964 discussion on "risk aversion and the utility function" are those of crucial studies from 19th century. These have been briefly summarized above. Nevertheless, the real official onset of behavioral finance is starting with D. Kahneman and A. Tversky's serial influential articles. The first study, they published together in 1971, *"Belief in the Law of Small Numbers"*, in which they conclude that *"People have erroneous intuitions about the laws of chance. In particular, they regard a sample randomly drawn from a population as highly representative"*. The initial step was to adapt psychological experiments in decision theory to real-world scenarios. They have tried to answer how investors make financial decisions in real financial markets, especially by examining the psychology factors of financial decisions. The psychologically aspects are more accurate description of decision making, compared to the expected utility theory's rational investor. A. Tversky's mathematical study on the normative theory and D. Kahneman's 'psychophysical emphasis on the difference between objective stimulus and subjective sensation' blended perfectly to serve the answering of decision-making problem.

It can be realized from the above literature that the studies on incorporating behavioral aspects to traditional finance theories started quite early. This field started gaining the importance especially in 1970's and 1980's. The studies of Simon (1955), Pratt (1964), Raiffa (1968) and Kahneman and Tversky (1979) presence an alternative to the expected utility theory. In later years, the expected utility theory wasn't the only theory which confront with many criticisms. Proponents of behavioral finance also found flaws in other standard finance theories like the CAPM, the Markowitz Mean-Variance model and the EMH. In the late 1990's and 2000's the EMH was also criticized by many researchers like A. Shleifer (2000) and R. Shiller (2000).

After that aforementioned literature, there have been many other articles which find anomalies of financial markets and proves the inefficiency of the markets.

The behavioral finance literature proves that the traditional finance theories alone isn't be able to answer the anomalies of financial markets. Recently, the researchers have realized the importance of incorporating behavioral factors into the traditional finance theories to achieve more realistic insight into the functioning of financial markets.

COMPARISON AND APPLICATION AREAS DISCUSSION

Behavioral Finance is not a branch of Traditional Finance, it's a *replacement.* It is built on the framework of traditional finance whereas provides a replacement for traditional finance as a descriptive theory. Behavioral finance reflects a different model of human behavior and consists of different components; prospect theory, cognitive errors, framing, overconfidence, self-attribution, conservatism and many other human feelings/emotions.

These behavioral factors help make sense of the real finance word including investor preferences, the design of modern financial products, and financial regulations by making sense of normal investor behavior. In Table 3, the basic differences between traditional finance and behavioral finance has been indicated.

Table 3. Traditional finance vs. behavioral finance

Traditional Finance vs. Behavioral Finance	
Traditional Finance	**Behavioral Finance**
Perfect rationality	Bounded rationality
Expected utility theory Risk aversion	Prospect theory Loss Aversion
Rational Investor Human and Investors behave rationally. Decision making depends heavly on facts. Investors behave in logic and independent judgement.	Normal Investors Investors suffer from cognitive biases that may lead to irrational decision making. Emotions and herd instincts play a vital role in decision making process. Challenges rational investor assumption. (Normal investors are not stupid, but neither are totally rational and rarely behave according to the assumptions made in traditional finance theory) Borrows from Cognitive Psychology
Rational economic man - make perfectly rational, unbiased decisions	Irrational exhibiting emotional & cognitive biases in observed behavior

continued on following page

Table 3. Continued

Traditional Finance vs. Behavioral Finance	
Traditional Finance	**Behavioral Finance**
People process data and information appropriately and correctly	People employ imperfect rules of thumb (heuristics) to process data which includes biases in their beliefs and predisposes them to commit errors.
People view all decisions through the transparent and objective lens of risk and return (inconsequential frame definition)	Perceptions of risk and return are significantly influenced by how decisions problems are framed (frame dependence).
Investors process new information quickly and correctly.	Investors may overreact or under-react to new information.
All investors are risk averse and utility maximizing. concave utility function with diminishing marginal utility (Utility Theory)	Investors value gains and losses differently. Some are risk averse to gains and risk seeking to losses. In general loss averse Convex Utility (Prospect Theory)
investors use "random" decision weights to model different outcomes which leads to lower probability events having higher weights than they deserve. (Utility Theory)	Probability weight all investment outcomes (i.e. use a Bayesian process) (Prospect Theory)
Normative – idealized behavior based on neo-classical economics	Descriptive – how we "actually" behave, based on human psychology
Uses Capital Asset Pricing Model (CAPM) Uses Arbitrage Price Theory (APT)	Uses Behavioral Asset Pricing Model (BAPM)
Markowitz Mean-Variance Model	Behavioral Portfolio Theory (BPT)
Construct and hold Minimum variance (MV) portfolios	Build layered portfolios – pyramids
the portfolio is evaluated as a whole, the risk attitude of the investors is accepted as consistent	the BPT model evaluates the different layers of all wealth, the risk attitude differs for different layers.
Markowitz mean variance model deal with the relations between each security in the whole portfolio and this is the most important factor in diversification process aiming to decrease risk at a certain return level.	The BPT theory investors do not deal with relations between different layers for different mental accounts. They all isolated each other.
Does not explain the anomalies	Explains anomalies that are unexplainable by rational means
Efficient market hypothesis	Adaptive market hypothesis
Markets are efficient: Quickly incorporate all known information Represent the true value of all securities Market price of each security is an unbiased estimate of its intrinsic value.	Markets are inefficient: May be difficult to beat in the long term There are anomalies and excesses in the short term Heuristic-driven biases and errors, frame dependence and effects of emotions and social influence often lead to discrepancy between market price and fundamental value.

CONCLUSION

According to evolution of finance theories in detail, it can be summarized that finance theories such as expected utility theory, the Markowitz Portfolio Selection Theory, the CAPM, the APT and the EMH in general revolve around four basic assumptions; rational investors; efficient markets; constructing portfolios depending on the rules of mean-variance portfolio theory and risk-return trade off. Expected returns on investments are explained by differences in risk.

However, Behavioral finance accepts that investors cannot be rational all the time and their decision making can be biased. Behavioral finance uses normal investor concept for irrational investor. This irrational investor leads to decay the market efficiency. So Behavioral finance accepts that financial market can be inefficient, although it is not very easy to beat those markets. In addition, according to behavioral finance, individuals conduct their portfolios by the principals of BPT instead of Markowitz Mean-Variance Model. Expected returns of securities are described by BAPM instead of CAPM. According to BAPM differences in expected returns are determined by more than differences in risk.

According to the traditional finance theory, the aim of the investors is maximum utility, and always behave in a non-prejudiced and rational manner for this purpose. Today, this aspect of finance has changed in dramatically. Research in this field has indicated that human psychology is very crucial in making financial decisions. The crises, panics, downfall, enthusiasm and bubbles that occur in the financial markets are the most important indicators that humans are not always rational. This area, which examines psychology, sociology, anthropology and finance together, is called behavioral finance. According to this behavioral finance theory, investors often show irrational behavior, unlike the traditional definition, and often prejudge investment decisions. "Why do investors make irrational decisions?" is the main field of study of behavioral finance. Cognitive errors and prejudices that investors often make are identified in studies conducted.

Today, strong psychology as well as financial literacy and market experience are among the basic requirements for being a leading investor. Learning the basic concepts of behavioral finance will enable the investor to become aware of the prejudices and cognitive errors of his / her feelings and thoughts.

As the studies in behavioral finance area develops, it becomes obvious that investor biases, irrational behavior of investors are very widespread. Since they are present wherever human is involved. In addition the impact of these human biases can be very costly. Thus, information about such human behavior becomes very crucial not just for investors, but also for the financial analysts and portfolio managers. By using this information both investors and financial experts can comprehend the market sensitivity, and financial experts are also able to advice the individuals the most profitable way. In this chapter, it has been tried to give basic concepts of both traditional finance and behavioral finance in historical order.

REFERENCES

Ball, R., & Kothari, S. (1989). Nonstationary Expected Returns: Implications for Tests of Market Efficiency and Serial Correlation in Returns. *Journal of Financial Economics*, *25*(1), 51–74. doi:10.1016/0304-405X(89)90096-2

Barberis, N., Shleifer, A., & Vishny, R. (1998). A model of investor sentiment. *Journal of Financial Economics*, *49*(3), 307–343. doi:10.1016/S0304-405X(98)00027-0

Barberis, N. C., & Thaler, R. H. (2003). A survey of behavioral finance. In Handbook of the Economics of Finance: Vol. 1B. Financial Markets and Asset Pricing. Elsevier.

Bem, D. J. (1967). Self-perception: An alternative interpretation of cognitive dissonance phenomena. *Psychological Review*, *74*(3), 183–200. doi:10.1037/h0024835 PMID:5342882

Bloomfield & Hales. (2002). *Predicting the next step of a random walk: experimental evidence of regime-shifting beliefs*. Academic Press.

Brabazon, T. (2000). *Behavioral finance: a new sunrise or a false dawn*. Department of Accountancy, University College Dublin. Available at: http://down.cenet.org.cn/upfile/36/20063711518134.pdf

Byrne, A., & Utkus, S. P. (n.d.). *Behavioural finance, Understanding how the mind can help or hinder investment success*. Retrieved from https://www.vanguard.co.uk/documents/portal/literature/behavourial-finance-guide.pdf

Causi, G. L. (2017). *Theories of investor behaviour: From the Efficient Market Hypothesis to Behavioural Finance* (Bachelor's Thesis). Tallinn University of Technology, School of Business and Governance, Department of Economics and Finance, Tallinn.

Charles, L. M. C., & Swaminathan, B. (2000). Price Momentum and Trading Volume. *The Journal of Finance*, *55*(5), 2017–2069. doi:10.1111/0022-1082.00280

Charles, M. K. (1996). *Memoirs of Extraordinary Popular Delusions*, 1841. In M. Fridson (Ed.), *Extraordinary Popular Delusions and the Madness of Crowds and Confusion de Confusiones*. New York: John Wiley.

Copur, Z. (2015). *Handbook of Research on Behavioral Finance and Investment Strategies: Decision Making in the Financial Industry*. Hacettepe University.

Daniel, K., Hirshleifer, D., & Subrahmanyam, A. (1998). Investor psychology and investor security market under- and overreactions. *The Journal of Finance*, *53*(6), 1839–1886. doi:10.1111/0022-1082.00077

De Bondt, W. F. M., & Thaler, R. H. (1985). Dose the stock market overreact? *The Journal of Finance*, *40*(3), 793–805. doi:10.1111/j.1540-6261.1985.tb05004.x

Fama, E. F. (1965). Random Walks in Stock Market Prices. *Financial Analysts Journal*, *21*(5), 55–59. doi:10.2469/faj.v21.n5.55

Fama, E. F. (1970). Efficient Capital Markets: A Review of Theory and Empirical Work. *The Journal of Finance*, *25*(2), 383–417. doi:10.2307/2325486

Fama, E. F. (1998). Market efficiency, long-term returns, and behavioral finance. *Journal of Financial Economics*, *49*(3), 283–306. doi:10.1016/S0304-405X(98)00026-9

Fama, E. F., Fisher, L., & Michael,, J.C., & Rol, R. (1969). The Adjustment of Stock Prices to New Information. *International Economic Review*, 10.

Festinger, L., Riecken, H. W., & Schachter, S. (1956). *When prophecy fails: A social and psychological study of a modern group that predicted the destruction of the world* (1st ed.). Minneapolis, MN: University of Minnesota Press. doi:10.1037/10030-000

Frank, C. (1973). The Behavior of Stock Prices on Fridays and Mondays. *Financial Analysts Journal*, *29*, 67–69.

Jensen, M. (1978). Some Anomalous Evidence Regarding Market Efficiency. *Journal of Financial Economics*, *6*(2), 95–101. doi:10.1016/0304-405X(78)90025-9

Kahneman, D., & Riepe, M. W. (1998). Aspects of Investor Psychology: Beliefs, preferences, biases investment advisors should know about. *Journal of Portfolio Management*, *24*(4), 52–65. doi:10.3905/jpm.1998.409643

Kahneman, D., & Tversky, A. (1973). On the psychology of prediction. *Psychological Review*, *80*(4), 237–251. doi:10.1037/h0034747

Kahneman, D., & Tversky, A. (1971). Belief in law of small numbers. *Psychological Bulletin*, *76*(2), 105–110. doi:10.1037/h0031322

Kahneman, D., & Tversky, A. (1972). Subjective Probability: A judgment of Representativeness. *Cognitive Psychology*, *3*(3), 430–454. doi:10.1016/0010-0285(72)90016-3

Kahneman, D., & Tversky, A. (1979). Prospect Theory: An Analysis of Decision under Risk. *Econometrica*, *47*(2), 263–291. doi:10.2307/1914185

Kahneman, D., & Tversky, A. (2000). *Choices, Values, and Frames*. Cambridge University Press.

Kahneman, D., & Tversky, A. (1984). Choices, values, and frames. *The American Psychologist*, *39*(4), 341–350. doi:10.1037/0003-066X.39.4.341

Kahneman, D., Slovic, P., & Tversky, A. (Eds.). (1982). *Judgment Under Uncertainty: Heuristics and Biases*. Cambridge University Press. doi:10.1017/CBO9780511809477

Knight, F. H. (1921). *Risk, Uncertainty and Profit*. Boston, MA: Hart, Schaffner & Marx, Houghton-Mifflin Co.

Matthew, R. (2000). Risk Aversion and Expected-Utility Theory: A Calibration Theorem. *Econometrica*, *68*(5), 1281–1292. doi:10.1111/1468-0262.00158

Maurice, A. (1953). Le Comportement de l'Homme Rationnel devant le Risque: Critique des Postulats et Axiomes de l'Ecole Americaine. *Econometrica*, *21*(4), 503–546. doi:10.2307/1907921

Nicholas, B., & Richard, T. (2003). *A survey of behavioral finance. Handbook of the Economics of Finance*. Elsevier Science B.V. doi:10.1016/S1574-0102(03)01027-6

Nofsinger, J. R. (2001). *Investment madness: how psychology affects your investing – and what to do about it*. Pearson Education.

Pratt, J. (1964). Risk aversion in the small and in the large. *Econometrica*, *32*(1/2), 122–136. doi:10.2307/1913738

Prelec, D., & Simester, D. (2001). Always leave home without it: A further investigation of the credit-card effect on willingness to pay. *Marketing Letters*, *12*(1), 5–12. doi:10.1023/A:1008196717017

Prosad, J. M., Kapoor, S., & Sengupta, J. (2015). Theory of Behavioral Finance. In Handbook of Research on Behavioral Finance and Investment Strategies: Decision Making in the Financial Industry. Academic Press. doi:10.4018/978-1-4666-7484-4.ch001

Rakow, T. (2010). Risk, uncertainty and prophet: The psychological insights of Frank H. Knight. *Judgment and Decision Making*, *5*(6), 458–466.

Rozeff, M., & Kinney, W. Jr. (1976). Capital market seasonality: The case of stock returns. *Journal of Financial Economics*, *3*(4), 379–402. doi:10.1016/0304-405X(76)90028-3

Schulmerich, M., Leporcher, Y.M., & Eu, C.H. (2015). Modern Portfolio Theory and Its Problems. *Applied Asset and Risk Management*, 101-173.

Schulmerich, M., Leporcher, Y.M., & Eu, C.H. (n.d.). Explaining Stock Market Crashes: A Behavioral Finance Approach. *Applied Asset and Risk Management*, 355-413.

Selden, G. C. (1912). *Psychology of the Stock Market: Human Impulses Lead To Speculative Disasters*. New York: Ticker Publishing.

Sewell, M. W. (2012). *The Application of Intelligent System Financial Time Series Analysis*. Department of Computer Science University College London.

Shefrin, H., & Statman, M. (1994). Behavioral capital asset pricing theory. *Journal of Financial and Quantitative Analysis*, *29*(3), 323–349.

Shefrin, H., & Statman, M. (1985). The disposition to sell winners too early and ride losers too long: Theory and evidence. *The Journal of Finance*, *40*(3), 777–790. doi:10.1111/j.1540-6261.1985.tb05002.x

Shefrin, H., & Statman, M. (2000). Behavioral Capital Asset Pricing Model. *Journal of Financial and Quantitative Analysis*, *35*(2), 127–151. doi:10.2307/2676187

Shefrin, H., & Statman, M. (2000). Behavioral Portfolio Theory. *Journal of Financial and Quantitative Analysis*, *35*(2), 127–152. doi:10.2307/2676187

Shefrin, H. (2000). *Beyond Greed and Fear: Understanding Behavioral Finance and the Psychology of Investing*. Boston, MA: Harvard Business School Press.

Shiller, R. J. (1981). Do Stock Prices Move Too Much to be Justified by Subsequent Changes in Dividends? *The American Economic Review*, *71*(3), 421–436.

Shiller, R. J. (2000). *Irrational Exuberance*. Princeton, NJ: Princeton University Press.

Shleifer, A. (2000). *Inefficient Markets: A Introduction to Behavioral Finance*. Oxford, UK: Oxford University Press. doi:10.1093/0198292279.001.0001

Simon, H. A. (1955). A behavioral model of rational choice. *The Quarterly Journal of Economics*, *69*(1), 99–118. doi:10.2307/1884852

Simon, H. A. (1956). Rational choice and the structure of the environment. *Psychological Review*, 63. PMID:13310708

Smith, A. (1759). *The theory of moral sentiments*. London: A. Millar. doi:10.1093/oseo/instance.00042831

Smith, A. (1776). *The Wealth of Nations*. London, W.: Strahan and T. Cadell.

Starmer, C. (2000). Developments in Non-Expected Utility Theory: The Hunt for a Descriptive Theory of Choice under Risk. *Journal of Economic Literature*, *38*(2), 332–382. doi:10.1257/jel.38.2.332

Statman, M. (1999). Behavioral Finance: Past Battles and Future Engagements. *Financial Analysts Journal, 55*(6), 18–27.

Statman, M. (2008). What is behavioral finance? In *Handbook of Finance* (Vol. 2). John Wiley & Sons, Inc. doi:10.1002/9780470404324.hof002009

Statman, M. (2014). Behavioral finance: Finance with normal people. *Borsa Istanbul Review*, *14*(2), 65–73. doi:10.1016/j.bir.2014.03.001

Subash, R. (2012). *Role of Behavioral Finance in Portfolio Investment Decisions: Evidence from India* (Master's thesis). Charles University in Prague, Faculty of Social Sciences Institute of Economic Studies.

Tekin, B. (2016). Beklenen Fayda ve Beklenti Teorileri Bağlamında Geleneksel Finans - Davranışsal Finans Ayrımı. *Journal of Accounting, Finance and Auditing Studies*, *2/4*, 75–107.

Thaler, R. H. (1985). Mental accounting and consumer choice. *Marketing Science*, *4*(3), 199–214. doi:10.1287/mksc.4.3.199

Thaler, R. H. (1999). Mental accounting matters. *Journal of Behavioral Decision Making*, *12*(3), 183–206. doi:10.1002/(SICI)1099-0771(199909)12:3<183::AID-BDM318>3.0.CO;2-F

Thaler, R. H. (2015). *Misbehaving: The making of behavioral economics*. New York: W. W. Norton & Company.

Thaler, R. H., & Johnson, E. J. (1990). Gambling with the house money and trying to break even: The effects of prior outcomes on risky choice. *Management Science*, *36*(6), 643–660. doi:10.1287/mnsc.36.6.643

Tversky, A., & Kahneman, D. (1974). Judgment Under Uncertainty: Heuristics and Biases. *Science*, *185*(4157), 1124–1131. doi:10.1126cience.185.4157.1124 PMID:17835457

Tversky, A., & Kahneman, D. (1981). The framing of decisions and the psychology of choice. *Science*, *211*(4481), 453–458. doi:10.1126cience.7455683 PMID:7455683

Tversky, A., & Kahneman, D. (1992). Advances in prospect theory: Cumulative representation of uncertainty. *Journal of Risk and Uncertainty*, *5*(4), 297–323. doi:10.1007/BF00122574

Yaari, M. E. (1987). The Dual Theory of Choice under Risk. *Econometrica*, *55*(1), 95–115. doi:10.2307/1911158

Zarowin, P. (1990). Size, seasonality and stock market overreaction. *Journal of Financial and Quantitative Analysis*, *25*(1), 113–125. doi:10.2307/2330891

ENDNOTE

1 The St. Petersburg paradox is a game of chance; after a certain entry fee has been paid, the money is thrown and checked if it is heads or tails. The player who thrown tails wins. When player changes in the game, the prize doubles. For example, after the first attempt to throw money, if the prize is one dollar, the prize for the second attempt is two dollars. There has been debate about how much the entrance fee should be for this game. This is because the expected reward is not finite. What will be if ever never comes tails?

Chapter 2
Linking Personal Values to Investment Decisions Among Individual Shareholders in a Developing Economy

Otuo Serebour Agyemang
University of Cape Coast, Ghana

ABSTRACT

This chapter examines the link between personal values and investment decisions among individual shareholders in a developing economy. It contributes to the knowledge on behavioral finance and decision sciences that individual shareholders' personal values have influence on their investment decisions and the choice of companies they invest in. It employs a grounded theory approach. The chapter highlights that individual shareholders hold value priorities and that honesty, a comfortable life and family security play a significant role in their lives and their investment decisions and the kind of companies they make investment in. In addition, to the individual shareholders, there is a clear distinction between a comfortable life and a prosperous life in the sense that they are not incentivized more by the latter but the former in their investment decisions.

INTRODUCTION

In this chapter, we respond to recent calls and discussions within broader social and economic perspectives to make a new contribution to the extant literature on behavioural finance and decisions sciences by examining how investment decisions of individual shareholders are influenced by their personal values. There is a clear distinction between ordinary shareholders and socially or ethically responsible shareholders in the sense that ordinary shareholders are always considered to be essentially interested in the financial gains of companies (Carroll & Buchholtz, 2003) or with the sole purpose of maximizing wealth or income (Lewis, 2002). Wärneryd (2001) professes that marketing financial services situates on the belief that all capital providers are keen and always ready to maximise their wealth or income.

DOI: 10.4018/978-1-5225-7399-9.ch002

The rationale for such notions of ordinary shareholders is that based on the neoclassical hypothesis of *Homo Economicus,* investors are self-centered human beings whose ultimate goal is to maximise wealth, which demands the maximisation of share price (Rivoli, 1995). However, this shallow hypothesis that investors are primarily self-interested and do not care about the well-being of other stakeholders (or non-shareholders) is flawed by the findings of Nair and Ladha (2014), Pasewark and Riley (2010), Chiu (2009), Hanson and Tranter (2006), Muller (2001) and Epstein (1992).

As contended by neoclassical economists, *Homo Economicus* is a rational man and yet perceived by others (for instance, Tomer, 2001; Kuran, 1995; Elster, 1985) as manipulative, self-centred, pitiless and making the very effort to gain personal pleasure or satisfaction. However, the belief that shareholders are shortsighted and are not supportive of their firms' socially responsible dealings appears to be in contradiction with the actual demeanor of ordinary individual shareholders. Studies reveal that small shareholders always take into consideration long-term view in periods of investments (Lease *et al.*, 1974; Muller, 2001; Ryan & Gist, 1995; Wärneryd, 2001) and their mind-sets are not entirely self-centered- that is increasing firm performance or profit to the detriment of other stakeholders (Muller, 2001; Epstein, 1992). In other words, individual shareholders seek both 'Utilitarian' (maximizing wealth) and 'expressive' gains (investment as a means of expressing their personal values) from their investment decisions (Nair & Ladha, 2014). Therefore, the traditional wealth maximization hypothesis that does not take into account personal values overlook a relevant factor that influences investment decisions (Pasewark and Riley, 2010).

Though shareholders may not agree on what the topmost Corporate Social Responsibility (CSR) is, they are becoming more conscious of the relevance of CSR. A study in Australia in 2007 divulges that seven out of ten investors in Australia point out that when investing in shares; they prefer firms that are both socially and environmentally responsible (Australian Securities Exchange, 2007). In addition, a survey conducted by Capgemini and RBC on wealth management[1] in 2014, divulged that more than half of the high net worth people surveyed expressed 'driving social influence' as extremely relevant and almost nine out of ten expressed it as relevant. This explicitly illuminates an aspect of investment preference behaviour that place emphasis on the neoclassical hypothesis that they are purely self-interested wealth maximisers. In fact, the Economic Man idea conspicuously lacks in providing an explanation and predicting human demeanor in that both the non-economic incentives and social facets of human life have been shunned from the concept (Tomer, 2001). A good example is cited by Frankfurt (1998) that, certain non-economic elements are included in the decision-making processes of individuals. The author proposes the view of caring- concerning our own principles, and in regards to those we love. The author postulates '[a] person who cares about something is, as it were, invested in it ... Thus he concerns himself with what concerns it, giving particular attention to such things and directing his behavior accordingly'.

As we are inescapably, a constituent of society, our decisions and demeanor cannot thus entirely leave out societal norms. From infancy, each person has a gamut of needs or goals created by socialization processes in a way and manner that comply or go hand in hand with societal needs (Rokeach & Regan, 1980). As argued by Etzioni (1991: 4) '[i]ndividuals do render the final decision, but usually within the context of values, beliefs, ideas and guidelines instilled in them by others, and reinforced by their social circles'. The interaction between social behaviour and economic behaviour helps people to make choices and preferences founded on their values and sentiments. Empirically, researchers on human values (Feather, 1995; Rokeach, 1973; Schwartz, 1992, 1994) contend persuasively for the sentimental and guiding roles of values in all facets of people's lives. Rokeach (1973) adds to his structure of universal human values, terminal values (end-states existence) that will probably be self-oriented or community-oriented, interpersonal or intrapersonal in nature. This is very much consistent with the perspective of Etzioni (1991) as stated earlier. In simple terms, societal values have a portion in the values a person possesses. In other words, human values whether self-centred or community-centred[2] play a key role in the lives of individuals as well as how they observe things.

A substantial number of studies carried out on managers and consumers backs the contention that values underpin people's behavioural processes, and that they are relevant drivers of our attitudes, behaviors and choices (Egri *et al.*, 2004; Lawrence & Collins, 2004; Connor & Becker, 2003; Mercer, 2003; Agle *et al.*, 1999; Homer & Kahle, 1988; Richins & Rudmin, 1994; Connor and Becker, 2003; Williams & Hall, 2006). The findings of these studies highlight that there is a relationship between a person's values and the relevance she/he attaches to certain aspects of corporate responsibility. However, the presence of the relationship is dependent on the kind of values-whether it is individually-based or others-oriented.

The line of reasoning put forth by Etzioni (1991) and others (for instance, Rokeach, 1973) and the empirical observations from extant studies (for example, Iyer & Kashyap, 2009; Egri *et al.*, 2004; Lawrence & Collins, 2004; Connor & Becker, 2004; Mercer, 2003; Agle *et al.*, 1999; Homer & Kahle, 1988) support three main points. First, values do seem to have a relevant role to play in shareholders' stock-buying decisions. Second, shareholders possess both self-centred values and community-centred values. Third, compared with the number of studies on managers and consumers' values, values of individual shareholders has received little attention, and almost no or little effort has been made to examine shareholder's perception of corporate responsibility in regards to the values they possess. By simply accepting that shareholders are rational self-centred individuals who are only interested in maximizing their wealth, we need to find out more about their values and attitudes that ultimately induce their decisions on investments. Based on the theoretical perspective that values underpin behavioural processes and influence our choice of actions (Connor & Becker, 1994), we argue that as individual shareholders are constructive members of society, their choices and behavioural processes may be guided by their personal values. In addition, this set of values may be relevant to them as a people. Thus, it is also natural that they may wish to include these strongly held personal values in their investment decisions. Therefore, the paper aims to examine the values that incentivize and guide stockholders- not only in their lives, but also when they make decisions on investment.

Ghana is a particularly interesting case to analyse. Ghana has a small, and yet diverse population in terms of ethnic origin (culture). Logically, it is an ideal research setting in that it offers easy access to a representative community of stockholders with diverse backgrounds and cultural profiles but with related demographic background in other developing countries. This heterogeneity not only results in a differing set of personal values among Ghanaians, but also results in numerous factors that incentivize them to invest and choose companies they deem appropriate to invest. In addition, recent developments in the country have added a lively impetus to the concept of corporate social responsibility concerning personal values of individual shareholders and their investment decisions. The 2010 Securities and Exchange Commission's guidelines on corporate governance point to the fact that corporate social responsibility and the stakeholder perspective of corporate governance are incrementally receiving the required attention in Ghana. Particularly, there are ample revelations concerning an increment in the number of activities of Ghanaian shareholders and the sort of companies Ghanaian shareholders desire to invest in.

Consequently, this chapter aims to make both theoretical and empirical contributions. First, the findings add to the extant literature on behavioural finance and decision sciences in developing countries especially, African countries, which lag behind in a study of this nature. This dearth of literature is more visible in regards to the association between personal values of individual shareholders and their investment decisions in sub-Saharan African economies. Second, the chapter makes the effort to contribute to the extant literature on the corporate social responsibility by establishing that personal values of individual shareholders influence their behavioural processes (that is, concerning their investment decisions) and their choices (concerning the sort of companies they invest). The chapter proceeds as follows: a review of related literature on values; the methodology employed; and a presentation of our findings and conclusions.

LITERATURE REVIEW

Defining Values

While many definitions are associated with human values, the majority of them are of related construct: values are conceptions of the desirable (Agle & Caldwell, 1999). Clyde Kluckhohn (1951:395) defines a value as 'a conception, explicit or implicit, distinctive of an individual, or characteristic of a group, of the desirable which influences the selection from available modes, means, and ends of action. In addition, Williams (1970: 442) defines values as 'those conceptions *of desirable states of affairs* that are utilized in selective conduct as *criteria* for preference or choice or as *justifications* for proposed or actual behaviour'. Rokeach (1973: 5) states:

[A] person has a value and a value system. A value is an enduring belief that a specific mode of conduct or end-state of existence is personally or socially preferable to an opposite or converse mode of conduct or end-state of existence. A value system is an enduring organization of beliefs concerning preferable modes of conduct or end-states of existence along a continuum of relative importance.

Further, Connor and Becker (1994:71) identify values as '(abstract) desirable modes of conduct or end states of existence – with the notion of desirability referring to the exercise of choice'. Moreover, Schwartz (1994: 21) in his work on the motivational kinds of values identifies values as 'desirable, trans-situational goals, varying in importance that serve as guiding principles in the life of a person'. More so, Schwartz and Bardi (2001) argued that the important facet that differentiates among values is the sort of motivational object they put across.

Inferring from all these definitions, we argue that values are the very principles that guide us and in the same vein, they possess a powerful motivational constituent in them. Collective terms employed to define values vary among researchers. Rokeach (1973) refers them as 'enduring beliefs'' for Kluckhohn (1951) and Williams (1970) they are termed 'conceptions'; they are considered 'transsituational goals' by Schwartz (1994) and they are 'abstract ideals' by Chiu (2009). Based on the aforementioned definitions, we follow the definition of value by Chiu (2009:14) as 'A person's abstract ideals, varying in importance, which guide and motivate their choice of actions'.

Based on Chiu's definition of values we argue that shareholders' values are the abstract ideals that incentivize and guide their actions. While best behaviours are guiding values, supreme goals in life are motivational issues (Chiu, 2009). Even though everyone has a painstaking system of values, in any specific circumstance we may well set in motion only a part of our entire value system. The system has been akin to a repertoire of television stations where the one that is immediately showing our favourite television show is selected and the rest is neglected for the particular moment. For the individual stockholder in a share-buying circumstance, it implies only those values important to making investment decisions are consulted and their entire inducement is dependent on the potency and strength of the principal value. Consequently, the chapter will examine the motivational and guiding values that direct stockholders when they make decisions on stock-buying decisions.

Classifying Values

Rokeach (1973) in his Universal system of values postulates that the total amount of values is comparatively small and in the 36 values he selects, there is an equal split between instrumental and terminal values (see Table 1). But Schwartz (1992) finds in his work that there is an insignificant support for the idea that the instrumental-terminal categorization is a relevant foundation upon which individuals put in order their values. However, Rokeach's values system offers an important basis in appreciating the differing groupings of values.

Rokeach (1973) differentiates between instrumental and terminal values. The latter are ultimate goals that possibly can be self-oriented or community-oriented, intrapersonal or interpersonal oriented. The former are principles that guide conduct of demeanor and comprises both moral and competence values. Moral values possess an interpersonal spotlight which, when despoiled, stimulates a twinge of conscience or thoughts of guilt for misconducts. On the other hand, competence values are individual-oriented. Their infringement leads to thoughts of shame about personal insufficiency rather than thoughts of guilt.

Although Rokeach groups values into social, personal, moral and competence constituents, he appears to be a little fuzzy in grouping each of the values into their sub-groups. In a work of the value orientations of American managers, Weber (1990) sub-grouped each terminal value as either social or personal, and each instrumental value as morals or competence. As can be noticed in the grouping column in Table 1, results of Weber's study reinforce Rokeach's conceptualization of the types of values.

Other studies have tested the Universal human values system by Rokeach (1973). Based on a varimax factor analysis of Rokeach's 36 values, Munson and Posner (1980) discover six (6) terminal elements (personal gratification, self-actualisation, security, love and affection, social harmony, and personal satisfaction or contentedness) and four (4) instrumental elements (integrity, sociality, compassion and competence). The authors revealed an insignificant intersect between the instrumental and terminal elements. Out of the six terminal elements, 'social harmony' is associated with social interest and is defined as attempts dedicated to ensuring a serene and harmonized social ambiance. The other five (5) elements are more associated with personal interest than communal interest.

Schwartz and Bilsky (1987) categorize the differences among the 36 values into seven motivational areas. Their 'achievement', 'self-direction' and 'enjoyment' concern personal interest, while 'restrictive-conformity; and 'prosocial values' concern collectivist interests. The outstanding two domains-'maturity' and 'security'- concern both personal interest and collectivist interest.

Though Schwartz and Bilsky (1987) classified Rokeach's 36 values into seven motivational areas, Schwartz (1994) modified Rokeach's list and fashioned out a set of 56 specified values that are categorized under ten (10) motivationally different types of values. The ten value types included five that concern basically, individual or personal interests (that is, accomplishment, hedonism, stimulation, power, and self-direction) and three that concern essentially collectivist interests. The outstanding two (security and universalism) serve both interests (Schwartz, 1992). Further, these ten types of values are categorized into two bipolar dimensions.

Table 1. Terminal values and instrumental values

Terminal Values	Classification*	Instrumental Values	Classification*
A comfortable life (a prosperous life)	P	Ambitious (hard-working, aspiring)	C
An exciting life (a stimulating active life)	P	Broadminded (Open-minded)	C
A sense of accomplishment (lasting contribution)	P	Capable (competent, effective)	C
A world at peace (free of war and conflict)	S	Cheerful (joyful, light-hearted)	M
A world of beauty (beauty of nature and the arts)	S	Clean (tidy, neat)	M
Equality (brotherhood, equal opportunity for all)	S	Courageous (stand up for your beliefs)	M
Family security (taking care of loved ones)	P	Forgiving (willing to pardon others)	M
Freedom (independence, free choice)	P	Helpful (working for the welfare of others)	M
Happiness (satisfaction/contentedness)	P	Honest (truthful, sincere)	M
Inner harmony (freedom from inner conflict)	P	Imaginative (creative, daring)	C
Mature love (sexual and spiritual intimacy)	P	Independent (Self-sufficient, self-reliant)	C
National security (protection from attack)	S	Intellectual (reflective, intelligent)	C
Pleasure (an enjoyable, leisurely life)	P	Logical (rational, consistent)	C
Salvation (saved, eternal life)	P	Loving (tender, affectionate)	M
Self-respect (self-esteem)	P	Obedient (respectful, dutiful)	M
Social recognition (respect, admiration)	P	Polite (well-mannered, courteous)	M
True friendship (close companionship)	P	Responsible (reliable, dependable)	C
Wisdom (a mature appreciation of life)	P	Self-controlled (self-disciplined, restrained)	Neither

*Classification by Weber (1990), **P**-Personal, **S**-Social, **C**-Competence, **M**-Moral.

The first dimension addresses 'openness to change' (particular emphasis on own independent thought and action and favouring change) which is in contradiction with 'conversation' (that is, highlighting on submissive self-restriction, preservation of conventional practices and protection of stability). The second dimension contradicts 'self-enhancement' values (that highlight the quest of one's own comparative success and control over others) with 'self-transcendence' values (that pay a particular attention to both the tolerance of others as equals and regard for their welfare). Self-enhancement values correspond to motivational objectives of 'power' and 'accomplishment'. Self-transcendence values are situated on 'universalism' and 'benignity' objectives (Schwartz, 1994). The second dimension is of direct importance to examining shareholders' values in that it portrays that human nature is much multifarious than the self-centred, *Homo Economicus*.

The categorization of values into their important groups (Weber, 1990), elements (Munson & Posner, 1980) and areas (Schwartz, 1994) has a common pattern. Within an individual's value structure, there are values that are essentially self-centred, and some that concentrate on others. For example, self-respect, pleasure, salvation and an exciting life are self-centred values; and a world at peace, a world of beauty, equality and safeguarding the environment are community-based (others-centred) values. Any study that examines shareholders' values thus ought not to be founded on just a proposition that they only possess self-centred values, which serve primarily to incentivize them to strive for economic contentment via wealth maximisation. Undoubtedly, investing for monetary return is the fundamental aim for ordinary shareholders, but this only forms a part of the whole picture. The need to identify the other values they possess, such as those that are community-oriented is imperative. In this way, the entire picture or appreciation of what incentivizes and directs individual shareholders' in their stock buying decision-making processes will be unearthed.

Hofstede (2001) conducted analyses on the bipolar dimensions and highlighted that most individuals simultaneously possess numerous contrasting values. The contradiction that is present between self-centered and community-centered (others-oriented) values can be described by Kuran's (1995) 'divided self' and Etzioni (1998) '*I and We*' model. The 'divided self' addresses 'a self with multiple, possibly competing, inner needs' (Kuran, 1995: 43). In regards to the '*I and We*' model, people encounter continuous inner contradictions created by conflict between a part of the self that always want them to be selfish and another part that wants to undertake activities for the benefit of society (Etzioni, 1988). Hence, shareholders, as a people, can anticipate encountering such inner contradictions, making it possible for one of these two inner contradictions to win at a particular point in time.

The categorization of values into self-centred or other-oriented has a powerful influence on shareholders' values. Schwartz (1994) posits that there is a vague impression about the borderline between terminal and instrumental values in that they both put across a variety of motivational goals. Nevertheless, we believe that there is a need to detach motivational values from guiding values in the sense that they perform differing roles in the lives of shareholders. Motivational values are crucial goals in life an individual makes the very effort to attain, and guiding values are preferred or most wanted conduct (Chiu, 2009). Lewin (1952), who employs the value of fairness as an illustration, argues this assertion. The author states that fairness is not a target in that a person does not strive to arrive at fairness, but fairness guides one's conduct. In sum, the importance of shareholders' values to this study is both motivational and guiding, and can be grouped as either 'self-centred[3] or others-centred.

Review of Recent Empirical Literature on Personal Values

Proponents of alternative investment decision hypotheses cite the move of funds into 'Socially responsible' and 'ethical' investments as evidence that persons seek investments in line with their individual values (Beal & Goyen, 1998; Social Investment Forum, 2008; Pasewark & Riley, 2010). Socially conscious investors hold the belief that they can invest and make money as well as make a meaningful difference by willfully investing in businesses that contribute to a healthy environment, treat persons fairly, champion equal opportunity, produce safe and relevant products, and strive to foster world peace (Pasewark

& Riley, 2010; Inglehart, 2000; Inglehart & Baker, 2001). Investors wish to put their funds to work in a way that is more closely connected to their personal values.

There are a few studies which examine the association between personal values and investment decisions; most notably Gold and Webster (1990), Inglehart (2000), Inglehart and Baker (2001), Ryan (1994), Australian Securities Exchange (2007), Pasewark and Riley (2010), Mackenzie and Lewis (1999), and Nair and Ladha (2014). Gold and Webster (1990) carried out a gamut of works, which traces how personal values of New Zealanders influence their investment decisions. They found out that there was a paradigm move from 'prosperous life', which was the most relevant objective among New Zealanders in the mid of 1980s, to an unambiguous precedence of 'security and stability' in the late 1980s. Inglehart (2000) addressed the values move that had taken place for the past 25 years and found out that in almost all developed industrial countries, interests of individuals in making effort to maximise economic benefits are diminishing and their desire for the sustainability of the environment is soaring. Inglehart and Baker (2001) further found out that post-industrial economies, instead of being materialistic with increased prosperity, are incrementally showing concern for safeguarding the environment, issues concerning quality of life and self-expression.

In a study on how personal values of Americans influence their investment decisions, Ryan (1994) pointed out that, shareholders in America rate and rank 'equality for all' ahead of 'happiness' and 'prosperous life'. Further, 'equality for all' is ranked highly by shareholders. A probable explanation is that Americans have moved from 'materialistic' values to the 'self-expression' values found by Inglehart and Baker (2001). Pasewark and Riley (2010) investigated the role of personal values in investment choices in a controlled experimental context. The participants of the study were asked to choose an investment in a bond issued by a tobacco firm or a bond issued by a non-tobacco firm that offered an equal or sometimes lower yield. Their study revealed that when the rate of return on a tobacco-related investment surpasses the rate of return on a non-tobacco investment by 1%, the strength of participants concerns about the societal impacts of their investment decisions was particularly, relevant in determining investment decisions and choices. In a related study by Mackenzie and Lewis (1999) concerning investors willingness to hold socially responsible investments given ex post evidence of investment return, it was revealed that most shareholders (94.8%) would not shift funds away from socially responsible funds if returns were two percentage points lower. In addition, only 35.8% would decrease socially responsible investments if returns were five percentage points lower. This unambiguously reveals that conventional wealth-maximization methods, which overlook personal values of shareholders, rule out a germane factor that influences investment choices and decisions.

Further, a study in Australia in 2007 divulges that seven out of ten investors in Australia point out that concerning investing in shares; they prefer firms that are both socially and environmentally responsible (Australian Securities Exchange, 2007). In addition, a survey conducted by Capgemini and RBC on wealth management[4] in 2014, divulged that more than half of the high net worth people surveyed expressed social influence as extremely relevant and almost nine out of ten expressed it as relevant. Nair and Ladha (2014) in their attempt to identify underlying values of Indian investors that influence their investment decisions found out that, there is a belief among Indian investors that one's action can bring up a change in society. Thus, most of them invest not for economic gains (ie. materialism) but for non-economic investment goals such as safeguarding the environment, improving the welfare of other people, enhancing the condition of the ecosystem and so on.

While the above discussion supports the view that some investors are willing to invest for non-economic benefits, there is no specific evidence concerning what sort of personal values influence their investment decisions and choices. For instance, certain values could probably persuade a socially responsible environmentalist to invest in a 'green' fund. Nevertheless, the same fund could possibly have an insignificant appeal to a socially responsible investor concentrated on values related to Child labour. However, there is a consensus on the assertion that personal values of people influence their decisions. Therefore, we argue that since personal values of people influence their decisions, there is a very high possibility that personal values of investors or shareholders could have influence on their investment decisions.

RESEARCH DESIGN AND METHODS

In examining how individual shareholders investment decisions are influenced by their personal values, this chapter employed grounded theory design (Charmaz, 2008; Creswell, 2003; Strauss & Corbin, 1998). Grounded theory, in the context of this chapter, ascertain those personal values possessed by individual shareholders that help them in their share-buying decision making. In simple terms, this chapter wants to ascertain the personal values that inform shareholders in their investment decisions. This design leans on discovery, grounds the resulting theoretic model in respondent realities and directly connects direction to firms as to those personal values that influence individual shareholders in making share-buying decisions.

Setting, Sample and Participants

As it was difficult to get hold of shareholders in small unlisted firms, the study concentrated only on large publicly-listed firms on the Ghana Stock Exchange (GSE)[5]. Individual shareholders who have absolute control over what firms they desire to invest in were selected as the study's participants. Further, in order to acquire a diverse category of shareholders with differing views on the qualities that directors should possess, companies representing different industries (ie. energy, financial, healthcare, information technology, materials and so on) in Ghana were selected. This is relevant in that qualitative researchers are to pursue sources that can provide them with catholic and rich data, instead of selecting a sample representative of the population (Strauss & Corbin, 1990). All the companies listed on the GSE were contacted to seek their consent on their readiness to participate in this research. Eventually, ten companies listed on the GSE expressed their willingness to participate in this study. Of these ten firms, six (6) firms, three (3) firms and one (1) firm came from the financial, manufacturing and consumer discretionary sectors respectively. Since there was no compulsion concerning the selection of the companies, we focused on these ten companies for the first stage of this study. Letters were then sent to the ten companies to release the list of their shareholders. Subsequently, two largest individual shareholders (who are residents of Ghana) from each of the companies were purposively selected to participate in this study, which eventually amounted to twenty-seven (27) individual shareholders. Accordingly, the resulting theoretical sample comprised 20 individual shareholders. These twenty (20) individual shareholders who were interviewed consisted of different professionals: teacher, manager, lecturer, nurse, financial analyst, accountant, journalist, architect, civil servant, banker and private businessperson.

Data Collection

Data collection involved interviews. We employed written interviews using open-ended, semi-structured questions (Kerlinger & Lee, 2000; Smith & Osborn, 2008). Questions are obtained from relevant extant studies (theoretic sensitivity), and fashioned out to achieve the purpose of the study. Follow-up interviews with eight (8) of the participants provided us with new insights and helped us to pursue emerging themes.

Data Analysis

We conducted the analysis employing grounded theory coding process (Strauss & Corbin, 1990) - open, axial and selective. Noted as an overlapping and a recursive process, it is an extensive exercise of matching up and organising data into emerging groups and sub-groups on the basis of the personal values that influence the selected individual's investment decisions. Recognised as constant comparison approach, the researcher asked questions of the data throughout the research process thereby illuminating categorical and thematic connections (Strauss & Corbin, 1990). Sticking to this painstaking coding approach aids to appreciation of shared participant similarities and their interconnections. The result and theoretic abstraction, grounded in participant similarities, instills findings with explanatory power (Charmaz, 2008; Parry, 2003). Actually, the explanatory power of grounded theory lays in its conceptual generalization.

In this chapter, we analyzed all twenty (20) interviews by sentence to ensure research meticulousness and data saturation. Open coding identified 137 values which fall under four guiding values and seven motivational values, representing a gamut of expressions of values individual shareholders depend on when making investment decisions. Next, we began by sorting out meaning units into like-categories based on shared properties. We initially constituted 15 tentative themes, but after allowing data to sit for a certain period of time, rethinking and reviewing initial meaning units, we started to resort units, alter and merge themes to make more sense of the available data. We were in the axial coding stage, "making connections between a category and its subcategories" (Straus & Corbin, 1997). This stage involved placing meaning units within a group or category into subgroups or subcategories by seeking significant definition of detail among properties shared by them. Our result: eleven (11) comprehensive categories, each composed of a handful of painstaking subcategories. These eleven categories were thus, grouped under guiding values and motivational values. Ensuing is the selective coding stage.

During the selecting coding stage, the central category became known by placing findings into a narrative account (Strauss & Corbin, 1990). At this point, we made some adjustments and polished the categorical connections among the eleven (11) categories. To remain grounded in participant viewpoints, initial findings were shared with individual shareholders for feedback and conceptual amplification. Consequently, member check helped us to do minor adjustments to our findings. The findings were presented with some peers multiple times to discuss, share perspectives, and to create the environment for them to ask questions. This helped us to rework the paper over a certain period (about 11 months).

Trustworthiness

Research rigor is one of the hallmarks of the grounded theory strategy. We attained research rigor by sticking to a set of well-accepted techniques provided by Strauss and Corbin (1990). The application of this research rigor helped us to gain the theoretic sensitivity needed to gather a catholic technique to relevant issues, construct the research strategy, interpret various kinds of data and compose findings that contribute to the extant literature on behavioural finance and decision sciences. Table 2 presents research techniques that contributed to research trustworthiness.

FINDINGS

We present the notions and behaviour of the individual stockholders who voluntarily partook in this study. We first, provide a short description of the participants. The 20 individual stockholders who were interviewed represent a differing range of professions: teacher, manager, lecturer, nurse, financial analyst, accountant, journalist, architect, civil servant, banker and private businessperson. To relate the responses of the participants in this study, each respondent is identified with his/her profession.

The demographic characteristics of the respondents in this study are fairly similar and as a matter of fact, are quite indifferent from the profiles usually found in individual shareholders in many countries: they fall within the older age categories (at least 45 years old), and a significant number of them has tertiary and/or professional certificates.

Out of the 20 interviewees, four were couples: the retired civil servant and nurse, and lecturer and banker. Two couples among the four couples jointly own their stocks, and even though each couple participated in the interview session together, each one of them expressed his/her own notions and was thus, considered as an individual stockholder. Surprisingly, though the interviews were carried out simultaneously, it did not prevent any of the interviewees to express his/her individual opinion about the study at hand. In some few instances, they were in agreement especially, about the fundamental values they possessed, but in voicing out what their value priorities were there was a significant variation between the couples. For instance, a couple held fundamental values and yet they were at variance in their value priorities. Whiles the husband emphasized on living a world of beauty and peace, and admiring the natural environment and arts surrounding him, the wife expressed being healthy or sound in mind and body was her motivational value. Figure 1 presents the 11 (4 guiding values and 7 motivational values), shareholder values that were obtained from the responses of the twenty participants who took part in the study.

Others-Oriented

As discussed in the literature section, our explanation of this figure will be founded on the bipolar 'self-enhancement' vis-à-vis 'self-transcendence' dimensions propounded by Schwartz (1994). Self-enhancement is geared towards an individual's own success and control over others; the self-transcendence addresses both the acknowledgement of others as equals and regard for their well-being. Our analysis will deviate a little from Schwartz's dimensions by referring to the values that is geared essentially towards oneself

Table 2. Research trustworthiness: Techniques for all stages of the research

Stage	Means
Collection	Interviews
Analysis	Coding notes, member checks, procedural rigor
Findings	Peer debriefing, field notes, thick and rich descriptions, theoretical sensitivity

Figure 1. Individual shareholders' values

	Guiding Values	Motivational Values
Self-oriented	Honesty (integrity, trustworthiness) Fairness (respect and dignity to persons)	Contribution to society (via involvement) A world of beauty (beauty of arts and culture) A world at peace (free of conflict and war)
Others-oriented	Excellence (quality, ultimate ability) Independence (Self-reliance, Self-sufficiency)	A comfortable life (financially sound, satisfaction) Family security (Looked after loved ones) An active life (sound in both mind and body) A Prosperous life (well-off, wealthy)

as 'self-oriented' and the values that is directed towards others as 'others-oriented'. As can be noticed in Figure 1, of the guiding values, honesty and fairness fall under others-oriented and they represent principles of demeanor of individuals anticipated by society; independence and excellence are categorized under self-oriented and they correspond to the principles a person sets for her/himself. Further, among the seven motivational values, four fall under the self-oriented dimension (a comfortable life, family security, an active life and a prosperous life) and three fall under the others-oriented (a world at peace, a world of beauty and contribution to society).

Ensuing is an in-depth discussion of how each one of the values is obtained from the responses of the participated stockholders and is in accordance with the evidence presented in figure 1 above, discussing the guiding values first, followed by the motivational values.

Guiding Values

Honesty (Integrity, Trustworthiness)

The guiding value that was more often than not expressed by the majority of the study's participants (14 participants) is *honesty.* Aside from the use of the word 'honest' by the participants, other similar words such as 'integrity', 'trustworthiness', 'virtue', 'uprightness', 'sincerity' and 'honor' were also always mentioned. Rokeach's (1973) *honesty* is a clear guiding value for most of the study's participants; and it is regarded as possessing the goal of 'benignity' that is to safeguard and improve the well-being of individuals with whom a person is always in contact with (Schwartz, 1994). *Honesty* has a powerful element of others and it is a principle of demeanor anticipated by society. A majority of the participants, who partook in the interview session, expressed that they always took 'honesty' for granted-as their guiding value-and that they required it in other people. For example, 'you normally think good of individuals, that they should be honest', 'my principle in life is to always be honest in that I will not concern myself with something else'.

Fairness (Respect and Dignity)

Of the participants, thirteen considered *fairness* as a relevant guiding value. The accountant voiced out that she considers 'fairness and equality' as her guiding value. Seven others expressed the popular Biblical quote, 'do unto others as you would have them do unto you' as their 'Golden rule'. Fascinatingly, three of the participants (the journalist, the retired civil servant and the private businessperson) consider *fairness* as transcending beyond relating to persons: 'show kindness to other persons and abide by the laws guiding the land'; 'exhibit fairness when dealing with others, behave morally towards persons, and not doing something to hurt them or the community, environment or other living creatures'.

Other respondents' anticipation of *fairness* cropped up from their expressions that they are unhappy about certain activities of some firms or industries in Ghana in the sense that they hold the view that companies in Ghana are exploitative and manipulative. This result is supported by the finding of Chiu (2009) that individual shareholders-on moral grounds- do not invest in companies they consider as manipulative. The context of 'social justice' (rectifying injustice, care for the vulnerable) under the 'universalism' kind of values propounded by Schwartz (1994) entails *fairness*. Further, Ng (1982) questioned the exhaustiveness of Rokeach's value items by suggesting that values like social power, social justice, equality, self-persistency/determination ought to be included in Rokeach's value items to mirror the importance of culture. Social justice, described as 'fairness, without any discrimination' was employed by Allen *et al* (2002) in their study on consumer attitudes.

In a discussion of business and ethical issues, Solomon (1997) argues that the free market is dependent on respect and dignity for people, respect for pacts and respect for the rules that ensure fair play. Most of the study's respondents linked *fairness* to respect and dignity for persons, to their observance of the golden rule as well as to their position against exploitation and manipulation by companies or industries. *Fairness* is obviously an others-oriented principle.

Excellence (Quality, Ultimate Ability)

Four respondents selected *excellence* as one of their guiding principles. Of the four, three described *excellence* as working to the utmost of their capability or ability that is likened to competence, considered as a 'personal virtue' by Ryan (1994). The architect expressed his '..ultimate goal in life is excellence in all spheres of life….making the very effort to often carry out everything', and the retired civil servant expressed: 'To be content, I have to undertake the best job'. But interestingly the nurse associated *excellence* with quality. She expressed that:

Excellence encompasses everything. Of course, quality. Nobody goes kaput making the very effort to achieve quality. I mean quality, I am not saying fashion or clear quality, I mean true quality, three-sided quality.

Taking into consideration all the three comments, it appears more suitable to illustrate *excellence* as 'quality, best of one's capability or ability' than just 'competence'. In the first place, the principle of *excellence* appears to be related to 'a sense of accomplishment' put forth by Rokeach (1973) and Kahle (1983). But the explanation of excellence expressed by the study's participants conflicts with the qualification 'lasting contribution' suggested by Rokeach. Excellence in working, to the best of a person's capability, is in a way and manner likened to 'successful (accomplishing goals)' by Schwartz (1994) in his self-enhancement 'accomplishment' kind of value. Yet *excellence*, essentially self-oriented, seems to have wider application.

Independence (Self-Reliance, Self-Sufficiency)

Three participants consider *independence* as their guiding value. Responses of the teacher and financial analyst were: 'I do not want to be dependent on others when doing things'. And 'it's relevant for me to fetch for myself and also not being a burden on other persons or even the country. The factors of self-reliance and self-sufficiency observed in the two shareholders' responses are consistent with Rokeach (1973) and Schwartz (1994). As a 'self-direction' kind of value (Schwartz, 1994), *independence* is a self-oriented guiding principle.

Motivational Values

Comfortable Life (Financially Sound, Satisfied)

The majority of the participants mentioned a comfortable life as their motivational value. In general, the participants describe a comfortable life as being financially sound and satisfied, in variance with the comfortable (prosperous) life mentioned by Rokeach (1973). Particularly, comfortable life is regarded by the participants as 'fetching for myself without experiencing abject poverty'; 'having an adequate amount'; having a sound and comfortable way of life- in logical decorum'; and 'a complete modest-class lifestyle, ability to purchase my wants'. The respondents who seek out to this motivational value do not seem to be worldly driven; this is mirrored in the undemonstrative or unadventurous way and manner in which they express their views on houses, automobiles, vacations, and primarily their views on money.

The retired civil servant and the accountant expressed that they are still using more than a 10-year-old car in that they 'didn't need' a new car. The retired civil servant also said that he does not need 'a flashy house'. The accountant said she is not a fan of persons who are unreasonably materialistic: 'They put up buildings that are far bigger than what they probably need; they ride in cars that are far bigger than they probably could drive'. Another respondent, the lecturer, who considers himself as 'not materialistic', expresses he does not need 'bigger mansion'. Some respondents selected vacations as 'an additional benefit' in life. One couple, agrees that their vacation trips since they went on pension are as a result of them being 'economical and cautious'. Other participants share their views. Another couple said: 'We do not particularly want to do gigantic things, a little bit of overseas trip is nice'.

Money is considered by most of the participants as the means to acquire the things they need: financial self-dependence, ability to cater for their loved ones and secure pension. The following responses from the study participants offer additional insight into the sentiments of most of the participants that suggest money as the means to an end instead of an end by itself.

Money isn't my ultimate goal. I am not gluttonous. I do not want to be the wealthiest man in the morgue. (Architect)

My priority is to educate my family and not to have money in a safe. (Nurse)

I am not a motivated individual and I do not want to be the wealthiest person in Ghana (manager)

Money is mere financial thing, not having to be worried about it. The fundamental aim is to make the very effort to accumulate wealth so that if we are to undertake certain activities, we can (Private businessperson)

I would only try to chase wealth to the point where it cannot enable me to do things I previously used to do.....security is the ultimate (teacher)

I believe it is of greater benefit in my case that I do not have money. I always give out money to the needy. After all, that is how God wants us to live (banker)

From the aforesaid comments by the respondents of their worldly needs (cars, mansions, vacation) and their notion about money, a comfortable life simply means to be most properly rendered as financially sound and satisfied. Rokeach described *a comfortable life* as a prosperous life. We grouped a prosperous life as well-off and wealthy. In his philosophical discussion of individuals' goals, objectives and ultimate goals from the viewpoint of means and ends, Solomon (1997) lists *wealth* and *a comfortable life* in isolation. Schwartz (1992: 61) suggests 'wealth (material possessions, money)' as a value that falls under the motivational objective of 'power'. The bottom-line is that certain values do not depict sameness to the description across cultures (Schwartz & Bardi, 2001) thus even if only from the cultural viewpoint of shareholders, we can distinguish between *a comfortable life* (financially sound, satisfaction) and *a prosperous life* (associated with wealth)

Family Security (Looking After Loved Ones)

Twelve respondents expressed the importance for them to cater for people they have affections for. Some of whom said that it is one of their ultimate goals of their stock investment: 'to invest for their kids'; 'has got to cater for my retirement and family'; 'to educate my family'; 'I will finance their education'; and 'I want my son to have a comfortable life'. Inferring from the responses by the shareholders, it is suitable to employ Rokeach's (1973) *family security* (catering for the needs of loved ones). Schwartz (1992) described *family security* as a relevant king of motivational principle.

Seven of the twelve shareholders who regard *family security* hold the notion that they invest so that they can provide for their children and grandchildren in regards to their educational needs. With 18 respondents having undergraduate and postgraduate degrees, it is not surprising that they consider family member's education as important.

Contribution to Society (via Involvement)

Ten respondents expressed that contributing to society is one of their goals in life. Some expressed simply- 'assisting other people'; a participation in voluntary activities'; and ' I give too much to others but I think that is not enough… when I contribute my quota to communal activities, I feel involved in the community'. The manager expressed his view on contribution to community: 'I am always enthused about educating people on managerial issues because it can ameliorate their lives'. The respondents who have a strong desire to contribute to community want full participation in the activities concerning the community rather than just financially contributing. Contribution to community and society (via involvement) is pretty close to Rokeach's (1973) 'helpful' categorized as a 'benignity' motivational goal. This community-oriented or others-oriented motivational principle is akin to Solomon's (1997: 152) 'doing something for my community'. This result is consistent with the findings of

Nair and Ladha (2014) that one's action can bring up a change in society and therefore, most investors invest not for economic gains but for non-economic investment goals such as improving the welfare of other people.

An Active Life (Sound in Mind and Body)

Of the shareholders, six believe in enjoying *an active life* and they consider it as 'staying sound', 'being mentally sound' and 'remain sound in mind and body'. In regards to these, *an active life* comprises being sound in both state of mind and body, therefore this is the most suitable means of explaining what these shareholders require in life.

Even though health value is not added to Rokeach's list, it is expressed by Schwartz (1992: 61) that; healthy (not being sick physically or mentally)' as a 'security' kind of goal. The exclusion of health as a value by Rokeach has received critique from Kitwood and Smithers (1975: 177) who contend that 'anything to do with health, vitality' is a relevant principle. The argument from the authors is consistent with the responses from the participants who expressed that they always make the very effort to have sound mind and body.

A World of Beauty (Beauty of Arts and Nature)

A quarter of the participants acknowledge the beauty of nature and arts, which is the same as *a world of beauty* in Rokeach (1973) Universal human values. The retired civil servant requires 'to do things properly for the environment', and the accountant made mention of a certain company she does not want to invest in because their activities adversely affect the environment, without putting measures in place to mitigate the negative effects. The lecturer and his wife, the banker, expressed their love for the natural environment. The wife said: 'I see nature as something that is greater than me, and it is the element that renews my liveliness'. The husband supports this response: 'My environment is very relevant to my contentment'.

Those five participants' acknowledgement of the beauty of the world corresponds to Rokeach's explanation. This supports the finding of Inglehart (2000) that interests of individuals in making effort to maximise economic benefits are diminishing and their desire for the sustainability of the environment is soaring. Schwartz (1992) groups a world of beauty as a 'universalism' sort of motivational goal and also categorizes 'safeguarding the environment (preservation of nature)' under the same group. Even though safeguarding the environment will probably be considered as a suitable explanation of the expressions of the shareholders, we found it too off-putting because it excludes the artistic traits of both artificial and natural surroundings. *A world of beauty* is others-oriented as it is related to both caring about and sharing the beauty of arts and nature with other people.

A World at Peace (Free of Conflict and War)

Four of the respondents mentioned that a *world at peace* is a relevant motivational principle. In their comments: 'Even at the global level, it could be thrashed out without applying force', 'I am in support of peaceful world' and 'we share an African belief that we are one people and should desist from wars and conflicts'. These expressions are in consistent with *a world at peace* in Rokeach (1973), which falls under others-oriented.

A Prosperous Life (Well Off, Wealthy)

Of the 20 participants, only one desire wealth. The youthful private businessperson throughout the interview made mention of his desire to become wealthy so that he can have a comfortable life, which he measured by 'going on vacations every year, having gigantic mansions' among others. He said the following:

I do not feel comfortable when I say this, but I must confess that I consider financial soundness as a priority.... I hate thinking about poverty. I want to have more [starts to laugh], I want to have everything; posh cars, big mansions, extravagant holidays and so on. I think I can only derive happiness when these things are at my disposal though I believe strongly that riches do not always result in happiness.

Even though financial soundness is also mentioned by the participants who consider *a comfortable life*, their desire for satisfaction is much more relevant to them. This contrasts the businessperson's view on money that, money is his source of happiness. For instance, the lecturer, who is a well to do person and wants to continue, living comfortably, perceives happiness as:

My objective now is to have a happy marriage and wonderful family life, and to help people around me...This is what I derive my happiness from.

Self-expression by shareholders in regards to satisfaction or material things obviously distinguishes between *a prosperous life* and the drive for *a comfortable life.* This paper highlights that the two values do not serve the same purpose to these shareholders. As said earlier, both Solomon (1997) and Schwartz (1992) regard 'wealth (material possessions)' as a singular notion. *A prosperous life* (Well off, wealthy) offers a better explanation for those who clamor for just a comfortable life and it obviously a self-oriented value.

CONCLUSION

Concerning the role values play in influencing our behavioural processes and choices, the chapter examined the role values play in the share-buying decision-making processes using Ghana as the research setting. The study highlights that Ghanaian shareholders possess value priorities and that *honesty, a comfortable life* and *family security* play the most relevant role in their lives and investment decisions. Howver, most Ghanaian individual shareholders are influenced by *a comfortable life* when it comes to share-buying decision-making processes. Another startling observation that cropped up from the comparison between Ghanaian shareholders' values and the values of Rokeach (1973) is that to Ghanaian individual shareholders, *a prosperous life* and *a comfortable life* stand for differing motivational values. However, these two values have differing influences on Ghanaian shareholders' attitudes, which eventually do have influence on their share-buying decision-making processes, and firms they choose to invest.

The study contributes to existing literature on behavioural decision and decision sciences on shareholders' personal values and their investment decisions. The outcome of the research gives further support to the contention that individual shareholders invest in companies not only for economic gains but for social gains as well. In addition, this study does not only offer Ghanaian corporate authorities (directors and management) with a comprehensive insight into how their shareholders' personal values influence their investment decision-making processes, but it also shows the relevance Ghanaian shareholders attach to their choice of companies they are willing to invest in.

Further, the study divulges some practical implications. The results can inform corporate directors and managers what values are considered in investment decisions, and that it is not purely financial. With these results, they can be informed that while some financial values are important- it is just to live a comfortable life and not a prosperous life. This may influence these directors and managers to have a more long-run focus and to have more of a CSR focus by putting implementable measures in place to tackle corporate responsibility issues and to take up a responsibility for their CSR feat. Also, the results can be used for public policy in that if regulators find out that more CSR type information is important to investors, they might require additional CSR-type disclosures in financial statements.

Limitation and Areas for Future Studies

However, our research in tandem with its conclusion suffers from a limitation. We have employed only a small sample of 503 individual shareholders thus making it difficult to generalize the findings to other Ghanaian shareholders. However, with the application of inductive analysis, our findings can be generalized to other individual shareholders who share similar characteristics and views with those who participated in this study. The current chapter also offers fertile areas for future research. Our chapter has revealed that personal values of individual shareholders influence their investment decision-making processes. However, shareholders in Ghana are increasingly becoming aware of the concept of corporate social responsibility thus it opens an avenue for a research to be carried out on individual shareholders' personal values and their perception on corporate social responsibility in Ghana. Also, appreciating the qualities individual shareholders expect of corporate directors has become a relevant issue in corporate governance discourse. Hence, it serves a fertile ground for a future research.

REFERENCES

Agle, B. R., & Caldwell, C. B. (1999). Understanding Research on Values in Business: A Level of Analysis Framework. *Business & Society*, *38*(3), 326–387. doi:10.1177/000765039903800305

Agle, B. R., Mitchell, R. K., & Sonnenfeld, J. A. (1999). Who Matters to CEOs? An Investigation of Stakeholder Attributes and Salience, Corporate Performance, and CEO Values. *Academy of Management Journal*, *42*(5), 507–525.

Allen, M. W., Ng, S. H., & Wilson, M. (2002). A Functional Approach to Instrumental and Terminal Values and the Value-attitude-behaviour System of Consumer Choice. *European Journal of Marketing*, *36*(1–2), 111–135. doi:10.1108/03090560210412728

Australian Securities Exchange. (2007). *2006 Australian Share Ownership Study*. Available at http://www.asx.com.au/about/pdf/2006_australian_share_ ownership_study.pdf

Carroll, A. B., & Buchholtz, A. K. (2003). *Business and Society: Ethics and Stakeholder Management* (5th ed.). Mason, OH: Thomson Learning.

Chiu, P. (2009). *Looking Beyond Profit: Small Shareholders and the Values Imperative*. Gower Publishing, Ltd.

Clark-Carter, D. (1997). *Doing Quantitative Psychological Research: From Design to Report*. East Sussex, UK: Psychology Press.

Connor, P. E., & Becker, B. W. (2003). Personal Value systems and Decision making Styles of Public Managers. *Public Personnel Management, 32*(1), 155–180. doi:10.1177/009102600303200109

Egri, C. P., Ralston, D. A., Milton, L., Naoumova, I., Palmer, I., & Ramburuth, P. (2004), *Managerial Perspectives on Corporate Environmental and Social Responsibilities in 22 Countries*, Paper presented at the Academy of Management. 10.5465/ambpp.2004.13857751

Elster, J. (1985). Introduction. In J. Elster (Ed.), *The Multiple Self* (pp. 1–34). Cambridge, UK: Cambridge University Press.

England, G. W. (1967). Personal Value Systems of American Managers. *Academy of Management Journal, 10*, 53–68.

Epstein, M. J. (1992). The Annual Report: Report Card. *Business and Society Review*, (81): 81–83.

Etzioni, A. (1988). *The Moral Dimension: Toward a New Economics*. New York: The Free Press.

Etzioni, A. (1991). Socio-Economics: A Budding Challenge. In A. Etzioni & P. R. Lawrence (Eds.), *Socio Economics Toward a New Synthesis* (pp. 3–7). New York: M.E. Sharpe.

Feather, N. T. (1995). Values, Valences, and Choice: The Influence of Values on the Perceived Attractiveness and Choice of Alternatives. *Journal of Personality and Social Psychology*, *68*(6), 1135–1151. doi:10.1037/0022-3514.68.6.1135

Frankfurt, H. G. (1988). *The Importance of What We Care About: Philosophical Essays*. Cambridge, UK: Cambridge University Press. doi:10.1017/CBO9780511818172

Gold, H., & Webster, A. (1990). *New Zealand Values Today*. Palmerston North, New Zealand: Alpha Publications.

Hanson, D., & Tranter, B. (2006). Who are the Shareholders in Australia and What are Their Ethical Opinions? An Empirical Analysis. *Corporate Governance*, *14*(1), 23–32. doi:10.1111/j.1467-8683.2006.00481.x

Hofstede, G. (2001). Culture's consequences (2nd ed.). Thousand Oaks, CA: Sage.

Homer, P. M., & Kahle, L. R. (1988). A Structural Equation Test of the Value attitude- behavior Hierarchy. *Journal of Personality and Social Psychology*, *54*(4), 638–646. doi:10.1037/0022-3514.54.4.638

Hussey, J., & Hussey, R. (1997). *Business Research: A Practical Guide for Undergraduate and Postgraduate Students*. London: MacMillan Press. doi:10.1007/978-1-349-25262-6

Inglehart, R. (2000). Culture and Democracy. In L. E. Harrison & S. P. Huntington (Eds.), *Culture Matters: How Values Shape Human Progress* (pp. 80–97). New York: Basic Books.

Inglehart, R., & Baker, W. E. (2001). Modernization's Challenge to Traditional Values: Who's Afraid of Ronald McDonald? *The Futurist*, *35*(2), 16–21.

Iyer, E. S., & Kashyap, R. (2009). Non economic goals of investors. *Journal of Consumer Behaviour*, *8*(5), 225–237. doi:10.1002/cb.281

Kahle, L. R. (1983). *Social Values and Social Change: Adaption to Life in America*. New York: Praeger Publishers.

Kahle, L. R., & Kennedy, P. (1989). Using the List of Values (LOV) to Understand Consumers. *Journal of Consumer Marketing*, *6*(3), 5–12.

Kilby, R. W. (1993). *The Study of Human Values*. Lanham, MD: University Press of America.

Kitwood, T. M., & Smithers, A. G. (1975). Measurement of Human Values: An Appraisal of the Work of Milton Rokeach. *Educational Research*, *17*(3), 175–179. doi:10.1080/0013188750170302

Kluckhohn, C. (1951). Values and Value-orientations in the Theory of Action. In T. Parsons & E. A. Shils (Eds.), *Toward a General Theory of Action* (pp. 388–433). Cambridge, MA: Harvard University Press. doi:10.4159/harvard.9780674863507.c8

Krippendorff, K. (1980). *Content Analysis: An Introduction to Its Methodology*. Newbury Park, CA: Sage Publications.

Kuran, T. (1995). *Private Truths, Public Lies: The Social Consequences of Preference Falsification*. Cambridge, MA: Harvard University Press.

Lawrence, S., & Collins, E. (2004). *Sustainability Practices of New Zealand Business*. Hamilton, New Zealand: Waikato Management School, University of Waikato.

Lease, R. C., Lewellen, W. G., & Schlarbaum, G. G. (1974). The Individual Investor: Attributes and Attitudes. *The Journal of Finance*, *29*(2), 413–433. doi:10.1111/j.1540-6261.1974.tb03055.x

Lewin, K. (1952). *Field Theory in Social Science: Selected Theoretical Papers*. London: Tavistock Publications.

Lewis, A. (2002). *Morals, Markets and Money: Ethical, Green and Socially Responsible Investing*. London: Pearson Education.

Mackenzie, C., & Lewis, A. (1999). Morals and Markets: The Case of Ethical Investing. *Business Ethics Quarterly*, *9*(3), 439–452. doi:10.2307/3857511

Mercer, J. J. (2003). *Corporate Social Responsibility and Its Importance to Consumers* (Unpublished doctoral dissertation). Claremont, CA: Claremont Graduate University.

Muller, D. (2001, August), *Shareholders Project: A Quantitative Study of Shareholder Attitudes to Investment-related Issues*. Available at http://www. ethics.org.au/our_services/ projects/shareholders_project

Mumford, M. D., Connelly, M. S., Helton, W. B., Van Doorn, J. R., & Osburn, H. K. (2002). Alternative Approaches for Measuring Values: Direct and Indirect Assessments in Performance Prediction. *Journal of Vocational Behavior*, *61*(2), 348–373. doi:10.1006/jvbe.2001.1860

Munson, J. M., & Posner, B. Z. (1980). The Factorial Validity of a Modified Rokeach Value Survey for Four Diverse Samples. *Educational and Psychological Measurement*, *40*(4), 1073–1079. doi:10.1177/001316448004000435

Nair, A. S., & Ladha, N. (2014). Determinants of non-economic investment goals among Indian investors. *Corporate Governance*, *14*(5), 714–727. doi:10.1108/CG-09-2014-0102

Ng, S. H. (1982). Choosing Between the Ranking and Rating Procedures for the Comparison of Values Across Cultures. *European Journal of Social Psychology*, *12*(2), 169–172. doi:10.1002/ejsp.2420120204

Pasewark, W. R., & Riley, M. E. (2009). It's a Matter of Principle: The Role of Personal Values in Investment. *Journal of Business Ethics*, *93*(2), 237–253. doi:10.100710551-009-0218-6

Patton, M. Q. (1990). *Qualitative Evaluation and Research Methods* (2nd ed.). Newbury Park, CA: Sage Publications.

Richins, M. L., & Rudmin, F. W. (1994). Materialism and economic psychology. *Journal of Economic Psychology*, *15*(2), 217–231. doi:10.1016/0167-4870(94)90001-9

Rivoli, P. (1995). Ethical Aspects of Investor Behavior. *Journal of Business Ethics*, *14*(4), 265–277. doi:10.1007/BF00871897

Rokeach, M. (1973). *The Nature of Human Values*. New York: The Free Press.

Rokeach, M., & Regan, J. F. (1980). The Role of Values in the Counseling Situation. *The Personnel and Guidance Journal*, *58*(9), 576–582. doi:10.1002/j.2164-4918.1980.tb00454.x

Ryan, L. V. (1994). *Reconcilable Differences: Goals, Values, and Virtues of American Shareholders and Executives* (Unpublished doctoral dissertation). University of Washington.

Ryan, L. V., & Gist, M. E. (1995). *An Innovative Approach to Business-values Measurement*. Paper presented at the Sixth Annual Meeting of the International Association for Business and Society.

Schwartz, S. H. (1992). Universals in the Content and Structure of Values: Theoretical Advances and Empirical Tests in 20 Countries. *Advances in Experimental Social Psychology*, *25*, 1–65. doi:10.1016/S0065-2601(08)60281-6

Schwartz, S. H. (1994). Are There Universal Aspects in the Structure and Contents of Human Values? *The Journal of Social Issues*, *50*(4), 19–45. doi:10.1111/j.1540-4560.1994.tb01196.x

Schwartz, S. H., & Bardi, A. (2001). Value Hierarchies Across Cultures: Taking a Similarities Perspective. *Journal of Cross-Cultural Psychology*, *32*(3), 268–290. doi:10.1177/0022022101032003002

Schwartz, S. H., & Bilsky, W. (1987). Toward a Universal Psychological Structure of Human Values. *Journal of Personality and Social Psychology*, *53*(3), 550–562. doi:10.1037/0022-3514.53.3.550

Solomon, R. C. (1997). *It's Good Business: Ethics and Free Enterprise for the New Millennium*. Lanham, MD: Rowman and Littlefield Publishers.

Tippet, J. (2000). 'Investors' Perceptions of the Relative Importance of Investment Issues'. *Accounting Forum*, *24*(3), 278–295. doi:10.1111/1467-6303.00042

Tomer, J. F. (2001). Economic Man vs. Heterodox Men: The Concepts of Human Nature in Schools of Economic Thought. *Journal of Socio-Economics*, *30*(4), 281–293. doi:10.1016/S1053-5357(01)00100-7

Wärneryd, K. E. (2001). *Stock-market Psychology: How People Value and Trade Stocks*. Cheltenham, UK: Edward Elgar Publishing.

Weber, J. (1990). Managerial Value Orientations: A Typology and Assessment. *International Journal of Value Based Management*, *3*(2), 37–54. doi:10.1007/BF01732412

Williams, R. M. Jr. (1970). *American Society: A Sociological Interpretation* (3rd ed.). New York: Alfred A. Knopf.

Williams, T. G., & Hall, P. (2006). Personal Values and Management Priorities: Marketing Students vs. Top Level Marketing Managers. *Marketing Management Journal*, *16*(1), 104–124.

ENDNOTES

1 The Capgemini, RBC Wealth Management, and Scorpio Partnership Global High Net Worth Insights Survey is the industry's biggest and most comprehensive investigation of high net worth persona. The survey was conducted over January - February 2014.

2 Community-oriented, others-oriented and others-centered are used interchangeably throughout this inquiry.

3 Self-centred and self-oriented are used interchangeably in this study.

4 The Capgemini, RBC Wealth Management, and Scorpio Partnership Global High Net Worth Insights Survey is the industry's biggest and most comprehensive investigation of high net worth persona. The survey was conducted over January - February 2014.

5 The GSE was established by the Stock Exchange Act in October 1990. Trading commenced on its floor in November 1990. Currently, thirty-five firms (comprising consumer discretionary, Energy, Financial, Healthcare, Industrials, Information technology and Materials sectors) are listed on it. It is worth noting that the GSE is dominated by the financial sector.

Chapter 3

Chicken-Egg Dilemma for the Relationship Between Price and Volume in Borsa Istanbul

Sadullah Çelik
Marmara University, Turkey

Ayben Koy
Istanbul Commerce University, Turkey

ABSTRACT

This chapter empirically examines the relationship between stock prices and stock volumes for Borsa Istanbul, the only stock exchange in Turkey. The price-volume debate has been a common focus in the literature as the chicken-egg dilemma probably since the financial markets started to operate in a competitive manner. This chapter employs Borsa Istanbul and also considers the sector indices of the market. The authors employ frequency domain causality analysis of Breitung and Candelon and wavelet coherence analysis of Grinsted et al. with comparisons of the results for each sector. The findings show that (1) it is hard to argue for the existence of a distinct pattern in an emerging stock market like Borsa Istanbul; (2) there are several periods that propose challenges like the increasing foreign share, foreign shocks transmitted to the domestic market, and local effects; and (3) speculation is an inherit part of stock markets; and it is not possible to get rid of but rather act timely to minimize the adverse consequences and to deter market-wide repercussions.

INTRODUCTION

The financial markets have been at the forefront of economic research since the early days of economic analysis. Nonetheless, the number of studies has increased to unprecedented levels since the Great Recession (Moderation). The stock exchange market occupies the central role in economic and financial research due to its well-known effects on an economy (through real, financial, monetary and survey-leading indicators-variables).

DOI: 10.4018/978-1-5225-7399-9.ch003

Since the financial markets started to operate in a competitive manner, the efficient markets theory has been tested and discussed. According to this theory, prices of securities should fully reflect all available information. In the weak form of efficient markets theory, the information on past prices, past returns and transaction volumes have already been reflected in the market prices. However in the real world, the relationship between price and volume of a stock is established in the stock market. Most of the previous studies focused on the advanced economies and therefore the price-volume literature deviated from its actual route into the analysis of existence of bubbles, which is now another strand of research in this sophisticated financial market analysis. It is not the advanced economies but rather the emerging markets which seem to present golden opportunities for economic and financial research. The main motivation of this chapter is to test the relationship between price (market index) and volume for one of the most dynamic emerging stock markets, Borsa Istanbul (BIST-100) in Turkey.

The chapter aims to examine whether the dynamics of the relationship between price and volume for the Turkish stock market carry any relevant information for the bullish-bearish behavior using unconventional econometric methodologies. Moreover, this chapter assesses the effects of the price-volume relationship through the econometric analysis of all the sub-indices. Some of the sub-indices in BIST-100 carry a higher weight in the calculation of the index as they contain stocks which are traded in volumes that are a lot higher than the smaller sub-indices which include only a few stocks with limited amount of trade volumes. The crucial findings are the increase in speculation for the higher volume sub-indices and the unexpected characteristics that the main index displays during periods of tranquility.

THEORY: EFFICIENT MARKETS

According to the efficient markets (EM) theory, securities prices fully reflect all available information. While it is impossible to obtain an economic profit with the current information-based transactions, the market is efficient. In an ideal market, prices give the right signals for resource allocation so firms can make production-investment decisions while investors are making investment decisions on the assumption that market prices always reflect "full knowledge" (Fama, 1970). The basic assumptions of EM are "the lack of information costs" and "the lack of transaction costs". However, new approaches to the market activity hypothesis have been developed in the real world because of the existence of the transaction costs. In an efficient market, a large number of investors have obtained information on securities at low cost; the transaction expenses are low, the liquidity is high. Thus, economic, social and political changes are spread rapidly in the market and reflected in the prices of the securities which change in an independent and random manner.

The initial definitions of EM are based on the random walk model. This model argues that any asset price cannot be estimated with the past price information. All of the available information in the market has been reflected in the price, and the existing price in the market is the real price. The efficiency have been tested empirically in three forms, as "Weak Form Efficiency", "Semi-Strong Form Efficiency" and "Strong Form Efficiency" (Fama, 1970).

Weak Form Efficiency

Fama (1970) defines weak form efficiency as prices of the securities cannot be predicted by using past information on returns. The information on past prices, past returns and transaction volumes have already been reflected to the market prices. For this reason, it is not possible to gain abnormal returns in a weak form efficient market. In 1991, Fama added information such as dividend, interest rate, profit/price ratio, etc. to forecast models in the context of the weak form efficiency. The first applications to test the weak form efficiency are serial correlation analysis, run test and filter test. In the literature, the major efficiency tests applied in the 2000s included a variety of models such as purchasing power parity, cointegration analysis, causality tests, regression analysis, VAR analysis, VECH/E-GARCH, VECH/FIE-GARCH.

Semi-Strong Form Efficiency

In a semi-strong form efficient market, it is not possible to obtain abnormal returns with information both in weak form efficient market (return, price, dividend, interest rate) as well as publicly disclosed information. The probability of gaining abnormal returns by using the corporate information such as merger, acquisition, dividend or the macroeconomic data are tested in the semi-strong form efficiency. The semi-strong form efficiency tests are named as "event studies" following Fama (1991). In event studies, the efficiency of the market is tested by calculating the abnormal returns before and after the event day when the information has reached the markets.

Strong Form Efficiency

Investors in the strong form efficient market will not get abnormal returns by the arrival of some specific information before the information reaches to the market, in addition to the information of past prices, transaction volume, interest rates and publicly disclosed information. The employees of the company, senior officials or top-level employees in the public can not gain abnormal returns with specific information they have. A strong market is also preventing unfair profit formation. The strong form efficiency tests are named as "private information tests" following Fama (1991). Professional fund managers (mutual funds and pension funds) have been tested for private information in Fama's study.

In the 1980s studies, with the discovery of anomalies in the financial markets, efficient markets hypothesis became a theory that was debated, rejected, or retested with new definitions. There are two separate views among scholars in rejecting the market activity with the reason of the existence of anomalies and interpreting the anomalies differently in terms of the way they take place as the duration and the result.

LITERATURE REVIEW

In the widening literature on examining the price-volume relationship, the early research shows evidence that the volume tends to be larger when the market moves rapidly (Osborne, 1959). Employing different techniques, studies have diverse evidence for the relationship content for different markets, observation periods or different frequencies. To date, a number of studies have examined both the effect of volume on price changes and the correlation between these two variables (Among others, Brock and Lebaron, 1995; Andersen, 1996; Bohl and Helke, 2003; Tambi, 2005; Wang and Chin, 2003).

Granger and Morgenstern (1963) is the primary research using cross-spectral analysis on the SEC composite index and total NYSE volume. Both Granger and Morgenstern (1963) and the following Granger, Morgenstern and Godfrey (1964) papers could not find any statistically significant relationship between price and volume. However, Ying (1966) improved the theory by some striking results as, (1) a small (large) volume is usually accompanied by a fall (rise) (2) a large increase in volume is usually accompanied by either a large rise in price or a large fall in price and (3) a large volume is usually followed by a rise in price.

A complementary model was introduced by Copeland (1976) and called the probabilistic model. It tried to explain the cause of the price-volume relationship according to the information flow to the market. If many of the investors evaluate the new information in the same direction, a highest price change will occur following the highest volume. The direction of this highest price change could be up or down.

Among many others, Karpoff (1987) is the seminal paper that summarizes the four reasons which led to the immense research on the relationship between price and volume of stocks in many markets through different models. First, it is possible to determine the underlying characteristics of the market when the price-volume relationship could be modelled, given that significant outcomes are obtained through econometric analysis. Second, the magnitude and sign of the relationship would be helpful especially when the stocks of the large firms that dominate the outcomes in the stock market are considered as event studies (Beaver, 1968; Kiger, 1972; Morse, 1981). Volume has been considered as the sum of the differences in traders' reactions to an announcement or might be a noisier indicator of information variables (Kim and Verrecchia, 1991). Third, price-volume relationship could provide useful information about the effects of the speculative price movements and their probability distributions. Last, spot markets-future markets debate could be enhanced through the empirical findings from the price-volume relationship.

The role of volume in prediction of stock prices is another studied area in literature (Bülmann, 1998; Lee and Swaminathan, 2000; Wang and Chin, 2003). Bülmann (1998), finding asymmetric relationship between return and volume, made predictions for extreme events in Dow Jones and NYSE. Lee and Swaminathan (2000) found that past trading volume predicts both the magnitude and the persistence of future price momentum over longer horizons for US market. Wang and Chin (2003) showed that low-volume stocks outperform high-volume stocks in terms of predictions for the future values of their prices for the Chinese stock market.

Qi (2001) found that the correlation associated with positive return and volume was greater than the correlation between negative return and volume for Argentina, Chile, Malaysia, Mexico, Singapore and Thailand by the threshold model.

In several studies, the trading volume, which is supposed to include the arriving information to the market, is included in the GARCH models for analyzing the "Mixture of Distribution Hypothesis" (MDH). In such models, trading volume is used as an explanatory variable for GARCH effects (Andersen, 1996, Bohl and Helke, 2003; Lucey, 2006). Andersen (1996) modelled the daily data of five stocks in the New York Stock Exchange (NYSE) between 1973 and 1991. It is assumed in the study that each information arrival causes a price discovery phase which includes dynamic learning, and each price discovery phase is followed by a stabilization phase. There is contrary evidence in literature if there is any decreasing estimation power of volume focused on explaining the strong conditional heteroskedasticity in stock returns. Using 20 Polish stocks (Bohl and Helke, 2003), 46 Irish stocks (Lucey, 2006) and 20 stocks in the Major Market Index (MMI) (Fleming et al. 2005) could not find a significant effect of volume in terms of heteroskedasticity.

In the causality context, there have been significant evidence on the existence of both unidirectional and bidirectional causal relationships between stock returns and volume. Samples used in many studies focus on one or more markets. Especially the analysis of samples with large number of stock markets clearly show that there are different results in different markets (Chen et al. 2001; Lee and Rui, 2002; Gunduz and Hatemi-J. 2005; Ajayi et al. 2006; Kamath and Wang, 2006, Pisedtasalasai and Gunasekarage, 2007). Unidirectional relationship is found for eight developed markets in Chen et al. (2001), two developed markets in Lee and Rui (2002), two markets in Gunduz and Hatemi-J. (2005) and six European markets in Ajayi et al. (2006). Same studies find less evidence on bidirectional relationships for the countries as Switzerland, the Netherlands, Canada and Hong Kong (Chen et al. 2001), Hungary and Poland (Gunduz and Hatemi-J. 2005) and Denmark, Portugal and Turkey (Ajayi et al. 2006).

Chuang et al. (2009) analyzed the casual relationship between stock return and volume based on quantile regressions and found that the causal effects of volume on return were usually heterogeneous across quantiles and those of return on volume were more stable. Additionally, an increase in the dispersion of return distribution has been found with lagged volume. Anifowose and Suleiman (2013) found unidirectional causality from stock return to trading volume for Nigerian stock market. Darwish (2012) found bidirectional relationship for Palestine Stock Exchange using GARCH and GC methodologies.

Some of the studies on the price-volume relationship for Borsa Istanbul are presented in Table 1. In general, the unidirectional causality from stock price to volume is the major finding through Granger Causality (GC) analysis. Even though the periods and indices (BIST-100 and Banking) used have been different, the results are similar in Gökçe (2002), Elmas and Yıldırım (2010) and Taş et al. (2016). Also, simple regression analysis (Kayalıdere, 2009 and Taş et al. 2016), GARCH models (Kıran, 2010 and Acar et al. 2010), Bounds testing by Pesaran et al. (2001), and ARDL (Okuyan and Erbaykal, 2011) are some other methodologies used to examine the price-volume relationship. For example, a negative relationship from volume to volatility is detected in a study using GARCH models (Acar et al. 2010) and a positive relationship is the finding in another one using a different methodology (Okuyan and Erbaykal, 2011). Besides applying different methodologies, monthly observations for two different indices for the same period are used in Acar et al. (2010) and Okuyan and Erbaykal (2011).

METHODOLOGY

The econometric methods employed are by Breitung and Candelon (2006) who propose a frequency domain (FD) causality test to determine whether the variables cause each other in all/some/any possible frequencies and the wavelet coherence analysis derived by Grinsted et al. (2004). These recently developed techniques are used to examine the relationships between variables in a non-linear world spectrum. Thus, they are econometric tools that are well equipped while helping us to assess the dynamics of the relationships between variables of interest better than conventional and rather ineffective measures.

Granger Causality in Frequency Domain

Granger causality (GC) is based on prediction with using past terms of variables. In GC, if a signal X_1 "Granger-causes" a signal X_2, then past values of X_1 should contain information that helps predicting X_2. The formulation of GC is based on linear regression modeling of stochastic processes (Granger, 1969).

FD is used to describe the domain for analysis of mathematical functions or signals according to frequency. One of the major concepts in the analysis is the transformation which is used to convert a time domain function to a FD function. Breitung and Candelon (2006) build a test for GC in the FD that is based on the Fourier transform of initial time series. This test investigates causal linkages at different frequencies. It is possible to capture the "causal clusters" in the time domain by Breitung and Candelon (2006)'s test.

Table 1. Summary of the literature on Borsa Istanbul

	# and Frequency of Observations	Period	Methodology	Result
Gökçe (2002)	IMKB-100, 3251 daily observations	1988-2001	GC	Unidirectional causality from stock prices to volume
Kayalıdere (2009)	IMKB-100, 1845 daily observations	2001-2008	Regression	Negative price changes are more sensitive to volume against positive price changes
Elmas and Yıldırım (2010)	IMKB Banking Index, Different # of daily observations	Three different periods 2001, 2006, 2008	GC	Unidirectional causality from stock prices to volume
Kıran (2010)	BIST100, 4612 daily observations	1990-2008	GARCH, TGARCH	The effect of trade volume on return volatility is significant in the statistical sense but not positive
Acar *et al.* (2010)	BIST100, 156 monthly observations	1997-2009	GARCH, VAR, GC	Long-term, negative relation running from trading volume to volatility Bilateral GC between return volatility and trading volume
Okuyan and Erbaykal (2011)	BISTTUM, 150 monthly observations	1997-2009	Bounds testing by Pesaran *et al.* (2001), ARDL	A positive relationship has been detected between the volume of foreign transactions and stock prices
Taş et al. (2016)	BIST100, 3700 daily observations	2000-2014	Regression, Granger, VAR, Johansen	Unidirectional causality from stock prices to volume

By using a Fourier transformation to VAR (p) model for x and y series, the Geweke's measure of linear feedback from y to x at frequency ω is defined as[1]:

$$M_{y\to x}(\omega) = \log\left[\frac{2\pi f_x(\omega)}{\left|\psi_{11}(e^{-i\omega})\right|^2}\right] = \log\left|1+\frac{\left|\psi_{12}(e^{-i\omega})\right|^2}{\left|\psi_{11}(e^{-i\omega})\right|^2}\right| \tag{3}$$

If $\left|\psi_{12}(e^{-i\omega})\right|^2=0$, then the Geweke's measure will be zero, and y will not Granger cause x at frequency ω. It is presented in Breitung and Candelon (2006) by reformulating the relationship between x and y in VAR equation:

$$x_t = \alpha_1 x_{t-1} + \ldots\ldots + \alpha_p x_{t-p} + \beta_1 y_{t-1} + \ldots\ldots + \beta_p y_{t-p} + \varepsilon_{1t} \tag{4}$$

The null hypothesis tested by Geweke, $M_{y \to x}(\omega) = 0$, corresponds to the null hypothesis of $H_0 : R(\omega)\beta = 0$ where β is the vector of the coefficients of y and x.

$$R(\omega) = \begin{bmatrix} \cos(\omega)\cos(2\omega)..........\cos(p\omega) \\ \sin(\omega)\sin(2\omega)............\sin(p\omega) \end{bmatrix}$$

This study uses Breitung and Candelon (2006) version of Geweke (1982) to be able to use a usual F-statistics. Breitung and Candelon (2006) simplify the Geweke's null hypothesis to test causality in FD.

Wavelet Analysis

The wavelet transform decomposes a time series in terms of some elementary functions, $\psi_{\tau,s}(t)$. Those functions are derived from a time-localized mother wavelet $\psi(t)$ by translation and dilation (see for example, Percival and Walden (2000)). Wavelets grow and rot in a finite time period, because they have limited energy and intensive support. They are defined as

$$\psi_{\tau,s}(t) = \frac{1}{\sqrt{s}}\psi\left(\frac{t-\tau}{s}\right) \tag{5}$$

In the formula, τ is the time position (translation parameter), s is the scale (dilation parameter), which is related with the frequency, and $\frac{1}{\sqrt{s}}$ is a normalization factor to ensure that wavelet transforms are comparable across scales and time series. To be a mother wavelet, $\psi(t)$, must fulfill certain criteria: it must have zero mean, $\int_{-\infty}^{+\infty} \psi(t)dt = 0$, its square integrates to unity, $\int_{-\infty}^{+\infty} \psi(t)^2 dt = 1$, which means that $_\psi(t)$ is limited to an interval of time; and it should also satisfy the so-called admissibility condition,

$$0 < C_\psi = \int_o^{+\infty} \frac{\left|\psi(\omega)\right|^2}{\omega} d\omega < +\infty$$

where $\hat{\psi}(\omega)$ is the Fourier transform of $\psi(t)$, that is, $\hat{\psi}(\omega) = \int_{-\infty}^{+\infty} \psi(t)e^{-i\omega\tau}dt$.

Torrence and Compo (1998) developed the approaches to estimating the cross-wavelet power, the cross wavelet coherency, and the phase difference. The phase difference can be evaluated as local variance, covariance and the time lag in the time-frequency space. The term "phase" implies the position in the pseudo-cycle of the series as function of frequency. "on the delay, or synchronization, between oscillations of the two time series (Aguiar-Conraria et al. 2008) is the given relation by the phase difference.

The methodological discussion in this chapter is based on the continuous wavelet transform which is suitable or preferable for orthogonal wavelet bases. The framework of wavelet coherence (WTC) is borrowed from Grinsted et al. (2004).[2]

Wavelet Coherence (WTC)

Coherence has importance in dealing with fluctuating quantities. If the degree of coherence between X and Y is close to its maximum value of unity, it indicates the linear transformation relation between two variables. The degree of coherence of two time series x(t) and y(t) with zero time-average values, is magnitude of their temporal correlation coefficient. The temporal correlation coefficient ranges from 0 (no correlation; completely incoherent) to 1 (perfect correlation; completely coherent). The caveat is that this correlation may not be contemporaneous, but may involve a lead or a lag, being the magnitude measured by the phase lead.

When compared with the cross wavelet power, the wavelet coherency has the advantage of being normalized by the power spectrum of the two time-series. In analogy with the concept of coherency used in Fourier analysis, given two time-series x(t) and y(t) one defines their wavelet coherency as:

$$R_{xy}(\tau,s)=\frac{\left|S\left(W_{xy}\left(\tau,s\right)\right)\right|}{\sqrt{S(\left|W_{xx}\left(\tau,s\right)\right|S(\left|W_{yy}\left(\tau,s\right)\right|}} \tag{10}$$

where S denotes a smoothing operator in both time and scale (Soares, 2010) . The cross-wavelet coherence gives an indication of the correlation between rotary components that are rotating in the same direction as a function of time and periodicity. It can be defined as the ratio of the cross-spectrum to the product of the spectrum of each series, and can be thought of as the local correlation between two CWTs (Mandelo-Pinho, 2012).

Sample and Data

The data set is defined as follows:

Main Index

BIST-100: 1995 – 2000; (6 Jan 1995 – 22 Dec 2000, weekly & in LOGs)
BIST-100: 2001 – 2007; (5 Jan 2001 – 28 Dec 2007, weekly & in LOGs)
BIST-100: 2008 – 2017; (4 Jan 2008 – 23 Jun 2017, weekly & in LOGs)

Sub Indices

2010 – 2017 (4 Jan 2010 – 23 Jun 2017, weekly & in LOGs)

These are in three groups and are defined as follows:

Group 1: Weekly volume over 10 billion TL per stock: Banking, Transportation, Financials, Telecommunications, Metal, Holding and Investment, Sports, Real Estate, Services.
Group 2: Weekly volume between 5.46 and 9.9 billion TL per stock: Tourism, Wood & Paper & Printing, Industrials, Chemicals, Textiles & Leather, Metal Products and Machinery, Leasing & Factoring

Group 3: weekly less than 5.45 TL per stock: Insurance, Whole Sale & Retail, Food and Beverage, Minerals, Technology, Electricity, Information Technology

The statistical data on the variables is in Table 2 and Table 3.

Validity of the Research

The validity of the research is already built in the econometric methodologies that are used to test the effectiveness of the stock exchange movements. In a non-linear world, using linear techniques would result in flawed outcomes and it has been a long time now that most of the variables of interest in economics, finance, business world and presumably most other social sciences have been categorized as non-linear in nature. Hence, to prevent the undesired outcomes that would only provide confusing results with no clear-cut answers to the questions that have been academically studied over several decades, this study prefers to choose the path that should lead to some answers that would be crucial and background for future studies.

Limitations of the Study

There are two main limitations of this study which are not really expected to be very effective on the empirical outcomes. The first of these is the span of data not being very long as it runs from January 2010 till June 2017. The data is weekly and there are 391 observations. This is a number which seems to be within the limits of plausible statistical and econometric analysis. On the other hand, the second limitation is the unavailability of comparison with similar studies as there is hardly any which uses unconventional methods to test the statistical significance of the well-known price-volume relationship.

Table 2. A short summary for different periods in BIST-100 stock exchange

<table>
<tr><th>Variables</th><th colspan="2">1995-2000</th><th colspan="2">2001-2007</th><th colspan="2">2008-2016</th></tr>
<tr><td>% Foreign
(Equity Investment)</td><td colspan="2">1995 – 22
1996 – 23
1997 – 33
1998 – 30
1999 – 55
2000 – 73</td><td colspan="2">2001 - 49
2002 - 51
2003 – 54
2004 - 71
2005 – 65
2006 – 65
2007– 72</td><td colspan="2">2008 – 67
2009 – 67
2010 – 66
2011 – 62
2016 - 63
2017 June – 67</td></tr>
<tr><td>Borsa Istanbul
Average Daily Trading Volume</td><td colspan="2">1995 Average
0,0095 (Billion TL)
0,2084 (Billion USD)
2000 Average
0,45 (Billion TL)
0,73 (Billion USD)</td><td colspan="2">2001 Average
0,375 (Billion TL)
0,324 (Billion USD)
2007 Average
1,5 (Billion TL)
1,2 (Billion USD)</td><td colspan="2">2008 Average
1,2 (Billion TL)
1,0 (Billion USD)
2016 Average
3,99 (Billion TL)
1,5 (Billion USD)</td></tr>
<tr><td>Number of Companies</td><td colspan="2">2000 – 201</td><td colspan="2">2007 – 332</td><td colspan="2">2016 - 405</td></tr>
<tr><td></td><td>Number of Stocks</td><td>Volume (000 TL)</td><td>Number of Stocks</td><td>Volume (000 TL)</td><td>Number of Stocks</td><td>Volume (000 TL)</td></tr>
<tr><td>BIST100</td><td>100</td><td>283,6</td><td>100</td><td>4676,58</td><td>100</td><td>11955,38</td></tr>
</table>

Table 3. A summary information for sub-indices of BIST-100 for the period of study

SUB-INDICES	Number of Stocks (23/06/2017)	Average Weekly Trading Volume (mil TL) 04/01/2010 – 23/06/2017	Average Weekly Trading Volume Per Stock (mil TL) 04/01/2010 – 23/06/2017
Banking	12	346030,59	28835,88
Transportation	7	180988,47	25855,50
Financials	84	2026217,19	24121,63
Telecommunications	2	42210,46	21105,23
Metal	16	284626,16	17789,14
Holding and Investment	36	505890,33	14052,51
Sports	4	54112,61	13528,15
Real Estate	26	295448,18	11363,39
Services	53	537875,96	10148,60
SUB-INDICES	Number of Stocks (23/06/2017)	Average Weekly Trading Volume (mil TL) 04/01/2010 – 23/06/2017	Average Weekly Trading Volume Per Stock (mil TL) 04/01/2010 – 23/06/2017
Tourism	6	55369,87	9228,31
Wood Paper Printing	13	97587,44	7506,73
Industrials	147	1071290,15	7287,69
Chemicals	23	164451,61	7150,07
Textiles and Leather	14	94488,87	6749,21
Metal Products and Machinery	27	168192,33	6229,35
Leasing and Factoring	4	21962,07	5490,52
SUB-INDICES	Number of Stocks (23/06/2017)	Average Weekly Trading Volume (mil TL) 04/01/2010 – 23/06/2017	Average Weekly Trading Volume Per Stock (mil TL) 04/01/2010 – 23/06/2017
Insurance	5	27220,01	5444,00
Wholesale and Retail	18	85280,00	4737,78
Food and Beverage	21	72613,45	3457,78
Minerals	26	83252,81	3202,03
Technology	15	44938,08	2995,87
Electricity	6	8012,41	1335,40
Information Technology	14	3810,87	272,20

FINDINGS AND EVALUATIONS

In the first part, we introduce our findings using the FD analysis and in the second part, we enhance our findings employing the wavelet coherence methodology.

Frequency Domain Granger Causality

Figures in the Appendix show the FD GC analysis results using price and volume analysis. The critical values are represented by the red (5%) and black (10%) lines. Green curves show FD GC from price to volume while blue ones represent the FD GC from volume to price.

For the BIST-100 index:

1995-2000: The main significant relationship is price causing volume in the long-run at 5% level.

2001-2007: Price is causing volume in all maturities (at 5% in the long and short-run and at 10% in the medium-term).

2008-2017: Price is causing volume in the long-run at 5% level and in the medium term at 10% level whereas volume causes price only at 10% level in the long-run.

For the first group of sub-indices:

- **Financials:** Volume is causing price in the long-run at 10% level.
- **Real Estate:** Volume is causing price in the medium-term at 10% level.
- **Transportation:** Volume is causing price in the medium-term and in the long-run at 5% level.

Figure 1. FD GC: BIST100

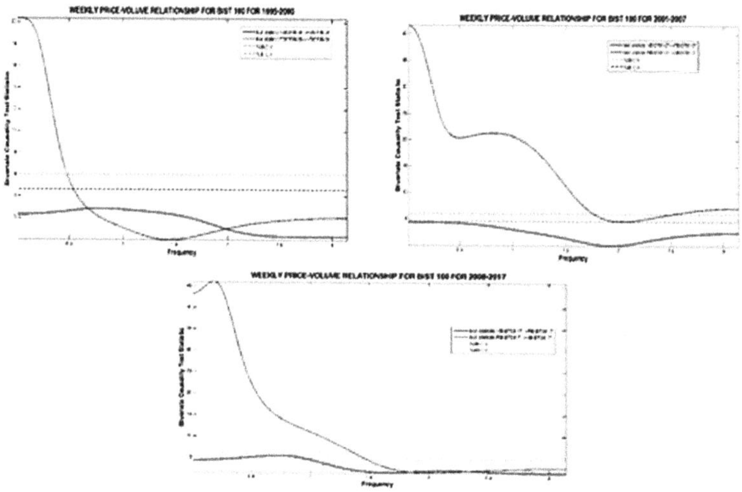

- **Banking:** Price is causing volume in the medium-term at 5% level and in the long-run at 10% level.
- **Metal:** Price is causing volume in the long-run and short-run at 5% level.
- **Telecommunications:** Price is causing volume in the long-run at 5% level.
- **Holding and Investment:** Price is causing volume in the medium-term at 5% level and in the long-run at 10% level. Volume is causing price in the medium-term at 5% level.
- **Services:** Price is causing volume in the long-run at 5% level. Volume is causing price in the medium-term and short-run at 5% level.
- **Sports:** Price is causing volume at all frequencies at 5% level. Volume is causing price in the long-run and medium-term at 10% level.

For the second group of sub-indices:

- **Chemicals, Metal Products & Machinery, Textiles & Leather and Tourism:** Price is causing volume in the long-run at 5% level and in the medium-term at 10% level.
- **Industrials:** Price is causing volume in the long-run and medium-term at 5% level.
- **Wood, Paper and Printing:** Price is causing volume in the long-run at 5% level and in the medium-term at 10% level. Volume is causing price in the medium-term and long-run at 5% level.
- **Leasing and Factoring:** No significant relationship

For the third group of sub-indices:

- **Wholesale & Retail:** Volume is causing price in the medium-term and in the long-run at 5% level.
- **Electricity and Minerals:** Price is causing volume in the long-run at 5% level and in the medium-term at 10% level.
- **Food & Beverage:** Price is causing volume in the long-run and in the medium-term at 5% levels.
- **Technology:** Price is causing volume in the long-run at 5% level and in the short-run at 10% level.

Figure 2. FD GC; Financials, Real Estate, Transportation, Banking

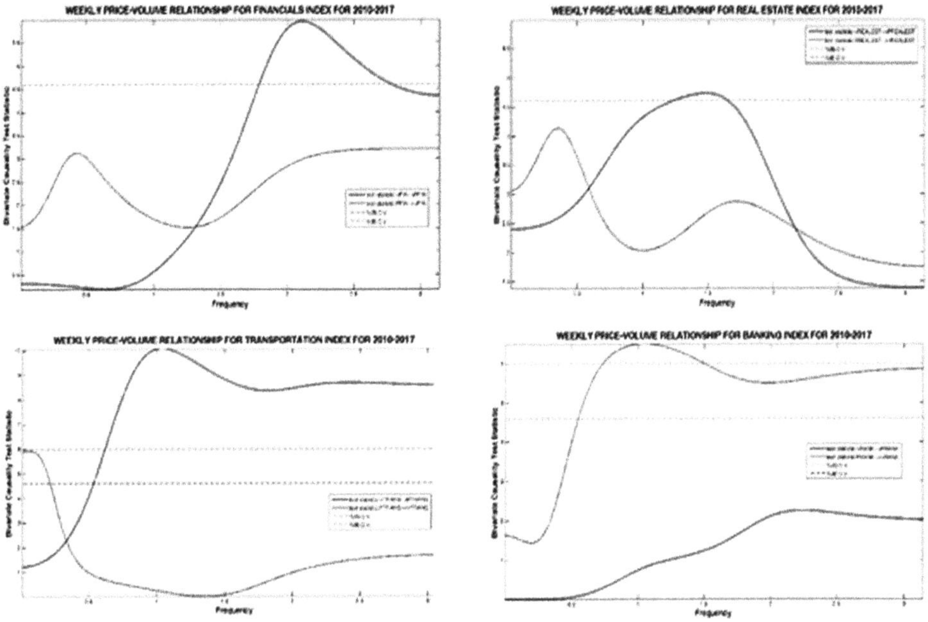

- **Information Technology:** Price is causing volume in the long-run at 5% level. Volume is causing price in the short-run at 5% level.
- **Insurance:** No significant relationship

Wavelet Coherence Analysis

The wavelet coherence is used to identify both frequency bands and time interval within which two variables are correlated.

It displays the coherence between price and volume of indices. The thick black contour designates the 5% significance level estimated from Monte Carlo simulations using phase randomized surrogate series. The cone of influence, which indicates the region affected by edge effects, is also shown with a light black line. The color code for coherency ranges from blue (low coherency-close to zero) to red (high coherency-close to one). The phase difference between the price and volume is indicated by arrows. Arrows pointing to the right mean that the variables are in phase. To the right and up price is lagging and to the right and down, price is leading the volume. Arrows pointing to the left mean that the variables are out of phase. Hence, they aren't on the same side of the business cycle (one is booming and the other is busting). To the left and up is where price is leading and to the left and down is where the price is lagging. In phase case indicates that variables are having cyclical effects on each other whereas out of phase or anti-phase underlines the case where variables are having anti-cyclical effects on each other.

For the BIST-100 index:

1995-2000: Price and volume lead each other at higher frequencies and are usually in phase during 1996 January-1999 May. Volume is leading price in a weekly period and price is leading volume over a week (both cases also in phase).

Figure 3. FD GC; Metal, Telecommunications, Holding & Investment, Services, Sports

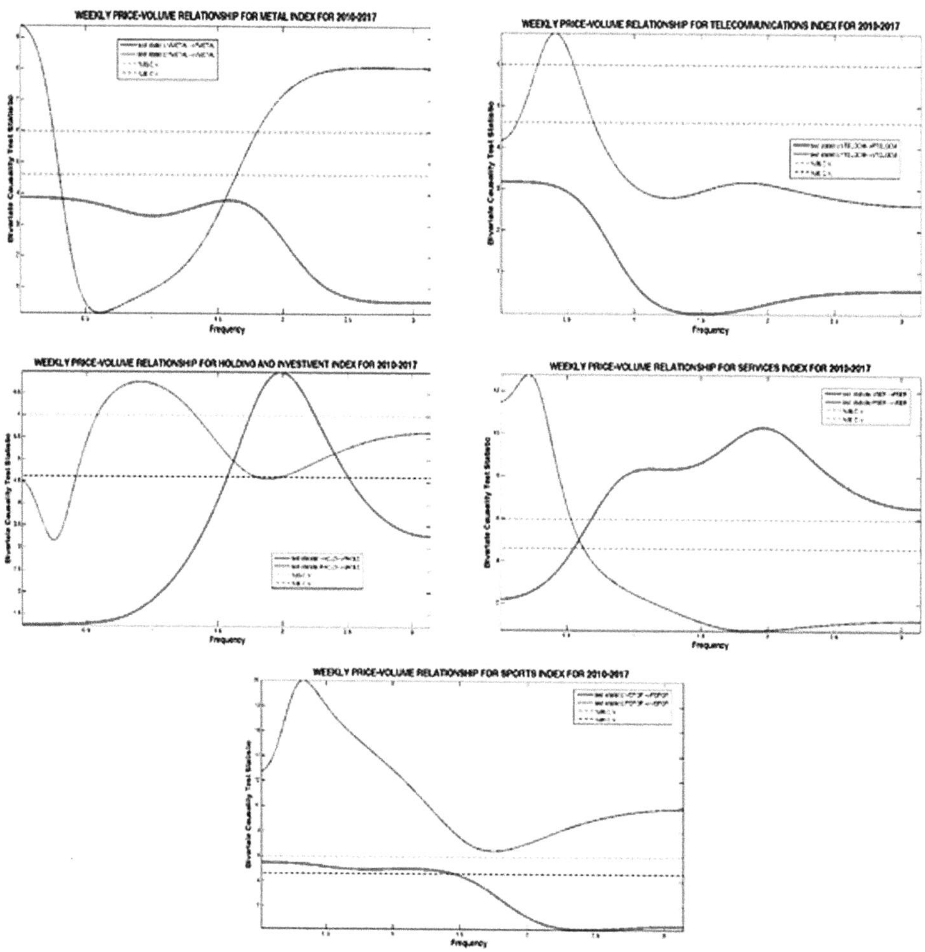

2001-2007: Price is leading volume at higher frequencies whereas volume is leading price in lower frequencies between 2003 January-2006 March and all are in phase.

2008-2017: There are a few instances where volume causes price at higher frequencies whereas price is leading volume at lower frequencies between 2011 January-2014 December (with in phase cases).

For the first group of sub-indices:

- **Banking:** Price is leading volume in high and low frequencies between 2013 January – 2015 January but most of the relationship is out of phase.
- **Transportation:** Price is leading volume at high frequencies and volume is leading price at low frequencies during 2015-2016 with the relationship usually in phase.
- **Financials:** There are very short lived relationships between price and volume (usually price leading) during 2013-2014 which are out of phase.

Figure 4. FD GC; Metal Products & Machinery, Chemicals, Textiles & Leather, Industrials

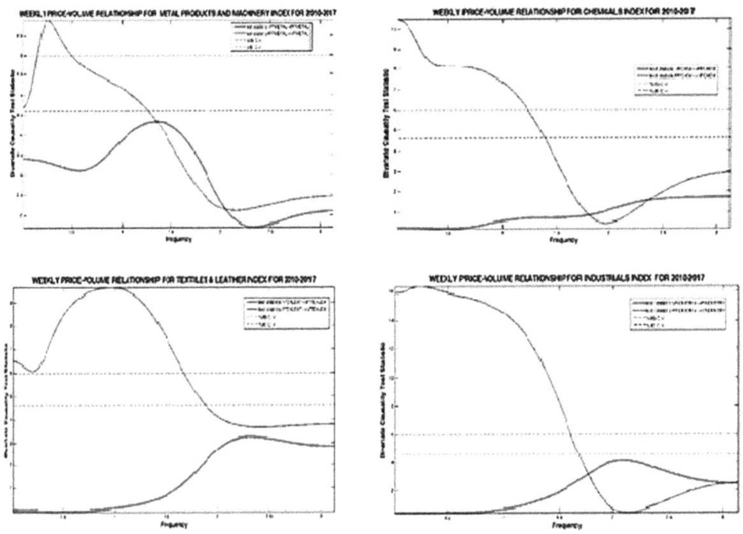

Figure 5. FD GC; Tourism, Wood & Paper & Printing, Leasing & Factoring

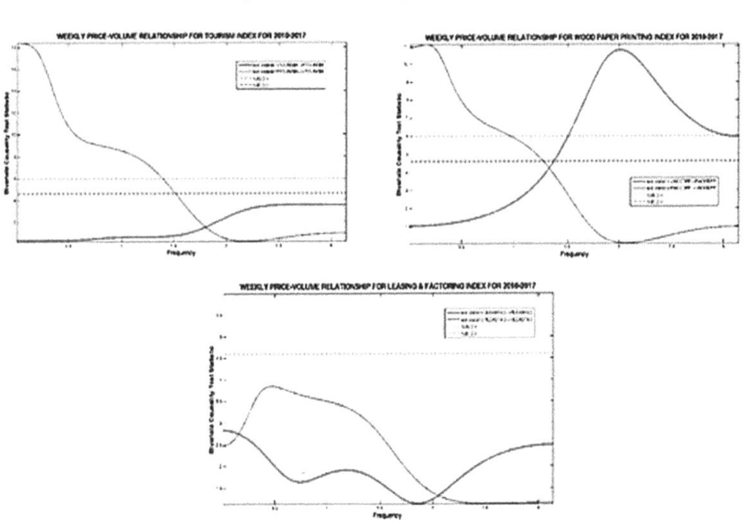

- **Telecommunications:** There are contradictory and very short life-span relationships between price and volume at higher frequencies. At lower frequencies, price is both lagging and leading volume for 2013-2015 and the relationship is in phase.
- **Metal:** There is hardly any descriptive pattern but price is lagging volume at higher frequencies during small intervals with usually in phase cases.
- **Holding and Investment:** At higher frequencies, the relationship is short span and at varying cases. Price is leading volume during 2013-2015 with an in phase relationship.
- **Sports:** At both high and low frequencies, volume is leading price at in phase cases.

Figure 6. FD GC; Wholesale & Retail, Electricity, Minerals, Food & Beverage

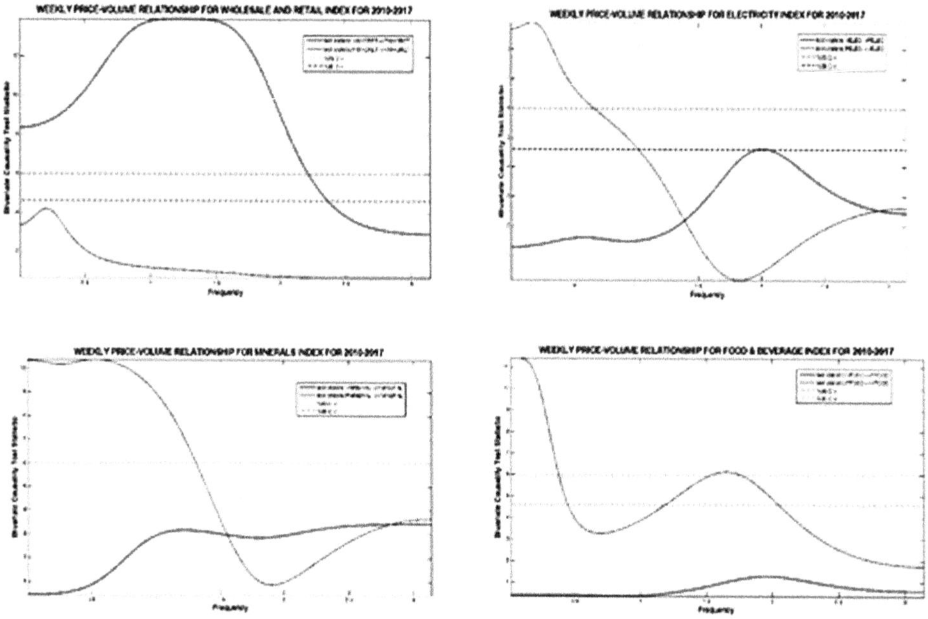

Figure 7. FD GC; Technology, Insurance

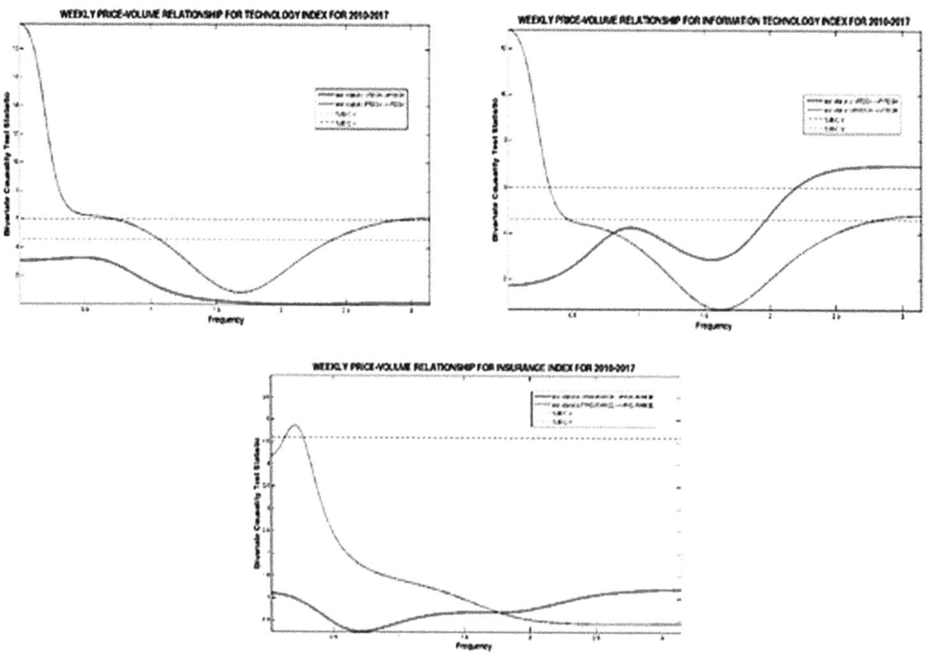

Figure 8. Wavelet Coherence Analysis: BIST100

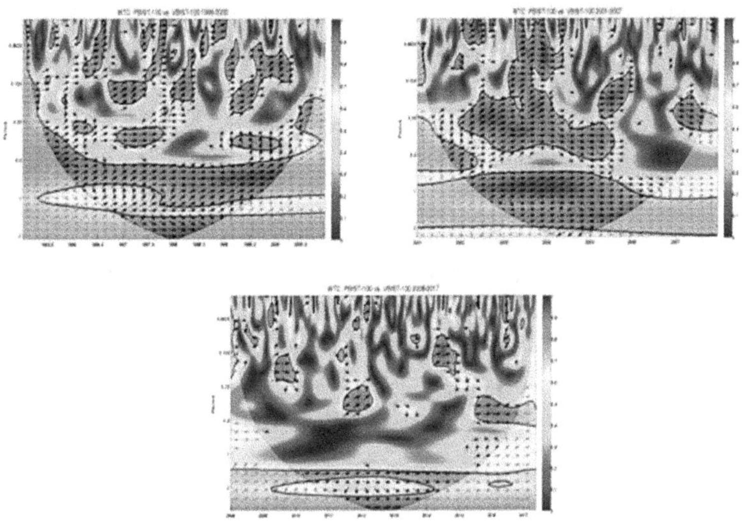

**For a more accurate representation see the electronic version.*

Figure 9. Wavelet Coherence Analysis; Banking, Transportation, Financials and Telecommunications

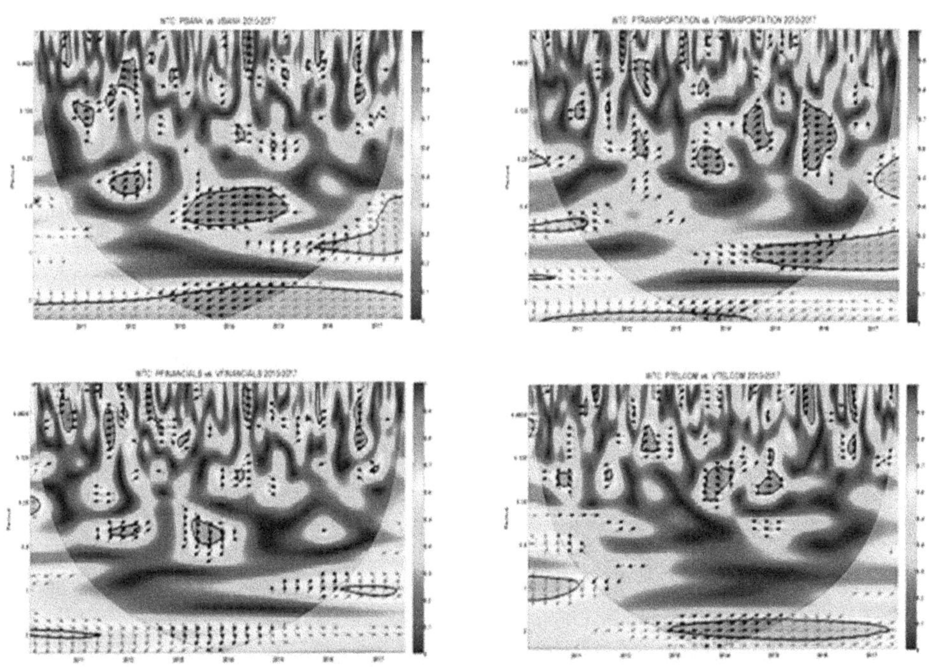

**For a more accurate representation see the electronic version.*

- **Real Estate:** Price is leading volume at higher frequencies whereas volume is leading price in lower frequencies and they are in phase.
- **Services:** At higher frequencies, the relationship varies. At low frequencies, volume is leading price and the relationship is in phase.

For the second group of sub-indices:

- **Tourism:** Price is lagging volume during 2012-2013 at higher frequencies and between 2011 May – 2014 March in lower frequencies. Volume is lagging price in higher frequencies between 2015 September – 2016 February (all cases are in phase).
- **Wood, Paper and Printing:** Price is lagging volume between 2012 September – 2013 March in higher frequencies with in phase case.
- **Industrials:** Volume is leading price between 2011 April – 2012 August in higher frequencies with in phase case.
- **Chemicals:** There is hardly any significant relationship.

Figure 10. Wavelet Coherence Analysis; Metal, Holding & Investment, Sports, Real Estate, Services

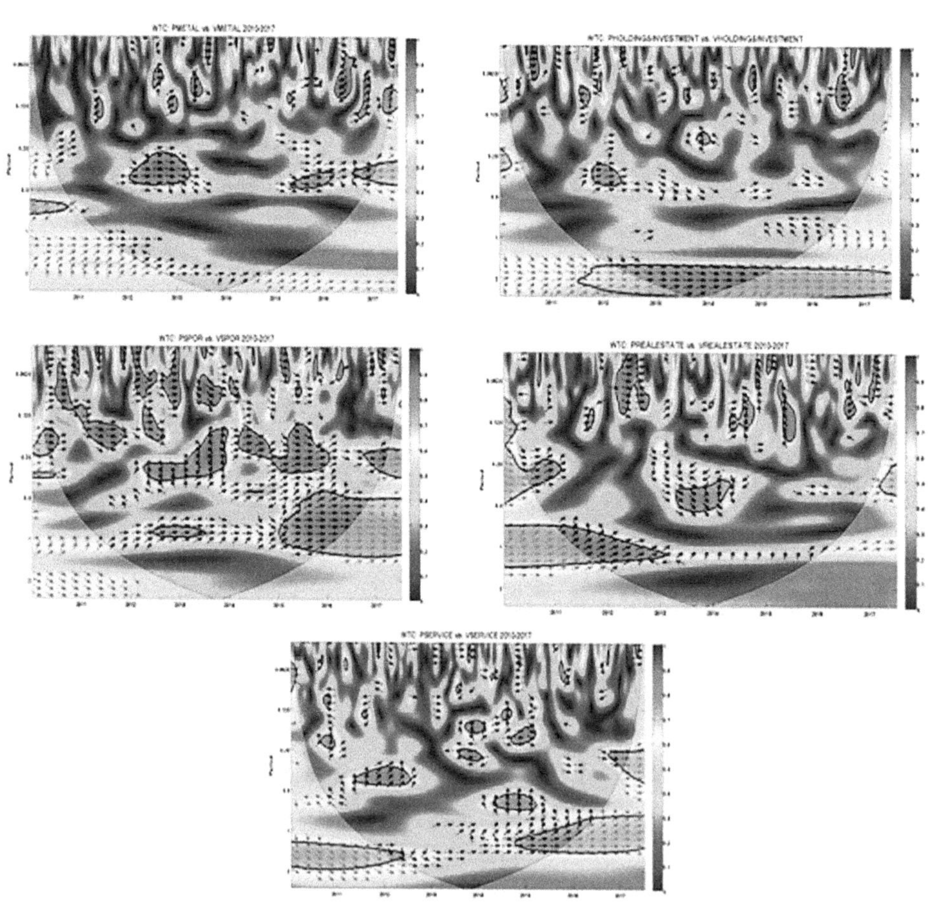

**For a more accurate representation see the electronic version.*

Figure 11. Wavelet Coherence Analysis; Tourism, Wood & Paper & Printing, Chemicals

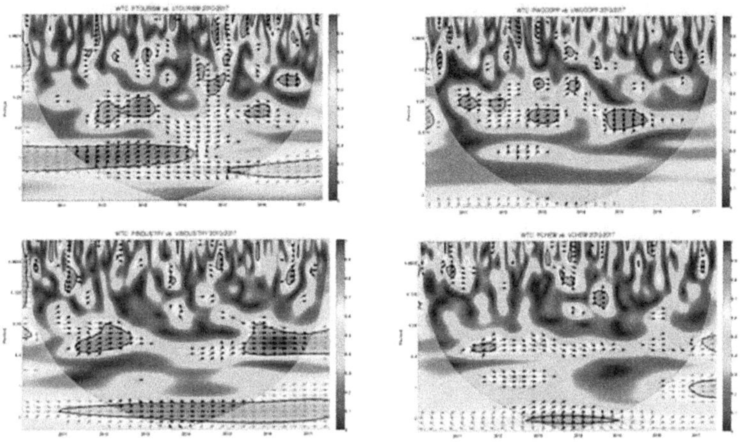

**For a more accurate representation see the electronic version.*

- **Textiles & Leather:** Volume is leading price between 2011 March – 2012 December in higher frequencies with in phase case.
- **Metal Products & Machinery:** Price is leading volume between 2012 January – 2015 February in lower frequencies and volume is leading price between 2011 June – 2012 May in higher frequencies, with both in phase cases.
- **Leasing & Factoring:** Volume is leading price in most of the period at higher frequencies with in phase case.

For the third group of sub-indices:

- **Insurance:** Volume is leading price in most of the period at higher frequencies with in phase case.

Figure 12. Wavelet Coherence Analysis; Textiles & Leather, Metal Products & Machinery, Leasing & Factoring

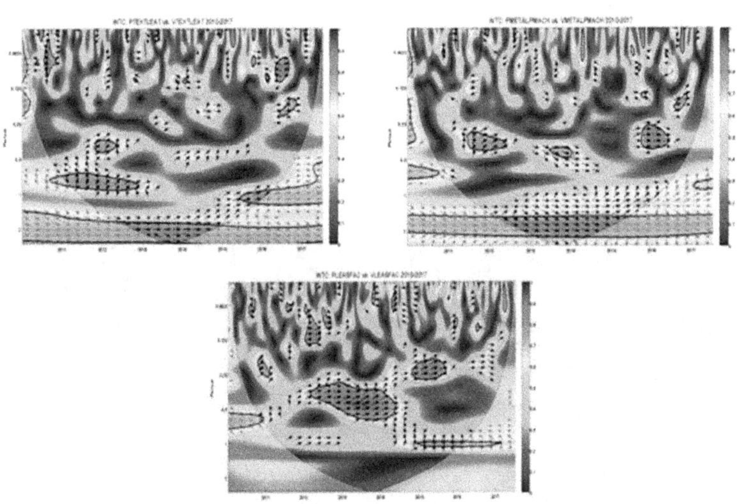

**For a more accurate representation see the electronic version.*

- **Wholesale & Retail:** There is hardly any significant relationship.
- **Food & Beverage:** There are some very small wavelets formed for higher frequencies in which volume is leading the price with in phase case.
- **Minerals:** Volume is leading price at higher frequencies between 2013 January – 2014 December and at lower frequencies between 2011 September – 2013 December. This is reversed for lower frequencies.
- **Technology:** Price is lagging volume in higher frequencies and volume is leading price at lower frequencies during small intervals with all cases in phase.
- **Electricity:** Price is lagging volume in both higher and lower frequencies during almost the whole period with all cases in phase.
- **Information Technology:** Volume is leading price in higher frequencies during 2012-2015 with in phase case.

CONCLUSION

This chapter tries to measure the relationship between price and volume for the emerging market of Turkey stock exchange, Borsa Istanbul. There are two new methods used and these produce results that are interesting not only in terms of the relationship but also the composition of the stock exchange.

Using the first method, the FD approach, we obtain that speculation dominates BIST-100 before the Great Recession whereas afterwards there is bi-directional causality in the long-run but still price is dominant compared to volume. For the 2010-2017 period, the dominant sub-indices show 3 of each V -> P, P -> V and bi-directional causality. The second category sub-indices display 5 of P -> V and 1 of each bi-directional and no causality. The lowest trading sub-indices result in 4 of P -> V, and 1 of each V -> P, bi-directional and no causality.

Figure 13. Wavelet Coherence Analysis; Insurance, Wholesale & Retail, Food & Beverage, Minerals

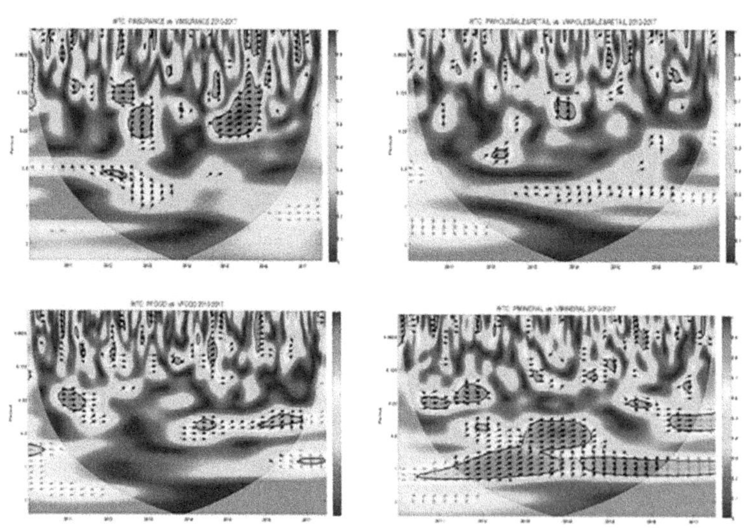

**For a more accurate representation see the electronic version.*

Figure 14. Wavelet Coherence Analysis; Technology, Electricity, Information Technology

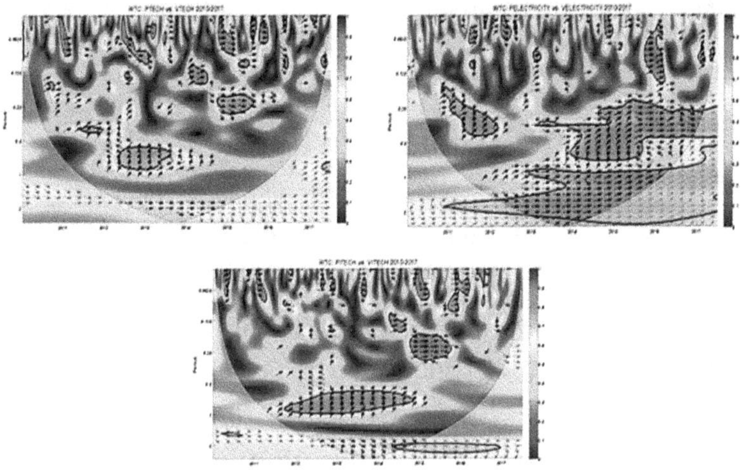

**For a more accurate representation see the electronic version.*

Employing the wavelet coherence methodology, before the Great Recession, volume is leading price at all frequencies whereas price is leading volume in higher frequencies for BIST-100. Afterwards price is leading in lower frequencies and volume is leading in higher frequencies. In all instances, the relationships are in case. For the 2010-2017 period, the dominant sub-indices show 1 of V -> P, 2 of P -> V and 3 of bi-directional and no causality. The second category sub-indices display 4 of V -> P, 2 of bi-directional and 1 of no causality. The lowest trading sub-indices result in 6 of V -> P, and 1 of no causality.

This chapter tries to bring a new perspective for the price and volume relationship in an emerging stock market. Unconventional methodologies are employed to assess the true nature of the relationship. The main BIST-100 index shows speculation before the Great Recession whereas this is reversed afterwards with both unconventional econometric methods. For BIST-100 sub-indices which analyze the 2010-2017 period, FD results emphasize the existence of speculation whereas wavelet coherence analysis display that volume is leading price in most cases.

In summary, the findings highlight that:

1. It is hard to argue for the existence of a distinct pattern in an emerging stock market like Borsa Istanbul.
2. There are several periods that propose challenges like the increasing foreign share, foreign shocks transmitted to the domestic market and local effects (which should be studied further).
3. Speculation is an inherit part of stock markets and it is not possible to get rid of but rather act timely to minimize the adverse consequences and to deter market-wide repercussions.

REFERENCES

Acar Boyacıoğlu, M., Güvenek, B. & Alptekin, V. (2010). Getiri volatilitesi ile işlem hacmi arasındaki ilişki. *Muhasebe ve Finansman Dergisi*, (48), 200-217.

Aguiar-Conraria, L., & Soares, M. J. (2010). *Business Cycle Synchronization and the Euro: A Wavelet Analysis*. Retrieved from http://www3.eeg.uminho.pt/economia/nipe/docs/2010/NIPE_WP_36_2010.pdf

Ajayi, R. A., Mehdian, S., & Mougoue, M. (2006). The empirical relation between price changes and trading volumes: Further evidence from European stock markets. *Alliance Journal of Business Research, 1*, 3–20.

Andersen, T. G. (1996). Return Volatility and Trading Volume: An Information Flow Interpretation of Stochastic Volatility. *The Journal of Finance, 51*(1), 169–204. doi:10.1111/j.1540-6261.1996.tb05206.x

Anifowose, M., & Suleiman, S. (2013). An analysis of casual relation between stock return and trading volume in Nigerian Capital Market. *International Journal of Social Sciences and Humanities Reviews, 4*(2), 137–147.

Beaver, W. H. (1968). The information content of annual earnings announcements. *Journal of Accounting Research, 6*, 67–92. doi:10.2307/2490070

Bohl, M. T., & Henke, H. (2003). Trading volume and stock market volatility: The Polish case. *International Review of Financial Analysis, 12*(5), 513–525. doi:10.1016/S1057-5219(03)00066-8

Breitung, J., & Candelon, B. (2006). Testing for Short and Long-run Causality: A FD Approach. *Journal of Econometrics, 132*(2), 363–378. doi:10.1016/j.jeconom.2005.02.004

Brock, W. A., & LeBaron, B. D. (1995). *A Dynamic Structural Model for Stock Returns Volatility and Trading Volume*. NBER Working Paper Series. No. 4988.

Bühlmann, P. (1998). Extreme events from the return-volume process: A discretization approach for complexity reduction. *Applied Financial Economics, 8*(3), 267–278. doi:10.1080/096031098333023

Chen, G., Firth, M., & Rui, O. M. (2001). The Dynamic relation between stock returns, trading volume, and volatility. *Financial Review, 38*(3), 153–174. doi:10.1111/j.1540-6288.2001.tb00024.x

Chuang, C. C., Kuan, C. M., & Lin, H. Y. (2009). Causality in quantiles and dynamic stock return–volume relations. *Journal of Banking & Finance, 33*(7), 1351–1360. doi:10.1016/j.jbankfin.2009.02.013

Copeland, T. E. (1976). A model of asset trading under the assumption of sequential information arrival. *The Journal of Finance, 31*(4), 1149–1168. doi:10.2307/2326280

Dar, A. B., Samantaraya, A., & Shah, F. A. (2014). The predictive power of yield spread: Evidence from wavelet analysis. *Empirical Economics, 46*(3), 887–901. doi:10.100700181-013-0705-6

Darwish, M. (2012). Testing the Contemporaneous and Causal Relationship between Trading Volume and Return in the Palestine Exchange. *International Journal of Economics and Finance, 4*(4), 182–192. doi:10.5539/ijef.v4n4p182

Dominitz, J., & Manski, C. F. (2004). How Should We Measure Consumer Confidence? *The Journal of Economic Perspectives, 18*(2), 51–66. doi:10.1257/0895330041371303

Elmas, B., & Yıldırım, M. (2010). Kriz Dönemlerinde Hisse Senedi Fiyatı ile İşlem Hacmi İlişkisi: İMKB'de İşlem Gören Bankacılık SEktör Hisseleri üzerine Bir Uygulama. *Atatürk Üniversitesi İktisadi ve İdari Bilimler Dergisi, 24*(2), 37–46.

Fama, E. F. (1970). Efficient Capital Markets: A Review of Theory and Empirical Work. *The Journal of Finance, 25*(2), 383–417. doi:10.2307/2325486

Fama, E. F. (1991). Efficient Capital Markets II. *The Journal of Finance, 46*(5), 1575–1617. doi:10.1111/j.1540-6261.1991.tb04636.x

Fleming, J., Kirby, C., & Ostdiek, B. (2005). *ARCH effects and trading volume.* Rice University and Clemson University Working Paper.

Geweke, J. (1982). Measurement of Linear Dependence and Feedback between Multiple Time Series. *Journal of the American Statistical Association, 77*(378), 304–324. doi:10.1080/01621459.1982.10477803

Godfrey, M. D., Granger, C. W., & Morgenstern, O. (1964). The random-walk hypothesis of stock market behavior. *Kyklos, 17*(1), 1–30. doi:10.1111/j.1467-6435.1964.tb02458.x

Gökce, A. (2002). IMKB'de Fiyat-Hacim İlişkisi: Granger Nedensellik Testi. *Gazi Üniversitesi İ.İ.B.F. Dergisi, 3*, 43–48.

Granger, C. W., & Morgenstern, O. (1963). Spectral analysis of New York stock market prices. *Kyklos, 16*(1), 1–27. doi:10.1111/j.1467-6435.1963.tb00270.x

Granger, C. W. J. (1969). Investigating causal relations by econometric models and cross-spectral methods. *Econometrica, 37*(3), 424–438. doi:10.2307/1912791

Grinsted, A., Moore, J.C. & Jevrejeva, S. (2004). Application of the Cross Wavelet Transform and Wavelet Coherence to Geophysical Time Series. *Nonlinear Processes in Geophysics, 11*, 561–566.

Günay, S. (2015). BİST100 Endeksi Fiyat ve İşlem Hacminin Fraktallık Analizi. *Doğuş Üniversitesi Dergisi, 16*(1), 35–50. doi:10.31671/dogus.2018.59

Gunduz, L., & Hatemi-J, A. (2005). Stock price and volume relation in emerging markets. *Emerging Markets Finance & Trade, 41*(1), 29–44. doi:10.1080/1540496X.2005.11052599

Kamath, R. R., & Wang, Y. (2006). The causality between stock index returns and volumes in the Asian equity markets. *Journal of International Business Research, 5*, 63–74.

Karpoff, J. M. (1987). The Relation between price Changes and Trading Volume: A Survey. *Journal of Financial and Quantitative Analysis, 22*(1), 109–126. doi:10.2307/2330874

Kayalıdere, K. (2009). Price-Volume Relationship in ISE – Asymmetric Interaction. *Yönetim ve Ekonomi., 16*(2), 49–62.

Kiger, J. (1972). An Empirical Investigation of NYSE Volume and Price Reactions to the Announcements of Quarterly Earnings. *Journal of Accounting Research, 10*(1), 113–128. doi:10.2307/2490222

Kim, O., & Verrecchia, R. E. (1991). Trading volume and price reactions to public announcements. *Journal of Accounting Research, 29*(2), 302–321. doi:10.2307/2491051

Kıran, B. (2010). Trade volume and return volatility in Istanbul Stock Exchange. *Doğuş Üniversitesi Dergisi, 11*(1), 98–108.

Lee, B. S., & Rui, O. M. (2002). The dynamic relationship between stock returns and trading volume: Domestic and cross – country evidence. *Journal of Banking & Finance, 26*(1), 51–78. doi:10.1016/S0378-4266(00)00173-4

Lee, C., & Swaminathan, B. (2000). Price momentum and trading volume. *The Journal of Finance, 55*(5), 2017–2070. doi:10.1111/0022-1082.00280

Lucey, B. M. (2005). Does volume provide information? Evidence from the Irish stock market. *Applied Financial Economics Letters, 1*(2), 105–109. doi:10.1080/08935690500047205

Mandelo, M., & Pinho, C. (2012). International stock market indices comovements: A new look. *International Journal of Finance & Economics, 17*(1), 89–102. doi:10.1002/ijfe.448

Morse, D. (1981). Price and Trading Volume Reaction Surrounding Earnings Announcements: A Closer Examination. *Journal of Accounting Research, 19*(2), 374–383. doi:10.2307/2490871

Oktay, T. A. Ş., Tokmakçıoğlu, K., & Çevikcan, G. (2016). Borsa İstanbul'da Pay Senedi Getirileri ile İşlem Hacmi arasındaki İlişki. *Dokuz Eylül Üniversitesi Sosyal Bilimler Enstitüsü Dergisi, 18*(1), 11–30.

Okuyan, H. A., & Erbaykal, E. (2011). İMKB'de yabancı işlemleri ve pay senedi getirileri ilişkisi. *Doğuş Üniversitesi Dergisi, 12*(2), 256–264. doi:10.31671/dogus.2018.141

Osborne, M. F. (1959). Brownian motion in the stock market. *Operations Research, 7*(2), 145–173. doi:10.1287/opre.7.2.145

Percival, D. B., & Walden, A. T. (2000). *Wavelet Methods for Time Series Analysis*. Cambridge University Press. doi:10.1017/CBO9780511841040

Pisedtasalasai, A., & Gunasekarage, A. (2007). Causal and dynamic relationships among stock returns, return volatility, and trading volume: Evidence from emerging markets in South-East Asia. *Asia-Pacific Financial Markets, 14*(4), 277–297. doi:10.100710690-008-9063-3

Qi, R. (2001). *Return-volume relation in the tail: evidence from six emerging markets.* Columbia Business School Working Paper.

Tambi, M. K. (2005). *An empirical study of return-volume relationship for Indian market.* Retrieved from http://econwpa.repec.org/eps/fin/papers/0504/0504013.pdf

Torrence, C., & Compo, G. P. (1998). A Practical Guide to Wavelet Analysis. *Bulletin of the American Meteorological Society, 79*(1), 61–78. doi:10.1175/1520-0477(1998)079<0061:APGTWA>2.0.CO;2

Twari, A. K., Mutascu, M. I., & Albulescu, C. T. (2013). The Influence of International Oil Prices on the Real Effective Exchange Rate in Romania in a Wavelet Transform Framework. *Energy Economics, 40*, 714–733. doi:10.1016/j.eneco.2013.08.016

Uddin, G. Z., Arouri, M., & Tiwari, A. K. (2014). *Co-movements Between Germany and International Stocks Markets: Some New Evidence from DCC-GARCH and Wavelet Approaches*. Working Paper Series. Retrieved from https://www.ipag.fr/wp-content/uploads/recherche/WP/IPAG_WP_2014_143.pdf

Wang, C., & Chin, S. (2004). Profitability of return and volume-based investment strategies in China's stock market. *Pacific-Basin Finance Journal, 12*(12), 541–564. doi:10.1016/j.pacfin.2003.12.002

Yıldırım, N., & Taştan, H. (2009). *Capital Flows and Economic Growth across Spectral Frequencies: Evidence from Turkey.* Turkish Economic Association Discussion Paper 2009/2.

Ying, C. C. (1966). Stock market prices and volumes of sales. *Econometrica, 34*(3), 676–685. doi:10.2307/1909776

ENDNOTES

1 For details of the computation of the measure, see Geweke (1982) and Breitung and Candelon (2006).

2 See Uddin et al. (2013) and Grinsted et al. (2004).

Chapter 4

Does Parasocial Breakup Affect the Stock Market Returns?

Evidence From an Emerging Market

İbrahim Bozkurt
Çankırı Karatekin University, Turkey

Mercan Hatipoğlu
Çankırı Karatekin University, Turkey

ABSTRACT

This chapter analyzes the impact of parasocial breakup on the stock returns in Borsa Istanbul as an emerging stock market. In this study, 129 Turkish TV series finales, broadcast between 2005 and 2015, are employed as a negative mood proxy. In line with the purpose of this chapter, GARCH-M model is used to obtain a more efficient parameter and alternative mood proxy dummies and other macroeconomic variables are incorporated into the analyses to examine the robustness of the effect of parasocial breakup on stock market returns. The analysis presents robust evidence that the negative mood increases the stock market returns. It also found that the effect of parasocial breakup on returns depends on the types of TV series and the channels they are broadcast on.

INTRODUCTION

In a latest study, for the first time in the literature, the number of individuals experiencing a parasocial breakup[1] is used as a mood proxy to investigate the power of exterior variations in the psychology of investor on stock market returns (Lepori, 2015). Lepori (2015) adopts that arise in the watcher of TV series finales causes the society to fall into the negative mood. However there is no data on the watcher numbers of Turkish TV serials and for this reason, it is assumed for Turkey that when the long-episode TV series end, negative mood dominates over the society (Eyal and Cohen, 2006). This view can be briefly stated as follows: Cohen (2003), Cohen (2004) and Eyal and Cohen (2006) reveal that if the parasocial relationship prior to breakup is powerful, the negative mood arising from a parasocial breakup is more severe. It is understood that the negative mood effect of the parasocial breakup on the society proceeds

DOI: 10.4018/978-1-5225-7399-9.ch004

from the power of the parasocial relationship. The longer a viewer watches a TV persona, the stronger the attachment and the parasocial relationship that he/she builds becomes (Rubin and McHugh, 1987); hence, the power of parasocial relationships, which affects the psyche of the society, grows stronger in long-running TV serials and the impact deepens by the tragic or happy endings of their popular characters.

This study examines the episode counts of the Turkish TV series that reached their finales to investigate the influence of parasocial breakup on market returns in Borsa Istanbul (BIST). This chapter, which presents forceful findings that are in concert with the few studies in the field of psychology however out of harmony with the studies in the field of behavioural finance, aims four major contributions to the literature. First off, this study examines the episode numbers of the TV series ended. Secondly; in this chapter, the effect of parasocial breakups on stock returns is also analyzed by considering the forms of the TV series and different TV channels. Thirdly; Generalized Autoregressive Conditional Heteroscedasticity in Mean (GARCH-M) model is employed to capture the effect of risk on return and also to obtain a more efficient parameter. Fourthly, this chapter presents evidence on the effects of parasocial breakups on the behaviour of investors in an emerging market (Turkey). Investigating the relationship between TV series finales and stock returns by using data from Turkey has various advantages (RTÜK, 2013; NTV, 2013): (i) the most preferred programs by the audience are the TV serials in Turkey, so they play an important role for both the society and the media. (ii) Most of the viewers in Turkey identify themselves with TV personae. (iii) Turkey is the second major TV series exporting country after the USA. (iv)Viewers from all of the geographic regions of Turkey allow us to observe the impact of TV series in the whole country.

The rest of this chapter is organized as follows. First, some of the studies in the literature related to parasocial breakup-mood and mood-investing in stocks are briefed. Thereinafter, the methodology and the data are introduced and then the results of the empirical findings are discussed. Finally, it is presented concluding remarks.

BACKGROUND

The Relationship Between Mood and Invest in Risky Asset

The decision maker reflects his / her mood at every stage of the decision-making process. The individual's mood affects the last choice in his judgement action in the same manner. (see in Bower 1981, Johnson and Tversky, 1983). In other words, an individual with a negative mood is more pessimistic than the individual who has a positive mood (see in Isen et al.1978, Kavanagh and Bower 1985, Wright and Bower, 1992). This can be described by the influence of mood congruency. The mood congruence term means the match between the individual's thought and his mood (Myer vd., 1992). According to the mood congruency, the individual keeps his mind in his mind; that is, if the investor feels himself or herself feeling psychologically bad, the mind constantly feels bad or fears (like fear of loss or bankruptcy) and therefore avoids the risk (ie the risk perception rises up and to avoid risk-taking). "Affect as information" theory can also help to determine the relationship between a person's mood and the decisions. According to this theory; before making an opinion, individuals generally make an assessment of themselves about the situation they are facing by asking themselves "What Do I Feel About It " and " How Do I Feel ?", and this is often the result of their emotions (Schwarz and Clore, 1983, 1988). In other words, an individual with a negative mood becomes more pessimistic in decisions than an individual with a certain state of mind. For example, Lee and Yeon (2003) made an experiment that missed the cheerfulness of the subjects through watching video clips. Afterwards, it was observed that the tendency of risk-taking was decreased. The final outcome of the first views is that individuals will tend to increase the risk perceptions if they feel in negative moods and tend to avoid risk. The more risk avoidance tendency will also lessen the interest on volatility assets (here equities). many of the studies support the strong anticipation that the positive (negative) mood will increase the risk-taking tendency (Yuen and Lee, 2003). Besides that, few studies partly or completely have rejected the direct perfect links between mood and risk-taking. They have put forward evidence that this relationship is negative. For example, some papers emphasized that depressed attendants bear a bigger risk (Raghunathan and Pham, 1999). On the other hand, Bruyneel et al. (2009) showed that individuals with negative moods tend to risky assets. Bozkurt and Hatipoglu (2017) claimed that the negative mood hikes the bidding for stocks by domestic investors.

Leith and Baumeister (1996) stated that investors in negative moods tend to prefer risky alternatives to safe options. Lin et al. (2007) implied that people who sense repentant for themselves at the decision moment are more likely to take risks and prefer options with more potential for earnings. Conte et al. (2013) provide the fact that sadness, anger, and fear situations lead individuals to risky behaviours. The idea of the second group is that the individuals with negative mood will tend to take more risks. The trends taking more risk will also increase the demand for risky assets. Mittal and Ross (1998) noticed that the reasons why individuals in negative moods are willing to take a higher risk are the possibility of repairing their negative emotions with higher earnings. According to Mick and Demoss (1990), those who feel depressed and have a negative mood tend to buy gifts for themselves; that is, individuals with negative moods want to be replaced by rewards of living negativity. Zillmann (1988), Isen and Geva, (1987) argue that individuals in negative moods will go to high-risk (high-return) preferences to correct their mental state. It is pointed out that the individuals in negative mood act with the motive of " mood repair ". Thaler and Johnson (1990) indicate that people with negative moods (ie those who had previously suffered losses) find the risky preferences more compelling, giving them the opportunity to make up for their damages (break-even effects). According to the third opinion, which is separated by a slight difference in the second opinion, individuals in negative moods will tend to take more risks as they increase their chances of compensating their harm. The fact that the trends to take risks will increase if the possibility of compensating the losses is increased, will also increase the demand for risky assets (stocks).

Mood Proxies Used in the Literature

According to experiments; to clarify the relationship between mood and decision-making, the moods of the subjects were changed in positive or negative directions; they were asked to watch short videos, listen to music, read short stories and were given small presents (e.g. Johnson & Tversky, 1983; Bruyneel, Dewitte, Franses & Dekimpe, 2009; Yuen & Lee, 2003). On the other hand, in field experiments, the individual's mood is represented with factors like weather and full moon. For instance, factors like (i) weather (Saunders, 1993), (ii) full moon (Bozkurt, 2015), (iii) football match results (Berument, 2006), (iv) daylight (Hirshleifer & Shumway, 2003), (v) TV series finales (Lepori, 2015), (vi) air pollution (Levy & Yagil, 2011), (vii) seasons (Cao & Wei, 2005) and (viii) religious festivals (Białkowski, Etebari & Wisniewski, 2012) are used as mood proxy variables to explain the effect of exogenous variations in investors' moods on stock market returns. In this section, parasocial separation is used as a representative of negative moods.

The Effect of Parasocial Breakup on Mood and Stock Market Return

Parasocial breakup describes a condition where the viewers' identification of themselves with certain TV personae ends with the TV series finale (Cohen, 2003). Parasocial breakup causes problems similar to the death of a close friend or break-ups between lovers (Cohen, 2004). These problems show themselves as psychological conditions such as depression, loneliness, anxiety, sleeplessness and stress (Field et al., 2009; Rhoades et al., 2011; Slotter, Gaedner & Finkel, 2010; McCarthy, Lambert & Brack, 1997). As a result, in times when the TV series reach their finale, it is prevalently supposed that the mood of the society is negative.

There are two studies examining the effect of the parasocial breakdown. One of these was made by Lepori (2015) for the United States and investigates the effect of parasocial breakup on stock exchange returns. The other was made by Bozkurt and Hatipoglu (2017) for Turkey and investigates the effect of parasocial breakup on the demand for stocks by domestic investors. In this study, the effect of the parasocial breakup on the stock return will be examined in the contex of Turkey.

Just as the lab counterparts, in the field studies above mentioned, it is confirmed that mood has an effect on the individual's risk perception and his decisions. Related studies have contradictory results on the effect of mood on investor behaviour and so this chapter tests the following two hypotheses:

H_1: The negative mood caused by parasocial breakup drops the stock market returns because negative mood prompts investors to decrease the demand for volatile assets (stocks).

H_2: The negative mood caused by parasocial breakup increases the stock market returns because negative mood prompts investors to buy the volatile assets (stocks).

THE EFFECT OF PARASOCIAL BREAKUP ON STOCK MARKET RETURNS

Data and Methodology

The daily data on the performance of the BIST-100 index is collected from BIST website[2] from December 7, 2005, to April 14, 2015. Daily returns for the BIST-100 index (R_t) are expressed in USD values and are calculated as shown in Eq.1. Turkey has had a high and volatile inflation rate, so investors evaluate the daily performance of the stock market by looking at its USD value (Berument, Ceylan & Eker, 2006).

$$R_t = \ln\left(\frac{BIST_t}{BIST_{t-1}}\right) - \ln\left(\frac{USD_t}{USD_{t-1}}\right) \tag{1}$$

BIST is defined as the daily closing price of BIST-100 index and USD is the value of US Dollar's exchange rate to Turkish Lira in equation 1.

Datum with regard to 129 Turkish TV series[3] that reached their finales between December 1, 2005, and April 30, 2015 (e.g., form of series, ending date, episode number and the TV channels that broadcasted these series) are also employed in this paper. These related data were acquired from different sources[4] in order to provide the dependableness of the related information. The finale dates of TV series expresses the dates when the negative mood dominates on investors and this study assumes that negative mood will affect the investor behaviours on the trading day following the airing date of the final episode[5]. The statistical summaries on the TV series and BIST-100 index returns are presented in Table 1. In Table 1, some descriptive statistics of other control variables which are used for robustness check are also reported. These variables are useful in controlling for calendar anomalies, macroeconomic factors and alternative mood proxies.

The GARCH-in-mean model of Engle, Lilien and Robins (1987) is employed to test the hypotheses of the study. The feature of the GARCH-M model is to include the conditional variance of return into the conditional mean equation. Since the model considers the time-varying effect of risk premium, it would establish a more robust parameter compared to OLS methods.

Table 1. Summary statistics of variables

	Period: December, 2005 – April, 2015	**Mean**	**St. Dev.**	**Median**	**Max.**	**Min.**
A -	Episode Counts	68.61	52.30	52	375	20
	R_t	-0.000058	0.01947	0.0009	0.0947	-0.1064
B-	Logarithmic change of the gold prices ($/Ons)	0.000306	0.01258	0.0006	0.0968	-0.0617
	Logarithmic change of the Brent oil prices ($ / Barrel)	0.000015	0.02116	0.0000	0.1981	-0.1683
	Macroeconomic Announcement 1- CPI (yes =1; no= 0)	0.0467	0.2110	0	1	0
	2- Foreign trade statistics (yes =1; no= 0)	0.0458	0.2091	0	1	0
	3- Labor statistics (yes =1; no= 0)	0.0535	0.2252	0	1	0
	4- GDP (yes =1; no= 0)	0.0155	0.1238	0	1	0
	5- Industrial production index (yes =1; no= 0)	0.0531	0.2243	0	1	0
	6- Retail sales volume index (yes =1; no= 0)	0.0087	0.0929	0	1	0
	7- Economic confidence index (yes =1; no= 0)	0.0013	0.0370	0	1	0
	8- Consumer confidence index (yes =1; no= 0)	0.0490	0.2159	0	1	0
	9- Construction turnover and prod. index (yes 1; no 0)	0.0105	0.1021	0	1	0
	10- Decision of the monetary policy com. (yes 1; no 0)	0.0485	0.2149	0	1	0
C-	Full moon $_{\text{from t-3 to t+3}}$ (yes = 1; no = 0)	0.232	0.422	0	1	0
	New moon $_{\text{from t-3 to t+3}}$ (yes = 1; no = 0)	0.234	0.423	0	1	0
	Average daily temperature in Istanbul (^{0}C)	14.447	7.550	14.20	30.70	-3.5
	Av. daily rate of cloudiness in Ist. (min:0 – max:10)	4.155	2.444	4.30	10.0	0.00
	Rainfall in Istanbul (mm = kg/m^2)	2.272	6.595	0.00	107.1	0.00
D-	January (yes = 1; no = 0)	0.0893	0.2852	0	1	0
	Holiday and observances $_{t-1}$ (yes = 1; no = 0)	0.0238	0.1525	0	1	0
	Holiday and observances $_{t+1}$ (yes = 1; no = 0)	0.0242	0.1539	0	1	0
	Monday (yes = 1; no = 0)	0.1914	0.3935	0	1	0

Note: (1) All variables are in daily frequency. Panel A shows the summary statistics of TV series and stock market return; Panel B shows the summary statistics concerning the macroeconomic control variables, Panel C displays some summary statistics related with alternative mood proxies and Panel D presents some summary statistics of most known calendar anomalies in the finance literature. (2) Because of space limitations, only the summary statistics of January and Monday are presented. (3) All meteorological variables data obtained from the Turkish State Meteorological Service via mail in 06.05.2015. (4) All dates related with macroeconomic announcement collected from Central Bank of the Republic of Turkey and Turkish Statistical Institute. (5) While gold prices are obtained from the Borsa Istanbul stock exchange database, oil prices from the US Energy Information Administration. (6) All data are stationary in level. (7) Some information with regard to TV series ended is as follows: 1- "A woman - A man", which is a 375-episode TV series, has the highest episode number. 2- TV series named "Aşk-ı Memnu" with a rating of 23.41% (and a share 58.55%) has the highest finale rating. 3- The series named "Fatih Harbiye", which was broadcasted at 02:00, has the latest ending hour.

We estimated the following specifications.

$$R_t = \beta_1 Z_{t\text{-}1} + \beta_2 Z_{t\text{-}1} \times \ln(EPISODE_{t-1}) + \sum_{k=1}^{5} \rho_k W_{kt} + \ell_1 R_{t-1} + \lambda h_t^2 + e_t, e_t \sim (0, h_t^2) \quad (2)$$

$$h_t^2 = \alpha_0 + \alpha_{1a} e_{t-1}^2 + \alpha_{1b} h_{t-1}^2 \quad (3)$$

Here, $Z_{t\text{-}1}$ = the dummy variable set (see, Table 2) of TV serials that finish after the closure of the exchange on day t-1. $EPISODE_{t\text{-}1}$ = the episode count of the series ended on day t-1. W_{kt} = the dummy variable related to the five days of the weekday. In this model, the dependent variable "R_t" is thought to follow an autoregressive path, therefore the study includes it to Eq. 2 as an independent variable until the 1st lag length[6]. Such analyses are known as transfer function analyses (Enders, 1995). h_t^2 denotes the conditional variance that is estimated by GARCH (1,1) and λ is the risk premium term which measures the risk and return relationship. While significant and positive λ implies that the investor is rewarded for taking additional risk, an insignificant λ means that risk does not affect the return process.

The dummy variables for the TV series finales are shown in Table 2, where description 1 is the most general model. Ensuing descriptions were thought out in order to consider the TV Channels and TV series forms for the purpose of providing the robustness of the analysis findings.

The model in Eq. 2 is estimated using the GARCH-M technique for descriptions 1–9 in Table 2. In Eq. 2, R_t follows an autoregressive path cut by $Z_{t\text{-}1}$ in each period. β_1 and β_2 coefficients are tested under the null hypothesis (H_0: $\beta_1 = \beta_2 = 0$) and both of them simultaneously measure the effect of TV series finales (parasocial breakup, in other words, negative mood) on stock market returns.

Empirical Results

The results revealing the effect of negative mood (TV series finales) on stock market returns are summarized in Table 3.

Table 2. Descriptions of dummy variables for the TV series finales

Description 1	Z = FINALE	=	The day when a TV Series ended = 1; 0
Description 2	Z = FINALE $_{\text{Drama}}$	=	The day when a TV Series ended = 1; 0 (for drama serials)
Description 3	Z = FINALE $_{\text{Action}}$	=	The day when a TV Series ended = 1; 0 (for action serials)
Description 4	Z = FINALE $_{\text{Comedy}}$	=	The day when a TV Series ended = 1; 0 (for comedy serials)
Description 5	Z = FINALE $_{\text{ATV}}$	=	The day when a TV Series broadcasted on ATV ended = 1; 0
Description 6	Z = FINALE $_{\text{ChannelD}}$	=	The day when a TV Series broadcasted on Channel D ended = 1; 0
Description 7	Z = FINALE $_{\text{Show-TV}}$	=	The day when a TV Series broadcasted on Show-TV ended = 1; 0
Description 8	Z = FINALE $_{\text{Star-TV}}$	=	The day when a TV Series broadcasted on Star-TV ended = 1; 0
Description 9	Z = FINALE $_{\text{Other}}$	=	The day when a TV Series broadcasted on other channels ended = 1; 0

Table 3. The effect of TV series finales on the BİST-100 index (Eq. 2 and description 1 – 9)

	Descriptions								
	1	2	3	4	5	6	7	8	9
Panel A: Estimates for Return Equation									
β_1 Finale	-0.0202[a]								
β_2 Finale×ln(Episode)	0.0050[a]								
β_1 F_{Drama}		-0.0037							
β_2 F_{Drama}×ln(Episode)		0.0009							
β_1 F_{Action}			-0.0626[b]						
β_2 F_{Action}×ln(Episode)			0.0150[b]						
β_1 F_{Comedy}				-0.0421[a]					
β_2 F_{Comed}×ln(Episode)				0.0097[a]					
β_1 F_{ATV}					-0.0259				
β_2 F_{ATV}×ln(Episode)					0.0058				
β_1 $F_{Chan\text{-}D}$						-0.0256[c]			
β_2 $F_{Chan\text{-}D}$×ln(Episode)						0.0067[c]			
β_1 $F_{Show\text{-}TV}$							-0.0030		
β_2 F_{Show}×ln(Episode)							0.0003		
β_1 $F_{Star\text{-}TV}$								-0.0121	
β_2 $F_{Star\text{-}TV}$×ln(Episode)								0.0036	
β_1 F_{Other}									-0.0379[c]
β_2 F_{Other}×ln(Episode)									0.0083[c]
Monday	0.0015[c]	0.0015[c]	0.0015[c]	0.0015[c]	0.0016[c]	0.0015[c]	0.0015[c]	0.0015[c]	0.0015[c]
Tuesday	0.0008	0.0007	0.0007	0.0007	0.0007	0.0008	0.0007	0.0007	0.0008
Wednesday	0.0005	0.0004	0.0004	0.0004	0.0004	0.0004	0.0004	0.0004	0.0004
Friday	-0.00004	-0.00005	-0.00007	-0.00003	-0.00008	-0.00006	-0.00006	-0.00006	-0.00005
R_{t-1}	0.1603[a]	0.1612[a]	0.1598[a]	0.1609[a]	0.1612[a]	0.1606[a]	0.1609[a]	0.1609[a]	0.1614[a]
(Risk) h^2_t	0.0140	0.0159	0.0174	0.0161	0.0188	0.0133	0.0161	0.0157	0.0155
Panel B: GARCH Parameters									
Constant	0.00004[a]	0.00004[a]	0.00004[a]	0.00004[a]	0.00004[a]	0.00004[a]	0.00004[a]	0.00004[a]	0.00004[a]
e^2_{t-1}	0.0797[a]	0.0797[a]	0.0780[a]	0.0811[a]	0.0795[a]	0.0802[a]	0.0798[a]	0.0802[a]	0.0800[a]
h^2_{t-1}	0.9077[a]	0.9081[a]	0.9100[a]	0.9064[a]	0.9083[a]	0.9078[a]	0.9083[a]	0.9075[a]	0.9079[a]
Log likelihood	6244.5	6241.1	6243.4	6245.6	6243.0	6243.6	6241.2	6241.7	6242.5
Panel C: Joint Test									
Wald-Test (H_0:β_1=β_2=0)	3.437[b]	0.054	33.157[a]	34.014[a]	1.192	2.298[c]	0.177	1.156	2.567[c]
Panel D: Autocorrelation Q-Statistics									
lags									
1	1.329	1.181	1.257	1.275	1.185	1.241	1.147	1.209	1.229

continued on following page

Table 3. Continued

	Descriptions								
	1	2	3	4	5	6	7	8	9
5	8.424	8.232	8.709	8.282	8.303	8.196	8.336	8.484	8.154
10	12.216	11.694	12.344	12.266	11.509	11.752	11.713	11.952	12.069
Panel E: ARCH-LM tests									
lags									
1	1.094	1.112	0.910	1.091	1.068	1.111	1.118	1.189	0.957
5	2.712[b]	2.656[b]	2.662[b]	2.642[b]	2.726[b]	2.625[b]	2.654[b]	2.614[b]	2.584[b]
10	1.518	1.477	1.473	1.491	1.502	1.466	1.477	1.474	1.441

Note: ([a]), ([b]) and ([c]) show that the coefficient estimations are statistically significant at 1%, 5%, and 10% levels respectively.

Description 1 of Table 3 shows statistically significant evidence that investors react positively to TV series finales. β_1 is estimated to be negative and statistically significant at 1% level (the null hypothesis "$H_0:\beta_1=0$" is rejected). β_2 is also statistically significant at the 1% level, but positive. The Wald test result shows that the null hypothesis ($H_0:\beta_1=\beta_2=0$) can be rejected at the 1% level. Regression coefficients β_1 and β_2 together suggest that negative changes in the investors' mood caused by the finales of long-running TV series (which have a stronger parasocial relationship) increase the stock market returns in the following trading day. When everything is stable, it is forecasted that an investor will response to the ending of a TV series with 25% more episodes by increasing stock market returns nearly 11 basis points on the next trading day[7]. From a different viewpoint, after the finale of a TV series with 20 episodes, the stock market return will be approximate -%0.5 in the next trading day. On the other hand, the finale of a TV series with 24 episodes, by reducing the loss of return by 10 basis points, provides the expected return nearly -%0.4 in the next trading day. The estimated coefficient for λ is positive but insignificant. These results show that there is no tradeoff between risk and return in Turkish financial market.

Descriptions 2-4 are designed to test if the findings related to description 1 will stay the same after the ended series are grouped according to types. For the same purpose, descriptions 5-9 also group the ended series according to TV channels. The purpose of this grouping is to establish the robustness of the study results. When coefficients (β_2) of the descriptions 2-9 in Table 3 are considered, it is seen that the results related to description 1 are still valid. Stock market returns respond positively to the finales (negative mood) of actions, comedies and the finales of series broadcasted on Channel D and other TV channels (except Show TV, Star TV and ATV), specifically. These findings are compatible with the survey of RTUK (The Radio and Television Supreme Council) which shows the most popular TV series is broadcasted by Channel D (RTUK, 2012: 21).

Panel D reports the autocorrelation Q statistics for the standardized residuals calculated to test the null hypothesis of zero autocorrelation up to 10 lags. Overall, we cannot reject the null hypothesis of no autocorrelation for any description.

To test the null hypothesis in order to prove that there is no ARCH effect for the standardized residuals, we apply Engle's (1982) ARCH-LM test. Test statistics for the standardized residuals are reported in Panel E. We regressed the squared standardized residuals on a constant term and on the first, fifth and tenth lags. The results show that the null of no ARCH effect is rejected only for all descriptions at five lags at the 5% significance level.

As for the remaining variables in Table 3, the Monday effects are positive and are statistically significant for all descriptions at 1% significance level. This result is not parallel to the findings in the literature on the day-of-the-week effects. One-day lagged returns have also a positive coefficient at 1% significance level in the case of all descriptions. The findings, which are not coherent with the results of studies in the behavioural finance literature, can make some readers suspicious because they are fairly interesting and surprising. Presenting robustness check results can eliminate probable suspicions.

Robustness Check

Quartile Analysis

The relationship between the negative mood and stock market returns, stated in Table 3, is also supported by quartile analysis[8]. Fig. 1 shows the quartile limits[9] calculated based on the episode count of ended TV series.

In the quartile analysis, first, the TV serials are divided into four groups, based on the episode counts in Fig. 1. Then, the mean changes in stock returns are calculated for each group on trading days following the final episodes (Fig. 2). Fig. 2a shows the average change in stock returns for each of the quartiles. Fig. 2b shows the cumulative average stock returns.

Fig. 2 shows that stock market returns rise when the long-running TV series end (i.e. negative mood dominates over the society). This relationship between the stock returns and the negative mood is also statistically significant (Table 4). Table 4 reports that the average stock returns are different from one another on a quartiles basis.

Figure 1. Box-Plot graphics related to the length of TV series on the episode number

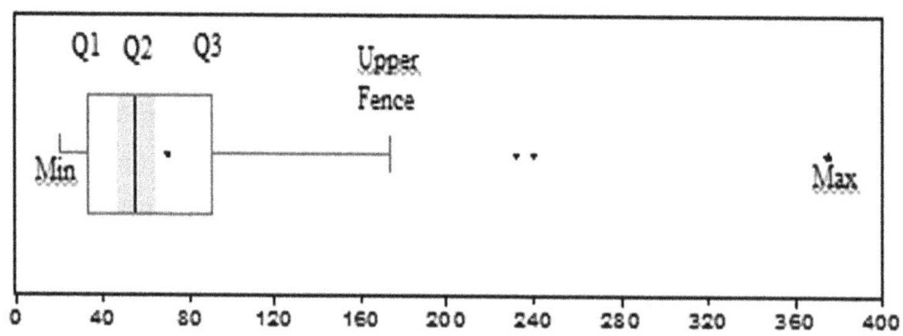

Figure 2. Changes in the BIST-100 index returns on quartiles basis

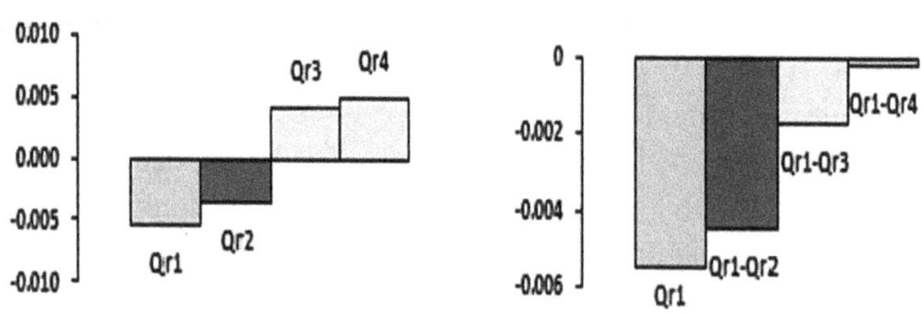

Table 4. Summary statistics of the changes in the numbers of stocks on quartiles basis

Panel A[d]	Qr1(low)	Qr2	Qr3	Qr4(high)
Mean	-0.0054	-0.0035	0.0041	0.0049
Maximum	0.0346	0.0291	0.0258	0.0356
Minimum	-0.0377	-0.0281	-0.0265	-0.0181
Std. Dev.	0.0165	0.0134	0.0123	0.0131
Jarque-Bera[f]	0.2273	0.7808	1.6168	0.9060
	F-Statistic = 4.3457[a]			
Panel B[e]	**Qr3**		**Qr4(high)**	
Qr1(low)	*t-Stat.*= -2.5836[b]		*t-Stat.*= -2.6827[a]	
Qr2	*t-Stat.*= -2.3327[b]		*t-Stat.*= -2.4648[b]	

Note: ([a]), ([b]) and ([c]) have been used to indicate that the coefficient estimations are statistically significant at 1%, 5% and 10% level, respectively. This means, ([a]), ([b]) and ([c]) imply that there is a statistically significant difference between the average stock returns belonging to the quartiles. ([d]) Panel A presents the summary statistics related to the stock returns for each quartile. Moreover, it includes the statistics which show whether or not the average returns differ on the quartiles basis. ([e]) Panel B presents the T-statistic values related to differences between the stock returns related to groups of TV series which have the most (Qr3 and Qr4) and the least (Qr1 and Qr2) episodes. ([f]) The null hypothesis "the related sample presents a normal distribution" cannot be rejected. Thus in this table, only the parametric (F and t-tests) test results are given.

Different Indicators as Controlled Variables

The purpose of this section is to provide robustness results for analysis by controlling for calendar anomalies, macroeconomic factors and alternative mood proxies in the behavioural finance literature. Gradually, we utilize three different models (Eq. 4, Eq. 5 and Eq. 6) by adding new variables.

$$\begin{aligned} R_t &= \beta_1 Z_{t\text{-}1} + \beta_2 Z_{t\text{-}1} \times \ln(EPISODE_{t-1}) + \ell_1 R_{t-1} + \omega_1 PRE_t \\ &+ \omega_2 POST_t + \sum_{n=1}^{12} \gamma_n M_{nt} + \sum_{k=1}^{5} \rho_k W_{kt} + \lambda h_t^2 + e_t \end{aligned} \tag{4}$$

$$\begin{aligned} R_t &= \beta_1 Z_{t\text{-}1} + \beta_2 Z_{t\text{-}1} \times \ln(EPISODE_{t-1}) + \ell_1 R_{t-1} + \omega_1 PRE_t + \omega_2 POST_t \\ &+ \sum_{n=1}^{12} \gamma_n M_{nt} + \sum_{k=1}^{5} \rho_k W_{kt} + \delta_1 GOLD_{t\text{-}1} + \delta_2 OIL_{t\text{-}1} + \sum_{m=1}^{13} \eta_m ANNOUNCE_{mt} + \lambda h_t^2 + \varepsilon_t \end{aligned} \tag{5}$$

$$
\begin{aligned}
R_t &= \beta_1 Z_{t-1} + \beta_2 Z_{t-1} \times \ln(EPISODE_{t-1}) + \ell_1 R_{t-1} + \omega_1 PRE_t + \omega_2 POST_t \\
&+ \sum_{n=1}^{12} \gamma_n M_{nt} + \sum_{k=1}^{5} \rho_k W_{kt} + \delta_1 GOLD_{t-1} + \delta_2 OIL_{t-1} + \sum_{m=1}^{13} \eta_m ANNOUNCE_{mt} + \\
&+ \xi_1 NMOON_t + \xi_2 FMOON_t + \xi_3 TEMP_t + \xi_4 CLOUD_t + \xi_5 RAIN_t + \lambda h_t^2 + \varepsilon_t
\end{aligned}
\tag{6}
$$

In Eq. 4, 5 and 6, PRE_t ($POST_t$) = the holiday and observances immediately before (after) the trading day; M_{nt} = the twelve months of the year; $NMOON_t$ ($FMOON_t$) = the three calendar days immediately before and after new (full) moon. These dummy variables take the value of 1 on the related days and 0 on the other days. $GOLD_{t-1}$ (OIL_{t-1}) is the logarithmic change of the prices of gold (Brent oil) in US Dollars on day t-1. $ANNOUNCE_{mt}$ is the set of dummies that take the value of 1 in case a macroeconomic announcement is made on day t, and otherwise 0 for each of ten macroeconomic indicators shown in Table 1. $RAIN_t$ = precipitation (mm) in Istanbul. $TEMP_t$ is temperature (^{0}C) in Istanbul; $CLOUD_t$ is the rate of cloudiness in Istanbul.

Since some TV series finales are shown until late hours, viewers (potential investors) may remain awake. Sleeplessness may affect all kinds of investment decisions. The model defined by Eq. 3 is designed to test if the proposed relationship between parasocial breakup (negative mood) and stock market returns is still valid, taking this sleepless state into consideration.

$$
\begin{aligned}
s_t^d &= \beta_1 FINALE_{t-1} + \beta_2 FINALE_{t-1} \times \ln(EPISODE_{t-1}) + \beta_3 FINALE_{t-1,LATE} \\
&+ \beta_4 FINALE_{t-1,LATE} \times \ln(EPISODE_{t-1}) + \ell_i s_{t-1} + \Phi + \varepsilon_t
\end{aligned}
\tag{7}
$$

$FINALE_{t-1,LATE}$ is the dummy variable that takes the value of 1 for TV series finales[10] that end after 22:30[11] and 0 otherwise. Φ represents all of the other variables in Eq. 6.

Lastly, we repeat all analysis with returns in Turkish Lira (TL) and the estimates are reported in column 6 of Table 5 for only Eq. 6 because of space limitations. The results are robust.

The results of Eq. 4, 5 and 6 in Table 5 show that despite the new additions, β_1 and β_2 are still statistically significant. Robust results reveal that TV series finales (parasocial breakup, i.e. negative mood) increase the stock market returns.

For Eq. 7 in Table 5, the coefficient β_3 is positive, whereas the coefficient β_4 is negative but both coefficients are statistically insignificant, individually and jointly. The results related to coefficients β_3 and β_4 do not confirm that the TV series ending at late hours negatively affect stock returns on the following trading day. Table 5 shows that even if the TV series ending at late hours are controlled, parasocial breakup (negative mood) still increases the stock market returns. In addition, we reach the same results by using stock returns expressed in Turkish Liras.

In Table 5, although it is assumed that rainy days have a negative impact on mood (Dowling & Lucey, 2005; Lepori, 2015), the coefficient on the RAIN is estimated to increase stock market returns by 14 basis points if the rainfall in Istanbul exceeds 20 mm in a day.

The magnitude and sign of the coefficient on Monday, RAIN and TV series finales (β_1 and β_2) in Table 5 confirm that negative mood increases the stock market returns in Turkey. This result is not consistent with previous literature which suggests that the relationship among negative mood and stock market return are in the opposite direction.

Table 5. Robustness test results (only for description 1)

	Eq. 4	Eq. 5	Eq. 6	Eq. 7	Return (TL)
Panel A: Estimates for Return Equation					
β_1 Finale	-0.1916^{a}	-0.1875^{a}	-0.0204^{a}	-0.0351^{b}	-0.0139^{b}
β_2 Finale×ln(Episode)	0.0047^{a}	0.0047^{a}	0.0051^{a}	0.0087^{b}	0.0033^{b}
β_3 $Finale_{LATE}$	-	-	-	0.0200	-
β_4 FinaleLATE×ln(Episde)	-	-	-	-0.0051	-
R_{t-1}	0.1527^{a}	0.1552^{a}	0.1556^{a}	0.1555^{a}	0.1597^{a}
(Risk) h^2_t	0.0150	0.0153	0.0025	0.0006	0.0173
Calendar Variables					
Monday	0.0015^{c}	0.0017^{c}	0.0015^{c}	0.0015^{c}	-
November	-	-	-0.0023^{c}	-0.0023^{c}	-0.0024^{c}
Economic Variables					
Gold	-	0.0477^{c}	0.0487^{c}	0.0480^{c}	0.0413^{c}
Oil	-	-0.0448^{a}	-0.0451^{a}	-0.0450^{a}	-0.0285^{c}
Foreign trade statistics	-	0.0034^{b}	0.0035^{b}	0.0034^{b}	0.0021^{c}
Industrial production index	-	-	-	-	-0.0026^{b}
Economic confidence index	-	-	-0.0123^{c}	-0.0122^{c}	-
Consumer confidence index	-	-	-	0.0022^{c}	0.0020^{c}
Alternative Mood Proxies					
Rain	-	-	0.00007^{c}	0.00007^{c}	0.00006^{c}
Panel B: GARCH Parameters					
Constant	0.00004^{a}	0.00004^{a}	0.00004^{a}	0.00004^{a}	0.00008^{a}
e^2_{t-1}	0.0793^{a}	0.0787^{a}	0.0782^{a}	0.0780^{a}	0.1087^{a}
h^2_{t-1}	0.9086^{a}	0.9100^{a}	0.9106^{a}	0.9109^{a}	0.8618^{a}
Log likelihood	6250.8	6261.9	6264.3	6265.0	6506.5
Panel C: Joint Test					
Wald-Test (H_0:β_1=β_2=0)	3.004^{b}	2.892^{b}	3.369^{a}	3.195^{b}	2.343^{c}
Panel D: Autocorrelation Q-Statistics					
lags					
1	1.437	1.224	1.272	1.264	1.819
5	7.516	6.56	6.408	6.397	3.993
10	10.692	9.809	9.703	9.699	8.937
Panel E: ARCH-LM Tests					
lags					
1	1.099	1.218	1.338	1.259	2.139
5	2.557^{b}	2.787^{b}	2.894^{b}	2.873^{b}	3.423^{b}
10	1.424	1.589	1.520	1.601	1.873

Note: (1) ^{a},^{b}and ^{c} indicate that the estimated coefficients are statistically significant at 1%, 5%, and 10% levels respectively. (2) In order to save space, only the statistically significant variables are included here. (3) To narrow the research to a smaller area, only the test results related to the description 1 shown in Table 2 are reported here. Description 1 is the most general model. (4) In TL model (in column 6), the dependent variable "R_t" includes it to Eq. 6 as an independent variable until the 6th lag length according to the FPE (Final Predict Error) criterion.

Besides, results in Table 5 imply that stock market returns reacted positively to the announcements of foreign trade statistics and consumer confidence index. However, the dummies of the industrial production index and economic confidence index are negative and statistically significant at the %5 and %10 levels respectively. Regarding the fundamental macroeconomic variables, we observe that the effect of gold prices on stock market returns is positive, while the effect of oil prices is negative.

SOLUTIONS AND RECOMMENDATIONS

Within our knowledge, this is the first study outside the US that investigates the relationship between stock market returns and the negative mood arising from the parasocial breakup. This study, which explores the effect of parasocial breakups on stock returns in an emerging market (Turkey), also includes the TV series types and TV channels in the analyses. The results of the analyses reveal that the negative mood from parasocial breakup affects stock returns positively and this positive effect of negative mood on stock market returns differs by the TV series forms and TV channels. With this aspect, this paper presents robust findings that are in accord with the few studies in the field of psychology but inconsistent with the studies in the field of behavioural finance. The common findings of behavioural finance reveal that negative mood affects the demand for stocks and stock market returns negatively (see, literature review). However, we reveal that negative mood proxy variables such as Monday and rainy days in addition to TV series finales (i.e. parasocial breakup) also have a positive effect on Turkish stock market performance.

The findings of this chapter may have a practical implication for diligent investors in an emerging market (Turkey). According to the findings, TV series finales may be used to forecast the stock market trend. Furthermore, this paper has an implication for policymakers, too. Towards the end of long-running TV series, if policymakers can get TV personae to act in commercial films accord with his/her role by exercising their power, market inefficiency can be reduced. Continuance of a TV persona by commercial films can minimize the negative psychological effects of parasocial breakup and thus chips away at the effect of TV series finales (i.e. negative mood) on stock market performance.

As a result of this chapter, stock market returns respond positively to the finales of actions, comedies and the finales of series broadcasted on Channel D in particular. These findings are compatible with the survey of RTUK which shows the most popular TV series is broadcasted by Channel D (RTUK, 2012: 21). These results have several important implications for media bosses and producers of TV series in Turkey. Media bosses in Turkey can prefer to serialize more action and comedy series to increase the ratings of their channels by strengthening the power of the parasocial relationship. Producers of TV series, on the other hand, prefer to represent their TV series to Channel D in order to be on the air their TV shows for a longer time by increasing the recognition potential of TV personae.

FUTURE RESEARCH DIRECTIONS

This chapter contributes to the existing literature by examining the data of an emerging market and revealing inconsistent results with Lepori (2015) who was conducted in the USA. However, we cannot generalize the results of this chapter to other emerging markets and cannot account for our opposite results to those revealed by Lepori (2015). To fill this gap, researchers should examine the effect of TV series finales on stock market performance in most emerging and advanced market. Results of such studies would be attracted with regards to revealing the effect of values and norms of investors on the relationship between stock return and negative mood. Our inconsistent results with Lepori (2015) can probably result from the cultural differences of investors in Turkey and the USA.

We have not empirical results related to abnormal returns in BIST, although we exhibit the positive effect of negative mood on stock market returns. Further researches should examine the impact of long-running TV series finales on abnormal returns using other quantitative approaches and methods (for example, event study methodology, APARCH model, Monte Carlo simulations).

This chapter assumes that the long-running TV series finales have a negative effect on the mood of society and the findings support the relationship between parasocial breakup and stock market performance. However, we do not examine the effect of parasocial breakup (i.e. negative mood) on the other economic consequences. It would also be nice to investigate the effect of TV series finales on the mood and productivity of workers or consumer behaviour.

At first glance, our results seem to be in accordance with hypothesis H_2. The basic foundation of H_2 is that investors in a negative mood tend to take the higher risk because they have the hope to repair their negative feelings by achieving higher gains (see, literature review). Unfortunately, we do not clarify that investors in a negative mood buy more stocks traded in BIST to get higher returns because our results show that there is no tradeoff between risk and return in BIST. Increasing in Turkish stock market performance may be based on preferences of investors towards safer stocks to decrease their level of risk-taking. Furthermore, it is also possible that investors increase their holdings in the number of stocks to increase their level of diversification, which also decreases risk. One way to test for these statements is to more carefully examine the characteristics of stocks (e.g. beta, standard deviation, lottery-type stocks, etc.) that are bought and sold by investors, although we do not know if the data of other emerging markets allow for this (data related to BIST do not allow our for this).

CONCLUSION

The parasocial breakups and consequent mood swings in human beings are evident from psychological studies on TV series, movies and theatre play. However, its effect on stock market returns is not analyzed for emerging stock markets and not fully understood yet. This paper uses parasocial breakup as a proxy variable of negative mood and analyzes how such a variable affects the stock market returns in Borsa Istanbul. This study presents robust evidence that long-running TV series finales influence the stock market returns in the context of parasocial breakup concept.

The results of the analyses reveal that (i) negative mood arising from parasocial breakup stunningly enhances stock market performance out of keeping with the findings in the field of behavioral finance (see, literature review), (ii) this positive effect of negative mood on stock market returns differs by the TV series types and TV channels, (iii) the other negative mood proxies such as Monday and rainy days affect the stock market returns positively and (iv) relationship between risk and return in BIST is positive but insignificant. The situation, where the TV series finales increase the stock market returns without the relationship between risk and return in BIST, shows that "investors are rational at the decision making" is a basic but paradoxical assumption of economic and financial theories.

REFERENCES

Berument, H., Ceylan, N. B., & Gozpinar, E. (2006). Performance of soccer on the stock market: Evidence from Turkey. *The Social Science Journal*, *43*(4), 695–699. doi:10.1016/j.soscij.2006.08.021

Berument, M. H., Ceylan, N. B., & Ogut-Eker, G. (2009). Soccer, stock returns and fanaticism: Evidence from Turkey. *The Social Science Journal*, *46*(3), 594–600. doi:10.1016/j.soscij.2009.06.001

Białkowski, J., Etebari, A., & Wisniewski, T. P. (2012). Fast profits: Investor sentiment and stock returns during Ramadan. *Journal of Banking & Finance*, *36*(3), 835–845. doi:10.1016/j.jbankfin.2011.09.014

Bower, G. H. (1981). Mood and memory. *The American Psychologist*, *36*(2), 129–148. doi:10.1037/0003-066X.36.2.129 PMID:7224324

Bozkurt, İ. (2015). Investigation of the Effects of the Moon on Stock Returns: An Empirical Application on ISE. *İktisat İşletme ve Finans, 30*(352), 55-78.

Bozkurt, I., & Hatipoglu, M. (2017). The Relationship between Parasocial breakup and Investor Behaviours. *International Journal of Academic Research in Accounting, Finance and Management Sciences*, *7*(3), 87–96.

Bruyneel, S., Dewitte, S., Franses, P. H., & Dekimpe, M. G. (2009). I felt low and my purse feels light: Depleting mood regulation attempts affect risk decision making. *Journal of Behavioral Decision Making*, *22*(2), 153–170. doi:10.1002/bdm.619

Cao, M., & Wei, J. (2005). Stock market returns: A note on temperature anomaly. *Journal of Banking & Finance*, *29*(6), 1559–1573. doi:10.1016/j.jbankfin.2004.06.028

Cohen, J. (2003). Parasocial Break-ups: Measuring Individual Differences in Responses to the Dissolution of Parasocial Relationships. *Mass Communication & Society*, *6*(2), 191–202. doi:10.1207/S15327825MCS0602_5

Cohen, J. (2004). Parasocial Break-up from Favorite Television Characters: The Role of Attachment Styles and Relationship Intensity. *Journal of Social and Personal Relationships*, *21*(2), 187–202. doi:10.1177/0265407504041374

Conte, A., Levati, M. V., & Nardi, C. (2013). *The role of emotions on risk preferences: An experimental analysis (No. 2013-046)*. Jena Economic Research Papers.

Dowling, M., & Lucey, B. M. (2005). Weather, biorhythms, beliefs and stock returns—Some preliminary Irish evidence. *International Review of Financial Analysis*, *14*(3), 337–355. doi:10.1016/j.irfa.2004.10.003

Enders, W. (1995). *Applied econometric time series*. John Wiley Sons Inc.

Engle, R. F., Lilien, D. M., & Robins, R. P. (1987). Estimating time varying risk premia in the term structure: The ARCH-M model. *Econometrica*, 391–407.

Eyal, K., & Cohen, J. (2006). When Good Friends Say Goodbye: A Parasocial Breakup Study. *Journal of Broadcasting & Electronic Media*, *50*(3), 502–523. doi:10.120715506878jobem5003_9

Field, T., Diego, M., Pelaez, M., Deeds, O., & Delgado, J. (2009). Breakup distress in university students. *Adolescence*, *44*(176), 705–727. PMID:20432597

Hirshleifer, D., & Shumway, T. (2003). Good day sunshine: Stock returns and the weather. *The Journal of Finance*, *58*(3), 1009–1032. doi:10.1111/1540-6261.00556

Isen, A. M., & Geva, N. (1987). The influence of positive affect on acceptable level of risk: The person with a large canoe has a large worry. *Organizational Behavior and Human Decision Processes*, *39*(2), 145–154. doi:10.1016/0749-5978(87)90034-3

Isen, A. M., Shalker, T. E., Clark, M., & Karp, L. (1978). Affect, accessibility of material in memory, and behavior: A cognitive loop? *Journal of Personality and Social Psychology*, *36*(1), 1–12. doi:10.1037/0022-3514.36.1.1 PMID:621625

Johnson, E. J., & Tversky, A. (1983). Affect, generalization, and the perception of risk. *Journal of Personality and Social Psychology*, *45*(1), 20–31. doi:10.1037/0022-3514.45.1.20

Kavanagh, D. J., & Bower, G. H. (1985). Mood and self-efficacy: Impact of joy and sadness on perceived capabilities. *Cognitive Therapy and Research*, *9*(5), 507–525. doi:10.1007/BF01173005

Leith, K. P., & Baumeister, R. F. (1996). Why do bad moods increase self-defeating behavior? Emotion, risk taking and self-regulation. *Journal of Personality and Social Psychology*, *71*(6), 1250–1267. doi:10.1037/0022-3514.71.6.1250 PMID:8979390

Lepori, G. M. (2015). Investor mood and demand for stocks: Evidence from popular TV series finales. *Journal of Economic Psychology*, *48*, 33–47. doi:10.1016/j.joep.2015.02.003

Levy, T., & Yagil, J. (2011). Air pollution and stock returns in the US. *Journal of Economic Psychology*, *32*(3), 374–383. doi:10.1016/j.joep.2011.01.004

Lin, C. H., Yen, H. R., & Chuang, S. C. (2007). The effects of emotion and need for cognition on consumer choice involving risk. *Journal of Business and Psychology*, *22*(1), 65–78.

Loewenstein, G., Weber, E., Hsee, C., & Welch, N. (2001). Risk As Feelings. *Psychological Bulletin*, *127*(2), 267–286. doi:10.1037/0033-2909.127.2.267 PMID:11316014

Mayer, J. D., Gaschke, Y. N., Braverman, D. L., & Evans, T. W. (1992). Mood-congruent judgment is a general effect. *Journal of Personality and Social Psychology*, *63*(1), 119–132. doi:10.1037/0022-3514.63.1.119

McCarthy, C. J., Lambert, R. G., & Brack, G. (1997). Structural model of coping, appraisals, and emotions after relationship breakup. *Journal of Counseling and Development*, *76*(1), 53–64. doi:10.1002/j.1556-6676.1997.tb02376.x

Mick, D. G., & DeMoss, M. (1990). Self-gifts: Phenomenological insights from four contexts. *The Journal of Consumer Research*, *17*(3), 322–332. doi:10.1086/208560

Mittal, V., & Ross, W. T. Jr. (1998). The impact of positive and negative affect and issue framing on issue interpretation and risk taking. *Organizational Behavior and Human Decision Processes*, *76*(3), 298–324. doi:10.1006/obhd.1998.2808 PMID:9878512

Raghunathan, R., & Pham, M. T. (1999). All negative moods are not equal: Motivational influences of anxiety and sadness on decision making. *Organizational Behavior and Human Decision Processes, 79*(1), 56–77. doi:10.1006/obhd.1999.2838 PMID:10388609

Rhoades, G. K., Kamp-Dush, C. M., Atkins, D. C., Stanley, S. M., & Markman, H. J. (2011). Breaking up is hard to do: The impact of unmarried relationship dissolution on mental health and life satisfaction. *Journal of Family Psychology, 25*(3), 366–374. doi:10.1037/a0023627 PMID:21517174

RTÜK. (2013). *Televizyon İzleme Eğilimleri Araştırması 2012*. Retrieved from http://www.rtuk.org.tr/Icerik/DownloadReport/13

Rubin, R. B., & McHugh, M. P. (1987). Development of Parasocial Relationships. *Journal of Broadcasting & Electronic Media, 31*(3), 279–292. doi:10.1080/08838158709386664

Saunders, E. M. (1993). Stock prices and Wall Street weather. *The American Economic Review*, 1337–1345.

Schwarz, N., & Clore, G. L. (1983). Mood, misattribution, and judgments of well-being: Informative and directive functions of affective states. *Journal of Personality and Social Psychology, 45*(3), 513–523. doi:10.1037/0022-3514.45.3.513

Schwarz, N., & Clore, G. L. (1988). How do I feel about it? The informative function of affective states. In K. Fiedler & J. Forgas (Eds.), *Affect, cognition, and social behavior* (pp. 44–62). Göttigen, Germany: Hogrefe.

Slotter, E. B., Gaedner, W. L., & Finkel, E. J. (2010). Who am I without you? The influence of romantic breakup on the self-concept. *Personality and Social Psychology Bulletin, 36*(2), 147–160. doi:10.1177/0146167209352250 PMID:20008964

Thaler, R. H., & Johnson, E. J. (1990). Gambling with the house money and trying to break even: The effects of prior outcomes on risky choice. *Management Science, 36*(6), 643–660. doi:10.1287/mnsc.36.6.643

Westbrook, R. A. (1980). Intrapersonal affective influences on consumer satisfaction with products. *The Journal of Consumer Research, 7*(1), 49–54. doi:10.1086/208792

Wright, W. F., & Bower, G. H. (1992). Mood effects on subjective probability assessment. *Organizational Behavior and Human Decision Processes, 52*(2), 276–291. doi:10.1016/0749-5978(92)90039-A

Yuen, K. S., & Lee, T. M. (2003). Could mood state affect risk-taking decisions? *Journal of Affective Disorders, 75*(1), 11–18. doi:10.1016/S0165-0327(02)00022-8 PMID:12781345

Zillmann, D. (1988). Mood management through communication choices. *The American Behavioral Scientist, 31*(3), 327–340. doi:10.1177/000276488031003005

ENDNOTES

1 Parasocial relationship is a sentimental relationship between watchers of TV and the TV persona/personae. Parasocial breakup is the ending of the related relationship.

2 Downloaded from; http://www.borsaistanbul.com/en/data/data/index-data. The stock exchange index gives information on the price movements of stocks in that index and has frequently been used in economic analyses to determine stock performances. An increase (decrease) in index shows that the investors in the market have decided to buy (sell) stocks.

3 Selection criteria of TV series in this chapter are as follows: (i) their finales must have a minimum rating of 1% and share of 2%. (ii)They must have reached their finales during the period between the opening and the former closing of the BIST. (iii)They must be broadcasted for at least 20 episodes to have enough parasocial relationship with viewers. In Turkey, the seasonal broadcasting of TV series is roughly 35-36 episodes. (iv)Finally, the TV series finales, broadcasted at the time of the Turkish National Team matches, are excluded from the study.

4 All the information (except ratings) related to the TV series was obtained from the web sites http://www.bizimhikayelerimiz.com/forum/forumdisplay.php?108-D%C4%B0Z%C4%B0-AR%C5%9E%C4%B0V%C4%B0, http://tr.wikipedia.org/wiki/Kategori:T%C3%BCrk_televizyon_dizileri and http://www.imdb.com/search/title?countries=tr&start=1&title_type=tv_series, http://www.ddizi1.com/; the ratings were obtained from the web sites http://www.ucankus.com/ratingler, http://www.canlitv.com/rating/ and http://www.tvaktuel.com/tv/tv-rating/ between 01.04.2015 – 07.06.2015.

5 For example, it is supposed that the effect on investors' psychology and behaviors of a TV series that reached its finale on Saturday will be observed on Monday.

6 The related lag length is determined according to the FPE (Final Predict Error) criterion. If there is an autocorrelation between error terms in a regression model, the reliability of the model decreases. At this point FPE criterion determines the lag length that diminishes the autocorrelation between error terms. The results were found robust, but not shown here due to the space limitations.

7 In fact, the intensity of the response changes according to a baseline episode count. In this calculation, the baseline number of the episodes are supposed to be equal to the average episode count "69". According to this supposition, a 25% increase in the episode count causes an increase in the stock returns on the day after finale of the TV series in question, which is $E(R_T)-E(R_t)=[\beta_1+\beta 2\times Finale\times \ln(Episode_T)]-[\beta_1+\beta_2\times Finale\times \ln(Episode_t)]=[-0.02 + 0.005\times 1\times \ln(69*1.25)]-[-0.02 + 0.005\times 1\times \ln(69)]=0.0011$.

8 This method analyzes the relationship between two series without considering time effect.

9 Min.=20 episodes; Qr1 (Lower Quartile)=33 episodes; Qr2 (Median)=55 episodes; Qr3 (Upper Quartile)=90 episodes; Maximum=375 episodes and Upper Fence=175.5 episodes. The episode counts of "Çocuklar Duymasın", "Sihirli Annem" and "Bir Kadın Bir Erkek" TV series are outliers (233, 240 and 375, respectively).

10 The ending hour of some TV series that reached their finales could not be obtained. Only of 85 of 129 TV series' ending hours were obtained. 42 of them ended their finale broadcasts after 22:30.

11 As a result of the Turkish Sleep Medicine Society research (TSMS), it is known that the vast majority of the population in Turkey (75%) has a habit of sleeping for 7-8 hours (http://www.tutd.org.tr/eng/nekadar.php). Since the finales that ended after 22:30 may have caused at least a minor sleep loss in a sizable portion of the population, we estimate the model (in Eq. 7) with two additional interaction terms.

Section 2
Psychological Concepts in Behavioral Finance

Chapter 5
Emotional Finance Plays an Important Role in Investment Decisions

Sarika Keswani
ITM University Gwalior, India

ABSTRACT

Most of the investors focus on human emotions not expressed openly while making investment decisions. Emotions have a powerful position in making investment decisions. They drive human behavior that is consistent with economic predictions while making investments. Emotions play a significant role while making decisions on investments just like any other business decisions. Behavioral finance tries to combine behavioral and cognitive psychological theory with conventional economics and finance to provide justifications for why people make irrational financial decisions. The aim of this chapter is to understand whether emotional phases affect investors' decisions in different investment situations basing on levels of uncertainty. Positive emotions like self-confidence, challenge, and hope increase the decision-makers tendency to exaggerate the commitment, and negative emotions, namely embarrassment and strain, do not.

INTRODUCTION

The vast majority of the financial specialists center around human feelings not communicating transparently while settling on venture choices. Feelings have an effective position in settling on speculation choices. It drives human conduct that is reliable with financial expectations while making ventures. Feelings assume a noteworthy part while settling on choices on speculations simply like some other business choices. Behavioral fund tries to consolidate behavioral and subjective mental hypothesis with customary financial aspects and back, to give avocations to why individuals settle on unreasonable money related choices.

The point of this section is to comprehend whether passionate stages influence speculators' choices in various venture circumstances basing on levels of vulnerability. Positive feelings like fearlessness, test, and expectation increment the leaders inclination to misrepresent the dedication and negative

DOI: 10.4018/978-1-5225-7399-9.ch005

feelings to be specific humiliation and strain don't. At the point when budgetary markets are at their sadness because of retreat all through the entire monetary world, the inquiry that emerges is to discover the relationship how the feelings like dread related with interest in money related markets impacts the speculation choices. Further, it centers around inspecting the effect of feelings on the arrangement and returns of the chose venture choices. This section likewise manages distinguishing the components that are the dynamic power of their speculation basic leadership process and the part of feelings behind such choices. This section considers the hypothetical viewpoints.

Traditional Finance

This hypothesis expect that business sectors are for the most part productive, that speculators are sound and very much educated processors of data, working in what they accept to be their own self-intrigue. The ideas of "hazard" and "vulnerability" are come down to factual elements of unpredictability and co-fluctuation. Seen wasteful aspects in advertise valuing are the after effect of the "cutoff points to arbitrage," and markets normally incline toward a condition of harmony. Choices by singular financial specialists (discerning or not) are never sufficiently extensive to affect the market all in all. An unfaltering movement of research prompted the improvement of Modern Portfolio Theory, the Capital Asset Pricing Model, the Arbitrage Pricing Theory and the Efficient Market Hypothesis.

Taken as an assortment of work, Traditional Finance is an exquisite hypothetical develop and a massively profitable commitment to the comprehension of the way advertises work. But then, it misses the mark concerning clarifying individual speculator conduct. Truth be told, the underlying foundations of conduct and inclination (natural, mental, moral and moral) – the very components that make us human – are thought to be settled and are deliberately let well enough alone for the model. Indeed, even at the total level, Traditional Finance has no clarification for showcase oddities like "force," considerably less resource value bubbles (e.g., the Dot-com madness) or sharp breaks in the ordinary working of business sectors (e.g., occasions encompassing the sub-prime home loan emergency).

Behavioral Finance

Generally, financial aspects and fund have concentrated on models that accept sanity. The behavioral bits of knowledge have risen up out of the application in back and financial matters of experiences from test brain science. Behavioral back is generally another field which tries to give clarification to individuals' monetary choices. It is a mix of behavioral and intellectual mental hypothesis with regular financial aspects and fund. . Powerlessness to amplify the normal utility (EU) of sound speculators prompts development of behavioral back research inside the effective market structure. Behavioral fund investigate is an endeavor to determine irregularity of Traditional Expected Utility Maximization of balanced speculators inside proficient markets through clarification in view of human conduct. For example, Behavioral back clarifies why and how markets may be wasteful.

A hidden supposition of behavioral fund is that, the data structure and attributes of market members deliberately impact the person's venture choices and in addition showcase results. Financial specialist, as an individual, forms data utilizing easy routes and passionate channels.

This procedure impacts money related leaders to such an extent that they demonstration apparently in silly way, and settle on problematic choice, disregard conventional back claim of discernment. The effect of this imperfect money related choice has consequence for the proficiency of capital markets, individual riches, and the execution of enterprises. Unreasonable choice could be either because of preparing of wrong data or understanding with conflicting choices.

Conduct fund centres upon how speculators translate and follow up on data to settle on educated venture choices. Financial specialists don't generally act in a normal, unsurprising and an impartial way showed by the quantitative models. Behavioral Finance puts an accentuation upon financial specialist conduct prompting different market oddities.

The rise of behavioral back has introduced another domain for investigating the manners by which financial specialists settle on choices that incorporates mental factors and also giving new grounds whereupon it question traditional techniques for demonstrating speculator conduct. The test that behavioral back amasses is pointed especially toward the effective market theory (EMH), which is the model that Statman alludes to standard fund Model. Behavioral fund challenge speculation that standard back model of on'how financial specialist choice is off base', as it neglects to incorporate mental and esteem expressive inclinations in calculations (Statman, 1999).

Concept of Behavioural Finance

Definition of Behavioural Finance

Linter G.(1998) has characterized behavioral back as being investigation of how human translates and follow up on data to settle on educated speculation choices. (Linter,1998).

Olsen R. (199828) attests that behavioral back looks to comprehend and foresee orderly budgetary market ramifications of mental choice process.

"Behavioral fund, as a piece of behavioral financial aspects, is that branch of back that, with the assistance of speculations from other behavioral sciences, especially brain research and human science, tries to find and clarify wonders conflicting with the worldview of expected utility of riches and barely characterized objective conduct. Behavioral financial aspects is generally exploratory, utilizing research techniques that are infrequently connected in the conventional, standard back literature".

Brabazon recommends that the limited parts of Behavioral back can be part into two diverse arrangement gatherings (Brabazon,2000) . The main gathering is the heuristic choice procedures, where an individual financial specialist through natural mental.

WHAT IS EMOTIONAL FINANCE?

Enthusiastic fund is another worldview in the comprehension of speculation action and forecast of advantage costs and market conduct. It contrasts both from conventional fund hypothesis which depends on the thought speculators are "discerning", and behavioral back which in spite of the fact that perceiving that financial specialists are inclined to predisposition all things considered verifiably accept they can at present figure out how to be balanced. Passionate back perceives that individuals are characteristically silly and to a great extent driven by their feelings, both those of which they are intentionally mindful and, all the more critically, those which are oblivious. These last are considerably more effective in light of the fact that they are not specifically available to the cognizant personality.

Neuroscientists call attention to that no less than 95% of our psychological action is oblivious and how, practically speaking, activity goes before thought and cognizant mindfulness. Passionate back draws expressly on the experiences of the psychoanalytic comprehension of the human personality to depict how oblivious procedures drive speculation choices and market elements, and are a necessary piece of all money related basic leadership. By specifically recognizing the indispensable part financial specialists' oblivious needs, dreams and drives play in their speculation judgments, enthusiastic fund gives an exceptionally down to earth system that can help clarify and foresee those parts of venture basic leadership and market action not open to discerning models and traditional points of view.

Some researches indicate how showcase members eventually feel choices as opposed to intentionally influence them regardless of what they to seem to accept. Enthusiastic back specifically perceives the essential part hallucination and the related want for wish-satisfaction play in this procedure. Speculation choices are, essentially, the result of a battle between oblivious sentiments of fervor, the pleasurable thought of potential future pick up, and nervousness, the torment of potential future misfortune. Related with this is the dissent of the trouble of beating, and its related oblivious consequences. In mystic reality the speculator goes into a glorified passionate association with a stock, other resource, or even firm administration, which can without much of a stretch let him or her down. Truth be told, an imperative understanding of passionate fund is the manner by which a few sorts of venture, referred to actually as phantastic objects, speak to outstandingly energizing and attractive transformational wish-satisfying dreams in oblivious terms.

Passionate fund additionally perceives how advertises constitute substantial virtual gatherings with conduct mirroring the cooperation of the frequently oblivious drives, needs, feelings and wants of their members as they attempt and manage the intrinsic vulnerability of the speculation procedure and related uneasiness. Markets go up against their own particular oblivious mental life and are inclined to showcase on indistinguishable feelings from singular speculators, for example, fervor, happiness, frenzy, sadness and craziness. Vitally, by drawing on the bits of knowledge of gathering psychodynamic hypothesis enthusiastic back can help clarify why markets act as they do and diverse market states including resource estimating bubbles, for example, the present rerun of dot.com lunacy and the Chinese securities exchange rise, and also numerous parts of the Global Financial Crisis.

An expanding assemblage of observational research confirm exhibits the useful commitment enthusiastic fund can make. For instance, it can enable us to comprehend what truly drives finance director speculation choices which is altogether different to what is expectedly thought and advised to their customers. Correspondingly, it clarifies why singular financial specialists keep on investing so effectively in spite of the subsequent misfortunes, and the oblivious dreams that support this. Passionate fund bits of knowledge are likewise enter in clarifying securities exchange oddities where stocks seem, by all accounts, to be deliberately mispriced and, for instance, why the market has incredible trouble in managing terrible news properly. Once more, much venture movement has betting like qualities with clear ramifications for showcase estimating, and by understanding the basic mental procedures at work enthusiastic fund is additionally ready to contribute here. In rundown, enthusiastic fund gives us an idea about what is genuinely essential to financial specialists and their conviction to contribute in spite of results being so unusual.

The commence of enthusiastic fund is that formal learning of the inconspicuous and complex ways our oblivious personality works and related oblivious gathering procedures can enable us to see better how resource valuations and speculation judgements are made, and how advertises work and why, now and again, they separate. This new comprehension can lead straightforwardly to better venture choices and more viable money related basic leadership all the more by and large, very separated from its suggestions for, among others, financial strategy producers and market controllers.

EMOTIONAL FINANCE IN PRACTICE

The past area outlined a portion of the fundamental hypothesis of passionate back; this segment investigates its significance to genuine capital markets. To begin with, the genuine importance of hazard is talked about; this is altogether different to how chance is ordinarily seen in fund instructing. Next, the key part the need to trust plays in venture choices, and a portion of the ramifications of this for financial specialist and market conduct, is depicted. The potential commitment of passionate back in clarifying securities exchange oddities is then viewed as; some psychodynamic parallels between speculation conduct and betting are additionally drawn. Next the subject of why people are regularly hesitant to spare sufficiently for their retirement is investigated, and whether what seniority speaks to in mystic reality could enable us to see such apparently "nonsensical" conduct. At last, this area portrays how passionate fund can help clarify how proficient speculators can go into irresolute protest relations with budgetary resources and stocks when results are to a great extent unusual and they can undoubtedly be let down. This is by means of the procedure of narrating.

Emotional Fund and the Genuine Importance of Hazard

"Our institutional customers some of the time characterize chance as following mistake. They are hoping to expand their data proportion, yet you can augment your data proportion and limit your following blunder and drive your portfolio appropriate off a 40% precipice. All things considered it is about vocation chance, isn't that so? … to me, the meaning of 'chance' isn't standard deviation, it's not unpredictability, it's not beta; it's what your danger of an emergency. What's the hazard that you delve your customer into an opening sufficiently extensive that they never recuperate, they never receive in return? That is chance.

Venture hazard is ordinarily estimated by such measurements as fluctuation of profits, following mistake, esteem in danger (VaR), stock beta and an expansive scope of trademark based factors, for example, measure, esteem/development, energy, yield and income inconstancy and so forth., and saw as target and quantifiable. The thought is that hazard can be fittingly overseen through the utilization of refined quantitative investigation and experience However, there is an unmistakable qualification amongst hazard and vulnerability. Hazard is conspicuous, quantifiable and known, being founded on the possibility that the past can, it might be said, be utilized foresee what's to come. Then again, vulnerability is unidentifiable, incomprehensible and obscure.

There are four chief concerns:

1. **Information Chance:** Stresses over the nature of the data support chiefs depend on to settle on venture choices and whether they can trust what organization administration is letting them know,
2. Anxiety (hazard) about the natural flightiness of the speculation undertaking,
3. **Business Hazard:** The threat of underperformance prompting customer misfortune, and
4. **Career Chance:** Dangers to remuneration and advancement, and even employment end, if the reserve director fails to meet expectations for any time allotment.

Emotional Back and the Need to Trust

As has been brought up above, venture is synonymous with vulnerability; financial specialists can't anticipate with any level of exactness the results of their speculation choices. This definitely prompts nervousness which is frequently stifled. Given such unpleasurable effects, how are speculators ready to go into irresolute protest associations with resources that would so be able to effortlessly and agonizingly disappointed them? Passionate fund sees this puzzle as far as the key part trust plays in the venture procedure.

Trust pervades all human movement with the capacity to trust established in the security of early newborn child encounters and securely in parental physical and enthusiastic reliance connections (Neri, 2005). Be that as it may, there are the unavoidable, and regularly oblivious, clashes amongst trust and doubt, and require and the related tension about being misdirected or let down, which are experienced as genuinely unnerving in clairvoyant reality. In any case, without the capacity to trust (and have confidence) venture isn't conceivable, prompting stasis. To contribute (act) is to trust. The capacity to trust when 'not knowing' the result creates the conviction to focus on an advantage or stock. Trust prompts powerlessness as it includes offering carefulness to, depending on, or being helpless against, another under states of vulnerability (Shapiro, 2012) regardless of whether, for our motivations, the "market", organization administration or the investigator who gave the first speculation thought. Essentially, it gives a "fantasy of control" (Pixley, 2004, pp.19– 20). Put stock in "trumps" nervousness and prompts activity; in passionate terms it interfaces the present and the future – it "makes" wanted future results.

Trust is likewise connected in venture to confidence which requires just conviction or "conviction", not check or affirmation, and depends on admiration (i.e., "flawlessness" as in the phantastic protest) and figment. Reality testing, as in venture for the most part, is stayed away from with fundamental suspicion aggregate reasoning commanding – confidence is encouraged inside the aggregate conviction of the gathering (Neri, 2005) in money related markets.

The need to trust to contribute regardless of the related tension about being foiled encourages us comprehend not exactly how financial specialists can take part in business sectors when future results are erratic, yet in addition why support directors put such a great amount of accentuation on meeting organization administration in spite of monitoring how effortlessly they can be misdirected. In spite of the fact that gathering administration prompts exchanging movement, there is no confirmation this is converted into prevalent longer term returns. Such gatherings appear to have as their primary reason the easing of (oblivious) tension by anticipating this on to firm administration to perform for the store director, and producing the sentiment trust (or individual preferring of the CEO or administration group) expected to put resources into the primary spot.

Enthusiastic fund sees the determination of the nervousness inalienable in the venture procedure related with the mysterious future as far as the key part trust and (visually impaired) confidence play simultaneously. To trust is to contribute!

Emotional Finance and Stock Market Anomalies

Securities exchanges are expectedly seen as "effective". In any case, a significant part of the back writing has concentrated on looking to distinguish exchanging systems that damage the Efficient Markets Hypothesis. This sub-segment proposes some enthusiastic back clarifications for why securities exchange peculiarities could exist by and by. Financial specialists acting exclusively and in addition together go into basically undecided question associations with stocks where what these speak to in clairvoyant terms may well command their relative engaging quality in view of customary basic resource valuation criteria. On this premise enthusiastic fund would, for instance, estimate with regards to the book/advertise (esteem/development) irregularity that high market to book stocks which are probably going to be "energizing" (pleasurable) could therefore be conceivably overrated prompting ensuing underperformance. Then again, low market to book stocks may well have unpleasurable or nervousness creating attributes prompting them being possibly underpriced in key terms, and resulting outperformance.

Investment and Gambling

Stock merchants and lottery purchasers have much in like manner. In his original section "Who Gambles in the Stock Market?" Its shows how the affinity to bet and the speculation choices of retail speculators are corresponded. State lotteries, used to intermediary for betting affinity, and stocks with comparative betting like attributes pull in fundamentally the same as customer bases. Specifically, the degree to which individuals' general state of mind towards betting impacts their stock speculation choices. In light of a scope of definite examinations Kumar reasons that there are "an arrangement of regular individual characteristics" which give confirmation of solid similitudes between the conduct of state lottery players and individual financial specialists who put resources into lottery-type stocks.

Emotional Finance and Retirement Saving Behavior

Once the worker is enlisted in the arrangement, a solid default inclination is seen with commitment rates tied down to the (normally low) default rate, instead of a more suitable one. Though programmed enrolment is presently expectedly used to support interest in retirement sparing plans along these lines essentially expanding investment rates, including since October 2012 by the UK government, in any case reserve funds levels stay low and lacking to give fitting benefits on retirement.

Be that as it may, this understanding disregards the capable feelings and phantasies related with retirement, for example, sick wellbeing, illness and, critically, the dread of death. This oblivious "signifying" of retirement and related requirement for sparing may along these lines prompt oblivious disavowal and not having any desire to know, separating from and quelling the ramifications of unavoidable seniority and passing from maybe an at present sound and dynamic early middle age. Strikingly, common assets appear to perceive these elements verifiably by advertising their annuity items with photos of an admired maturity in this way advancing disavowal and the not looking of reality. The hazard is this can bolster into an isolated perspective, additionally promising dissent of the related hidden apprehensions and frenzy, and prompt inaction so individuals can evade or deny undesirable reality. Such oblivious dynamic procedures are profoundly attached and should be legitimately recognized; enthusiastic fund recommends it isn't sufficient just to leave annuity sparing choices to the use of paternalistic libertarianism utilizing behavioral standards.

Emotional Finance and the Conviction to Invest

Reserve administrators can't outflank different supervisors or their separate benchmarks after expenses and especially in later periods. Likewise, regardless of whether specific chiefs do have better capacities it is exceptionally troublesome than recognize them ex bet and, all the more for the most part, recognize ability from fortunes Fund directors are settled on the horns of an issue. They "know" on one level that there is minimal observational proof they can do what is (unreasonably) expected of them. Be that as it may, then again, it is to trust it is in any case conceivable to convey prevalent profits for a predictable premise as requested by their customers. Passionate back proposes that reserve directors manage the vacillation expected of them by doing what we as a whole do, which is by recounting stories. This is both to themselves intentionally and unknowingly, and to others. Critically, having the capacity to clarify conceivably why venture choices both worked out and did not enables the obscure future to seem unsurprising, and by forcing significance can enable the reserve administrator to feel ready to control the inalienably dubious world he needs to manage and the related fundamental tension.

THEORIES OF EMOTIONAL FINANCE

Neuroscientists call attention to how most mental movement happens outside of cognizant mindfulness. Present day investigate in neuropsychology is progressively affirming Freud's unique bits of knowledge into the workings of the human mind and the developmental part early newborn child connections and encounters play in grown-up mental procedures. Feeling and oblivious mystic procedures are focal in the way individuals manage the world. In any case, the part individuals' oblivious needs, dreams and drives may play in their monetary choices is expectedly overlooked by money related scientists.

Venture showcase results are characteristically eccentric and such vulnerability prompts enthusiastic reactions of both a neurological and mental nature. Enthusiastic back specifically investigates how oblivious procedures help drive speculator and market conduct. The critical part of figment in venture, which from a psychoanalytic point of view is seen as any conviction intensely affected by wish satisfaction and the bending of the truth, is unequivocally perceived. Individuals unwittingly feel what they need to be valid, as opposed to what really is. The clairvoyant, or subjective, reality, of the "internal world", the universe of oblivious dreams and wishes, is altogether different to the material universe of outside reality, the undeniable realities of the issue, with which back customarily tries to bargain.

Ambivalence and Unconscious Conflict

Therapy sees considerations made by emotions as eventually being of two kinds: pleasurable (energizing) or unpleasurable (agonizing, nervousness creating, or misfortune inciting). Mental working mirrors the result of a progressing and never completely settled battle between the joy guideline and the truth standard, the ability to detect reality as it truly seems to be, however agonizing, as opposed to how individuals may wish it to be. Speculation choices make sentiments of both fervor (the joy of envisioned future pick up) and tension (the torment or unpleasure of potential future misfortune). The way toward putting implies that the speculator goes into an enthusiastic connection, regardless of whether cognizant or not, with something, a stock or other resource, which can prompt both pick up or torment. The financial specialist winds up subject to its future value, something which is inalienably unverifiable. There is the desire and expectation the stock will go up, which is pleasurable or energizing, however then again it can without much of a stretch let the speculator down, the possibility of which is unpleasurable and anxiety generating. Essentially, since both pleasurable and unpleasurable sentiments are produced in the meantime, this prompts subjectively agonizing enthusiastic clash or inner conflict.

Unconscious Phantasies

Comprehensively, the term oblivious alludes to the psychological procedures of which the individual is unconscious however which in any case apply an immediate impact on cognizant experience. The term is related with the manner by which individuals are driven by thoughts, clashes and sentiments past their cognizant mindfulness. Phantasies are the essential building squares of oblivious mental life and in this way profound drivers of human conduct and subjective idea. Such unrecognized feelings are intense in light of the fact that they stay obscure and in this manner not open to cognizant idea and reflection. The term phantasy with a 'ph' is utilized customarily by psychoanalysts to allude to oblivious occasions and dream to more cognizant developed ones, for example, wanders off in fantasy land or impractical reasoning.

Phantastic Objects

As has been called attention to above, venture incites sentiments of both energy about pick up (delight) and uneasiness about misfortune (unpleasure). Passionate back expressly consolidates the part of energy in the investigation of financial specialist and market conduct by perceiving that any venture can have an extraordinarily energizing and transformational significance in oblivious reality. This animates a condition of high fervor and related romanticizing prompting the want to have. The term phantastic question is gotten from the Freudian idea of protest which is utilized to portray the disguised "portrayals" of individuals, thoughts or things in our oblivious personality, and phantasy as characterized previously. It portrays the oblivious mental portrayal of something (or a thought) that satisfies the person's most profound (and soonest) wants to have precisely what they need precisely when they need it. Ownership of such phantastic objects permits speculators unwittingly to feel all-powerful, similar to Aladdin whose light could summon the genie, or the anecdotal bond dealer, Sherman McCoy, in The Bonfire of the Vanities (Wolfe, 1987) who felt himself to be an ace of the universe.

Judgments and States of Mind

As we have seen inner conflict is at the core of clairvoyant life. Every passionate relationship are in some sense irresolute, we make both great (pleasurable) and terrible (unpleasurable) emotions driving definitely to mental clash of which we are typically ignorant. We can manage this in a pretty much coordinated perspective where both the great and terrible sentiments are recognized and endured, indecision is felt and perceived and vulnerability acknowledged, i.e., in all actuality. Or on the other hand in a partitioned perspective by abstaining from, overlooking or legitimizing endlessly any sentiments that may cause mental torment and ruin the positive or pleasurable ones, trying to be left with just the pleasurable, i.e., in falsity. Here everything is it might be said dark or white, there is no vulnerability. Great and awful emotions are kept rationally isolate with the last denied and put onto others. Be that as it may, what is curbed and no longer specifically available to cognizant mindfulness, obviously, keeps on existing "behind" the scenes influencing what we do and feel.

Markets as Large Groups

Enthusiastic fund sees advertises as virtual extensive gatherings with conduct mirroring the collaboration of the frequently oblivious drives, needs, feelings and phantasies of their members as they manage the innate inner conflict and vulnerability of the speculation procedure. Markets, as a result, go up against a dynamic oblivious "passionate" existence of their own which pundits regularly recognize by review Benjamin Graham's Mr. Market in a human path as being inclined to such human feelings as frenzy, rapture and lunacy, and much of the time being "unreasonable". Passionate fund considers markets to be agreeable to investigation drawing on the psychoanalytic comprehension of oblivious gathering flow. Gathering forms don't require their individuals to be in a similar room; markets are comprised of heap people all communicating with each other on various levels and in various ways. Recognizes two essential gathering forms, work gatherings and fundamental presumption gatherings, which carry on in altogether different ways. In a work assemble its individuals cooperate imaginatively to a typical end utilizing data properly, both positive and negative, in this undertaking. Then again, when an essential suspicion assemble is working, the reason for the gathering is to give great (i.e., pleasurable) sentiments through the oblivious protections the gathering all in all receives against uneasiness, instead of through reality-based idea and cooperating for a typical reason. For this situation the gathering doesn't think about the established truths. Data is utilized to advance solace and fervor in an isolated perspective with the negative viewpoints denied and split off.

THE ROLE OF EMOTIONS IN INVESTMENT DECISIONS

Reserve supervisors work in an exceptionally candidly charged condition and need to go into irresolute protest associations with the advantages they purchase and offer, which can undoubtedly disappoint them, and where future results are indeterminate. Tension and disavowal overwhelm intheir endeavor to comprehend what they do. At last they are required to separate from and subdue what they would prefer not to "know", i.e., "turning a visually impaired eye".

In this last area before the section finishes up the idea of the store administration industry is broke down from a passionate fund viewpoint. In the first place, the Catch 22 of the business being based on the thought it is conceivable to accomplish something which isn't conceivable is investigated; the accompanying sub-area at that point talks about what truly drives resource director conduct.

1. Fund supervisors as phantastic objects Stock markets are situations in which financial specialists' cognizant needs and oblivious phantasies are played out. Members go into sincerely reliant and undecided associations with their benefits, regardless of whether intentionally mindful of this or not, that render them powerless and can without much of a stretch prompt them being let down. The very idea of the flighty condition in which subsidize chiefs need to work and the absurd requests set on them to accomplish something which it isn't conceivable to do prompt feelings which waver persistently between fervor (delight) and tension (unpleasure). Sentiments of put stock in, expectation and love (i.e., fascination) are consistently hollowed against those of stress, frustration, dread and detest (i.e., repugnance).

What isn't regularly perceived is the manner by which finance administrators are being utilized by the benefit administration industry to make impossible desires among financial specialists. The business is based on the possibility that in any event some store chiefs can beat reliably after some time which is the thing that customers, accordingly, agree to accept. To have the capacity to do this store directors need to trust they can discover phantastic objects, stocks which will procure them exceptional yields with low or no hazard which different speculators have not yet found.

In parallel, support supervisors themselves are in some sense being utilized as phantastic objects. They are the specialists that their customers, businesses, monetary counsels, venture advisors and the media unknowingly need to have faith in to reduce the tension related with the way that speculation results are unverifiable. On one level, the entire business is unwittingly intriguing in essential presumption bunch thinking in the hallucination that it is conceivable to accomplish something which is exceptionally troublesome if certainly feasible. Reserve administration is an industry based on a separated perspective in which fundamental reality (the impossibility of reliably outflanking the market) is held under control. Oblivious conspiracy and the quality of gathering forms repress any legitimate examination of this Catch 22. This means the essential part the reserve director plays in meeting the genuine needs of his customers in a wide range of ways is disregarded.

2. Excitement, tension and dissent According to speculation old stories the feelings of covetousness, dread and expectation drive money related markets. In any case, this is a poor portrayal of what truly vitalizes subsidize chiefs. A few investigations demonstrated that what propels genuine cash chiefs isn't eagerness however a mission for fervor, the scan for and envisioned joy in finding the "ideal" speculation (or phantastic protest). Additionally it isn't fear however nervousness at the possibility of misfortune which is typically denied and subdued, and consequently a much more capable impact on genuine conduct since it isn't thought. At long last, the term trust is utilized to cover foreswearing of the way that venture results are unverifiable. In some capacity support administrators "know", yet can't recognize the truth that what they are required to do is to a great degree troublesome if certainly feasible. Expectation cover refusal.

Passionate back accordingly sees financial specialists as not being driven by ravenousness, dread and expectation as regularly negligently accepted, however determined by a particular arrangement of energies, nerves and disavowals. A comprehension of the key part such normally oblivious feelings play in all venture movement should be consolidated straightforwardly in any hypothesis that looks to clarify this present reality of the reserve supervisor.

THE IMPACT OF EMOTIONS ON THE COMPOSITION AND RETURNS OF THE SELECTED INVESTMENT DECISIONS

If you think that emotions don't affect financial planning, you'll be surprised. As negative emotions will affect your mental state, they can result in bad investment options. One Research has found that fear and sadness are experienced at a more intense level than positive emotions. In fact, both feelings can be felt 2.5 times stronger. This means you are more likely to splurge when feeling low as compared with having a good day. When you are feeling a negative emotion, a biological response creates an urgent need to deal with it. Since making financial decisions are often difficult, it's only natural that the process involves unsettling emotions.

Balance Your Emotions and Financial Decisions

The good news is once you have identified these negative feelings, it can motivate you to come up with creative solutions to correct any financial problem. Some of these negative emotions are listed:

Sadness

According to the study, sadness induces impatience and narrow-mindedness. When making decisions on financial planning, this emotion can cause a person to have 'present bias', where they end up favouring immediate gratification over future rewards. The skewed decision rests on short-term gains instead of long-term benefits.

Anxiety

People often hesitate when it comes to making investment decisions. One reason for this is fear. They are afraid that their decisions will result in a loss of capital and that they will have to rely on family and friends for money. Another reason is their lack of awareness. Their limited knowledge on personal financial planning lowers their confidence when it comes to making such decisions.

Envy

It's natural to be envious of other people's possessions. But sometimes this emotion can lead to jealousy, embarrassment, and the need to measure up, causing you to spend beyond your means, while affecting your personal financial planning disastrously.

Over-Confidence

Some people tend to be too optimistic when it comes to their investment decisions. They have no concept of investment planning, often because they don't believe in the system or think that their investment will somehow work out.

Finance may be the stuff of numbers but emotions can create chaos in this realm. Once your negative emotions have been identified, you can take the appropriate steps to ensure the practicality of your financial decision.

SUMMARY AND CONCLUSION

This section recommends we can expand the comprehension of budgetary markets and speculator conduct gave by customary monetary models and behavioral fund on the off chance that we are likewise ready to perceive all the more formally how perception and feeling are personally connected. In particular, drawing on the psychoanalytic comprehension of the human personality, this article investigates the part oblivious phantasies, needs, and drives play in all speculation movement.

The initial segment of the section traces passionate fund hypothesis. It depicts how contributing incites clashing sentiments of both energy and nervousness, and the enthusiastic outcomes of the speculator engaging in an essentially undecided association with a benefit that can without much of a stretch let him or her down. It additionally demonstrates how speculation choices can be made in two swaying fundamental perspectives named coordinated and partitioned with hidden reality separately either recognized or denied, and the unfortunate outcomes on account of the last mentioned. How all monetary resources can conceivably assume the part of energizing and transformational phantastic protests in financial specialists' clairvoyant reality in everyday exchanging action, not simply in resource estimating bubbles, is next investigated. The section additionally proposes how markets can be seen as virtual extensive gatherings driven by their own oblivious procedures. It is simple for financial specialists to be gotten up to speed in energized and deceitful fundamental suspicion gather conduct including aggregate foreswearing of hidden reality with the mystic objective of influencing everybody to feel "great". The accompanying areas at that point apply these thoughts by and by to help clarify particular speculator and market practices, resource valuing bubbles and related wonders, and the idea of the advantage administration industry.

Initially regular measures of hazard utilized as a part of capital markets are indicated additionally to fill an alternate need in clairvoyant terms, this is of guarding against the way that what's to come is naturally erratic, i.e., genuine hazard. The key part the capacity to trust plays in the speculator having the capacity to focus on a benefit or a stock when the result in indeterminate is next viewed as, together with the unavoidable clash that emerges amongst trust and doubt. The section at that point investigates potential correlative enthusiastic fund based clarifications for why securities exchange irregularities could exist by and by. Specific spotlight is put on showcase underreaction to awful news occasions when it requires investment for reality to overpower speculators' oblivious barriers against acknowledging the enthusiastic agony of misfortune. The parallels between parts of securities exchange contributing and betting are next explored with clairvoyant energy and refusal of reality, despite the fact that in various degrees, inalienable in the two exercises.

The part likewise indicates how a comprehension of the oblivious "signifying" of retirement and related foreswearing of what it speaks to may cause disclose individuals' hesitance to spare sufficiently for their annuities. At long last, the procedure by which support supervisors can produce the conviction to contribute when results are questionable is investigated, and how narrating assumes a key part in mitigating the related oblivious nervousness.

The accompanying segment of the section gives a passionate back point of view on the website and the later and significantly bigger Chinese securities exchange resource evaluating bubbles. The worldwide money related emergency, with apparently very comparable way subordinate procedures at work, is additionally investigated. Specifically, the part proposes how both website and Chinese stocks seemed to have all the alluring properties of phantastic objects. As costs shot up any drawback hazard or nervousness was cleared from mindfulness in essential supposition bunch showcase wide deceitful foreswearing of reality trying to leave the massively fulfilling wish satisfaction phantasy in place. At last, reality couldn't be closed out for ever and the procedure ran quickly into turn around with the phantastic question now despised and criticized. Fault of, and outrage with, those felt in charge of the value fall substituted for hyper fervor with no clear learning by financial specialists about how they had been gotten up to speed in the phantasy conceivable. In parallel, the part demonstrates how the carrying on of hugely energizing oblivious phantasies related with the possibility that house costs could just keep on going up for ever seems to have assumed a critical part in the beginning of the worldwide monetary emergency. Specifically, governments, national banks, and controllers appeared to have been made up for lost time readily with venture banks and other market members in tremendously fulfilling starry-eyed reasoning that there was no drawback to hypothesis as uneasiness and hazard had been vanquished by the phantastic protest spoke to by "new thousand years back." Emotional fund hypothesis predicts that business sectors (and economies) in which such oblivious deceitful conduct is permitted to overwhelm, and may even be in a roundabout way supported, are intrinsically insecure.

At long last the section takes a gander at the speculation business and the oddity it constitutes. Instead of appropriately perceiving the imperative part the store director plays in meeting speculators' genuine budgetary and passionate needs, the industry and its customers give off an impression of being regarding cash administrators as phantastic objects with fundamental reality held under control.

In parallel, the section contends recognize that the genuine feelings driving speculation are those of fervor, tension and refusal, regularly experienced by advertise members on an oblivious level. The basic start in passionate back is that learning of the unobtrusive and complex ways our regularly oblivious sentiments, dreams and needs decide clairvoyant reality may enhance our comprehension of both how resource valuations and venture judgments are made, and how markets can separate. Venture choices are driven together by insight and feeling with most related mental action oblivious. Gathering elements likewise assume a fundamental part in what goes on. This part draws on a progression of cases to represent how receiving a correlative psychodynamic viewpoint could well be useful and give extra comprehension of money related action and market practices as of now not all around clarified by existing monetary standards and models. Actually, it is even conceivable to guess that notwithstanding their "truth" esteem these last may likewise be being utilized unknowingly by speculators to reduce uneasiness and enable them to trust the dubious future is in any case in some sense unsurprising.

REFERENCES

Brabazon, T. (2000). Behavioural Finance: A new sunrise or a false dawn? Coil Summer School 2000, University of Limerick.

Dickason, Z., & Ferreira, S. (2018). Establishing a link between risk tolerance, investor personality and behavioural finance in South Africa. *Cogent Economics & Finance*, *6*(1), 1–13. doi:10.1080/23322039.2018.1519898

Frankfurter, G. M., & McGoun, E. G. (2002). Resistance is futile: The assimilation of behavioral finance. *Journal of Economic Behavior & Organization*, *48*, 375–389.

Kahneman, D., & Tversky, A. (1979). Prospect theory: An analysis of decision making under risk. *Econometrica*, *47*(2), 263–291. doi:10.2307/1914185

Lintner, G. (1998). Behavioral finance: Why investors make bad decisions. *The Planner*, *13*(1), 7–8.

Mathews. (2005). A situation-based Decision-making process. *The ICFAI Journal of Organisation Behaviour, 4*(3), 19-25.

Neri, C. (2005). What is the function of faith and trust in psychoanalysis? *The International Journal of Psycho-Analysis*, *86*(1), 79–97. doi:10.1516/H27X-L81H-PPLM-MNVG PMID:15859223

Olsen, R. A. (1998). Behavioural Finance and its implications for Stock-Price volatility. *Financial Analysts Journal*, *54*(2), 2, 10–17. doi:10.2469/faj.v54.n2.2161

Pixley, J. (2004). *Emotions in finance: Distrust and uncertainty in global markets*. Cambridge University Press. doi:10.1017/CBO9781139195041

Shapiro, S. (2012). The grammar of trust. In *New Perspectives on Emotions in Finance* (pp. 115–134). Routledge.

Shefrin, H. (2000). *Beyond Greed and Fear: understanding behavioural finance and the psychology of investing*. Boston: Harvard Business School Press.

Slovic, P. (1972). Psychological study of human judgement: Implications for investment decision making. *The Journal of Finance*, *27*(4), 779–801. doi:10.1111/j.1540-6261.1972.tb01311.x

Thaler, R., & Shefrin, H. (1981). An economic theory of self control. *Journal of Political Economy*, *89*(2), 392–410. doi:10.1086/260971

Thaler. (1999). Mental Accounting Matters. *Journal of Behavioural Decision Making, 12*, 183-206.

Tversky, A., & Kahneman, D. (1974). Judgement under uncertainty: Heuristics and biases. *Science*, *185*(4157), 1124–1131. doi:10.1126cience.185.4157.1124 PMID:17835457

Venkatesh, B. (2002, December 1). What is Loss Aversion? *Business Line*.

Chapter 6
Individual Factors Affecting the Participation of Turkish People in the New Individual Pension System

Emine Ebru Aksoy
Ankara Hacı Bayram Veli University, Turkey

ABSTRACT

In Turkey, the first step of the individual pension system was based on volunteerism, but the voluntary system resulted in limited participation. Thus, the second step of the system has started to be implemented mandatorily since 2017, and participants were allowed to opt-out the system within two months. More than half of participants in the system preferred to leave the system. Therefore, this study aims to examine individual factors affecting their decision of staying in this system. A survey study was conducted with 374 people selected using the random sampling method. As a result of the study, a positive relationship was found only between the dependent variable and gender, but a significant relationship was determined only between the dependent variable and education level. Based on the results of this study, it is suggested that if the system will need to be improved, the low-performing fund management of the new individual pension system should be re-audited, and the confidence in the system should be increased in this way.

INTRODUCTION

People are exposed to many risks throughout their life and this situation has led people to pursue ways to protect themselves against risks. For this reason, they tend to avoid these risks by saving money when they earn income. However, social problems can arise if the saving rate is low. In this case, one of the ways to protect people from risks is social security. According to article 22 of the Universal Declaration of Human Rights (UDHR) everyone being a member of society has the social security right. Moreover, article 25 emphasizes that everyone has the right to a standard of living adequate for their health, well-being and family. It is also underlined in this article that food, clothing, housing, medical care, necessary

DOI: 10.4018/978-1-5225-7399-9.ch006

social services, and the right of security in the event of unemployment, sickness, disability, widowhood, old age or other lack of livelihood in circumstances beyond everyone's control are the rights granted to everyone in society.

Social security for the purpose of increasing social welfare provides people with an assurance against occupational risks, physiological risks, and socio-economic risks that individuals may encounter throughout their life. These risks include occupational accidents, occupational diseases, illness, maternity, invalidity, old age, death, unemployment, etc. However, the rapid aging of the population, deterioration of the birth rate, increasing unemployment and economic instability cause social security problems in countries. Therefore, it is not expected that social security systems around the world will be able to maintain the same standard of living for individuals during their pension (Antolin et.al., 2012, p.29). This situation forces countries to revise their social security systems and individual pension systems are generally seen as the solution to the problems in the social security system.

Pension systems have a significance for economic, social and political perspectives for countries. The practices of countries' pension system vary from each other. It can be seen that the triple system has been applied generally. The first part constitutes the compulsory social security system, whereas the second part constitutes the occupational pension system and the last part constitutes the individual pension system. Recently, countries have been using the second and third part to support social security systems. In particular, the individual pension system is used as a complement to the social security system. The purpose of the individual pension system is to enable participants to continue their working life standard during their pension. Moreover, the pension system offers the opportunity for individuals to invest their current savings in financial assets and earn income during their pension period. In addition, it offers a wide range of different options for participating in the assessment of savings. In this way, both social goals can be realized and a fund accumulation is created for the economy.

While the individual pension system is mandatory in developed countries and it is voluntary in developing countries. In Turkey, as a developing country, the first application of the individual pension system was based on volunteerism. Voluntary participation in the system had resulted in limited participation for the country with a very low income level. This situation limited the achievement of the social and economic goals that form the basis of the system. The individual pension savings and investment system law in Turkey was accepted on 28 March 2001 within the scope of social security reform and enforced on 7 October 2001. In addition to the social security system, the individual pension system began to be implemented on the basis of volunteerism on October 27, 2003. However, to implement mandatory enforcement of the system as a result of changing social and economic conditions, the gradual transition to the individual pension system with automatic enrollment was accepted in 2017. Employees of 45 years old and under were included in the scope of the new individual pension system, which has become mandatory to increase the savings of the individual. Moreover, automatic enrollment is mandatory, and participants are allowed to opt-out decision the system within 2 months. It is aimed that 14 million people save money with this system. 3% contribution will be automatically deducted from employee earnings, and the government contribution will be 25% of the employee payment. Collected funds are managed by professional managers to secure the pension period.

The importance of the individual pension system is increasing because of the high population density of young people in Turkey. The introduction of automatic enrollment for the development of the individual pension system is an important step, but allowing individuals to leave the system has limited the system development. More than half of the participants in the system have preferred to leave the system. Thus, the expected benefit from the new individual pension system cannot be obtained. In this context, determining the factors that affect the decisions of the individuals to stay in the system is important in terms of system efficiency. If the cause of the problem can be understood, the solution can be found accordingly. Determining the factors that trigger exiting from this new system has great importance in terms of guiding policy makers. Therefore, individual factors affecting the continuation of the new individual pension system will be examined in this study. Herewith, the factors that prevent the development of the system can be exposed, and the obstacles hinder the system development can be detected. In addition, it can guide for the measures to be taken . The rest of the study was organized in 4 sections. Section 2 presents some previous research and their results on factors affecting individual preferences in pension and pension funding. Section 3 includes an empirical application and its results. Section 4 concludes the study.

LITERATURE REVIEW

People who are not over 45 years old have to join the system automatically, with the new pension system implemented in Turkey. If people wish, they have the right to leave within two months of entering the system. However, as a result of the large number of people leaving the system, the expected benefit cannot be provided from the system in terms of country economy. Accordingly, it is necessary to identify the factors that cause individuals to leave the system. In other words, the identification of the individual characteristics that make it possible to stay in the system has a great precaution for the continuity of the system. In this context, the purpose of this study is to analyses the individual factors affecting the opt-out decision from the individual pension system with automatic enrollment. To determine the variables to be used in the analysis, many studies on the pension systems of other countries have been examined in the literature. There are a variety of studies in the literature to find out the factors that affect individuals' preferences in term of pension and pension funding. Factors considered in these studies can be ordered as gender, age, income level, marital status, education level, etc. Identifying these factors is a prerequisite for the development of the pension system. Therefore, it can become easier to identify the effective factors for the pension system of a country to take measures to improve the system.

It is expected that one of the most important factors affecting the pension and pension fund preferences of individuals is gender. Gender has two effects the first of which is the status distinction in the society, whereas the second is the difference in risk perceptions. In line with this, a study emphasizing men's social status differences was carried out by Ginn and Albert (1993). They specified that men were more likely to reach pension alternatives than women. On the other hand, a study aimed at revealing the differences between the views of men and women was presented in Schubert et al. (1999). In this study, they showed that there was not gender differences in risk attitudes regarding insurance choices. On the contrary, Hubermen et al (2007) did a study revealing that gender was an effective factor. They found women's participation probability in pension plan was 6.5% higher than men's. According to them, women saved more than men because they lived more than men and they earned lower than men. Another study including only women was carried out by Peggs (2000) in which she examined women's perceptions of pension choice and pension risks. It was found that material circumstances, cultural capital, extent and quality of pension information and habitus affected pension choice and pension risks. Moreover, she suggested that poverty increased among many women in later life, because the expansion of pension choice had a negative effect.

Gender difference also influences the pension plan choice. One of the studies in this context was done by Bajtelsmit et.al.(1999).They examined gender differences in allocation of household wealth to defined contribution pensions, and it was found that women had greater relative risk aversion in their allocation of wealth into defined contribution pension assets. Similarly, Bernasek and Shwiff (2001) and Gerrans and Murphy (2004) pointed out that gender differences was an important factor in explaining individual investments in pension.

There are also a number of studies in which some of individual factors are evaluated together to determine the factors that affect the choice of pension and pension fund preference. In one of these kinds of studies, Bassett et.al. (1998) examined how workers use 401(k) individual pension plans by examining their participation, contribution, and withdrawal decisions. The employee participation in the plan increases with income, age, job opportunities, education, and employers also make contributions, but low-income workers did not use 401(k) individual pension plans to save for pension. Similarly, Munnell et.al. (2002) examined the factors that affect the decisions of individuals to participate in the 401k individual pension plan in the USA. In this study, 1698 participant data were used, and it was found that while income level increased, participation in the individual pension system also increased. They found that employees' participation and contribution decisions were most affected by their planning horizon. The availability of an employer match and the ability of employees to gain access to their funds before pension through withdrawal or borrowing were the most important determinants. They expected to low-income individuals had less participation in the individual pension system because they might exposure to liquidity risk in the short run. Moreover, it might even be possible for low-incomes to protect their current living standards with state-pensions during the pension period. Additionally, the increase in the wealth level also positively affected the entry into the individual pension system. Because people with low-income had limited financial resources, they focused on day-to-day operations and their future point of view was short term (Hershey et.al., 2007). In another study, Clark and Strauss (2008) examined the impact of socio-demographic characteristics on individuals' pension preferences. They showed that the gender, age and income could give rise to distinctive risk preference. Moreover, marital status, and whether a spouse also had a pension plan made a significant effect for household risk preferences.

The level of education, especially financial literacy, is another factor that is expected to influence pension preference. In this context, the effects of employer-based financial education on individual saving and pension were investigated by Bernheim and Garrett (2003). Their result indicated that financial education increased the rates of participation in 401(k) individual pension plans. Low literacy and lack of information were suggested to be very important factors for the ability to save and to secure a comfortable pension. In a similar study, Hershey and Mowen (2000) studied the factors affecting the financial preparation of individuals for pension, and they found that personality constructs and financial literacy were significant predictors. Moreover, it was claimed that lack of basic financial concepts could be attributed to the lack of pension planning by Lusardi (2008). In a research conducted in Italy, Fornero and Monticone (2011) examined the link between financial information and participation in the pension plan. They revealed that most individuals lack of basic financial information, and financial literacy had a positive impact on the pension plan participation probability. In another study in Italy, Zanghieri (2013) investigated the effect of pension income expectation and financial literacy on decision of joining a pension fund. It was found that education was more effective than pension income expectation. A study obtaining similar results in Russia was done by Klapper and Panos (2011). They studied the relationship between financial literacy and pension planning, and found that financial literacy was related significantly and positively to individual pension planning.

Many studies regarding Turkey have been conducted to determine the factors that influence individual pension choices. A study was conducted in the period when the individual pension system was based on voluntary system by Elveren and Hsu (2007). They examined the effect of gender differences on the decision to participate in individual pension, and it was found that women were more disadvantaged than men. Main reasons for this result were the lower salary and the fewer full-time job opportunities for women. On the other hand, in the other study on voluntary participation in the individual pension system, Ozer and Cınar (2012) aimed to determine the opinions of the academicians at a Turkish university about the individual pension system. A significant relationship between their point of view regarding individual pension and age, gender, working year, level of income was found. Kara, Yildiz and Karan (2015) analyzed the risk taking behavior of individual pension system participants in Turkey. They found that the duration of participation was the most influential factor on the risk taking behavior.

DATA SET AND METHODS

This study aims to examine the individual factors affecting the decision of the participants to remain in or leave the new individual pension system. For this purpose, a survey study was conducted with 374 people selected according to the random sampling method. The survey includes participants who did not turn into 45, working under the social security, and taken into the new individual pension system automatically in Turkey. The ones who did not meet these requirements were not included in the study. The participants were asked about their decision to stay in or leave the new pension system and this was taken as a dependent variable.

Dummy variables were used as '0' for exiting, and as '1' for remaining in the new system. In addition, each participant was asked about their age, gender, marital status, salary, education level, so their personal characteristics was tried to be determined and these personal characteristics were taken as independent variables. The effects of the independent variables on the dependent variable were attempted to determine. Logistic regression analysis was used because both the dependent variable and some independent variables were nominal.

If the dependent variable is nominal, it is not possible to use the least squares analysis. Because the variances cannot be expressed as a minimum, in other words, it is not possible to provide the normal distribution feature of the data belonging to the dependent variable. In this case, the discriminant and logistic regression analysis can be used. Discriminant analysis requires normal distribution of independent variables, and the covariance of the independent variables must be equal at each group level. If one of the independent variables is nominal, these assumptions cannot be provided, for this reason, discriminant analysis cannot be used in this study. However, the logistic regression can be applied on both the nominal dependent variable and the independent nominal variables and the specified assumptions are not required. Logistic regression provides a nonlinear relationship between categorical dependent variables and independent variables. It also reveals the possibility of one of the possible values of the dependent variable. In a logistic regression model based on probability, probability is expressed as odds. Odds ratio is calculated by using the division of the probability in which the event occurs by the probability in which the event does not occur. This calculation is expressed as follows(Osborne, 2008, p.365):

$$Odds = \frac{P(x)}{1 - P(x)}$$
$$P(x) = Probability\, of\, Occurrance \qquad (1)$$
$$1 - P(x) = Probability\, of\, Non - Occurrance$$

The logistic regression model is a nonlinear logarithmic model and is constructed as follows:

$$L = \ln\left[\frac{P_i}{1 - P_i}\right] = b_0 + b_1 X_i + e_i \qquad (2)$$

As can be understood from this equation, it can be difficult to interpret model results because a logarithmic function is calculated in the logistic regression model. For this reason, the exponential logistics coefficients are used and are calculated as follows (Yildiz, 2014, p.81):

$$\frac{P}{1 - P} = e^{(b_0 + b_1 X_1)} \qquad (3)$$

In this study, the logistic regression model is constructed as follows:

$$L = \ln\left[\frac{P_i}{1 - P_i}\right] = \ln(odds) = b_0 + b_1 A + b_2 G + b_3 MS + b_4 S + b_5 EL + e_i \qquad (4)$$

A = Age
G = Gender
MS = Marital Status
S = Salary
EL = Education Level

In the model, decision to stay in or leave the new pension system, which is a categorical variable, was taken as a dependent variable, the participants' age, gender, marital status, salary, education level were taken as independent variables. Moreover, Binary Logistic Regression analysis was used because the dependent variable has two values as '0' and '1'.

RESULTS

As a result of the Binary Logistic Regression analysis, the -2LL (Log likelihood) value for the first model including the only constant was calculated in the first step. The obtained results were summarized in Table 1.

Table 1. Iteration History-Step 0

Iteration	-2 Log Likelihood	Coefficients
		Constant
1	513,286	-,235
2	513,286	-,236
3	513,286	-,236

In the second step, when independent variables were added to the model, 2LL in Table 1 could be interpreted. If there is a decrease in the 2LL calculated in the second step, this indicates an increase in the model harmony. Table 2 shows only the classification success of the model in which the only constant coefficient was included.

All observations were given in Table 2, which shows the classification success of the model with the only constant coefficient, according to the category where the number of observations was high. Because yes answers were more than no answers, the table was created according to yes categories. The total number of participants is 374 and 209 of the participants who wanted to leave the system were classified correctly, but 165 of them who said no were classified wrongly. The coefficient result of the model with the only fixed term and significance test result was shown in Table 3.

According to Table 3, the constant coefficient is -0,236, and it was found significant (sig<0,05). Statistical significance of other variables not included in the model were shown in the following table.

According to Table 4, education level and salary were significant, but other variables were not significant. Because the score of education and the salary are higher, it shows that these variables are expected to make more contributions to the model. Gender, age and marital status are insignificant and have low scores.

Table 2. Classification Table-Step 0

Observed		Predicted		
		Did You Exit the New Individual Pension System?		Percentage Correct
		Yes	No	
Did you exit the new individual pension system?	Yes	209	0	100,0
	No	165	0	,0
Overall Percentage				55,9

Table 3. Variables in the Equation-Step 0

	B	S.E.	Wald	df	Sig.	Exp(B)
Constant	-,236	,104	5,152	1	,023	,789

Table 4. Variables not in the Equation-Step 0

	Score	df	Sig.
Gender	,011	1	,916
Age	,090	1	,764
Marital Status	,005	1	,946
Educational Level	119,652	1	,000
Salary	26,460	1	,000
Overall Statistics	120,226	5	,000

Table 5. Omnibus Tests of Model Coefficients-Step 1

	Chi-Square	df	Sig.
Step	136,105	5	,000
Block	136,105	5	,000
Model	136,105	5	,000

While the first model was only generated for the constant, all independent variables were added in the second model. In Table 5, the omnibus test was performed to examine the suitability of the second model for variables. The test measures the power of all independent variables to predict dependent variables. Because the significance value was smaller than 0.05, it shows that at least one of the independent variables had a significant relation and, the model was suitable for variables.

In the second model, where the independent variables were added, the 2LL value decreased from 513,286 to 377,180. The decrease in the value was regarded as an indication of the increase in model harmony. Cox-Snell R^2 and Nagelkerke R^2 introduced the explained variance in dependent variable by the logistic model. Accordingly, While Cox-Snell R^2 revealed that the logistic model could explain 30,5% of variance in the dependent variable, Nagelkerke R^2 revealed that the new model could explain 40,9% of variance in the dependent variable.

Hosmer and Lemeshow test was used to evaluate the suitability of the model as a whole. The null hypothesis in the test means that there is no difference between the observed and the predicted model values. If the test result is not significant, it shows that the model and the data compatibility are acceptable. In the light of our Hosmer and Lemeshow test result, the model and the data compatibility were acceptable because the significance value was greater than 5% in this model.

Table 6. Model Summary- Step 1

-2 Log Likelihood	Cox & Snell R Square	Nagelkerke R Square
377,180	,305	,409

Table 7. Hosmer and Lemeshow Test-Step 1

Chi-Square	df	Sig.
10,884	8	,208

Table 8. Classification Table-Step 1

Observed		Predicted		
		Did You Exit the New Individual Pension System?		Percentage Correct
		Yes	No	
Did you exit the new individual pension system?	Yes	187	22	89,5
	No	49	116	70,3
Overall Percentage				81,0

The classification success of the second model with all the variables were shown in Table 8. Accordingly, 187 participants who wanted to leave the system were classified correctly, but 22 of them were classified wrongly. Moreover, 116 of the ones who did not want to leave the system were classified correctly, but 49 participants were classified wrongly. According to the data presented in the table, 89.5% of participants who want to leave the system, and 70.3% of participants who did not want to leave the system were predicted correctly. The results of the model obtained in Binary Logistic Regression analysis were summarized in Table 9.

According to the table above, a positive relationship was found only in gender and other variables had a negative relationship; however, a significant relationship was determined only with education level. The binary logistic regression equation could be written as follows:

$$L = \ln\left[\frac{P_i}{1-P_i}\right] = \ln(odds) \qquad (5)$$
$$= 3.824 + 0,022 * G - 0,095 * A - 0,028 * MS - 1,593 * EL - 0,046S$$

Table 9. Variables in the Equation –Step 1

	B	S.E.	Wald	df	Sig.	Exp(B)
Gender	,022	,262	,007	1	,933	1,022
Age	-,095	,226	,176	1	,675	,909
Marital Status	-,028	,306	,009	1	,926	,972
Education Level	-1,593	,190	70,663	1	,000	,203
Salary	-,046	,151	,093	1	,760	,955
Constant	3,824	,563	46,082	1	,000	45,806

Gender had a positive relationship, this result shows that men want to leave the system more than women, and this result is consistent with the results of Hubermen et al (2007). In Turkey, because of the low participation of women in the workforce, their low status in business life and long lifespan, they feel obliged about saving more than men for their future life. For these reasons, it is expected that women tend to stay longer in the new individual pension system.

There is a negative relationship with age, and this result means that older people want to leave the system more than young ones. This result is consistent with the results of Elveren ve Hsu (2007), but inconsistent with the results of Bassett et. Al. (1998). The reason for this result is that older people may think that the system will not be useful to them because of the short time spent in the system and their possibility to evaluate their fund for a short period.

A negative relationship was found with the marital status and this shows that married people tend to leave the system more than single people. The reason why married people quit more the new pension system is that the necessity of compulsory consumption due to spouses and children of the married people is high and as a result of this situation, their saving power reduces.

A negative relation was found with salary, which shows that participants with high salary level quit the system more than the participants with low salary levels. This result is not consistent with Bassett et. Al. (1998) and Munnel et. al. (2002). However, the obtained result could mean that the participants with low salary have more future concern, because they expect a low future salary. This situation increases the need to save more money and secure the future with their limited salary.

The significance relationship was determined only with education level in the second model. According to the result of this model, as the education level increases, so does the level of quitting the new individual pension system. Besides, the ratio of the participants with low education level quitting the system accounts for 20,3% ($e^{-1,593}$=0,203) of the participants with high education level. In other words, the exiting tendency of the participants with a high education level from the system was 4.926 (1 / 0,203=4,926) times higher than those with a low education level. This result differs from the study of Bassett (1998), Bernheim and Garrett (2003), Fornero and Monticone (2011), Lusard (2008), Klapper and Panos (2011); however, the result in question is similar to the study of Fornero and Monticone (2011). The main reason for this result is the low performance of individual pension funds in the past years in Turkey, and that the high educated participants are aware of this situation, as for low educated participants, they are not said to be aware of this situation. The participants with low education levels can be claimed not to have the knowledge or skills to assess their own savings; therefore, they are thought to see the management of their savings by professional managers both more reliable and profitable. On the other hand, individuals with high education levels can be speculated to have the knowledge and skills about managing their savings, so it can be claimed that leaving the fund management to professional managers is thought to be more risky by these individuals. Moreover, these participants could recognize, evaluate and analyze the system. They may not find it logical to continue within this system because the performance of the fund management in the individual pension system was low in the past. If the system is to be improved, individuals with a high level of education can be attracted to the system for the development of the new individual pension system using the increased fund performance. For this purpose, the fund management of the individual pension system should be re-audited, corrected for its errors, and improved for the reliability of the system. Thus, both the confidence in the system can be increased and the individual can be convinced that the system will be useful to them.

CONCLUSION

Social security for the purpose of increasing social welfare provides people with an assurance against risks. However, the rapid aging of population, deterioration of the birth rate, increasing unemployment and economic instability have led countries to experience in social security problems. Therefore, countries revise their social security systems and the individual pension system is viewed as the solution to the problems in the system. Similarly, the individual pension system was accepted based on volunteerism at first in Turkey. However, this voluntary participation resulted in limited participation; hence, this situation limited the achievement of the social and economic goals that form the basis of the individual pension system. In the second stage, the gradual transition to the new individual pension system with automatic enrollment has been implemented to implement mandatory enforcement of the system since 2017. The 45-year-old and under were included in the scope of the new individual pension system mandatorily, and participants were allowed to opt-out decision from the system within two months. Accordingly, determining the factors that affect the decisions of the individuals to stay in the system has become important in terms of the development of this system. In this study, individual factors affecting the participants' decision of continuing within the new individual pension system were examined. In this way, the factors that prevent the development of the system can be exposed, and the obstacles in front of the system development can be detected.

In this study, a survey study was conducted with 374 people, who were taken into the new individual pension system automatically, selected according to the random sampling method. Both nominal dependent and independent variables were used, so the binary logistic regression was applied. As a result of the study, a positive relationship was found between only gender, and others had a negative relationship, but a significant relationship was determined only with education level.

In the light of the findings of this research, the women participants wanted to quit the system less than the man did because of the low level of participation of women in the workforce, their low status in business and having a longer lifespan. On the other hand, the elderly people wanted to leave from the system more than the younger ones, because the elderly people stay in the system for a shorter time. Similarly, since the married people had more compulsory consumption for their family, they tended to leave the system more than the single people. Moreover, participants with low income had more future concern because they expected a low level future returns. For this reason, the individuals with low incomes levels quit the system less than those with high income levels. In terms of education, which is a significant variable in the model, the high education level increases quitting the system. The main reason for this result is the low performance of individual pension funds in the past years in Turkey. On the other hand, individuals with high education levels have knowledge about managing their savings. Therefore, the fund management of the new individual pension system should be re-audited and corrected for errors, and the confidence in the system should be increased by this way. This study has a great importance in terms of determining individual perspectives for the development of the new individual pension system. Moreover, after a certain period of time from the implementation of the new individual pension system, the relationship between fund performance and participation in the system may also be examined in subsequent studies.

REFERENCES

Antolin, P., Payet, S., & Yermo, J. (2012). Coverage of Private Pension Systems: Evidence and Policy Options. *OECD Working Papers on Finance, Insurance and Private Pensions*, (20).

Bajtelsmit, V. L., Bernasek, A., & Jianakoplos, N. A. (1999). Gender differences in defined contribution pension decisions. *Financial Services Review*, *8*(1), 1–10. doi:10.1016/S1057-0810(99)00030-X PMID:11481724

Bassett, W. F., Fleming, M. J., & Rodrigues, A. P. (1998). How workers use 401 (k) plans: The participation, contribution, and withdrawal decisions. *National Tax Journal*, 263–289.

Bernasek, A., & Shwiff, S. (2001). Gender, risk, and retirement. *Journal of Economic Issues*, *35*(2), 345–356. doi:10.1080/00213624.2001.11506368

Bernheim, B. D., & Garrett, D. M. (2003). The effects of financial education in the workplace: Evidence from a survey of households. *Journal of Public Economics*, *87*(7-8), 1487–1519. doi:10.1016/S0047-2727(01)00184-0

Clark, G. L., & Strauss, K. (2008). Individual pension-related risk propensities: The effects of socio-demographic characteristics and a spousal pension entitlement on risk attitudes. *Ageing and Society*, *28*(6), 847–874. doi:10.1017/S0144686X08007083

Elveren, A. Y., & Hsu, S. (2007). *Gender gaps in the individual pension system in Turkey* (No. 2007-06). Working Paper, University of Utah, Department of Economics.

Fornero, E., & Monticone, C. (2011). Financial literacy and pension plan participation in Italy. *Journal of Pension Economics and Finance*, *10*(4), 547–564. doi:10.1017/S1474747211000473

Gerrans, P., & Clark-Murphy, M. (2004). Gender differences in retirement savings decisions. *Journal of Pension Economics and Finance*, *3*(2), 145–164. doi:10.1017/S1474747204001477

Ginn, J., & Arber, S. (1993). Pension penalties: The gendered division of occupational welfare. *Work, Employment and Society*, *7*(1), 47–70. doi:10.1177/095001709371003

Hershey, D. A., Jacobs-Lawson, J. M., McArdle, J. J., & Hamagami, F. (2007). Psychological foundations of financial planning for retirement. *Journal of Adult Development*, *14*(1-2), 26–36. doi:10.100710804-007-9028-1

Hershey, D. A., & Mowen, J. C. (2000). Psychological determinants of financial preparedness for retirement. *The Gerontologist*, *40*(6), 687–697. doi:10.1093/geront/40.6.687 PMID:11131085

Huberman, G., Iyengar, S. S., & Jiang, W. (2007). Defined contribution pension plans: Determinants of participation and contributions rates. *Journal of Financial Services Research*, *31*(1), 1–32. doi:10.100710693-007-0003-6

Kara, S., Yildiz, Y., & Karan, M. B. (2015). Analysis of risk-taking behavior of individual pension system participants: The case of turkey. *Journal of Economics Finance and Accounting*, *2*(3), 375–396.

Klapper, L., & Panos, G. A. (2011). Financial literacy and retirement planning: The Russian case. *Journal of Pension Economics and Finance*, *10*(4), 599–618. doi:10.1017/S1474747211000503

Lusardi, A. (2008). *Household saving behavior: The role of financial literacy, information, and financial education programs (No. w13824)*. National Bureau of Economic Research. doi:10.3386/w13824

Munnell, A. H., Sunden, A., & Taylor, C. (2001). What determines 401 (k) participation and contributions? *Social Security Bulletin*, *64*(3), 64–75. PMID:12655741

Osborne, J. W. (Ed.). (2008). *Best practices in quantitative methods*. Sage. doi:10.4135/9781412995627

Özer, Ö., & Çınar, E. (2012). Evaluation of a foundation university academic personal perspective to private pension system. *Mustafa Kemal Üniversitesi Sosyal Bilimler Enstitüsü Dergisi*, *9*(19).

Peggs, K. (2000). Which pension? Women, risk and pension choice. *The Sociological Review*, *48*(3), 349–364. doi:10.1111/1467-954X.00220

Schubert, R., Brown, M., Gysler, M., & Brachinger, H. W. (1999). Financial decision-making: Are women really more risk-averse? *The American Economic Review*, *89*(2), 381–385. doi:10.1257/aer.89.2.381

Yildiz, A. (2014). Corporate ratings based on the corporate governance index and altman z score applying with the logistic regression method. *Suleyman Demirel University The Journal of Faculty of Economics and Administrative Sciences*, *19*(3), 71–89.

Zanghieri, P. (2013). *Participation to Pension Funds in Italy: The Role of Expectations and Financial Literacy*. Academic Press.

Chapter 7
Comparative Analysis of Service Quality Perception Between Public Sector and Private Sector Banks of India

Deepika Singh Tomar
Amity University, India

Rohit Singh Tomar
Symbiosis Institute of Health Sciences, India

ABSTRACT

The chapter deals with the study of customers' expectations as well as their perceptions for service quality in banking sector. Again, the study focuses on the influence of major demographic variables such as age, income, education, and occupation on customers' expectations and perceptions for service quality. Moreover, this research work has been carried out with the help of primary data collected through a survey of 300 retail banking customers (i.e., 150 ICICI Bank customers and 150 SBI customers of Agra region). In India, retail banking is one of the fastest growing industries. The present study has endeavored to examine the service quality aspects of the two leading banks in Agra region and will also help the other private and public sector banks and financial institutions to have a better understanding of customer needs and the booming opportunities in retail banking in India.

INTRODUCTION

Concept of Service Quality

Recognition of service quality as a competitive weapon is relatively a recent phenomenon in the Indian Banking sector. Prior to the liberalization era the banking sector in India was operating in a protected environment and was dominated by nationalized banks. Banks at that time did not feel the need to pay attention to service quality issues and they assigned very low priority to identification and satisfaction

DOI: 10.4018/978-1-5225-7399-9.ch007

of customer needs. After liberalization as a result of partial implementation of the Narasimham Committee Report the nationalized banks and old generation private banks started facing competition from the new private and foreign banks that had international banking standards. These new generation banks were characterized by the usage of modern information technology endorsed services like ATM, tele banking, online systems etc. Clients, for the first time in India were able to choose from a number of banks offering a wide range of services and delivering quality service.

Purohit, H.C. & Pathardikar, Avinash, D. (2007), studied the Measurement of service quality and Consumer Perception about the Services of Banking Institutions' specially in the Nationalized Banks of India. As per their study, the need of the hour in the Indian banking sector is to build up competitiveness through enhanced service quality, thus making the banks more market oriented and customer friendly.

Quality in services is an elusive concept because of the intangible nature of the service offering and the definition of quality may vary from person to person and from situation to situation. Even though a universally accepted definition of quality does not exist till now, most writers on service quality support a customer-centered definition with the reservation that customer expectations are not necessarily consistent and predictable.

The definition produced by Howcraft (1991) that service quality in banking implies consistently anticipating and satisfying the needs and expectations of the customer. Hence, service quality is the conformance of services to the customer specifications and expectations. The quality of service therefore depends on the ability of the server to meet the expectations of the customer.

Quality has been defined in many ways by quality gurus like Juran, Deming, Crosby and Taguchi, among others Joshep Juran has defined quality as fitness for use. Deming believes quality has to satisfy the needs of customers, both present and future. Crosby holds that conformance to requirements is quality. The essence of these definitions is the same. As applicable to banking, quality may be defined as the ability to satisfy the customer's requirements and needs to the fullest and to replicate this on an ongoing basis.

Delivering higher levels of service quality is the strategy that is increasingly being offered as a key to service provider's efforts to position themselves more effectively in the marketplace. Almost all banks perform same functions. Therefore, customer takes into account the relative efficiency while choosing a particular bank. Moreover, banks carry on business with public money and, therefore, customers expect better services from them. Under such circumstances, customer's decision to patronize one and not the other is based on quality service offered to him. Firms, therefore, prosper or decline, depending upon the quality of service they provide to their customers. Because of this widespread belief, service organizations have placed service quality at the top of the list of strategic constructs.

The service sector contributes a major portion of the Gross Domestic Product of developed countries. In developing countries too, the contribution of the service sector (which comprise services relating to transport, communications, trade, banking, insurance, other financial services, medical and hospital services, public administration and defense and miscellaneous services) has been growing rapidly. The service sector now contributes over 40% of India's GDP. In the service sector, the banking segment has been amongst the fastest growing segment as can be seen from the Table 1.

Table 1. Annual Growth Rate of Different Services

Service	Annual Rate of Growth*
Banking and Insurance	7.9%
Transport (other than Rail)	6.8%
Communication	6.5%
Hotels and Restaurants	5.1%
Real Estate and Business Services	4.4%
Railways	3.4%
Services	4.9%

*For the period of 1950-1995
Source: CMIE

REVIEW OF LITERATURE

Quality is especially important in the banking sector because duplication of products and services is relatively easy. Further, differentiation of product is difficult and hazy. Thus, quality becomes the only differentiator and the only key to continuing success. Quality service can be used as a tool for differentiation and can provide a competitive edge. Service quality is also crucial for developing loyal customers and is hence responsible for the success of any service organization (Kandampully, 1998; 2000). The customers at the time of service delivery interact closely with the service providers and get an inside knowledge of the service organization. This knowledge gives them an opportunity to critically assess the service provided and the service provider. Thus service quality plays an important role in adding value to the overall service experience. Also customers seek organizations that are service loyal i.e. aim to provide consistent and superior quality of service for present and long term and organizations aiming for this are bound to get customers' loyalty.

Because services are intangible, consumers are more likely to use extrinsic cues to infer service quality prior to the actual purchase and consumption of the service. As a result, cues such as price, brand, advertising, word-of-mouth, and certain tangible service elements are important to consumers as they attempt to judge the quality of a service prior to consumption.

In a study of quality in four consumer service industries: long distance telephone, banking, credit cards, and an appliance repair and maintenance, Parasuraman et al. (1998) found consistent attributes of perceived quality across the four service industries. These abstract attributes included reliability, responsiveness, assurance, empathy, and tangibles. In a period during the service delivery process, the customer is directly interacting with the personnel, physical facilities and other elements such as communication materials. Because services are intangible, consumers use tangible clues as proxies in evaluating the quality of services. If consumer perceives that the appearance of physical facilities, equipment, personnel, and communication materials are good, then his or her judgment will be positively affected. We refer to this as "tangibles". The attribute termed "reliability" is associated to the ability of the service provider to perform the promised services dependably and accurately. Reliability is closely related to the concept of technical quality of service. The other attributes such as tangibles, responsiveness, assurance, and empathy are related to the concept of functional quality.

The "responsiveness" attribute of service quality refers to whether the service provider has the willingness to help customers and provide prompt service. When the service provider provides prompt service to its customers, the customer perceives that he or she is receiving good quality.

Customers frequently find difficult to evaluate the quality of the service if they have not experienced yet the particular service. It is believed that the level of the customer's trust plays important role in assessing the quality of the service provided by the service provider. The more the customer trusts the service provider, the better the customer's perception on the service quality. The attribute termed "assurance" is associated with the ability of the service provider to convey trust and confidence to the customers.

Finally, if customers perceive that they are not receiving concerned, personal, or individual attention from the service provider, then their quality judgment will be negatively affected. This is called "empathy". A brief description of each attribute is presented in Table 2.

These above five attributes are widely accepted in the literature, although they suffer from at least two major shortcomings. Firstly, they are very broad and lack specificity in serving as cues that consumer can use to infer service quality. For example, a problem with a service's "reliability" does not indicate the particular attribute that was unreliable. Secondly, the particular attributes or cues that comprise each dimension vary across service contexts. Some researchers suggested that the dimensionality of service quality might depend on the type of services under study. Many researchers conducted service quality research in retail banking setting, in which they modified the service quality dimensions to fit the bank specific characteristics.

Service Quality Attributes of Retail Banking

Israel, D., Sudhakar J.C. and Selvam M. (2004) concluded that, in order to develop marketing strategy, service marketers, especially bank marketers need to understand the service attributes that are used by consumers in selecting banks. For example, consumers would use bank reputation, bank reliability, bank assurance, and physical facilities of the bank in selecting bank services. If marketers can understand which attributes are used to evaluate a service, they will be better able to manage and influence the customer's evaluations and perception of the offering.

Table 2. Definition of the five service quality attributes

Attributes	Definition
Tangibles	Appearance of physical facilities, equipment, personnel, and communication materials
Reliability	Ability to perform the promised service dependably and accurately
Responsiveness	Willingness to help customers and provide prompt service.
Assurance	Knowledge and courtesy of employees and their ability to convey trust and confidence.
Empathy	Caring, individualized attention the firm provides its customers.

The exploratory study conducted by Stafford (1996) reported the distinct elements (attributes) of bank service quality as perceived by customers. Seven attributes were found in assessing bank service quality. The first attribute, named "bank atmosphere"; included cleanliness, as well as an overall positive and courteous attitude by employees (kindness, friendliness, and pleasantness). The second attribute, 'relationship", indicates the importance of a personal relationship with the bank employees, where customers are recognized easily by long-term employee. The third attribute, "rates and charges", indicates that low costs and high interest rates can affect an individual's perception of bank service quality. The fourth attributes, "available and convenient services", indicates a full array of services that available, easily accessible and convenient. The fifth attribute, "ATMs", indicates available, convenient, and working automatic teller machines. The sixth attribute, "reliability/honesty", indicates the importance of a solid bank rating and honest, reliable employee. The seventh attribute, "teller", indicates adequate and accessible teller.

Angur et al. (1999) examined the applicability of alternative measures of service quality in the banking industry in India. Data were gathered from customers of two major banks in the retail banking industry (a leading public sector bank and a leading private sector multinational bank). The results suggested that the service quality concept in the retail banking of India as one of the developing economy is a multidimensional construct of service quality. Although the five-factor conceptualization of service quality proposed by Parasuraman et Al.(1985, 1988) did not entirely hold, the results reinforce their proposal that the five dimensions are of varying importance, with reliability and responsiveness dimensions being the most important. In addition, the SERVQUAL scale appeared to provide much greater diagnostic information about service quality than the SERVPERF did. Although SERVQUAL is not without its critics, the result of Angur et al.'s showed that SERVQUAL is a better instrument for measuring service quality.

Bahia and Nantel (2000) conducted a study to develop a reliable and valid scale for the measurement of the perceived service quality of retail banking in Canada. They argued that the universality of the five dimensions of SERVQUAL across different types of services had been questioned in a number of subsequent studies. They also argued that these five dimensions are not fully generic. It is often necessary to incorporate additional items to dimensions because they are particularly important for some service categories. Another critique addressed to SERVQUAL since it has focused on the first marketing mix element (i.e. product) to improve quality. Further they developed a measurement of perceived service quality with reference to Parasuraman et al.' (1985) original ten dimensions and some additional items which are important to retail banking service, then they remodeled and tested the measurement scale.

Based on this procedure, they proposed a scale that was called as bank service quality (BSQ). The BSQ comprises 31 items, which span six dimensions: effectiveness and assurance, access, price, tangibles, service portfolio, and reliability.

Sureschandar, Rajendran, and Anantharaman (2002) aspired to develop an empirical model of service quality with a specific focus on the banking sector. The objectives of their study are: (1) to identify the critical factors of service quality from the customers' perspective; (2) to develop an instrument to measure customer-perceived service quality based on the identified factors with a specific focus on the banking sector; (3) to empirically test the proposed instrument for unidimensionality, reliability and validity using a confirmatory factor analysis approach. They proposed the 5 critical factors of service quality from the customers' perspective i.e. human element of service delivery, core service or service product, systematization of service delivery, tangibles of service (servicescapes), and corporate social image.

These factors resulted from modifying the original SERVQUAL instrument, by adding and/or reducing other relevant factors. The five-dimensional structure could possibly serve as a meaningful framework for tracking a firm's service quality performance over time and comparing it against the performance of competitors. The wording of some individual items may need to be customized to each service setting. Items on some dimensions should be expanded if that is necessary for reliability. Thus, the banking industries must continuously measure and improve these dimensions in order to gain customers' loyalty.

With increasing competition, banks that survive and succeed will be the one that provide quality service. Research studies have repeatedly proved that customers are willing to pay for the quality. Banks that wish to succeed and stay ahead must, therefore, systematically build a structure that aims at providing Total Quality Service. As with the bank's financial goals, success can be achieved only with proper analysis and suitable goals.

Service quality is about meeting customers' needs and requirements, and how well the service level delivered matches customer expectations. Service quality in banking implies consistently anticipating and satisfying the needs and expectations of customers (Howcroft 1991). Data from the Profit Impact of Market Strategy (PIMS) research show that a perceived quality advantage leads to higher profits (Buzzell and Gale 1987). Berry and Parasuraman (1991) also hold the view that high quality service gives credibility to the field sales force and advertising, stimulates favourable word-of-mouth communications, enhances customers' perception of value, and boosts the morale and loyalty of employees and customers alike. Heskett *et al.* (1990) observed that across a wide range of businesses, the pattern is the same: the longer a company keeps a customer, the more money it stands to make. Increased competition, slower growth, and mature markets are also forcing many businesses to review their customer service strategy. Many businesses are channeling more efforts to retain existing customers rather than to acquire new ones. There is enough evidence that demonstrates the strategic benefits of quality in contributing to market share and returns on investment (Adrian 1995; Bateson 1995; Berry and Parasuraman 1991; Reichheld and Sasser 1990) and lowering manufacturing cost and improving productivity (Garvin 1983; Kotlar, 1999; Leonard and Sasser, 1982). Maximizing customer satisfaction through quality customer service has been described as the 'the ultimate weapon" by Davidow and Uttal (1989). According to them, "in all industries, when competitors are roughly matched, those that stress customer service will win".

In the light of the above research findings, interest in service quality is, thus, unarguably high. Poor quality places a firm at a competitive disadvantage. If customers perceive quality as unsatisfactory, they may be quick to take their businesses elsewhere. Thus, it is clear that service quality offers a way of achieving success among competing services, particularly in the case of firms that offer nearly identical services, such as banks, where establishing service quality may be the only way of differentiating oneself. Such differentiation can yield a higher proportion of consumers' choices and, hence, mean the difference between financial success and failure.

Increased competition, slower growth and mature markets are also forcing many businesses to review their customer service strategy. Many businesses are channeling more efforts to retain existing customers rather than to acquire new ones. It has been estimated that the cost of acquiring a new customer is about five to eight times more than retaining an existing one. Maximizing customer satisfaction through quality customer service has been described as "the ultimate weapon" by Davidow and Uttal (1989) in their book "Total Customer Service".

Another driving force to place more attention on service quality is the emergence of a new breed of customers. Not only are today's consumers better educated, they also travel extensively and read widely.

These characteristics influence their buying behaviour in that they are becoming more sophisticated, more discerning and have higher expectations.

High service quality would result in higher customer satisfaction with the product or service. These satisfied customers are likely, through word-of-mouth communication; promote the company products/ services to others. Thus, the customer base will gradually expand. The benefit of this form of promotion is the high degree of credibility of the information transmitted. Further, a satisfied is likely to be a loyal customer who will give repeat business to the company.

So, as competition increases, quality will become the only true differentiator. Successful banks will be those that compete on quality. We must realize that competition on price means we are dependent on what the competition is doing - for our success. Competing on quality means, staying ahead of the competition. Banks that wish to surge ahead successfully into the new millennium would need to in-grain a quality culture. Every aspect of the bank functioning would have to be governed by the quality principles. As we head into the new millennium, technology will be the backbone of many aspects of our lives. In India most of the banks with their sophisticated technology have been able to provide superior service. ATMs help customers reach the bank even after closing hours. In the future, too, banks that wish to provide quality service will have to make investments in technology. Technology can help banks deliver superior service and provide better management information systems and decision support systems. Technology can help banks better analyze and manage various risks, and this will become increasingly important in tomorrow's global market.

Service Quality can also be thought of as having two dimensions: Technical quality and Functional quality. Technical Quality refers to 'what' the bank gives the customer. Functional Quality refers to 'How' the bank's services are provided to the customer.

1. **Technical Quality:** To ensure that it delivers technical quality, the bank must ensure that
    a. Its products and services are closely aligned with customer needs.
    b. Customers are adequately informed about the bank's products and services.
    c. The bank's staff, especially front-line staff, have thorough knowledge of the bank's products and services.
    d. The bank's branch has a suitable mix of people with experience in banking, finance, accounting and legal aspects, so as to ensure that the branch is adequately equipped to deliver technical quality.
    e. The bank's staff should adequately communicate with customer queries.
    f. The bank's staff is able to effectively communicate with customers –staff should also be able to converse in the local language, if required.
    g. The bank's staff is able to provide professional advice to its customers.
    h. The bank's staff, especially front –line staff, has been adequately trained to deal with 'difficult' customers and with customer complaints.
    i. Handling of customer grievances is the overall responsibility of a senior official who is not directly involved with the routine branch banking operations.
2. **Functional Quality:** Functional quality is concerned with how the service is provided to the bank's customer. A few elements that affect a banking service's functional quality include:
    a. Attitude of the bank's staff members.
    b. Importance given to the bank's customers over routine work.
    c. Perceived credibility of the bank's officials to customer queries.

d. Ambience at the bank.
e. Ability to hold discussions with senior officials with a suitable degree of privacy.
f. Image of the bank as a whole.

A bank must be equipped to deliver both Technical and Functional quality thus ensuring that it provides its customers with total quality service. Relevant qualitative determinants could be set up for a few technical and functional quality parameters, but most of these remain difficult to quantify. A bank could set up appropriate policies and procedures, for example recruitment policies, to create enabling conditions for providing technical and functional quality to its customers. The ultimate focus should firmly be on providing quick and cost-effective quality banking services.

The most crucial and perhaps, the most difficult part of the exercise is customer satisfaction. The best way to determine what satisfies the customer is to ask the customer. Several organizations regularly send out questionnaires and direct mailers to their customers (both internal and external), analyze the feedback received and initiate appropriate action. 'Customer', who is central to the banking service, is not a homogeneous class. They come from varying socio-economic and cultural backgrounds. The perception of the Quality of Banking Services provided will differ from customer to customer and even for the same customer at different points of time, depending on the mood and mind-set of the same user at a particular point of time. A customer who needs money and comes to an ATM on a Sunday to find that it is not working is likely to be much more dissatisfied than if she or he were to find the same ATM temporarily out of order on a day when they happen to have popped in to the ATM on their way to work. Some other factors that may influence perceptions of banking service quality are:

- Overall ambience at the bank.
- Past experiences with the bank.
- Familiarity with the services offered by the bank, the procedures followed etc.
- Knowledge of or experience with competitor's products and services.
- Banking with a particular bank which may be regarded as a status symbol
- Interaction with and/ or opinions of other customer's rights etc.

These factors make the measurement of banking service quality difficult and subjective. Despite of all the efforts and initiatives of last two decades, the quality of service offered to the bank customers can vary enormously. There is, however, growing evidence that quality programs can lead to real improvements in customer satisfaction, cross selling, business growth and profitability. With many financial services products becoming relatively commoditized and new ones easily replicated, excellence service can be a key differentiator. Any quality program needs total commitment; a top down approach with clear, effective communications, training and continuous measurement. It's imperative that employee's incentives are linked directly to quality measurements such as customer satisfaction. Ongoing measurement of customer satisfaction is time consuming and expensive, but is absolutely necessary- even on a branch by branch basis- to help ensure continuous improvement. Share of wallet is one of the holy grails of banking, leading to a greater profitability and customer loyalty. Each customer touch point is an opportunity not only to sell but also to enhance the overall brand experience.

Parasuraman et al. (1988) found consistent attributes of perceived quality across all the four service industries. These abstract attributes included Tangibility, Reliability, Responsiveness, Assurance and Empathy. In a period during the service delivery process, the customer is directly interacting with the personnel, physical facilities and other elements such as communication materials. Because services are intangible, consumers use tangible clues as proxies in evaluating the quality of services. If consumer perceives that the appearance of physical facilities, equipment, personnel, and communication materials are good, then his or her judgment will be positively affected. We refer to this as "Tangibility". The attribute termed "Reliability" is associated with the ability of the service provider to perform the promised services dependably and accurately. Reliability is closely related to the concept of technical quality of service. The other attributes such as Tangibility, Responsiveness, Assurance, and Empathy are related to the concept of functional quality.

The "Responsiveness" attribute of service quality refers to whether the service provider has the willingness to help customers and provide prompt service. When the service provider provides prompt service to its customers, the customer perceives that he or she is receiving good quality.

Customers frequently find it difficult to evaluate the quality of the service if they have not experienced yet the particular service. It is believed that the level of the customer's trust plays important role in assessing the quality of the service provided by the service provider. The more the customer trusts the service provider, the better the customer's perception on the service quality. The attribute termed "Assurance" is associated with the ability of the service provider to convey trust and confidence to the customers.

Finally, if customers perceive that they are not receiving concerned, personal, or individual attention from the service provider, then their quality judgment will be negatively affected. This is called "Empathy".

RESEARCH METHODOLOGY

Objectives of the Study

Following are the major objectives of the present study

1. To measure, analyze and compare service quality perception for private and public sector banks (i.e. ICICI Bank and State Bank of India).
2. To suggest ways and means for improving service quality in banks on the basis of the study results.

Hypothesis to Be Tested

Our null hypothesis for the present study is

Ho: There is no significant difference between the service quality perceptions for private and public sector banks.

Research Methodology

This research study is the study of the service quality perceptions of the customers of private and public sector banks. In order to conduct this study I have surveyed 150 SBI customers and 150 ICICI customers. The surveys have been conducted at the various branches of these two banks and various other localities of Agra region.

Sources of Data

All the data required for this purpose have been obtained mainly from the primary sources but at the times of requirement I have also referred to the secondary sources of data also.

Data Collection Method

The data collection method used to obtain the desired information from primary sources has been the direct interview and the instrument used has been a questionnaire.

Sampling Plan

For ICICI Customer Survey

- **Target Population or Universe:** Customers of ICICI Bank.
- **Sampling Unit:** An individual customer of ICICI Bank.
- **Sampling Method:** Judgement Sampling.
- **Sample Size:** 150
- **Area of Survey:** Agra region

For SBI Customer Survey

- **Target Population or Universe:** Customers of State Bank of India.
- **Sampling Unit:** An individual customer of SBI.
- **Sampling Method:** Judgement Sampling
- **Sample Size:** 150
- **Area of Survey:** Agra region

Statistical Tools and Techniques

For measuring various phenomena and analyzing the collected data effectively and efficiently so that sound conclusions may be drawn, I have used a no. of statistical tools and techniques ranging from simple differences, percentages, mean and standard deviation to sophisticated statistical

Designing the SERVQUAL instrument is very much important as data will de captured through this instrument. The genetic questionnaire with 22 statements under 5 dimensions (i.e. Tangibility, Reliability, Responsiveness, Assurance and Empathy) as used by Parasuraman et al. (1988) has also been used here for measuring service quality expectations and perceptions. The responses have been captured in 7-point Likert scale and the difference (E-P) between these expectations (E) and perceptions (P) is the gap score which is then averaged. Simple descriptive statistics are used for data analysis. Moreover, at the time of data collection, proper care has been given to the demographic profiles of the users to ensure that the results are free from any sort of bias.

The use of SERVQUAL is analyzed here in greater detail with logical sequences. It starts with all of the 22 original statements categorized into five dimensions in the form of a questionnaire and a 7-point Likert scale is used to collect the customers' expectations and perceptions.

Tangibility

Analysis of data in Table 3 brings to light that as far as "Tangibility" is concerned, in case of ICICI Bank, total mean expectation score is 24.22, mean perception score is 22.84 and average gap score is 0.34.

It is quite evident from data given in Table 4 that as far as "Tangibility" is concerned, in case of SBI, total mean expectation score is 23.44, mean perception score is 19.16 and average gap score is 1.07.

Table 3. Tangibility gap score analysis for ICICI bank

Tangibility Expectations	Mean Score (E)	Tangibility Perceptions	Mean Score (P)	Gap Score (E-P)
E-1. Banks should have up to date equipments.	6.48	**P-1.** ICICI Bank has up to date equipments.	6.00	0.48
E-2. Banks' physical facilities should be visually appealing	5.90	**P-2.** ICICI Bank's physical facilities are visually appealing	5.80	0.10
E-3. Banks employees should be well dressed and appear neat.	6.06	**P-3.** ICICI Bank's employees are well dressed and appear neat.	5.86	0.20
E-4. The appearance of physical facilities of banks should be in keeping with the types of services provided.	5.78	**P-4.** The appearance of physical facilities of ICICI Bank is in keeping with the types of services provided.	5.18	0.60
Total	**24.22**		**22.84**	**1.38**
Average Gap Score				**1.38/4 =0.34**

Source: Primary Data

Table 4. Tangibility gap score analysis for SBI

Tangibility Expectations	Mean Score (E)	Tangibility Perceptions	Mean Score (P)	Gap Score (E-P)
E-1. Banks should have up to date equipments.	6.26	**P-1.** SBI has up to date equipments.	5.44	0.82
E-2. Banks' physical facilities should be visually appealing	5.76	**P-2.** SBI's physical facilities are visually appealing	4.80	0.66
E-3. Banks employees should be well dressed and appear neat.	5.76	**P-3.** SBI's employees are well dressed and appear neat.	4.62	1.14
E-4. The appearance of physical facilities of banks should be in keeping with the types of services provided.	5.66	**P-4.** The appearance of physical facilities of SBI is in keeping with the types of services provided.	4.30	1.36
Total	**23.44**		**19.16**	**4.28**
Average Gap Score				**4.28/4 =1.07**

Source: Primary Data

It can be observed from the ensuing Table 5 that as far as "Tangibility" is concerned, in case of ICICI bank, combined mean & combined S.D. for perception scores are 5.71 and 1.1116 respectively; and in case of SBI, combined mean & combined S.D. for perception scores are 4.79 and 1.3549 respectively.

Further, in this case Z- test is applied to test the null hypothesis,

H_0: $\mu_1 = \mu_2$ (i.e. There is no significant difference between the two types of the banks as far as the customer perception for tangibility dimension is concerned).

Here, $n_1 = n_2 = 150$, $\bar{x}_1 = 5.71$, $\bar{x}_2 = 4.79$, $s_1 = 1.1116$ and $s_2 = 1.3549$

Now test statistic,

$$z = \frac{\bar{x}_1 - \bar{x}_2}{\sqrt{\frac{s_1^2}{n_1} + \frac{s_2^2}{n_2}}} = 6.42, \text{ i.e. } Z_{cal.} = 6.42$$

At 5% level of significance, for two-tailed test, the critical value of Z, $Z_{tab.} = 1.96$.

Since, $Z_{cal.} > Z_{tab.}$, so we reject the null hypothesis and conclude that there is a significant difference between the two types of the banks as far as the customer perception for tangibility dimension is concerned.

Reliability

Table 6 clearly depicts that as far as "Reliability" is concerned, in case of ICICI Bank, total mean expectation score is 30.18, mean perception score is 26.52 and average gap score is 0.73.

Similarly, it is also clear from Table 7 that as far as "Reliability" is concerned, in case of SBI, total mean expectation score is 30.34, mean perception score is 25.70 and average gap score is 0.92.

Table 5. Comparison of tangibility perceptions for ICICI bank & SBI

Tangibility Perceptions (ICICI)	Mean Score (P)	S.D.	Tangibility Perceptions (SBI)	Mean Score (P)	S.D.
P-1. ICICI Bank has up to date equipments.	6.00	0.9165	**P-1.** SBI has up to date equipments.	5.44	1.1164
P-2. ICICI Bank's physical facilities are visually appealing.	5.80	0.9591	**P-2.** SBI's physical facilities are visually appealing	4.80	1.3416
P-3. ICICI Bank's employees are well dressed and appear neat.	5.86	1.1315	**P-3.** SBI's employees are well dressed and appear neat.	4.62	1.3840
P-4. The appearance of physical facilities of ICICI Bank is in keeping with the types of services provided.	5.18	1.2278	**P-4.** The appearance of physical facilities of SBI is in keeping with the types of services provided.	4.30	1.3000
Combined Mean Combined S.D.	**5.71**	**1.1116**		**4.79**	**1.3549**

Source: Primary Data

Table 6. Reliability gap score analysis for ICICI bank

Reliability Expectations	Mean Score (E)	Reliability Perceptions	Mean Score (P)	Gap score (E-P)
E-5. When banks promise to do something by a certain time, they should do so.	6.20	**P-5.** When ICICI Bank promises to do something by a certain time, it does so.	5.30	0.90
E-6. When customers have problems; these banks should be sympathetic and reassuring.	5.88	**P-6.** When customers have problems; ICICI Bank is sympathetic and reassuring.	4.98	0.90
E-7. These banks should be dependable.	5.50	**P-7.** ICICI Bank is dependable.	4.96	0.54
E-8. Banks should provide their service at the time they promise to do so.	6.02	**P-8.** ICICI Bank provides its service at the time it promises to do so.	5.14	0.88
E-9. Banks should keep their records accurately.	6.58	**P-9.** ICICI Bank keeps its records accurately.	6.14	0.44
Total	**30.18**		**26.52**	**3.66**
Average Gap Score				**3.66/5= 0.73**

Source: Primary Data

Table 7. Reliability gap score analysis for SBI

Reliability Expectations	Mean Score (E)	Reliability Perceptions	Mean Score (P)	Gap score (E-P)
E-5. When banks promise to do something by a certain time, they should do so.	6.26	**P-5.** When SBI promises to do something by a certain time, it does so.	4.94	1.32
E-6. When customers have problems; these banks should be sympathetic and reassuring.	5.80	**P-6.** When customers have problems; SBI is sympathetic and reassuring.	4.60	1.20
E-7. These banks should be dependable.	5.76	**P-7.** SBI is dependable.	5.60	0.16
E-8. Banks should provide their service at the time they promise to do so.	5.92	**P-8.** SBI provides its service at the time it promises to do so.	4.64	1.28
E-9. Banks should keep their records accurately.	6.60	**P-9.** SBI keeps its records accurately.	5.92	0.68
Total	**30.34**		**25.70**	**4.64**
Average Gap Score				**4.64/5 = 0.92**

Source: Primary Data

Again, the ensuing Table 8 shows that as far as "Reliability" is concerned, in case of ICICI bank, combined mean & combined S.D. for perception scores are 5.71 and 1.1116 respectively; and in case of SBI, combined mean & combined S.D. for perception scores are 4.79 and 1.3549 respectively.

Further, in this case Z- test is applied to test the null hypothesis,

H_o: $\mu_1 = \mu_2$ (i.e. There is no significant difference between the two types of the banks as far as the customer perception for reliability dimension is concerned).

Table 8. Comparison of reliability perceptions for ICICI bank & SBI

Reliability Perceptions (ICICI)	Mean Score (P)	S.D.	Reliability Perceptions (SBI)	Mean Score (P)	S.D.
P-5. When ICICI Bank promises to do something by a certain time, it does so.	5.30	1.3304	**P-5.** When SBI promises to do something by a certain time, it does so.	4.94	1.3024
P-6. When customers have problems; ICICI Bank is sympathetic and reassuring.	4.98	1.2882	**P-6.** When customers have problems; SBI is sympathetic and reassuring.	4.60	1.6248
P-7. ICICI Bank is dependable.	4.96	1.3410	**P-7.** SBI is dependable.	5.60	1.5231
P-8. ICICI Bank provides its service at the time it promises to do so.	5.14	1.2650	**P-8.** SBI provides its service at the time it promises to do so.	4.64	1.3965
P-9. ICICI Bank keeps its records accurately.	6.14	1.0950	**P-9.** SBI keeps its records accurately.	5.92	1.2302
Combined Mean Combined S.D.	**5.30**	**1.4069**		**5.14**	**1.5177**

Source: Primary Data

Here $n_1 = n_2 = 150$, $\overline{x}_1 = 5.30$, $\overline{x}_2 = 5.14$, $s_1 = 1.4069$ and $s_2 = 1.5177$

Now test statistic,

$$z = \frac{\overline{x}_1 - \overline{x}_2}{\sqrt{\frac{s_1^2}{n_1} + \frac{s_2^2}{n_2}}} = .95, \text{ i.e. } Z_{cal.} = .95$$

At 5% level of significance, for two-tailed test, the critical value of Z, $Z_{tab.} = 1.96$.

Since, $Z_{cal.} < Z_{tab.}$, so we accept the null hypothesis and conclude that there is no significant difference between the two types of the banks as far as the customer perception for reliability dimension is concerned.

Responsiveness

Analysis of data in Table 9 reveals that as far as "Responsiveness" is concerned, in case of ICICI Bank, total mean expectation score is 19.66, mean perception score is 18.06 and average gap score is 0.40.

Again, it is quite evident from data given in Table 10 that as far as "Responsiveness" is concerned, in case of SBI, total mean expectation score is 19.24, mean perception score is 14.77 and average gap score is 1.11.

It can be observed from the ensuing Table 11 that as far as "Responsiveness" is concerned, in case of ICICI bank, combined mean & combined S.D. for perception scores are 4.51 and 1.6641 respectively; and in case of SBI, combined mean & combined S.D. for perception scores are 3.69 and 1.7634 respectively.

Further, in this case Z- test is applied to test the null hypothesis,

Table 9. Responsiveness gap score analysis for ICICI bank

Responsiveness Expectations	Mean Score (E)	Responsiveness Perceptions	Mean Score (P)	Gap Score (E-P)
E-10. Employees of the banks should tell the customers exactly, when the services will be performed.	5.06	**P-10.** Employees of ICICI Bank tell the customers exactly, when the services will be performed.	4.30	0.76
E-11. Employees of the banks should give prompt service to the customers.	4.70	**P-11.** Employees of ICICI Bank give prompt service to the customers.	4.52	0.18
E-12. Employees of the banks should always be willing to help the customers.	5.38	**P-12.** Employees of ICICI Bank are always willing to help the customers.	4.98	0.40
E-13. Employees of the banks should never be too busy to respond the customers.	4.52	**P-13.** Employees of ICICI Bank are never too busy to respond the customers.	4.26	0.26
Total	**19.66**		**18.06**	**1.60**
Average Gap Score				**1.60/4= 0.40**

Source: Primary Data

Table 10. Responsiveness gap score analysis for SBI

Responsiveness Expectations	Mean Score (E)	Responsiveness Perceptions	Mean Score (P)	Gap Score (E-P)
E-10. Employees of the banks should tell the customers exactly, when the services will be performed.	4.96	**P-10.** Employees of SBI tell the customers exactly, when the services will be performed.	3.98	0.98
E-11. Employees of the banks should give prompt service to the customers.	4.72	**P-11.** Employees of SBI give prompt service to the customers.	3.47	1.25
E-12. Employees of the banks should always be willing to help the customers.	5.06	**P-12.** Employees of SBI are always willing to help the customers.	4.06	1.00
E-13. Employees of the banks should never be too busy to respond the customers.	4.50	**P-13.** Employees of SBI are never too busy to respond the customers.	3.26	1.24
Total	**19.24**		**14.77**	**4.47**
Average Gap Score				**4.47/4= 1.11**

Source: Primary Data

H_0: $\mu_1 = \mu_2$ (i.e. There is no significant difference between the two types of the banks as far as the customer perception for responsiveness dimension is concerned).

Here $n_1 = n_2 = 150$, $\overline{x}_1 = 4.51$, $\overline{x}_2 = 3.69$, $s_1 = 1.6641$ and $s_2 = 1.7634$

Now test statistic,

Table 11. Comparison of responsiveness perceptions for ICICI bank & SBI

Responsiveness Perceptions (ICICI)	Mean Score (P)	S.D.	Responsiveness Perceptions (SBI)	Mean Score (P)	S.D.
P-10. Employees of ICICI Bank tell the customers exactly, when the services will be performed.	4.30	1.7000	**P-10.** Employees of SBI tell the customers exactly, when the services will be performed.	3.98	1.7491
P-11. Employees of ICICI Bank give prompt service to the customers.	4.52	1.7348	**P-11.** Employees of SBI give prompt service to the customers.	3.47	1.4534
P-12. Employees of ICICI Bank are always willing to help the customers.	4.98	1.4627	**P-12.** Employees of SBI are always willing to help the customers.	4.06	1.6900
P-13. Employees of ICICI Bank are never too busy to respond the customers.	4.26	1.6469	**P-13.** Employees of SBI are never too busy to respond the customers.	3.26	1.9267
Combined Mean Combined S.D.	**4.51**	**1.6641**		**3.69**	**1.7634**

Source: Primary Data

$$z = \frac{\overline{x_1} - \overline{x_2}}{\sqrt{\frac{s_1^2}{n_1} + \frac{s_2^2}{n_2}}} = 4.14, \text{ i.e. } Z_{cal.} = 4.14$$

At 5% level of significance, for two-tailed test, the critical value of Z, $Z_{tab.} = 1.96$.

Since, $Z_{cal.} > Z_{tab.}$, so we reject the null hypothesis and conclude that there is a significant difference between the two types of the banks as far as the customer perception for responsiveness dimension is concerned.

Assurance

Table 12 reveals that as far as "Assurance" is concerned, in case of ICICI Bank, total mean expectation score is 24.4, mean perception score is 21.04 and average gap score is 0.84.

Similarly table 13 shows that as far as "Assurance" is concerned, in case of SBI, total mean expectation score is 24.22, mean perception score is 20.74 and average gap score is 0.87.

From the ensuing Table 14 we can easily observe that as far as "Assurance" is concerned, in case of ICICI bank, combined mean & combined S.D. for perception scores are 5.26 and 1.3791 respectively; and in case of SBI, combined mean & combined S.D. for perception scores are 5.18 and 1.5813 respectively.

Further, in this case Z- test is applied to test the null hypothesis,

H_o: $\mu_1 = \mu_2$ (i.e. There is no significant difference between the two types of the banks as far as the customer perception for assurance dimension is concerned).

Here $\overline{x_1} = 5.26$, $\overline{x_2} = 5.18$, $s_1 = 1.3791$ and $s_2 = 1.5813$

Now test statistic,

Table 12. Assurance gap score analysis for ICICI Bank

Assurance Expectations	Mean Score (E)	Assurance Perceptions	Mean Score (P)	Gap Score (E-P)
E-14. Customers should be able to trust the employees of these banks.	5.90	**P-14.** Customers are able to trust the employees of ICICI Bank.	4.82	1.08
E-15. Customers should be able to feel safe in their transactions with bank employees.	6.22	**P-15.** Customers are able to feel safe in their transactions with ICICI Bank employees.	5.12	1.10
E-16. Employees of the banks should be polite.	6.18	**P-16.** Employees of ICICI Bank are polite.	5.86	0.32
E-17. Employees should get adequate support from the banks to do their job well.	6.10	**P-17.** Employees get adequate support from ICICI Bank to do their job well.	5.24	0.86
Total	**24.4**		**21.04**	**3.36**
Average Gap Score				**3.36/4= 0.84**

Source: Primary Data

Table 13. Assurance gap score analysis for SBI

"Assurance" Expectations	Mean Score (E)	Assurance Perceptions	Mean Score (P)	Gap Score (E-P)
E-14. Customers should be able to trust the employees of these banks.	5.78	**P-14.** Customers are able to trust the employees of SBI.	5.54	0.24
E-15. Customers should be able to feel safe in their transactions with bank employees.	6.38	**P-15.** Customers are able to feel safe in their transactions with SBI employees.	5.82	0.56
E-16. Employees of the banks should be polite.	6.12	**P-16.** Employees of SBI are polite.	4.46	1.66
E-17. Employees should get adequate support from the banks to do their job well.	5.94	**P-17.** Employees get adequate support from SBI to do their job well.	4.92	1.02
Total	24.22		20.74	**3.48**
Average Gap Score				**3.48/4= 0.87**

Source: Primary Data

Table 14. Comparison of "Assurance" Perceptions for ICICI bank & SBI

Responsiveness Perceptions (ICICI)	Mean Score (P)	S.D.	Responsiveness Perceptions (SBI)	Mean Score (P)	S.D.
P-14. Customers are able to trust the employees of ICICI Bank.	4.82	1.4654	**P-14.** Customers are able to trust the employees of SBI.	5.54	1.6273
P-15. Customers are able to feel safe in their transactions with ICICI Bank employees.	5.12	1.4232	**P-15.** Customers are able to feel safe in their transactions with SBI employees.	5.82	1.5451
P-16. Employees of ICICI Bank are polite.	5.86	1.0200	**P-16.** Employees of SBI are polite.	4.46	1.4171
P-17. Employees get adequate support from ICICI Bank to do their job well.	5.24	1.3499	**P-17.** Employees get adequate support from SBI to do their job well.	4.92	1.3541
Combined Mean Combined S.D.	**5.26**	**1.3791**		**5.18**	**1.5813**

Source: Primary Data

$$z = \frac{\overline{x_1} - \overline{x_2}}{\sqrt{\frac{s_1^2}{n_1} + \frac{s_2^2}{n_2}}} = 0.46, \text{ i.e. } Z_{cal.} = 0.46$$

At 5% level of significance, for two-tailed test, the critical value of Z, $Z_{tab.} = 1.96$.

Since, $Z_{cal.} < Z_{tab.}$, so we accept the null hypothesis and conclude that there is no significant difference between the two types of the banks as far as the customer perception for assurance dimension is concerned.

Empathy

Analysis of data in Table 15 brings to light that as far as "Empathy" is concerned, in case of ICICI Bank, total mean expectation score is 23.62, mean perception score is 22.08 and average gap score is 0.30.

It is quite evident from data given in Table 16 that as far as "Empathy" is concerned, in case of SBI, total mean expectation score is 22.22, mean perception score is 20.30 and average gap score is 0.38.

It can be observed from the ensuing Table 17 that as far as "Empathy" is concerned, in case of ICICI bank, combined mean & combined S.D. for perception scores are 4.42 and 1.8980 respectively; and in case of SBI, combined mean & combined S.D. for perception scores are 4.06 and 1.8482 respectively.

Further, in this case Z- test is applied to test the null hypothesis,

H_0: $\mu_1 = \mu_2$ (i.e. There is no significant difference between the two types of the banks as far as the customer perception for empathy dimension is concerned).

Here $\overline{x_1} = 4.42$, $\overline{x_2} = 4.06$, $s_1 = 1.8980$ and $s_2 = 1.8482$

Table 15. Empathy gap score analysis for ICICI bank

Empathy Expectations	Mean Score (E)	Empathy Perceptions	Mean Score (P)	Gap Score (E-P)
E-18. Banks should give individual attention to the customers.	4.38	**P-18.** ICICI Bank gives individual attention to the customers.	4.00	0.38
E-19. Banks should have employees who give customers personal attention.	4.74	**P-19.** ICICI Bank has the employees who give customers personal attention.	4.24	0.50
E-20. Employees of the banks should understand the specific needs of their customers.	4.52	**P-20.** Employees of ICICI Bank understand the specific needs of their customers.	4.16	0.36
E-21. Banks should have their customers' best interests at heart.	4.66	**P-21.** ICICI Bank has its customers' best interests at heart.	4.52	0.14
E-22. Banks should have operating hours convenient to all its customers.	5.32	**P-22.** ICICI Bank has operating hours convenient to all its customers.	5.16	0.16
Total	**23.62**		**22.08**	**1.54**
Average Gap Score				**1.54/5 = 0.30**

Source: Primary Data

Table 16. Empathy gap score analysis for SBI

Empathy Expectations	Mean Score (E)	Empathy Perceptions	Mean Score (P)	Gap Score (E-P)
E-18. Banks should give individual attention to the customers.	4.52	**P-18.** SBI gives individual attention to the customers.	3.64	0.88
E-19. Banks should have employees who give customers personal attention.	4.64	**P-19.** SBI has the employees who give customers personal attention.	4.08	0.56
E-20. Employees of the banks should understand the specific needs of their customers.	4.30	**P-20.** Employees of SBI understand the specific needs of their customers.	4.06	0.24
E-21. Banks should have their customers' best interests at heart.	4.64	**P-21.** SBI has its customers' best interests at heart.	4.50	0.14
E-22. Banks should have operating hours convenient to all its customers.	4.12	**P-22.** SBI has operating hours convenient to all its customers.	4.02	0.10
Total	**22.22**		**20.30**	**1.92**
Average Gap Score				**1.92/5 = 0.38**

Source: Primary Data

Table 17. Comparison of empathy perceptions for ICICI bank & SBI

Empathy Perceptions (ICICI)	Mean Score (P)	S.D.	Empathy Perceptions (SBI)	Mean Score (P)	S.D.
P-18. ICICI Bank gives individual attention to the customers.	4.00	1.8330	**P-18.** SBI gives individual attention to the customers.	3.64	1.6584
P-19. ICICI Bank has the employees who give customers personal attention.	4.24	1.8172	**P-19.** SBI has the employees who give customers personal attention.	4.08	1.8956
P-20. Employees of ICICI Bank understand the specific needs of their customers.	4.16	1.7590	**P-20.** Employees of SBI understand the specific needs of their customers.	4.06	1.7936
P-21. ICICI Bank has its customers' best interests at heart.	4.52	2.0222	**P-21.** SBI has its customers' best interests at heart.	4.50	1.9416
P-22. ICICI Bank has operating hours convenient to all its customers.	5.16	1.8260	**P-22.** SBI has operating hours convenient to all its customers.	4.02	1.8274
Combined Mean Combined S.D.	**4.42**	**1.8980**		**4.06**	**1.8482**

Source: Primary Data

Now test statistic,

$$z = \frac{\bar{x}_1 - \bar{x}_2}{\sqrt{\frac{s_1^2}{n_1} + \frac{s_2^2}{n_2}}} = 1.66 \text{ i.e. } Z_{cal.} = 1.66$$

At 5% level of significance, for two-tailed test, the critical value of Z, $Z_{tab.} = 1.96$.

Since, $Z_{cal.} < Z_{tab.}$, so we accept the null hypothesis and conclude that there is a significant difference between the two types of the banks as far as the customer perception for empathy dimension is concerned.

CONCLUSION AND SUGGESTIONS

The major findings of the present study are as follows

1. As far as the perception of customers for Tangibility dimension of service quality is concerned, results of Z-test reveal that there is a significant difference between the two types of banks (i.e. Private and Public sector Banks).

Moreover, average gap score between Tangibility Expectations and Tangibility Perceptions for ICICI Bank (i.e. 0.34) is less than the average gap score between Tangibility Expectations and Tangibility Perceptions for SBI (i.e. 1.07). It implies that as far as Tangibility dimension of service quality is concerned, private sector banks are far ahead of public sector banks.

2. In case of customer perception for Reliability dimension of service quality, results of Z-test show that there is no significant difference between the two types of banks (i.e. Private and Public sector Banks).
3. Results of Z-test also reveal that there is a significant difference between the two types of banks (i.e. Private and Public sector Banks), as far as the perception of customers for Responsiveness dimension of service quality is concerned.

Furthermore, average gap score between Responsiveness Expectations and Responsiveness Perceptions for ICICI Bank (i.e. 0.40) is less than the average gap score between Responsiveness Expectations and Responsiveness Perceptions for SBI (i.e. 1.11). It implies that as far as Responsiveness dimension of service quality is concerned, private sector banks are far ahead of public sector banks.

4. As far as the perception of customers for Assurance dimension of service quality is concerned, results of Z-test shows that there is no significant difference between the two types of banks (i.e. Private and Public sector Banks).
5. In case of customer perception for Empathy dimension of service quality, results of Z-test imply that there is no significant difference between the two types of banks (i.e. Private and Public sector Banks).

On the basis of the above findings, following are some of the important suggestions for private and public sector banks:

a. It is quite evident from the study results that public sector banks are legging behind the private sector banks in terms of Tangibility and Responsiveness dimensions of service quality. So, it is suggested to the public sector banks that they should adopt a futuristic approach and thus should strive hard to improve upon the customer services related to these two dimensions.
b. Both the private and public sector banks are advised to have the updated database containing data related to important demographic variables such as age, education and occupation etc. of all the existing and potential customers. Analysis of this data may help the banks to cater the diverse banking needs of the customers in a better way and may also help in increasing the customer-base.

REFERENCES

Adrian, P. (1995). The Essence of Service Marketing. Prentice-Hall of India.

Angur, M.G., Natrajan, R., & Jaherea, J.S., Jr. (1999). Service Quality in the Banking Industry: An Assessment of Developing Economy. *International Journal of Marketing, 17*(3), 116-125.

Bahia, K., & Jacques, N. (2000). A Reliable and Valid Measurement Scale for the Perceived Service Quality of Banks. *International Journal of Bank Marketing, 18*(2), 84–91. doi:10.1108/02652320010322994

Bateson. (1995). SERVQUAL: review, critique, research agenda. *European Journal of Marketing, 30*(1), 8-32.

Buzzel, R., & Gale, B. (1987). *The PIMS Principles: Linking Strategy to Performance.* New York: Free Press.

Crosby, P. B. (1979). *Quality is free.* New York: McGraw-Hill.

Davidow, A., & Uttal, B. (1989). *Total Customer Service: The Ultimate Weapon.* New York: Harper & Row.

Garvin, D. A. (1983). Quality on the line. *Harvard Business Review, 61*, 64–75.

Heskett, J., Sasser, E., & Hart, C. (1990). *Services Breakthrough: Changing the Rules of the Game.* New York: Free Press.

Howcraft. (1991). Customer Satisfaction in Retail Banking. *The Service Industries Journal, 11*, 11-17.

Israel, D., Sudhahar, J.C., & Selvam, M. (2004, October). The Measurement of Service Quality Perception in Banking Sector. *SCMS Journal of Indian Management*, 37-51.

Juran, J. M. (1974). *Quality Control Handbook.* London: McGraw Hill Publications.

Kanadampully, J. (1998). Service Quality to Service Loyalty: A Relationship which goes beyond Customer Services. *Total Quality Management, 9*(6), 431–433. doi:10.1080/0954412988370

Kanadampully, J. (2000). The impact of demand fluctuation on the quality of service: A tourism industry example. *Managing Service Quality: An International Journal, 10*(1), 10–19. doi:10.1108/09604520010307012

Kotler, P., Ang, S. H., Leong, S. M., & Tan, C. T. (1999). *Marketing Management: An Asian Perspective*. Prentice Hall Inc.

Leonard, F. S., & Sasser, W. E. (1982). The incline of quality. *Harvard Business Review*, *60*(5), 163–171.

Narasimham Committee on Banking Sector Reforms (Narsimham Committee II). (n.d.). Retrieved from https://www.rbi.org.in/scripts/PublicationReportDetails.aspx?ID=251

Parasuraman, A., Zeithaml, V. A., & Berry, L. L. (1998). SERVQUAL: A Multiple Item Scale for Measuring Consumer Perceptions of Service Quality. *Journal of Retailing*, *64*(1), 12–40.

Purohit, H.C., & Pathardikar, A.D. (2007, March). Service Quality Measurement and Consumer Perception about the Services of Banking Institutions. *Indian Journal of Marketing*, 12-18.

Reichheld, F. F., & Sasser, E. (1990). Zero Defections: Quality Comes to Services. *Harvard Business Review*, *68*, 105–111. PMID:10107082

Stafford, M. R. (1996). Demographic Disriminations of Service Quality in Banking Industry. *Journal of Services Marketing*, *10*(4), 6–22. doi:10.1108/08876049610124554

Sureshchander, G. S., Rajendran, C., & Ananthraman, R. N. (2002). Determinants of Customer-Perceived Service Quality: A Confirmatory Factor Analysis Approach. *Journal of Services Marketing*, *16*(1), 9–32. doi:10.1108/08876040210419398

Chapter 8
Personality and Emotional Biases

Sezen Güngör
Namik Kemal University, Turkey

Engin Demirel
Trakya University, Turkey

Nihan Tomris Küçün
Eskisehir Osmangazi University, Turkey

ABSTRACT

Over the past decades, Cloninger et al. have developed a biosocial model of personality based on four temperaments and three characteristics. This multidimensional psychobiological model of personality presents in the temperament and character inventory – revised (TCI-R) form. Temperament subscales are novelty seeking (NS), harm avoidance (HA), reward dependence (RD), and persistence (P), and character subscales are self-directedness (SD), cooperativeness (CO), and self-transcendence (ST). The study has been used in different disciplines of science, especially in psychology. Behavioral finance is one of these disciplines of science. TCI is frequently used, especially for investor biases. In this chapter, TCI is used to examine the relationship between investor biases and personality. The first three chapters are about personality. Personality, personality approaches, and personality measurement methods examined in these sections. In the fourth part, emotional biases in financial investment decisions searched. In the fifth part, literature studies showing the relationship between personality and financial decisions included. Finally, a field survey is conducted, and findings are revealed.

DOI: 10.4018/978-1-5225-7399-9.ch008

INTRODUCTION

Personality

Personality is a sequence of behaviors, attitudes, and experiences that explain the reactions of one person to other persons and their surroundings (Stuart-Hamilton, 2007). The concept of personality, which thought to derived from masks called "persona" used by classical Roman theater players, is used to describe the differences between individuals (Evrim, 1967). Shiffman and Kanuk also define personality as follows: "the distinctive and characteristic patterns of thought and behavior that define the individual's interaction with the physical and social environment" (Shiffman and Kanuk, 2004).

In his study titled 'Personality: A Psychological Commentary' (1937), Allport mentioned nearly 50 definitions, and he also suggested a definition of the personality phenomenon in the same work. According to Allport, personality is "the dynamic structuring of psychophysical systems that determine the individual's own thinking and behavior" (Inanç and Yerlikaya, 2012).

Although there is not an absolute consensus on the definition of personality, it is possible to define the notion as 'coherent patterns of behavior and intrapersonal processes originating from the individual himself' (Dal, 2009). The definition which is advocated by Flexner and Stein (1982) is that "personality is the sum of physical, mental, emotional and social characteristics of the individual." Ewen also proposed a similar definition in 2003. According to Ewen; personality is in a relationship with human behavior in a broad range spectrum. Personality involves many things about the individual such as mental, emotional, social and physical aspects. Some phenomena which belong to a human being (such as dreams and thoughts) are not observable. Despite that, the physical behavior and manifestations of the person are observable. Personality includes all aspects in which the individual has a conscious or unconscious form.

While the concept of 'personality' is sometimes defined as 'the sum of all features' or as a 'process,' almost all of these definitions draw attention to the environmental variables because a person is always in an interaction with the inner and outer environmental factors. The individual's personality is a concept that determines the scope of the relation established by the inner and outer environmental factors (Cuceloglu, 2007). Furthermore, an individual is directed to be a sum of the national, religious, political and economic values of the society in which he lives (Büyükdüvenci, 2013).

PERSONALITY THEORIES

The concept of personality is described in many different ways because psychology is a very young discipline, and also a human being is a very complex creature and is not adequately suitable for being objectively studied (İnanç and Yerlikaya, 2012).

Personality development studies are the studies that try to explain the differences and development of individuals who focus on the goal of life-long self-realization in addition to the development of individual differences (Van Lieshout, 2000). Some of the approaches that explain personality development explain the formation of personality with the obvious physiological and psychological stages of life, and some with social incidents in the environment (Isır, 2006). Some theoreticians tend to search for an essential feature of personality, while others try to understand the personality differences and their causes.

Hence, as is seen, the predictions about the personality development of each theory are different. These different approaches discussed in the literature with six personality theories (Şenyuva, 2007).

Structural Approach

The structural approach is the approach that begins with Plato and continues with Hippocrates, which initially includes philosophical contents and later on transformed into the field of medical research. However, today there are no studies on this approach. The psychopathology suggested by this approach is related to body structure and about some fluids which thought to found in the body within different amounts. Hippocrates (B. C. 460-357) and Galenos (131- 201) thought that the four essential elements in the world (water, air, soil, and fire) and four different body fluids (blood, sputum, yellow and black bile) connected to four different personality types (optimistic, melancholic, calm and temperamental). According to this view, four elements or four liquids which were abundant in the body indicate the type of personality. (Van Lieshout, 2006).

These kinds of personality categories criticized regarding trying to fit human beings into a few groups. Moreover, also the hypothesis that advocates the relation between body structure and personality structure is not proven (Şenyuva, 2007).

Psychoanalytic: Psychodynamic Approach

The psychodynamic approach is one of the approaches which mostly focus on personality development (Şenyuva, 2007). This theory also called the Freudian approach because its most important representative is himself.

There are two notable names in theory. One of them, Freud, describes human behavior with innate instincts, that is, biological impulses, while Adler, the second important name, bases behavior on social grounds (Yörükan, 2006). For example, according to Adler, the most critical factor underlying human behavior is the effort of success or superiority. In other words, according to Adler, people are motivated both by their successes and by the success of other people (Feist and Feist, 2009). Freud is the scientist who designed the first personality theory and the first psychoanalysts. According to Freud, the majority of our personality is unconscious, and we are living creatures who tend to hide some unpleasant facts about ourselves from ourselves by using our defensive mechanisms. Moreover, we are provoked continuously by desires, beliefs, fears, and memories of which we are unaware. (Ewen, 2003). Freud has criticized for explaining the causes of personality development often with sexual and aggressive impulses. An important critique of Freud came from Jung, another prominent name in theory.

Jung states that psychoanalytic approach places unnecessary emphasis on sexual instincts than it does; on the contrary, it implies that individuals need an analytical approach to demonstrate their individuality and attitudes to reach various goals, and not to mention a single cause like Freud (Cüceloğlu, 2007).

We can divide the typical characteristics of the scholars of this approach into two groups. First, they argued that the most crucial factor in shaping the personality is the motivation of the subconscious. Secondly, they asserted that personality had shaped the conflict between opposing motivations and the defense mechanism (Isır, 2006). The common point in these two groups is that unconsciousness explains many essential aspects of the personality notion. In other words, psychodynamic theories emphasize unconsciousness in personality (Ewen, 2003).

Distinctive Features Approach (Trait Theory)

Distinctive features approach attempts to explain the human behavior with conscious and concrete concepts instead of describing it concerning unconscious and metaphysics concepts. The approach also based on empirical research rather than clinical observations (Ewen, 2003).

Trait approach based on two assumptions. First; personality traits do not change over time. In other words, the results from personality measurements will be consistent with the results achieved during adulthood. Second, personality traits do not vary in different situations. That is, a personality attribute that the individual has been identified to possess (e.g., aggression) will manifest itself in all cases, regardless of the circumstances or conditions (Dal, 2009).

Allport did the first known study on the trait in 1921. Personality defined as a dynamic organization of psychophysical systems that determines the individual's behavior and thoughts, while its distinctive characteristics define characteristics that include specific situations that often associated with how one behaves in many cases (Şenyuva, 2007). According to this approach, people have personality traits that reflect the tendency to act in a certain way (Isır, 2006).

In his 1946 work, Cattell states that the distinctive features can be analyzed correctly and that the analysis must be considered as structural and environmental patterns. Thus, in describing phenotypic changes, the concept of behavioral genetics can be mentioned (Revelle, 2009).

Cloninger, the most contemporary name of the Trait Approach, created a psychobiological model and tried to understand personality in this perspective (Şenyuva, 2007). 'Temperament and Character Inventory' which is developed by Cloninger in this concept will be explained in detail in the following sections.

Behavioral Approach

Behavioral approach is the result of persistent studies by Watson and Skinner, two of the most important names in Psychology, to detect subjective and unobservable features. Researchers in behavioral personality theory emphasizes the concept of social learning. This theory advocates that an individual's behavior shaped by the opinions of him about his behavior (Funder, 2001).

The behaviorist approach ignores the concepts that almost all theorists emphasized before such as internal causes, wishes, needs, thoughts, feelings, memories, inner spiritual conflicts, beliefs, expectations, preferences, prejudices, unconscious processes, and dreams. Therefore, behaviorism is not another approach to personality theories but an alternative method to all of them (Ewen, 2003).

Cognitive Approach

The cognitive approach, one of the personality theories, emphasizes the importance of thinking. According to theory, the behavior is defined not by innate instincts, but by interpreting and analyzing events, estimating possibilities and evaluating them. Researchers like George Kelly and Albert Bandura are among the advocates of this theory (Ewen, 2003).

According to cognitive theory, the way individual constructs and interprets his experiences influences how he feels and behaves. The view of theory on the concept of personality is related to some schemes and fundamental beliefs in information processing and behavior formation (Taymur and Türkçapar, 2012). Kelly's way of explaining behavior is about these schemas and underlying assumptions. According to

Kelly (1955), ordinary people exhibit some hypotheses and test these hypotheses with some experimental methods just like scientists (Ewen, 2003).

Humanistic Approach

The humanistic approach revealed by the researchers such as Abraham Maslow, George Kelly and Carl Rogers who are influenced by the streams such as existentialism in Europe and Zen Buddhism in Asia. (Funder, 2001). In the humanistic approach, psychologists act on the assumption that every human being has a unique way of perceiving and understanding the world, and advocates that all behaviors realized in this way. The advocates of humanistic inquiry ask different questions from other approaches. For example; the advocates of other approaches ask the question, "How is this person?", while the advocates of the humanitarian approach ask the question "How is such a person?" by trying to understand the subjectivities of people (Sammons, REF).

The humanistic theory argues that we have an innate potential for healthy growth and development. Rogers, one of the most well-known scholars of the approach, rejects the pessimism of Freud's human nature and says that our internal potential is always positive. He also says that we have an innate tendency to develop the positive part of ourselves. Another vital representative of the theory is Maslow. As Maslow points out in his work on the Essential Hierarchy of Needs, individuals will not care about the goals at a higher level without satisfying their needs in their current position. Because needs arise hierarchically, and when one is convinced, the lack of need at the higher level arises. The point at which Maslow left Freudian thought was to reject certain structural formations. However, acceptance of issues such as inhibition, projecting, reaction formation and rationalization is considered to be similar to Freudian thought (Ewen, 2003).

PERSONALITY MEASUREMENT METHODS

Woodworth Personal Data Sheet, which was developed to determine the level of personality and adaptability of soldiers during the First World War, is considered a prototype of personality inventories. The inventory consists of 116 items and measures the behavioral deviation, abnormal fears, obsessions, obsessions, obsolescence and other sleep disturbances, excessive fatigue, and other psychosomatic symptoms, hallucinations, psychomotor disturbances. Cornell made a similar study during World War II. In this study, Cornell developed an inventory with a yes or no system consisting of 101 questions; fear, inadequacy, depression, aggression, anxiety, hypersensitivity and suspicion, pathological fear reactions, and numerous psychosomatic symptoms. (Isır, 2006).

All personality inventories try to measure different personality traits. For example; Multidimensional Personality Questionnaire, also known as MPQ, measures 11 different personality traits. (Carey, Chapter 22, 2002). Cloninger's Temperament and Character Inventory examines personality in 7 dimensions. The model, which described as a five-factor model in the literature, argues that personality consists of five essential characteristics and used in research that measures these five factors. The question that psychologists have been asking for so many years is the explanation of the numerous and detailed studies in that field: "Why is this difference in personality traits and how are these different traits related to each other?"

Personality measurement efforts under the title of psychological evaluation aim to reveal the differences and similarities between individual's and the other individuals' characteristics. For this reason, psychological evaluation practices involve many different methods that serve this purpose. (Weiner, 2003).

Today, candidates in the recruitment process often subjected to personality tests. Before employing employees, employers use these tests to know whether the candidates have the personality characteristics required for the job (outreach, team member, sociability) and to place the right person in the right job. It seems that many personality inventories shaped according to the necessity. Also, financial advisors or investment specialists, who serve in the financial investment process, are now beginning to take into consideration the individual's personality.

Schmidt and Hunter (1998) conducted a meta-analysis study of personality measures used in recruitment decisions. They concluded that cognitive ability measures are the most critical determinants of performance and work-related learning (Klimoski and Zukin, 2003).

Personal psychology surrounded by the chaotic and highly variable nature of our personality. The use of different tools to measure similar features or the use of similar tools to measure different features explained by that cause (Funder, 2001).

Typical personality tests are used to measure similar personalities. Some of these tests based on concepts (such as Five Factor Models) and others have neurobiological bases (such as Cloninger's three-dimensional personality study with dopamine, serotonin, and norepinephrine systems) (Benjamin et al., 2008). In the literature, it is possible to classify personality tests as objective personality tests and projective personality tests (Isır, 2006).

Objective Personality Tests

Objective personality tests can be exemplified as paper-pencil tests or self-explanatory inventory. Among the most commonly used personality tests are personal assessment inventories. Personal assessment inventories specify whether individuals participate in various expressions of their personality traits. Answer options are often true-false, yes-no or agree or disagree (Isır, 2006).

Among the most frequently used personality inventories are 'Personality Five-Factor Model,' Zuckermann and Kuhlman's 'Personality Scale,' Eysenck's 'Personality Inventory,' and Cloninger's 'Temperament and Character Inventory.'

Eysenck Personality Survey

Eysenck suggests a dimensional approach to personality in his theory. Eysenck defines personality in four primary dimensions. These are neuroticism - stability and extroversion - introversion. In his later work, he added two more aspects as psychoticism and lie (Lewis et al., 2002). Eysenck stated that these distinctive personality traits are independent of each other.

There are 'inward' and 'outward' horizontal dimensions, 'neurotic' and 'normal' vertical dimensions. Personality structures of all people located somewhere between these two dimensions. Observation and tests determine this point. The vertically and horizontally placed items of personality placed at four separate levels that are separate but interconnected (Goodworth, 1988). These four levels are schematized by Eysenck and Wilson (1998) as shown in Figure 1.

After Eysenck, a large number of personality scales developed by his followers. These were Maudsley Medical Questionnaire (MTA, 40 items), Maudsley Personality Inventory (MKE, 48 items), Eysenck

Figure 1. Eysenck's Personality Types
(Eysenck and Wilson, 1998, s.17)

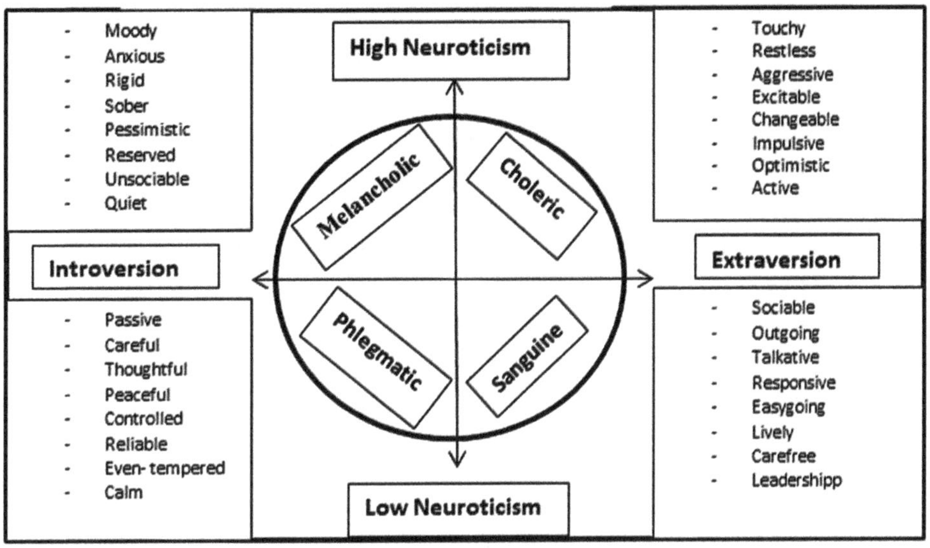

Personality Inventory (EKE, 57 items), Eysenck Personality Questionnaire (EKA, 90 items), Observed Eysenck Personality Questionnaire) and the Eysenck Personality Questionnaire Survey-Short Form (EKA-GGK 48 items). (Karancı, Dirik, and Yorulmaz, 2007).

Five Factors Model

Despite all the repeated critics in literature 'Five Factors Model' (Funder, 2001) which accepted as a classification model of personality characteristics, persists in explaining personality with five factors; openness, conscientiousness, neuroticism, extraversion, and agreeableness.

Despite its popularity, the theory has two main problems: First, all five factors regarded as independent of each other. In other words, it assumed that there are five independent factors from the viewpoint of factor weights. But are these five factors completely independent? In some measurements, the elements seem to be related to each other. The second and more critical problem is that all personality traits of the individual are limited to these five factors. It is not realistic that each personality structure shaped by only these five factors (Funder, 2001).

Cloninger's Temperament and Character Inventory

Temperament, character, and personality are different phenomena. Temperament is a structural feature that passes through heredity and changes slightly in life. The character is a learned attitude under the influence of the environment and culture, and therefore includes features that can be changed over time. Personality is the combination of genetically derived character and later acquired character (Sayın and Aslan, 2005). Cloninger describes personality as a dynamic formation that exists within the individual's psychobiological system through changing patterns and constantly changing internal and external environmental conditions (Fahlgren et al., 2015).

According to Cloninger, human personality has evolved through three primary systems of learning and memory in large part of the steps taken by humankind during evolution. The first primary system is the procedural system. The procedural system regulates different emotional reactions such as anger, passion, disgust, and ambition, which is the temperament of this person. The second system of learning and memory is the proportional system. This system is about living together and self-managing in a social environment. The third system is known as the episodic system. The episodic system is only seen among people and is based on self-awareness, which allows the autobiographical memory to perform subjective observation and recall actions (Fahlgren et al., 2015).

Cloninger's personality theory has the potential to provide comprehensive information in a wide range of contexts ranging from the genetic basis of the person to the neurobiological basis of behavior, the cognitive and emotional nature and development of personality, the behavioral ties of individual differences in personality dimensions, the interaction of personality constructs with developmental factors, and psychiatric disorders (Köse, 2003). In other words, it deals with three dimensions of your personality: body, soul, and mind (Fahlgren, 2015).

Cloninger has developed a general psychobiological theory to describe the structure and development of personality (Cloninger 1987, Cloninger et al., 1993). Cloninger's personality model also gives the opportunity to connect behavioral views and neurotransmitters. It has been reported that there is a relationship between novelty seeking (behavioral activation) and dopamine, harm avoidance (behavioral inhibition), serotonin and reward dependence (maintaining behavior), and norepinephrine and persistence (persistence in behavior) and glutamatergic activity (Köse, Sayar et al., 2004).

Temperament and Character Inventory is a self-assessment scale designed to measure individual differences in each of the temperament and character dimensions (Svrakic, 2002). Cloninger's temperament dimensions reflect individual differences in perceptual knowledge and skills and are genetically homogeneous and mutually independent. The components of the character dimension convey that as the age progresses, the concept of self-develops, or that it develops with the personal and social effects of adulthood (Köse, Sayar et al., 2004).

The inventory is a self-report scale including 240 items. The scale has translated into many languages (Turkish work Köse, Sayar et al. in 2004). Temperament and Character Inventory divides temperament and character into sub-dimensions as follows;

- **Temperament:** While Buss and Plomin (1984) described the temperament as a biological personality component, Rothbart and Derry Berry (1981) described a structural basis as differences in self-control and reactivity. According to Fahlgren (2015), temperament defined as relational learning involving automatic responses to perceptual stimuli. Temperament is dealt with in 4 basic dimensions (Hansenne et al., 2005).
- **Novelty Seeking:** It linked to the behavioral activation system. When responding to a new stimulus, an exploratory-searching activity refers to a hereditary predisposition to see behaviors such as impulsive decision-making, overbearing, rapid anger, and active avoidance when the probability of a reward is high (Köse, Sayar et al., 2004. Arkar, 2005).
    - Exploratory excitability
    - Impulsiveness
    - Extravagance
    - Disorderliness

- **Harm Avoidance:** Behavioral inhibition is related to the system. Pessimistic concerns for future problems manifest themselves in passive avoidance behaviors such as fear of uncertainty, shame from strangers, and rapid fatigue, and it is a hereditary tendency to prevent or halt behavior (Arkar, 2005. Köse Sayar et al., 2004).
    - Anticipatory worry
    - Fear of uncertainty
    - Shyness
    - Fatigability
- **Reward Dependence:** It is about the behavioral maintenance system. It is a hereditary tendency that manifests itself with extreme emotionality, dependence upon others' approval, and continuity of social attachment behaviors (Arkar, 2005. Köse, Sayar et al., 2004).
    - Sentimentality
    - Openness to warm communication
    - Attachment
    - Dependence
- **Persistence:** It refers to a hereditary predisposition to persistence against frustration and fatigue. (Arkar, 2005. Köse, Sayar et al., 2004).
    - Persistence
- **Character:** Cloninger's personality theory includes temperament and dimensions, which are described as hereditary predispositions, as well as the maturing character and dimensions of personal and social activity that comes with adulthood as the individual grows older (Köse, Sayar et al., 2004.).
- **Self-Directedness:** The self-governing individual is an autonomous individual, who is responsible, skillful, has goals, and has mission awareness (Köse and Sayar et al., 2004).
    - Responsibility
    - Purposefulness
    - Resourcefulness
    - Self-acceptance
    - Enlightened second temperament
- **Cooperativeness:** Cooperativeness means social acceptance, empathy, compassion, virtue, and conscience. People who make cooperation are tolerant, empathic, loving and virtuous people. (Köse and Sayar, 2004).
    - Social acceptance
    - Empathy
    - Helpfulness
    - Compassion
    - Pure-hearted nature
- **Self-Transcendence:** Self-transcendence means getting away from individualism, showing empathy and having spiritual acceptance. These people can be described as idealistic individuals who exhibit intense, non-selfish creative behavior in their beliefs and spiritual feelings. (Köse and Sayar, et al., 2004).
    - Self-loss-Self awareness
    - Self – forgetful

- Transpersonal identification
- Spiritual acceptance

During the inventory's evaluating process, some items coded as positive, and others coded as negative. Individual questions for each sub-dimension included in the score (Köse, Sayar, 2004).

Cloninger (1987) explains the evaluation of these dimensions as shown in Table 1 (Fahlgren, 2015).

Projective Tests

A projective test used by Lawrence for the first time in 1939 (Alibal, 1974) now seen as a method of measuring personality and helping to understand the unknowns of personality. In this method, uncertain stimuli are given to the subject, and they are asked to react. The test is not clearly explained to the participant, so it is expected that the reaction of the participant reflects his unconscious desires and feelings. A numeric value does not evaluate the answers. Usually, Freud's dream interpretation methods are used in the evaluation process (Akkoyun, 1983).

The most commonly used tests in projective tests can be listed as follows; 'Rorschach Inkblot Test' (1920), 'Jung's Word Association Test' (1904) and 'Murray's Story Telling Test' (1935). As seen in the literature, there are many different opinions on projective tests. Unlike Rorschach, some researchers have called these tests as just 'imagination.' Eysenck also rejected this method of testing and defined projective tests as "unstructured tests" (Alibal, 1994. Dal, 2009).

Table 1. Description of the temperament and character dimensions

Dimensions		High Scores	Low Scores
Temperament	Novelty Seeking	Exploratory and curious; impulsive; extravagant and enthusiastic; disorderly.	Indifferent; reflective; frugal and detached; orderly and regimented.
	Harm Avoidance	Worrying and pessimistic; fearful and doubtful; shy; fatigable.	Relaxed and optimistic; bold and confident; outgoing; vigorous.
	Reward Dependence	Sentimental and warm; dedicated and attached; dependent.	Practical and cold; withdrawn and detached; independent.
	Persistence	Industrious and diligent; hard-working; ambitious and overachiever; perseverant and perfectionist.	Inactive and indolent; gives up easily; modest and underachiever; quitting and pragmatist.
Character	Self-Directedness	Mature and strong; responsible and reliable; purposeful; resourceful and effective; self-accepted; habits congruent with long term goals.	Immature and fragile; blaming and unreliable; purposeless; inert and ineffective; self-striving; habits incongruent with long term goals.
	Cooperativeness	Socially tolerant; empathic; helpful; compassionate and constructive; ethical and principled.	Socially intolerant; critical; unhelpful; revengeful and destructive; opportunistic.
	Self-Transcendence	Wise and patient; creative and self-forgetful; united with the universe.	Impatient; unimaginative and self-conscious; pride and lack of humility.

EMOTIONAL BIASES IN FINANCIAL DECISIONS

Some of the economics and finance theorists denominate people as rational entities with complete knowledge, while others call them the irrational or limited rationale. In particular, it appears that many different theories have emerged in decision-making under uncertainty. These theories mainly divided into two main headings. The first of these is the traditional finance theories that outline the rational investor, and the second is behavioral finance theories that suggest that decision makers are under the influence of many biases (Sezer, 2013). In traditional finance theories, investor behavior generally based on rationality. The investor's primary objective is to increase the ultimate wealth. When making financial decisions, they only take into account the risk and return of the alternative investment. According to behavioral finance theories, an investor is a person who influenced by rumors in the market, his feelings, the behavior of his surroundings and many other things. He may not be interested in the only risk and return.

In the financial decision process, individuals are sometimes affected differently by different factors and may make incorrect decisions. These factors sometimes originate from false financial calculations, and sometimes they become psychological. The impact of psychological factors on the capital market instruments was initially set forth by Kahneman and Tversky. Intuition and feelings play a significant role in investment decisions (Şenkesen, 2009), and it observed that phenomena defined as tendencies or biases in behavioral finance are useful in the formation of the intuition and feelings about decision making entity.

In understanding the effects of behavioral biases in the investment process, it is important for the investor and the investment adviser to reach pre-determined financial targets and raise the economic results (Pompian, 2012a). The financial consequences of investment decisions of individuals will also maximize through the adoption of the effect in the decision process of behavioral prejudices, which is the natural consequence of human behavior which not considered in traditional financial approaches.

Pompian (2012a) handled these short-cuts, which are used by individual investors who act irrationally under uncertainty, under two main headings: cognitive biases and emotional biases. Emotional biases corrections are difficult because these biases depend on temperament, character, and personal characteristics. Emotional biases are derived from impulsions, intuitions, and emotions, and can lead to decisions that are not based on reason. In this case, focusing on the cognitive aspects of biases may be more effective than trying to change the emotional response (Pompian, 2012a).

Psychologists and economists have done a number of studies that demonstrate that emotions manifest themselves in different forms, especially in the financial decision-making process. In these studies, for example, it has been seen that when the soccer team that is being supported has won, it has made the person a good mood, and this good mood can be effective in making investment decisions. One of these studies was done by Lo et al. in 2005. They studied the moods and investments of 80 participants in the study. They used the University of Wales Institute of Science and Technology (UWIST) Mood Adjective Checklist (MACL) for mood detection (Lo, Repin and Steenbarger, 2005). Researchers have found that investors with intense emotional reactions to financial gains and losses exhibit significantly worse investment performance. Likewise, good and bad moods can sometimes surprise investors who use traditional finance theories cause them to make miscalculations. For example, in the Gordon Model (PV = D1 / (k-g)), the user has to estimate g (growth rate in dividends).

Pompian (2012a) classifies emotional biases as follows:

- **Loss Aversion Bias:** Loss aversion tendency has come to the fore with the Expectation Theory published by Kahneman and Tversky in 1979. They discuss loss aversion in the context of the

S-shaped, utility representative value function that models the entire evaluation stage in prospect theory. According to Kahneman and Tversky, people weigh all potential gains and losses in relation to some benchmark reference point (the point of origin on the graph in next Figure. The value function that passes through this point is asymmetric; and risk-seeking behavior prevails in the domain of losses (below the x axis), while risk-averse behavior prevails in the domain of gains (above the x axis) (Pompian, 2012a). Adam Smith's book titled "Theory of Moral Sentiments" describes the avoidance of loss, which is often used today in behavioral economics or finance; "The pain we feel when we fall into a bad situation from a good situation is more than the joy we feel when we rise from a bad situation to a good situation, and this avoids a loss" (Nofsinger, 2011. Gazel, 2014).

- **Overconfidence Bias:** Researchers and academics working in the field of psychology and behavioral finance have examined the issue of excessive trust, and they say that as humans we tend to exaggerate our skills and predictions (Ricciardi, Simon, 2000). People have a lot of confidence in their talents. Especially entrepreneurs are expected to have such overconfidence (Ritter, 2003). Excessive confidence studies have revealed that this bias has led investors to make erroneous decisions. One of these mistakes reflected in the investor as the decline in net income due to excessive transaction costs arising from excessive trading. Moreover, investors with this bias can sell high-performance financial assets and to buy low-performance assets (Nofsinger, 2012. Gazel, 2014). Another mistake of investors who has overconfidence bias is explaining the performance success of financial assets that valued because of the rise in the market with their abilities. Statman et al. (2006) examined the monthly share earnings and transaction numbers during a 40 year period, and they determined the high transaction numbers followed by the high-yielding months (Statman, 2006).
- **Self-Control Bias:** In the simplest sense, the tendency to self-control is related to spending today, rather than saving for retirement because of lack of self-discipline. The most typical behavior of an investor with this tendency is to make much higher risk investments for short-term returns rather than making less risky investments for long-term financial success.

Figure 2. Prospect Theory

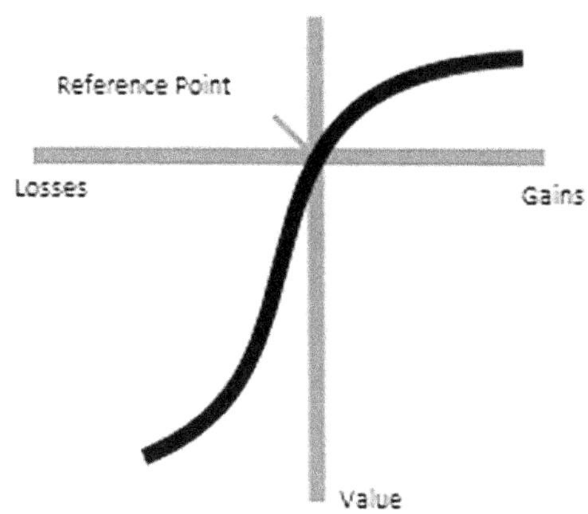

- **Status-Quo Bias:** The concept of status quo bias is defined as the motive to protect the current situation. In terms of behavioral financing, the status quo bias shows protecting the investor's current financial position and showing a tendency to escape from changes. This tendency becomes bias when the investor displays irrational behavior and is deprived of potential gains. The status quo bias often arises when investment options increase. In other words, the more alternatives investors have, the less they do. Considering unlimited investment opportunities in the real world, it seems likely that the prejudice of status quo protection will emerge (Nofsinger, 2012. Gazel, 2014).
- **Endowment Bias:** Endowment bias is described as a mental process in which a differential weight is placed on the value of an object. That value depends on whether one possesses the object and is faced with its loss or whether one does not possess the object and has the potential to gain it (Pompian, 2012a). According to Kahneman et al. (1991), people tend to overestimate things that he has regardless of their objective market values. People are reluctant to be separated from what they have, despite getting in exchange cash money. In simpler terms, people tend to overestimate, even for a commodity that can easily be bought and sold in the marketplace, if they attach empirical, emotional or symbolic importance to that commodity. Endowment bias is a form of status quo bias and can be explained by the tendency to lose aversion (Kahneman et al., 1991).
- **Regret Aversion Bias:** Regret is an emotional pain caused by previous decisions becoming a wrong decision. Regret Aversion Bias can explain as the tendency of investors to sell their winning shares early and to hold long-lived share securities (Shefrin and Statman 1985). Another exciting investor behavior about regret aversion is re-buying behavior. Strahilevitz, Odean and Barber (2011) put forward a decision tree showing their investor behavior on this subject. Accordingly, two situations may arise when a financial asset is acquired; the price of the asset may increase, and the price of the asset may decrease. When an increasing price is concerned, the investor may sell the asset due to the influence of the regret aversion. In this case, if the price of that asset continues to increase after the sale, then the investor may have a tendency to purchase again. Or if the price drops after the asset sold, then the investor will have the pleasure of making the right decision. However, in the coming period, an increase in the price of the asset will drive the investor to buy again (Strahilevitz et al., 2011).
- **Affinity Bias:** The affinity bias defined as a familiarity bias or a tendency to prefer familiar ones in some sources. These biases can set as the preference of investment alternatives that are more familiar to individuals. The studies show that investors who have affinity bias tend to invest the well-known company's stocks that they feel close to themselves or emotionally close to them. For example, Coca-Cola's 16% stake acquired by the Georgia-ABD public, where the company headquarters located. Also, Ivkovic and Weisbenner's study showed that US households tend to invest in companies that are no more than 250 miles away from their homes (Nofsinger, 2012. Gazel, 2014).

STUDIES THAT EXPLAIN THE RELATIONSHIP FINANCIAL DECISIONS AND PERSONALITY

There are many studies in financial decision-making that examine investors' personality patterns and reveal various models. Some of these studies have been referred to as the "Psychographic Models" in literature.

Psychographic models are designed to categorize people according to specific characteristics, tendencies or behaviors. Psychological classifications are particularly important regarding individual strategy and risk tolerance (Pompian, 2012a). Investors' compliance with specific psychographic profiles may increase their tendency to show certain investment biases. In other words, psychographic models try to define these biases in investment decisions by dividing them into classes according to the individual, personality, sex, age, marital status, and many other psychographic traits, and associating these variables with specific investor biases.

The most popular models among psychographic models are the ones developed by Barnewall (1987) and Bailard, Biehl, and Kaiser (1986). These models are often used in behavioral financing." Other than these, there are Myers and Briggs's study at the beginning of the 1940s, Pompian and Longo's study (2004) at the beginning of the 2000s and Sadi, Ghalibaf, Rostami and Gholipour's study in 2011.

The Barnewall (1987) model is one of the oldest and most common psychographic models. Barnewall categorizes investors into two classes: passivity in creating wealth or activity in creating wealth. Active investors are individuals who have taken an active role in gaining their fortunes during their lifetime and risking their own capital. Inactive investors, the security requirement has less importance than the risk tolerance and exhibits higher tolerance to risk, because they have higher confidence. They have a part in investment decisions with their advisors. They feel they have minimized the risk to an acceptable level thanks to their participation and inspections. Passive investors also have wealth by inheritance or by risking the capital of others instead of risking their own capital. These investors have a more security requirement than risk tolerance. According to Barnewall, the smaller the economic resources of an investor, the higher the likelihood that a person is a passive investor. Resource deficiency provides individuals with greater security and lower risk tolerance. Thus, a large percentage of the middle and lower socioeconomic classes are passive investors (Barnewall, 1987).

In the psychographic model developed by Bailard, Biehl, and Kaiser (1986), there are some principles of the Barnewall model. Also, the investor classifies the personality into two axes (level of confidence and method of action) and presents an additional dimension of analysis. In the model known as the Five-Way Model, investors classified into two dimensions: Confidence level and Action method. The first (the aspect of personality) deals with how confidently the investor approaches life, regardless of whether it is his approach to his career, his health, or his money. These are essential emotional choices, and they are dictated by how confident the investor is about some things or how much he tends to worry about them. The second element deals with whether the investor is methodical, careful, and analytical in his approach to life or whether he is emotional, intuitive, and impetuous. These two elements can be thought of as two "axes" of individual psychology; one axis is called the "confident–anxious" axis, and the other is called the "careful–impetuous" axis (Zaidi and Tauni, 2012). The dimensions of the model can be shown as shown in Figure 3.

Adventurers may hold highly undiversified portfolios because they are confident and willing to take chances. Their confidence leads them to make their own decisions and makes them reluctant to take advice. Celebrities like to be the center of attention. They may hold opinions about some things but to a certain extent recognize their limitations and may be willing to seek and take advice about investing. Individualists are independent and confident. They like to make their own decisions but only after careful analysis. Guardians are cautious and concerned about the future. As people age and approach retirement, they may become guardians. They are concerned about protecting their assets and may seek advice from those they perceive as being more knowledgeable than themselves. Straight arrows are sensible and

Figure 3. Bailard, Biehl, and Kaiser Model

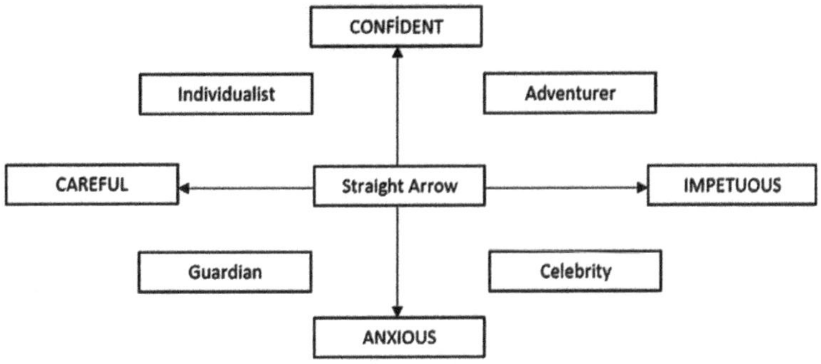

secure. They fall near the center of the graph. They are willing to take on some risk in the expectation of earning a commensurate return (Pompian, 2012a).

Another popular psychographic model is the Myers-Briggs Personality Type Inventory (MBTI) developed by Isabel Briggs Myers and Katherine Briggs. Based on the idea that different occupational groups are related to different personality orientations, and according to MBTI, which planned to use in recruitment processes, there are natural preferences that define how each person behaves in a given situation. Pompian and Longo (2004) used MBT in their studies and found that investors who have different gender and different personality types, succumbed to various investment biases such as overconfidence. It also suggests that investment advisor should consider gender and investor personality as an important factor in customer profiling and should use these elements in creating investment programs that will minimize the negative effects of investment factors (Pompian and Longo, 2004).

The other research that discusses investor personality and behavioral tendency in investment with personality analysis studied by Lin (2011). In this study, Lin investigated personality traits with the Five Factor Personality Model. According to Lin, some personality traits and demographic characteristics significantly related to each other. For example, he discovered that neuroticism is related to loss aversion, which known as "losses loom larger than gains" (Kahneman and Tversky, 1979), while there is no relation to the overconfidence bias. Another study that tried to investigate investor behavior using the Five Factor Personality Model was conducted by Sadi, Ghalibaf, Rostami, and Gholipour in 2011. They found a positive relationship between extroversion and hindsight bias, negative correlation with a tendency of randomness. They also found that there are positive relationships between neuroticism and randomness and between hindsight bias and overconfidence bias (Zaidi and Tauni, 2012. Sadi et al., 2011).

PRACTICE

Data Collection

In this study, TCI-Temperament and Personality Inventory, which frequently used in personality studies, was used in its original form with 240 items. The original form was not translated into Turkish. Instead, Turkish TCI prepared by Kose, Sayar et al. (2004) used. The validity and reliability study of the inventory was carried out using the Cronbach alpha method. Accordingly, the minimum values for temperament, character and their subscales range from 0.44 to 0.85. The values in this study varied between 0.45 and 0.76. The overall Cronbach's alpha value of the 240 items was 0.87. In the detection of emotional biases, diagnostic tests conducted by Pompian (2012a and 2012b), Kahneman and Tversky (1979) and Cesarini et al. (2011) used. Experiments have been translated into one-to-one Turkish and are organized to be understood better by participants. The prepared test is given to all participants as the questionnaire.

Participants

For this study, 120 healthy participants interviewed in Turkey. Because of some problems with answering the survey, 18 participants eliminated, and eventually, the study completed with 102 subjects between the ages of 18-55 (Mean=28.18and SD= 10.27). A total of 33 women and 69 men participated in the survey of all participants. 72 of the participants are married, 30 are single. Also, 29 people stated that they had at least one child, while 73 people said they didn't have any children. The average monthly income of 24 people is less than 1000 TL, the income of 51 people is in the range of 1001-2000 TL, and 27 people have a higher rate than 2001 TL.

Statistical Analyzes

In the study, firstly, the relationship between personality and emotional biases and age, gender, marital status, parental status, education level and income level were examined. Chi-Square analysis investigated this relationship. Then the correlations between emotional prejudices and temperament and character inventory were tested, and Chi-Square analysis was used to determine whether there was a relationship between these variables. Finally, the participants grouped into those with and without bias, and the difference in the mean scores of the personality traits among these groups was analyzed. This analysis was performed using the Mann Whitney U test, a non-parametric test.

Results and Conclusion

120 healthy individuals participated in the study. It is important for individuals to be over 18 years old to have financial decision-making competence and to sign a consent form that they have agreed to participate in the work. 18 participants were excluded from the study because they responded incompletely to the questionnaire, or they answered "yes" to TCI's statement "I lied in this questionnaire."

33 women and 69 men participated in the study. The average age of all participants was found to be 28.18 ± 10.27. 72 participants were single, 30 were married; 29 people have at least one child, 73 people are not children; 17 people graduated from primary school, 44 graduates from high school and 41 people graduated from higher education. Also, participants stated that 24 people had a monthly income of less than 1.000 TL, 51 people had an income between 1.000 and 2.000 TL and 27 people had an income higher than 2.000 TL.

In Table 1, the relationship between personality dimensions and emotional prejudices and demographic characteristics analyzed. Results indicate that gender is related to reward dependence, loss aversion and overconfidence (respectively; 9.877, p=.002; 3.146, p=.046; 5.371, p=.020). With regard to marital status, there is a relationship with only harm avoidance (10.470, p=.001). Another demographic feature that associated with the search for novelty seeking is parenthood (6.589, p=.010). The level of education connected with two demographic features: novelty seeking (12.492, p=.014) and self-directedness

Table 2. Personality, Emotional Biases and Demographic Characteristics

Chi-Square Test	Gender		Marital Status		Parenthood		Education		Income	
	Value	p	Value	p	Value	p	Value	p	Value	p
Novelty Seeking	0,001	0,970	**10,470**	**0,001**	**6,589**	**0,010**	**12,492**	**0,014**	7,098	0,131
Harm Avoidance	0,569	0,451	0,216	0,642	0,047	0,828	5,782	0,216	1,069	0,899
Reward Dependence	**9,877**	**0,002**	0,000	1,000	0,385	0,535	3,755	0,440	4,624	0,328
Persistence	0,082	0,775	0,455	0,500	0,656	0,418	6,424	0,170	5,190	0,206
Self-Directedness	0,321	0,571	0,672	0,412	0,008	0,929	**20,517**	**0,000**	4,730	0,319
Cooperativeness	0,122	0,727	0,550	0,458	0,947	0,331	6,909	0,141	6,592	0,159
Self-Transcendence	0,202	0,653	0,850	0,357	0,385	0,535	8,350	0,080	**10,262**	**0,036**
Loss Aversion	**3,146**	**0,046**	3,079	0,079	1,323	0,250	5,373	0,251	7,895	0,096
Overconfidence	**5,371**	**0,020**	2,953	0,086	2,105	0,147	4,793	0,309	1,265	0,867
Status-Quo	0,094	0,760	0,108	0,743	0,421	0,517	2,177	0,703	6,761	0,149
Endowment	0,226	0,635	0,053	0,817	0,226	0,634	1,462	0,833	2,429	0,657
Regret Aversion	0,224	0,636	0,003	0,956	0,151	0,698	1,294	0,862	2,706	0,608
Self-Control	1,120	0,290	0,000	1,000	0,048	0,826	3,459	0,484	**14,405**	**0,006**
Affinity	0,050	0,822	0,237	0,627	0,081	0,776	7,185	0,126	3,177	0,529

(20.517, p=.000). Concerning income level, the relationship with self-transcendence (10.262, p=.036) and with self-control (14.405, p=.006) is statistically significant.

When the correlations between emotional biases and all sub-dimensions of temperament and character dimensions of personality are examined, the following conclusions emerge.

The tables above show correlations between personality dimensions and emotional prejudices.

Table 3. The Correlations between Emotional Biases and Personality -1

	Loss Aversion	p	Overconfidence	p	Status-Quo	p
Impulsiveness			-0,271	0,006	-0,261	0,008
Extravagance			-0,211	0,034		
Novelty Seeking			-0,202	0,042	-0,246	0,013
Anticipatory worry	0,251	0,011				
Harm Avoidance	0,225	0,023				
Dependence			-0,201	0,043	0,215	0,030
Persistence					0,218	0,028
Responsibility	-0,197	0,047				
Purposefulness			0,195	0,049		
Resourcefulness			0,256	0,009		
Self-Directedness			0,217	0,028		
Social acceptance	-0,205	0,039				

Table 4. The Correlations between Emotional Biases and Personality -2

	Endowment	p	Regret Aversion	p	Self-Control	p	Affinity	p
Novelty Seeking	-0,228	0,021						
Fear of uncertainty			0,248	0,012				
Harm Avoidance			0,253	0,010				
Sentimentality							0,334	0,001
Reward Dependence			0,206	0,038			0,309	0,002
Persistence	0,311	0,001						
Purposefulness	0,206	0,037						
Resourcefulness	0,200	0,044						
Helpfulness					-0,261	0,008	0,196	0,049
Transpersonal identification							0,213	0,032
Self-Transcendence							0,232	0,019

When the tables examined, it can be seen that loss aversion correlated with harm avoidance and anticipatory worry. Individuals high in loss aversion have a significant concern, fear, trepidation one feels when facing new or unknown situations. On the other hand, individuals who have loss aversion bias avoid responsibility and social acceptance.

According to results in the above tables, individuals low in novelty seeking and its subscales (impulsiveness and extravagance) tend to be overconfident in financial decisions. When considered from this point of view, it can be said that if one has overconfidence bias, because of self-confidence, he/she does not feel outgoing, impulsive or willing to explore behaviors. Also, the overconfidence emotion blocks the dependence behavior, because of the negative correlation between these two variables. However, self-directedness impulse will be expected to be high in those who have overconfidence bias.

When we look at the results of the correlation with status-quo bias, we can say that individuals who have this bias are far from novelty seeking and impulsiveness, and do not behave impulsively in financial decisions. Besides, these people act in a perseverant manner, because of the positive correlations with dependence and persistence. The negative correlation of the endowment bias with the search for novelty seeking and the positive correlation this bias with persistence can be similarly resolved.

Another correlation analysis made between regret aversion and personality traits. According to the results of this analysis, there are positive correlations between regret aversion and harm avoidance, fear of uncertainty and reward dependence. Regret Aversion is the trend to avoid making decision due to the fear of experiencing the hurt of regrets. Investors avoid taking decisive actions due to regret aversion because they fear that, in perception, whatever course they select will prove less than optimal (Singh and Singh, 2015). For this reason, individuals who avoid regret will also have harm avoidance and reward dependence as personality traits.

Finally, according to the correlations between endowment bias and personality traits, individuals high in endowment have high reward dependence and self-transcendence.

REFERENCES

Akkoyun, F. (1983). Kişiliğin Projektif Testlerle Değerlendirilmesi. *Ankara Üniversitesi Eğitim Bilimleri Fakültesi Dergisi, 2*(16), 397-408.

Alibal, M. (1974). Projektif Testlerle Kişilik Değerlendirilmesi Özellikler ve Materyal. *Ankara Üniversitesi Eğitim Bilimleri Fakültesi Dergisi, 1*(7), 193-209.

Allport, F. H., & Allport, G. W. (1921). Personality Traits: Their Classification and Measurement. *Journal of Abnormal and Social Psychology, 16*(1), 6–40. doi:10.1037/h0069790

Allport, G. W. (1937). The Functional Autonomy of Motives. *The American Journal of Psychology, 50*(1/4), 141–156. doi:10.2307/1416626

Arkar, H. (2005). Cloninger'in Psikobiyolojik Kişilik Kuramı. *Türk Psikoloji Bülteni, 36*, 82–94.

Bailard, T. E., Biehl, D. L., & Kaiser, R. W. (1986). *Personal Money Management*. Chicago: Science Research Associates Inc.

Barnewall, M. M. G. (1987). Psychological Characteristics of the Individual Investor. In W. Droms (Ed.), *Asset Allocation for the Individual Investor.* The Institute of Chartered Financial Analysts. doi:10.2469/cp.v1987.n2.7

Benjamin, D. J., Chabris, C. F., Glaeser, E. L., Gudnason, V., Harris, T. B., Laibson, D. I., Launer, L. J. & Purcell, S. (2008). *Genoeconomics*. National Research Council (Us) Committee On Advances in Collecting And Utilizing Biological Indicators And Genetic Information in Social Science Surveys.

Buss, A. H., & Plomin, R. (1984). *Temperament: Early developing personality traits*. Hillsdale, NJ: Erlbaum.

Büyükdüvenci, S. (2013). *Kişi, Kişilik, Kimlik ve Toplum. 3.* Ilgaz Felsefe Günleri Sempozyumu.

Carey, G. (2002). *Human Genetic for Social Sciences*. London: Sage Publication.

Cesarini, D., Johannesson, M., Magnusson, P. K. E., & Wallace, B. (2011). The Behavioral Genetics of Behavioral Anomalies. *Management Science, 58*(1), 21–34.

Cloninger, C. R. (1987). A Systematic Method for Clinical Description and Classification of Personality Variants. *Archives of General Psychiatry, 44*(6), 573–588. doi:10.1001/archpsyc.1987.01800180093014 PMID:3579504

Cloninger, C. R., Svrakic, D. M., & Przybeck, T. R. (1993). A Psychobiological Model of Temperament and Character. *Archives of General Psychiatry, 50*(12), 975–990. doi:10.1001/archpsyc.1993.01820240059008 PMID:8250684

Cüceloğlu, D. (2007). *İnsan ve Davranışı: Psikolojinin Temel Kavramları. Remzi Kitabevi, 16.* Basım.

Dal, V. (2009). *Farklı Kişilik Özelliklerine Sahip Bireylerin Risk Algılarının Tüketici Davranışı Açısından İncelenmesi: Üniversite Öğrencileri Üzerine Bir Araştırma.* Yayınlanmamış Yüksek Lisans Tezi, Süleyman Demirel Üniversitesi Sosyal Bilimler Enstitüsü İşletme Anabilim Dalı.

Evrim, S. (1967). *Psikoloji Açısından Bir Buud Olarak İçedönüklük-Dışa Dönklük (İntroversion-Extraversion) Sorunu Üzerine Bir Araştırma*. İstanbul Üniversitesi Edebiyat Fakültesi Yayınları, No: 1284.

Ewen, R. B. (2003). *An Introduction to Theories of Personality. Lawrence Erlbaum Associates, Inc.* doi:10.4324/9781410607287

Eysenck, H. J., & Wilson, G. (1998). *Kişiliğinizi Tanıyın*. Basım.

Fahlgren, E., Nima, A. A., Archer, T., & Garcia, D. (2015). Person-Centered Osteopathic Practice: Patients' Personality (Body, Mind, and Soul) and Health (İll-Being and Well-Being). *PeerJ, 27*(3), E1349.

Feist, J., & Feist, G. J. (2009). *Theoriest of Psychology*. McGraw-Hill Education Learning Technology.

Flexner, S. B., & Stein, J. (Eds.). (1982). *The Random House College Dictionary*. New York: Random House.

Funder, D. C. (2001). Personality. *Annual Review of Psychology, V*, 52, 197–221. PMID:11148304

Goodworth, C. (1988). *The Secrets of Successful Leadership and People Management*. London: Heinemann Pub. Ltd.

Hansenne, M., Delhez, M., & Cloninger, C. R. (2005). Psychometric Properties of the Temperament and Character Inventory Revised (TCI-R) in a Belgian Sample. *Journal of Personality Assessment, 85*(1), 40–49. doi:10.120715327752jpa8501_04 PMID:16083383

İnanç, B. Y., & Yerlikaya, E. E. (2012). *Kişilik Kuramları. Pegem Akademi, 6*. Baskı.

Isır, T. (2006). *Örgütlerde Personel Seçim Süreci: Bir Kamu Kuruluşundaki Yönetici Personelin Kişilik Özelliklerinin Tespit Edilerek Personel Seçim Sürecinin İyileştirilmesi Üzerine Bir Araştırma*. Çukurova Üniversitesi Sosyal Bilimler Enstitüsü İşletme Anabilim Dalı, Yayınlanmamış Doktora Tezi.

Kahneman, D., Knetsch, J. L., & Thaler, R. H. (1991). The Endowment Effect, Loss Aversion, and Status Quo Bias. *The Journal of Economic Perspectives, 5*(1), 193–206. doi:10.1257/jep.5.1.193

Kahneman, D., & Tversky, A. (1979). Prospect theory: An analysis of decisions under risk *Econometrica. Cilt, 47*, 313–327.

Karancı, N., Dirik, G., & Yorulmaz, O. (2007). Eysenck Kişilik Anketi- Gözden Geçirilmiş Kısaltılmış Formunun (Eka-Ggk) Türkiye'de Geçerlik ve Güvenirlik Çalışması. *Türk Psikiyatri Dergisi, 18*, 3.

Kelly, G. (1991). *The psychology of personal constructs. London: Routledge.*

Klimoski, R. J., & Zukin, L. B. (2003). *Psychological Assessment in Industrial Organizational Settings* (I. B. Weiner, Ed.). doi:10.1002/0471264385.wei1014

Köse, S. (2003). A Psychological Model of Temperament And Character: TCI. *Yeni Symposium: Psikiyatri, Nöroloji ve Davraniş Bilimleri Dergisi, 41*(2), 86–97.

Köse, S., Sayar, K., Ak, İ., Aydın, N., Kalelioğlu, Ü., Przybeck, T. R., & Cloninger, C. R. (2004). Mizaç ve Karakter Envanteri (Türkçe TCI): Geçerlik, Güvenirliği ve Faktör Yapısı. *Klinik Psikofarmakoloji Bülteni, 14*, 107–131.

Lawrence, F. K., & Josiah, M. (1939). *Projective Methods for the Study of Personality. The New York Academy of Sciences, 1(8).*

Lewis, C. A., Francis, L. J., Shevlin, M., & Forrest, S. (2002). Confirmatory factor analysis of the French translation of the abbreviated form of the Revised Eysenck Personality Questionnaire (EPQR-A). *European Journal of Psychological Assessment, 18*(2), 79–85. doi:10.1027//1015-5759.18.2.179

Lin, H. W. (2011). Elucidating the Influence of Demographics and Psychological Traits on Investment Biases. *World Academy of Science, Engineering and Technology.*

Lo, A. W., Repin, D. V., & Steenbarger, B. N. (2005). Fear and Geed in Financial Markets: A Clinical Study of Day-Traders. *The American Economic Review, 95*(2), 352–359. doi:10.1257/000282805774670095

Nofsinger, J. (2011). The Psychology of Investing (3rd ed.). Pearson.

Pompian, M. (2012a). *Behavioral Finance and Wealth Management; How to Build Investment Strategies That Account For Investor Bias* (2nd ed.). John Wiley & Sons, Inc. doi:10.1002/9781119202400

Pompian, M. (2012b). *Behavioral Finance And Investor Types: Managing Behavior To Make Better Investment Decisions* (1st ed.). John Wiley & Sons, Inc. doi:10.1002/9781119202417

Pompian, M., & Longo, J. (2004). A New Paradigm For Practical Application of Behavioral Finance: Creating Investment Programs Based On Personality Type And Gender To Produce Better Investment Outcomes. *The Journal of Wealth Management, 7*(2), 9–15. doi:10.3905/jwm.2004.434561

Revelle, W. (2009). Personality Structure and Measurement: The Contributions of Raymond Cattell. *British Journal of Psychology, V*, 100, 253–257. PMID:19351450

Ricciardi, V., & Simon, H. K. (2000). What's Behavioral Finance? *Business. Education and Technology Journal, 2*(2), 1–9.

Ritter, J. R. (2003). Behavioral Finance. *Pacific-Basin Finance Journal, 11*(: 4), 429–437. doi:10.1016/S0927-538X(03)00048-9

Rothbart, M. K., & Derryberry, D. (1981). Development of İndividual Differences İn Temperament. In M. E. Lamb & A. Brown (Eds.), *Advances in developmental psychology* (Vol. 1, pp. 37–86). Hillsdale, NJ: Erlbaum.

Sadi, R., Ghalibaf, H., Asl, R., Mohammad, R., Gholipour, A., & Gholipour, F. (2011). Behavioral Finance: The Explanation of Investor's Personality and Perceptual Biases Effects on Financial Decisions. *International Journal of Economics and Finance, 3*(5).

Sammons, A. (n.d.). Eysenck's theory of the criminal personality. In *Eysenck's Personality Theory of Offending. Criminological Psychology.* Available from: http://www.psychlotron.org.uk/newresources/criminological/AZ_AQB.Crim.EysenckTheory.pdf

Sayın, A., & Aslan, S. (2005). Duygudurum Bozuklukları ile Huy, Karakter ve Kişilik İlişkisi. *Türk Psikiyatri Dergisi, 16*(4), 276–283. PMID:16362847

Schmidt, F. L., & Hunter, J. E. (1998). The Validity and Utility of Selection Methods in Personnel Psychology: Practical and Theoretical Implications of 85 Years of Research Findings. *Psychological Bulletin, 124*(2), 262–274. doi:10.1037/0033-2909.124.2.262

Şenkesen, E. (2009). *Davranışsal Finans ve Yatırımcı Duyarlılığının Tahvil Verimi Üzerindeki Etkisi: İMKB Tahvil ve Bono Piyasasında Bir Uygulama*. Basılmamış Doktora Tezi, İstanbul Üniversitesi Sosyal Bilimler Enstitüsü İşletme Bölümü.

Şenyuva, H. (2007). *Aydın İlinden Alınan Normal Bir Örneklemde Kişilik Bozukluklarının Yaygınlık Çalışması*. Yayınlanmamış Doktora Tezi, Adnan Menderes Üniversitesi Sağlık Bilimleri Enstitüsü Psikiyatri Anabilim Dalı.

Sezer, D. (2013). *Yatırımcı Davranışlarının Etkinliği ve Psikolojik Yanılsamalar*. Adnan Menderes Üniversitesi Sosyal Bilimler Enstitüsü İşletme Anabilim Dalı, Doktora Tezi.

Shefrin, H., & Statman, M. (1985). The Disposition To Sell Winners Too Early And Ride Losers Too Long: Theory And Evidence. *The Journal of Finance, 40*(3).

Shiffman, L. G., & Kanuk, L. L. (2004). *Consumer Behavior* (8th ed.). Pearson Prentice Hall.

Singh, T., & Singh, S. G. (2015). The Influence of Investor Psychology on Regret Aversion. *Global Journal of Management and Business Research: C Finance, 15*(2), 55-69.

Skinner, B. F. (1966). *The Behavior of Organisms: An Experimental Analysis*. New York: Appleton-Century -Crofts. (Original work published 1938)

Statman, M., Thorley, S., & Vorkink, K. (2006). Investor Overconfidence and Trading Volume. *The Review of Financial Studies, 19*(4), 1531–1565.

Strahilevitz, M. A., Odean, T., & Barber, B. M. (2011). Once Burned, Twice Shy: How Naive Learning, Counterfactuals and Regret Affect The Repurchase of Stock Previously Sold. *JMR, Journal of Marketing Research, 48*(SPL), 102–120. doi:10.1509/jmkr.48.SPL.S102

Stuart-Hamilton, I. (2007). *Dictionary of Psychological Testing, Assessment and Treatment 2*. Jessica Kingsley Publishers.

Svrakic, D. M., Draganic, S., Hill, K., Bayon, C., Przybeck, T. R., & Cloninger, C. R. (2002). Temperament, Character, and Personality Disorders: Etiologic, Diagnostic, and Treatment Issues. *Acta Psychiatrica Scandinavica, 106*(3), 189–195. doi:10.1034/j.1600-0447.2002.02196.x PMID:12197856

Taymur, İ., & Türkçapar, M. H. (2012). Kişilik: Tanımı, Sınıflaması ve Değerlendirmesi. *Psikiyatride Güncel Yaklaşımlar-Current Approaches in Psychiatry, 4*(2), 154–177. doi:10.5455/cap.20120410

Van Lieshout, C. F. M. (2000). Lifespan Personality Development: Self-Organising Goal-Oriented Agents and Developmental Outcome. *International Journal of Behavioral Development, 24*(3), 276–288. doi:10.1080/01650250050118259

Watson, J. B. (1913). Psychology as the behaviorist views it. *Psychological Review, 20*(2), 158–177. doi:10.1037/h0074428

Weiner, I. B. (2003). *The Assessment Process*. Handbook of Psychology. doi:10.1002/0471264385.wei1001

Yörükan, T. (2006). *Alfred Adler Sosyal Roller ve Kişilik. Türkiye İş Bankası Yayınları, 2.*

Zaidi, F. B., & Tauni, M. Z. (2012). Influence of Investor's Personality Traits and Demographics on Overconfidence Bias. *Interdisciplinary Journal of Contemporary Research in Business*, *4*(6).

Section 3

Behavioral Approach to Financial Issues and Investment

Chapter 9
Determinants of Market Capitalization in India and Its Impact

Chandrika Prasad Das
Khallikote University, India

Rabindra Kumar Swain
Utkal University, India

ABSTRACT

The purpose of this chapter is to study the determinants of market capitalization and to investigate the impact of determinants of market capitalization. This chapter uses secondary data from 2003-2016 relating to market capitalization, income per capita, stock market liquidity, etc. The study employed descriptive test and normality test to describe the basic features of data and their distribution. The multicollinearity test has also been used to check the interdependence among independent variables. Multiple regression statistics has been used to determine the impact of independent variables on dependent variable. The results show that there is a positive impact of determinants on development of stock market except political risk and inflation. The findings will help stock market authority, individuals, and companies to understand the factors that affect share prices.

INTRODUCTION

Financial market plays a vital role in the economic development of any country. They are the intermediaries that facilitate the flow of funds from surplus areas to deficit areas. They provide an institutional financial intermediation done by commercial banks mechanism for mobilizing savings and channel it effectively into productive investments. Basically financial intermediation is done by commercial banks between borrowers and savers. They provide finance for investments. The alternative method of intermediation is equity financing. It can be achievable through the growth of stock market. Stock market which deals with buying and selling of shares and bonds are one of the way to raise money from market.

DOI: 10.4018/978-1-5225-7399-9.ch009

The stock market is an important place for companies to raise funds. In addition, stock markets can increase the efficiency of the financial system through competition among different financial instruments. So, the main objective of this paper is to discover the determinants of stock market and their impact on market capitalization.

REVIEW OF LITERATURE

Jahur et al. (2014) studied the determinants of stock market and their performance in Bangladesh. The study used secondary data sources, and applied descriptive measures and linear regression model to analyse the data. The study found that all macro-economic variables like Interest Rate and Exchange Rate, Consumer Price Index have significant impact on stock market performance.

Kimani and Mutuku (2013) examined the impact of deposit rate, GDP, inflation, Central Depository System on stock market performance under Nairobi Stock exchange. They found a negative association between stock market performance and inflation in Kenya and the Central Depository System have a significant impact on stock market performance.

Mehwish (2013) conducted a study on Determinants of Stock Market Performance in Pakistan. The data was analysed quantitatively through regression analysis using E– views. With the use of time series data the study established a negative relationship between stock market performance and real interest rate, whereas the banking sector development has no significant influence on stock market performance.

Aduda et al. (2012) investigated the determinants of stock market development. The regression results stated that stock market liquidity, income per capita, institutional quality, bank development and domestic savings are significant determinants of stock market development in the Nairobi Stock Exchange.

Songole (2012) examined the relationship between stock return and selected macroeconomic variables at the Nairobi securities exchange. The study based on market interest rate, Consumer price index, Foreign exchange rate and Industrial Production Index. The study concluded consumer price index, market interest rate and exchange rate have a negative relationship with stock return, while industrial production index showed a positive relationship.

Garcia and Liu (1999) made a study on market capitalization as a determinant of stock market development. The study established that saving rate, real income, stock market liquidity and financial intermediary development are significant determinants of stock market capitalization

STATEMENT OF THE PROBLEM

The performance of stock market is a strong index of economic growth of India. So the problem of this study is what are the stock market determinants and whether they contribute positively or negatively towards stock market development.

VALUE OF THE STUDY

- **Stock Market Authority:** The findings will help to know the factors affecting the stock market and which factors are contributing towards market capitalization.

- **Individual and Companies:** The study will help to understand the factors which affect share prices and they will take care of that while investing.

OBJECTIVES OF THE STUDY

The objectives of the study are:

- To study the determinants of Market Capitalization.
- To analyze the impact of determinants on market capitalization.

RESEARCH METHODOLOGY

- **Sources of Data:** The required data have been collected from World Bank data base, ICRG rating system. Secondary data have been used for the study.
- **Sample Design:** A study period of 14 years has been taken. We have selected dependent and independent variables from literature review.
- **Variables:**
  - **Dependent Variables:** Market Capitalization
  - **Independent Variables:**
    - Income per Capita
    - Stock Market Liquidity
    - Macro-economic Stability (Inflation)
    - Foreign Direct Investment
    - Political Risk (Institutional Quality)
    - Market Liquidity

Econometric Model

$Y_e = \beta_0 + \beta_1 IC + \beta_2 SML + \beta_3 MS + \beta_4 FDI + \beta_5 IQ + \mu e$

where,

Y_e = Market Capitalization
β_0 = constant or the value of Y when all values of X are zero
$\beta_1, \beta_2, \ldots\ldots$ = Slope of the independent variables
IC = Income per Capita
SML = Stock Market Liquidity
MS = Inflation
FDI = Foreign Direct Investment
IQ = Institutional Quality (Political Risk)
μe = The error term

Statistical Measures

- **Descriptive Statistics:** It helps to describe the basic features of the data in our study. SPSS test have used to calculate descriptive statistics.
- **Test of Normality:** This test is used to determine whether data has been taken from a normally distributed population or not. This test calculated by using Excel STATA software.
- **Multicollinearity Test:** This test have been used to find out the Multicollinearity between independent variables. Excel NUM test helps to calculate this test.
- **Multiple Regression:** It helps to analyse the impact of independent variables on dependent variable. E-views 9.5 student version helps to find out regression result.

Software Used for Data Processing

- **Excel STATA:** This software have been used for Normality test.
- **Eviews9.5:** It helps to determine regression analysis and DW test.
- **SPSS:** SPSS helps to find out Descriptive statistics.
- **Excel NUM:** It has been used to establish Multicollinearity test between independent variables.

HYPOTHESIS

H^1_0: There is no association between market capitalization and per capita income.
H^2_0: Market capitalization does not influenced by stock market liquidity.
H^3_0: Market capitalization is not significantly associated with foreign direct investment.
H^4_0: Market capitalization is not affected by macro-economic stability (Inflation).
H^5_0: There is no significant relationship between market capitalization and institutional quality (Political risk).
H^6_0: Independent variables have no impact on dependent variable.

DETERMINANTS OF MARKET CAPITALIZATION

Income Per Capita

The study uses GDP per capital in India to measure the income of people. Per capital income shows the purchasing power parity of people. The income per capita can be calculated by dividing total income with total population. Figure 1 shows that per capita income is highest in the year 2017 and lowest in 2003. In 2008 the per capita income reduced due to financial crisis.

STOCK MARKET LIQUIDITY

This study uses value of shares traded as a percentage of GDP to measure the stock market liquidity. It measures the liquidity position of the company's share which can be recorded at the time of share bought

Figure 1. Income per capita
Source: Self Compiled

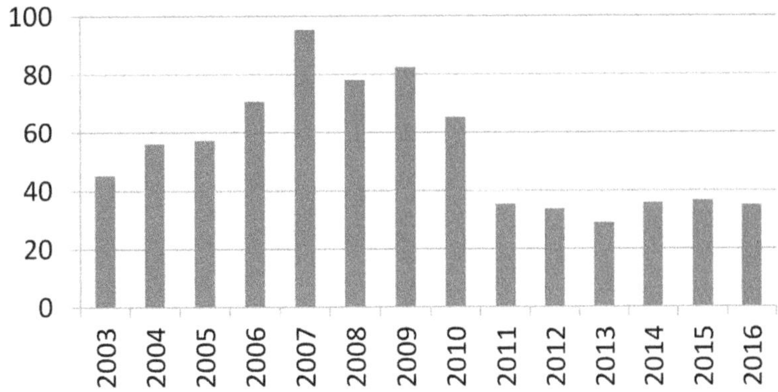

Table 1. Income per capita

Year	IPC (US $)
2003	541.1352
2004	621.3184
2005	707.008
2006	792.026
2007	1018.166
2008	991.4846
2009	1090.318
2010	1345.77
2011	1461.672
2012	1446.985
2013	1452.195
2014	1573.118
2015	1613.189
2016	1709.388

and sold. The stock market liquidity achieves highest in the year 2007 and lowest in 2013. In 2008 it was reduced due to financial crisis and again the value has increased.

MACROECONOMIC STABILITY

Macroeconomic variable shows the inflation, growth, fiscal deficit, current account deficit in India. The macroeconomic environment is characterized by low and predictable inflation. This study measured inflation rate as macroeconomic variable. The inflation rate is high in 2010 and less in 2004. It was in increasing trend from 2005 to 2010.

Figure 2. Stock market liquidity
Source: Self Compiled

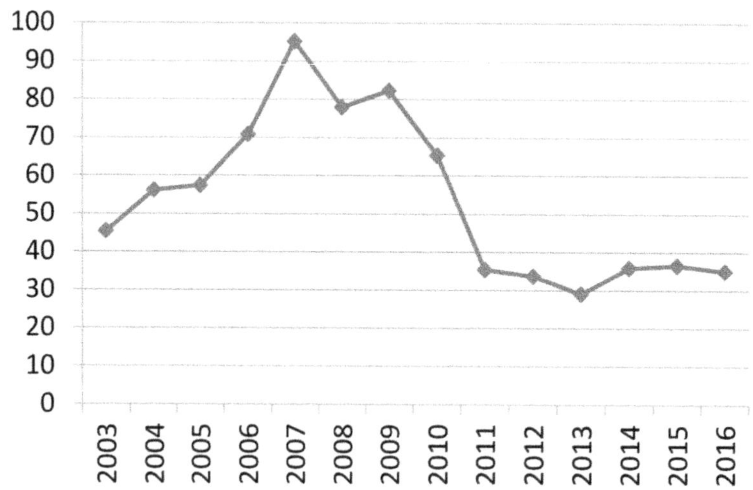

Table 2. Stock Market Liquidity

Year	sml (US $)
2003	45.36966
2004	56.13484
2005	57.34444
2006	70.82165
2007	95.19378
2008	77.96896
2009	82.37199
2010	65.25686
2011	35.40469
2012	33.70874
2013	28.9638
2014	35.89988
2015	36.55724
2016	34.98968

FOREIGN DIRECT INVESTMENT

FDI plays an important role in developing countries. It can have a positive influence on growth of the nation. FDI is an investment that made by a company or an individual in one country in business interests in another country. FDI inflow in India is highest in 2008 and lowest in 2003. In 2007 FDI has decreased.

Figure 3. Macroeconomic Stability
Source: Self Compiled

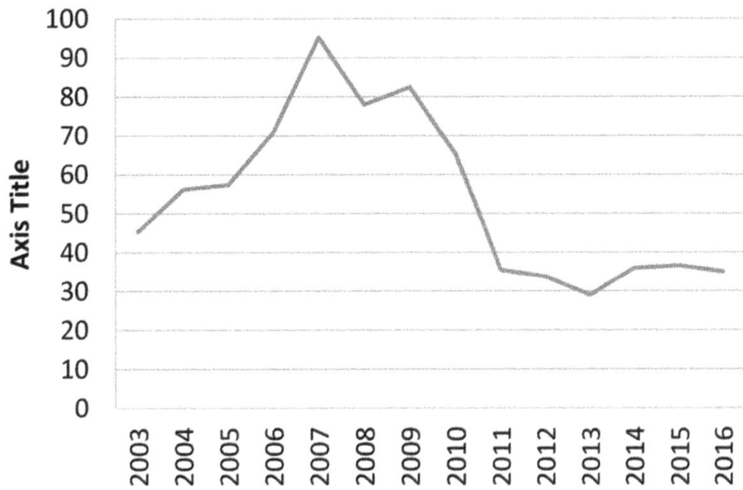

Table 3. Macroeconomic Stability

Year	Inflation (%)
2003	3.81
2004	3.77
2005	4.25
2006	5.79
2007	6.39
2008	8.32
2009	10.83
2010	12.11
2011	8.87
2012	9.3
2013	10.92
2014	6.37
2015	5.88
2016	4.97

INSTITUTIONAL QUALITY

This study used political risk to measure the institutional quality. It includes bureaucratic quality, law and order, corruption index and democratic accountability. Political risk has been calculated by using international country risk guide. In table number 5, political risk shows mix trend all over the years.

Figure 4. Foreign Direct Investment
Source: Self Compiled

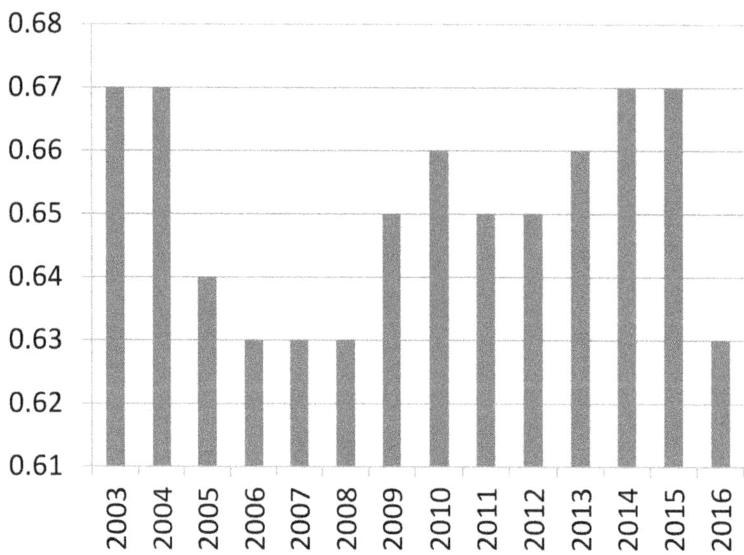

Table 4. FDI

Year	FDI (%)
2003	0.614081
2004	0.775952
2005	0.898677
2006	2.176329
2007	2.100366
2008	3.656951
2009	2.687536
2010	1.653785
2011	2.002066
2012	1.312934
2013	1.516276
2014	1.69877
2015	2.084028
2016	1.964132

MARKET CAPITALIZATION

Capital market development is measured by market capitalization as a proportion of GDP. The stock market provides buying and selling of shares in the secondary market. A stock exchange can influence the growth of an economy. The market capitalization is more in 2007 and less in 2003. In 2008 it was reduced due to financial crisis.

Figure 5. Institutional Quality
Source: Self Compiled

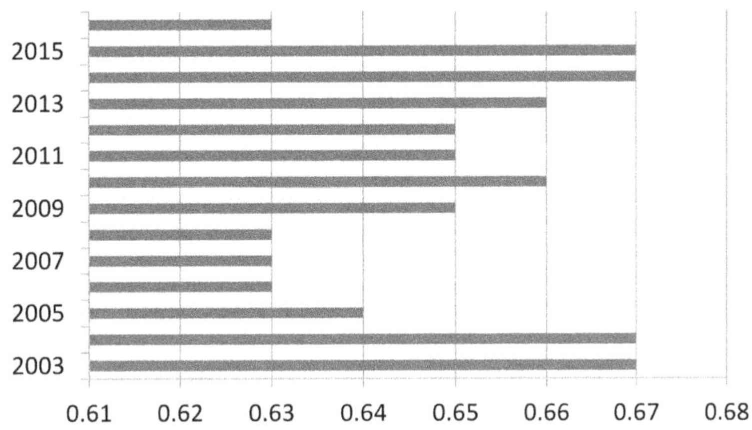

Table 5. Institutional Quality

Year	Political Risk (%)
2003	0.67
2004	0.67
2005	0.64
2006	0.63
2007	0.63
2008	0.63
2009	0.65
2010	0.66
2011	0.65
2012	0.65
2013	0.66
2014	0.67
2015	0.67
2016	0.63

DATA ANALYSIS

Table 7 shows the summary of the descriptive statistics. Income per capita, Stock market liquidity, FDI are represented as a ratio of GDP. The macroeconomic variable inflation is measured in percentage. Institutional quality is an index that is reported by World Bank showing how political risk affects the financial sector.

The above table depicts that the mean value of income per capita is 1168.84 and standard deviation is 395.86. It shows there is no consistency in income per capita. The stock market liquidity is not consistent to some extent as the standard deviation is more with comparison to mean value. Inflation, FDI, Political

Figure 6. Market Capitalization
Source: Self Compiled

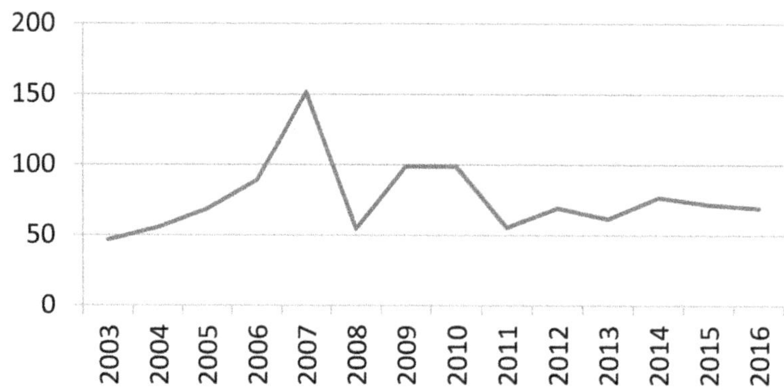

Table 6. Market Capitalization

Year	MC (US %)
2003	46.54705
2004	55.43195
2005	68.37347
2006	88.97793
2007	151.4514
2008	54.52658
2009	98.68423
2010	98.50373
2011	55.24714
2012	69.12395
2013	61.33573
2014	76.56012
2015	71.79903
2016	69.21427

Table 7. Descriptive Statistics

	Income	SML	INF	FDI	IQ	Marketcap
Mean	1168.8410	53.9990	7.2557	1.7958	.6507	76.1269
Std. Deviation	395.86153	21.40077	2.79479	.79580	.01639	26.95995

Source: Self Compiled

risk shows consistency as their standard deviation is satisfactory. Market capitalization has mean value of 76.12 and standard deviation of 26.95. It means there is no consistency.

NORMALITY TEST

The data is normally distributed as we found all the independent variables satisfy the normal distribution in Jarque – Bera test and dependent variable satisfies Kolmogorov – Smirnov test. The P value of all the variables is more than 5% level of significance which depicts normal distribution of data.

From this report it is observed that VIF vale of independent variables is less than the rule of thumb i.e. 10. Here there is no interdependence among the independent variables and all the variables are eligible for running regression equation.

The top panel includes the dependent variable i.e. Market Capitalization, the least square method for estimation of data, the sample period from 2003-2016 and total number of observations i.e. 14 years.

Market capitalization = 11.79+0.07IC+1.96SML-25.57FDI-119.05IQ-0.94INF+μe

Table 8. Independent Variables

Variables	Jarque-Bera
IC	0.542
SML	0.535
INF	0.576
FDI	0.640
IQ	0.516

Table 9. Dependent Variable

Variables	Kolmogorov-Smirnov[a]
MARKETCAP	.103

Source: Self Compiled

Table 10. Multicollinearity Test

Variables	VIF (Rule of Thumb: 10)
Income	3.102
SML	3.369
INF	1.606
FDI	2.553
IQ	1.703

Source: Self Compiled

Table 11. Regression result

Dependent Variable: MC
Method: Least Squares
Date: 12/15/17 Time: 06:08
Sample: 2003 2016
Included observations: 14

Variable	Coefficient	Std. Error	t-Statistic	Prob.
C	11.79422	164.3191	0.071776	0.9445
IC	0.075874	0.013429	5.649862	0.0005
SML	1.960779	0.258897	7.573595	0.0001
FDI	-25.57741	6.060311	-4.220478	0.0029
IQ	-119.0565	240.3235	-0.495401	0.6336
MS__INF_	-0.940898	1.368805	-0.687387	0.5113

R-squared	0.899719	Mean dependent var	76.12690
Adjusted R-squared	0.837043	S.D. dependent var	26.95995
S.E. of regression	10.88319	Akaike info criterion	7.909842
Sum squared resid	947.5501	Schwarz criterion	8.183724
Log likelihood	-49.36890	Hannan-Quinn criter.	7.884490
F-statistic	14.35510	Durbin-Watson stat	1.781593
Prob(F-statistic)	0.000805		

Source: Self Compiled

The middle panel shows the coefficient values. Here C is the estimated constant of the regression and the value of C is 11.79. The other coefficients measure their contribution towards market capitalization. Here Income per capita and stock market liquidity shows positive contribution towards market capitalization. The income per capita coefficient is 0.07, it means 1 unit change in income per capita leads to 0.07 unit change in market capitalization. Stock market liquidity contributes more than income per capita towards market capitalization. The stock market liquidity coefficient is 1.96. Thus, 1% change in Stock market liquidity leads to 1.96% change in market capitalization. The other three variables Foreign direct investment, Political risk and Inflation contributes negatively to market capitalization. The coefficient of Foreign direct investment is -25.57%. It denotes -25.57% change in market capitalization if 1% change in foreign direct investment. The political risk has highest negative impact on market capitalization. The inflation coefficient measures the marginal contribution of inflation to market capitalization i.e. -0.94%.

$H^1_{0,}$ null hypothesis was that there is no association between market capitalization and income per capita but as per our statistical tools P value is 0.0005 which is less than 0.05 the probability norm. Therefore our alternative hypothesis is accepted i.e. there is an association between market capitalization and income per capita.

H^2_0, hypothesis was there is no relationship between market capitalization and stock market liquidity. Here P value is 0.0001 i.e. < 0.05. it means null hypothesis is rejected and alternative hypothesis is accepted i.e. there is a significant relationship between market capitalization and stock market liquidity.

H^3_0, was market capitalization does not influenced by stock market liquidity but here the P value is 0.0029 i.e. <0.05 which depicts null hypothesis is rejected and alternative hypothesis i.e. market capitalization is influenced by stock market liquidity.

H^4_0, the hypothesis was market capitalization is not affected by macro-economic stability (Inflation). The regression result shows P value i.e 0.6336 which is more than standard 0.05. So, null hypothesis is accepted. It is proved that market capitalization is not affected by macro-economic stability variable i.e. Inflation.

H^5_0, there is no significant relationship between market capitalization and institutional quality (Political risk). Here P value is 0.5113. The null hypothesis is accepted because standard value of P is 0.05 which is less than the calculated value. So, there is no significant relationship between market capitalization and political risk.

The third panel revealed r squared which shows the success of the regression equation in forecasting the values of dependent variable. Here all the independent variables predicting 0.89% of dependent variable i.e. market capitalization. Adjusted r-squared will conform the number of independent variables by punishing r-squared for additional variables. Here Adj r-squared is 0.83.

$H^6_{0,}$ null hypothesis was Independent variables have no impact on dependent variable but our results shows P value is 0.0008 i.e. $P < 0.05$. It means null hypothesis is rejected. It means independent variables influences dependent variable.

Durbin Watson Statistics depicts the auto correlation in the data i.e. 1.78 which lies between the rule of thumb i.e. 1.7 to 2.3.

FINDINGS

- Stock market liquidity and Income per capita contributes positively to stock market development.
- FDI influences Market capitalization negatively.
- There is no association between political risk and inflation with the stock market development in India.
- Independent variables significantly influence the dependent variable.

CONCLUSION

This study has investigated empirically the main determinants of stock market development by using a panel data from 2003 – 2016. The paper also analyzed whether the determinants helps to explain the growth of the stock market in India or not. We choose market capitalization to measure stock market development. We have taken 5 determinants i.e. per capita income, stock market liquidity, political risk, inflation and FDI to examine their contribution on stock market. First, Stock market liquidity and Income per capita contributes positively to stock market development. Second, FDI has negatively associated market capitalization. Third, Political risk and Inflation have no contribution towards stock market growth in India. The result shows that income per capita and security market lending have significant contribution on stock market development in India.

REFERENCES

Aduda, J., Masila, J. M., & Onsongo, E. N. (2012). The Determinants of Stock Market Development: The Case for the Nairobi Stock. *International Journal of Humanities and Social Science*, *2*(9), 214–227.

Agyre-Tetty, K.F. & Kyereboah-Coleman. (2008). Impact of macroeconomic indicators on stock market performance. *The Journal of Risk Finance*, *9*(4), 71–81.

Aurangzeb. (2012). Factors affecting performance of stock market: Evidence from South Asian Countries. *International Journal of Academic Research in Business and Social Sciences, 2*(9).

Beck, T., & Levine, R. (2004). Stock markets, banks and growth: Panel evidence. *Journal of Banking & Finance*, *28*(3), 423–442. doi:10.1016/S0378-4266(02)00408-9

Chen, N., Richard, R., & Stephen, A. R. (1986). Economic forces and the stock market. *The Journal of Business*, *59*(3), 383–403. doi:10.1086/296344

Demirguc-Kunt, A., & Levine, R. (1996). Stock markets, corporate finance and economic growth: An overview. *The World Bank Economic Review*, *10*(2), 223–239. doi:10.1093/wber/10.2.223

Garcia, V. F., & Liu, L. (1999). Macroeconomic Determinants of Stock. *Journal of Applied Econometrics*, *2*(1), 29–59.

Jahur, M. S., Quadir, S. M., & Khan, M. A. (2014). Determinants of stock market performance in Bangladesh. *Indonesian Management and Accounting Research*, *13*(1), 16–28.

Kimani, D. K., & Mutuku, C. M. (2013). Inflation Dynamics on the Overall Stock Market Performance: The Case of Nairobi Securities Exchange in Kenya. *Economics and Finance Review*, *2*(11), 1–11.

Mehwish, Z. (2013). Determinants of Stock Market Performance in Pakistan. *Interdisciplinary Journal of Contemporary Research in Business*, *4*(5), 1017–1018.

Songole, R. K. (2012). *The Relationship between Selected Macroeconomic Variables and Stock Return at the Nairobi Securities Exchange*. Nairobi: University of Nairobi.

Chapter 10
Macroeconomics and Its Impact on Stock Markets of India, China, and Japan: ASIAN Markets

Amith Vikram Megaravalli
University of Naples Federico II, Italy

ABSTRACT

The objective of this chapter is to examine the long-run and the short-run relationship between India, China, and Japanese stock markets and key macroeconomic variables such as exchange rates and inflation (proxied by consumer price index) of ASIAN 3 economies (India, China, and Japan). Monthly time series data spanning the period from 2008 January to November 2016 has been used. The unit root test, the cointegration test, Granger causality test, and pooled mean group estimator have been applied to derive the long-run and short-run statistical dynamics. The findings of pooled estimated results of ASIAN 3 countries show that exchange rate has a positive and significant long-run effect on stock markets while the inflation has a negative and insignificant long-run effect. In the short run, there is no statistically significant relationship between macroeconomic variables and stock markets. This study emphasizes the impact of macroeconomic variables on the stock market performance of a developing economy (India and China) and developed economy (Japan).

INTRODUCTION

From past few decades, international investors and researchers have focused on emerging financial markets, especially in ASIAN markets. Stock markets in these nations have provided attractive investment opportunities to foreign investors. The effectiveness of the growing markets presumes more significant as the pattern of investments is hastening in the secondary market because of political and legal changes and liberalising all other blockades has opened the market for foreign investors. Effective Market Hypothesis advocated by Eugene F. FAMA in 1970, the stock price is a proficient market indicator which will respond to all information and facts about the changes in macroeconomic variables.

DOI: 10.4018/978-1-5225-7399-9.ch010

Globalisation and extensive growth in trade investment and integration of international financial markets and participation of foreign institutional investors have enhanced the relationship between global stock markets and foreign exchange markets and thereby strengthening the relationship between exchange rate changes and stock market fluctuations. This phenomenon has been the subject matter of study by scholars during various financial crises, such as the 1997 Asian financial crisis, the sub-prime mortgage crisis, and the recent European debt crisis. Therefore, a thorough understanding of the long- and short-run interactions between the global stock markets and foreign exchange markets can be effective in enabling governments in various countries to develop relevant financial policies and investment portfolios and to reduce any possible adverse impacts on a country's economy.

India's economy has been one of the stars of global economies (Economy watch, 2008), as it is among the fastest growing and fourth largest economy in terms of purchasing power parity in the world. The capital investment boom in the country drives the current growth phase of the Indian economy. Markets react promptly to any news, at times even any forms of instability including but not limited to escalating political tensions or even war rumours of war, change in regulatory environment (business), deemed as negative by the business (investing) community and interest rate fluctuations in general performance of the economy (Moneybiz, 2008). Some other variables like population, movements in global markets, money supply growth, manufacturing sector growth and aggregate deposits of scheduled banks that affect the various economic changes (Gera, 2007).

During last decade China has been demonstrating the quite significant growth of economics. This attracted quite a lot of investors. The study of Luo, Gan, Hu, Tzu-Hui Kao (2009) showed that Chinese stock market has experienced a rapid growth and has played important roles in the growth and development of the Chinese economy since the launching of the Shanghai and Shenzhen Exchange in early 1990. According to Degan (2009) investing in Chinese stocks is finding the right way of profiting from China's expected exceptional and unique future growth in the twenty-first century, and at the same time avoiding the risks represented by corruption, murky corporate financial statements, shady corporate governance, and complicated opaque government bureaucracy. With such risks, it is not surprising that the Chinese stock markets are extremely volatile.

For Japanese stock market, Hamao (1988) concludes that changes in expected inflation, unanticipated changes in risk premia, and the term structure of interest rates significantly affect the Japanese stock returns. Mukherjee and Naka (1995) observe a long run relationship between the Japanese stock market and six macroconomic variables.

Many studies focused on studying the relationship between macroeconomic variables and stock markets or stock returns of individual countries. However, in this study, we attempt to do the cross-country analysis of developed and developing economies of Asian countries like India, China and Japan. In this study, we contribute to the existing literature by studying the asymmetric effects of monetary policy on real output in the ASIAN-3 countries in a panel setting by using the recently formulated pooled mean group (PMG) estimator proposed by Pesaran et al. (1999).

In this paper, we examine the relationships between the ASIAN Stock index and macroeconomic variables (Inflation, measured by consumer price index and exchange rate) on a monthly data from 2008 to 2016 using Granger Causality Test, cointegration tests and the pooled estimated results. Specifically, the main objective of the study is to understand how the stock markets and macroeconomic indicators (exchange rate and inflation) are integrated in India, China and Japan. Secondly, to describe the 'causal relationships between stock markets and macro-economic variables. Finally, we use panel autoregressive distributive lag (ARDL) to estimate the long-run and short-run association between stock markets and macroeconomic variables of 3 ASIAN countries.

In this backdrop, the intent of this study is to probe into the course of the relationship existing among macroeconomic variables (Exchange rate and Consumer Price Index) in ASIAN-3 countries and stock market returns of India, China and Japan with reference to NSE (NIFTY INDEX), Shanghai stock exchange and Nikkei stock exchange.

REVIEW OF LITERATURE

Relationship Between Stock Market and Exchange Rate

Bahmani and Sohrabian (1992) considered S&P 500 and USD exchange rate as the variables for studying causal relationship for the short period of time. They ascertained that bidirectional causality relationship exists between the selected variables. On the contrary, the co-integration analysis was abortive to recognize the long-term association between the two selected factors. Studies on the stock market and its impact on macroeconomic factors are not nascent in the world. It is always being considered that macroeconomic events have a specific quantity of pressure on the stock markets. In a study by Büyüksalvarci et.al (2010) studied stock prices and its impact on macroeconomic variables of Turkey, the result of the study confirmed that there is a unidirectional long-run relationship between stock price and macro-economic variables.

The study of Kyereboah and Agyire (2008) showed that macroeconomic factors adversely affect the performance of stock market.It appeared from the analysis that only money supply has a significant relationship on the Turkish Stock Index. Singh (2010) tried to explore an affiliation among three macroeconomic factors and BSE Sensex using unit root tests, correlation, and Granger causality test. The outcome of the study revealed that the market index, exchange rate, Index of Industrial Production and wholesale price index hold a unit root and was integrated.

Moreover, the result of the Granger causality showed that bilateral causality exists between Index of Industrial Production and Sensex, on the other hand, Sensex is having unilateral causality. In a study of Adjasi (2009) showed that higher volatility in cocoa prices and interest rates increases the volatility of the stock prices.

Inflation of country is determined by the alteration in the Consumer Price Index. Higher the inflation there will be an obvious increase in the living expenses and shifting of resources from investments to consumption. High inflation has an effect on corporate profits amalgamated with the rise in the cost of borrowing of the organisations, which in turn forces dividend downward and thereby lowering stock prices. In view of that, it is said that equity prices are negatively related to inflation.

Relationship Between Stock Market and Consumer Price Index

Fama (1981) recommended proxy hypothesis which shows the negative connection between inflation rate and stock prices. The negative stock returns with inflation are defined by the positive connection between stock returns and basic determinants of equity values, such as the cost of capital, the average real rate of return capital and productivity of a firm (Fama, 1981). Feldstein (1980) also confirmed the effect of inflation on stock prices through corporate income taxation, cost depreciation and taxation of nominal capital gains. When inflation rate increases, the cost depreciation affects firm profits.

Since the depreciation is determined based on historical cost, which is not affected by the increase in inflation rate. The depreciation is less than it is supposed to drive the real taxable earnings to go up (Hong, 1977). Omran et.al (2000) analyse the effect of the inflation rate on the performance of the Egyptian stock market.

Relationship Between India, China and Japan Markets

Numerous studies have been done to investigate stock market linkages, integration or interdependence. The Stock market is said to be integrated when correlation exists between markets. While the results of these studies are mixed, inconsistent and often oppose with each other, the ultimate determination behind the studies are the advantages of diversification. If evidence of stock market linkage were found, it would imply that there is a common force that brings these markets together. Hence, the benefit of diversification would be limited.

Two developing markets, China and India have been called the Asian tigers due to the remarkable economic growth experienced by both markets in recent years. During the last decade, China's economy as measured by GDP has grown at the average of 10 percent per annum while India's at 7 percent per annum. During this period, the trade level, capital flows and common economic contracts with other markets have also improved rapidly. Having large economic size, huge population and dynamic economic growth, China and India emerge as two major prominent emerging markets which contribute to the world economy. Singh (2010) analysed the linkage between China and India with four major developed markets and concluded that both Indian and Chinese stock market are cointegrated with all the four developed markets and also there exists a bilateral causality between India and China.

Chen et.al. (2006) examines the bilateral relations between three pairs of stock markets, namely India-U.S., India-China and China-U.S. The result of the study show that markets are fractionally co-integrated with each other. A Study done by Chattopadhyay and Behera (2006) did not find any causality between the Japanese stock market and Indian stock market. Miyakoshi (2003), examined the magnitude of return and volatility Spillovers from Japan and the US to seven Asian equity markets.

The result of the study showed that US was important for Asian market returns and there was no influence from Japan. Thus, this study aims at providing some insight on the linkage of Indian, Japanese and Chinese markets.

SOURCE OF DATA AND DESCRIPTION

With a vision to achieve the predetermined goal of the study macroeconomic variables such as Exchange rate (US Dollar/Indian Rupee), (USD/Chinese Yuan) and (USD/JPY), Consumer Price Index were selected to examine the impact of these factors on stock market with reference to NSE, Shanghai stock exchange and Nikkei stock exchange (Dependent Variables). The previous research studies indicated that there is no any set yardstick for prices and inflation, but in maximum studies wholesale price index (WPI) and consumer price index (CPI) have been used single or simultaneously both indices (e.g., Czapkiewicz, Stachowicz 2016; Abraham, Harrington 2016; Sibanda et al. 2015; etc.). In the present study, we use consumer price index as the proxy for inflation for all the three markets selected in the study.

Monthly data from January 2008 to November 2016 is used in this study from January 01, 2008 to November 30, 2016, which consists of 107 observations. Data on NSE (India) has been obtained from NSE website, inflation and exchange rate of India has been obtained from global-rates dot com and investing dot com; Data on Shanghai stock exchange and exchange rate has been obtained from investing dot com; inflation data of China has been obtained from global-rates dot com; data of Japanese stock market (Nikkei) and exchange rate has been obtained from Investing dot com and inflation has been obtained from global-rates dot com. (More details on data source refer appendix 1).

METHODOLOGY

This paper employs Granger-causality test and Johansen cointegration to determine whether selected macroeconomic variables are cointegrated (hence possibly causally related) with stock markets of India, China and Japan. Furthermore, PMG (Pooled mean group) estimator is used to investigate the possible asymmetries between macroeconomic indicators and Indian, Chinese and Japanese stock markets. For time series analysis, it is essential to determine whether the dataset is stationary or not. If the data set mean variance is constant then it is said to be stationary over a period of time. Time series data is stationary if the data characteristics such as mean and variance, do not change over time. Stationary nature of the data set is tested using ADF test proposed by Dickey Fuller (1981).

1. **ADF Test Is on the Basis of the Null Hypothesis That H0:** Yt is not I (0), thus H (0) specifies the data of the specified variable is not stationary or got unit root.

The entire model with trend and intercepts is shown in equation 1:

Table 1. Brief description of variables

Variables	Variables Description
Dependent Variable	
Stock Market (SM1)	Nifty
Stock Market (SM2)	Shanghai stock exchange
Stock Market (SM3)	Nikkei stock exchange
Independent Variables	
Exchange Rate (ER1)	INR vs USD
Exchange Rate (ER2)	CNY vs USD
Exchange Rate (ER3)	JPY vs USD
Consumer Price Index (CPI1)	CPI, India
Consumer Price Index (CPI2)	CPI, China
Consumer Price Index (CPI3)	CPI, Japan

Note: Overview of variables used in the study

$$\Delta Y_t = \alpha + \beta T + \rho Y_{t-1} + \sum_{i=1}^{k} \gamma_i \Delta Y_{t-i} + e_t \tag{1}$$

H0: Y_t has unit root test or not stationary
H1: Y_t is stationary

Y_t is the variable selected for the period t, Δ is the difference operator, T denotes a time trend, e_t is an error term disturbance with mean 0 and variance as σ^2, and k corresponds to the number of lags of the differences in the ADF equation.

2. **Granger Causality Test:** Granger Causality method developed by Engle and Granger (1987) has been used to locate the path of causality among the variables. It is a tool for discovering if one-time series data is substantial in estimating another set of selected variables or not. Cointegration indicates the existence of a long-run relationship between variables. To test the Granger causality, the following regression equation (2) and (3) can be applied:

$$Y_t = \beta_0 + \sum_{k=1}^{M} \beta_k Y_{t-k} + \sum_{l=1}^{N} \propto_l X_{t-1} + u_t \tag{2}$$

$$X_t = \gamma_0 + \sum_{k=1}^{M} \gamma_k X_{t-k} + \sum_{l=1}^{N} \delta_l Y_{t-1} + v_t \tag{3}$$

3. **Johansen Cointegration Test:** The Johansen's co-integration test is being considered as compact maximum likelihood test that assists for examining co-integration in a whole system of equations. Johansen co-integration test through Co-integration Rank Test has been used to determine if there subsist long-run association between the change in the stock index and the four macroeconomic variables. There could be more than one cointegrating vector in a system of variables and the Johansen method can discover all such cointegrating relations [Juselius (2006), Johansen and Juselius (1990), Kasa (1992)].

The trace statistics test is being specified by the following equation (4):

$$Trace(r,k) = -T \sum_{i=r+1}^{k} \ln(1 - \lambda_i) \tag{4}$$

H0: No cointegration among variables
H1: There is cointegration among variables

4. **Pooled Mean Group Estimator (PMG):** This study used the Pooled mean group method proposed by Pesaran et al. (1999) to contemplate a lower degree of heterogeneity, as it imposes homogeneity in the long-run coefficients while still enabling heterogeneity in the short-run coefficients and er-

ror variances. The basic presumptions of the PMG estimator are: first, the error terms are serially uncorrelated and are distributed independently of the regressors, that is, the independent variables can be treated as exogenous; second, there is a long-run connection between the dependent and independent variables; and third, the long-run factors are the same across countries. This method also provides a long-run coefficient homogeneity over a single nation or regressors. Through this estimation technique, we can provide the multiplicity between the stock markets and macroeconomic indicators.

In the present study following panel error correction model is used:

$$\Delta X_{i,t} = \alpha_i + \theta_i (X_{i,t-1} \beta_i \Delta z'^{s}_{i,t}) + \sum_{j=1}^{p-1} yi, j \Delta z'^{s}_{i,t} + \sum_{j=1}^{Q-1} \varphi i, j \Delta X_{i,t} + \mu_i + \varepsilon_{i,t} \quad (5)$$

where β_i is the long-term parameter, θ_i = equilibrium parameter, $X_{i,t}$ = a stock market index of India, China and Japan, z as the macroeconomic variables, i represents countries and t refers to time.

Pesaran et al. (1999) recommend two various estimators, which are consistent when both T and N are large. The difference between Mean group (MG)and pooled mean group (PMG) is that MG estimator appears to be more constant under the presumption that both the slope and intercepts can change across the countries, whereas the PMG estimator is constant under the presumption of long-run slope homogeneity.

An alternative estimator is established under the presumption of the homogeneous slope is dynamic fixed effects (DFE), wherein the slopes are fixed and the intercepts can change across countries.

EMPIRICAL FINDINGS

Table 2 represents an outline of descriptive statistics of all the variables (country-wise). The results of the Descriptive study show the number of observations, maximum and minimum values, the sample mean and standard deviation.

The descriptive statistics for the three variables of India, China and Japan have been obtained for empirical analysis and are presented in Table 2.

The variables are exchange rate, inflation (CPI), Nifty, Shanghai stock exchange and Nikkei stock exchange. The results of Skewness and kurtosis suggest that the distribution is symmetry. Additionally, if Skewness and kurtosis have values 0 and three, it is noticed that the given data sequence is normally distributed.

The primary and easiest method for identifying whether the data sequence is stationary is the graphical representation of each variable which is presented in Figure 1 which notices the facts of mean, variance, autocorrelation and seasonality. The existence of these patterns in the time series confirms the truth that the data frame is non-stationary. The graphical representation of Nifty, Shanghai stock exchange, Nikkei, exchange rates and inflation rate shows the trend of these variables.

Figure 1 represents the unusual vertical variation of the series indicates that one part of series varies greatly from the other. Thus, showing non-constant mean, variance and making the data frame non-stationary. The graphical representation of Nifty and exchange rate shows a downward and upward trend which could be an indication of non-constant mean and variance. On the other hand, India CPI is highly

Table 2. Descriptive Statistics

Overview of Indian Markets				
	Nifty	**Exchange Rate (USD/ INR)**	**CPI**	**Obs**
Mean	6021.46	54.25	49.45	107
SD	1585.01	8.57	28.56	107
Min	2755.10	39.28	1.00	107
Max	8901.85	68.60	99	107
Skewness	0.16	0.12	0.0039	107
Kurtosis	2.32	1.62	1.81	107
Overview of Chinese Markets				
	Shanghai	**Exchange Rate (USD/ CNY)**	**CPI**	**Obs**
Mean	2706.75	6.49	52.56	107
SD	606.85	0.29	29.84	107
Min	1728.79	6.05	1.00	107
Max	4611.74	7.18	104	107
Skewness	0.97	0.24	-0.004	107
Kurtosis	3.88	1.74	1.82	107
Overview of Japanese Markets				
	Nikkei	**Exchange Rate (USD/ YEN)**	**CPI**	**Obs**
Mean	12789.11	97.35	43.54	107
SD	3695.15	13.83	26.36	107
Min	7568.42	76.23	1	107
Max	20585.24	124.14	91	107
Skewness	0.46	0.22	0.11	107
Kurtosis	1.89	2.06	1.8	107

volatile and show higher fluctuation. Further, Shanghai stock exchange shows upward-downward and then less volatile and again upward trend and exchange rate of CNY vs USD upward and downward trend and China inflation rate is downward-upward which makes less volatile when compared to Indian inflation rate. Lastly, Japan Nikkei showing a downward and upward trend, Yen vs USD also show downward and upward trend which indicates that series can be stationary as they do not show much fluctuation.

But Japan inflation rate is slightly volatile downward upward and again upward trend. These facts are further established by the ADF test, which is a suitable and proper testing technique for determining the stationary or non-stationary nature of the data frame.

The ADF statistics shown in Table 3 reveal that except CPI of India all other variables of China and Japan found to be non-stationary in levels, with intercept and lagged 0. All other variables of respective countries found to be non-stationary because they failed to reject the null hypothesis, which shows all other variables except CPI of India has the presence of unit root.

Figure 1. Graphical presentation of dataset

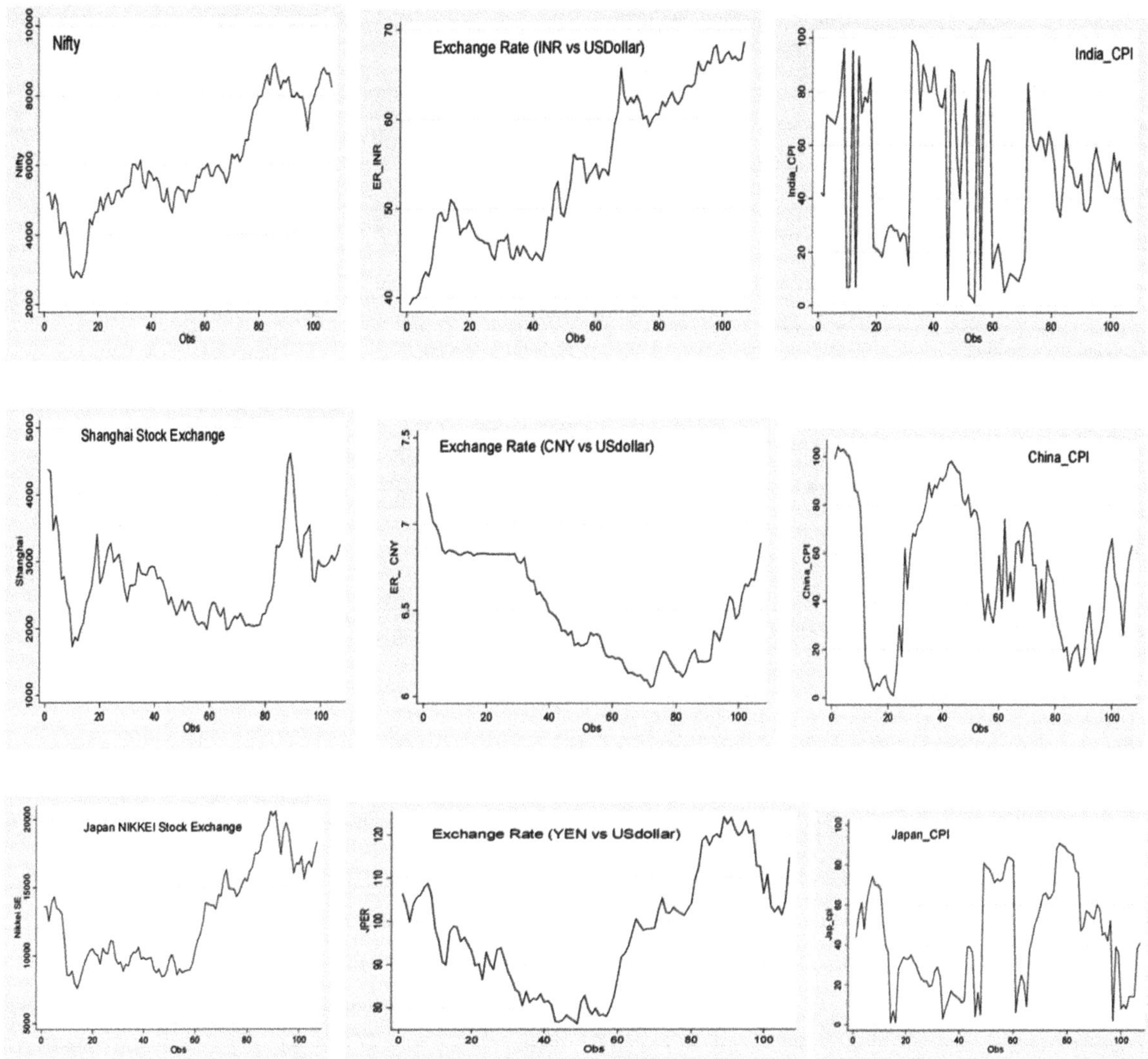

Table 4 illustrates the result of the ADF test after taking the first difference. The resultant value of the ADF test statistics is compared with critical values for the above variables. All the variables after taking the first difference to the time series found to be stationary. Thus, after employing ADF test, now Johansen's cointegration test and Granger causality test has been applied further to test the long-term integration between the variables of India, China and Japan.

The result from Table 5 indicates that demonstrates the result of Johansen co-integration test. The principle discussed in Johansen (1992) is based on the principle of Panthula (1989). As per the same principle if the test statistic is less than the critical value at 5% significant level, then the null hypothesis of no cointegration cannot be rejected. The result from Table 5 it can be noted that all the pairs except Nifty – CPI (India) and Shanghai stock exchange – CPI (China) does not have cointegration among the selected pairs in the study. But it can be noted that India stock market (Nifty) and Chinese market

Table 3. Augmented Dickey-Fuller Unit Root Test: Model 1(Without First Difference)

No of Observations: 107 Exogenous: Constant Dickey-Fuller Test for Unit Root			**lags (0)**
Variables	**ADF Test**	**Null Hypothesis**	**Result**
Indian Market			
Nifty	-0.703*	Failed to reject h0	Variable is not stationary
CPI	-6.630	Reject H0	Variable is stationary
Exchange rate	-0.920*	Failed to reject h0	Variable is not stationary
Chinese Market			
Shanghai stock market	-3.060*	Failed to reject h0	Variable is not stationary
CPI	-2.437*	Failed to reject h0	Variable is not stationary
Exchange rate	-2.004*	Failed to reject h0	Variable is not stationary
Japanese Market			
Nikkei	-0.575*	Failed to reject h0	Variable is not stationary
CPI	-3.158*	Failed to reject h0	Variable is not stationary
Exchange rate	-0.898*	Failed to reject h0	Variable is not stationary

Notes: * indicate acceptance of the null hypothesis of variable is not stationary at 1 percent significant levels. A null hypothesis is accepted if Test statistic < Critical value.

Table 4. Augmented Dickey-Fuller Unit Root Test: Model 2 (First Difference)

No of Observations: 107 Exogenous: Constant Dickey-Fuller Test for Unit Root			**lags(0)**
Variables	**ADF Test**	**Null Hypothesis**	**Result**
Indian Market			
Nifty	-10.273	Reject H0	Variable is stationary
Exchange rate	-9.763	Reject H0	Variable is stationary
Chinese Market			
Shanghai stock market	-8.950	Reject H0	Variable is stationary
CPI	-17.592	Reject H0	Variable is stationary
Exchange rate	-7.282	Reject H0	Variable is stationary
Japanese Market			
Nikkei	-8.888	Reject H0	Variable is stationary
CPI	-8.808	Reject H0	Variable is stationary
Exchange rate	-9.002	Reject H0	Variable is stationary

Notes: The Null hypothesis is rejected if Test statistic > Critical value

(Shanghai stock market) has cointegration with the inflation, which means they have a long-term association or they have a long-term association or they move collectively in long-run.

The result is also supported by Adam and Tweneboah (2008) where the result of the study shows the long-term relationship exists among Ghana stock exchange and macroeconomic variables. The Granger-causality test is conducted to study the lead-lag relationship between 3 ASIAN markets and macroeconomic variables. Table 6 presents the results of the Granger causality test for the pairwise, the decision whether to reject or not to reject the null hypothesis is based on the p-values. Bidirectional Granger causality is found between Nifty and exchange rate, unidirectional causality is found Nikkei and exchange rate. Whereas relationship does not exist between Inflation (India) and Nifty and Inflation (Japan) and Nikkei implies that short-run-run differences between the markets are sufficient for investors to achieve gains by portfolio diversification.

Results of Pooled Estimates

To identify the impact of the variables of the exchange rate and inflation, error correction based on autoregressive distributed lag ARDL (p,q) model has been used, with focus on the pooled mean group. Table 7 reports the results of PMG estimates of the long-run coefficients, error correction term, short-term coefficients and Hausman test statistics for all the three countries (India, China and Japan) used in the study. The Hausman test statistics fail to decline the homogeneity of long-run coefficients. Hence the PMG estimator is more efficient than the MG estimator. Table 8(a) and 8(b) reports individual countries results of PMG along with Hausman h-test to measure the comparative efficiency and consistency of PMG and MG model.

Table 5. Johansen's Cointegration Test

	Pairs	Null	Trace Statistics (Critical Value)	Max Statistics (Critical Value)
Indian Market (Lag 1)				
1	Nifty - Exchange rate (INR vs USD)	r = 0	9.31* (15.41)	9.31 (14.07)
		r = 1	0.00 (3.76)	0.00 (3.76)
2	Nifty - CPI (India)	r = 0	38.24 (15.41)	37.78 (14.07)
		r = 1	0.45* (3.76)	0.45(3.76)
Chinese Market (Lag 2)				
1	Shanghai - Exchange rate (CNY vs USD)	r = 0	15.13* (15.41)	11.90 (14.07)
		r = 1	3.23 (3.76)	3.23(3.76)
2	Shanghai - CPI (China)	r = 0	32.88 (15.41)	22.11(14.07)
		r = 1	10.77(3.76)	10.77(3.76)
Japanese Market (Lag 1)				
1	Nikkei - Exchange rate (Yen VS USD)	r = 0	10.11* (15.41)	9.35 (14.07)
		r = 1	0.75 (3.76)	0.75 (3.76)
2	Nikkei - CPI (Japan)	r = 0	10.50* (15.41)	10.17 (14.07)
		r = 1	0.33 (3.76)	0.33 (3.76)

Notes: Null hypothesis is accepted, if Test statistic < Critical value, Critical value considered at 5%

Table 6. Granger Causality Test

	Pairs	Df	F. Test	p Value	Conclusion
Indian Market (Lag 1)					
1	Nifty does not Granger cause Exchange rate	1	8.86	0.00*	
	Exchange rate does not Granger cause NIFTY	1	3.67	0.05**	Bidirectional relation exists
2	Nifty does not Granger Cause Inflation (India CPI)	1	0.89	0.34	
	Inflation (CPI) does not Granger Cause Nifty	1	0.35	0.55	Relationship does not exist
Chinese Market (Lag 2)					
1	Shanghai stock exchange does not Granger cause Exchange rate	2	0.27	0.75	
	Exchange rate does not Granger cause Shanghai stock exchange	2	1.10	0.33	Relationship does not exist
2	Shanghai Stock exchange does not Granger Cause Inflation (China CPI)	2	5.38	0.00*	
	Inflation (CPI) does not Granger cause Shanghai Stock exchange	2	3.23	0.04**	Bidirectional relation exists
Japanese Market (Lag 1)					
1	Nikkei does not Granger cause Exchange rate	1	1.26	0.26	
	Exchange rate does not Granger cause Nikkei	1	7.55	0.00*	Unidirectional Relation
2	Nikkei does not Granger Cause Inflation (Japanese CPI)	1	0.00	0.95	
	Inflation (CPI) does not Granger cause Nikkei	1	0.44	0.50	Relationship does not exist

Notes: *, ** indicate rejection of null hypothesis at 1, 5 percent significant levels.

Table 7. Pooled mean group (PMG)

Pooled Mean group of 3 Countries		
Variables	**Coef**	**Std. Error**
Long run coefficient		
Exchange rate	1.4360* (0.00)	0.2760
Inflation (CPI)	-0.0743(0.11)	0.0473
Error correction term	-0.2184* (0.00)	0.0681
Short run Coef		
Exchange rate Inflation (CPI)	1.4614 (0.42) 0.0451(0.13)	0.0681 0.0299
Constant Log Likelihood Hausman Test	0.9855** (0.04) 275.1331 2.08 (0.35)	0.4878 - -

Notes: *, ** indicates significant at 1% and 5%. Estimations are done by using (xtpmg) routine in Stata. The Pooled mean group, all controlling for country and time effects, while the panel (LR) shows long-run effects. The second panel reports short-run effects (SR) and the speed of adjustment (ec). Monthly data 2008-2016. The total number of observation for each variable 321 (107 from each country for individual variable)

Table 8a. Pooled mean group (PMG)

Variables	Pooled Mean Group for India		Pooled Mean Group for China	
	Coef	Std. Error	Coef	Std. Error
Long run coefficient				
Exchange rate	1.4360*(0.00)	0.2760	1.4360* (0.00)	0.2760
Inflation (CPI)	-0.0743(0.11)	0.0473	-0.0743(0.11)	0.0473
Error correction term	-0.3517*(0.00)	0.6310	-0.1760*(0.00)	0.0534
Short run Coef				
Exchange rate Inflation (CPI)	4.7068 * (0.00) 0.1019*(0.00)	0.9106 0.0356	-1.6767*(0.00) 0.0001*(0.01)	0.2137 0.0284
Constant Log Likelihood Hausman Test	1.9544*(0.00) 275.1331 2.08 (0.35)	0.3989 - -	0.6004**(0.03) 275.1331 2.08(0.35)	0.2760- - -

Table 8b. Pooled mean group (PMG): Continued

Variables	Pooled Mean Group for Japan	
	Coef	Std. Error
Long run coefficient		
Exchange rate	1.4360* (0.00)	0.2760
Inflation (CPI)	-0.0743(0.11)	0.0473
Error correction term	-0.1274* (0.01)	0.4923
Short run Coef		
Exchange rate Inflation (CPI)	1.3541* (0.00) 0.0332*(0.00)	0.1588 0.0079
Constant Log Likelihood Hausman Test	0.4018** (0.03) 275.1331 2.08 (0.35)	0.3989 - -

Notes: *, ** indicates significant at 1% and 5%. Estimations are done by using (xtpmg full, to obtain each individual country results) routine in Stata. Pooled mean group, all controlling for country and time effects, while the panel (LR) shows long -run effects. The second panel reports short-run effects (SR) and the speed of adjustment (ec). Monthly data 2008-2016. The total number of observation for each variable 107 for each country. Hausman test is indicating that PMG is consistent and efficient estimation than MG (the p-value of Hausman test is >5% and hence we report only PMG results in the study).

Table 7 shows that exchange rate has a positive and significant relationship with the stock market in the long run for all the three countries and stock market and inflation have no significant relationship in the long run. This result is also found in Pal and Mittal (2011), the study reveals that exchange rate and stock market have a significant relationship and stock market and inflation rate showed an insignificant relationship in the long run. The result of the study agrees with Erdem et al. (2005) where the result of this study found a negative relationship between inflation and Istanbul Stock Exchange's index. The short-run association between the stock market and the exchange rate is also positive and statistically significant and inflation and stock market relationship are insignificant. The error correction term is negative and statistically significant. This confirms that the co-integration relationship according to Engle and Granger representation theorem. Particularly, it shows that any deviation from the long-run expected value is adjusted by 21.84%.

Table 8(a) and 8(b) shows the result of individual country-wise where it can be noted that stock market index is positively associated with the exchange rate for all the three countries in short run. The positive association between exchange rate and stock market can also be found in Aggarwal (1981). Inflation showed a negative and insignificant association between India, China and Japan.

CONCLUSION AND FUTURE STUDY

The research has made an effort towards the evaluation of the effect of exchange rate and inflation on stock markets of India, China, and Japan. In the present globalised era, where capital markets are becoming significantly integrated, it has become essential to understand the underlying fundamentals influencing the markets at domestic and global level. Thus, variables like inflation, the exchange rate of India, China and Japan are taken as the independent variable and Nifty, Shanghai stock market and Nikkei are taken as an explanatory variable.

The objective of the study was to examine the relationships between the ASIAN Stock index and macroeconomic variables (Inflation, measured by consumer price index and exchange rate) on a monthly data from 2008 to 2016 using Granger Causality Test, cointegration tests and the pooled estimated results. The PMG estimation indicated that exchange rate has a positive and significant relationship with the stock market in the long run for all the three countries and stock market and inflation have no significant relationship in the long run. The short-run association between the stock market and exchange rate is also positive and statistically significant and inflation and stock market relationship are insignificant.

The result of Johansen integration test reveals that all the pairs except Nifty – CPI (India) and Shanghai stock exchange – CPI (China) does not have cointegration among the selected pairs in the study. But it can be noted that India stock market (Nifty) and Chinese market (Shanghai stock market) has cointegration with the inflation, which means they have a long-term association or they have the long-term association or they move collectively in long-run and supporting the previous studies done by Ahmed (2008). The test of the Granger causality test reveals that Bidirectional Granger causality is found between Nifty and exchange rate, unidirectional causality is found Nikkei and exchange rate. Whereas relationship does not exist between Inflation (India) and Nifty and Inflation (Japan) and Nikkei implies that short-run-run differences between the markets are sufficient for investors to achieve gains by portfolio diversification. The results of VECM showed some interesting result where inflation (CPI) showed long-run causality between exchange rate and Nifty and Shanghai stock exchange showed negative long-run (Short-run run) causality among exchange rate and inflation (long-run). Whereas Nikkei showed short-run-run negative causality with inflation and positive short-run-run causality with the exchange rate.

The present study has further scope for comprehensive results. It can be extended over a longer period and with several countries and by including various macroeconomic variables, it will be more interesting to see how the stock market is affected by macroeconomic variables in European, US and other developed market. Future study can also focus on comparative study of developing and developed markets. The major implication of the study can be to governments of India, China and Japan and for the individual and institutional investors.

REFERENCES

Abraham, R., & Harrington, C. (2016). Determinants of oil futures prices. *Theoretical Economics Letters, 6*(4), 742–749. doi:10.4236/tel.2016.64078

Adam, A. M., & Tweneboah, G. (2008). *Macroeconomic factors and stock market movement: Evidence from Ghana*. Academic Press.

Adjasi, C. K. (2009). Macroeconomic uncertainty and conditional stock-price volatility in frontier African markets: Evidence from Ghana. *The Journal of Risk Finance, 10*(4), 333–349. doi:10.1108/15265940910980641

Aggarwal, J. K., Davis, L. S., & Martin, W. N. (1981). Correspondence processes in dynamic scene analysis. *Proceedings of the IEEE, 69*(5), 562–572. doi:10.1109/PROC.1981.12025

Ahmed, S. (2008). Aggregate economic variables and stock markets in India. *International Research Journal of Finance and Economics, 14*, 141–164.

Bahmani-Oskooee, M., & Sohrabian, A (1992) Stock prices and the effective exchange rate of the dollar. *Applied Economics, 24*(4), 459-464.

Büyüksalvarci, A., & Abdioglu, H (2010). The causal relationship between stock prices and macroeconomic variables: A case study for Turkey. *International Journal of Economic Perspectives, 4*(4), 601.

Chattopadhyay, S. K., & Behera, S. R. (2006, March). Financial integration for Indian stock market. *Annual Conference on Money & Finance held at IGIDR*.

Chen, H., Lobo, B. J., & Wong, W. K. (2006). *Links between the Indian, US and Chinese stock markets*. National University of Singapore, Department of Economics, Working Paper, 602.

Czapkiewicz, A., & Stachowicz, M. (2016). The long-run relationship between the stock market and main macroeconomic variables in Poland. *Managerial Economics, 17*(1), 7. doi:10.7494/manage.2016.17.1.7

Degan, R. J. (2009). *Understanding China's historical development: The profit and the risk that China's stock market provides investors*. Globadvantage, Center of research in international business & strategy. Available from: http://globadvantage.ipleiria.pt/files/2009/07/working_paper-35_globadvantage.pdf

Dickey, D. A., & Fuller, W. A. (1981). Likelihood ratio statistics for autoregressive time series with a unit root. *Econometrica, 49*(4), 1057–1072. doi:10.2307/1912517

Economywatch. (2008). Available at: www.economywatch.com/indianeconomy

Engle, R. F., & Granger, C. W. (1987). Co-integration and error correction: Representation, estimation, and testing. *Econometrica, 55*(2), 251–276. doi:10.2307/1913236

Erdem, C., Arslan, C. K., & Sema Erdem, M. (2005). Effects of macroeconomic variables on Istanbul stock exchange indexes. *Applied Financial Economics, 15*(14), 987–994. doi:10.1080/09603100500120365

Evaluating Mutual Fund Performance. (n.d.). Alliance Business School, Bangalore. Available at: www.indianmba.com/Occasional_Papers/OP158/op158.html

Fama, E. F. (1981). Stock returns, real activity, inflation, and money. *The American Economic Review*, *71*(4), 545–565.

Feldstein, M. S. (1980). *Inflation, tax rules, and investment: some econometric evidence*. Academic Press.

Hamao, Y. (1988). An empirical examination of the arbitrage pricing theory: Using Japanese data. *Japan and the World Economy*, *1*(1), 45–61.

Hong, H. (1977). Inflation and the market value of the firm: Theory and tests. *The Journal of Finance*, *32*(4), 1031–1048. doi:10.1111/j.1540-6261.1977.tb03307.x

Johansen, S. (1995). Identifying restrictions of linear equations with applications to simultaneous equations and cointegration. *Journal of Econometrics*, *69*(1), 111–132. doi:10.1016/0304-4076(94)01664-L

Johansen, S., & Juselius, K. (1990). Maximum likelihood estimation and inference on cointegration—With applications to the demand for money. *Oxford Bulletin of Economics and Statistics*, *52*(2), 169–210. doi:10.1111/j.1468-0084.1990.mp52002003.x

Juselius, K. (2006). *The cointegrated VAR model: methodology and applications*. Oxford University Press.

Kasa, K. (1992). Common stochastic trends in international stock markets. *Journal of Monetary Economics*, *29*(1), 95–124. doi:10.1016/0304-3932(92)90025-W

Kyereboah-Coleman, A., & Agyire-Tettey, K. F. (2008). Impact of macroeconomic indicators on stock market performance: The case of the Ghana Stock Exchange. *The Journal of Risk Finance*, *9*(4), 365–378. doi:10.1108/15265940810895025

Luo, J., Gan, C., Hu, B., & Kao, T. K. (2009). An empirical analysis of Chinese stock price anomalies and volatility. *Investment Management and Financial Innovations*, *6*(1), 1–18.

Miyakoshi, T. (2003). Spillovers of stock return volatility to Asian equity markets from Japan and the US. *Journal of International Financial Markets, Institutions and Money*, *13*(4), 383–399. doi:10.1016/S1042-4431(03)00015-5

Moneybiz. (2008). Available at: www.moneybiz.co.za/personal_finance/jse_6.asp

Mukherjee, T. K., & Naka, A. (1995). Dynamic relations between macroeconomic variables and the Japanese stock market: An application of a vector error correction model. *Journal of Financial Research*, *18*(2), 223–237. doi:10.1111/j.1475-6803.1995.tb00563.x

Omran, M., & Pointon, J. (2004). The determinants of the cost of capital by industry within an emerging economy: Evidence from Egypt. *International Journal of Business*, *9*, 3.

Pal, K., & Mittal, R. (2011). Impact of macroeconomic indicators on Indian capital markets. *The Journal of Risk Finance*, *12*(2), 84–97. doi:10.1108/15265941111112811

Pantula, S. G. (1989). Testing for unit roots in time series data. *Econometric Theory*, *5*(02), 256–271. doi:10.1017/S0266466600012421

Pesaran, M. H., Shin, Y., & Smith, R. P. (1999). Pooled mean group estimation of dynamic heterogeneous panels. *Journal of the American Statistical Association*, *94*(446), 621–634. doi:10.1080/01621459.1999.10474156

Sibanda, K., Hove, P., & Murwirapachena, G. (2015). Oil prices, exchange rates, and inflation expectations in South Africa. *The International Business & Economics Research Journal (Online)*, *14*(4), 587.

Singh, T. (2010). Does international trade cause economic growth? A survey. *World Economy*, *33*(11), 1517–1564. doi:10.1111/j.1467-9701.2010.01243.x

APPENDIX

Data Sources Used in the Study

1. India:
    a. INR vs USD: https://in.investing.com/currencies/usd-inr-historical-data
    b. Nifty (NSE): https://in.investing.com/indices/s-p-cnx-nifty-historical-data
    c. India CPI: http://www.global-rates.com/economic-indicators/inflation/2008.aspx (Each year downloaded separately from Jan 2008 to Nov 2016 monthly data)
2. China:
    a. CNY vs USD: https://www.investing.com/currencies/usd-cny-historical-data
    b. Shanghai: https://in.investing.com/indices/shanghai-composite-historical-data
    c. China CPI: http://www.global-rates.com/economic-indicators/inflation/2008.aspx (Each year downloaded separately from Jan 2008 to Nov 2016 Monthly data)
3. Japan:
    a. YEN vs USD https://www.investing.com/currencies/usd-jpy-historical-data
    b. Nikkei: https://www.investing.com/indices/japan-ni225-historical-data
    c. Japan CPI: http://www.global-rates.com/economic-indicators/inflation/2008.aspx (Each year downloaded separately from Jan 2008 to Nov 2016 Monthly data)

Note: NSEindia.com, English.sse.com.cn (Shanghai stock exchange), indexes.nikkei.co.jp/en/nkave (Nikkei 225) has been also referred for additional information.

Chapter 11
Digital Financial Inclusion in India:
A Review

Gaurav Agrawal
Indian Institute of Information Technology and Management Gwalior, India

Pooja Jain
Jiwaji University, India

ABSTRACT

Financial inclusion is a multidimensional approach. With technology intervention in financial inclusion, electronic banking activity in rural India leads to increased use of financial services and better living standards. In the rising market, many people using mobile phones still are not able to access banking products and financial services. This indicates a huge untouched market for commercial banks. In India, mobile banking services are still in the early stages of development. Thus, the main objective of the chapter is to understand the factors that would act as drivers towards the adoption of mobile financial services and understand people's intention to adopt and use of mobile banking services which lead to increases accessibility towards financial products among rural people as well improve standards of living and overall development of the nation. The study focuses on utilizing secondary sources which is related to financial inclusion to understand the new banking technology and identifies people's behavior towards adoption and uses of banking services.

INTRODUCTION

India has the second largest unbanked population in the world with more than half of its population considered as financially excluded or underserved (World Bank, 2017). Indian culture is low risk taking culture, so banks are very important financial institution which protects the cash related risk of the general public. Technological advancement helped banking organization in replacement of physical cash into cost effective and less risky flexible payment system. Emerging and fast growing innovations in banks and financial institution have changed the whole process of banking industries. Digital financial

DOI: 10.4018/978-1-5225-7399-9.ch011

service is the backbone of economic development of any country. Mobile banking and mobile money are some new emerging concept which changes mass services into customized services. By this digital financial inclusion come into existence which promotes efficient interconnection among participants in economic activities. Digital financial inclusion is considered a success when a poor, and thus far unbanked, customer starts transacting digitally with his/her family and friends, formal banking and financial institutions and utility companies, and receives government to-person (G2P) payments directly into his/her bank account. In the current scenario globally, around 1.7 billion adults remain unbanked (Global Findex Database, 2017) i.e. without an account of any financial institution and banks or through any mobile banking and mobile money provider. As we seen in figure1, China has the world's largest unbanked population, followed by India (190 million), Pakistan (100 million), and Indonesia (95 million). Apart, these four countries, Nigeria, Mexico, and Bangladesh has also unbanked population but ratio is less as compare to China, India, Pakistan and Indonesia (Global Findex Database, 2017). In the line, figure 2 reflect that 56% women and 44% men adult has unbanked population by gender, mostly per cent of women not having an account (Global Findex Database, 2017).

Figure 1. Adults without an account by economy in % (2017)
Source: Global Findex Database, 2017

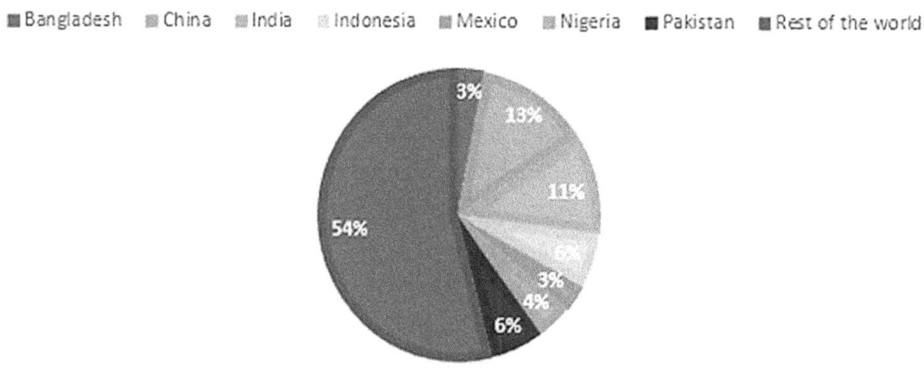

Figure 2. Adult without an account by gender in % (2017)
Source: Global Findex Database, 2017

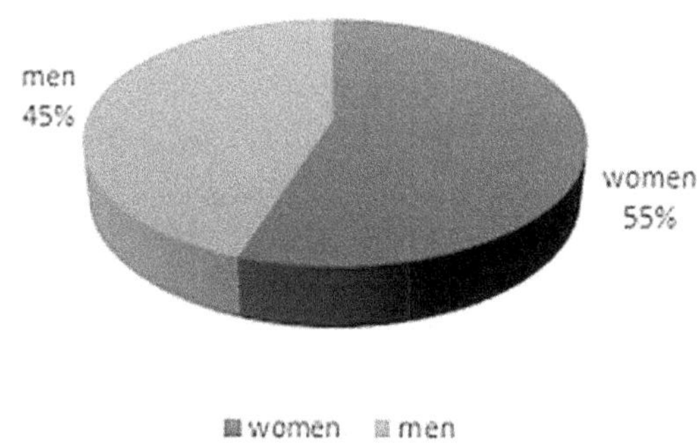

As we seen in figure 3, around 5.6% customers had registered to mobile money services on December-2012 and it has increased by 34% on December 2017 in South Asia, 3.1% increase in Latin America & Caribbean and 1.7% increase in Europe & Central Asia (Global System for Mobile Communication Association (GSMA) survey report, 2017)

This figures indicate that customer adoption towards mobile banking or mobile money is still low. Hence, it is very important to investigate factors that positively or negatively would affect customers toward the adoption or rejection of mobile banking services. Furthermore, this study also exploring the most influencing factors that have been used for adoption behavior intention towards mobile banking services. The study uses diffusion of innovation as a base-line theory to investigate factors that may influence mobile banking adoption and use. More specifically, the main objective of the study is to examine the potential factors of mobile banking adoption which provide a comprehensive understanding of their impacts toward the adoption of mobile banking applications

LITERATURE REVIEW

Various number of previous studies has been done to understand the individual behavior towards adoption of mobile banking as a technological invention. Maximum number of researchers have come across different types of models to identify behaviour intention of customers towards adoption of mobile banking services by suggesting some factors or attributes that could affect an individual's decisions to adopt mobile banking services. Here various models and frameworks like Technology acceptance model (TAM) (Davis, Bogozzi and Warshaw, 1989), Innovation diffusion theory (IDT) (Rogers, 1995), Theory of planned behaviour (TPB) (Ajzen, 1991), Unified Theory of Acceptance and Use of Technology (UTAUT) (Venkatesh et al. in 2003), Self-developed model (SDM) (Sultan, Al-Baltah, & Abdulrazzak, 2017). All of these models are very helpful in determining the adoption intention of customers toward mobile banking services. Rogers define most popular theory of innovation is Innovation Diffusion Theory that have tried to explain various factors that affect an individual behavior to adopt an innovation or a technology. Innovation Diffusion Theory is a theory that try to find out what, how and why new ideas, innovation and technology spread over beliefs and cultures. Theory identified several attributes or traits of an innovation that are significantly influences on adoption behavior of individuals. Conferring to Rogers, these attributes or factors are:

Figure 3. Global spread of registered mobile money customers from December 2012-December 2017
Source: GSMA (Global System for Mobile Communication Association) Report, 2017

Relative Advantage

Relative advantage refers to the degree to which an innovation is perceived as providing more benefits than its predecessor (Moore & Benbasat 1991). It effects in increased efficiency, enhanced status and economic benefits (Rogers 2003). Previous study has found that relative advantage of an innovation is positively significant related to the rate of adoption (Moore & Benbasat 1991). Study proposes that when user identifies relative advantage of an innovative technology over an old one, they have a tendency to adopt and uses of technology (Rogers 2003). In the perspective of mobile banking adoption, customers have stated various benefits such as convenience, affordability and immediacy (Lin 2011) as well as they are more likely to adopt it.

Complexity

Cheung et al. (2000) defined complexity as the extent to which an innovation can be considered relatively difficult to understand and use. Study reveals that complexity is a factor which negatively influences the adoption of internet usage. Complexity is the opposite of ease of use and it is a major factor in adoption of mobile banking. There is extensive amount of empirical study on the mobile technology to suggest that consumers' intention to adopt mobile banking is reserved by the perceived complexity of the innovation (Au & Kauffman 2008; Mallat 2007; Ondrus & Pigneur 2006). Complexity in use, technical structure, and design of technology are reported as individual barriers in a number of studies (Bouwman et.al 2007). Whereas there is a strong and significant impact of perceived ease of use of new technology on mobile banking adoption (Luarn & Lin 2005; Venkatesh & Davis 2000). Mobile banking services have very consumer friendly interface, users see them as easy to use, and hence to form positive attitudes towards them (Lin 2011). Ample of literature on barriers of mobile banking adoption is mostly related to technical complexity. Users will be reserved to use mobile banking if they find it requires more mental and technical effort as well as time-consuming or frustrating. Customers try to adopt that technology which is not complex and consume less physical and mental effort to work with. They adopted new technology which feel easy and simple to use. If any new technology is very complex, difficult and consumer not able to learn, acquire and use it easily, there is fewer chances of adoption (Davis 1989). Ease of use is a critical success factor in technology adoption in India as many people have less knowledge of innovative and developed technology Kolodinsky et.al (2004). Eriksson (2005) have also reported in their studies about Ease of use as an important construct.

Compatibility

Compatibility refers to the degree to which a service is perceived as consistent with users' existing values, beliefs, habits and present and previous experiences (Chen et al. 2013). It is a vibrant attribute of innovation as adaptable by consumer's lifestyle where can drive a rapid rate of adoption (Rogers 2003). Study has shown that compatibility is a positive significant factor to determine consumers' attitude towards internet banking adoption in Malaysia (Ndubisi & Sinti 2006). Compatibility has also been found significantly influential attribute in the adoption of virtual store (Chen et al. 2004), m-payment (Chen 2008), and mobile banking (Lin 2011). Al-Gahtani (2003) found that compatibility had significant positive correlation with computer adoption in Saudi Arabia. Many studies have also provided supporting evidence. Thus, it is also likely that the relationship between compatibility and adoption of innovation and technology will hold in the context of mobile banking. Associated study demonstrated that compatibility is a significant antecedent in determining consumer attitudes towards adopting internet banking (Ndubisi and Sinti, 2006). Obviously, Diffusion innovation theory has clarified how compatibility affects consumer willingness to adopt an innovation (Rogers, 1995).

Observability

Observability of an innovation describes the extent to which an innovation is visible to the members of a social system, and the benefits can be easily observed and communicated (Rogers 2003). In the context of mobile banking, observability defined that users' can access the banking services at any time, place and from any location without any interruption or delay, and seeing the effect of mobile banking transactions instantly and conveniently to users. Through such exposure, customers gain knowledge about mobile banking and its benefits, thereby facilitating adoption. It simplified the original construct by redefining observability into two constructs: visibility and result demonstrability (Moore & Benbasat 1991).

Trialability

Trialability denotes the capacity to experiment with new technology and innovation before adoption. Potential consumers who are allowed to test with an innovation will feel more comfortable with it and are more likely to adopt it (Agarwal & Prasad 1998; Rogers 2003). Further support is given by Tan & Teo (2000) who discuss that if customers are given a chance to try the new innovation that will lead to minimize certain unidentified fears and also lead to adoption. If banks provide help, assistance support and demonstrations on services of mobile banking usage in the trial period then fears about mobile banking usage can be minimized and this will also motivate potential adopters to use mobile banking.

Perceived Risk

Perceived risk states that degree of risks in using an innovation (Rogers 2003). Generally, perception on risk arise due to doubt related to the degree of unpredictability between customers' judgment and technology failing to deliver its expected outcome and its subsequent loss (Chen 2008). In technology adoption, there is research evidence of the importance of the perception of risk in deploying new technology or services (Ndubisi & Sinti 2006). In the perspective of mobile banking, the perception of consumers towards risk is more important due to the threat of privacy and security concerns (Luarn & Lin 2005). Furthermore, fear of loss of PIN codes may also pose security threats (Kuisma et al. 2007). Next, some users also anxiety and fear that hackers may access their bank accounts as well as stolen PIN codes. Finally, some users may also have a fear of loss or theft of a mobile device with stored data (Coursaris et al. 2003). Therefore, perceived risk is more likely to negatively affect the mobile banking adoption. Consumer trust is key factor in adoption of m-banking (Mukherjee 2003) (Gu et.al 2009). (Sathye 1999, Chiou et.al 2012) have said security and privacy is main concern while using mobile banking. Security is one of the major problem confronted by consumer while making online transactions. Consumers always try to avoid disclose and share their personal information online because of online privacy matter (Sathye 1999). (Poon 2007) suggested that bank should develop trust with their customers to ensure secure online service as well as value added services, which will lead to create better customer satisfaction.

METHODOLOGY

Data has been collected by academics and non-academic studies published between 1991 and 2017, which stated various challenges and factors related to the adoption of mobile banking by developed and developing countries. Using Global Findex database, GSMA (Global System for Mobile Communication Association) survey report and World bank to identify users and non-users of mobile banking as well as identified unbanked countries. Data has been collected from project reports, opinion pieces' articles, field notes and blogposts published by the World Bank and peer-reviewed research articles appeared in top-tier journals where using key words mobile banking adoption and financial inclusion discipline were considered for data analysis.

FINDINGS AND CONCLUSION

Based on the conducted review, it can be clearly seen that the adoption of mobile services in both developed and developing countries has not reached to the expected amount of intention and usage toward customers. Hence it becomes an important goal for banks and service providers to increase the rate of adoption of mobile banking users. Thus, some important recommendations are banks should also explain the advantages of the new values added services for adapting to mobile banking, such as customers don't have to go to a branch to do their transaction, and explain a new value for them such as saving their time and cost, inconvenience of travelling to a bank or branch, and the avoidance of long queues. Banks can investigate the concept of mobile banking is valuable and it will give them greater control over their banking transactions. With the help of literature review most studies consistently concluded or examined factors i.e. relative advantage, trialability, and compatibility has significant impact on the attitude of customers whereas the perceived risk and complexity both factors are negative influence the adoption of mobile banking. The conclusion found from the literature reveals that adoption of mobile banking is reserved by the perceived complexity of technology adoption and it has a huge possibility to change the people behavior specially who lives in a rural area if they believe that mobile banking is easy to use, clear, and useful to them. Further, the study also suggests that banks should form a web site with features or give information about new value of added services to facilitate users towards mobile banking and thus minimize the perceived risk and maximize the perceived ease of use banking services. Hence, the main attention of banks should be focused on the development of ease of use and usefulness of system because it found that customers will adopt mobile banking services if they find it easy to use, clear, and useful to them that it will create greater financial inclusion for the un(der)banked consumers with greater access to the benefits of traditional banking institutions and lower cost alternative financial services are expected to enable digital financial inclusion.

REFERENCES

Agarwal, R., & Prasad, J. (1998). The antecedents and consequents of user perceptions in information technology adoption. *Decision Support Systems*, *22*(1), 15–29. doi:10.1016/S0167-9236(97)00006-7

Ajzen, I. (1991). The theory of planned behavior. *Organizational Behavior and Human Decision Processes, 50*(2), 179–211. doi:10.1016/0749-5978(91)90020-T

Al-Gahtani, S. S. (2003). Computer technology adoption in Saudi Arabia: Correlates of perceived innovation attributes. *Information Technology for Development, 10*(1), 57–69. doi:10.1002/itdj.1590100106

Al-Jabri, I., & Sohail, M. S. (2012). *Mobile banking adoption: Application of diffusion of innovation theory*. Academic Press.

As-Sultan, S. Y., Al-Baltah, I. A., & Abdulrazzak, F. A. H. (2017). A Survey on Mobile Banking Applications and the Adopted Models. *International Journal (Toronto, Ont.), 7*(2).

Au, Y. A., & Kauffman, R. J. (2008). The economics of mobile payments: Understanding stakeholder issues for an emerging financial technology application. *Electronic Commerce Research and Applications, 7*(2), 141–164. doi:10.1016/j.elerap.2006.12.004

Bouwman, H., Carlsson, C., Molina-Castillo, F. J., & Walden, P. (2007). Barriers and drivers in the adoption of current and future mobile services in Finland. *Telematics and Informatics, 24*(2), 145–160. doi:10.1016/j.tele.2006.08.001

Chen, C. (2013). Perceived risk, usage frequency of mobile banking services. *Managing Service Quality: An International Journal, 23*(5), 410–436. doi:10.1108/MSQ-10-2012-0137

Chen, L. D. (2008). A model of consumer acceptance of mobile payment. *International Journal of Mobile Communications, 6*(1), 32–52. doi:10.1504/IJMC.2008.015997

Chen, L. D., & Tan, J. (2004). Technology Adaptation in E-commerce: Key Determinants of Virtual Stores Acceptance. *European Management Journal, 22*(1), 74–86. doi:10.1016/j.emj.2003.11.014

Cheung, W., Chang, M. K., & Lai, V. S. (2000). Prediction of Internet and World Wide Web usage at work: A test of an extended Triandis model. *Decision Support Systems, 30*(1), 83–100. doi:10.1016/S0167-9236(00)00125-1

Chiou, J. S., & Shen, C. C. (2012). The antecedents of online financial service adoption: The impact of physical banking services on Internet banking acceptance. *Behaviour & Information Technology, 31*(9), 859–871. doi:10.1080/0144929X.2010.549509

Coursaris, C., Hassanein, K., & Head, M. (2003). M-commerce in Canada: an interaction framework for wireless privacy. *Canadian Journal of Administrative Sciences/Revue Canadienne des Sciences de l'Administration, 20*(1), 54-73.

Davis, F. D. (1989). Perceived usefulness, perceived ease of use, and user acceptance of information technology. *Management Information Systems Quarterly, 13*(3), 319–340. doi:10.2307/249008

Davis, F. D., Bagozzi, R. P., & Warshaw, P. R. (1989). User acceptance of computer technology: A comparison of two theoretical models. *Management Science, 35*(8), 982–1003. doi:10.1287/mnsc.35.8.982

Eriksson, K., Kerem, K., & Nilsson, D. (2005). Customer acceptance of internet banking in Estonia. *International Journal of Bank Marketing, 23*(2), 200–216. doi:10.1108/02652320510584412

Gu, J. C., Lee, S. C., & Suh, Y. H. (2009). Determinants of behavioral intention to mobile banking. *Expert Systems with Applications*, *36*(9), 11605–11616. doi:10.1016/j.eswa.2009.03.024

Kolodinsky, J. M., Hogarth, J. M., & Hilgert, M. A. (2004). The adoption of electronic banking technologies by US consumers. *International Journal of Bank Marketing*, *22*(4), 238–259. doi:10.1108/02652320410542536

Kuisma, T., Laukkanen, T., & Hiltunen, M. (2007). Mapping the reasons for resistance to Internet banking: A means-end approach. *International Journal of Information Management*, *27*(2), 75–85. doi:10.1016/j.ijinfomgt.2006.08.006

Laura, B., & Kate, S. (2002). A Delphi study of the drivers and inhibitors of Internet banking. *International Journal of Bank Marketing*, *20*(6), 250–260. doi:10.1108/02652320210446715

Lin, H. F. (2011). An empirical investigation of mobile banking adoption: The effect of innovation attributes and knowledge-based trust. *International Journal of Information Management*, *31*(3), 252–260. doi:10.1016/j.ijinfomgt.2010.07.006

Luarn, P., & Lin, H. H. (2005). Toward an understanding of the behavioral intention to use mobile banking. *Computers in Human Behavior*, *21*(6), 873–891. doi:10.1016/j.chb.2004.03.003

Mallat, N. (2007). Exploring consumer adoption of mobile payments–A qualitative study. *The Journal of Strategic Information Systems*, *16*(4), 413–432. doi:10.1016/j.jsis.2007.08.001

Moore, G. C., & Benbasat, I. (1991). Development of an instrument to measure the perceptions of adopting an information technology innovation. *Information Systems Research*, *2*(3), 192–222. doi:10.1287/isre.2.3.192

Mukherjee, A., & Nath, P. (2003). A model of trust in online relationship banking. *International Journal of Bank Marketing*, *21*(1), 5–15. doi:10.1108/02652320310457767

Ndubisi, N., & Sinti, Q. (2006). Consumer attitudes, system's characteristics and internet banking adoption in Malaysia. *Management Research News*, *29*(1/2), 16–27. doi:10.1108/01409170610645411

Ondrus, J., & Pigneur, Y. (2006). Towards a holistic analysis of mobile payments: A multiple perspectives approach. *Electronic Commerce Research and Applications*, *5*(3), 246–257. doi:10.1016/j.elerap.2005.09.003

Poon, W. C. (2007). Users' adoption of e-banking services: The Malaysian perspective. *Journal of Business and Industrial Marketing*, *23*(1), 59–69. doi:10.1108/08858620810841498

Rogers, E. M. (1995). Diffusion of Innovations: modifications of a model for telecommunications. In *Die diffusion von innovationen in der telekommunikation* (pp. 25–38). Berlin: Springer. doi:10.1007/978-3-642-79868-9_2

Rogers, E. M. (2003). The diffusion of innovation (5th ed.). New York: Free Press.

Sathye, M. (1999). Adoption of Internet banking by Australian consumers: An empirical investigation. *International Journal of Bank Marketing*, *17*(7), 324–334. doi:10.1108/02652329910305689

Tan, M., & Teo, T. S. (2000). Factors influencing the adoption of Internet banking. *Journal of the AIS, 1*(5).

Venkatesh, V., & Davis, F. D. (2000). A theoretical extension of the technology acceptance model: Four longitudinal field studies. *Management Science, 46*(2), 186–204. doi:10.1287/mnsc.46.2.186.11926

Venkatesh, V., Morris, M. G., Davis, G. B., & Davis, F. D. (2003). User acceptance of information technology: Toward a unified view. *Management Information Systems Quarterly, 27*(3), 425–478. doi:10.2307/30036540

Chapter 12
Employees Perception Regarding CSR Initiatives of the Companies in India

Vikrant Vikram Vikram Singh
Amity University, India

Manoj Pandey
Amity University, India

Anil Vashisht
Amity University, India

ABSTRACT

This chapter is an attempt to understand the impact of CSR on a very important stakeholder of the company (i.e., an employee of the company). Employees are an integral part of the company, and at the same time, they can be the costumer of the company if using the product or services offered by the company. This thing makes him a powerful tool to analyze the impact of various initiatives of the organization which will have long lasting impact on the company as well as on the society as a whole. This study is conducted through a survey by preparing questionnaire for obtaining information from the employees of different organizations regarding their perception w.r.t. CSR activities. The result of the report shows that CSR engagement of the company has positive impact on the employee. But, the report also suggests that companies are lacking in terms of their CSR initiatives from last few years. It further suggests that inputs and methods of the CSR activities by the organizations should improve in order to increase the productivity and belongingness of the employees.

DOI: 10.4018/978-1-5225-7399-9.ch012

INTRODUCTION

Corporate social responsibility (CSR, additionally called corporate citizenship) is a type of corporate self-control; coordinated into a plan of action. CSR strategy works as a self-administrative system whereby a business screens and guarantees its dynamic consistence with the soul of the law, moral gauges and national or universal norms. Corporates are trying different things with different regions in CSR; aside from what is expressed in their vision proclamations. They are additionally teaming up with NGOs, neighborhood self-government bodies; or the administration to guarantee better achieve, better system definition and contributions from the legislature. It is crucial for an organization to view and center CSR as a wellspring of upper hand; instead of a routine with regards to charity. CSR is the proceeding with responsibility by business to carry on morally and add to monetary improvement while enhancing the personal satisfaction of the workforce and their families and also of the nearby group and society on the loose. Immature assets for execution have made enormous crevices and have expanded the cost for CSR usage. Furthermore, there are additionally no for the most part acknowledged norms; for measuring the accomplishment of the variety of group advancement programs that are presently set up.

Corporate Social Responsibility (CSR); has cleared organizations universally and has been guaranteed to be a basic piece of the present day organizations. CSR mirrors an organization's objectives, vision, mission, culture and the procedures. It characterizes; what and how an organization looks past benefits. Various organizations today; are starting to consolidate CSR into their long haul arranging forms, recognizing particular objectives and measures of advance since it assumes an exceptionally critical part; in the business, some of which can be clarified as under:

- **Lift in Brand Building and Reputation:** Clients are regularly drawn; to brands and organizations with great notoriety in CSR-related regions. An organization considered socially dependable can profit; both from its improved notoriety with general society and also inside the business group, expanding an organization's capacity to draw in capital and exchanging accomplices. "
- **Increased Sales and Customer Loyalty:** A number of studies have 386 The Indian Journal of Industrial Relations, Vol. 44, No. 3, Jan. 2009; suggested a large and growing market for the products; and services of companies who are perceived to be socially responsible."
- **Diminishment in Working Costs:** CSR activities help, decrease working expenses drastically. For instance, numerous activities went for enhancing natural execution, for example, diminishing contaminations that add to worldwide environmental change or lessening utilization of agrochemicals additionally bring down expenses. Many reusing activities cut waste-transfer costs and create salary by offering reused materials.
- **Higher Profitability and Quality:** An organization's endeavors to enhance working conditions; diminish ecological effects or increment representative association in basic leadership regularly prompt expanded efficiency and decreased blunder rate. For instance; organizations that enhance working conditions and work rehearses among their providers frequently encounter, a lessening in stock that is blemished or can't be sold.
- **Draw In and Hold Representatives:** Organizations saw to have solid CSR duties regularly think that its less demanding to select and hold workers; bringing about a decrease in turnover; related enrollment and preparing costs. Indeed, even in troublesome work markets; potential representatives assess an organization's CSR execution to decide if it is the right "fit".

- **Lessened Administrative Oversight:** Organizations that evidently fulfill; go past administrative consistence necessities are given all the more free rule by both national and nearby government elements."

CSR is not just another idea in India. As far back as their commencement, corporates like Tata Group, the Aditya Birla Group, and Indian Oil Corporation, to give some examples, have been included in serving the group. Through gifts; and philanthropy occasions, numerous different associations have been doing their part for the general public. The fundamental goal of CSR in nowadays is to boost the organization's general effect; on the general public and partners. CSR strategies, practices and projects are by and large exhaustively coordinated by an expanding number of organizations all through their business operations and procedures. A developing number of corporates feel that CSR is not simply one more type of aberrant cost but rather is imperative for securing the goodwill and notoriety, shielding assaults and expanding business intensity.

Organizations have specific CSR groups; that detail arrangements, methodologies and objectives for their CSR projects and put aside spending plans to support them. These projects are regularly dictated by social reasoning; which have clear goals and are all around characterized and are lined up with the standard business. "The programs are put into practice by the employees who are crucial to this process. A CSR program ranges from community development to development in education, environment and healthcare etc."

Although, there is much awareness about the CSR concept, much has to be still done to reach the lower hierarchy of the organization. Many employees still think that the revenue and profits of the organization have not shooted up.

Companies can also indulge itself in other domains when it works for the society apart from donation to various institutions and cause related marketing like taking up environmental issues.

CSR has brought a paradox change in the organizational scenario. It has gathered a overwhelming response from the employees perception, however future prediction is unreliable and fraught process and any kind of prediction is even more unreliable. We can only be sure of the fact that it will be a steady process because government has made it mandatory. However, whatever is achieved is indeed a positive change for the society and has changes the way organization and civil society stand.

It is legitimate to challenge claims about the ineluctable beneficence of the pursuit of economic or financial well-being in a way which has been considered almost heretic for far too long.

REVIEW OF LITERATURE

Andrea Pe´rez et al(2014)" have offered few comprehensive models; to understand the benefits of corporate social responsibility image, in terms of customer behaviour, the authors of this paper propose a hierarchy of effects model to study how customer perceptions of the social responsibility of companies; influence customer affective responses in a service context.'The authors test a structural equation model; using information collected directly from 1,124 customers; of banking services in Spain. The findings demonstrate that corporate social responsibility image influences customer identification with the company, the emotions evoked by the company and satisfaction positively."

Austin(2000) gave the concept of Cooperation Continuum. He clarified the improvement of coordinated effort between non-benefits and organizations. As indicated by him, such joint effort starts from a generous stage, where, the nature of the relationship is like that of a beneficent benefactor brings about authoritative incorporation, where the equivalency of shared advantages is completely captured by firms. The Collaboration Continuum subsequently, gives firms more motivations to be socially dynamic. Organizations can take after this idea by supporting societal causes, and rousing different organizations thus. Benefit organizations ought to have an unequivocal approach to shape their societal contribution and their corporate generosity.

Zahler(2015) proposed and tested a hypothesis of social flexibility; to exogenous stuns. The hypothesis set that excellent corporate social obligation (CSR) divulgence advances the view of authoritative authenticity, making social versatility to exogenous stuns (outer occasions outside administration control). Utilizing a way model and information from 100 experienced, nonprofessional speculators, we inspect whether the nature of an enterprise's intentional CSR revelation expands its apparent hierarchical authenticity.

Gilmore(2012) has principally centered around the cooperative energies amongst social and monetary execution, our comprehension of how (and the conditions under which) organizations utilize CSR to deliver arrangement results that conflict with open welfare has remained similarly immature. This investigation tends to this issue utilizing inside tobacco industry records to investigate British-American Tobacco's (BAT) thinking on CSR and its impacts on the organization's CSR Program. The article displays a three-arrange model of CSR advancement, in light of Sykes and Matza's hypothesis of procedures of balance.

Christopher J Bamber(2004) concentrates on usage of the CSR motivation in little to-medium ventures (SMEs) and reports on inquire about findings from an activity look into contextual analysis that has been led in a UK based SME. The contextual investigation explore exhibits how the CSR plan has been executed utilizing ISO 9001:2000 as a stage and what benefits the contextual investigation association has picked up from this approach. These outcomes are contrasted and a UK study on plausibility of CSR for SMEs directed by the UK's Department of Trade and Industry and parallels are drawn."

Nez-Camplillo(2010) draws consideration on the Agency–Stewardship approach, which proposes that supervisor profile may run from the operator model to the steward show, this article means to look at how vital CEOs are to corporate social obligation (CSR). Specifically, this exploratory study proposes the existence of a relationship between manager profile and CSR practices and that this relation is mediated by the perceived role of ethics and social responsibility.Results show that those closer to the steward model are more inclined to attach great importance to ethics and social responsibility, and to implement CSR practices in their companies."

Susan Cholette(2014) concentrates on Social entrepreneurial venture (SEVs) which encounter one of a kind social and ecological issues that test their missions. For instance, little rising firms ordinarily outsource a large portion of their generation and dispersion capacities to store network accomplices, without much use. What parts of corporate social responsibility (CSR) are most effectively grasped by SEVs, and what store network administration issues do they confront? How would they prevail with regards to unraveling esteem clashes with their social mission, and when are CSR store network exchange offs essential? These inquiries are researched through an exploratory different cases investigation of four such little farming ward SEVs situated in the San Francisco Bay Area. From the graphic bits of knowledge picked up by concentrate the arrangements and common focal points little SEVs have, and also the exchange offs made, he proposed potential administrative ramifications for comparative rising SEVs and make recommendations for additionally explore on these sorts of organizations.

Wim Dubbinik(2008) talks about the points of interest and inconveniences of two regular approach procedures: the assistance arrangement and the summon and control methodology. Utilizing three criteria, (proficiency, opportunity and ethicalness) we reason that the two procedures are faulty. Most consideration is paid' to the assistance system since governments these days basically utilize this. In assessing this methodology we break down the Dutch case. As an option he presented a third government arrangement: the improvement of an automatic sub-framework.

Ewa Stawicka(2015) showcased business entities interest in implementing the CSR practices; using aid programs and discuss the issues of various approaches to the dissemination of CSR practices in the SME sector. "Almost all the business entities interested in the PARP aid program and implementing socially responsible actions declared an activity in two areas: employees and natural environment." CSR implementation within the market and society is a less frequent and common action and it occurs as planned or under development."

Matthias G Will et al (2014) took both a theoretical and an observational way to deal with answer the inquiry in the matter of how Corporate Social Responsibility (CSR) can be associated with the organization's part as an operator of social esteem creation. To build up a utilitarian outline for an exact examination, we draw on the idea of ordonomics, which gives a heuristics to capable business exercises in the public arena.

David Evans (2010) explains why corporate social responsibility, is vital. Giving a three-letter acronym (CSR) to the enormous area of social responsibility concerns me because it risks becoming just another corporate badge, heavily displayed but lightly borne."

W. Michael Hoffman et al (2007) explored how senior members and executives at the best 50 worldwide MBA programs react to inquiries regarding the incorporation and scope of the points of morals, corporate social duty, and supportability at their particular foundations. This work intentionally researches each of the three points independently.

Alan Muller et al (2008) concentrated on created nations. The sparse writing on the subject, which generally recommended that CSR was moderately immature in developing markets, has as of late investigated the setting specificity, proposing that it is extraordinary and mirrors the particular social and political foundation." This would especially apply to nearby organizations, less to outside backups of multinationals dynamic in developing markets. Hitherto, exact research that methodically archives a scope of CSR exercises of neighborhood organizations and their execution has been rare. This paper reports the aftereffects of a review led among organizations in the Mexican vehicle industry. "

Wayne Visser (2015) focused on Integrated Value Creation, or IVC, is an important evolution of the corporate responsibility; and sustainability movement. More than a new concept, IVC is a methodology for turning the proliferation of societal aspirations and stakeholder expectations, including numerous global guidelines, codes, and standards covering the social, ethical, and environmental responsibilities of business, into a credible corporate response without undermining the viability of the business. Practically, IVC helps a company integrate its response to stakeholder expectations (using materiality analysis) through its management systems (using best governance practices) and value chain linkages (using life cycle thinking)."

Claire Johnson (2015) concentrated on corporate volunteering (CV) is known to be a compelling representative engagement activity. Notwithstanding, in spite of the unmistakable quality of corporate social responsibility (CSR) in the scholarly community and practice, look into is yet to explore whether and how CV may influence purchaser impression of CSR picture and resulting shopper conduct. Information gathered utilizing an online review in Australia; demonstrate saw recognition with an organization's

CV program to decidedly affect CSR picture and firm picture, halfway interceded by others-focused attributions. CSR picture, thusly, fortifies full of feeling and subjective steadfastness and additionally verbal. Advance examination uncovers the directing impact of saw utilizing of the corporate volunteering program, client status and the esteem people put on CSR. The paper closes with hypothetical and administrative ramifications, and additionally a plan for future research."

Dirk Michael Boehe(2010) analyzed how multinational companies (MNCs); from the retail area manage four difficulties they confront while receiving Corporate Social Responsibility (CSR) strategies: the test of growing great performing CSR activities and projects, building upper hands in view of CSR, reacting to neighborhood partner issues in the host nations and gaining from various CSR encounters; on an overall premise. In light of top to bottom contextual analyses of two all around driving retail MNCs (with solid operations in Latin America), the idea of Transverse CSR Management rose. Transverse CSR Management is defined as a particular type of authoritative configuration that crosses diverse useful regions, nation operations, and the limits of the firm.

Vidhi A. Chaudhri(2009) exhibited a system; of organizing alternatives accessible to worldwide companies. To better elucidate the difficulties required in sorting out worldwide CSR, some characteristic factors that may affect the level of globalization or potentially restriction of an enterprise's CSR activities are likewise talked about. The examination infers that, in conceptualizing worldwide CSR, it is hard to give programs a role as being completely worldwide or nearby; rather, contingent upon their remarkable nature and the extent of execution, worldwide CSR activities may fall along a continuum.

Benedict Sheehy (2014) swung to approach the issue of definition; utilizing the theory of science. It applies a scientific definition approach of sort, differential and species to touch base at a definition of CSR as universal private business self-control. The article gives a diagram of the ramifications of this definition on CSR as a field of study, an administration rehearse and a way to deal with enhancing the discourse concerning the social commitment of business.

RESEARCH METHODOLOGY

This study on "Study on Employees Perceptive regarding CSR Initiatives of the Companies in India" is a small effort through a primary research wherein a questionnaire was prepared with 13 questions and the sample size was 30 employees of different companies across India.

Objectives of the Study

The main objective of the research is to study and analyze the perception and awareness of the employees with respect to CSR activities of the company.

Hypothesis

- **Null Hypothesis:** Employees has significant awareness about CSR activities of the company.
- **Alternate Hypothesis:** Employees have significant awareness about CSR activities of the company.

For the purpose of this study data was conducted through survey among the top employees of the following companies in India:

- Orient Paper and Industries Limited
- South Eastern Coal Fields Limited
- Thermal Power Plant, Chachai
- Thermal Power Plant, Jaithari
- Gujarat National Fertilizer Corporation
- Bhilai Steel Plant
- Infosys
- Tata Consultancy Services
- Wipro
- Accenture
- SRF limited
- Cadbury
- Hindustan Unilever

DATA ANALYSIS AND INTERPRETATION

Based on the questionnaire and response received from the employees of various companies following interpretations were concluded in this study:

Figure 1 Analysis

We can analyse from the pie chart in Figure 1 that almost sixty percent of the employees have the knowledge about CSR activities and abide to them in their respective companies. This means that most of the employees have awareness about the CSR activities in the organizational scenario.

Figure 1. Knowledge about the theme of corporate social responsibility of the company

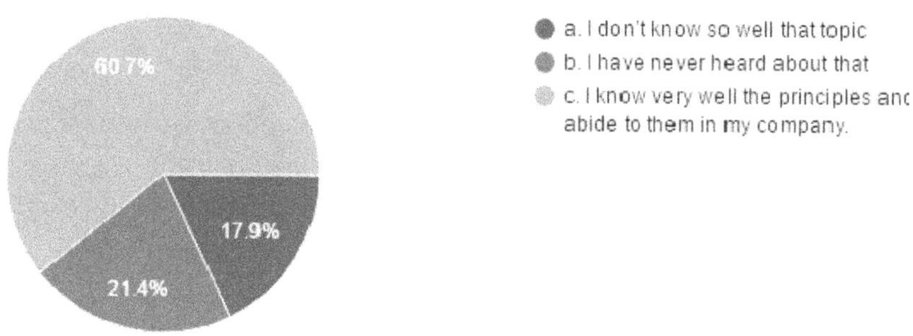

Figure 2. Area of social responsibility which is more significant for the company in CSR

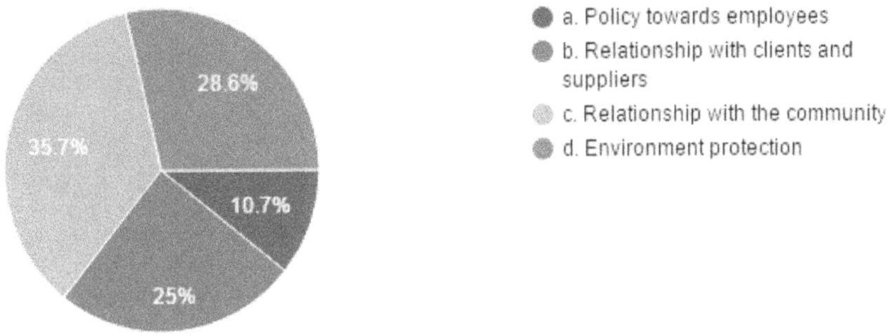

Figure 2 Analysis

From the representation in Figure 2, we can analyse that CSR operations vary from firm to firm, like for some relationship with community is significantly focused on; wherein some focus on environmental protection while others can focus on suppliers or clients.

Figure 3 Analysis

Most of the employee's i.e around 50 percent of them thinks positive about the fact that profit has shooted up due CSR activities while around 25 percent feel neutral about the fact. It means CSR has positive impact on the profitability of the company in India.

Figure 4 Analysis

Most of the employees' i.e more than 50 percent thinks positive about the fact that revenue of the company has also increased due to involvement of the company in CSR activities, while 30 percent are neutral with this statement that revenue has taken an upsurge.

Figure 3. Profit generated by the company shooted due to CSR activities

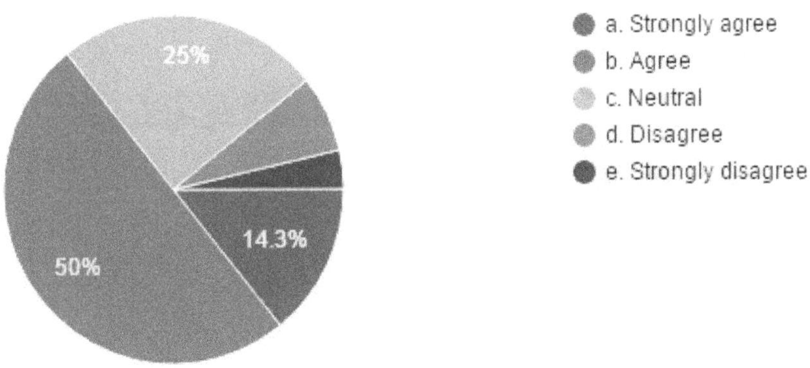

Figure 4. If revenue of the company for the particular year has taken an upsurge due to CSR initiatives

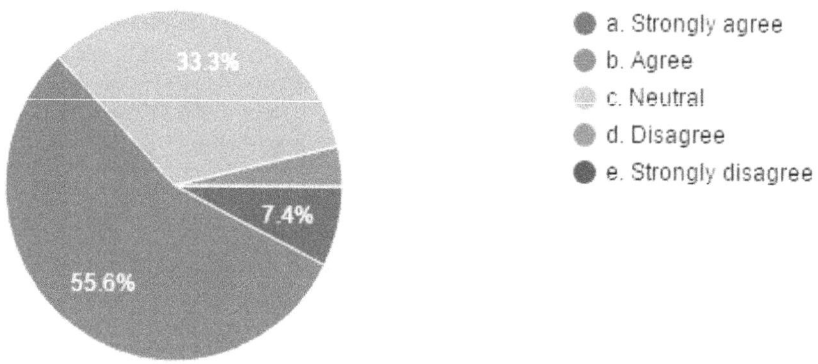

Figure 5 Analysis

More than 50 percent of the people support the fact that practices of responsible business have helped the company in realizing significant operations. According to survey 51% of the respondents think that most of the CSR operations are in the field of practices of responsible business, 33 percent activities are in the area of health and development of employees. According to our survey 22% of the CSR activities are dedicated towards climate change.

Figure 6 Analysis

Most of the companies use social budget and intangible capital budget for their operations.

Figure 7 Analysis

Most of the companies think that employee retention and overtime are the major problematic areas of the company according to the graph.

Figure 5. In which of the following areas your company has realized significant operations?

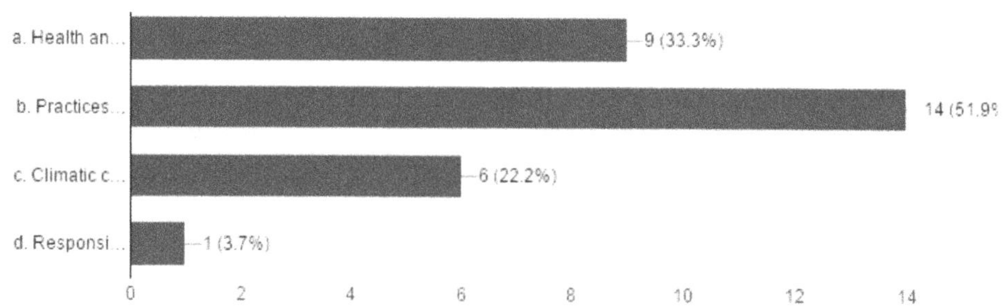

Figure 6. CSR activities used by the companies in India

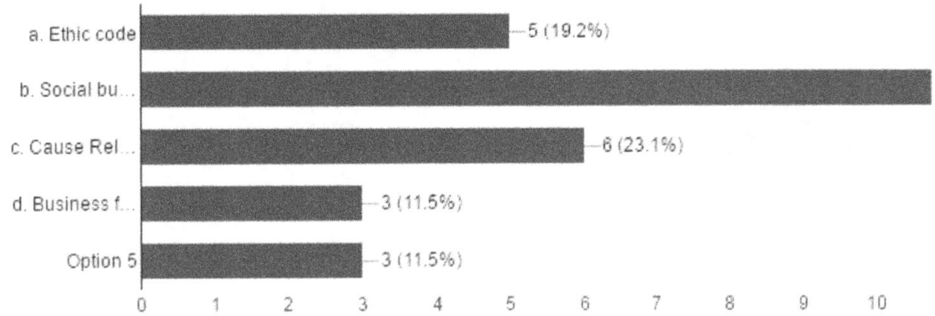

Figure 7. Major problematic areas of your companies in India

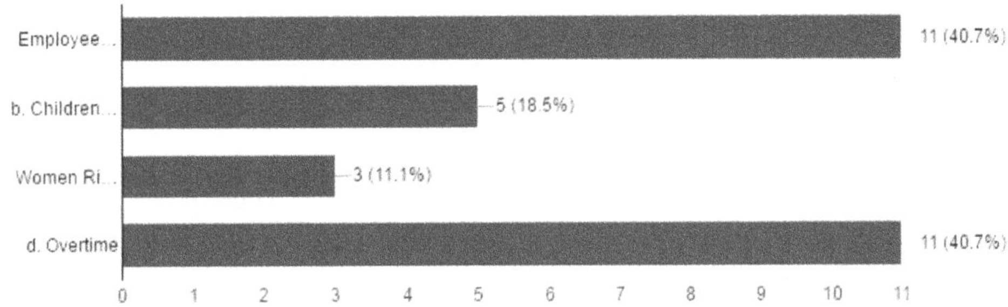

Figure 8 Analysis

We can see that most of the companies use energy saving techniques while many of them use waste recycling methods.

Figure 9 Analysis

Most of the companies, as we can see from the pie chart indulge in donations to various institutions while some of them work for cause related marketing. Thus this is all community oriented in most of the cases.

Figure 8. Measures adopted by the companies to reduce environmental impact in India

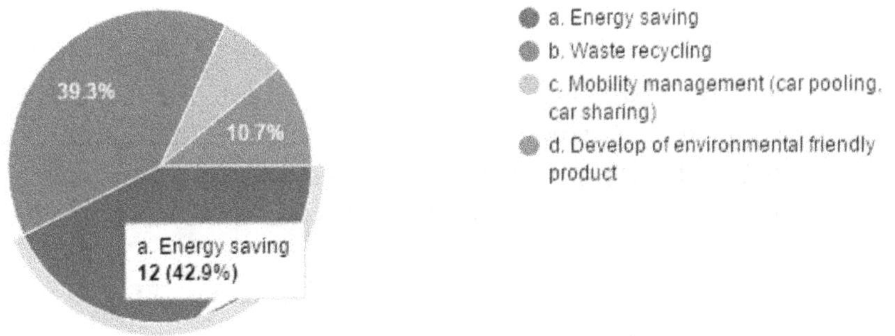

Figure 9. Concrete contributions towards community which the companies are doing in India

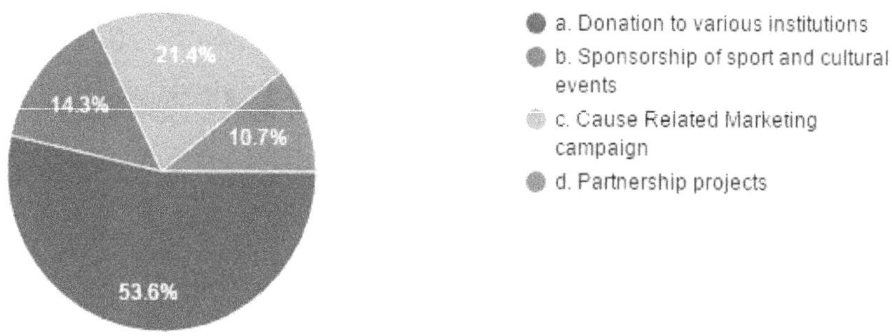

Figure 10 Analysis

For greater transparency most of the companies try to communicate clear information about their product and services.

Figure 11 Analysis

As seen from Figure 11, the main benefit of social responsibility can be improved relations with suppliers, institutions, donors and community.

Figure 12 Analysis

Major problematic areas are lack of specific legislation on CSR, for some business may take time to set up and benefits are not immediate while lack of knowledge can also be one of the major problems.

Figure 13 Analysis

From Figure 13, we can see that that most of the companies are taking innovative measures to go eco-friendly and develop new products and services which help them to reduce environmental problems.

CONCLUSION

From above study we can conclude following point's w.r.t. employees' awareness about CSR practices of the companies in India

1. Since most of the employees have the knowledge about CSR activities and abide to them in their respective companies, there is awareness about the CSR activities in the organisational scenario.
2. CSR operations vary from firm to firm, like for some relationship with community is significantly focused on, wherein some focus on environmental protection while others can focus on suppliers or clients.

Figure 10. For greater transparency of the market in which you operate, practices companies has started using in India

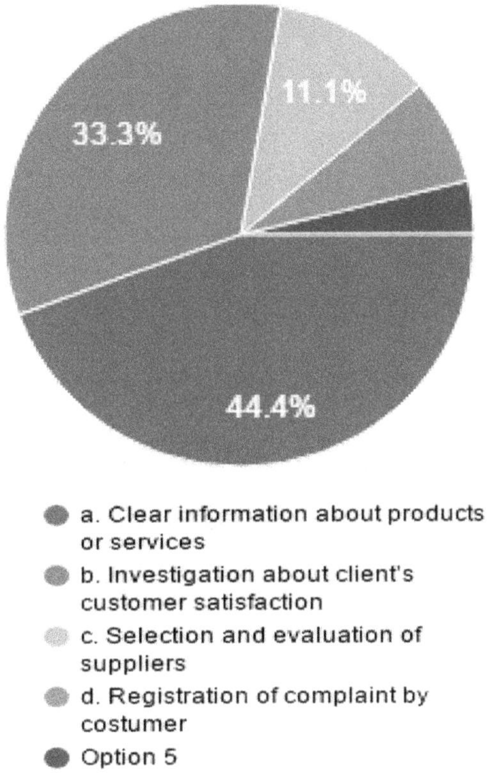

Figure 11. Main benefit of the adoption of measures for social responsibility

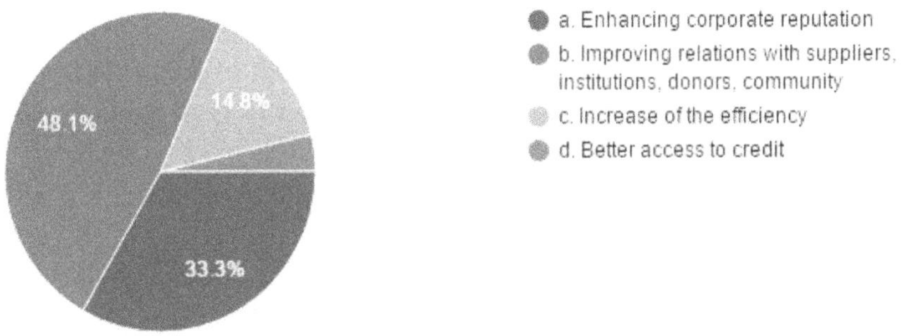

3. Most of the employees think positive about the fact that profit has shooted up due CSR activities.
4. Most of the employees think positive about the fact that revenue has taken an upsurge while some of them are neutral.
5. More than 50% of the people support the fact that practices of responsible business have helped the company in realising significant operations.
6. Most of the companies use social budget and intangible capital budget for their operations as CSR action.

Figure 12. Problems related to the development of initiatives in the field of social responsibility by the companies in India

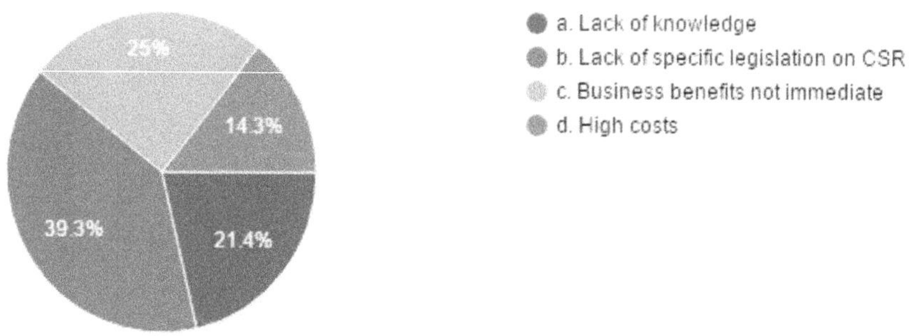

Figure 13. CSR activities we want to realize in the upcoming years in our company

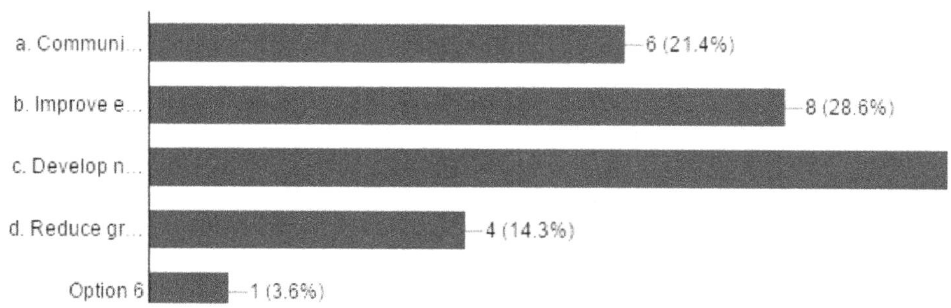

7. Most of the employees think that employee retention and overtime are the major problematic areas of the company.
8. We can see that most of the companies use energy saving techniques while many of them use waste recycling methods.
9. Most of the companies, as we can see from the pie chart indulge in donations to various institutions while some of them work for cause related marketing. Thus this is all community oriented in most of the cases.
10. For greater transparency most of the companies try to communicate clear information about their product and services..
11. Major problematic areas are lack of specific legislation on CSR, for some business may take time to set up and benefits are not immediate while lack of knowledge can also be one of the major problems.

REFERENCES

Alessandra, M. (2014). Backshoring, Local Sweatshop Regimes and CSR in India. Competition and Change, 18(4), 327–44.

Austin. (2000). Do Corporates Have Social Responsibility? A Case Study of TVS Motor Company. *The Icfai University Journal of Corporate Governance, 8*(3-4), 131-138.

Ghosh. (2015). Proactive Communication of CSR in India: A Distant Dream or Reality? *Paradigm, 19*(2), 115–136. Retrieved from http://par.sagepub.com

Gilmore. (2012). CSR Communication in Emerging Economies: Need for a New Paradigm: A Case Study of a Multinational and an Indian Trans National's CSR Communication in India. *IJBIT, 6*(4), 66-77.

Johnson. (2015). MNC CSR in Emerging Economy Conflict Zones A Case Study of HUL's North East Operations in India. *Vikalpa, 38*(4), 69-82.

Madhavi. (2015). A Study of the CSR Policies and Practices of Indian Companies. *DAWN: Journal for Contemporary Research in Management*, 17-26.

Muller & Kolk. (2009, October). Economic Empowerment Through Microfinance: An Assessment of CSR Activity run by Forbes Marshall Ltd. *International Journal of Business Insights & Transformation*, 64-74.

Nair, N. K., & Sodhi, J. S. (2012, April). CSR Practices by SMEs in India: Lessons from Five Case Studies. *Indian Journal of Industrial Relations, 47*(4).

Philippa, W. (2013). Corporate Sustainability/CSR and the Influence of the Independent Director: "100% Pure." *European Conference on Management, Leadership & Governance*, 372-380.

Zahler. (2015). An Analysis of CSR Expenditure by Indian Companies. *Indian Journal of Corporate Governance, 7*(2), 82-94.

Zhao. (2012). Efficient Water Management through Public Private Partnership Model: An Experiment in CSR by Coca Cola India. *Vikalpa, 38*(4), 97.

Section 4
Behavioral Corporate Finance

Chapter 13
The Impact of Tax Policies on Behavior of Albanian Taxpayers

Dorina Plaku
Epoka University, Albania

Eglantina Hysa
Epoka University, Albania

ABSTRACT

The Albanian state has experienced many changes of this system over the years due to the policies and different regimes that have followed, but there has always been a tendency for improvement. The tax system and the informality are the mirror of the economy of the country, especially the favorable tax/fiscal policies that have been adapted to the economy, which bring economic development and integration of all the gaps to a proper economic environment. The chapter aims to find the effects of tax changes on the taxpayers. Furthermore, the study focuses on how the business performance has been indicated from the tax control. The data is collected from a survey which was focused in small and big businesses that operates in the capital city of Albania, in Tirana. The questionnaire is realized during April 2018. The main finds of the study are the different perception of businesses for the tax control and the impact of the fiscal changes on these businesses. All these fiscal changes that the businesses faced were more in disfavor of the small businesses.

INTRODUCTION

The tax system has always been treated as one of the most important factors in the economy of the country. It has created a strong relationship between the system, the state, the economy, businesses and taxpayers. The burial system has never shifted to its rustic form but it has always been in line with the changes. Moreover, the tax system is seen as a kind of harmonization between different countries. By using preferential and stimulating policies, has developed a fair and profitable trade for each of the two trading partners. The way that one country decides to develop the tax system, shows clearly the economy of the country and that's why the developed countries give a big boost to it. They believe that through this system they can create a sustainable economy and government. With the economic changes of our

DOI: 10.4018/978-1-5225-7399-9.ch013

country, of the regions and the countries which are in the process of being part of the EU, fiscal policies remain the only macroeconomic policies with which government can operatory within their territory.

Over the years like any other aspect of the economy, concepts and features of the fiscal system began to be improved and more detailed. Practices have shown that the fiscal system is a stratification of rules. From time to time or year to year the fiscal system needs to be updated but always in the way to reach an optimal fiscal system. An optimal fiscal system will be optimal when the fiscal burden is fairly distributed through tax payers, when taxes do not cause distortions in taxpayer behavior or in investors in different sectors or in industries. The tax system in the Republic of Albanian state has had a continuous sustainable development during the development period of the Albanian state up to the present day. The study and the analysis of this system are really crucial not only at its doctrinal level but above all in the practical aspect of this concept. Our country has gone through all of the political systems that could have passed and each one has left a culture somewhere developed and somewhere not developed. However, we try to decrease the level of the informality and to increase the level of the development of the fiscal system. Even the fiscal policies that have been set up have a great deal of power, and all the theories that exist for them or the precise establishment of an optimal system were clearly shown that favoring policies do not bring unnecessary consequences to the economy and to a wage. Favorable policies are all those policies that do not express a tax burden or a high tax obligation, any changes that may be made to this policy are the first that they are reacting to and are skeptical, where they are normally always expected a response from the most important part of a tax system. Fiscal policies and their changes have a major impact on increasing or decreasing the level of GDP in the world, affecting inflation, unemployment, and the well-being of a single person. Therefore, the level of taxes should be kept at the allowed rates which can negatively affect all the above elements. Nowadays the countries all over the world are in an open struggle between them to have a developed economy and are competing with each other to increase as much as the number of foreign investors. Hence favoring and developing the appropriate tax policies would help to attract foreign investors and affect the growth of the economy. Taxpayers are also interested in more favorable policies, but they do not pose a high level of trust in the entire tax system, perhaps from the point of view of how this system has developed and the drastic changes it has had, or perhaps even from a non-developed culture of how the whole system works. None of the taxpayers have the proper for the way that their money is administrated, no one has the confidence that this money is a return and investment for them, or even that will ever have compensation. All these uncertainties have begun earlier, at a time when the system was not set up to the fullest extent possible and brought the informality that taxpayers were adapted to it and all this tax audit that took place in the period 2014-2015 and that continues today, found no-prepared all the taxpayers and businesses.

Albania is the country with the lowest level of tax revenues, compared to most of the countries in the region. The key findings of this research were mainly regarding the perception of big and small businesses about the frequent changes of the fiscal policies. The whole situation that was created for this issue makes small businesses to trust less the law, the inspectors and the tax legislation. From the data collection, it can be said that small businesses believe that all the tax action was realized for them. Moreover, from the survey it comes out that both categories of businesses need to be trained for the tax policies and they believe that such frequent changes on tax policies have e negative impact on the businesses' performance and in the entire economy.

Objectives and Purpose

The purpose of choosing this topic, besides being one of my favorite fields, is moreover a modest study of all this change in the Albanian tax system. What I'm most interested in is about how taxpayers have responded to all of this tax control that has been made to them. Are they able to adapt all this change in the fastest possible way and at the same time in the right way? Are these taxpayers aware of the evasion they have caused throughout these years? Even the Albanian tax system, along with all its competent bodies, throughout the tax audit seemed to exert pressure on the business and slow down its activity.

The research question of the chapter is more focused on how taxpayers have understood all this change in the tax system. More specifically, the study's research question consists: how the perception of the major groups of the businesses is (small and big businesses) related to all this tax control and fiscal changes.

Objectives: Apart from the main goal of the study, there are some objectives that are very helpful to the research question:

The perception of the Big Businesses and Small Businesses in the changes of tax policies

1. To take a general look at how the tax system has changed in Albania
2. To compare Albanian tax system with the region
3. To study the overall perception of the businesses that operates in the Albanian market.

BACKGROUND

Tax System in Albania and Changes Though the Time

The fiscal system is a mechanism that has existed since the early days where people lived in communion. Even if the payments of the fiscal policies were not in monetary terms, the philosophy remains the same. After that period, we had a more advanced system from the creation of ancient Greece, followed then by Ottoman Emperors and continuing further whuch has take a great importance that continues to his days. While modern fiscal systems appeared in Western Europe and North-America during the mid-century. A that time we can not say that it was the proper fiscal system but it could be called the beginning of a new area in the fiscal aspect and onlu in the 11th century was created the basic legal framework for imposing taxes at the right way. One of the oldest books for tax systems that says a little more contemporary at that time, and which continues to be the benchmark for creating more moderate systems is that of researcher Casey, where the book titled is Tax planning ideas, 1966. The tax system in various parts of the world has had very important evolutions and major changes, always in its continuous improvement. In practice there is no perfect tax system in any part of the world, although economic analysis is mainly focused on how taxes should be imposed to boost economic efficiency and promote a fair distribution of income to the state and at the same time as public spending. Although there are no "perfect" systems, the ways these systems are designed have essentially economic prosperity (Mirrlees et al., 2011). Yet due to the complexity of the tax planning, it cannot be said to have a unified and very clear definition (Spitz, B., 1972) for the taxation system but based on all the knowledge adopted during the development of various causes related to the fiscal system, we can reach an all-inclusive definition of the tax system:

- **Tax System:** is been defined as the entirety of harmonized, rational, effective, flexible and appropriate forms of taxation in the realization of the economic, social development goals of a state.

The tax system is the base for creating a state budget, because in the end, modern and industrialized societies do not have a budget-free state, and there is no budget without a public revenue system or a tax-free system. Tax planning is legal from a legal point of view but is more necessary from an academic point of view (Rieger, H 1978).

Creating a tax system by itself is not creating some rules or institutions that merely serve to collect taxes. Practice has shown that the fiscal system is a stratification of the right rules. Year after year, the fiscal system around the world has needed important adjustments, always taking into account the fact or aiming at achieving the creation of an optimal system. It will be called optimal when the fiscal policy is fairly distributed through taxpayers or is more explicit when taxes do not cause distortions in taxpayer behavior or decisions or investors in different sectors or industries. The first initiative to create an optimal fiscal system (Ramsey, 1927) and (Atkinson 1971). Two other researchers such as Mirrles (1971) and Vicrey (1996) model formula and economic equations based on a system where economic information is asymmetric or ubiquitously incomplete, sending to what is called "Hazard Moral".

Creating a proper tax system would mean creating a better economy and a better prosperity for the population of a country (Scharpf, F. W., & Schmidt, V. A. (Eds.). (2000). We have to say that tax planning has a very important role in any financial organization, industrial enterprises, but also in oriented services. It is very difficult to compare financial systems between countries, because it may indicate different factors on it, such as macroeconomic, geographic, or why not the history of the country. The number of population, the taxpayer behavior, the geographical and the historical conditions are elements that affect the type and nature of taxes. Normally, to have a proper tax system, there are some standards that should be part of the system and these standards are: economic effectiveness, simplicity, flexibility, transparency and justice. However, we have to say that tax systems in all countries of the world had and have the same basis in which they focused on creating a unified system and it is not very different from other countries (Board, J., Sutcliffe, C., Ziemba, WT, 2003). Despite the differences between the countries, due to the factors mentioned above, we can say that the states have always established among themselves several favorable multinational policies to help different businesses invest where they want (Finnerty, CJ, Merks, P., Petriccione, M., Russo, R., 2007). Two other authors have shown that appropriate international fiscal policies and policies may have and have had a positive effect on increasing foreign direct investment and increasing the economy of many countries.

In the foreign literature one of whom was titled "Equity and Tax Planning", which was developed for the tax system in Spain, the authors clearly indicated that the clear design of a tax system is in most cases a scary tax. Economies have become and are becoming increasingly complex, which causes the fiscal system to change frequently and consistently to suitably taxpayers (Duran-Cabre.J and Esteller-More, A, 2014). It is not so important how the fiscal policies are drafted for an optimal system, the more important is the way they understand these policies than those directly affected by those that are neither less nor more than the taxpayer. To talk about the advantages or disadvantages of a system, you should compare the country and the taxpayer's reaction before deciding this policy and also after imposing a fiscal policy (Schanz.S, 2008).

Tax Policies as Part of the Fiscal System

In some countries of the European Union, some studies have been carried out on how the fiscal system changes indicate in the state budget. This is about the way of how a state achieves a harmony between the costs and revenues that generates a system of a given state (Wagner, 1976, Pommerehne 1978). A country that has the most revenue and a certain level of public spending indicates a good future for that country and a sovereign state budget, which is not possible for any country in European countries and moreover, because the frequent changes in fiscal policies and other financial policies (Roig-Alonso, M. (1998). Fiscal system is not just a term that needs to be updated or improved at all times. But it is such a subtle economic process, as it has many fiscal and tax policies, taxpayers, agents, etc. or we can call it as one of the most important processes of a country's economic planning, which means that to this system should be given a very great importance. At the beginning the tax system was mainly built for corporations. Generally, in all countries of the world, there were more corporations than other business units. And since corporations had profits or even high earnings during the economic activity, the politicians of the respective states began to use them as way of generating the most revenue in the state budget, so they created the right policies for set a balance between public spending and revenues generated by corporations Oates, W. E. (1969).

The optimum tax system, or a system that has no irregularities and no deficiencies, still does not exists, even in countries such as the United States or Germany that are a world superpower, frequent changes in the fiscal system and fiscal policies have led to many irregularities and quite dissatisfaction for the taxpayer. To create a proper fiscal system, or at least rely on some rules that need to be taken into account by states when designing the system, and those rules are (Smith, S. 1992)

- Each subject should contribute in order to support its government as much as possible in the means of revenue that it will generate.
- The tax that everyone has to pay must be fair, safe, in favor of entities or taxpayers, and not arbitrary.
- Each of the taxes or any other tax liability should be taken at those times that are most appropriate for the contributor to pay.
- Each of the taxes should be taken and kept out of the system as little as possible.

The power of a tax system does not depend only on the number of entities that one country has, but on the income that the state generates. The tax resource consists mostly: incomes, rent, profit, land, property (Kryeziu R, 2014) etc. and all this should be factual in order to give to the legislator the opportunity to decide in which form he/she will apply the taxes (Leibfritz.W, Thornton, J and Bibbee, 1997). It is not only the creation of a tax system that is important but also the administration of a particular tax system because the proper administration brings wide system consistency and a harmonization for all system components. The administration of the tax system requires a recognition of the costs incurred by it. Recognized direct costs are costs of the operation of the tax authorities. Indirect costs include a variety of forms such as: the cost of time used to collect tax declaration forms, the costs of keeping accounting records, the cost of tax consultants' rewards.

Until now we have mentioned fiscal policies that are an integral part, or that they are the epicenter of a tax system. Monetary policy and fiscal policies have been the most discussed and analyzed topics from many different scholars around the world, showing very clearly that establishing or creating appropriate fiscal policies would be the future of a country. For fiscal policies, many different studies were conducted in the Eurozone, pointing to the importance of the latter for this continent, but not only for the Eurozone, but also for developing countries, a study has been carried out to see the effect of tax policies on their development.

The most important principle of fiscal policy is described by the following authors:

The primary purpose of the taxation process, or so-called fiscal policy, is to transfer the control of resources from one group to another in a society and realized in such a way that it does not compromise, but rather helps in realizing other economic goals (Break.G. F 1975). But fiscal policies also include taxes, agents, taxation rates, tax obligations, but above all, taxpayers who are the most disadvantaged in this tax system. In a study conducted in Romania, after the 2008 crisis, all fiscal policies were changed so as to make possible the recovery of the economy in general, but they also came to another conclusion that fiscal policies are not merely a main objective simply economic growth, but also the consolidation of public finances (Dinu, M., & Marinaş, M. C. (2014)). For the planning of appropriate tax policies, it is also necessary to look at the composition of the policy or government of a state (Welsch, G.A., Anthony, R.N., 1974). But fiscal policies are also discrete, and the primary purpose of these policies is their impact on the economy of a country.

Discrete fiscal policies are supposed to help to achieve some macroeconomic parameters such as the optimal level of employment, price stability and economic growth, and they consist of executive and legislative powers of the state through government spending programs and taxes. Fiscal policies are part of a law process and the state budget and these discrete policies cannot act immediately (Auerbach, A. J., & Gale, W. G. 2009). After the global crisis that generally caught up in all countries, we can say that discretionary policies are not giving the proper effect and stabilizing various macroeconomic cycles (Feldstein, 2009). According to Colbert, "The art of taxation consists of such a level of taxation in order to provide a multitude of possible revenue, with the minimum of taxpayer response. For taxes and fees there is a division of the specifications under clearly defined laws, they appear to be the same, but they really have other meanings, because each one is designed for a particular purpose. The tax according to Law no. 9920 is hereby amended as follows:

According to James.S, 2001, the tax has certain characteristics such as: that the tax lacks the condition of direct return or compensation or are such unanticipated inputs in the case general.

It should be said that taxes are the element that has changed more in a particular fiscal system, for every given exchange there is a certain tax and every source or profit has a set tax and that is paid by all. While the tax has another definition in law 9920, but very close to that of tax, with small differences:

- **Tax:** It is a compulsory and irrevocable payment in the state budget, but also in the budget of certain local government organs, established by law and it is paid by any person who benefits from a public right or even benefits one public service in the Republic of Albania.

The tax has its own characteristics, such as: they are mainly monetary revenues in local state organs, are also voluntary, and from a financial point of view the role of taxes is less important than that of taxation. Many scholars have taken over the review and study of any tax, because they are among the most numerous. We can start with the dividend that is made on taxes and where a general dividend is given as direct taxes and indirect taxes. Direct taxes are all taxes that impede income, real ownership, dividends and these taxes are paid directly by the responsible persons and are deposited in the state budget. Direct taxes are divided into progressive taxes and proportional taxes, each of which has its own characteristics, because progressive tax has a different percentage of tax base application, while the other tax has a different percentage of tax base application. However, in the history of taxes, different forms of taxation are known as proportional, progressive, regressive and flat. Each of these systems is distinguished by the type of fee that is applied to the tax object for its calculation (Liaropoulos, L., & Tragakes, E. (1998). Indirect taxes or indirect taxation, which is mainly due to taxation of consumption, where this is realized by taxation of the price of products and services and is paid by consumers in their indirect way because the introduction of these taxes into the state budget is done by the subject itself or entity that carries out other actions with the fiscal system.

For all types of tax, have been conducted a lot of different studies, ranging from direct and indirect taxation. We can say that studies have started with income taxes, which are seen as one of the most important direct taxes and which occupy a large volume of revenues accruing from taxes to the state budget (Madura, 2004). Exactly is the consumption tax, a typical example of indirect taxation (Hall.R E and Rabushka, 1983). But not just for consumption but also for other taxes such as taxation on international investment and savings (Gordon.R.H, 1986) Gordon 1992 also conducted a study on how different countries applied income tax. Profit tax and dividends are studied by (Chow, JF, 1974), while capital structure tax has been studied by Modigliani and Miller (Modigliani, F., Miller, MH, 1958), whereas in Europe the study of interest rate tax with cross-border strategies (Janeba, E. and Peters, W, 1999), while VAT has been studied by (Gordon.R.H, 1986). However, in the European Union, which is the cradle of tax, VAT is one of the most criticized by academics because of its frequent change and the many exemptions made for it, bringing a large reduction in state budget revenues.

Changes in Fiscal Policies and its Impact on the Economy

Fiscal policies have always been formed primarily for all large companies in a country and not for small businesses. Big corporations, or more precisely since corporations were best known, when creating a tax system, we can say that every policy was originally created and then generalized and regulated for medium companies, reaching even in small businesses. Fiscal policies have a huge impact on the performance of a country's economy and are among the key factors affecting any kind of small or small business. Normally taxes and fees for large businesses are more numerous and larger in size than tax obligations that small businesses (Chown J, 2000), at least in the countries of the world and mainly in Europe, this is visible. In various studies I've read mainly developed in Europe, we can say that often on big businesses there has been a pressure to pay tax obligations on the part of big companies and a liberalization or let's say a favor towards businesses small. Talking just about how the financial system affects businesses means that you've talked about much of the economy of a country. Throughout the review of the literature, I noticed that the fiscal policy and the tax system itself have a strong link to GDP and a certain place. In the study titled "Aggregate Demand, in Macroeconomics", it is mentioned very clearly the link between GDP and established taxes. There is a positive relationship between them.

$$AD = GDP = C + G + NX + I \quad (1)$$

Looking at the above formula we can clearly observe the way in which taxes affect the GDP of a state. All this is related to the types of fiscal policies (Mankiw, G, 2008). In the knowledge adapted to the development of different subjects, we have seen that we have two types of fiscal policies that are bound to fiscal policies, each of which has a certain use and importance. As noted by the formula consumption is indirectly taxed by the VAT, investments can be considered as a source and can be taxed at source and net exports include both imports and exports, where gross exports are not taxed, while imports have certain exceptions but mostly they are taxed.

According to many different authoritative policy makers, it means:

↓ t(taxation) / ↓ VAT / ↓ Excise => ↑ C and ↑ G => ↑ GDP,

but we are lowering taxes in general we have a ↑ I and we will have an unemployment ↓, in the budget deficit of the state. While restrictive fiscal policy is the opposite, that would mean a ↓ of GDP and a ↓ I and an increase in inflation and unemployment and (Mikesell, J). As it is mentioned above one of the most important taxes and that many studies have been done by many different, we can say that is income taxes. One of these studies had to do with the method of amortization of the tax evasion of monetary flows that are uncertain in the future (Berg, M., Waegenaere, A.D., Wielhouwer, J.L., 2001). This study clearly stated the fact that taxpayers interact with tax agents to enable them to intervene in the amortization of their income, so that the tax burden they have to pay is lower, so they do not believe they will have, any major returns and by the state after the payment of tax liabilities at the disposal of these taxpayers

Taxpayers

The effect of the notice is the impact on the economy of introducing a new tax that is not absorbed instantly. Some tax effects can be recognized and before the introduction of a tax change only through the relevant notice. The fact that the effects of the announcement, otherwise known as the effects of the impact, may be very important explains the statement according to which: “An old tax is a good tax” (Buchanan J, 1999). Not only does the notification effect give rise to problems related to tax law, but even the anticipation of a future announcement may also provoke an increase in the spreading effect on prices or other tax-affected variables. In a study conducted in Spain in 2012, as its economy was not at the right levels and local taxes and fees had changed a lot, it was noted that taxpayers, both large and small, felt some kind of insecurity and some kind of consent to such frequent changes in the tax system and fiscal policies. In the unilaterally distributed questionnaires, taxpayers stated that these changes are not in favor of the businesses or entities they have, but they are in favor of the failed Spanish policy and setting as much change as possible in these policies is more borer issues (Jose.D and Alejandro.M, 2014). Taxpayers are generally susceptible to any taxes and taxes imposed, they want to be highly informed and be prepared for any change in the fiscal system of the country they operate, but at the same time they require to have information about other countries where they can operate.

Different theories such as empirical and economic ones are the necessary and useful tools to study the behavior of taxpayers when there is a change in taxes, but also all other economic policies (Crawford and Fredman, 2010). A tax system should be transparent in order the citizens to recognize the tax burden they have to pay. Many well-known economists advise that it would be very positive that the state aims to be transparent to the contributors and does not misinform the taxpayers. According to this view, those types of taxation in which are clearly defined the subjects that will pay the tax liability are most preferable. For example, one of the taxes that can be considered as a good tax is the tax on profit, because the tax-paying companies are anonymous in carrying the burden. But from the aspect of transparency, profit tax is one of the most obvious because it is not visible to the one who actually pays the tax. Taxes are paid by people, not by institutions and are the shareholders, employees, clients and others who bear the tax burden on such a case.

Albanian Tax System During the Period 1991 Until Now

After the collapse of the communist regime, the economy of our country had a very different culture from those of the surrounding countries, even having a culture and economy even worse than all of its neighboring countries that also had a certain communist regime. Albania's economic and financial situation in this period is characterized by:

- Deep economic crisis and lack of legal certainty for the market economy.
- Lack of ownership right
- The "cultivated" psychology that Albania was the only country without taxes and taxes
- Lack of tax legislation and fiscal culture

In Albania, the first legal acts for the establishment of the tax system have their origin in 1991, a period corresponding to the drafting of tax legislation in the country, which was concrete with its announcement in January 1992, and then with issuing the Law on Income Tax on July 14, 1992. Tax legislation, which began to be implemented in 1992, can be considered as the foundation of the modern tax system. We can say that in these years there was a huge development and a significant improvement in the tax system, at least based on the laws that were read out for the tax system. At this time, the concepts of direct taxes and indirect taxes began to appear for the first time, each of which is included in certain taxes or fees. It was also understood and increased the importance of the revenue collected from the tax system and the impact of these in the economy of a country.

During the following years we can say that the Albanian state had a good performance of the cashier's system, but in 1997 it suffered a great financial crisis because of the pyramid schemes and the consequences of a disruption of the economy, were followed year after year onwards. The flat tax has been applied in Albania since 2007, having an immediate effect on revenue growth in 2008, before the outbreak of the global financial crisis. However, 2012 proved unsuccessful in its implementation because less than 10% of individuals actually reported income tax. From 2014 we have the progressive tax. Somewhat between 2007 and 2014, sometimes referred to as the years of restructuring and modernization of the tax system. In this period, a number of different laws for the reform of the financial system were drafted and adopted, among which we can mention the Law on Value Added Tax, the Law on Securities, the Law on Insurance and Reinsurance Activity, the Law on income tax, the law on tax procedures in the Republic of Albania, etc. These laws, together with the directives and recommendations of the European Union, are at the basis of the current legislation on the tax system in the Republic of Albania. Later in 2015, the big action is already known to avoid tax evasion and the increase in tax revenues that have been missing for years, sending a rise in the debt level, which still receives very high figures today a country like Albania.

EMPIRICAL RESULTS ON IMPACT OF TAX POLICIES ON BEHAVIOUR OF TAXPAYERS

Data Collection and Methodology

In order to measure the perception of the taxpayers regarding the fiscal changes, it is realized a questionnaire. All the questionnaires have been distributed in a direct contact with the finance chief or the company's financier and in indirect through accounting studios. The number of questionnaires sent was 230 in total, which 204 of them found valid, while the rest 26 were invalid for various factors that are not directly related to the disputed questionnaire but with the refusal to respond or the inability to complete the questionnaire by responsible persons such as financiers. The questionnaire is abandoned by 24 questions, where six of the first questions require general business information, while the rest of the questions are in line with the perception of the businesses regarding the tax policies. Out of these twenty-four questions, 15 of them are closed questions, one of them open questions and only 5 have a degree of appreciation, otherwise called liqueur degrees. The first, second and third questions are general information about entities. The four and fifth questions relate to each other in order to notice when the entities have started their activity and when they are made aware of the registration at QKB. The other questions are related to the tax action developed in this period and the type of penalties the entities have received, the tens of questions is a question that is different from the first because between accounting and fiscal laws there are many differences that often for many businesses have made possible the generation of different fines. The next and beyond are questions about which taxpayers think or allude to what is required, e.g. if they need training or not, which of the taxes think that there is a high burden on them and how much high, how have all this tax assessment been exercised, etc. This is a questionnaire based on a few readings and at the same time as the most recent reports of economic portals such as the IMF and a media outbreak of all this delayed initiative.

The questionnaires have been spread to small and big business and have been completed from responsible people during April 2018. The data which were taken from them was divided in two major groups (small and big businesses). The data has been excelled. After that, it is used SPS software to build ANOVA model in order to analyze them and to compare the results in the groups that previously were mentioned. Firstly, we will see the overall perception and then the impact of size on the perception. The study's variables are SB and BB independent variables and the perception is the dependent variable. Analysis variance (ANOVA) is used to analyze the differences among groups. Many authors state that ANOVA model is appropriate for comparing groups for statistical significance. In other words, it helps to determine whether there are statistically significant differences between groups. It is suited to a wide range of practical problems.

The tax system and the fiscal policies are widely dealt with by many different scholars in different perspective. Taxpayers have also developed studies of different types to study how these are affected and respond to any possible change in fiscal policies and laws. In this study will be analyzed the historical part of the tax system and more concretely the perception of the fiscal changes.

Questionnaire Analysis

The questionnaire is designed to have an argument and answer the research question and all the other questions that are have raised in order to achieve the results and the conclusions drawn. As it is shown above, this questionnaire is distributed in Tirana, with specified areas. In the 220 dispersed questionnaires, 204 of them are properly filled out by the responsible persons and are valid at the same time, while only 16 of them are not valid. Most of the entities from which the questionnaires were distributed were mainly in Tirana city. They were almost 204 completed questionnaires. They were split in an equal way: 86 big business and 118 small business.

As can be seen from the following chart it can be said that 45% of the entities that answered me in the questionnaire were retail trade, where most of them were small businesses, while the rest went to large businesses, followed by 37% of the entities have their wholesale trading activity, while in the smallest number of respondents were the production activities, with a 10% percentage and the service activity which, based on the responses received, results in a percentage of 8%. Production and service activity was very difficult for me to have direct contact with company financiers for different factors, who did not depend entirely on me.

The fifth and sixth questions are very related to each other, because in those two questions we will see when companies have actually started their activity and when they are registered at the National Registration Center. Most of the companies which were contacted, they state that they have a foreign capital and always show that they want to be ok with all the decisions and changes that the state has taken so they preferred to register in time in order to not create problems. Businesses that had operate for a short time in our market, which they were somewhere between 0 and 3 years, showed very clearly that their registration had taken place after the first tax audit, which means about 6% of them. While the businesses that had been operating for many years in the market showed that most of them in Tirana were registered in time, at the national business registration center where among them can be mentioned: Kosmonte Foods Albania, Delta Sh.pk, Neranxi, Albtelecom Albania, while another part in Tirana were registered after the tax action or were registered much later than when they initially started the activity.

The following graph indicates that the units were controlled by tax inspectors of the area but also by other responsible taxpayers as controllers who are not necessarily related to external inspectors. As can be seen in the graph above we can see that somewhere in 27 business units are checked only once by tax inspectors, this generally based on the generated questionnaires were more large and consolidated businesses and timely acting on the market ours, which means they had gained a trust from the tax authorities.

Figure 1. The kind of the business activity
Source: Authors

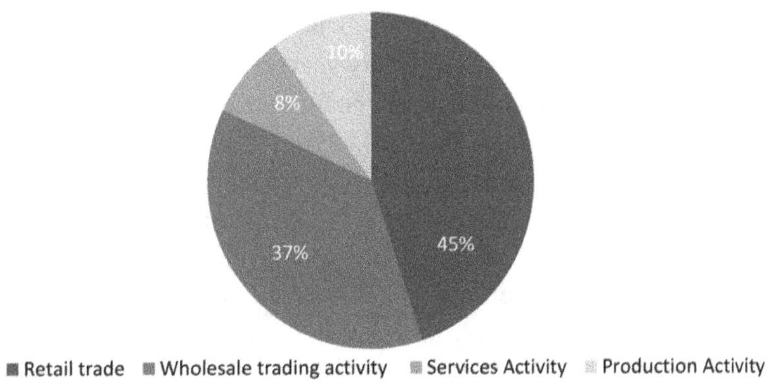

Figure 2. The duration that businesses have operated in the market
Source: Authors

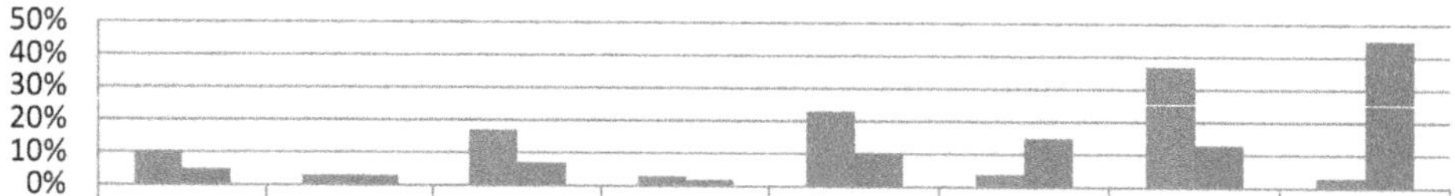

	Lower the number of employees	Lower the trading level	Increase the level of declarations	Accrue responsibilities	Create chaos until the procedures are set	Lower the level of investment in business	All the above	There was no impact
SB	10%	3%	17%	3%	23%	4%	37%	3%
BB	5%	3%	7%	2%	10%	15%	13%	45%

Figure 3. How many times the businesses have been controlled
Source: Authors

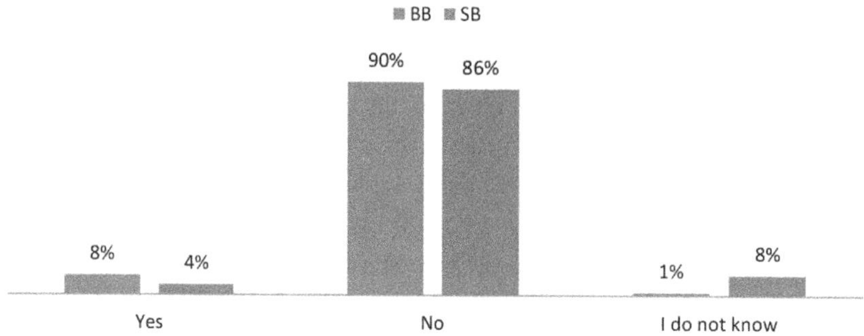

Most of the businesses were controlled more than twice, about 107 of the economics units within a specific period because we have to say it was more a control against small businesses. The entities that were controlled twice were the lowest in number, somewhere in 66 of them, whereas the entities that gave no response, since they were not controlled for this period were somewhere in 6 of them. Controlling each entity for a period of one year, more than twice is an inadequate economic policy or action, because frequent assignments exert a lot of pressure on the entity, preventing the continuation of the activity in a properly way.

Based on the graph above we notice that large financial units or businesses that are considered big have a lower number of fines. Businesses with a penalty are mostly the big businesses that most of them, which have made it possible to distribute the questionnaire, we can say that they have been operating in this market for years and are more careful about all the fiscal incentive systems. Even for businesses that have only received two more penalties are the SB. Based on this data it can be said that now that all this movement and this tax action has been taken by the government and the competent fiscal organization has aimed at the largest and at the same time fierce control of the SMEs that appear to be is not that they generate tax revenues for the state budget over the years for many factors. The number of fines imposed on small and medium-sized businesses can be said to be too high and at the same time very costly for these businesses.

Figure 4. The number of the penalties that the subjects have took
Source: Authors

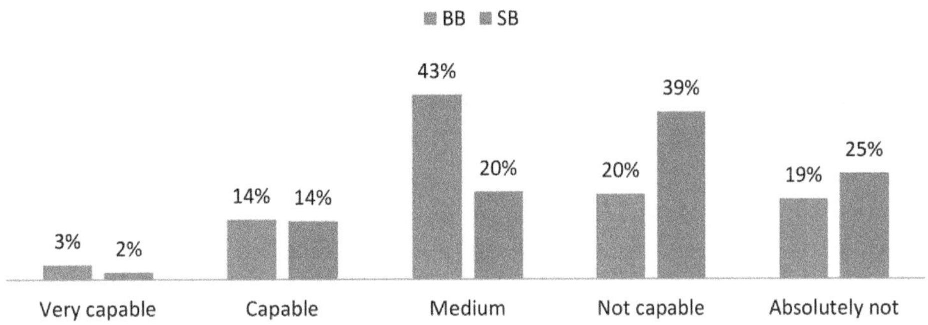

From all this it seems as if these entities are the cause of the low tax revenues, but this can not be left at the expense of these units, as many large businesses that have the operating hours in the market cause the highest percentages of fiscal evasion and it seems that they are not penalized and even continue to operate smoothly and providing even greater profits. But the question arises which are some of the penalties that big businesses provide and what are some of these penalties for small businesses?

Figure 5 shows clearly that a number of different penalties are taken by different entities based on the turnover they generate during the year. Clearly there are some penalties that both large and small businesses have in common. Failure to declare the obligation within the deadlines set out in the fiscal law seems to have been a common offense but that the big businesses were penalized, which showed that they often overlooked this penalty even because they saw it as a small cost and many of them showed that this was also due to the lack of time for all the actions that are being done in businesses. While the penalty that is almost equal for both large and small businesses is the penalty related to the non-payment of the tax liability within the deadline set in the fiscal laws for any tax.

It seems that the highest penalties for small and medium businesses have been related to not issuing a tax coupon, something that for big businesses is not a problem. The only penalty that has not been selected by all of my units in the study is not allowing tax control. The penalties that have only affected the large and non-cash business are the following: the failure to issue a tax invoice for goods that they can buy or sell, unaccompanied goods. Which means there are only two fines that have touched the big

Figure 5. Types of penalties received by entities
Source: Authors

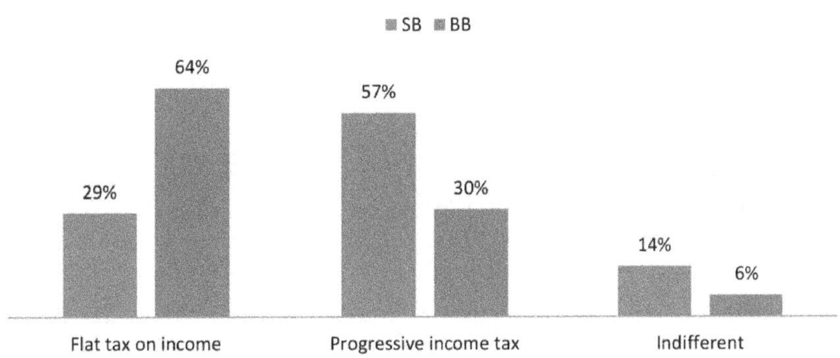

business, as opposed to the amount of penalties that have touched the small business. While the taxes that have affected SB and have not affected the big business are as follows: Failure to keep the right documents or purchase and sale books; no display of the price of traded products, no declaration of employees or even payments or receipts with amounts greater than 150000 ALL

The penalties that an entity can take are many, even though they may not have a direct link with the entire tax system. It has been heard for a long time by Albanian taxpayers, is a complaint about the level of this fine and the mistrust they have in its value, as well as the entire tax system, for many reasons by the most diverse but point of the first cultural one and not the proper development of this system over the years. Precisely with this tax audit that was developed, it is still believed by the entities that the level of fines generated for this period is simply a value set on an unrealistic and proper basis, but on the basis of the unknowns of the responsible persons.

The chart gives a summary of the evaluation of the respective people who have done the controll, where by filling out the questionnaire for the question of whether the level of penalties received is in full compliance with the rules and tax laws. Some entities (especially big busninesses) that had received a penalty thought that the level of the fine was in full compliance with the fiscal laws and at the same time affordable for the entity. While the rest of the entities have a lower estimation of how these high costs for the entity are met, especially small businesses.

Most of the entities in our country think that these penalties are of a very high value and cause very high costs for the unit, hindering the economic development of the entity as a whole. This shows some sort of untrustworthiness of businesses against persons involved in the development of relevant duties in the tax system and some kind of underestimation of the knowledge of these persons, perhaps because of other factors or due to delays in return of the response to these taxpayers. A very small proportion of financial analysts gave a positive rating to these individuals, while the rest of the financiers gave a moderate and lower estimate.

Regarding the question whether the entities have addressed to the Tirana Appeal Directorate for fines, based on the statistics and answers provided in the questionnaire, most of the entities have filed a petition for a fine in this competent body. About 23% of the entities did not consider it necessary to appear in this body or other bodies to apologize for the penalties or reductions. While the rest of 77%

Figure 6. The evaluation of the ability of tax authorities's employees
Source: Authors

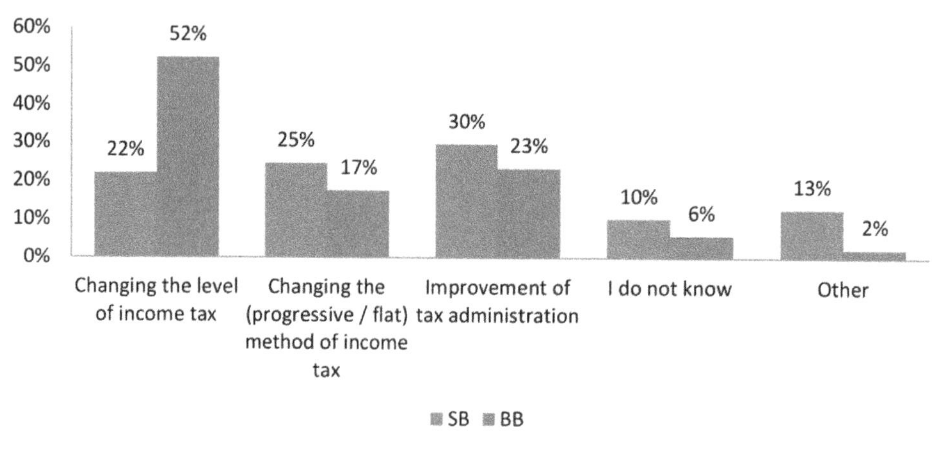

of entities thought it necessary to file claims to reduce the level of penalties received, as most of them are medium or small entities, but also large ones that have been penalized twice or more than twice at very high and unmanageable values.

All of these fiscal changes are often too unconcerned, very unexplained and not very quickly adapted to taxpayers, both businesses and taxpayers. Everyone needs to be well-behaved for any kind of change that will occur in a tax system, because, according to many taxpayer studies, "an old tax is a good tax", so an old system for them is a system of good. Businesses are taxpayers who require a great deal of time in making changes required by the tax system, so a question posed to the taxpayers involved in the study is as is it necessary for the taxpayers to be trained for the fiscal changes. Based on the answers provided and collected, they presented this result:

The graph shows that most of the financiers of the entities feel much needed to develop different trainings in the fiscal system for any change that the face. Most of the entities have an average rating for these trainings.While businesses that were only penalized for a kind of penalty, we can say that it was not necessary to carry out fiscal trainings because they were very well informed about these changes and because their businesses had been operating for years in the level of professionalism. However it was very necessary to inform the taxpayers in due time for any new initiative. Big businesses are taxed in a different way from small businesses.

Figure 9 shows the significance of taxes for entities. Based on the results of the graph, it is shown that most of the entities have an average rating for the heavy weight that these taxes and taxes charge for them. About 38% of the entities value all the severity of tax liabilities as important, while 28% think these liabilities are important at the medium level and about 26% of other businesses specify them as very importamt for the entity. Only 1% of the entities state that the taxation is not important at all.

Small taxpayers (businesses) expressed the impression that large businesses did not suffer much from all this tax action, and they were also greatly favored by all this tax audit and small taxpayers believed that all this control has been done especially for them, for the a lot of reasons, among them due to high tax evasion. About 15% of the entities that are a very small percentage are very positive about all this control over the businesses, which is to say that it is a negligible percentage that have confidence in the development of the entire tax system in general. While most taxpayers in the business format, both large

Figure 7. How much is necessary for taxpayers to be trained for the fiscal changes?
Source: Authors

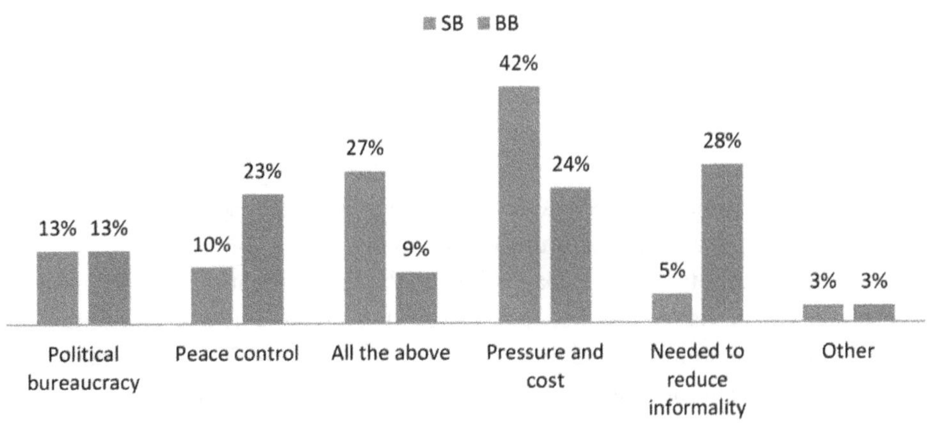

Figure 8. The importance of taxation for the businesses
Source: Authors

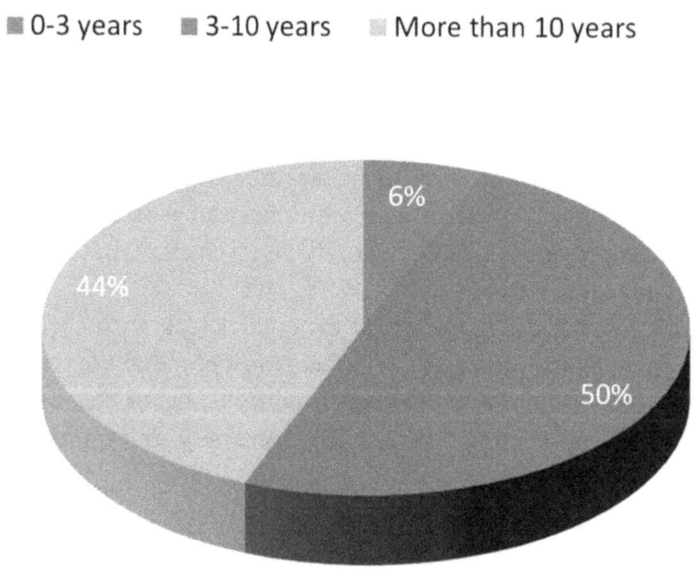

Figure 9. How equal do you believe that the controls from the respective persons have been?
Source: Authors

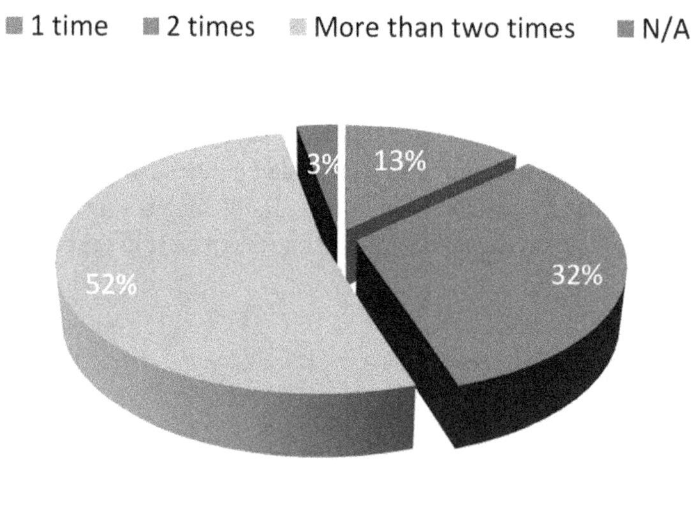

and small, expressed some sort of untruth about the fiscal system and the way this system operated in general, not to mention all this control against informality. This is a negative sign to the entire tax system in our country, showing that many taxpayers do not believe in it because it comes as a result of other chain factors, which do not disappear or eliminate very soon.

The way in which all recent tax changes have affected the selected entities are different for big small businesses. Normally, such divisions are expected between businesses, and in view of the mission, vision and objectives they have. It is well known that most of the businesses that are consolidated and operating in Tirana are more regular than some of the businesses that operate in some of the most sprawling cities.

Figure 10. The impact of the tax controll on the businesses
Source: Authors

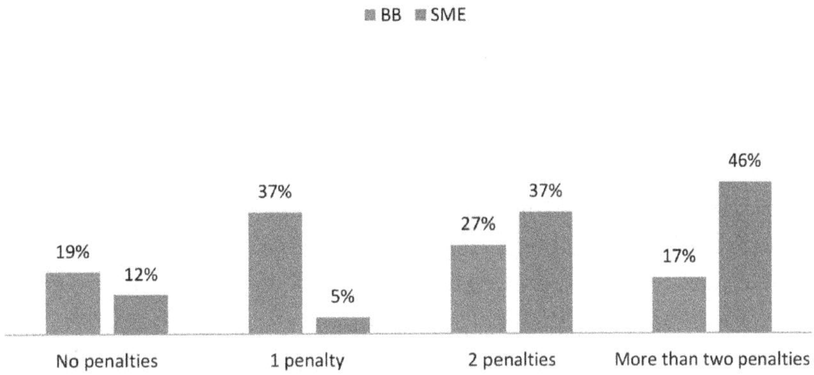

This graph shows how all this tax control and constant tax changes have influenced their activity and continuity simultaneously. The differences between big and small businesses are apparent. Big businesses in the largest proportion filled in distributed questionnaires have shown that this tax control is not having a major impact on those with a 45% share, as they had been operating in the market for years and it is not that they were affected by tax audits, this only sometimes in special cases, which concerned the preparation of final reports, or mistakes that could be made during declarations. The rest of the big businesses indicated that they had had an impact on their activity, frequent control, causing many unnecessary breaks. 15% had lowered the level of investment in their business during this period, while other large economic entities indicated that their controls were mostly carried out for political reasons against them rather than as a genuine fiscal checkpoint, while as far as other alternatives are concerned, a very small percentage of these businesses makes their choice.

Otherwise, it happens with small businesses that view all of this tax audit as a quasi-political and not too functional or frustrating action for the fiscal system itself as a whole 37% of small and medium-sized enterprises show that with the implementation of tax control within a very short period of time, they have had the effect of: reducing the number of employees, lowering the level of trade at lower rates. Only 23% of the respondents responded that these frequent tax changes and a very inexpensive tax control have created a chaos for their economic unit, until all procedures are properly regulated, creating a lot of cost for and even interruption of their economic activity for a while.

Annova Results

Above we saw an overeall pereption from the businesses about the fiscal policies and the changes on it. The second part of the results will be focused on the impact of size devided in two major groups: for Big Businesses and Small Businesses. In order to compare and analyze the results for this two groups we will use ANOVA Model. The study's aim is to test the significant differences within groups. Below we will see the results of ANOVA model fro the questions which were related with the perception/behavior of the businesses Obviously the perception for the tax sytem is different regarding the type of business.

A general finding about the perception of this two categories of the businesses is that the small businesses believe less in the fairness of the tax controls and tax policies compared to the big businesses. Small businesses have less information about the tax legislation of our country. Most of them they do not have informtion at the medium level. While a very small portion of the small businsses 6/118 knows the legislacion well. Menawhile the big businesses are more well informed. The frequent changes in the tax policies are not are not efective for the businesses due to the businesses.

Some of the businesses had request a decrease in the penalties that they had received and the answer that they had regarding their opinion was in egeneral fair. However if we compare this answer between big and small entities there is a difference. Big businesses were not satisfiedrelated with the compesations that they should took from the gorvernment.

From ANOVA model the results of this question seems to be significant $P<0.05$. Meaning that the difference is significant between the groups. However, 90% of BB believe that frequent changes are not effectiv and 86% of SB have the same opinion. Even if for this alternative both categories of businesses aswered almost the same, we have a differencce in the other two alternatives of the question. From the raph we can notice that 8% of SB do not know if the frequent changes of the tax policies favor or disfavor the business. From this point we can understand that SB do not have enough information to judge what is apropriate or not for the unity compared to BB. In the question above we observed that SB have less ifnformation than BB and here we can notice a link between this two questions. The main findg of this graph is that both kind of unities state that the frequent change in tax policies does brings any benefit to the unities.

Another point where we can underline from the results of ANOVA model is the businesses's perception about the capability of the inspectors. The evaluation of this capability is based in the contacts, controlls that thi unities have had with the inpectors.

The results are significant P= 0.018, the perception of the unities is different. From data is shown that BB trust and evaluate more positively the inspectors who have done the controlls. From the graph above is noticed 43% of BB underline that the inspectors are in a medium level capabel. Meanwhile the SB that attached to this opinion are the half in number. Maybe this reaction may come from the fact that all the intensive tax controll that was made was seeking more SB than BB.

The entities were asked in the questionaire about the percption of the tax regiomatics system and their results were as follow:

Figure 11. Do you think that such frequent changes on tax policies are effective?
Source: Authors

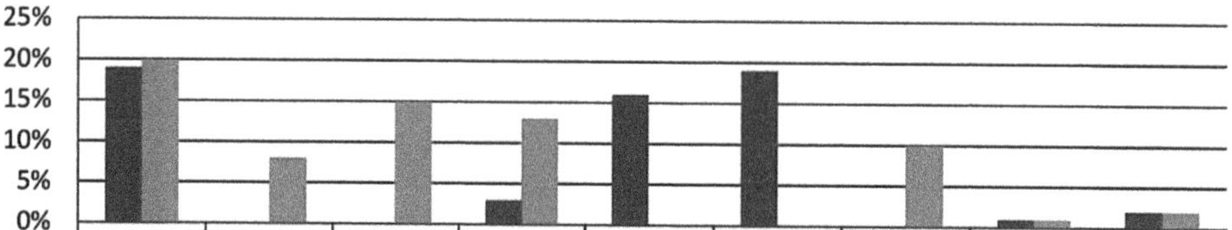

	Not declaring the obligation within the deadlines set out...	Do not buy sale's/purchase's books	Do not display product prices	Wrong price declarations	Not issuing tax bills	Unsupported Goods with Documents	Do not declare the employees	Other	N/A
BB	19%	0%	0%	3%	16%	19%	0%	1%	2%
SB	20%	8%	15%	13%	0%	0%	10%	1%	2%

Figure 12. Evaluation of inspectors
Source: Authors

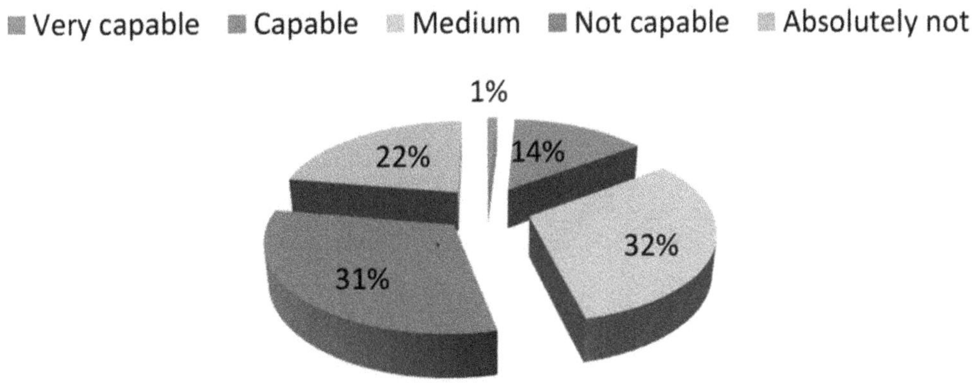

Figure 13. Tax regiomatics system
Source: Authors

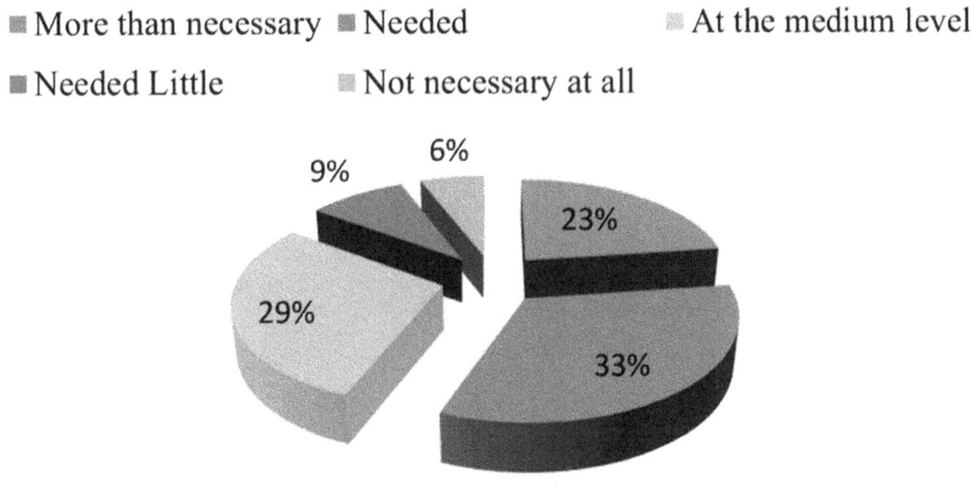

From ANOVA Model, we observed that the result is significant between SB and BB 0.000. Meaning that the perception regarding the the tax regiomatics system is quite different among the groups. Big business prefer more the flat tax on income than the progressive income tax. The progressive income tax is based on how much you earn thats why the big businesses tend to avoid it. Menawhile for the small businesses is totally the different. They state that who earns more should pay more. A small percentage of both kind of entities were indifferent in this quetion.

The conclude question is related with the alternative that it would be more apropriate for the tax system in the albanian condistions.

In the graph is shown that 52% of the BB prefer to change the level of income tax and 17% of them to change the kind of the tax which is applied in Albania. A considerable percentage beliveve that it should be a change in the tax administration. As about the SB, if we list from the importance the want an improvement in the tax administration, then a change in the kind of the tax.

Figure 14. The apropriate alternative for the tax system in Albanian conditions
Source: Authors

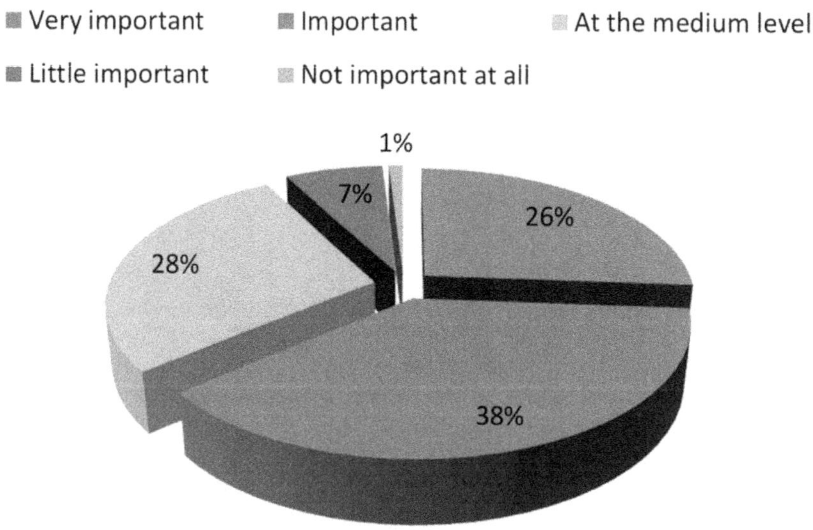

Figure 15. How was the entity's assessment of all this tax audit?
Source: Authors

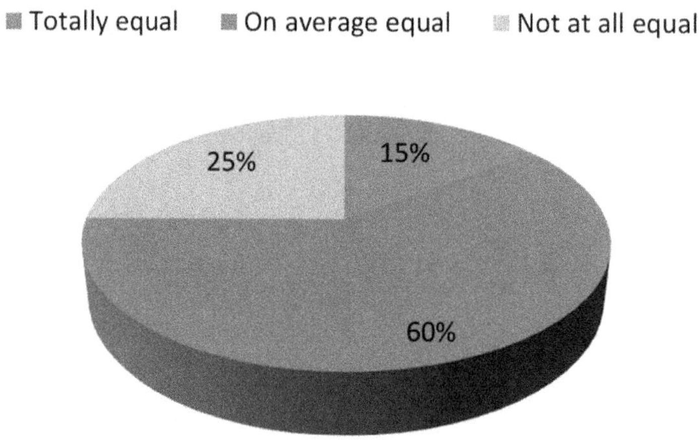

This is a question that is related to or wanting to know how the whole fiscal system looks, the whole of its policies. Albania is the only country in the Balkans that has developed a very liberal policy towards businesses that allowed them to develop all their activity by not paying tax obligations or not configuring at all times registered with the competent authorities. Even Kosovo, which is one of the newest Balkan states, has for some years been developing a somewhat appropriate fiscal policy, also as a result of a culture adored by Yugoslav or Serbian occupations. In the many comparisons over the years for the Balkan countries, Albania was listed as one of the last countries in the development of appropriate tax policies, or for the lowest GDP, or for unemployment, inflation etc.

As a conlusion of the ANOVA model findgs, BB and SB in some points they have totally different perceptions regarding the tax polices, inspectors, the fairness of the tax system. From the survey, is mentioned that SB were in focus of the tax controlls more than BB. This may be a reason why the results of some questions were significant in ANOVA model. The model states that there is a lack of trust from the small unities to the all tax system. Moreover small and big unities prefer a different regiomatic system. SB tend to choose more the progressive tax of income, menawhile the BB the flat tax of income.

SOLUTIONS AND RECOMMENDATIONS

Tax controls should be developed, both for big and small businesses and for all types of taxpayers, so that we can familiarize the entities with them so that this whole step is not restored intensive from the beginning. Training at fiscal institutions for any possible tax evasion is very important, both as a consequence of a not very developed fiscal culture, but also of a significant lack of proper functioning of this system and its competent bodies.

Develop appropriate controls with the right people in order to create a highly functional and effective link between the fiscal system bodies and taxpayers. On the part of the tax authorities, there should be no room for taxpayers to judge the professionalism and the way of doing so, although even in the most developed countries the taxpayer are skeptical of any change that occurs in the whole system and any undesired outcome attributes it to the latter. Tax controls should be effectively organized and exercised equally in all entities.

Tax controls should not be exercised within a very short period of time, but they must be extended in time, leaving sufficient space for businesses to develop their entire activity without unnecessary pressure or pressure increase business costs and also bring no benefits to either party.

Albania needs to create a wealth fiscal system whose development will bring benefits, such as the level of GDP growth, unemployment and inflation decline. Appropriate tax policies are one of the best choices for every country, taxpayers, but also for foreign investors. Today the struggle between countries is to attract as many foreign investors as possible, pushing them through favorable fiscal policies and eliminating double taxation.

Reduction of some tax rates is very necessary, especially for VAT, or other taxes that are not very encouraging for our taxpayers. VAT is one of the taxes most affecting the consumer and is at a very high level compared to many countries in the region and at the same time a high tax on the minimum vital products. The fiscal system is not to be seen as separate on its own but as a very important link to the whole economic system of a country. All systems within an economic system, including the fiscal system, are very important to interact with one another in order to achieve those objectives that make for any economic system

FUTURE RESEARCH DIRECTIONS

There were some limitations for realizing this study. The literature review was limited for the Albanian case. A key limitation of this research was that the businesses which were contacted, were sceptic regarding the questionnaires and as a result this makes the results to be less trustfull. Another point of limitaions was the lack of informacion for secondary data regarding the number of the businesses that were regjistrated to the NRC. This informacion was important in order to compare the primary data with the secondary one.

CONCLUSION

The tax system in Albania has undergone many political changes, some of which have provided the basic form of a modest fiscal system, while other policies have eradicated it, causing major problems for this system that until recently was very unworkable. Taxpayers, both businesses and individuals, are the only ones who are affected or are sensitive to any kind of change in fiscal policies.

From the data collection seems that the recent tax controls that took place in our country to businesses seemed to have had a lot of impact on the them: increasing the number of businesses registered in NRC, increasing the tax declaration and paying them, made it possible to create a other culture, how a business should operate in a developing society, and increase taxpayer responsibilities to tax authorities. The most numerous penalties according to the analysis and completion of the distributed questionnaires are addressed to small businesses, such as: not installing fiscal equipment, not issuing a tax receipt, not paying the tax liability in time etc. While for the big business the number of penalties was small, but in higher value such as: failure to issue a tax invoice, no tax declarations on time, payment or collection of customers or suppliers with values greater than 150000 ALL. All tax control exercised on different entities had different impacts. Most major businesses showed that the whole action was not having a major impact on them, while for small businesses there was a huge impact on reducing employee numbers, increasing claims on the online system, increasing cost, numerous checks carried out often had led to the termination of economic activity.

According to the finding of this study, taxpayers do not have a strong belief in the entire fiscal system, how fiscal policies are deployed or changed, the way they operate with businesses, they are mostly driven by political bureaucracy that does not serve them. As about the small businesses during the development of the questionnaires expressed the idea that all this tax or action control was developed towards them and not to big businesses that do not pay the obligations as much as they need and are still not penalized. Few of the businesses think this control as a task that should have been realized before, extending in time and needed to reduce informality and tax evasion.

REFERENCES

Alm, J. (2014). Does an uncertain tax system encourage "aggressive tax planning"? *Economic Analysis and Policy*, *44*(1), 30–38. doi:10.1016/j.eap.2014.01.004

Atkinson, A. B., & Stiglitz, J. E. (1976). The design of tax structure: Direct versus indirect taxation. *Journal of Public Economics*, *6*(1-2), 55–75.

Auerbach, A. J., & Gale, W. G. (2009). *The economic crisis and the fiscal crisis: 2009 and beyond.* Urban-Brookings Tax Policy Center.

Auerbach, A. J., & Gale, W. G. (2009). *The economic crisis and the fiscal crisis: 2009 and beyond.* Urban-Brookings Tax Policy Center.

Batini, N., Guerreiro, J., & Callegari, G. (2011). An Analysis of US Fiscal and Generational Imbalances: Who Will Pay and How? (No. 11-72). International Monetary Fund.

Berg, M., De Waegenaere, A., & Wielhouwer, J. L. (2001). Optimal tax depreciation with uncertain future cash-flows. *European Journal of Operational Research, 132*(1), 197–209. doi:10.1016/S0377-2217(00)00132-6

Black, J. (1995). Phillip T. Hoffman and Kathryn Norberg (eds.), Fiscal Crises, Liberty, and Representative Government, 1450-1789 (Book Review). Parliamentary History, 14(3), 349.

Board, J., Sutcliffe, C., & Ziemba, W. T. (2003). Applying operations research techniques to financial markets. *Interfaces, 33*(2), 12–24. doi:10.1287/inte.33.2.12.14465

Break, G. F. (1957). Income taxes and incentives to work: An empirical study. *The American Economic Review, 47*(5), 530–549.

Buchanan, J. M., & Musgrave, R. A. (1999). *Public finance and public choice: two contrasting visions of the State*. MIT Press. doi:10.7551/mitpress/5688.001.0001

Chown, J. (2000). Monetary Union and tax harmonization. *Intertax, 28*(3), 102–109. doi:10.1023/A:1005625820708

Dinh, H. D. (2014). *Optimization in finance: approaches for modeling and solving the multi-period loss offset problem in German income tax system*. Academic Press.

Dinu, M., & Marinaş, M. C. (2014). Testing the impact of the fiscal policy with the SVAR model in seven CEE economies. *Economic Computation and Economic Cybernetics Studies and Research, 48*(1).

Durán Cabré, J. M., & Esteller Moré, A. (2014). *Tax professionals' view of the Spanish tax system: efficiency, equity and tax planning*. IEB Working Paper 2014/04.

Durán-Cabré, J. M., Esteller-Moré, A., & Salvadori, L. (2015). Empirical evidence on horizontal competition in tax enforcement. *International Tax and Public Finance, 22*(5), 834–860. doi:10.100710797-014-9333-0

Edwards, C., & Mitchell, D. J. (2008). *Global tax revolution: the rise of tax competition and the battle to defend it*. Cato Institute.

Feldstein, M. (2009). Rethinking the role of fiscal policy. *American Economic Review (Kansas City, Mo.), 99*(2), 556–559.

Finnerty, C., Merks, P., Petriccione, M., & Russo, R. (2007). *Fundamentals of international tax planning*. Ámsterdam: IBFD.

Gale, W., & Auerbach, A. (2009). *The economic crisis and the fiscal crisis: 2009 and beyond*. Academic Press.

Galuszka, J. (2013). The Fiscal Union as a Remedy For the economic and Financial Crisis in the european Union. *Equilibrium, 8*(1), 49–67. doi:10.12775/EQUIL.2013.003

Gjyli, K. (2009). *Shkenca mbi financat dhe e drejta e financave*. Academic Press.

Gordon, R. H. (1986). Taxation of investment and savings in a world economy. *The American Economic Review*, 1086–1102.

Hall, R. E., & Rabushka, A. (1983). *Low tax, simple tax, flat tax*. McGraw-Hill Companies.

Hong, Q., & Smart, M. (2010). In praise of tax havens: International tax planning and foreign direct investment. *European Economic Review*, *54*(1), 82–95. doi:10.1016/j.euroecorev.2009.06.006

Janeba, E., & Peters, W. (1999). Tax evasion, tax competition and the gains from nondiscrimination: The case of interest taxation in Europe. *Economic Journal (London)*, *109*(452), 93–101. doi:10.1111/1468-0297.00393

Jara, H. X., & Tumino, A. (2013). Tax-benefit systems, income distribution and work incentives in the European Union. *The International Journal of Microsimulation*, *6*, 27–62.

Joumard, I. (2001). *Tax systems in European Union countries*. Academic Press.

Knirsch, D., & Niemann, R. (2007). *Allowance for shareholder equity: implementing a neutral corporate income tax in the European Union* (No. 34). Arqus-Diskussionsbeiträge zur quantitativen Steuerlehre.

Leibfritz, W., Thornton, J., & Bibbee, A. (1997). *Taxation and economic performance*. Academic Press.

Liaropoulos, L., & Tragakes, E. (1998). Public/private financing in the Greek health care system: Implications for equity. *Health Policy (Amsterdam)*, *43*(2), 153–169. doi:10.1016/S0168-8510(97)00093-6 PMID:10177616

Mankiw, N. G. (2008). *Principles of Macroeconomics* (5th ed.). South-Western: Cengage Learning.

Mikesell, J. (2013). *Fiscal administration*. Cengage Learning.

Mirrlees, J., Adam, S., Besley, T., Blundell, R., Bond, S., Chote, R., & Poterba, J. (2011). The Mirrlees Review: Conclusions and recommendations for reform. *Fiscal Studies*, *32*(3), 331–359. doi:10.1111/j.1475-5890.2011.00140.x

Modigliani, F., & Miller, M. H. (1958). The cost of capital, corporation finance and the theory of investment. *The American Economic Review*, *48*(3), 261–297.

Oates, W. E. (1969). The effects of property taxes and local public spending on property values: An empirical study of tax capitalization and the Tiebout hypothesis. *Journal of Political Economy*, *77*(6), 957–971. doi:10.1086/259584

Peachman, J. B. (1975). *Anatomy of Fiscal Crisis*. University of Michigan.

Pommerehne, W. W., & Schneider, F. (1978). Fiscal illusion, political institutions, and local public spending. *Kyklos, 31*(3), 381-408.

Poterba, J. M., & Rueben, K. S. (2001). Fiscal news, state budget rules, and tax-exempt bond yields. *Journal of Urban Economics*, *50*(3), 537–562. doi:10.1006/juec.2001.2233

Ramsey, F. P. (1927). A Contribution to the Theory of Taxation. *Economic Journal (London)*, *37*(145), 47–61. doi:10.2307/2222721

Rieger, H. (1978). *Prinzipien des internationalen Steuerrechts als Problem der Steuerplanung in dr multinationalen Unternehmung* (Vol. 4). Erich Schmidt.

Roig-Alonso, M. (1998). Fiscal visibility in the European Union member countries: New estimates. *International Advances in Economic Research*, *4*(1), 1–15. doi:10.1007/BF02295231

Romer, C. (2011). What do we know about the effects of fiscal policy? Separating evidence from ideology. Speech at Hamilton College.

Ross, E. B. (1991). *Management control of Aviation Career Incentive Pay for selected reservists of the Naval Reserve* (Doctoral dissertation). Naval Postgraduate School.

Schanz, S. (2008). *Strategien optimaler Repatriierung*. Springer-Verlag.

Scharpf, F. W., & Schmidt, V. A. (Eds.). (2000). Welfare and work in the open economy: volume II: diverse responses to common challenges in twelve countries. OUP Oxford. doi:10.1093/0199240922.001.0001

Smith, J. P. (2014). *Taxpayer effects of immigration*. IZA World of Labor. doi:10.15185/izawol.50

Smith, S. (1992). Taxation and the environment: A survey. *Fiscal Studies*, *13*(4), 21–57. doi:10.1111/j.1475-5890.1992.tb00505.x

Spitz, B. (1972). *International tax planning*. Butterworths.

Taylor, J. B. (2000). Reassessing discretionary fiscal policy. *The Journal of Economic Perspectives*, *14*(3), 21–36. doi:10.1257/jep.14.3.21 PMID:15179965

Vickrey, W. (1939). Averaging of income for income-tax purposes. *Journal of Political Economy*, *47*(3), 379–397. doi:10.1086/255390

Virkola, T. (2014). *Exchange Rate Regime, Fiscal Foresight and the Effectiveness of Fiscal Policy in a Small Open Economy (No. 20)*. The Research Institute of the Finnish Economy.

Welsch, G. A., & Anthony, R. N. (1974). *Fundamentals of Financial Accounting*. Richard D. Irwin.

Ziu & Fishta. (2004). Historia e ekonomisw sw Shqipwrisw (1944-1960). *Shtepia botuese Dita.*

KEY TERMS AND DEFINITIONS

ANOVA: Analysis variance is used to analyze the differences among groups and their statistical significance.

Big Business in Albania: A large business is classified as any natural or legal person who carries out an economic activity (business), whereby a gross annual income (turnover) of more than 8,000,000 (eight million) ALL is realized during the fiscal year.

National Registration Center in Albania: The main characteristic of the NRC is that it concentrates all the registration related issues (including work inspectorate, healthcare and social security, tax registration, and the National Statistics Institute).

Small Business in Albania: A small business is classified as any natural or legal person who performs an economic activity (business), whereby a gross annual income (turnover) of less than or equal to ALL 8,000,000 (eight million) is realized during the year fiscal.

Tax: It is a compulsory and irrevocable payment to the state budget, or it is also done for exchange of goods and services.

Tax in Albania: It is a compulsory and irrevocable payment in the state budget, but also in the budget of certain local government organs, established by law and it is paid by any person who benefits from a public right or even benefits one public service in the Republic of Albania.

Tax System: the entirety of harmonized, rational, effective, flexible and appropriate forms of taxation in the realization of the economic, social development goals of a state.

APPENDIX 1

This appendix contains the Questionnaire used in the study.

1. What is your current job position in the company?
   a. Economist
   b. Manager
   c. Economist Specialist (Approved Accountant, Certified Accounting Expert)
   d. Other *
2. What is your experience in this position?
   a. I have no experience
   b. Less than 1 year
   c. 1-5 years
   d. 5-10 years
   e. Over 10 years
3. What is your highest level of educational qualification?
   a. High school
   b. Bachelor
   c. Master
   d. PHD
   e. Other ____________________
4. What kind of business is the subject where you work?****
   a. Big business
   b. Small business
5. What is the activity of the economic unit that you work for?
   a. Wholesale
   b. Retail
   c. Manufacturing
   d. Service
6. How many years is the economic unit operating in the Albanian market?
   a. 0-3 years
   b. 3-10 years
   c. 10 years and over
7. When was the entity registered to the National Registration Center?
   a. At the beginning of the activity
   b. 0-1 years
   c. 1-3 years
   d. 3 years and over
8. Which was the reason for encouraging the subject to registration to the National Registration Center?
   a. For Correctness
   b. Due to tax control
   c. Other reason

9. How well do you know the tax legislation of our country?
    a. Very well
    b. Good
    c. Fair
    d. Slightly
    e. Nothing at all
10. Do you think that such a frequent change of tax legislation is effective?
    a. Yes
    b. No
    c. I do not know
11. How many times has the entity been controlled from the tax audit?
    a. 1 time
    b. 2 times
    c. More than two times
    d. Never
12. Have you ever been subject to penalties for errors? If so, how many times have you been penalized?
    a. time
    b. 2 times
    c. More than two times
    d. Never
13. Which are some of the penalties provided by large businesses and which small businesses (Please note after the BM (Large Business) or BV (Small Business) Answer?
    a. Not declaring the obligation within the deadlines set out in the fiscal law
    b. Do not buy sale's/purchase's books
    c. Do not display product prices
    d. Failure to meet the tax obligations within the deadline
    e. Wrong price declarations
    f. Not issuing tax bills
    g. Unsupported Goods with Documents
    h. Do not declare the employees
    i. Other
    j. N/A
14. How capable do you think are the employees of state bodies?
    a. Very capable
    b. Capable
    c. Medium
    d. Not capable
    e. Absolutely not
15. Has the company ever request forgiveness for penalties from the Appointment Unit of the Appellate Body?
    a. Yes
    b. No

16. How do you think was the assessment made by the fiscal authorities to change the level of penalties?
    a. Very correct
    b. Correct
    c. Fairly correct
    d. No corrected
    e. Not at all correct
17. How much do taxpayer need to be trained on fiscal changes?
    a. More than necessary
    b. Needed
    c. at the medium level
    d. Needed Little
    e. not necessary at all
18. How important are the taxes and fees for the economic unit?
    b. very important
    c. important
    d. at the medium level
    e. little important
    f. Not important at all
19. How equal do you believe that the controls from the respective persons have been?***
    a. Totally equal
    b. On average equal
    c. Not at all equal
20. Which was the impact of tax control on businesses?
    a. Lower the number of employees
    b. Lower the trading level
    c. Increase the level of declarations
    d. Accrue responsibilities
    e. Create chaos until the procedures are set
    f. Lower the level of investment in business
    g. All the above
    h. There was no impact
21. How was the entity's assessment of all this tax audit?
    b. Political bureaucracy
    c. Peace control
    d. All the above
    e. Pressure and cost
    f. Needed to reduce informality
    g. Other
22. What model of income tax appears to be most appropriate for you to apply in Albania's terms?***
    a. Flat tax on income
    b. Progressive income tax
    c. Indifferent

23. Please specify the type of income you think is appropriate to submit to the tax model selected in the above question:
    a. Flat / progressive tax only on personal income
    b. Flat / Progressive Taxes only on business incomes
    c. Flat / progressive taxes on personal income and on business incomes
24. Under the current conditions in Albania, which of the following alternatives would be more appropriate for the tax system?**
    a. Changing the level of income tax
    b. Changing the (progressive / flat) method of income tax
    c. Improvement of tax administration
    d. I do not know
    e. Other

, *: Questions in asterisks have been used in the ANOVA analysis.

APPENDIX 2

Table 1.

ANOVA						
		Sum of Squares	**df**	**Mean Square**	**F**	**Sig.**
Q2	Between Groups	.829	1	.829	.996	.320
	Within Groups	168.166	202	.833		
	Total	168.995	203			
Q3	Between Groups	.001	1	.001	.001	.970
	Within Groups	166.994	202	.827		
	Total	166.995	203			
Q5	Between Groups	4.594	1	4.594	6.082	.014
	Within Groups	152.582	202	.755		
	Total	157.176	203			
Q6	Between Groups	.048	1	.048	.130	.719
	Within Groups	73.889	202	.366		
	Total	73.936	203			
Q7	Between Groups	62.953	1	62.953	62.725	.000
	Within Groups	202.733	202	1.004		
	Total	265.686	203			
Q8	Between Groups	3.990	1	3.990	8.604	.004
	Within Groups	93.672	202	.464		
	Total	97.662	203			
Q9	Between Groups	7.476	1	7.476	9.027	.003
	Within Groups	167.284	202	.828		
	Total	174.760	203			
Q10	Between Groups	.626	1	.626	5.649	.018
	Within Groups	22.370	202	.111		
	Total	22.995	203			
Q11	Between Groups	22.376	1	22.376	48.068	.000
	Within Groups	94.031	202	.466		
	Total	116.407	203			
Q12	Between Groups	11.372	1	11.372	13.268	.000
	Within Groups	173.138	202	.857		
	Total	184.510	203			
Q14	Between Groups	6.143	1	6.143	5.639	.018
	Within Groups	220.029	202	1.089		
	Total	226.172	203			

continued on following page

Table 1. Continued

ANOVA						
		Sum of Squares	df	Mean Square	F	Sig.
Q15	Between Groups	.745	1	.745	5.592	.019
	Within Groups	26.917	202	.133		
	Total	27.662	203			
Q16	Between Groups	10.009	1	10.009	6.360	.012
	Within Groups	317.912	202	1.574		
	Total	327.922	203			
Q17	Between Groups	2.458	1	2.458	1.941	.165
	Within Groups	255.836	202	1.267		
	Total	258.294	203			
Q18	Between Groups	.719	1	.719	.824	.365
	Within Groups	176.203	202	.872		
	Total	176.922	203			
Q19	Between Groups	.273	1	.273	.554	.458
	Within Groups	99.648	202	.493		
	Total	99.922	203			
Q20	Between Groups	86.296	1	86.296	19.857	.000
	Within Groups	877.875	202	4.346		
	Total	964.172	203			
Q21	Between Groups	1.597	1	1.597	.896	.345
	Within Groups	360.065	202	1.783		
	Total	361.662	203			
Q22	Between Groups	9.149	1	9.149	23.637	.000
	Within Groups	78.184	202	.387		
	Total	87.333	203			
Q23	Between Groups	.472	1	.472	3.228	.074
	Within Groups	29.509	202	.146		
	Total	29.980	203			
Q24	Between Groups	32.559	1	32.559	23.123	.000
	Within Groups	284.436	202	1.408		
	Total	316.995	203			

Source: Author

Chapter 14
Credit Rating and Its Interaction With Financial Ratios:
A Study of BSE 500 Companies

Shraddha Mishra
IILM University, India

Reenu Bansal
IILM University, India

ABSTRACT

Credit rating evaluates credit worthiness of corporate and securities issued by government. It provides investors with unbiased reviews and opinion about the credit risk of various securities. The main aim of the chapter is to identify the relationship between the financial ratios and rating symbols. The sample of 158 firms is taken into consideration that discriminates best ratings given by credit rating firms. In order to examine the variability in ratings issued by various rating agencies, the time period of eight years starting from April 2009 to March 2017 has been selected. The study employed the multinomial logistic regression model to explain the relationship among the variables. The analysis suggests that variables such as debt to equity ratio, profit after tax, returns on capital employed, and return on net worth are those having the highest impact on ratings and thus there is also discriminating power among Indian rating agencies.

INTRODUCTION

- **Purpose:** Credit rating agencies have bought revolutionary changes in Indian capital market by introducing various innovations. Credit rating evaluates credit worthiness of corporate and securities issued by government. It provides investors with unbiased reviews and opinion about the credit risk of various securities. The main aim of the study is to identify the relationship between the financial ratios and rating symbols.

DOI: 10.4018/978-1-5225-7399-9.ch014

- **Design:** Out of various rating agencies in India only four are taken into consideration for the purpose of analysis i.e. CRISIL, ICRA, CARE and FITCH. The short-term liquidity ratio considered in the study is Current Ratio; long-term solvency ratio includes gearing ratio, Total Indebtedness Ratio and Interest Coverage Ratio. The profitability ratio includes Profit before interest and tax; Net cash accruals to total debt; profit after tax (PAT) margin; Return on capital employed and Return on Net worth.
- **Methodology:** The sample of one hundred and fifty eight firms is taken into consideration that discriminates best ratings given by credit rating firms. The selections of these companies were as per the market capitalization from the list of BSE 500 as on 31st March, 2017. In order to examine the variability in ratings issued by various rating agencies; the time period of eight years starting from April, 2009 to March, 2017 has been selected. The study employed the multinomial logistic regression model to explain the relationship among the variables.
- **Findings:** Arora (2003) had used anova model to predict the inconsistency. The anova result signifies that the methodologies of all four credit rating companies are inconsistent in nature. The analysis suggests that variables such as debt to equity ratio, profit after tax; returns on capital employed and return on Net worth are those having the highest impact on ratings and thus there is also discriminating power among Indian rating agencies. The results are consistent with the following studies; Pinches and Mingo (1973), Ang and Patel (1978), Wingler and Watts (1980), Belkaoui (1980) and Altman and Katz (1976), and Novotná (2012).
- **Practical Implications:** This article will help the investor to evaluate the efficiency of credit rating assigned by all the four credit rating agencies in India. Taking into consideration, the fundamental analysis of stock valuation, analyst would be able to define the competent agency among all. The study will also help the credit rating firms to know their performance in long term.

The economic scene in the post-independence period has seen a sea change, the result being that the economy has made enormous progress in diverse fields. Indian economy has expanded quantitatively and diversifies its economic activities. The experiences of 1980s have led to the conclusion that needs efficient financial systems to rely on market based decision making.

The financial system is the most important institutional and functional vehicle for economic transformation. The financial system is a set of inter-related activities which aims at establishing and providing a regular, smooth, efficient and effective linkage between depositors and investors. Indian financial system comprises of financial institutions, financial services, financial markets and financial instruments which influence the generation of savings, investments, capital formation and growth.

Van Horne James C (2002) defined the financial system as the purpose of financial markets to allocate savings efficiently in an economy to ultimate users either for investment in real assets or for consumption. Christy, G. C. (2009) has opined that the objective of the financial system is to "supply funds to various sectors and activities of the economy in ways that promote the fullest possible utilization of resources without the destabilizing consequence of price level changes or unnecessary interference with individual desires." According to Robinson, J. (1933) the primary function of the system is "to provide a link between savings and investment for the creation of new wealth and to permit portfolio adjustment in the composition of the existing wealth."

A financial system includes components that are essential in a modern economy. Within the financial system, financial services not only help in raising the funds but also ensure their efficient utilization. The financial services industry serves the primary sectors of the economy by transmitting the flow of funds and providing financial services. Among the other financial services, credit rating is of most recent origin. Credit rating is a financial service which is helpful to investors in taking their investment related decisions. The expansion of financial markets and ever increasing number of financial instruments provides both borrowers and investors with large number of funding and investing options. Due to multiplicity of instruments and fund raisers, it is very difficult for the investors to make a right choice of funds. Therefore, the investors feel a growing need for an independent and credible agency which judges the credit quality of debt obligations of various issuers impartially, thereby assisting investors, individuals and institutions in making the sound investment decisions.

Credit rating agencies (CRAs) play a very important role in helping the investors to take their investment decisions by providing comparable information on credit risk based on standard rating scales regardless of the specifics of the companies. Their primary function is to assess the credit worthiness of a company and its' debt obligations. These ratings greatly influence the ability of the issuers of securities to raise capital by lowering their costs and also influence the decisions of some fiduciaries to invest. CRAs have been rating instruments and subjecting them to periodic review, sometimes necessitating a transition to a lower or higher grade. In some cases opinions of these agencies are important in structuring transactions which involve financial products like credit derivatives and asset-backed securities. Further, the advanced use of credit ratings in individual contracts has increased their importance.

The Credit Rating Agencies evaluate the intrinsic worth of a company and assign ranks to the companies accordingly. These agencies have become important in view of the increasing number of companies going to the public for funds and also due to government stipulating that corporate bodies wanting to raise funds from the market should have their debt instrument rated. The main objective of these agencies is to restore the confidence in the capital market and to provide unbiased assessment of credit worthiness of the companies issuing debt instruments. Credit Rating Agencies are essentially corporations with specialized functions, namely, assessment of the likelihood of the timely payments by an issuer on a financial obligation (known as 'credit rating'). Thus, 'credit rating' is essentially the task of determining the strength and prospects of a security offered in the market and thereupon place it amongst a band having predetermined standards called 'grades'.

The credit rating agencies are not only involved in the rating activities instead they all are engaged in multiplicity of operations. The wide range of operations makes the arena of rating agencies very broad. All the rating agencies use similar basic symbols from "AAA" to "D" to rate the long term instruments. In order to differentiate their symbols, the rating agencies use various prefixes and suffixes and '+' and '-' signs. The rating agencies rate different instruments and issues after taking into consideration various quantitative and qualitative factors. Since various qualitative factors like history of the company, business profile, quality of management, competitive standing, strength of brand names, etc. can't be quantified for analysis purpose, thus only some of the quantitative factors, being commonly used by all credit rating agencies for rating purposes, are considered for the study. The quantitative factors include nine financial ratios related to short-term liquidity and long-term solvency as well as profitability of the companies.

The main aim of the study is to identify the relationship between the financial ratios and rating symbols. The brief review of the credit rating agencies in India and development of traditional ratios for investigating the corporate performance is presented in section one. Section two deals with the brief literature review on the topics related to ratios and rating of the companies. Research gap has also been analyzed in this section. In the next section, the data collection and the methodology are introduced with the emphasis centering on the credit ratings and its compatibility with ratio analysis. The multinomial logistic regression model is developed in section four, where an initial sample of one hundred and fifty eight firms is utilized to establish a function which best discriminates between ratings given by credit rating firms. The model's adaptability to practical decision-making situations and its potential benefits in a variety of situations are suggested in section five. The final section summarizes the findings and conclusions of the study, and assesses the role and significance of traditional ratio analysis within a modern analytical context.

LITERATURE REVIEW

Previous research analyzes how the rating agencies use public information in setting quality ratings. The need for reliable financial statement data and the importance of financial ratios for analysis and prediction is well established in the literature.

Beginning with Blume et al (1998) contention that standard financial ratios can predict the long term issuer's credit ratings, many subsequent studies have attempted to demonstrate the predictive value of various techniques for estimating credit ratings. Several techniques were used including multiple regression analysis (Horrigan, 1966; Pogue and Soldofsky, 1969; West, 1970), multiple discriminant analysis (Pinches and Mingo, 1973; Altman and Katz, 1976), ordered linear probit model (Kaplan and Urwitz, 1979; Poon, 2003; Cheng et al, 2009; Hwang et al, 2010), ordered and unordered linear logit models (Ederington & Yawitz, 1985), bayesian networks (Wijayatunga et al, 2006), support vector machines and neural networks (Huang et al., 2004).

Pinches and Mingo (1973) use factor analysis to arrive at a set of six factors considered determinants of bond issues ratings: subordination, years of consecutive dividends, issue size and three financial ratios. These factors differ significantly from those considered determinants of issuer ratings defined as firms' size, financial leverage, coverage, cash flow, profitability, liquidity, market-driven variables and industry variables (Hwang et al., 2010).

Kanagaraj and Murugesan (2006) tried to evaluate the relationship between financial variables and credit ratings. Manufacturing firms whose debentures were rated by CRISIL was taken as sample. The time period of study was a period of six years from 1996-1997 to 2001-2002. The financial variables were grouped into nine dimensions i.e. profitability, liquidity, activity, debt service coverage, liabilities structure, size, firm's age, leverage and sales turnover. The author revealed a positive relation between the financial performance and credit rating of the firm. Also it was revealed that variables such as debt coverage, profitability and leverage hold a dominant position in credit rating classifications.

Bheemanagauda and Madegowda (2010) made an attempt to evaluate the performance of Indian credit rating agencies including CRISIL, ICRA, CARE and FITCH. For the purpose of the study, data relating to the long-term debt instruments was taken as sample. The time period of study was a period of 8 years from 2000-2008. The author revealed that during the period of study, there was a substantial increase in rating business in India. The study also depicted that the downgrades were more than double the upgrades both in terms of number of instruments and the volume of debt which shows that the ratings were issuer biased. Based on the findings, author suggested that stringent methods should be adopted to avoid frequent downgrades.

Arora, M. (2003) made an attempt to evaluate the credit rating system in India. The main objective was to study the factors affecting bond ratings, their relevant weightage in rating and to develop a model for testing bond rating by various agencies. The study depicted that both qualitative and quantitative factors were important for bond rating. The findings showed that the post-rating performance of companies did not justify initial ratings assigned to them. Further, the external inconsistency and variability in rating of bonds was observed due to changing corporate business environment and poor forecasting abilities of the analysts.

Credit rating agencies act as the information providers for credit related opinions. The comprehensive research pertaining to credit rating for bonds is a well researched topic in India as well as in other nations. However, the linkage of credit ratings assigned to the shares and its financial ratios are still not much explored. In this study, we look for to answer the question that "Are the ratings assigned to the shares by the credit rating agencies are implicit and found useful by the individual investors in India?" We want to explore that if there is any linkage between the credit ratings given by the credit rating agencies and financial performance. We have considered financial ratios as the proxy of financial performance. (Opler, T. C., & Titman, S. 1994).

RESEARCH METHODOLOGY

The analysis of a company's financial ratios is core to the rating process by the rating agencies as these ratios help judging a company's overall financial risk profile. The study assesses the consistency in shares rating methodology of four rating agencies including CRISIL, ICRA, CARE and FITCH. The rating agencies rate on the basis of various factors like history of the company, quality of management, competitive standing, strength of brand names, short-term liquidity and long-term solvency and profitability of the companies etc. We have only considered the quantitative factors on the basis of previous studies like Pogue and Soldofsky (1969), Blume et al. (1998), Kaplan and Urwitz (1979), Raghunathan and Varma (1993), Bhattacharyya (2009). The relative importance of the ratios may vary on a case-specific basis. CRISIL does not adopt an arithmetic approach in using these ratios while assessing financial risk; instead, CRISIL makes a subjective assessment of the importance of the ratios for each credit. A detailed discussion on each of the nine parameters is presented in Figure 1.

Rating agencies usually considers nine crucial financial parameters while evaluating a company's credit quality: capital structure, interest coverage ratio, debt to equity ratio, net worth, profitability, return on capital employed, net cash accruals to total debt ratio, and current ratio. The data regarding various rating grades has been collected from the reports of the rating agencies including various issues of CRISIL Rating Scan, ICRA Rating Profile, CARE Rating View, FITCH's India Ratings Monthly and websites of these rating agencies. Further, the data relating to various financial ratios during the given period has been collected from PROWESS database of CMIE.

The primary motive of the study is to assess the consistency in the rating methodology of selected rating agencies. The secondary objective is to know the dependence of ratings on the mix of financial risks borne by the entity and financial performance.

The sample of one hundred and fifty eight firms is utilized to establish a relation which best discriminates between ratings given by credit rating firms and financial ratios. The selections of these companies were as per the market capitalization from the list of BSE 500 as on 31st March, 2017. In order to examine the variability in ratings by various rating agencies the time period of eight years starting from April, 2009 to March, 2017 has been selected. The study employed the multinomial logistic regression model to explain the relationship among the variable. Literature supports the application of the model as they have applied the following: ordered linear probit model (Kaplan and Urwitz, 1979; Poon, 2003; Cheng et al, 2009; Hwang et al, 2010), ordered and unordered linear logit models (Ederington, 1985),

Figure 1. Use of Financial Risk Analysis in Rating Decisions
Source: www.crisil.com

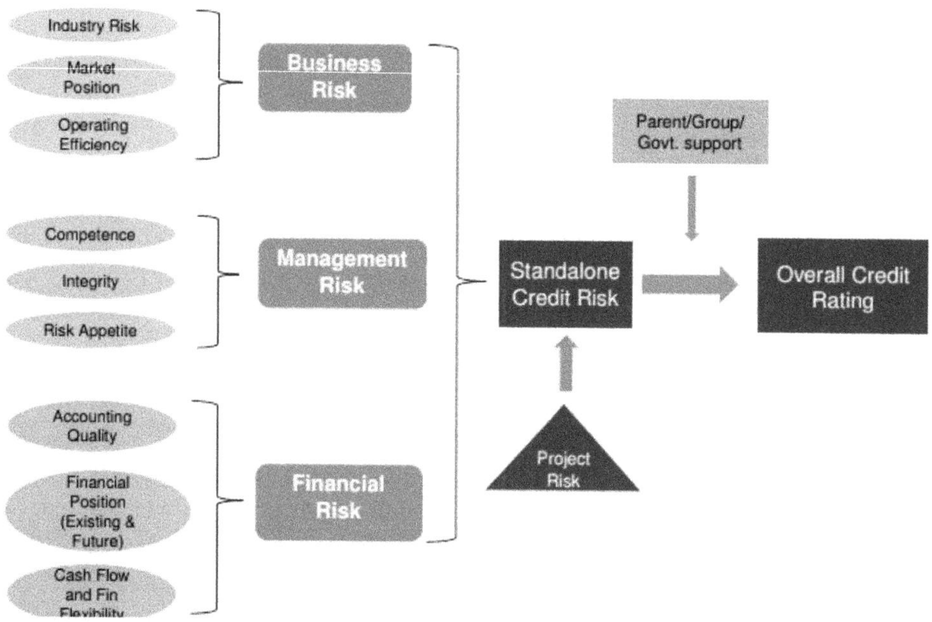

bayesian networks (Wijayatunga et al, 2006), support vector machines and neural networks (Huang et al., 2004). The details of the variables used in the study are as shown in Table 1.

A credit rating informs investors about the probability of timely servicing of the rated debt obligation. Therefore, financial risk in the form of high gearing adversely affects an entity's credit rating. The rating also depends on the mix of business and financial risks borne by the entity. For instance, entities that are highly susceptible to industry cycles, such as sugar and cement companies cannot afford high gearing. On the other hand, companies in stable industries may choose to operate with higher debt without unduly straining their financial position. The codes assigned to each ratings are: AAA Rating -1, AA Rating -2, A Rating -3, BBB Rating -4, BB Rating -5, B Rating - 6, C Rating -7, D Rating - 8, No Rating- 0. The descriptive statistics of the variables used in the study are as follow:

The data set used in the study shows the highest mean for Interest coverage ratio and lowest for FITCH. Standard deviation and variance is highest for the Interest coverage ratio. Two variables used in the study are following the distribution with kurtosis less than 3 and are said to be platykurtic in nature. The rest all variables are following the distributions with kurtosis greater than 3 are said to be leptokurtic.

EMPIRICAL RESULTS AND DISCUSSION

A company's capital structure--commonly referred to as gearing, leverage, or debt-to-equity ratio--reflects the extent of borrowed funds in the company's funding mix. The equity component in the capital employed by a company has no fixed repayment obligations; returns to equity shareholders depend on the profits made by the company. Debt, on the other hand, carries specified contractual obligations of interest and principal. These will necessarily have to be honored, in full and on time, irrespective of the

Table 1. Details of variable used

Abbreviations	Variable Used	Formula Used
DERTO	Gearing	Total debt /Tangible net worth
LTDERTO	Total Indebtedness Ratio	Total Outside Liability / Tangible Net Worth
CurRTO	Current ratio	Current assets (including marketable securities)/Current liabilities (including current portion of long-term debt i.e. CPLTD)
IntCov_RTO	Interest coverage ratio	Profit before depreciation, interest, and tax (PBDIT)/ Interest and finance charges
PBITM	Profit before interest and tax	PBDIT includes recurring non-operating income, however excludes one time, extra ordinary income or expense
CPM	Net cash accruals to total debt	[PAT - Dividend + Depreciation] / Total debt (short and long term, including off-balance-sheet debt)
APATM	PAT margin	Profit after tax / Operating income
ROCE	Return on capital employed	Profit before interest and tax (PBIT) / [Total debt + Tangible net worth + Deferred tax liability]
RONW	Return on Net worth	Profit before interest and tax (PBIT) / Net tangible net worth - reserves and Surplus - miscellaneous expenditure

Source: www.crisil.com
https://www.crisil.com/mnt/winshare/Ratings/SectorMethodology/MethodologyDocs/criteria/CRISILs%20Approach%20to%20Financial%20Ratios.pdf

Table 2. Descriptive Statistics

Variables	Minimum	Maximum	Mean	Std. Deviation	Variance	Skewness	Kurtosis
CARE	0	8	.66	1.214	1.473	1.905	2.931
CRISIL	0	8	1.98	1.887	3.560	1.555	2.591
ICRA	0	8	.82	1.349	1.820	2.453	8.851
FITCH	0	8	.27	.993	.986	4.819	27.598
DERTO	.0000	25.8820	1.148797	2.4292476	5.901	7.341	69.516
LTDERTO	.0000	18.4400	.684190	1.6658486	2.775	8.171	83.164
CurRTO	.2600	9.8920	1.512506	1.2905929	1.666	4.234	22.629
IntCov_RTO	-481.9480	10726.2340	217.651089	1050.9843244	1104568.050	7.642	68.057
PBITM	-131.8840	1510.2060	31.636025	121.5311780	14769.827	11.606	141.959
CPM	-181.8380	1354.5780	22.559101	108.9356583	11866.978	11.749	144.959
APATM	-194.5220	1353.0160	18.227570	109.3472053	11956.811	11.679	143.978
ROCE	-1.7620	124.1800	19.405468	15.3309018	235.037	2.693	13.485
RONW	-17.9800	103.5600	17.850139	14.2429447	202.861	1.796	8.009

Source: Author's Compilation

volatility witnessed in the business. A company's capital structure is invariably a function of the strategy adopted by its management. Although high dependence on borrowed funds (and thus, high gearing) may result in a higher return on shareholders' funds, it translates into high fixed costs in terms of the interest burden, which may adversely affect the company's financial position. In fact, in situations of weak business performance, high gearing may weaken profitability, constraining a company's ability to repay debt. Gearing, therefore, denotes the extent of financial risk taken by a company: the larger the quantum of debt, the higher the gearing, and the more difficult it will be for the company to service its debt obligations. Arora (2003) had used anova model to predict the inconsistency and we have implied anova analysis to check the significant difference among the credit rating agencies. Analysis shows that ROCE and RONW are the consistent variable for CRISIL, ICRA and FITCH. However, for CARE, DERTO and LTDERTO are the variables that are significant. The anova result signifies that the methodologies of all four credit rating companies are inconsistent in nature. Hence, to make more clarity in results we have used Multinomial logistic regression.

A multinomial logit model fits the full factorial model or a user-specified model. Multinomial logistic regression is known as polytomous logistic regression, softmax regression, maximum entropy (MaxEnt) classifier, multinomial logit, and conditional maximum entropy model. In this model, parameter estimation is performed through an iterative maximum-likelihood algorithm. To obtain the maximum likelihood estimate of B, Newton-Raphson iterative estimation method is used. Notice that this method is the same as Fisher Scoring iterative estimation method in this model, since the expectation of the second derivative of the log-likelihood with respect to B is the same as the observed one. In natural language processing, multinomial LR classifiers are commonly used as an alternative to naive Bayes classifiers because they do not assume statistical independence of the random variables (commonly known as features) that serve as predictors. Martina Novotná (2012) has employed multinomial logit model for credit rating prediction.

Table 3. Anova Analysis

Rating Agencies	CRISIL		ICRA		CARE		FITCH	
Variables	**F**	**Sig.**	**F**	**Sig.**	**F**	**Sig.**	**F**	**Sig.**
DERTO	1.560	.142	1.560	.142	16.140	**.000**	1.475	.201
LTDERTO	1.256	.271	1.256	.271	18.216	**.000**	.896	.485
CurRTO	.592	.784	.592	.784	.349	.882	1.038	.398
IntCov_RTO	.383	.928	.383	.928	.351	.881	.435	.824
PBIDTM	.510	.848	.510	.848	2.016	.079	.061	.997
PBITM	.533	.830	.533	.830	1.961	.088	.065	.997
PBDTM	.552	.816	.552	.816	2.132	.065	.082	.995
CPM	.563	.807	.563	.807	2.066	.073	.067	.997
APATM	.595	.781	.595	.781	2.004	.081	.075	.996
ROCE	3.343	**.002**	3.343	**.002**	1.443	.212	3.401	**.006**
RONW	2.895	**.005**	2.895	**.005**	2.096	.069	2.982	**.013**

Source: Author's Compilation

The results for CRISIL[1] credit ratings have been mentioned in Table 4. Debt to equity ratio along with its log variable and profit after tax margin are the ratios which are statistically significant in the model. Three out of nine variables are found significant. The R square of Cox and Snell is .508, R square statistics of Nagelkerke is .524 and McFadden's statistics for Pseudo R-Square is .204. The overall correct predicted percentage of the model is 44.9 percent for CRISIL credit ratings. This signifies that the model can be classified as approx 44.9 percent actual versus predicted. Overall model for CRISIL is statistically significant at 0.05 level.

CARE[2] credit rating is the next CRA to enter into the Indian market after Crisil. The MNL results for CARE have been mentioned in Table 5. Debt to equity ratio along with its log variable, Return on capital employed, Return on Net worth and profit after tax margin are the ratios which are statistically significant in the model. Five out of nine variables are found significant. The R square of Cox and Snell is .408, R square statistics of Nagelkerke is .467 and McFadden's statistics for Pseudo R-Square is .253. The overall correct predicted percentage of the model is 71.5 percent for CARE credit ratings. Overall model for CARE is statistically significant at 0.05 level.

ICRA's ratings is well known for its investment grade, it convey the probability of default and relative likelihood of loss on default. The results for ICRA[3] credit ratings have been mentioned in Table 6. Profit after tax margin is the ratio which is statistically significant in the model. One out of nine variables are found significant. The R square of Cox and Snell is .357, R square statistics of Nagelkerke is .397 and McFadden's statistics for Pseudo R-Square is .193. The overall correct predicted percentage of the model is 65.8 percent for ICRA credit ratings. Overall model for ICRA is statistically significant at 0.05 level.

Internationally, Fitch Ratings is considered as one of the 'Big three credit rating agencies' in the world. Fitch has gained this position after Moody's and Standard & Poor's credit rating agencies. The results for FITCH[4] credit ratings have been stated in Table 7. Profit after tax margin and Return on net worth are the ratios which are statistically significant in the model. Two out of nine variables are found significant. However, overall model for ICRA is not statistically significant at 0.05 level. The R square of Cox and Snell is .255, R square statistics of Nagelkerke is .425 and McFadden's statistics for Pseudo R-Square is .322. The overall correct predicted percentage of the model is 91.1 percent for FITCH credit ratings. The reason behind this is, may be that Fitch is taking the help of Business risk and Market risk in place of financial risk.

FUTURE GUIDELINES

Credit rating establishes a link between risk and return, thereby, providing a yardstick to measure the risk inherent in any financial instrument. The investors use the ratings to assess the risk level and compare the rate of return offered with the expected rate of return to optimize their risk-return trade-offs.

In the absence of a credit rating system, it is not feasible for the investors to undertake a detailed risk evaluation. The investors largely depend upon their familiarity with the promoters and collaborators to arrive at a uniform conclusion towards relative quality of the instrument. Therefore, the need of the credit ratings cannot be overemphasized. In today's changing environment, credit ratings are playing an important role in the financial ecosystem.

Thus, this article will help the investor to evaluate the efficiency of credit ratings assigned by all the credit rating agencies selected under the study. Taking into consideration, the fundamental analysis of stock valuation, analyst would be able to define the competent agency among all.

Table 4a. Multinomial logistic regression: CRISIL likelihood ratio tests

Likelihood Ratio Tests			
Effect	**-2 Log Likelihood of Reduced Model**	**Chi-Square**	**Sig.**
Intercept	448.989	12.602	.126
DERTO	451.581	15.194	.053**
LTDERTO	454.970	18.583	.017**
CurRTO	442.652	6.265	.618
IntCov_RTO	442.303	5.916	.657
PBITM	443.096	6.709	.568
CPM	447.523	11.137	.194
APATM	452.427	16.041	.042**
ROCE	448.448	12.061	.148
RONW	443.904	7.517	.482
Model Fitting Information			
Intercept Only	548.295	111.908	.002**
Final	436.387		
Pseudo R-Square			
Cox and Snell			.508
Nagelkerke			.524
McFadden			.204

Table 4b. Multinomial logistic regression: CRISIL classification

Classification: Actual V/s Predicted										
Observed	**Predicted**									
	0	**1**	**2**	**3**	**4**	**5**	**6**	**7**	**8**	**Percent Correct**
0	14	2	18	0	0	0	0	0	0	41.2%
1	5	10	16	1	1	0	0	1	0	29.4%
2	4	7	40	0	1	0	0	0	0	76.9%
3	3	1	10	0	1	0	1	0	1	0.0%
4	1	1	1	0	2	0	0	0	0	40.0%
5	2	0	2	0	1	0	0	0	1	0.0%
6	0	0	1	0	0	0	1	0	0	50.0%
7	0	1	0	0	0	0	0	1	0	50.0%
8	1	0	2	0	0	0	0	0	3	50.0%
Overall Percentage	19.0%	13.9%	57.0%	0.6%	3.8%	0.0%	1.3%	1.3%	3.2%	44.9%

Source: Author's Compilation

Table 5a. Multinomial logistic regression: CARE likelihood ratio tests

Likelihood Ratio Tests			
Effect	**-2 Log Likelihood of Reduced Model**	**Chi-Square**	**Sig.**
Intercept	254.062	10.091	.073
DERTO	258.880	14.909	.011**
LTDERTO	259.343	15.372	.009**
CurRTO	253.128	9.158	.103
IntCov_RTO	247.398	3.428	.634
PBITM	247.655	3.685	.596
CPM	253.990	10.019	.075
APATM	254.672	10.701	.052**
ROCE	263.326	19.356	.002**
RONW	258.646	14.676	.012**
Model Fitting Information			
Intercept Only	326.765	82.794	.001**
Final	243.970		
Pseudo R-Square			
Cox and Snell			.408
Nagelkerke			.467
McFadden			.253

Table 5b. Multinomial logistic regression: CARE classification

Classification: Actual V/s Predicted										
Observed	**Predicted**									
	0	**1**	**2**	**3**	**4**	**5**	**6**	**7**	**8**	**Percent Correct**
0	107	1	3	0	0	0	0	0	0	41.2%
1	13	0	1	0	1	0	0	0	0	29.4%
2	15	0	2	0	0	0	0	0	0	76.9%
3	4	0	0	3	0	0	0	0	0	0.0%
4	2	0	1	1	1	0	0	0	0	40.0%
5	2	0	0	0	1	0	0	0	0	0.0%
6	0	0	0	0	0	0	0	0	0	0.0%
7	0	0	0	0	0	0	0	0	0	0.0%
8	0	0	0	0	0	0	0	0	0	0.0%
Overall Percentage	90.5%	0.6%	4.4%	2.5%	1.9%	0.0%	0.0%	0.0%	0.0%	71.5%

Source: Author's Compilation

Table 6a. Multinomial logistic regression: ICRA likelihood ratio tests

Likelihood Ratio Tests			
Effect	**-2 Log Likelihood of Reduced Model**	**Chi-Square**	**Sig.**
Intercept	293.667	3.136	.679
DERTO	295.169	4.638	.462
LTDERTO	294.097	3.566	.613
CurRTO	297.751	7.220	.205
IntCov_RTO	292.745	2.214	.819
PBITM	294.248	3.717	.591
CPM	299.997	9.466	.092
APATM	302.631	12.100	.033**
ROCE	297.096	6.565	.255
RONW	297.376	6.845	.232
Model Fitting Information			
Intercept Only	360.226	69.695	.011**
Final	290.531		
Pseudo R-Square			
Cox and Snell			.357
Nagelkerke			.397
McFadden			.193

Table 6b. Multinomial logistic regression: ICRA classification

Classification: Actual V/s Predicted										
Observed	**Predicted**									
	0	**1**	**2**	**3**	**4**	**5**	**6**	**7**	**8**	**Percent Correct**
0	96	1	1	1	0	0	0	0	0	97.0%
1	14	3	0	0	0	0	0	0	0	17.6%
2	23	0	3	1	0	0	0	0	0	11.1%
3	9	0	1	0	0	0	0	0	0	0.0%
4	3	0	0	0	0	0	0	0	0	0.0%
5	0	0	0	0	0	0	0	0	0	0.0%
6	0	0	0	0	0	0	0	0	0	0.0%
7	0	0	0	0	0	0	0	0	0	0.0%
8	0	0	0	0	0	0	0	0	2	100.0%
Overall Percentage	91.8%	2.5%	3.2%	1.3%	0.0%	0.0%	0.0%	0.0%	1.3%	65.8%

Source: Author's Compilation

Table 7a. Multinomial logistic regression: FITCH likelihood ratio tests

Likelihood Ratio Tests			
Effect	**-2 Log Likelihood of Reduced Model**	**Chi-Square**	**Sig.**
Intercept	101.352	3.446	.632
DERTO	107.810	9.904	.078
LTDERTO	106.781	8.875	.114
CurRTO	99.187	1.281	.937
IntCov_RTO	101.786	3.881	.567
PBITM	104.025	6.119	.295
CPM	106.841	8.935	.112
APATM	120.467	22.561	.000**
ROCE	101.015	3.109	.683
RONW	125.329	27.423	.000**
Model Fitting Information			
Intercept Only	144.363	46.457	.412
Final	97.906		
Pseudo R-Square			
Cox and Snell			.255
Nagelkerke			.425
McFadden			.322

Table 7b. Multinomial logistic regression: FITCH classification

Classification: Actual V/s Predicted										
Observed	**Predicted**									
	0	**1**	**2**	**3**	**4**	**5**	**6**	**7**	**8**	**Percent Correct**
0	142	0	0	1	0	0	0	0	0	99.3%
1	4	0	0	0	0	0	0	0	0	0.0%
2	4	0	0	0	0	0	0	0	0	0.0%
3	2	0	0	0	0	0	0	0	0	0.0%
4	3	0	0	0	1	0	0	0	0	25.0%
5	0	0	0	0	0	0	0	0	0	0.0%
6	0	0	0	0	0	0	0	0	0	0.0%
7	0	0	0	0	0	0	0	0	0	0.0%
8	0	0	0	0	0	0	0	0	1	100.0%
Overall Percentage	98.1%	0.0%	0.0%	0.6%	0.6%	0.0%	0.0%	0.0%	0.6%	91.1%

Source: Author's Compilation

The most significant change in the recent relates to emphasize on accountability of the rating agencies and more importantly, the caution in regulator's use of ratings.

The study will also help the credit rating firms to know their performance in long term. In European economies studies has given much importance to the financial performance for knowing the rating and their pattern (Kaplan and Urwitz, 1979; Poon, 2003; Cheng et al, 2009; Hwang et al, 2010). Few have found a systematic relation amongst them (Ederington, 1985), (Wijayatunga et al, 2006), (Huang et al., 2004).

In India, ratings are a more recent phenomenon, but changes in the global perspectives impact the financial system. Credit rating agencies specialize in analysing and evaluating the creditworthiness of corporate and sovereign issuers of debt securities. Moreover, ratings determine the eligibility of debt and other financial instruments to be included in the portfolios of the investors.

Therefore, further analysis can be done by taking into consideration the impact of pre and post news announcements on the share prices of the issuers of debt and financial instruments.

CONCLUSION AND POLICY IMPLICATIONS

Safety and risk are two sides of the same coin. Understanding and interpreting the rating scale is not easy. Ratings agencies in India use "safety" as a description for the upper rating symbols and "certainty" for the lower rating symbols. "Inadequate" description for a rating symbol offers no precise estimate of the risk involved except on a relative scale. Rating agencies gathers sufficient data to be able to publish probability estimates of instrument's default under various rating categories. The rating agencies considered for the study are not only the largest and most experienced of the ratings agencies in India, but are also by most accounts, the best of the lot. Therefore, it can be safely said that our conclusions would, in fact apply to the entire Indian credit rating industry.

The rating agencies under the study considered almost the similar parameters for the rating methodology. The methodologies and criteria used for determining the rating levels are created and revised by the analytical groups. As far as consistency in the rating methodology is concerned, all the rating agencies follow the same methodology to some extent while assigning a particular rating grade. We attempted to assess the impact of financial ratios on the rating symbols given by the Indian credit rating agencies and their performance in term of rating methodology.

The important policy issues relate to what can be done to improve the quality of the ratings in India. It is highly instructive to examine the international experience on how rating agencies have been able to maintain their well-deserved reputation for independence and expertise. Internationally, the good debt instruments are rated by two independent agencies and the market tends to follow the lower of the two ratings. Also, the rating agencies have developed the technique of unsolicited rating, in which rating is made by the rating agency without being requested or being paid to do so by the issuer. If these factors can be adopted, they can eliminate the problem of competitive relaxation of norms. In this context, there needs to be much greater competition among the credit rating agencies so that raters can be kept on their toes and help the ratings more meaningful and useful than they are today.

Every credit rating agency has its own unique approach for adding value to the business world. The role played by the rating agencies in India is very critical in determining the investment portfolio of individual as well as institutional investors. Thus, these agencies play a significant role in the development of overall economy of the country.

It must be stressed that this article is not intended to describe the rating process or the particular financial ratios favoring any of the rating agencies, but rather uses the standard ratios to explore the quantitative content of ratings by the selected credit rating agencies. Moreover, while some industry and issuer specific judgments have been made to these ratios, they are not always the precise ratios used by the credit rating agencies in India for evaluating the credit.

While the nine parameters mentioned above are crucial in analyzing a company's credit quality, they do not by themselves capture the company's financial health in its entirety. Ratio analysis is only one part of the rating process. To assess a company's overall financial risk profile, qualitative and forward looking considerations are also important. Thus, even as an entity may report strong financials, its credit rating may still be constrained if its business risk is high or it follows a less transparent corporate governance structure. On the other hand, strong financial flexibility or backing from stronger group entities could mitigate the impact of weak financials and support an entity's credit profile.

The result for analysis of variance shows that ICRA CRISIL AND FITCH is adopting consistent rating methodology for the companies. However, CARE has shown a different result for adoption of rating methodology. Through the results of Multinomial logistic regression we can say that if any investor wants to draw any conclusion by looking at rating methods then the variables are different for different rating agencies. We had considered only those ratios which were shown by the CRISIL in their reports or available literatures. The regression result shows a inter-linkage of all credit rating firms with financial ratios, except the FITCH credit rating. The reason behind this is, may be that Fitch is taking the help of Business risk and Market risk in place of financial risk. Another reason may be that FITCH is new in the Indian financial market and hence, their rating may not be that appropriate for the investors in terms of their dependence on financial performance. The analysis suggests that variables such as debt to equity ratio, profit after tax; returns on capital employed and return on Net worth are those with the highest impact on rating agencies and thus there is also discriminating power among rating agencies. The results are consistent with the following studies; Pinches and Mingo (1973), Ang and Patel (1978), Wingler and Watts (1980), Belkaoui (1980) and Altman and Katz (1976), and Novotná (2012).

The results were predicted as the financial ratios used by the credit rating agencies for credit rating differ across companies and so their methodologies. Overall this paper provides a better understanding of the relationship between financial ratios and credit ratings. Applying such relationship to the data sample consisting of sector specific and industry firms is however left for the future research.

Future Guidelines

This article will help the investor to evaluate the efficiency of credit rating assigned by all the four credit rating agencies in India. Taking into consideration, the fundamental analysis of stock valuation, analyst would be able to define the competent agency among all. The study will also help the credit rating firms to know their performance in long term. In European economies studies has given much importance to the financial performance for knowing the rating and their pattern (Kaplan and Urwitz, 1979; Poon, 2003; Cheng et al, 2009; Hwang et al, 2010). Few have found a systematic relation amongst them (Ederington, 1985), (Wijayatunga et al, 2006), (Huang et al., 2004). The analysis will show better results, if the pre and post impact of news announcement related to Credit ratings on the Indian share prices may be looked into.

Conclusion and Policy Implications

At the corporate level, it is usually in the best interest of a company to look for a credit rating agency to rate their debt. Investors often times base part of their decision to buy bonds, or even the stock, on the credit rating of the company's debt. Major credit agencies, such as Moody's or Standard and Poor's, perform this rating service for a fee. Usually, investors will look at the credit rating given by these international credit rating agencies as well as ratings given by domestic rating agencies before deciding to invest. Hence, the linkage of credit ratings assigned to the shares and its financial ratios becomes important issue. In this study, we look for to answer the question that "Are the ratings assigned to the shares by the credit rating agencies are implicit and found useful by the individual investors in India?" We explored that if there is any linkage between the credit ratings given by the credit rating agencies and financial performance.

The result for analysis of variance shows that ICRA CRISIL AND FITCH is adopting consistent rating methodology for the companies. However, CARE has shown a different result for adoption of rating methodology. Through the results of Multinomial logistic regression we can say that if any investor wants to draw any conclusion by looking at rating methods then the variables are different for different rating agencies. We had considered only those ratios which were shown by the CRISIL in their reports or available literatures. The regression result shows a inter-linkage of all credit rating firms with financial ratios, except the FITCH credit rating. The reason behind this is, may be that Fitch is taking the help of Business risk and Market risk in place of financial risk. Another reason may be that FITCH is new[5] in the Indian financial market and hence, their rating may not be that appropriate for the investors in terms of their dependence on financial performance. The analysis suggests that variables such as debt to equity ratio, profit after tax; returns on capital employed and return on Net worth are those with the highest impact on rating agencies and thus there is also discriminating power among rating agencies. The results are consistent with the following studies; Pinches and Mingo (1973), Ang and Patel (1978), Wingler and Watts (1980), Belkaoui (1980) and Altman and Katz (1976), and Novotná (2012).

Credit ratings are also important at the country level. Many countries rely on foreign investors to purchase their debt, and these investors rely heavily on the credit ratings given by the credit rating agencies. The benefits for a country of a good credit rating include being able to access funds from outside their country, and the possession of a good rating can attract other forms of investment to a country, such as foreign direct investment. For instance, a company looking to open a factory in a particular country may first look at the country's credit rating to assess its stability before deciding to invest. Hence, it becomes essential to know the relevance of rating agencies and their way of rating the firms.

REFERENCES

Altman, E. I. (1968). Financial Ratios, Discriminant Analysis and the Prediction of Corporate Bankruptcy. *The Journal of Finance*, *23*(4), 889–609. doi:10.1111/j.1540-6261.1968.tb00843.x

Altman, E. I., & Katz, S. (1976). Statistical bond rating classification using financial and accounting data. In *Proceedings of the conference on topical research in accounting* (pp. 205-239). New York: University Press New York.

Arora, M. (2003). *Credit Rating in India: Institutions, Methods and Evaluation.* Delhi: New Century Publications.

Beaver, W. (1967). Financial Ratios as Predictor of Failure. *Empirical Research in Accounting, Empirical Studies, Journal of Accounting Research, 4*, 71–111. doi:10.2307/2490171

Bhattacharyya, M. (2009). A Study of Issuer Rating Service with an Appraisal of ICRA's Rating Model. *Indian Journal of Accounting, 39*(2), 53–60.

Bheemanagauda & Madegowda, J. (2010). Performance of Credit Rating Agencies in India. *The Indian Journal of Commerce, 63*(3), 50-62.

Blume, M. E., Lim, F., & MacKinlay, A. C. (1998). The declining credit quality of US corporate debt: Myth or reality? *The Journal of Finance, 53*(4), 1389–1413. doi:10.1111/0022-1082.00057

Cheng, H., Lu, Y. C., & Sheu, C. (2009). An ontology-based business intelligence application in a financial knowledge management system. *Expert Systems with Applications, 36*(2), 3614–3622. doi:10.1016/j.eswa.2008.02.047

Christy, G. C. (2009). The Accounting Fog Machine. *Free Cash Flow: Seeing Through the Accounting Fog Machine to Find Great Stocks*, 15-24.

Ederington, L. H., & Yawitz, J. B. (1985). *The bond rating process.* Washington University. Institute of Banking and Financial Markets.

Gray, S., Mirkovic, A., & Ragunathan, V. (2006). The determinants of credit ratings: Australian evidence. *Australian Journal of Management, 31*(2), 333–354. doi:10.1177/031289620603100208

Horrigan, J. O. (1966). The determination of long-term credit standing with financial ratios. *Journal of Accounting Research, 4*, 44–62. doi:10.2307/2490168

Horrigan, J. O. (1966). The determination of long-term credit standing with financial ratios. *Journal of Accounting Research, 4*, 44–62. doi:10.2307/2490168

Huang, Z., Chen, H., Hsu, C. J., Chen, W. H., & Wu, S. (2004). Credit rating analysis with support vector machines and neural networks: A market comparative study. *Decision Support Systems, 37*(4), 543–558. doi:10.1016/S0167-9236(03)00086-1

Hwang, R. C., Chung, H., & Chu, C. K. (2010). Predicting issuer credit ratings using a semiparametric method. *Journal of Empirical Finance, 17*(1), 120–137. doi:10.1016/j.jempfin.2009.07.007

Kanagaraj, A., & Murugesan, B. (2006). Evaluation of Financial Information Content in Credit Rating using Binary Logistic Regression. *The ICFAI Journal of Applied Finance, 12*(10), 40–64.

Kaplan, R. S., & Urwitz, G. (1979). Statistical models of bond ratings: A methodological inquiry. *The Journal of Business, 52*(2), 231–261. doi:10.1086/296045

Opler, T. C., & Titman, S. (1994). Financial distress and corporate performance. *The Journal of Finance, 49*(3), 1015–1040. doi:10.1111/j.1540-6261.1994.tb00086.x

Pinches, G. E., & Mingo, K. A. (1973). A multivariate analysis of industrial bond ratings. *The Journal of Finance*, *28*(1), 1–18. doi:10.1111/j.1540-6261.1973.tb01341.x

Pogue, T. F., & Soldofsky, R. M. (1969). What's in a Bond Rating. *Journal of Financial and Quantitative Analysis*, *4*(2), 201–228. doi:10.2307/2329840

Poon, J. P. (2003). Hierarchical tendencies of capital markets among international financial centers. *Growth and Change*, *34*(2), 135–156. doi:10.1111/1468-2257.00211

Raghunathan, V., & Varma, J. R. (1993). *When AAA means B: The State of Credit Rating in India*. Working Paper No. 1141, Indian Institute of Management, Ahmedabad. Available at www.rediff.com

Robinson, J. (1933). A Parable on Savings and Investment. *Economica*, (39), 75–84. doi:10.2307/2548862

Van Horne James, C. (2002). *Financial Management and Policy* (12th ed.). Pearson Education.

West, R. R. (1970). An alternative approach to predicting corporate bond ratings. *Journal of Accounting Research*, *8*(1), 118–125. doi:10.2307/2674717

Wijayatunga, P., Mase, S., & Nakamura, M. (2006). Appraisal of companies with Bayesian networks. *International Journal of Business Intelligence and Data Mining*, *1*(3), 329–346. doi:10.1504/IJBIDM.2006.009138

ENDNOTES

1 CRISIL, India's first credit rating agency, is incorporated on the 29th Jan 1987, promoted by the erstwhile ICICI Ltd along with UTI and other financial institutions. Mr. N Vaghul and Mr. Pradip Shah are CRISIL's first Chairman and Managing Director, respectively. (Source: https://www.crisil.com/en/home/about-us/our-history.html)

2 CARE, a credit rating agency set up in 1993 and promoted by the Industrial Development Bank of India (IDBI), Canara Bank, Unit Trust of India (UTI) in association with other domestic banks and financial service companies. (Source: http://expressindia.indianexpress.com/fe/daily/20000713/fco13044.html)

3 ICRA Limited (formerly Investment Information and Credit Rating Agency of India Limited) was set up in 1991 by leading financial/investment institutions, commercial banks and financial services companies as an independent and professional investment Information and Credit Rating Agency. (Source: https://www.icra.in/Home/Profile)

4 Fitch India got established in 2000, after acquisition of 33 per cent stake in credit rating agency Duff & Phelps Credit Rating India Pvt Ltd. (Source: http://expressindia.indianexpress.com/fe/daily/20000713/fco13044.html)

5 Fitch India got established in 2000, after acquisition of 33 per cent stake in credit rating agency Duff & Phelps Credit Rating India Pvt Ltd. (Source: http://expressindia.indianexpress.com/fe/daily/20000713/fco13044.html)

Chapter 15
An Impact Assessment of Goods and Services Tax in India Through Strategic Analysis Approach (SAA)

Tripti Tripathi
Jiwaji University, India

Manoj Kumar Dash
Indian Institute of Information Technology and Management Gwalior, India

ABSTRACT

This chapter focuses on the need, requirements, implementation, challenges, and impact of the goods and services tax on the Indian economic scenario. The major stakeholders in the process are the Government of India (GOI), the individual states, the industry, the businesses, and the biggest tax reform since independence of India in 1947. Often considered as overdue, it seeks to remove the various shortcomings and the loopholes in the existing system of indirect taxation in the country. The GST bill saw more than a decade of political and economic upheaval in the country. Subsequently, it became an act on 8th September 2016. The various strategic analysis approach (SAA) of the GST mechanism (e.g., SWOT analysis, value chain analysis, PEST analysis, and SAP-LAP analysis) give an in-depth account of the various issues and potential challenges in the implementation of the GST.

INTRODUCTION

The reform process of indirect taxes in India began with the Central Value Added tax (CENVAT) replacing the central excise duties of the central government, and the VAT replacing the sales tax of the state governments (Ehtisam & Nicholas 1984). Shantayanan & Hossain (1998) says that it mitigated the cascading effect due to a multiplicity of taxes to a great extent. This led to a major simplification of the tax structure and broadening the tax base, with more people coming under the tax –net. But both the CENVAT and the VAT proved to be inadequate .Tarun (2012) suggested that the CENVAT lacks the

DOI: 10.4018/978-1-5225-7399-9.ch015

inclusion of the value addition in the distributive stage and the absorption of many central indirect taxes like the additional excise and custom duties, surcharges etc. Thus, making the utility of comprehensive input tax and service tax set-off absolutely futile. Similarly, Harry, Sophie & Wim (1996) explained that the state wise VAT will bear the cascading effect of multiplicity of taxes and fails to absorb many state level taxes like the entertainment tax, luxury tax, etc. Therefore even after repeated policy- steps to simplify the indirect tax regime, it remains cumbersome, complicated and not business friendly. Klaus (2000) suggested that the GST is a scientific, simplified and modern but unified system of taxation in consonance with the developed nations.

The GST is broad based, single and comprehensive tax Douglas& Terry (2001) levied on goods and services at each stage of the sale of goods or the provision of services. The seller or the service provider at each stage will be eligible to claim the input credit of tax which he has already paid while purchasing the goods or availing the service. Thus, the final consumer will only pay the GST charged by the last dealer in the supply chain of the goods and service.

GST Time –Line in India

Since for a developing country Parash Upreti (2015), tax to GDP ratio should be approximately equal to 18% and for a developed country, the ratio should be in a range of 70% in order to ensure sustainable economic growth (Edward, 1987). At 16.49%, India has one of lowest GDP tax to GDP ratio among developing and emerging countries. The tax to GDP ratio for direct and indirect taxes stood at 5.97 and 10.52, respectively, for the financial year 2016-2017.

This work studies and analyses the impact of post- implementation and policy mix of other countries for successful implementation of the GST. It brings out the practices that can be applied to the Indian scenario as well as the identification of the Indian challenges.

Table 1. Tax to GDP Ratio since Indian Independence (1950-51 to 2016-2017)

Tax	1950-51	1960-61	1970-71	1980-81	1990-91	2000-01	2005-06	2010-11	2016-17
Direct tax to GDP ratio	2.22	2.24	2.12	2.8	2.09	3.31	4.5 4	5.78	5.97
Indirect tax to GDP ratio	3.81	4.86	9.22	9.22	11.09	9.23	9.98	9.35	10.52
Total tax to GDP ratio	6.03	7.10	11.40	11.40	13.18	12.54	15.52	15.13	16.49

(Source: Public Finance Statistics, 2017)

Table 2. Tax Rate of GST for Some Selected Countries

Country	Australia	France	Canada	Germany	Japan	Singapore	Sweden	New Zeland
Rate of GST	10%	19.6%	5%	19%	5%	7%	25%	15%

The work also studies the different nuances and details of the GST through the principals of SWOT Analysis (Marylin & Judy, 2010), Value Chain Analysis (Gary John, Raphael &Timothy, 2009), PEST Analysis (Guo & Miguel, 2009) and SAP- LAP Analysis (Sachin, Pradeep & Mukesh 2014), and gives appropriate recommendations.

Until and unless any reform (here the Goods and Services Tax) is well accepted by the people (here, the tax payers) and is consistent with the prevailing social structure and economic level, it cease to be an efficient and effective reform. Therefore, it is imperative to assist in the better implementation of the radical tax reform. In order to begin a systematic mode of study, firstly, the currently available literature on GST and its implications is reviewed in the following section.

Post Implementation GST Study of Some Selected Countries

Shefali (2016) explained that GST has been implemented in one form or the other in more than 140 countries of the world. Some of the countries have very peculiar features in their format of the GST. These described as follows:

In Canada, Richard & Pierre (2010) suggested that the GST replaced the existing Manufacturer's Sales Tax. Products such as groceries, residential rent, and medical services, and services such as financial services are exempted from payment of any tax. Malaysia introduced the GST as a better and more effective tax to replace the inefficient and archaic sales tax and service tax (Kraal & Kasipillai, 2015). In the European Union, the GST (known as the value Added Tax in the EU) has two components – output VAT (i.e. VAT on its output supplies) and input VAT (i.e. VAT paid by a business to another business on the supplies it receives). A business recovers the tax it paid either by adjusting it against the output VAT or if it is in excess, then, by claiming a repayment from the government for the tax component already paid.

Liu, Benjamin, Huang & Allen (2012) investigated that when GST was implemented in Australia there was a corresponding reduction in other taxes. Treasurer Peter Costello to claim that people were effectively paying no extra tax. The tax authorities provide the use of a GST calculator, which is available on ASIC's (Australian Securities and Investment Commission) Money Smart website to calculate the GST. The GST is worked out on the basis of an Australian Business Number (ABN). In New Zealand GST is levied on the prices of most of the goods and services sold or availed in New Zealand. This include most imported goods and some imported Services. The New Zealand tax department clearly specifies activities as taxable and nontaxable.

Analysis of GST Implementation Policies

The following section attempts a comparative study of the different policies and implementation strategies adopted by the above mentioned countries. The various policies are categorized into effective policies, situational policies and detrimental policies.

Geetanjali & Miriam (2017) suggested that GST rate structure should be rational such that it levies optimal taxes. Neither the government should lose any revenue nor are the consumers or businesses unduly burdened. A reasonable GST rate structure is, thus imperative to ensure its successful implementation. Abbas (2004) identified that GST may be inflationary in the short term as the products having current tax rates lower than the proposed rates are bound to get costlier. For example, restaurant services and entertainment modes will initially be costlier. But in the long term as the tax base widens and compliance increases, the government may reduce the tax rates. Palil & Ibrahim (2011) analyzed that that if

Table 3. Analysis of GST policies of selected countries

SN	Effective Policies	Situational Policies	Detrimental Policies
1.	Businesses need to start early with the implementation process to be GST ready	In some countries, VAT is the substitute for GST, but conceptually it is a destination based tax on consumption of goods and services	An aspect encountered and accepted by most of the GST countries lies in the statistic that GST will be inflationary, especially if the effective tax rate is higher than what prevailed before.
2.	The release of sector specific guidance paper(s) on tax treatment concerning each business sector. It aids in addressing the to be tax practice associated with a particular business segment.	Similar to Indian context, it is only Canada and Brazil that has the concept of dual GST. The Government of Canada has been pragmatic and worked towards reducing the GST rate a couple of times post implementation	It would be a mistake to assume that IT software with GST capability from other countries may be adopted wholesale in India, due to peculiarities embedded in the proposed Indian dual GST model.

the businesses adopt a casual attitude or are resistant, they may lag behind the inevitable implementation of GST. This will lead to unnecessary and unavoidable losses for the businesses concerned. Hence, they need to prepare themselves for the new indirect tax regime (Shah, 2006) well in advance. Mishkin (1999) explained that there should be some release of sector specific guidance papers on tax treatment. The government must release sector specific manuals and other documents to suitably guide the different business segments. This will ensure their proper assimilation into the updated indirect tax regime. Mary, Stephen & Matthew (2000) suggested automation and use of IT system for the successful implementation of GST will require a robust information Technology infrastructure to handle the enormous quantity of data, its processing and provision of adequate security. Businesses should be given necessary time and their concerns must be taken into account through dialogue and the industry should be engaged. This will lead to proper, efficient and effective roll out of GST.

Every stakeholder has some prime task at hand in the successful implementation of the GST the GST rate structure should be reasonable keeping in view of the great economic diversity in the country. The businesses should be GST ready and be cooperative with the authorities concerned. All documents are to be thoroughly referred to. The processes and changes required for GST compliance need to be automated with liberal use of latest information and Communication Technology (ICT).

REVIEW OF LITERATURE

The opportunity to bring about a radical change in a countries tax- administration does not come along very often. Particularly when the stakes are high and the consequences are far reaching. This may very well be a life- time opportunity. Thus, every decision should be a well thought of and the technicalities involved should be suitably taken care of.

It is matter of fact that different stakeholders are indeed willing to cooperate to bring about a drastic change in the indirect tax administration of India. Almost everybody is convinced that the present system of tax administration is mired with inefficiency. This is not only hampering the progress of the society but also adversely affecting the economic growth. It is, therefore, imperative for 21st Century India to get unified economically with a unified taxation regime.

The literature pertaining to the various nuances of the Goods and Services focus on the need and basis for reforms in the indirect tax structure in India. Vasanthagopal (2011) states that though the positive impacts of the GST implementation are enormous, the need is to take along the opinions of all the stakeholders who will be getting affected by it. The implementation of a fool proof GST will be a big leap in the indirect taxation regime. It will boost economic growth. Because of these reasons, many countries around the world are introducing the GST in some form or the other. The experience of such countries has so far been mostly positive. Sehrawat, et at (2015) state that the business in the country (India) is growing to cater to the demands of the growing population. This has led to an enormous increase in the consumption level in the country, which is expected to grow further in the coming future. The growing level of consumption will lead to an increase in the taxable income of people and businesses. Thus, the need of the hour is to have a simplified taxation system which is robust and prevent undue leakages. This is essential for the sustenance and gradual increase in the government's revenue. It will also provide the domestic producers a level playing field in the local as well as international market. The same taxation- system across the country will also lead to the better management of the same. Khurana, et at (2016) state that GST will be beneficial not only to the producers and consumers, but also to the economical scenario in the country. It will lead to a better utilization of available resource. It will have a conducive effect on the various sectors of the economy and enhance tax- compliance. However, the efficient implementation of the GST requires concerted efforts by all stakeholders.

The following four research papers focus on the consequences of GST implementation in India.

The consequences of GST implementation in India is well explained by Shaik, et at (2015) state that tax policies play a crucial role on the economy through their impact on the efficiency, the effectiveness and the equity in the country. The GST will accord equal status to all goods and services. It will be a significant improvement of the current taxation scenario in the country. The main areas to be kept in focus are the national income, per capita income and the status of international trade. A unified system of dispute redressal will also bring down the level of litigation burden on the government and the judiciary. On the same lines Herekar (2012) highlighted the change in the Indian economy form closed to open, from public sector based to dominated by the private sector, and from a welfare state to gradual market economy. The GST implementation will widen the tax base and increase revenue for the government and thus, improve the level of infrastructure in the country. This will be highly beneficial to the economy in the long run.

Gupta (2014) states that although CENVAT and State VAT were a step forward in the direction of reforms in the indirect tax regime. Both of these had some inherent deficiencies. As a result, the benefit were not being translated into the overall economic growth and the consumers remained burdened. There were certain limitations which needed to be overcome. Thus, GST is expected to eliminate all these short- comings and remove the distortions. In the same way Ahmad, et al (2009) states that GST will give a modern taxation system is coherence with the changing times. It cites the examples of different countries to draw the point that GST is a more neutral and efficient tax structure. It will lead to increased output and enhanced productivity in the Indian economic environment. The paper does an empirical study to highlight the potential that the GST carries. But all this will require through research and meticulous planning to initiate what is correctly regarded as the biggest taxation reform since independence.

Existing literature do not say anything about, let only focus on getting the common man (Consumer for whose ultimate benefit GST is being implemented) have a grip of the new tax regime. There are no efforts, as of now, of generating adequate awareness among the masses; so that they can make informed choices related to their consumption behavior/pattern. Unless they are made to know the actual and underlying benefits of GST, The task remains incomplete.

The past researches have not delved into much and did not found out the causes for lack of necessary awareness among the masses, influence of GST on policy formulation, the regional diversity in terms of development and other parameters, probable response of different sectors to the new regime which the researcher in this study tried to find out.

On the basis of the prior studies and gap the objective is to compare and analyze the impact of GST among different countries, and policy analyses from their post-implementation experiences and also to identify policies and policy mix for effective implementation of GST in India.

RESEARCH METHODOLOGY

As a means of scientific inquiry into the GST framework, various managerial analysis are used. The important one used in the work are- SWOT (Strengths, Weaknesses, Opportunities, Threats Matrix), SAP- LAP (Situation, Actor, Process- Learning, Action, Performance), Value-chain and PEST (Political, Economic, Social, Technological) Analysis. These are performed on the GST one by one as follows:

Goods and Services Tax in India: SWOT Analysis

The strength and the main characteristics of a business or a project (here GST) that give it an advantage over others are profitability, less tax burden on consumers and it will also drive high GDP growth. The weakness that include characteristics of the business or the project that place the business or project at a disadvantage relative to others are High investments in research and development are being done and uncertain future productivity. The opportunities are the elements in the external environment that the business or project can exploit to its advantage such as growing economy, increasing demand, new and global markets, new products and services and less tax burden on consumers. The threats comprises of those elements in the external environment that can cause trouble for the business or the project such as when financial capacity is unknown, effects of demonetization on cash flows, effect of increased rates of interest for certain goods and services, technological problems, increasing costs and related price changes.

Goods and Service Tax in India: Value Chain Analysis

It is need of the hour for visionary companies to start working on the impact analysis of GST on its business model and industry, to ideate their best foot forward and take the transition to their advantage. As it will have impact on business by reduction on multiplicity of taxes, cascading effects and overall costs. It will affect Government as increased in tax collections due to wide tax base will help in better compliance. Finally it will also have an impact on final consumers if Government tax collection increases then it will reduce the price and reduction in taxes for the end consumers.

Good and Services Tax in India: PEST Analysis

The basic PEST analysis includes four factors i.e. political, economic, social and technological. Political factors are basically how the government intervenes in the economy. As Consensus- building has become a chronic issue. Vested, regional interests are hampering national interests and political opportunism is a diminishing factor. Economic factors include economic growth, interest rates, exchange rates, and the inflation rate. By implementing GST economic unification of the country will be achieved. Enhanced tax-compliance will lead larger tax base and lesser burden on existing tax payers. Greater revenue generated can be used to improve the infrastructure of the economy. Social factors include the cultural aspects and health consciousness, population growth rate, age distribution, career attitudes and emphasis on safety of the stakeholders. As tax-evasion will become minimal it will lead to employment generation. Increased government revenue will translate into better social amenities, with increased expenditure on education, health and infrastructure. Technological factors include technological aspects like RD activity, automation, technology incentives and the rate of technological change. GSTN supplements the digital India initiatives and the digitization drive of the government. Boost to domestic IT companies for software and logistics development. This will boost IT- based innovation among the people.

Goods and Service Tax in India: SAP-LAP Analysis

The SAP- LAP paradigm, is the basis of flexible system management (Sushil,1997). "It considers three basic entities in any management context, viz., situation, actor and processes. A situation can be dealt with by an actor or set of actors via a process or a set of processes. Out of the three basic entities, the freedom of choice exists with the actor, who can be an individual, a group, a department, or the whole organization. Depending upon the context, first of all, the relevant actors need to be identified. The situation for different actors can be different. What a process for an actor can be the situation for the other actor or vice versa."

Models of SAP-LAP Paradigm:

Model 1: General Problem Solving
Model 2: Change
Model 3: Flexibility

Applying Change Model of SAP- LAP Paradigm to GST

A general model of inquiry into the change (i.e. since the GST is a reform process) is:

- **Situation:** The major opportunities for the GST project in India are growing economy (Mike, Igor, Robert & Peng, 2005), Increasing demand (Johanna, Juha & Patrik, 2003) new and global markets (Gillian & Jay,2006), new products and services and less tax burden on consumers. The major threats of GST project are financial capacity is unknown, cash flows effects of demonetization, increased rates of interest for certain goods and services, technological problems, increasing cost and related price changes. The seeds of reform for the GST project are undue burden for cascading of taxes and uneven tax regime within the same country (Monika & Upasna, 2015).
- **Actor:** A guiding coalition been formed for the proper implementation. First paper, empowered committee report, recommendations of different stakeholders, as well as, research papers by the government and private agencies have been the guiding path. The values and beliefs to move towards GST are reduction in multiplicity of taxes, mitigation of cascading/double taxation, more efficient neutralization of taxes especially for exports, development of common national market, simpler tax regime, reduction in prices of goods/ services due to elimination of cascading of taxes, uniform prices throughout the country, transparency in the taxation system and it will increase in

the employment opportunities. Robert & Vijay (1995) discussed that the level of reform process has been communicated as the vision of change encompass all possible levels of economic hierarchy, viz. Government, procedure, manufacturers, dealers, retailers, customers and consumers.

- **Process:** Entire existing tax structure and collection regime needs to be overhauled. Dahal (2010) suggested that the reform process of the indirect taxes in India began with the Central Value Added Tax. (CENVAT) replacing the central excise Duties of the central government, and the VAT replacing the sales tax of the State governments. It mitigated the cascading effect due to the multiplicity of taxes to a great extent. This led to a major simplification of the tax structure and broadening of the tax base, with more people coming under the tax-net. But both CENVAT and the State VAT proved to be inadequate.

The CENVAT lacks the inclusion of the value added chain in the distributive stage and the absorption of many other Central indirect taxes like additional excise and custom duties, surcharges, etc. Thus, making the utility of comprehensive input tax and service tax set-off absolutely futile in the longer run. Similarly, the State wise VAT still bear the cascading effect of multiplicity of taxes and fails to absorb many State-level taxes like the entertainment tax, luxury tax, etc. therefore even after repeated policy-steps to simplify the indirect tax regime, it remains cumbersome, complicated and non-business friendly. The GST is a scientific, simplified and modern but unified system of taxation in consonance with the developed nations.

- **Learnings:** The introduction of GST will not only subsume most of the existing indirect taxes levied in the country but also charge the consumer only for the incremental value of the value-addition done prior to his purchase. There is unanimous support as far as a common market. However major points of disagreement were/are capping the limit of double taxation to 18% constitutionally, dropping of additional levy of 1% (a major demand of surplus states) and providing for a separate dispute redressal mechanism. More or less wide acceptance among the industry, businessmen and consumers, enhance the potential of the change.
- **Action:** Massive awareness generation of at least the basic nuances, as common people are oblivious to the concept of GST. To initiate the structural change, training of related personnel, regular evaluation and conditioning of policies, and making sure that the target-benefits are being accomplished. To be ahead of the change transparent monetary infrastructure to begin with, along with an emphasis on digitization and cashless economy, will help in keeping ahead of the incoming change.
- **Performance:** The change affect the performance of indirect tax administration by enhanced tax compliance, wider tax base, and increased state revenue at lower rates of taxation.

ANALYSIS AND FINDINGS OF GST IMPLEMENTATION IN INDIA

The inference drawn from the comparative study of the above three analysis, namely SWOT, Value chain based, PEST and SAP-LAP, as well experiences from other countries can be summarized as the tax administration- simpler and more transparent, significant compliance in voluntary compliance, yield significant dividend to economy in terms of increased output and productivity and substantial consensus among all stakeholders for a genuine reform.

The Good and service Tax may be aimed at simplifying the existing indirect tax structure, but its implementation demands require companies businesses to assertively prepare themselves to completely adapt to the new GST rules and regulations. Taking quick initial steps will be a matter of Competitive advantage over rival firms. The businesses need to take important decisions across all domains and sections of their supply chain. The choice of site selection for manufacturing bargaining power of suppliers, supplier contractual agreements, legal documentation, type of purchase and cost settlements form the main issues under this. The issues concerning the factor/ plant such as location, set up, expansion or closure; contract- manufacturing as compared to self-manufacturing and the implications of the evolving business environment. Transportation and distribution as this is the core of supply- chain with challenges posed by the location and operation of distribution centers, flow of goods and services, and the availability of logistics providers in the country at large. The inter play of market forces, demand forecasting, working capital and pricing strategies. The choice between own warehousing and lease warehousing as well the optimization problems of inventory management.

The manufacturing units should be located according to the location of the current and prospective customers. The choice regarding procurements and business partners should be suitably strategized. The locational factors should be decided based on the GST framework. The issues concerning capacity building and competency development should be suitably supplemented. All legal formalities and procedural requirements must be fulfilled regularly and at appropriate times.

One of the remarkable features of the GST framework is its availability as a shared service. The GST will be encapsulated in a common and shared IT infrastructure. This will provide a platform to all stakeholders like the government, businesses and tax payers and so on. It will be, therefore, a common platform for the registration, returns and payment of taxes. The creation of an efficient and user friendly GST Eco- system is the ultimate aim of this initiative. To achieve this, the government is open to collaboration with external agencies as well. Continuing the governments "Maximum Governance, Minimum Government" vision, the services are bound to get more and more simplified. Due research is being carried out in this field. The relevant agencies are extracting best practices from the experiences of others. The training of relevant personnel is simultaneously going on. In order to implement GST hassle-free tax payer profiling Utility (TPU) is being created. All this will make the Tax administration more transparent and improve tax compliance Customization of service for consumers is also on the cards.

The overall impact of GST on businesses shall be in the three main domains- interstate transactions will become tax neutral, ease of doing business will improve, and the rationalization of warehouses and Transport networks will lead to a better and more efficient utilization of resources.

The GST implementation in India has to be executed in the context of a reasonable GST tax rate inflationary perception of the GST, businesses need to start early, release of sector specific guidance papers on tax treatment, automation and use of IT systems and deft planning process. The capital flow compared for pre and post implementation of GST can be understood from Table 4.

Unanimity and consensus- building has been the key. This must be carried forward. It should be remembered that GST will be an evolving tax structure and will require constant reviewing. The ultimate goal of widening the tax base, increase tax compliance and reduction of tax rates in the longer term must be adhered to.

The scope is plenty in this domain as explained earlier. The future researches may pertain to thorough, quantitative and qualitative studies that explain actual implementation assessments. The future researchers will benefit from the fact that the GST would be in execution stage by then.

Table 4. Cash- Flow during pre and post GST implementation

Element of Outflow	Pre GST Outflow	Post GST Outflow
Number of warehouses	23	17
1 day service level	81.10%	80.60%
Days of Inventory	45	32
Total Sales	676	676
Primary Freight Cost	4.82	4.62
Secondary Freight Cost	3.42	4.16
CST	0.88	
Excise	57	
VAT	85	
GST		135

(Sources: Taking Advantage of GST (2015), Redseer Consulting)

The GST Council had cleared the model State GST (SGST) Bill on 16th March, 2017. According to press information bureau of India, eight states had passed the State GST Bill in their respective assemblies, as on 4th May, 2017. The order of these first eight states is Telangana (9th April 2017), Bihar (24th April 2017), Rajasthan (26th April, 2017), Jharkhand (27th April, 2017), Chhattisgarh (28th April, 2017), Uttarakhand (2nd May, 2017), Madhya Pradesh (3rd May, 2017) and Haryana (4th May, 2017).

The Central Government has already set the target for the roll out of the GST, which is 1st July, 2017. The enthusiastic response and swift passage of the State GST Act in different State Assemblies in a time bound manner displays the robustness on the part of the State Governments to ensure that implementation of the GST in letter and spirit is done without any further delay. In order to create general awareness among the people at large and stakeholders in particular and remove their doubts about the various of GST and its related legislations, an outreach programme has been commenced.

CONCLUSION

GST in indeed the order of the day. The entire indirect tax administration will become more robust, efficient, transparent, effective, and the tax- leakages will be plugged. It will go a long way in eliminating the various shortcomings of the previous indirect tax structures. It will also assist the nation in its fight against corruption and black- money. The tax base will widen, thereby, increasing the revenue for the government. This may lead to a reduction in the direct taxes in the future.

REFERENCES

Ahmad, E., & Poddar, S. (2009). *GST Reforms and intergovernmental Considerations in India*. LSE Asia Research Centre, LSE Asia Research Centre.

Ahmad, E., & Stern, N. (1984). The theory of reform and indian indirect taxes. *Journal of Public Economics*, *25*(3), 259–298. doi:10.1016/0047-2727(84)90057-4

Arshinder, K., Kanda, A., & Deshmukh, S. G. (2007). Supply chain coordination issues: An SAP-LAP framework. *Asia Pacific Journal of Marketing and Logistics*, *19*(3), 240–264. doi:10.1108/13555850710772923

Barbier, E. (1987). The Concept of Sustainable Economic Development. *Environmental Conservation*, *14*(02), 101. doi:10.1017/S0376892900011449

Bird, R. M., & Gendron, P.-P. (2019). *Sales Taxation in Canada: The GST-HST-QST-RST 'System'*. Revision of paper present at American Tax Policy Institute Conference on Structuring a Federal VAT: Design and Coordination Issues, Washington, DC. Retrieved from http://ssrn.com/abstract=1413333

Bitner, M., Brown, S., & Meuter, M. (2000). Technology Infusion in Service Encounters. *Journal of the Academy of Marketing Science*, *28*(1), 138–149. doi:10.1177/0092070300281013

Charan, P. (2012). Supply chain performance issues in an automobile company: A SAP-LAP analysis. *Measuring Business Excellence*, *16*(1), 67–86. doi:10.1108/13683041211204680

Dani, S. (2016). A Research Paper on an Impact of Goods and Service Tax (GST) on Indian Economy. *Business and Economics Journal, 7*(4). doi:10.4172/2151-6219.1000264

Devarajan, S., & Hossain, S. (1998). The combined incidence of taxes and public expenditures in the Philippines. *World Development*, *26*(6), 963–977. doi:10.1016/S0305-750X(98)00032-1

Gereff, J. G., Humphrey, J., Kaplinsky, R., & Sturgeon, T. (2009). *Introduction: Globalisation, Value Chains and Development*. Academic Press.

Gupta, N. (2014). Goods and Services Tax: It's impact on Indian Economy. *International Research Journal Of Commerce Arts And Science*, *5*(3), 126–133.

Harmonized 'Goods and Service Tax' in India: A Backgrounder. (n.d.). *SSRN Electronic Journal*. doi:10.2139srn.1267066

Helms, M., & Nixon, J. (2010). Exploring SWOT analysis – where are we now? *Journal Of Strategy And Management*, *3*(3), 215–251. doi:10.1108/17554251011064837

Herekar, M. (2012). Evaluation of impact of Goods and Services Tax (GST. *Indian Streams Research Journal*, *2*(I), 1–4.

Huang, A., & Liu, B. (2012). The Impact of the Goods and Services Tax on Mortgage Costs: Evidence from Australian Mortgage Corporations. *International Journal Of Financial Research*, *4*(1). doi:10.5430/ijfr.v4n1p54

Khurana, A., & Sharma, A. (2016). Goods and Services Tax in India – A Positive Reform for Indirect Tax System. *International Journal Of Advanced Research*, *4*(3), 500–505.

Kraal, D., & Kasipillai, J. (2015). *Finally, a Goods and Services Tax for Malaysia: A Comparison to Australia's GST Experience*. SSRN Electronic Journal. doi:10.2139srn.2804416

Mangla, S., Kumar, P., & Barua, M. (2014). Monte Carlo Simulation Based Approach to Manage Risks in Operational Networks in Green Supply Chain. *Procedia Engineering, 97*, 2186–2194. doi:10.1016/j.proeng.2014.12.462

Mishkin, F. (1999). International experiences with different monetary policy regimes). Any views expressed in this paper are those of the author only and not those of Columbia University or the National Bureau of Economic Research. *Journal of Monetary Economics, 43*(3), 579–605. doi:10.1016/S0304-3932(99)00006-9

Palil, M. R. (2011). Factors affecting tax compliance behaviour in self assessment system. *African Journal of Business Management, 5*(33). doi:10.5897/ajbm11.1742

Peng, G., & Nunes, M. (2009). Using PEST Analysis as a Tool for Refining and Focusing Contexts for Information Systems Research. *ECRM 2007: 6Th European Conference On Research Methodology For Business And Management Studies*. Retrieved from http://file:///C:/Users/hp/Downloads/SSRN-id1417274.pdf

Rennings, K. (2000). Redefining innovation— Eco-innovation research and the contribution from ecological economics. *Ecological Economics, 32*(2), 319–332. doi:10.1016/S0921-8009(99)00112-3

Sapienza, H., Manigart, S., & Vermeir, W. (1996). Venture capitalist governance and value added in four countries. *Journal of Business Venturing, 11*(6), 439–469. doi:10.1016/S0883-9026(96)00052-3

Sehrawat, M., & Dhanda, U. (2015). GST in India: A Key Tax Reform. *International Journal Of Trad-Granthaalayah, 3*(12), 133-141.

Shackelford, D., & Shevlin, T. (2000). *Empirical Tax Research in Accounting*. SSRN Electronic Journal. doi:10.2139srn.235796

Shah, A. (2006). *Fiscal Incentives for Investment and Innovation*. Available at SSRN: https://ssrn.com/abstract=896144

Shaik, S., Sameera, S., & Firoz, S. (2015). Does Goods and Services Tax (GST) Leads to Indian Economic Development? *Journal of Business and Management, 17*(12), 1-5.

Sharma, D., & George, M. (2017). GST-A Game Changer in Indian Tax Structure. *IOSR Journal Of Business And Management, 19*(04), 55–62. doi:10.9790/487X-1904015562

Sharma, M. (2014). A Study on Goods and services Tax in India. *International Journal's Research Journal Of Social Science And Management, 3*(10), 119–123.

Valadkhani, A., & Layton, A. (2004). Quantifying the Effect of the GST on Inflation in Australia's Capital Cities: An Intervention Analysis. *The Australian Economic Review, 37*(2), 125–138. doi:10.1111/j.1467-8462.2004.00314.x

Vasanthagopal, R. (2011). GST in India: A Big Leap in the Indirect Taxation System. *International Journal of Trade Economics and Finance, 144-146*. doi:10.7763/ijtef.2011.v2.93

Chapter 16
A Review on Role of Macro and Micro Banking Environment on Non-Performing Assets Management

Biswajit Prasad Chhatoi
Khallikote University, India

Sharada Prasad Sahoo
Khallikote University, India

ABSTRACT

In a self-resilient economy, banking system assumes importance in imparting momentum to economic growth and prosperity through mobilization of financial assets. Performance of banks, irrespective of their nature and function, is germane to their asset creation and maintenance capacity. In a neo-liberal regime, radical policy changes have crept into loan mechanism, thereby subjecting the banks to efficiently recover the loans, which is a vital asset for any banking firm. In this context, the authors through intensive review of literature identified micro and macro banking factors responsible for productive NPA management. The macro banking factors refer to the economic environment whereas the micro banking factors refer to the bank and branch-specific factors. The authors identified the critical role of organizational structure, involvement of employees, and organizational efficiency in driving prudent NPA management. The authors have found that the efficiency in managing NPAs differ in public and private banks, which is attributed to involvement of employees.

INTRODUCTION

In an emerging economy like India, for the rapid growth of the economy and industrialization most influential role is played by the banking sector (Gerschenkron 1965, Sylla 1969, Mayer 1990) because banks are intermediary between the providers of fund and users of the fund (Mayer 1988, 1990). The financial stability of an economy to great extent is dependent on efficiency and effectiveness of bank-

DOI: 10.4018/978-1-5225-7399-9.ch016

ing/financial sector (Schumpeter 1912, Gurley and Shaw 1960, Goldsmith 1969, and McKinnon 1973). The financial crisis of 2008 leads to a 'great recession'[1] in the world economy, is due to the debt accumulation, (Bezemer 2009 a, b), housing bubble (Shiller 2008) insolvency of few investment banks in the western country (Verick, & Islam, 2010). Always the banks and financial institutions are one of the most important pillars of a stable economy and play a vital role in growth and development of the economy(Mowery, 1998, Khan and Senhadji, 2000). In the era of globalisation, Indian Banking Sector struggled with restriction from regulatory bodies (Sáez, 2009), quality management, and fast changing norms and so on. The economic crisis of 2008 has increased the quantum of Non-Performing Assets (NPA) and deteriorated revenue of banks (Baselga-Pascual & Orden-Olasagasti, 2015) throughout the world. NPA also applicable to asset including a leased asset of banks, and these lease assets becomes non-performing when they cease to generate income for the bank (RBI, 2010). In general, NPA means an asset relating to the account of the borrower, which has been classified by the bank as sub-standard, doubtful or loss making asset, in accordance with the directions or guidelines relating to asset classification issued by Reserve Bank of India (RBI). NPA otherwise called as non-performing loans (NPLs) and defined as those loans on which payment are due more than one year and no repayment made. Dimitros, et.al, (2016), reported that loans past due more than 90 days are called NPLs. Out of several factors of credit risk for the banking sector, NPA is one of the most important factors which contribute a lot for enhancement of credit risk of banks.

The balance sheet is a summary sheet of Assets and Liabilities held by any organisation[2]. As per the principle of accounting equation, at any point of time, the aggregate of assets is equals to aggregate of liabilities of an organisation (Mann,1994). The performing assets have a positive impact on cash flow whereas the non-performing assets have a negative impact on cash flow. For a bank generally, the net income is the difference between interests received on loan and paid on the deposits. NPAs/NPLs are the asset/loans on which bank fails to collect interest as well as the principal given to the borrower. The concept of NPAs coined by the banking experts in India in light of financial sector reforms took place during the 1990s.

1. Rampell (2009) traces the evolution of the term and points out with some irony that it has also been used to describe all post-war recessions.
2. *The balance sheet explained: The basics of finance II, in basics of finance.* . (2001, Jan 01).[Video/DVD] Retrieved from https://search.proquest.com/docview/1822829890?accountid=175698

Banking sector reforms in India has progressed promptly on aspects like interest rate deregulation, reduction in statutory reserve requirements, and prudential norms for interest rates, asset classification, income recognition, provisioning and adoption of BASEL norms. During pre-nationalization period and after independence, the banking sector remained in private hands and managed by large industries. The government of India nationalized the banks in phase-wise to make them as an instrument of economic and social changes and the mandate given to the banks was top expand their networks in rural areas.

The ever-increasing trends in deposits and credit speak volumes for the performance of Indian banks. However, the NPAs in the credit portfolios have become a throne in the flesh during the last decade. NPAs not only affect the productivity but also sully the image of Indian banking system. Changes required tackling the NPA problem would have to span the entire gamut of Judiciary, polity and the bureaucracy to be truly effective.

The quality of loan assets is the most important factor for the basic viability of the banking system. NPAs not only eat into profitability and hamper their ability to recycle funds but also shake the public confidence, which is crucial for the existence of any financial institution. The present trend of NPAs is alarming and calls for rigorous and concerted efforts by banks and government.

CONCEPT AND MEANING OF NPA

An asset called NPA when the borrower fails to repay the interest and/or principal amount on agreed terms. An NPA is defined as a credit facility in respect of which the interest and /or instalment or principal amount has remained 'past due' for a specified period of time. If the borrower has failed to make interest or principal payments for 90 days or one quarter then the loan is considered as NPA. The norms and guide lines for NPA is decided by RBI in India. These norms are dynamic in nature and change according to national and international requirement. To cope with international best banking practices as well as to ensure transparency in Indian banking system, RBI has adopted the '90 days' overdue' norm for identification of NPA, from the year ending March 31, 2004. Accordingly, with effect from March 31, 2004, the norms for different types of advances to be declared as NPA are given below.

Classification of Non-Performing Assets

The Securitization and Reconstruction of Financial Assets and Enforcement of Security Interest (SARFAESI) Act, 2002 defines Non Performing Assets as "an asset or account of a borrower, which has been classified by a bank or financial institution as sub-standard, doubtful or loss assets in accordance with the direction and guidelines relating to asset classification issued by the RBI". From 31st March 2004, an asset is considered to have gone bad when the borrower has defaulted on principal and interest repayment for more than one-quarter or 90 days. The following are the RBI guidelines for NPA classification and provisioning:

Table 1. Norms of NPA for different types of loan

Types of Advance	Overdue Details	Time period
Term loan	Interest and/or instalment of principal	More than 91 days
Overdraft/Cash Credit	Out of order	More than 90 days
Bills purchased and discounted	Bill	More than 90 days
Advance granted for agricultural purposes	Interest and/or instalment of principal	2 harvest seasons but for a period not exceeding 2 half years
Cash Credit Facility		Non submission of Stock Statements for 3 Continuous Quarters
Cash Credit/Over Draft /EPC / PCFC		No active transactions in the account for more than 91days

Source: RBI

Standard Assets

Standard assets are not considered as NPAs but do not carry more than normal risk attached to the business. Thus, in general, all the current loans, agricultural and non-agricultural loans may be treated as standard assets. It requires a minimum of 25% provision on global portfolio but .4% provision for standard assets at the corporate level on the domestic portfolio.

Sub-Standard Assets

Sub-Standard Assets have been classified as NPA for a period less than or equal to 18 months. The general provision of 10% of total outstanding principal plus entire outstanding interest should be made on sub - standard assets. A Non-performing asset may be classified as sub-standard on the basis of the following criteria.

1. An asset which has remained overdue for a period not exceeding three years in respect of both agricultural and non-agricultural loans should be treated as sub-standard.
2. In the case of all types of term loans, where instalments are overdue for a period not exceeding three years, the entire outstanding in term loan should be treated as sub-standard.
3. An asset, where the terms and conditions of the loans regarding payment of interest and repayment of principal have been renegotiated or rescheduled, after the commencement of production, should be classified as sub-standard and should remain so in such category for at least two years of satisfactory performance under the renegotiated or rescheduled terms. In other words, the classification of an asset should not be upgraded merely as a result of rescheduling unless there is satisfactory compliance with the conditions.

Doubtful Assets

Doubtful assets have remained as NPAs for a period exceeding 18 months. On these assets, the banks are required to provide 100% for the unsecured portion and additional provision of 20% to 50% advances, if doubtful for 3 and above 3 years in respect of both agricultural and non-agricultural loans. As in the case of substandard assets, rescheduling does not entitle a bank to upgrade the quality of advance automatically. A loan classified as doubtful has all the weakness inherent as that of a substandard account. There is also a problem of weakness in the collection or liquidation of the outstanding dues in such an account in full

Loss Assets

Loss assets are those where the loss is identified by the bank but the amount has not been written off wholly or partly. Such loss assets will include overdue loans in cases (a) where decrees or execution petitions have been time barred or documents are lost which are legal proof to claim the debt, (b) where the members and their sureties are declared insolvent or have died leaving no tangible assets, (c) where the members have left the area of operation of the society leaving no property and their sureties have also no means to pay the dues (d) amounts which cannot be recovered in case of liquidated societies.

Provisioning Norms on the Basis of NPAs Classification

Provisioning is important considering the breakup in the value of security charged to the banks over a period of time. Therefore, after the assets are classified into various categories (viz. standard, substandard doubtful and loss assets) necessary provision has to be made for them. The details of provisioning requirements in respect of the various categories of assets are:

Provision for Standard Assets

Banks are required to make provision for standard assets at a minimum of 0.25 per cent of the total outstanding in this category. The provision made on standard assets may not be reckoned as erosion in the value of assets and will form part of owned funds of the bank. The advances granted against term deposits, National Savings Certificates (NSC) eligible for surrender, Kisan Vikas Patras (KVP), Indira Vikas Patras (IVP), Life policies, staff loans would attract the provision of 0.25 per cent prescribed for standard assets. The provision towards standard assets need not be netted from gross advances and should be shown separately as "Contingent provision against standard assets" under "other liabilities and other provisions".

Provision for Sub-Standard Assets

Since it is probable that a bank incurs some loss in such accounts, a general provision of 15 to 25 per cent is required to be made on the total outstanding amount in the case of all loan accounts categorized as substandard.

Provision for Doubtful Assets

1. A provision of 100 per cent of the advances is to be made to the extent to which the advance is not covered by the realizable value of securities to which the bank has valid recourse and the realizable value is estimated on a realistic basis.
2. Over and above the provision of the unsecured portion, a provision of 25 per cent 40 per cent and 100 per cent of the secured portion has to be made depending upon the period for which an asset has remained overdue (Table 1).

REVIEW OF LITERATURE

Banking Sector Growth and General Causes of NPA

Talwar (2001) mentioned that after the nationalization, the banks were given freedom to expand their branch network, increase the savings rate and extend credit to the rural and SSI sectors. This mandate has been achieved admirably. However, since the early 90's the focus has shifted towards improving the quality of assets and better risk management. The 'directed' lending approach has given way to more market driven practices.

Table 2. Criteria for Provision for Doubtful Assets

Sl. No	Type of Assets	Provision
1	Standard Assets	0.25% for all type of Standard Assets
2	Sub-Standard Assets	25% for Unsecured and 15% for Secured Sub-Standard Assets
3	Doubtful Assets	
3.A	Doubtful assets up to 1 year (DA 1)	100% of Unsecured Advances and 25% of Secured Advances
3.B	Doubtful assets 1 to 3 years (DA 2)	100% of Unsecured Advances and 40% of Secured Advances
3.C	Doubtful assets more than 3 years (DA 3)	100% of Unsecured and Secured Advances
4	Loss Assets	100% of Unsecured and Secured Advances

Source: RBI

RBI (2002) reports that a change in from the past income recognition is now not on an accrual basis but when it is actually received. Past problems faced by banks were top a great extent attributable to this. Classification of what an NPA is has changed with tightening of prudential norms. Currently, an asset is "non-performing" if interest or instalments of principal due remain unpaid for more than 180 days which was reduced to 90 days (RBI 2004) from 1st April 2004.

Muniappan (2002) adds that there have been noticeable improvements in the financial health of banks in terms of asset quality. Further, he pointed out that the pre and post reform NPA levels are not comparable as there has been a significant change and tightening of accounting norms for NPA in post reform period.

In the context of increase in NPA, the main culprits are not the priority sectors or PSU's but are the large industries. According to Ram Mohan (2002) the problem India faces is not lack of strict prudential norms but (1) the legal impediments and time consuming nature of asset disposal process, (2) 'Postponement' of the problem in order to report higher earnings; (3) Manipulation by the debtors using political influence. Reddy (2002), recommends that strengthening of legal norms is required and suggested creation of prudence norms should cope with international standards to reduce bad loans of big industrial houses.

Batra and Dass (2003) in their paper titled "Developing the Asian Markets for Non performing Assets: Developments in India", concluded that there is the practice of 'ever greening' of advances in Indian banking sector, through subtle techniques which is one of the reasons for an increase in NPA. Further, they pointed out that effective recovery of defaulters and overdue of borrowers was hampered on account of a sizeable overhand component arising from infirmities in the existing process of debt recovery, inadequate legal provision: and too much time-consuming formalities for foreclosure, bankruptcy and in the execution of court decrees.

Biswas and Deb (2004) identified and distinguished between random and non-random reasons of NPA formation. The non-random reasons go beyond the conventional paradigm of interim, ex-ante and ex-post information asymmetries and incomplete contracts. The financial notion of NPA as a mere risk phenomenon is inadequate because a number of reasons leading to the non-random generation of NPA is related to the dimension of uncertainty.

Shah (2006) concluded that to get command on Non Performing Assets, the co-operative bank has instituted a unique screening system for loan sanctioning to identify NPA at the initial stage of receipt of the loan application.

Nitsure (2007) contends that once there is a slowdown in private expenditure and corporate earnings growth, companies on the banks' books will not be in a position to service their debts on time and there is a strong likelihood of generation of new NPAs. He suggested that with rising interest rates in the government bond market, the banks' treasury incomes have declined considerably. So banks will not have enough profits to make provisions for NPAs.

Srinivasan (2009) observes that over the last few years Indian Banking, in its attempt to integrate itself with the global banking. In a developing country like India, banking is seen as an important instrument of development, while with the strenuous NPAs banks have become helpless burden on the economy. Looking to the worldwide changing scenario, the problem becomes more ironical because Indian banking cannot afford to remain unresponsive to the global requirements. The banks are, however, aware of the grim situation and are trying their level best to reduce the NPAs ever since the regulatory authorities (i.e., Reserve Bank of India) and the Government of India are seriously chasing up the issue.

Hunkar (2009) denies the forecast of April 2010, by the rating agency Crisil that gross NPA of banks in India may reach 5% by 2011. Hunker argues that despite the rating agency's warning, the NPA ratios of Indian banks are small and manageable even if they grow to 5%. This is because historically the NPA has decreased over the past few years. NPA is projected to double by 2011 from last year's 2.4%. However, the NPA ratio has fallen continuously from 9% in 2003 to less than 3% in 2008. So the rise to 5% in 2011 may not be a severe hit to the banks. While rising NPA due to problems with commercial loans is a cause for concern, it may not derail the growth of the banking sector in India, and it will be manageable as banks have adequate capital reserves.

Lele Abhijit (2010), stated that the commercial banks have tried to show healthy balance sheets by reducing NPA. The banks are practising one-time settlement (OTS) schemes for small and medium enterprises and trying to sell non-performing assets (NPAs).

Jain and Bhuria (2010), identified the causes of increasing NPA of Indian banking sector are lack of experience, disposal of recovery cases under the public Debt Recovery Act, non-settlement of claims by the corporation on flimsy grounds, unrealistically ambitious targets under priority sector lending, general slowdown in the economy, depressed capital markets, frequent adverse changes in the government. Jaynal Ud-din Ahmed (2010) opined that the level of NPAs of banks is an important criterion to assess the financial health of banking sector.

Prasad and Veena (2011), examined that the reason behind the falling revenues of Indian banks and concluded that 78% of the revenue of Public Sector Banks comes from traditional sources like the lending activity. With the increase in NPA, the decrease in performing assets leads to a reduction of revenue and profitability of the banks. Hosmani & Jugdish (2011), identified an inverse relation between asset quality and volume of NPA. They pointed out that NPA is an improvement scale for assessing the financial performance of Indian banks. The increased volume of NPA will adversely affect the financial performance of banks.

Macroeconomic Factors and NPA

The earlier studies classify determinants/causes of NPA into two different groups such as "macroeconomic causes" and "microeconomic or bank-specific causes". The macroeconomic factors are those factors on which the banks have no control. Fofack (2005) stated that macroeconomic variable like interest rate and inflation is a particularly have a positive relationship with default risk whereas GDP has a negative relation with default risk. Castro (2013) concluded that external factors which are beyond the boundary of bank-specific factors such as macroeconomic condition have a strong impact on the increase in default risk and NPA. Festić et.al (2011) proposed that the boost in macroeconomic factors like; export and production increases earning of the firm which minimises the default risk of banks, enhance the stability and performing assets. Chaibi et.al (2015) documented in their study that the macroeconomic factors having a strong impact on the financial environment as well as the efficiency of financial intuitions. Poudel (2013) pointed out that the macroeconomic variables having an insignificant impact on operating efficiency, credit risk and NPA level of the bank. Nkusu (2011) reported that macroeconomic environment is responsible for the efficiency of the banking sector and due to adverse macroeconomic condition the default risk of banking sector increases along with an increase in the volume of NPA. Bonfim et.al (2009) concluded that economic growth strongly attached by credit growth of banking sector and reduces default risk and NPA of banks. Aver (2008) identified that macroeconomic variables have a significant impact on the level NPA of banks, credit risk is directly proportionate to the interest rate. Fainstein and Novikov (2011) argued that macroeconomic predictors like GDP, interest rate have a significant influence on non-performing loans. Bonfim et al. (2009) concluded that economic growth strongly attached by credit growth of banking sector and reduces default risk and NPA of banks. Zaib et al. (2014) proposed that during the decline in GDP giving importance on enhancing credit increases the level of NPA.

Bank-Specific Factors and NPA

Bank-Specific characteristics like management behaviour, policies of banks, regulations and internal framework increases the profitability of banks and help in increasing goodwill of the banks. Chaibi et al. (2015) in their study use 5 years data of French and Germany economy, applied panel data model and concluded that Germany economy is bank-based economy and banks-specific variables having a significant impact on the credit risk of the banks, the regulatory bodies should concentrate on default risk, performance management, and estimation to identify financial instability and problems loans. Andriani and Wiryono (2015) collected financial data on 69 banks in Indonesian over for 10 years i.e. 2002 to 2013 and concluded that bank-specific factors like ownership structure, economic policy can lead to high level of credit risk in the banking sector and also leads to high level of NPAs. Further, Tehulu and Olana (2014), Louzis et al. (2012), Gonzalez-Hermosillo et al. (1997) in their study concluded that performance reduction and inefficiency are internal factors which have a significant impact on non-performing loans. Abid et al. (2014), analysis the impact of microeconomics and macroeconomics variables on non-performing loans of Tunisian banks and concluded that bank-specific characteristics indicate the measurement of the efficiency of banks.

Comparison of NPA and Performance of Private and Public Sector Banks

Several studies have been made on comparing the NPA of domestic commercial banks operate in India. Indian banking sector is dominated by public sector banks (Chhatoi, 2016), but the presence of private and foreign banks cannot ignore. The volume of advances, as well as NPA of Public sector banks, is higher than the private banks (Gupta, 2012; Veerakumar, 2012; Patidar et al. 2012; Paul et.al 2011; Chakrabarti 2005). The quality of asset and efficiency in managing NPA of private sector banks is better than the quality of asset of public sector bank (Joo, 2014; Paul et.al 2011). Samir and Kamra (2013) concluded that the performance of public sector banks is affected by increasing level of NPA. They pointed out that poor post loan sanction follow-up, politically motivated policy framework and poor recovery are some of the causes for which the NPA level of Public Sector Bank is high.

Organisational Structure, Involvement of Employee and Efficiency of Organisation

The category of organisation, their formation and development; and reasons responsible for success or failure is a subjective issue. The story of growth, success and survival of any organisation depend on a number of factors and contribution of each of the factors cannot be denied (Easterly 2002). The growth and survival of any business organisation is dependent on organisational policy (Easterly and Levine 2003); social capital of organisation (Fukuyama 1995), institutional design (Fukuyama 2006) informal networks and involvement of managers (Fukuyama 1995, Guiso et al 2004).

CONCLUSION

The economic development and financial security is a mirage in absence of a healthy banking system. A stable banking system and development of economy are interdependent on each other. Banks are generating revenue for themselves by providing financial assistance to the economy whereas economy is growing with the financial assistance of banks. A trust and success of provider of fund (bank) and end user of fund (customer) is the motivational factor for the growth of the both parties. The inability of banks to manage its resources and the difficulties of customers to repay the loan produces large amount of non-performing assets. The banks are more responsible for Management of own resources as it is an issue related to the internal environment of the banks. In the current article we have explained the views of different researchers on issues like normal causes pertaining to Non-Performing Assets, impact of Macro and Micro Banking Factors on NPAs as well as Organisational Structure and Efficiency on NPA management.

Further research may be carried out in the critical areas like Impact of macroeconomic variable and bank specific factors on NPA in India Context on NPA in Indian context, Factors responsible for control and reduction of NPA under the preventative and corrective measures, Involvement of bank managers across different category of Banks in implementing preventive and corrective measures and prioritising the measure which is more important for control and management of NPAs.

REFERENCES

Abhijit, L. (2010, March 17). Banks try to clean books through settlements, NPA sales. *Business Standard*. Retrieved from www.business-standard.com

Abid, L., Ouertani, M. N., & Zouari-Ghorbel, S. (2014). Macroeconomic and bank-specific determinants of household's non-performing loans in Tunisia: A dynamic panel data. *Procedia Economics and Finance*, *13*, 58–68. doi:10.1016/S2212-5671(14)00430-4

Ahmed. (2009). Management of non-performing assets of commercial banks in India. *Management Accountant, 44*(6), 470-478. Retrieved from https://search.proquest.com/docview/197653940?accountid=175698

Andriani, V., & Wiryono, S. K. (2015). Bank-specific determinants of credit risk: Empirical evidence from Indonesian banking industry. *International Journal of Technical Research and Applications*, *21*, 1–4.

Aver, B. (2008). An empirical analysis of credit risk factors of the Slovenian banking system. *Managing Global Transitions*, *6*(3), 317.

Baselga-Pascual, L., & del Orden Olasagasti, O. (2015). *Revenue Diversification and Asset Quality of Eurozone Banks*. Social Science Research Network. doi:10.2139srn.2687965

Batra, S., & Dass, K. (2003). *Developing the Asian Markets for Nin-Performing assets: Developments in India*. Paper presented at the Third Forum on Asia Insolvency Reform.

Bezemer, D. (2009a). *'No One Saw This Coming': Understanding Financial Crisis through Accounting Models*. Groningen University.

Bezemer, D. (2009b, September 7). Why some economists could see the crisis coming. *Financial Times*.

Biswas, P. K., & Deb, A. T. (2004). Determinants of NPAs in the Indian Public Sector Banks: A Critique of Policy Reforms. *The IUP Journal of Bank Management*, *III*(3), 11–41.

Bonfim, D. (2009). Credit risk drivers: Evaluating the contribution of firm-level information and of macroeconomic dynamics. *Journal of Banking & Finance*, *33*(2), 281–299. doi:10.1016/j.jbankfin.2008.08.006

Castro, V. (2013). Macroeconomic determinants of the credit risk in the banking system: The case of the GIPSI. *Economic Modelling*, *31*, 672–683. doi:10.1016/j.econmod.2013.01.027

Chaibi, H., & Ftiti, Z. (2015). Credit risk determinants: Evidence from a cross-country study. *Research in International Business and Finance*, *33*, 1–16. doi:10.1016/j.ribaf.2014.06.001

Chakrabarti, R. (2005). *Banking in India: Reforms and Reorganization*. Indian School of Business, Working Paper Series.

Chhatoi, B. P. (2016). SMSE Financing by Domestic Commercial Banks and its Growth in India: An Analysis of Two Indicators. In Issue and challenges in business management. Himalaya Publishing House.

Dimitrios, A., Helen, L., & Mike, T. (2016). Determinants of non-performing loans: Evidence from Euroarea countries. *Finance Research Letters*, *18*, 116–119. doi:10.1016/j.frl.2016.04.008

Easterly, W. (2002). *The elusive quest for growth*. Cambridge, MA: MIT Press.

Easterly, W., & Levine, R. (2003). Tropics, germs and crops: How endowments influence economic developemnt. *Journal of Monetary Economics*, *50*(1), 3–40. doi:10.1016/S0304-3932(02)00200-3

Fainstein, G., & Novikov, I. (2011). The comparative analysis of credit risk determinants in the banking sector of the Baltic States. *Review of Economics & Finance, 1*(3), 20-45.

Festić, M., Kavkler, A., & Repina, S. (2011). The macroeconomic sources of systemic risk in the banking sectors of five new EU member states. *Journal of Banking & Finance, 35*(2), 310–322. doi:10.1016/j.jbankfin.2010.08.007

Fofack, H. (2005). *Nonperforming loans in Sub-Saharan Africa: causal analysis and macroeconomic implications*. World Bank Policy Research Working Paper (3769).

Fukuyama, F. (1995). *Trust: The social virtues and the creation of prosperity*. New York: Free Press.

Fukuyama, F. (2006). *Development and the limits of institutional design*. St. Peterbersburg.

Gerschenkron, A. (1965). *Economic Backwardness in Historical Perspective*. New York, NY: Praeger.

Goldsmith, R. W. (1969). *Financial Structure and Development*. New Haven, CT: Yale University Press.

González-Hermosillo, B., Pazarbaşioğlu, C., & Billings, R. (1997). Determinants of banking system fragility: A case study of Mexico. *Staff Papers, 44*(3), 295–314. doi:10.2307/3867561

Guiso, L., Sapienza, P., & Zingales, L. (2004). Does local financial development matter? *The Quarterly Journal of Economics, 119*(3), 929–969. doi:10.1162/0033553041502162

Gupta, B. (2012). A comparative study of non-performing assets of SBI & associates & other public sector banks. *SIT Journal of Management, 2*(2), 175-189.

Gurley & Shaw. (1960). *Money and Theory of Finance*. The Booking Institution.

Hosmani & Hudagi. (2011). Unearthing the epidemic of non-performing assets: A study with reference to public sector banks in India. *International Journal of Multidisciplinary Research, 1*(8).

Hunkar, D. (2009). Rising NPAs of Indian Banks Not a Cause for Concern. *The Wisdom Tree*. Retrieved from http:// seekingalpha.com/ article/

Jain & Deepti. (2010). A Study of NPAs in Nationalized Banks of Madhya Pradesh. *International Research Journal, 1*(3).

Joo, B. A. (2014). Asset quality and accounting jugglery in Indian banks. *Indian Journal of Commerce and Management Studies, 5*(1), 105–112. Retrieved from https://search.proquest.com/docview/1511107407?accountid=175698

Louzis, D. P., Vouldis, A. T., & Metaxas, V. L. (2012). Macroeconomic and bank-specific determinants of non- performing loans in Greece: A comparative study of mortgage, business and consumer loan portfolios. *Journal of Banking & Finance, 36*(4), 1012–1027. doi:10.1016/j.jbankfin.2011.10.012

Mann, G. (1994). The origins of double-entry. *Australian Accountant, 64*(6), 17. Retrieved from https://search.proquest.com/docview/211265265?accountid=175698

Mayer, C. (1988). New issues in corporate finance. *European Economic Review, 32*(5), 1167–1183. doi:10.1016/0014-2921(88)90077-3

Mayer, C. (1990). Financial systems, corporate finance and economic development. In R. Glenn Hubbard (Ed.), *Asymmetric Information, Corporate Finance and Investment*. Chicago, IL: The University of Chicago Press.

McKinnon, R. (1973). *Money and Capital in Economic Development*. Washington, DC: Brookings Institution.

Mowery, D. C. (1998). The Changing Structure of the US National Innovation System: Implications for International Conflict and Cooperation in R&D Policy. *Research Policy*, *27*(6), 639–654. doi:10.1016/S0048-7333(98)00060-2

Muniappan, G. P. (2002). *Indian Banking: Paradigm Shift – A regulatory point of view*. Address at the Bank Economist Conference, Kolkata, India.

Nitsure, R. R. (2007). Corrective Steps towards Sound Banking. *Economic and Political Weekly*, *42*(13).

Nkusu, M. (2011). *Nonperforming loans and macrofinancial vulnerabilities in advanced economies*. St. Louis, MO: Federal Reserve Bank of St Louis. doi:10.5089/9781455297740.001

Patidar, S. (2012). *Analysis of NPA in priority sector lending: A comparative study between public sector banks and Private sector banks of India*. Academic Press.

Patnaik, B., Satpathy, I., & Mohapatra, A. (2011). NPA's side effect and curative mantra. *International Journal of Research in Commerce and Management*, *2*(7), 77–80.

Paull, P., Bose, S. K., & Dhalla, R. S. (2011). Efficiency measurement of Indian public sector banks: Non-performing assets as negative output. *Asia Pacific Journal of Finance and Banking Research*, *5*(5), 38–46.

Poudel, R. P. S. (2013). Macroeconomic Determinants of credit risk in Nepalese banking industry. In *Proceedings of 21st International Business Research Conference* (pp. 10-11). Academic Press.

Prasad, B. G., & Veena, V. D. (2011). NPAS in Indian banking sector- trends and issues. *Journal of Banking Financial Services and Insurance Research*, *1*(9), 67–84.

Ram Mohan, T.T. (2002). *Banking Reform in India*. Lecture at the Indian Institute of Management, Ahmedabad, India.

RBI. (2001). *Prudential Norms on Income Recognition, Asset Classification and Provisioning Pertaining to Advances*. Reserve Bank of India.

RBI. (2002a). *Selected Ratios of Scheduled Commercial Bankis: 2000 and 2001*. Retrieved from www.rbi.org.in

RBI. (2002b). *Financial Institutions*. Retrieved from www.rbi.org.in

RBI. (2010). *Prudential Norms on Income Recognition, Asset Classification and Provisioning Pertaining to Advances*. Reserve Bank of India.

Reddy, P. K. (2002). A *comparative study of Non Performing Assets in India in the Global context – Similarities and dissimilarities, remedial measures*. The Indian Institute of Management, Ahmedabad, unpublished report.

Reserve Bank of India. (2002). *Financial Institutions*. Retrieved from www.rbi.org.in

Sáez, L. (2009). The political economy of financial services reform in india: Explaining variations in political opposition and barriers to entry. *The Journal of Asian Studies*, *68*(4), 1137. doi:10.1017/S0021911809990805

Samir & Kamra. (2013). A Comparative Analysis of Non- Performing Assets (NPAs) of Selected Commercial Banks in India. *International Journal of Management*, *3*(1), 68–80.

Schumpeter, J. (1912). The Theory of Economic Development. Cambridge, MA: Harvard University Press.

Shah, T. (2006). *Attaining zero Non-Performing Asset (NPA) by Transparency, Trust and & Service* (Unpublished paper). Indian Institute of Planning and Management (IIPM).

Shiller, R. J. (2008). *The Subprime Solution: How Today's Global Financial Crisis Happened, and What to Do about It*. Princeton, NJ: Princeton University Press.

Srinivasan, R. (2009). *Performance measurement of Banks - NPA analysis & credentials of Parameters*. Retrieved from www.articlesbase.com/banking -articles/performance measurement-of-banks-NPA-analysis

Sylla, R. (1969). Federal policy, banking market structure and capital mobilization in the United States, 1863-1913. *The Journal of Economic History*, *29*(04), 657–686. doi:10.1017/S002205070007193X

Talwar, S.P. (2001). *Financial Stability and the Role of Banks*. Address at the Ban Economists' Conference, New Delhi, India.

Tehulu, T.A., & Olana, D.R. (2014). Bank-specific determinants of credit risk: Empirical evidence from Ethiopian banks. *Research Journal of Finance and Accounting, 5*(7), 80-85.

Vandenberghe, C., Bentein, K., & Michon, R. (2007). An examination of the role of perceived support and employee commitment in employee-customer encounters. *Journal of Applied Psychology, 92*(4), 1177. Retrieved from https://search.proquest.com/docview/213938270?accountid=175698

Veerakumar, K. (2012). Non-performing assets in priority sector: A threat to Indian scheduled commercial banks. *International Journal of Finance & Economics*, (93): 6–23.

Verick, S., & Islam, I. (2010). The Great Recession of 2008-2009: Causes, Consequences and Policy Responses. Institute for the Study of Labour, (4934), 3–61.

Willam, E. C. (1976). *Business Research Methods*. Homewood, IL: Richard D. Irwin.

Zaib, A., Farid, F., & Khan, M. K. (2014). Macroeconomic and bank-specific determinants of non-performing loans in the banking sector in Pakistan. International Journal of Information. *Business and Management*, *6*(2), 53.

ADDITIONAL READING

Arora, A., & Kohli, H. K. (2017). Soundness indicators of public and private sector banks: A comparative study. Vinimaya, 37(1), 47-64. Retrieved from https://search.proquest.com/docview/1861256976?accountid=175698

Bodla, B. S., & Bajaj, R. V. (2010). An analysis of the efficiency of private sector banks in india. IUP Journal of Bank Management, 9(1), 60-82. Retrieved from https://search.proquest.com/docview/365883865?accountid=175698

Chaudhary, K., & Sharma, M. (2011). Performance of Indian public sector banks and private sector banks: A comparative study. *International Journal of Innovation, Management and Technology*, *2*(3), 249. doi:10.7763/IJIMT.2011.V2.140

D'Silva, S., D'Silva, B., & Gandhi, R. A. (2012). Evaluation of nonperforming assets in public and private sector banks in India: A comparative study. *Indian Journal of Economics and Business*, *11*(3). Retrieved from https://search.proquest.com/docview/1629919469?accountid=175698

Haselmann, R., Pistor, K., & Vig, V. (2005). How law affects lending. *Columbia University Working Paper.*

Helge, E. J., & Padhye, P. (2016). Non-performing assets of public sector and private sector banks in india: An empirical analysis. *Journal of Commerce and Management Thought*, *7*(2), 298–308. doi:10.5958/0976-478X.2016.00020.3

Makesh, K. G. (2008). Financial Performance Analysis of Commercial Banks: A Comparison of Federal Bank, Dhanalaxmi Bankand SBI. *Professional Banker*, *8*(9), 34–44.

Makesh, K. G. (2008). Financial Performance Analysis of Commercial Banks: A Comparison of Federal Bank, Dhanalaxmi Bankand SBI. *Professional Banker*, *8*(9), 34–44.

Millissa, F. Y. (2010). Management commitment to service quality and organizational outcomes. *Managing Service Quality*, *20*(3), 259–272. doi:10.1108/09604521011041970

Rahman, M. M., Uddin, K. M. K., & Moudud-Ul-Huq, S. (2015). Factors Affecting the Risk-taking Behavior of Commercial Banks in Bangladesh. *Applied Finance and Accounting*, *1*(2), 96–106. doi:10.11114/afa.v1i2.850

Compilation of References

Abhijit, L. (2010, March 17). Banks try to clean books through settlements, NPA sales. *Business Standard*. Retrieved from www.business-standard.com

Abid, L., Ouertani, M. N., & Zouari-Ghorbel, S. (2014). Macroeconomic and bank-specific determinants of household's non-performing loans in Tunisia: A dynamic panel data. *Procedia Economics and Finance*, *13*, 58–68. doi:10.1016/S2212-5671(14)00430-4

Abraham, R., & Harrington, C. (2016). Determinants of oil futures prices. *Theoretical Economics Letters*, *6*(4), 742–749. doi:10.4236/tel.2016.64078

Acar Boyacıoğlu, M., Güvenek, B. & Alptekin, V. (2010). Getiri volatilitesi ile işlem hacmi arasındaki ilişki. *Muhasebe ve Finansman Dergisi*, (48), 200-217.

Adam, A. M., & Tweneboah, G. (2008). *Macroeconomic factors and stock market movement: Evidence from Ghana*. Academic Press.

Adjasi, C. K. (2009). Macroeconomic uncertainty and conditional stock-price volatility in frontier African markets: Evidence from Ghana. *The Journal of Risk Finance*, *10*(4), 333–349. doi:10.1108/15265940910980641

Adrian, P. (1995). The Essence of Service Marketing. Prentice-Hall of India.

Aduda, J., Masila, J. M., & Onsongo, E. N. (2012). The Determinants of Stock Market Development: The Case for the Nairobi Stock. *International Journal of Humanities and Social Science*, *2*(9), 214–227.

Agarwal, R., & Prasad, J. (1998). The antecedents and consequents of user perceptions in information technology adoption. *Decision Support Systems*, *22*(1), 15–29. doi:10.1016/S0167-9236(97)00006-7

Aggarwal, J. K., Davis, L. S., & Martin, W. N. (1981). Correspondence processes in dynamic scene analysis. *Proceedings of the IEEE*, *69*(5), 562–572. doi:10.1109/PROC.1981.12025

Agle, B. R., & Caldwell, C. B. (1999). Understanding Research on Values in Business: A Level of Analysis Framework. *Business & Society*, *38*(3), 326–387. doi:10.1177/000765039903800305

Agle, B. R., Mitchell, R. K., & Sonnenfeld, J. A. (1999). Who Matters to CEOs? An Investigation of Stakeholder Attributes and Salience, Corporate Performance, and CEO Values. *Academy of Management Journal*, *42*(5), 507–525.

Aguiar-Conraria, L., & Soares, M. J. (2010). *Business Cycle Synchronization and the Euro: A Wavelet Analysis*. Retrieved from http://www3.eeg.uminho.pt/economia /nipe/docs /2010 / NIPE_WP_36_2010.pdf

Agyre-Tetty, K.F. & Kyereboah-Coleman. (2008). Impact of macroeconomic indicators on stock market performance. *The Journal of Risk Finance*, *9*(4), 71–81.

Ahmad, E., & Poddar, S. (2009). *GST Reforms and intergovernmental Considerations in India*. LSE Asia Research Centre, LSE Asia Research Centre.

Ahmad, E., & Stern, N. (1984). The theory of reform and indian indirect taxes. *Journal of Public Economics, 25*(3), 259–298. doi:10.1016/0047-2727(84)90057-4

Ahmed. (2009). Management of non-performing assets of commercial banks in India. *Management Accountant, 44*(6), 470-478. Retrieved from https://search.proquest.com/docview/197653940?accountid=175698

Ahmed, S. (2008). Aggregate economic variables and stock markets in India. *International Research Journal of Finance and Economics, 14*, 141–164.

Ajayi, R. A., Mehdian, S., & Mougoue, M. (2006). The empirical relation between price changes and trading volumes: Further evidence from European stock markets. *Alliance Journal of Business Research, 1*, 3–20.

Ajzen, I. (1991). The theory of planned behavior. *Organizational Behavior and Human Decision Processes, 50*(2), 179–211. doi:10.1016/0749-5978(91)90020-T

Akkoyun, F. (1983). Kişiliğin Projektif Testlerle Değerlendirilmesi. *Ankara Üniversitesi Eğitim Bilimleri Fakültesi Dergisi, 2*(16), 397-408.

Alessandra, M. (2014). Backshoring, Local Sweatshop Regimes and CSR in India. Competition and Change, 18(4), 327–44.

Al-Gahtani, S. S. (2003). Computer technology adoption in Saudi Arabia: Correlates of perceived innovation attributes. *Information Technology for Development, 10*(1), 57–69. doi:10.1002/itdj.1590100106

Alibal, M. (1974). Projektif Testlerle Kişilik Değerlendirilmesi Özellikler ve Materyal. *Ankara Üniversitesi Eğitim Bilimleri Fakültesi Dergisi, 1*(7), 193-209.

Al-Jabri, I., & Sohail, M. S. (2012). *Mobile banking adoption: Application of diffusion of innovation theory*. Academic Press.

Allen, M. W., Ng, S. H., & Wilson, M. (2002). A Functional Approach to Instrumental and Terminal Values and the Value-attitude-behaviour System of Consumer Choice. *European Journal of Marketing, 36*(1–2), 111–135. doi:10.1108/03090560210412728

Allport, F. H., & Allport, G. W. (1921). Personality Traits: Their Classification and Measurement. *Journal of Abnormal and Social Psychology, 16*(1), 6–40. doi:10.1037/h0069790

Allport, G. W. (1937). The Functional Autonomy of Motives. *The American Journal of Psychology, 50*(1/4), 141–156. doi:10.2307/1416626

Alm, J. (2014). Does an uncertain tax system encourage "aggressive tax planning"? *Economic Analysis and Policy, 44*(1), 30–38. doi:10.1016/j.eap.2014.01.004

Altman, E. I., & Katz, S. (1976). Statistical bond rating classification using financial and accounting data. In *Proceedings of the conference on topical research in accounting* (pp. 205-239). New York: University Press New York.

Altman, E. I. (1968). Financial Ratios, Discriminant Analysis and the Prediction of Corporate Bankruptcy. *The Journal of Finance, 23*(4), 889–609. doi:10.1111/j.1540-6261.1968.tb00843.x

Andersen, T. G. (1996). Return Volatility and Trading Volume: An Information Flow Interpretation of Stochastic Volatility. *The Journal of Finance, 51*(1), 169–204. doi:10.1111/j.1540-6261.1996.tb05206.x

Andriani, V., & Wiryono, S. K. (2015). Bank-specific determinants of credit risk: Empirical evidence from Indonesian banking industry. *International Journal of Technical Research and Applications, 21*, 1–4.

Angur, M.G., Natrajan, R., & Jaherea, J.S., Jr. (1999). Service Quality in the Banking Industry: An Assessment of Developing Economy. *International Journal of Marketing, 17*(3), 116-125.

Anifowose, M., & Suleiman, S. (2013). An analysis of casual relation between stock return and trading volume in Nigerian Capital Market. *International Journal of Social Sciences and Humanities Reviews, 4*(2), 137–147.

Antolin, P., Payet, S., & Yermo, J. (2012). Coverage of Private Pension Systems: Evidence and Policy Options. *OECD Working Papers on Finance, Insurance and Private Pensions*, (20).

Arkar, H. (2005). Cloninger'in Psikobiyolojik Kişilik Kuramı. *Türk Psikoloji Bülteni, 36*, 82–94.

Arora, M. (2003). *Credit Rating in India: Institutions, Methods and Evaluation.* Delhi: New Century Publications.

Arshinder, K., Kanda, A., & Deshmukh, S. G. (2007). Supply chain coordination issues: An SAP-LAP framework. *Asia Pacific Journal of Marketing and Logistics, 19*(3), 240–264. doi:10.1108/13555850710772923

As-Sultan, S. Y., Al-Baltah, I. A., & Abdulrazzak, F. A. H. (2017). A Survey on Mobile Banking Applications and the Adopted Models. *International Journal (Toronto, Ont.), 7*(2).

Atkinson, A. B., & Stiglitz, J. E. (1976). The design of tax structure: Direct versus indirect taxation. *Journal of Public Economics, 6*(1-2), 55–75.

Auerbach, A. J., & Gale, W. G. (2009). *The economic crisis and the fiscal crisis: 2009 and beyond.* Urban-Brookings Tax Policy Center.

Aurangzeb. (2012). Factors affecting performance of stock market: Evidence from South Asian Countries. *International Journal of Academic Research in Business and Social Sciences, 2*(9).

Austin. (2000). Do Corporates Have Social Responsibility? A Case Study of TVS Motor Company. *The Icfai University Journal of Corporate Governance, 8*(3-4), 131-138.

Australian Securities Exchange. (2007). *2006 Australian Share Ownership Study.* Available at http://www.asx.com.au/about/pdf/2006_australian_share_ ownership_study.pdf

Au, Y. A., & Kauffman, R. J. (2008). The economics of mobile payments: Understanding stakeholder issues for an emerging financial technology application. *Electronic Commerce Research and Applications, 7*(2), 141–164. doi:10.1016/j.elerap.2006.12.004

Aver, B. (2008). An empirical analysis of credit risk factors of the Slovenian banking system. *Managing Global Transitions, 6*(3), 317.

Bahia, K., & Jacques, N. (2000). A Reliable and Valid Measurement Scale for the Perceived Service Quality of Banks. *International Journal of Bank Marketing, 18*(2), 84–91. doi:10.1108/02652320010322994

Bahmani-Oskooee, M., & Sohrabian, A (1992) Stock prices and the effective exchange rate of the dollar. *Applied Economics, 24*(4), 459-464.

Bailard, T. E., Biehl, D. L., & Kaiser, R. W. (1986). *Personal Money Management.* Chicago: Science Research Associates Inc.

Bajtelsmit, V. L., Bernasek, A., & Jianakoplos, N. A. (1999). Gender differences in defined contribution pension decisions. *Financial Services Review, 8*(1), 1–10. doi:10.1016/S1057-0810(99)00030-X PMID:11481724

Ball, R., & Kothari, S. (1989). Nonstationary Expected Returns: Implications for Tests of Market Efficiency and Serial Correlation in Returns. *Journal of Financial Economics*, *25*(1), 51–74. doi:10.1016/0304-405X(89)90096-2

Barberis, N. C., & Thaler, R. H. (2003). A survey of behavioral finance. In Handbook of the Economics of Finance: Vol. 1B. Financial Markets and Asset Pricing. Elsevier.

Barberis, N., Shleifer, A., & Vishny, R. (1998). A model of investor sentiment. *Journal of Financial Economics*, *49*(3), 307–343. doi:10.1016/S0304-405X(98)00027-0

Barbier, E. (1987). The Concept of Sustainable Economic Development. *Environmental Conservation*, *14*(02), 101. doi:10.1017/S0376892900011449

Barnewall, M. M. G. (1987). Psychological Characteristics of the Individual Investor. In W. Droms (Ed.), *Asset Allocation for the Individual Investor.* The Institute of Chartered Financial Analysts. doi:10.2469/cp.v1987.n2.7

Baselga-Pascual, L., & del Orden Olasagasti, O. (2015). *Revenue Diversification and Asset Quality of Eurozone Banks.* Social Science Research Network. doi:10.2139srn.2687965

Bassett, W. F., Fleming, M. J., & Rodrigues, A. P. (1998). How workers use 401 (k) plans: The participation, contribution, and withdrawal decisions. *National Tax Journal*, 263–289.

Bateson. (1995). SERVQUAL: review, critique, research agenda. *European Journal of Marketing, 30*(1), 8-32.

Batini, N., Guerreiro, J., & Callegari, G. (2011). An Analysis of US Fiscal and Generational Imbalances: Who Will Pay and How? (No. 11-72). International Monetary Fund.

Batra, S., & Dass, K. (2003). *Developing the Asian Markets for Nin-Performing assets: Developments in India.* Paper presented at the Third Forum on Asia Insolvency Reform.

Beaver, W. (1967). Financial Ratios as Predictor of Failure. *Empirical Research in Accounting, Empirical Studies, Journal of Accounting Research*, *4*, 71–111. doi:10.2307/2490171

Beaver, W. H. (1968). The information content of annual earnings announcements. *Journal of Accounting Research*, *6*, 67–92. doi:10.2307/2490070

Beck, T., & Levine, R. (2004). Stock markets, banks and growth: Panel evidence. *Journal of Banking & Finance*, *28*(3), 423–442. doi:10.1016/S0378-4266(02)00408-9

Bem, D. J. (1967). Self-perception: An alternative interpretation of cognitive dissonance phenomena. *Psychological Review*, *74*(3), 183–200. doi:10.1037/h0024835 PMID:5342882

Benjamin, D. J., Chabris, C. F., Glaeser, E. L., Gudnason, V., Harris, T. B., Laibson, D. I., Launer, L. J. & Purcell, S. (2008). *Genoeconomics*. National Research Council (Us) Committee On Advances in Collecting And Utilizing Biological Indicators And Genetic Information in Social Science Surveys.

Berg, M., De Waegenaere, A., & Wielhouwer, J. L. (2001). Optimal tax depreciation with uncertain future cash-flows. *European Journal of Operational Research*, *132*(1), 197–209. doi:10.1016/S0377-2217(00)00132-6

Bernasek, A., & Shwiff, S. (2001). Gender, risk, and retirement. *Journal of Economic Issues*, *35*(2), 345–356. doi:10.1080/00213624.2001.11506368

Bernheim, B. D., & Garrett, D. M. (2003). The effects of financial education in the workplace: Evidence from a survey of households. *Journal of Public Economics*, *87*(7-8), 1487–1519. doi:10.1016/S0047-2727(01)00184-0

Berument, H., Ceylan, N. B., & Gozpinar, E. (2006). Performance of soccer on the stock market: Evidence from Turkey. *The Social Science Journal*, *43*(4), 695–699. doi:10.1016/j.soscij.2006.08.021

Berument, M. H., Ceylan, N. B., & Ogut-Eker, G. (2009). Soccer, stock returns and fanaticism: Evidence from Turkey. *The Social Science Journal*, *46*(3), 594–600. doi:10.1016/j.soscij.2009.06.001

Bezemer, D. (2009b, September 7). Why some economists could see the crisis coming. *Financial Times*.

Bezemer, D. (2009a). *'No One Saw This Coming': Understanding Financial Crisis through Accounting Models*. Groningen University.

Bhattacharyya, M. (2009). A Study of Issuer Rating Service with an Appraisal of ICRA's Rating Model. *Indian Journal of Accounting*, *39*(2), 53–60.

Bheemanagauda & Madegowda, J. (2010). Performance of Credit Rating Agencies in India. *The Indian Journal of Commerce, 63*(3), 50-62.

Białkowski, J., Etebari, A., & Wisniewski, T. P. (2012). Fast profits: Investor sentiment and stock returns during Ramadan. *Journal of Banking & Finance*, *36*(3), 835–845. doi:10.1016/j.jbankfin.2011.09.014

Bird, R. M., & Gendron, P.-P. (2019). *Sales Taxation in Canada: The GST-HST-QST-RST 'System'*. Revision of paper present at American Tax Policy Institute Conference on Structuring a Federal VAT: Design and Coordination Issues, Washington, DC. Retrieved from http://ssrn.com/abstract=1413333

Biswas, P. K., & Deb, A. T. (2004). Determinants of NPAs in the Indian Public Sector Banks: A Critique of Policy Reforms. *The IUP Journal of Bank Management*, *III*(3), 11–41.

Bitner, M., Brown, S., & Meuter, M. (2000). Technology Infusion in Service Encounters. *Journal of the Academy of Marketing Science*, *28*(1), 138–149. doi:10.1177/0092070300281013

Black, J. (1995). Phillip T. Hoffman and Kathryn Norberg (eds.), Fiscal Crises, Liberty, and Representative Government, 1450-1789 (Book Review). Parliamentary History, 14(3), 349.

Bloomfield & Hales. (2002). *Predicting the next step of a random walk: experimental evidence of regime-shifting beliefs.* Academic Press.

Blume, M. E., Lim, F., & MacKinlay, A. C. (1998). The declining credit quality of US corporate debt: Myth or reality? *The Journal of Finance*, *53*(4), 1389–1413. doi:10.1111/0022-1082.00057

Board, J., Sutcliffe, C., & Ziemba, W. T. (2003). Applying operations research techniques to financial markets. *Interfaces*, *33*(2), 12–24. doi:10.1287/inte.33.2.12.14465

Bohl, M. T., & Henke, H. (2003). Trading volume and stock market volatility: The Polish case. *International Review of Financial Analysis*, *12*(5), 513–525. doi:10.1016/S1057-5219(03)00066-8

Bonfim, D. (2009). Credit risk drivers: Evaluating the contribution of firm-level information and of macroeconomic dynamics. *Journal of Banking & Finance*, *33*(2), 281–299. doi:10.1016/j.jbankfin.2008.08.006

Bouwman, H., Carlsson, C., Molina-Castillo, F. J., & Walden, P. (2007). Barriers and drivers in the adoption of current and future mobile services in Finland. *Telematics and Informatics*, *24*(2), 145–160. doi:10.1016/j.tele.2006.08.001

Bower, G. H. (1981). Mood and memory. *The American Psychologist*, *36*(2), 129–148. doi:10.1037/0003-066X.36.2.129 PMID:7224324

Bozkurt, İ. (2015). Investigation of the Effects of the Moon on Stock Returns: An Empirical Application on ISE. *İktisat İşletme ve Finans, 30*(352), 55-78.

Bozkurt, I., & Hatipoglu, M. (2017). The Relationship between Parasocial breakup and Investor Behaviours. *International Journal of Academic Research in Accounting, Finance and Management Sciences, 7*(3), 87–96.

Brabazon, T. (2000). *Behavioral finance: a new sunrise or a false dawn.* Department of Accountancy, University College Dublin. Available at: http://down.cenet.org.cn/upfile/36/20063711518134.pdf

Brabazon, T. (2000). Behavioural Finance: A new sunrise or a false dawn? Coil Summer School 2000, University of Limerick.

Break, G. F. (1957). Income taxes and incentives to work: An empirical study. *The American Economic Review, 47*(5), 530–549.

Breitung, J., & Candelon, B. (2006). Testing for Short and Long-run Causality: A FD Approach. *Journal of Econometrics, 132*(2), 363–378. doi:10.1016/j.jeconom.2005.02.004

Brock, W. A., & LeBaron, B. D. (1995). *A Dynamic Structural Model for Stock Returns Volatility and Trading Volume.* NBER Working Paper Series. No. 4988.

Bruyneel, S., Dewitte, S., Franses, P. H., & Dekimpe, M. G. (2009). I felt low and my purse feels light: Depleting mood regulation attempts affect risk decision making. *Journal of Behavioral Decision Making, 22*(2), 153–170. doi:10.1002/bdm.619

Buchanan, J. M., & Musgrave, R. A. (1999). *Public finance and public choice: two contrasting visions of the State.* MIT Press. doi:10.7551/mitpress/5688.001.0001

Bühlmann, P. (1998). Extreme events from the return-volume process: A discretization approach for complexity reduction. *Applied Financial Economics, 8*(3), 267–278. doi:10.1080/096031098333023

Buss, A. H., & Plomin, R. (1984). *Temperament: Early developing personality traits.* Hillsdale, NJ: Erlbaum.

Büyükdüvenci, S. (2013). *Kişi, Kişilik, Kimlik ve Toplum. 3.* Ilgaz Felsefe Günleri Sempozyumu.

Büyüksalvarci, A., & Abdioglu, H (2010). The causal relationship between stock prices and macroeconomic variables: A case study for Turkey. *International Journal of Economic Perspectives, 4*(4), 601.

Buzzel, R., & Gale, B. (1987). *The PIMS Principles: Linking Strategy to Performance.* New York: Free Press.

Byrne, A., & Utkus, S. P. (n.d.). *Behavioural finance, Understanding how the mind can help or hinder investment success.* Retrieved from https://www.vanguard.co.uk/documents/portal/literature/behavourial-finance-guide.pdf

Cao, M., & Wei, J. (2005). Stock market returns: A note on temperature anomaly. *Journal of Banking & Finance, 29*(6), 1559–1573. doi:10.1016/j.jbankfin.2004.06.028

Carey, G. (2002). *Human Genetic for Social Sciences.* London: Sage Publication.

Carroll, A. B., & Buchholtz, A. K. (2003). *Business and Society: Ethics and Stakeholder Management* (5th ed.). Mason, OH: Thomson Learning.

Castro, V. (2013). Macroeconomic determinants of the credit risk in the banking system: The case of the GIPSI. *Economic Modelling, 31*, 672–683. doi:10.1016/j.econmod.2013.01.027

Causi, G. L. (2017). *Theories of investor behaviour: From the Efficient Market Hypothesis to Behavioural Finance* (Bachelor's Thesis). Tallinn University of Technology, School of Business and Governance, Department of Economics and Finance, Tallinn.

Cesarini, D., Johannesson, M., Magnusson, P. K. E., & Wallace, B. (2011). The Behavioral Genetics of Behavioral Anomalies. *Management Science*, *58*(1), 21–34.

Chaibi, H., & Ftiti, Z. (2015). Credit risk determinants: Evidence from a cross-country study. *Research in International Business and Finance*, *33*, 1–16. doi:10.1016/j.ribaf.2014.06.001

Chakrabarti, R. (2005). *Banking in India: Reforms and Reorganization*. Indian School of Business, Working Paper Series.

Charan, P. (2012). Supply chain performance issues in an automobile company: A SAP-LAP analysis. *Measuring Business Excellence*, *16*(1), 67–86. doi:10.1108/13683041211204680

Charles, L. M. C., & Swaminathan, B. (2000). Price Momentum and Trading Volume. *The Journal of Finance*, *55*(5), 2017–2069. doi:10.1111/0022-1082.00280

Charles, M. K. (1996). *Memoirs of Extraordinary Popular Delusions*, 1841. In M. Fridson (Ed.), *Extraordinary Popular Delusions and the Madness of Crowds and Confusion de Confusiones*. New York: John Wiley.

Chattopadhyay, S. K., & Behera, S. R. (2006, March). Financial integration for Indian stock market. *Annual Conference on Money & Finance held at IGIDR*.

Chen, H., Lobo, B. J., & Wong, W. K. (2006). *Links between the Indian, US and Chinese stock markets*. National University of Singapore, Department of Economics, Working Paper, 602.

Chen, C. (2013). Perceived risk, usage frequency of mobile banking services. *Managing Service Quality: An International Journal*, *23*(5), 410–436. doi:10.1108/MSQ-10-2012-0137

Chen, G., Firth, M., & Rui, O. M. (2001). The Dynamic relation between stock returns, trading volume, and volatility. *Financial Review*, *38*(3), 153–174. doi:10.1111/j.1540-6288.2001.tb00024.x

Cheng, H., Lu, Y. C., & Sheu, C. (2009). An ontology-based business intelligence application in a financial knowledge management system. *Expert Systems with Applications*, *36*(2), 3614–3622. doi:10.1016/j.eswa.2008.02.047

Chen, L. D. (2008). A model of consumer acceptance of mobile payment. *International Journal of Mobile Communications*, *6*(1), 32–52. doi:10.1504/IJMC.2008.015997

Chen, L. D., & Tan, J. (2004). Technology Adaptation in E-commerce: Key Determinants of Virtual Stores Acceptance. *European Management Journal*, *22*(1), 74–86. doi:10.1016/j.emj.2003.11.014

Chen, N., Richard, R., & Stephen, A. R. (1986). Economic forces and the stock market. *The Journal of Business*, *59*(3), 383–403. doi:10.1086/296344

Cheung, W., Chang, M. K., & Lai, V. S. (2000). Prediction of Internet and World Wide Web usage at work: A test of an extended Triandis model. *Decision Support Systems*, *30*(1), 83–100. doi:10.1016/S0167-9236(00)00125-1

Chhatoi, B. P. (2016). SMSE Financing by Domestic Commercial Banks and its Growth in India: An Analysis of Two Indicators. In Issue and challenges in business management. Himalaya Publishing House.

Chiou, J. S., & Shen, C. C. (2012). The antecedents of online financial service adoption: The impact of physical banking services on Internet banking acceptance. *Behaviour & Information Technology*, *31*(9), 859–871. doi:10.1080/0144929X.2010.549509

Chiu, P. (2009). *Looking Beyond Profit: Small Shareholders and the Values Imperative*. Gower Publishing, Ltd.

Chown, J. (2000). Monetary Union and tax harmonization. *Intertax*, *28*(3), 102–109. doi:10.1023/A:1005625820708

Christy, G. C. (2009). The Accounting Fog Machine. *Free Cash Flow: Seeing Through the Accounting Fog Machine to Find Great Stocks*, 15-24.

Chuang, C. C., Kuan, C. M., & Lin, H. Y. (2009). Causality in quantiles and dynamic stock return–volume relations. *Journal of Banking & Finance*, *33*(7), 1351–1360. doi:10.1016/j.jbankfin.2009.02.013

Clark-Carter, D. (1997). *Doing Quantitative Psychological Research: From Design to Report*. East Sussex, UK: Psychology Press.

Clark, G. L., & Strauss, K. (2008). Individual pension-related risk propensities: The effects of socio-demographic characteristics and a spousal pension entitlement on risk attitudes. *Ageing and Society*, *28*(6), 847–874. doi:10.1017/S0144686X08007083

Cloninger, C. R. (1987). A Systematic Method for Clinical Description and Classification of Personality Variants. *Archives of General Psychiatry*, *44*(6), 573–588. doi:10.1001/archpsyc.1987.01800180093014 PMID:3579504

Cloninger, C. R., Svrakic, D. M., & Przybeck, T. R. (1993). A Psychobiological Model of Temperament and Character. *Archives of General Psychiatry*, *50*(12), 975–990. doi:10.1001/archpsyc.1993.01820240059008 PMID:8250684

Cohen, J. (2003). Parasocial Break-ups: Measuring Individual Differences in Responses to the Dissolution of Parasocial Relationships. *Mass Communication & Society*, *6*(2), 191–202. doi:10.1207/S15327825MCS0602_5

Cohen, J. (2004). Parasocial Break-up from Favorite Television Characters: The Role of Attachment Styles and Relationship Intensity. *Journal of Social and Personal Relationships*, *21*(2), 187–202. doi:10.1177/0265407504041374

Connor, P. E., & Becker, B. W. (2003). Personal Value systems and Decision making Styles of Public Managers. *Public Personnel Management*, *32*(1), 155–180. doi:10.1177/009102600303200109

Conte, A., Levati, M. V., & Nardi, C. (2013). *The role of emotions on risk preferences: An experimental analysis (No. 2013-046)*. Jena Economic Research Papers.

Copeland, T. E. (1976). A model of asset trading under the assumption of sequential information arrival. *The Journal of Finance*, *31*(4), 1149–1168. doi:10.2307/2326280

Copur, Z. (2015). *Handbook of Research on Behavioral Finance and Investment Strategies: Decision Making in the Financial Industry*. Hacettepe University.

Coursaris, C., Hassanein, K., & Head, M. (2003). M-commerce in Canada: an interaction framework for wireless privacy. *Canadian Journal of Administrative Sciences/Revue Canadienne des Sciences de l'Administration, 20*(1), 54-73.

Crosby, P. B. (1979). *Quality is free*. New York: McGraw-Hill.

Cüceloğlu, D. (2007). *İnsan ve Davranışı: Psikolojinin Temel Kavramları. Remzi Kitabevi, 16.* Basım.

Czapkiewicz, A., & Stachowicz, M. (2016). The long-run relationship between the stock market and main macroeconomic variables in Poland. *Managerial Economics*, *17*(1), 7. doi:10.7494/manage.2016.17.1.7

Dal, V. (2009). *Farklı Kişilik Özelliklerine Sahip Bireylerin Risk Algılarının Tüketici Davranışı Açısından İncelenmesi: Üniversite Öğrencileri Üzerine Bir Araştırma*. Yayınlanmamış Yüksek Lisans Tezi, Süleyman Demirel Üniversitesi Sosyal Bilimler Enstitüsü İşletme Anabilim Dalı.

Dani, S. (2016). A Research Paper on an Impact of Goods and Service Tax (GST) on Indian Economy. *Business and Economics Journal, 7*(4). doi:10.4172/2151-6219.1000264

Daniel, K., Hirshleifer, D., & Subrahmanyam, A. (1998). Investor psychology and investor security market under- and overreactions. *The Journal of Finance, 53*(6), 1839–1886. doi:10.1111/0022-1082.00077

Dar, A. B., Samantaraya, A., & Shah, F. A. (2014). The predictive power of yield spread: Evidence from wavelet analysis. *Empirical Economics, 46*(3), 887–901. doi:10.100700181-013-0705-6

Darwish, M. (2012). Testing the Contemporaneous and Causal Relationship between Trading Volume and Return in the Palestine Exchange. *International Journal of Economics and Finance, 4*(4), 182–192. doi:10.5539/ijef.v4n4p182

Davidow, A., & Uttal, B. (1989). *Total Customer Service: The Ultimate Weapon*. New York: Harper & Row.

Davis, F. D. (1989). Perceived usefulness, perceived ease of use, and user acceptance of information technology. *Management Information Systems Quarterly, 13*(3), 319–340. doi:10.2307/249008

Davis, F. D., Bagozzi, R. P., & Warshaw, P. R. (1989). User acceptance of computer technology: A comparison of two theoretical models. *Management Science, 35*(8), 982–1003. doi:10.1287/mnsc.35.8.982

De Bondt, W. F. M., & Thaler, R. H. (1985). Dose the stock market overreact? *The Journal of Finance, 40*(3), 793–805. doi:10.1111/j.1540-6261.1985.tb05004.x

Degan, R. J. (2009). *Understanding China's historical development: The profit and the risk that China's stock market provides investors*. Globadvantage, Center of research in international business & strategy. Available from: http://globadvantage.ipleiria.pt/files/2009/07/working_paper-35_globadvantage.pdf

Demirguc-Kunt, A., & Levine, R. (1996). Stock markets, corporate finance and economic growth: An overview. *The World Bank Economic Review, 10*(2), 223–239. doi:10.1093/wber/10.2.223

Devarajan, S., & Hossain, S. (1998). The combined incidence of taxes and public expenditures in the Philippines. *World Development, 26*(6), 963–977. doi:10.1016/S0305-750X(98)00032-1

Dickason, Z., & Ferreira, S. (2018). Establishing a link between risk tolerance, investor personality and behavioural finance in South Africa. *Cogent Economics & Finance, 6*(1), 1–13. doi:10.1080/23322039.2018.1519898

Dickey, D. A., & Fuller, W. A. (1981). Likelihood ratio statistics for autoregressive time series with a unit root. *Econometrica, 49*(4), 1057–1072. doi:10.2307/1912517

Dimitrios, A., Helen, L., & Mike, T. (2016). Determinants of non-performing loans: Evidence from Euroarea countries. *Finance Research Letters, 18*, 116–119. doi:10.1016/j.frl.2016.04.008

Dinh, H. D. (2014). *Optimization in finance: approaches for modeling and solving the multi-period loss offset problem in German income tax system*. Academic Press.

Dinu, M., & Marinaş, M. C. (2014). Testing the impact of the fiscal policy with the SVAR model in seven CEE economies. *Economic Computation and Economic Cybernetics Studies and Research, 48*(1).

Dominitz, J., & Manski, C. F. (2004). How Should We Measure Consumer Confidence? *The Journal of Economic Perspectives, 18*(2), 51–66. doi:10.1257/0895330041371303

Dowling, M., & Lucey, B. M. (2005). Weather, biorhythms, beliefs and stock returns—Some preliminary Irish evidence. *International Review of Financial Analysis, 14*(3), 337–355. doi:10.1016/j.irfa.2004.10.003

Durán Cabré, J. M., & Esteller Moré, A. (2014). *Tax professionals' view of the Spanish tax system: efficiency, equity and tax planning*. IEB Working Paper 2014/04.

Durán-Cabré, J. M., Esteller-Moré, A., & Salvadori, L. (2015). Empirical evidence on horizontal competition in tax enforcement. *International Tax and Public Finance, 22*(5), 834–860. doi:10.100710797-014-9333-0

Easterly, W. (2002). *The elusive quest for growth*. Cambridge, MA: MIT Press.

Easterly, W., & Levine, R. (2003). Tropics, germs and crops: How endowments influence economic developemnt. *Journal of Monetary Economics, 50*(1), 3–40. doi:10.1016/S0304-3932(02)00200-3

Economywatch. (2008). Available at: www.economywatch.com/indianeconomy

Ederington, L. H., & Yawitz, J. B. (1985). *The bond rating process*. Washington University. Institute of Banking and Financial Markets.

Edwards, C., & Mitchell, D. J. (2008). *Global tax revolution: the rise of tax competition and the battle to defend it*. Cato Institute.

Egri, C. P., Ralston, D. A., Milton, L., Naoumova, I., Palmer, I., & Ramburuth, P. (2004), *Managerial Perspectives on Corporate Environmental and Social Responsibilities in 22 Countries*, Paper presented at the Academy of Management. 10.5465/ambpp.2004.13857751

Elmas, B., & Yıldırım, M. (2010). Kriz Dönemlerinde Hisse Senedi Fiyatı ile İşlem Hacmi İlişkisi: İMKB'de İşlem Gören Bankacılık SEktör Hisseleri üzerine Bir Uygulama. *Atatürk Üniversitesi İktisadi ve İdari Bilimler Dergisi, 24*(2), 37–46.

Elster, J. (1985). Introduction. In J. Elster (Ed.), *The Multiple Self* (pp. 1–34). Cambridge, UK: Cambridge University Press.

Elveren, A. Y., & Hsu, S. (2007). *Gender gaps in the individual pension system in Turkey* (No. 2007-06). Working Paper, University of Utah, Department of Economics.

Enders, W. (1995). *Applied econometric time series*. John Wiley Sons Inc.

England, G. W. (1967). Personal Value Systems of American Managers. *Academy of Management Journal, 10*, 53–68.

Engle, R. F., & Granger, C. W. (1987). Co-integration and error correction: Representation, estimation, and testing. *Econometrica, 55*(2), 251–276. doi:10.2307/1913236

Engle, R. F., Lilien, D. M., & Robins, R. P. (1987). Estimating time varying risk premia in the term structure: The ARCH-M model. *Econometrica*, 391–407.

Epstein, M. J. (1992). The Annual Report: Report Card. *Business and Society Review*, (81): 81–83.

Erdem, C., Arslan, C. K., & Sema Erdem, M. (2005). Effects of macroeconomic variables on Istanbul stock exchange indexes. *Applied Financial Economics, 15*(14), 987–994. doi:10.1080/09603100500120365

Eriksson, K., Kerem, K., & Nilsson, D. (2005). Customer acceptance of internet banking in Estonia. *International Journal of Bank Marketing, 23*(2), 200–216. doi:10.1108/02652320510584412

Etzioni, A. (1988). *The Moral Dimension: Toward a New Economics*. New York: The Free Press.

Etzioni, A. (1991). Socio-Economics: A Budding Challenge. In A. Etzioni & P. R. Lawrence (Eds.), *Socio Economics Toward a New Synthesis* (pp. 3–7). New York: M.E. Sharpe.

Evaluating Mutual Fund Performance. (n.d.). Alliance Business School, Bangalore. Available at: www.indianmba.com/Occasional_Papers/OP158/op158.html

Evrim, S. (1967). *Psikoloji Açısından Bir Buud Olarak İçedönüklük-Dışa Dönklük (İntroversion-Extraversion) Sorunu Üzerine Bir Araştırma*. İstanbul Üniversitesi Edebiyat Fakültesi Yayınları, No: 1284.

Ewen, R. B. (2003). *An Introduction to Theories of Personality. Lawrence Erlbaum Associates, Inc.* doi:10.4324/9781410607287

Eyal, K., & Cohen, J. (2006). When Good Friends Say Goodbye: A Parasocial Breakup Study. *Journal of Broadcasting & Electronic Media, 50*(3), 502–523. doi:10.120715506878jobem5003_9

Eysenck, H. J., & Wilson, G. (1998). *Kişiliğinizi Tanıyın*. Basım.

Fahlgren, E., Nima, A. A., Archer, T., & Garcia, D. (2015). Person-Centered Osteopathic Practice: Patients' Personality (Body, Mind, and Soul) and Health (İll-Being and Well-Being). *PeerJ, 27*(3), E1349.

Fainstein, G., & Novikov, I. (2011). The comparative analysis of credit risk determinants in the banking sector of the Baltic States. *Review of Economics & Finance, 1*(3), 20-45.

Fama, E. F. (1965). Random Walks in Stock Market Prices. *Financial Analysts Journal, 21*(5), 55–59. doi:10.2469/faj.v21.n5.55

Fama, E. F. (1970). Efficient Capital Markets: A Review of Theory and Empirical Work. *The Journal of Finance, 25*(2), 383–417. doi:10.2307/2325486

Fama, E. F. (1981). Stock returns, real activity, inflation, and money. *The American Economic Review, 71*(4), 545–565.

Fama, E. F. (1991). Efficient Capital Markets II. *The Journal of Finance, 46*(5), 1575–1617. doi:10.1111/j.1540-6261.1991.tb04636.x

Fama, E. F. (1998). Market efficiency, long-term returns, and behavioral finance. *Journal of Financial Economics, 49*(3), 283–306. doi:10.1016/S0304-405X(98)00026-9

Fama, E. F., Fisher, L., & Michael,, J.C., & Rol, R. (1969). The Adjustment of Stock Prices to New Information. *International Economic Review*, 10.

Feather, N. T. (1995). Values, Valences, and Choice: The Influence of Values on the Perceived Attractiveness and Choice of Alternatives. *Journal of Personality and Social Psychology, 68*(6), 1135–1151. doi:10.1037/0022-3514.68.6.1135

Feist, J., & Feist, G. J. (2009). *Theoriest of Psychology*. McGraw-Hill Education Learning Technology.

Feldstein, M. S. (1980). *Inflation, tax rules, and investment: some econometric evidence*. Academic Press.

Feldstein, M. (2009). Rethinking the role of fiscal policy. *American Economic Review (Kansas City, Mo.), 99*(2), 556–559.

Festić, M., Kavkler, A., & Repina, S. (2011). The macroeconomic sources of systemic risk in the banking sectors of five new EU member states. *Journal of Banking & Finance, 35*(2), 310–322. doi:10.1016/j.jbankfin.2010.08.007

Festinger, L., Riecken, H. W., & Schachter, S. (1956). *When prophecy fails: A social and psychological study of a modern group that predicted the destruction of the world* (1st ed.). Minneapolis, MN: University of Minnesota Press. doi:10.1037/10030-000

Field, T., Diego, M., Pelaez, M., Deeds, O., & Delgado, J. (2009). Breakup distress in university students. *Adolescence, 44*(176), 705–727. PMID:20432597

Finnerty, C., Merks, P., Petriccione, M., & Russo, R. (2007). *Fundamentals of international tax planning*. Ámsterdam: IBFD.

Fleming, J., Kirby, C., & Ostdiek, B. (2005). *ARCH effects and trading volume*. Rice University and Clemson University Working Paper.

Flexner, S. B., & Stein, J. (Eds.). (1982). *The Random House College Dictionary*. New York: Random House.

Fofack, H. (2005). *Nonperforming loans in Sub-Saharan Africa: causal analysis and macroeconomic implications*. World Bank Policy Research Working Paper (3769).

Fornero, E., & Monticone, C. (2011). Financial literacy and pension plan participation in Italy. *Journal of Pension Economics and Finance*, *10*(4), 547–564. doi:10.1017/S1474747211000473

Frank, C. (1973). The Behavior of Stock Prices on Fridays and Mondays. *Financial Analysts Journal*, *29*, 67–69.

Frankfurter, G. M., & McGoun, E. G. (2002). Resistance is futile: The assimilation of behavioral finance. *Journal of Economic Behavior & Organization*, *48*, 375–389.

Frankfurt, H. G. (1988). *The Importance of What We Care About: Philosophical Essays*. Cambridge, UK: Cambridge University Press. doi:10.1017/CBO9780511818172

Fukuyama, F. (1995). *Trust: The social virtues and the creation of prosperity*. New York: Free Press.

Fukuyama, F. (2006). *Development and the limits of institutional design*. St. Peterbersburg.

Funder, D. C. (2001). Personality. *Annual Review of Psychology*, *V*, 52, 197–221. PMID:11148304

Gale, W., & Auerbach, A. (2009). *The economic crisis and the fiscal crisis: 2009 and beyond*. Academic Press.

Galuszka, J. (2013). The Fiscal Union as a Remedy For the economic and Financial Crisis in the european Union. *Equilibrium*, *8*(1), 49–67. doi:10.12775/EQUIL.2013.003

Garcia, V. F., & Liu, L. (1999). Macroeconomic Determinants of Stock. *Journal of Applied Econometrics*, *2*(1), 29–59.

Garvin, D. A. (1983). Quality on the line. *Harvard Business Review*, *61*, 64–75.

Gereff, J. G., Humphrey, J., Kaplinsky, R., & Sturgeon, T. (2009). *Introduction: Globalisation, Value Chains and Development*. Academic Press.

Gerrans, P., & Clark-Murphy, M. (2004). Gender differences in retirement savings decisions. *Journal of Pension Economics and Finance*, *3*(2), 145–164. doi:10.1017/S1474747204001477

Gerschenkron, A. (1965). *Economic Backwardness in Historical Perspective*. New York, NY: Praeger.

Geweke, J. (1982). Measurement of Linear Dependence and Feedback between Multiple Time Series. *Journal of the American Statistical Association*, *77*(378), 304–324. doi:10.1080/01621459.1982.10477803

Ghosh. (2015). Proactive Communication of CSR in India: A Distant Dream or Reality? *Paradigm*, *19*(2), 115–136. Retrieved from http://par.sagepub.com

Gilmore. (2012). CSR Communication in Emerging Economies: Need for a New Paradigm: A Case Study of a Multinational and an Indian Trans National's CSR Communication in India. *IJBIT*, *6*(4), 66-77.

Ginn, J., & Arber, S. (1993). Pension penalties: The gendered division of occupational welfare. *Work, Employment and Society*, *7*(1), 47–70. doi:10.1177/095001709371003

Gjyli, K. (2009). *Shkenca mbi financat dhe e drejta e financave*. Academic Press.

Godfrey, M. D., Granger, C. W., & Morgenstern, O. (1964). The random-walk hypothesis of stock market behavior. *Kyklos*, *17*(1), 1–30. doi:10.1111/j.1467-6435.1964.tb02458.x

Gökce, A. (2002). IMKB'de Fiyat-Hacim İlişkisi: Granger Nedensellik Testi. *Gazi Üniversitesi İ.İ.B.F. Dergisi*, *3*, 43–48.

Gold, H., & Webster, A. (1990). *New Zealand Values Today*. Palmerston North, New Zealand: Alpha Publications.

Goldsmith, R. W. (1969). *Financial Structure and Development*. New Haven, CT: Yale University Press.

González-Hermosillo, B., Pazarbaşioğlu, C., & Billings, R. (1997). Determinants of banking system fragility: A case study of Mexico. *Staff Papers*, *44*(3), 295–314. doi:10.2307/3867561

Goodworth, C. (1988). *The Secrets of Successful Leadership and People Management*. London: Heinemann Pub. Ltd.

Gordon, R. H. (1986). Taxation of investment and savings in a world economy. *The American Economic Review*, 1086–1102.

Granger, C. W. J. (1969). Investigating causal relations by econometric models and cross-spectral methods. *Econometrica*, *37*(3), 424–438. doi:10.2307/1912791

Granger, C. W., & Morgenstern, O. (1963). Spectral analysis of New York stock market prices. *Kyklos*, *16*(1), 1–27. doi:10.1111/j.1467-6435.1963.tb00270.x

Gray, S., Mirkovic, A., & Ragunathan, V. (2006). The determinants of credit ratings: Australian evidence. *Australian Journal of Management*, *31*(2), 333–354. doi:10.1177/031289620603100208

Grinsted, A., Moore, J.C. & Jevrejeva, S. (2004). Application of the Cross Wavelet Transform and Wavelet Coherence to Geophysical Time Series. *Nonlinear Processes in Geophysics, 11*, 561–566.

Guiso, L., Sapienza, P., & Zingales, L. (2004). Does local financial development matter? *The Quarterly Journal of Economics*, *119*(3), 929–969. doi:10.1162/0033553041502162

Gu, J. C., Lee, S. C., & Suh, Y. H. (2009). Determinants of behavioral intention to mobile banking. *Expert Systems with Applications*, *36*(9), 11605–11616. doi:10.1016/j.eswa.2009.03.024

Günay, S. (2015). BİST100 Endeksi Fiyat ve İşlem Hacminin Fraktallık Analizi. *Doğuş Üniversitesi Dergisi*, *16*(1), 35–50. doi:10.31671/dogus.2018.59

Gunduz, L., & Hatemi-J, A. (2005). Stock price and volume relation in emerging markets. *Emerging Markets Finance & Trade*, *41*(1), 29–44. doi:10.1080/1540496X.2005.11052599

Gupta, B. (2012). A comparative study of non-performing assets of SBI & associates & other public sector banks. *SIT Journal of Management,* 2(2), 175-189.

Gupta, N. (2014). Goods and Services Tax: It's impact on Indian Economy. *International Research Journal Of Commerce Arts And Science*, *5*(3), 126–133.

Gurley & Shaw. (1960). *Money and Theory of Finance*. The Booking Institution.

Hall, R. E., & Rabushka, A. (1983). *Low tax, simple tax, flat tax*. McGraw-Hill Companies.

Hamao, Y. (1988). An empirical examination of the arbitrage pricing theory: Using Japanese data. *Japan and the World Economy*, *1*(1), 45–61.

Hansenne, M., Delhez, M., & Cloninger, C. R. (2005). Psychometric Properties of the Temperament and Character Inventory Revised (TCI-R) in a Belgian Sample. *Journal of Personality Assessment*, *85*(1), 40–49. doi:10.120715327752jpa8501_04 PMID:16083383

Hanson, D., & Tranter, B. (2006). Who are the Shareholders in Australia and What are Their Ethical Opinions? An Empirical Analysis. *Corporate Governance*, *14*(1), 23–32. doi:10.1111/j.1467-8683.2006.00481.x

Harmonized 'Goods and Service Tax' in India: A Backgrounder. (n.d.). *SSRN Electronic Journal*. doi:10.2139srn.1267066

Helms, M., & Nixon, J. (2010). Exploring SWOT analysis – where are we now? *Journal Of Strategy And Management*, *3*(3), 215–251. doi:10.1108/17554251011064837

Herekar, M. (2012). Evaluation of impact of Goods and Services Tax (GST. *Indian Streams Research Journal*, *2*(I), 1–4.

Hershey, D. A., Jacobs-Lawson, J. M., McArdle, J. J., & Hamagami, F. (2007). Psychological foundations of financial planning for retirement. *Journal of Adult Development*, *14*(1-2), 26–36. doi:10.100710804-007-9028-1

Hershey, D. A., & Mowen, J. C. (2000). Psychological determinants of financial preparedness for retirement. *The Gerontologist*, *40*(6), 687–697. doi:10.1093/geront/40.6.687 PMID:11131085

Heskett, J., Sasser, E., & Hart, C. (1990). *Services Breakthrough: Changing the Rules of the Game*. New York: Free Press.

Hirshleifer, D., & Shumway, T. (2003). Good day sunshine: Stock returns and the weather. *The Journal of Finance*, *58*(3), 1009–1032. doi:10.1111/1540-6261.00556

Hofstede, G. (2001). Culture's consequences (2nd ed.). Thousand Oaks, CA: Sage.

Homer, P. M., & Kahle, L. R. (1988). A Structural Equation Test of the Value attitude- behavior Hierarchy. *Journal of Personality and Social Psychology*, *54*(4), 638–646. doi:10.1037/0022-3514.54.4.638

Hong, H. (1977). Inflation and the market value of the firm: Theory and tests. *The Journal of Finance*, *32*(4), 1031–1048. doi:10.1111/j.1540-6261.1977.tb03307.x

Hong, Q., & Smart, M. (2010). In praise of tax havens: International tax planning and foreign direct investment. *European Economic Review*, *54*(1), 82–95. doi:10.1016/j.euroecorev.2009.06.006

Horrigan, J. O. (1966). The determination of long-term credit standing with financial ratios. *Journal of Accounting Research*, *4*, 44–62. doi:10.2307/2490168

Hosmani & Hudagi. (2011). Unearthing the epidemic of non-performing assets: A study with reference to public sector banks in India. *International Journal of Multidisciplinary Research, 1*(8).

Howcraft. (1991). Customer Satisfaction in Retail Banking. *The Service Industries Journal, 11*, 11-17.

Huang, A., & Liu, B. (2012). The Impact of the Goods and Services Tax on Mortgage Costs: Evidence from Australian Mortgage Corporations. *International Journal Of Financial Research*, *4*(1). doi:10.5430/ijfr.v4n1p54

Huang, Z., Chen, H., Hsu, C. J., Chen, W. H., & Wu, S. (2004). Credit rating analysis with support vector machines and neural networks: A market comparative study. *Decision Support Systems*, *37*(4), 543–558. doi:10.1016/S0167-9236(03)00086-1

Huberman, G., Iyengar, S. S., & Jiang, W. (2007). Defined contribution pension plans: Determinants of participation and contributions rates. *Journal of Financial Services Research*, *31*(1), 1–32. doi:10.100710693-007-0003-6

Hunkar, D. (2009). Rising NPAs of Indian Banks Not a Cause for Concern. *The Wisdom Tree*. Retrieved from http:// seekingalpha.com/ article/

Hussey, J., & Hussey, R. (1997). *Business Research: A Practical Guide for Undergraduate and Postgraduate Students*. London: MacMillan Press. doi:10.1007/978-1-349-25262-6

Hwang, R. C., Chung, H., & Chu, C. K. (2010). Predicting issuer credit ratings using a semiparametric method. *Journal of Empirical Finance, 17*(1), 120–137. doi:10.1016/j.jempfin.2009.07.007

İnanç, B. Y., & Yerlikaya, E. E. (2012). *Kişilik Kuramları. Pegem Akademi, 6.* Baskı.

Inglehart, R. (2000). Culture and Democracy. In L. E. Harrison & S. P. Huntington (Eds.), *Culture Matters: How Values Shape Human Progress* (pp. 80–97). New York: Basic Books.

Inglehart, R., & Baker, W. E. (2001). Modernization's Challenge to Traditional Values: Who's Afraid of Ronald McDonald? *The Futurist, 35*(2), 16–21.

Isen, A. M., & Geva, N. (1987). The influence of positive affect on acceptable level of risk: The person with a large canoe has a large worry. *Organizational Behavior and Human Decision Processes, 39*(2), 145–154. doi:10.1016/0749-5978(87)90034-3

Isen, A. M., Shalker, T. E., Clark, M., & Karp, L. (1978). Affect, accessibility of material in memory, and behavior: A cognitive loop? *Journal of Personality and Social Psychology, 36*(1), 1–12. doi:10.1037/0022-3514.36.1.1 PMID:621625

Isır, T. (2006). *Örgütlerde Personel Seçim Süreci: Bir Kamu Kuruluşundaki Yönetici Personelin Kişilik Özelliklerinin Tespit Edilerek Personel Seçim Sürecinin İyileştirilmesi Üzerine Bir Araştırma.* Çukurova Üniversitesi Sosyal Bilimler Enstitüsü İşletme Anabilim Dalı, Yayınlanmamış Doktora Tezi.

Israel, D., Sudhahar, J.C., & Selvam, M. (2004, October). The Measurement of Service Quality Perception in Banking Sector. *SCMS Journal of Indian Management*, 37-51.

Iyer, E. S., & Kashyap, R. (2009). Non economic goals of investors. *Journal of Consumer Behaviour, 8*(5), 225–237. doi:10.1002/cb.281

Jahur, M. S., Quadir, S. M., & Khan, M. A. (2014). Determinants of stock market performance in Bangladesh. *Indonesian Management and Accounting Research, 13*(1), 16–28.

Jain & Deepti. (2010). A Study of NPAs in Nationalized Banks of Madhya Pradesh. *International Research Journal, 1*(3).

Janeba, E., & Peters, W. (1999). Tax evasion, tax competition and the gains from nondiscrimination: The case of interest taxation in Europe. *Economic Journal (London), 109*(452), 93–101. doi:10.1111/1468-0297.00393

Jara, H. X., & Tumino, A. (2013). Tax-benefit systems, income distribution and work incentives in the European Union. *The International Journal of Microsimulation, 6*, 27–62.

Jensen, M. (1978). Some Anomalous Evidence Regarding Market Efficiency. *Journal of Financial Economics, 6*(2), 95–101. doi:10.1016/0304-405X(78)90025-9

Johansen, S. (1995). Identifying restrictions of linear equations with applications to simultaneous equations and cointegration. *Journal of Econometrics, 69*(1), 111–132. doi:10.1016/0304-4076(94)01664-L

Johansen, S., & Juselius, K. (1990). Maximum likelihood estimation and inference on cointegration—With applications to the demand for money. *Oxford Bulletin of Economics and Statistics, 52*(2), 169–210. doi:10.1111/j.1468-0084.1990.mp52002003.x

Johnson. (2015). MNC CSR in Emerging Economy Conflict Zones A Case Study of HUL's North East Operations in India. *Vikalpa, 38*(4), 69-82.

Johnson, E. J., & Tversky, A. (1983). Affect, generalization, and the perception of risk. *Journal of Personality and Social Psychology, 45*(1), 20–31. doi:10.1037/0022-3514.45.1.20

Joo, B. A. (2014). Asset quality and accounting jugglery in Indian banks. *Indian Journal of Commerce and Management Studies*, *5*(1), 105–112. Retrieved from https://search.proquest.com/docview/1511107407?accountid=175698

Joumard, I. (2001). *Tax systems in European Union countries*. Academic Press.

Juran, J. M. (1974). *Quality Control Handbook*. London: McGraw Hill Publications.

Juselius, K. (2006). *The cointegrated VAR model: methodology and applications*. Oxford University Press.

Kahle, L. R. (1983). *Social Values and Social Change: Adaption to Life in America*. New York: Praeger Publishers.

Kahle, L. R., & Kennedy, P. (1989). Using the List of Values (LOV) to Understand Consumers. *Journal of Consumer Marketing*, *6*(3), 5–12.

Kahneman, D., Knetsch, J. L., & Thaler, R. H. (1991). The Endowment Effect, Loss Aversion, and Status Quo Bias. *The Journal of Economic Perspectives*, *5*(1), 193–206. doi:10.1257/jep.5.1.193

Kahneman, D., & Riepe, M. W. (1998). Aspects of Investor Psychology: Beliefs, preferences, biases investment advisors should know about. *Journal of Portfolio Management*, *24*(4), 52–65. doi:10.3905/jpm.1998.409643

Kahneman, D., Slovic, P., & Tversky, A. (Eds.). (1982). *Judgment Under Uncertainty: Heuristics and Biases*. Cambridge University Press. doi:10.1017/CBO9780511809477

Kahneman, D., & Tversky, A. (1971). Belief in law of small numbers. *Psychological Bulletin*, *76*(2), 105–110. doi:10.1037/h0031322

Kahneman, D., & Tversky, A. (1972). Subjective Probability: A judgment of Representativeness. *Cognitive Psychology*, *3*(3), 430–454. doi:10.1016/0010-0285(72)90016-3

Kahneman, D., & Tversky, A. (1973). On the psychology of prediction. *Psychological Review*, *80*(4), 237–251. doi:10.1037/h0034747

Kahneman, D., & Tversky, A. (1979). Prospect Theory: An Analysis of Decision under Risk. *Econometrica*, *47*(2), 263–291. doi:10.2307/1914185

Kahneman, D., & Tversky, A. (1979). Prospect theory: An analysis of decisions under risk *Econometrica. Cilt*, *47*, 313–327.

Kahneman, D., & Tversky, A. (1984). Choices, values, and frames. *The American Psychologist*, *39*(4), 341–350. doi:10.1037/0003-066X.39.4.341

Kahneman, D., & Tversky, A. (2000). *Choices, Values, and Frames*. Cambridge University Press.

Kamath, R. R., & Wang, Y. (2006). The causality between stock index returns and volumes in the Asian equity markets. *Journal of International Business Research*, *5*, 63–74.

Kanadampully, J. (1998). Service Quality to Service Loyalty: A Relationship which goes beyond Customer Services. *Total Quality Management*, *9*(6), 431–433. doi:10.1080/0954412988370

Kanadampully, J. (2000). The impact of demand fluctuation on the quality of service: A tourism industry example. *Managing Service Quality: An International Journal*, *10*(1), 10–19. doi:10.1108/09604520010307012

Kanagaraj, A., & Murugesan, B. (2006). Evaluation of Financial Information Content in Credit Rating using Binary Logistic Regression. *The ICFAI Journal of Applied Finance*, *12*(10), 40–64.

Kaplan, R. S., & Urwitz, G. (1979). Statistical models of bond ratings: A methodological inquiry. *The Journal of Business*, *52*(2), 231–261. doi:10.1086/296045

Karancı, N., Dirik, G., & Yorulmaz, O. (2007). Eysenck Kişilik Anketi- Gözden Geçirilmiş Kısaltılmış Formunun (Eka-Ggk) Türkiye'de Geçerlik ve Güvenirlik Çalışması. *Türk Psikiyatri Dergisi, 18*, 3.

Kara, S., Yildiz, Y., & Karan, M. B. (2015). Analysis of risk-taking behavior of individual pension system participants: The case of turkey. *Journal of Economics Finance and Accounting, 2*(3), 375–396.

Karpoff, J. M. (1987). The Relation between price Changes and Trading Volume: A Survey. *Journal of Financial and Quantitative Analysis, 22*(1), 109–126. doi:10.2307/2330874

Kasa, K. (1992). Common stochastic trends in international stock markets. *Journal of Monetary Economics, 29*(1), 95–124. doi:10.1016/0304-3932(92)90025-W

Kavanagh, D. J., & Bower, G. H. (1985). Mood and self-efficacy: Impact of joy and sadness on perceived capabilities. *Cognitive Therapy and Research, 9*(5), 507–525. doi:10.1007/BF01173005

Kayalıdere, K. (2009). Price-Volume Relationship in ISE – Asymmetric Interaction. *Yönetim ve Ekonomi., 16*(2), 49–62.

Kelly, G. (1991). *The psychology of personal constructs. London: Routledge.*

Khurana, A., & Sharma, A. (2016). Goods and Services Tax in India – A Positive Reform for Indirect Tax System. *International Journal Of Advanced Research, 4*(3), 500–505.

Kiger, J. (1972). An Empirical Investigation of NYSE Volume and Price Reactions to the Announcements of Quarterly Earnings. *Journal of Accounting Research, 10*(1), 113–128. doi:10.2307/2490222

Kilby, R. W. (1993). *The Study of Human Values*. Lanham, MD: University Press of America.

Kimani, D. K., & Mutuku, C. M. (2013). Inflation Dynamics on the Overall Stock Market Performance: The Case of Nairobi Securities Exchange in Kenya. *Economics and Finance Review, 2*(11), 1–11.

Kim, O., & Verrecchia, R. E. (1991). Trading volume and price reactions to public announcements. *Journal of Accounting Research, 29*(2), 302–321. doi:10.2307/2491051

Kıran, B. (2010). Trade volume and return volatility in Istanbul Stock Exchange. *Doğuş Üniversitesi Dergisi, 11*(1), 98–108.

Kitwood, T. M., & Smithers, A. G. (1975). Measurement of Human Values: An Appraisal of the Work of Milton Rokeach. *Educational Research, 17*(3), 175–179. doi:10.1080/0013188750170302

Klapper, L., & Panos, G. A. (2011). Financial literacy and retirement planning: The Russian case. *Journal of Pension Economics and Finance, 10*(4), 599–618. doi:10.1017/S1474747211000503

Klimoski, R. J., & Zukin, L. B. (2003). *Psychological Assessment in Industrial Organizational Settings* (I. B. Weiner, Ed.). doi:10.1002/0471264385.wei1014

Kluckhohn, C. (1951). Values and Value-orientations in the Theory of Action. In T. Parsons & E. A. Shils (Eds.), *Toward a General Theory of Action* (pp. 388–433). Cambridge, MA: Harvard University Press. doi:10.4159/harvard.9780674863507.c8

Knight, F. H. (1921). *Risk, Uncertainty and Profit*. Boston, MA: Hart, Schaffner & Marx, Houghton-Mifflin Co.

Knirsch, D., & Niemann, R. (2007). *Allowance for shareholder equity: implementing a neutral corporate income tax in the European Union* (No. 34). Arqus-Diskussionsbeiträge zur quantitativen Steuerlehre.

Kolodinsky, J. M., Hogarth, J. M., & Hilgert, M. A. (2004). The adoption of electronic banking technologies by US consumers. *International Journal of Bank Marketing, 22*(4), 238–259. doi:10.1108/02652320410542536

Köse, S. (2003). A Psychological Model of Temperament And Character: TCI. *Yeni Symposium: Psikiyatri, Nöroloji ve Davraniş Bilimleri Dergisi*, *41*(2), 86–97.

Köse, S., Sayar, K., Ak, İ., Aydın, N., Kalelioğlu, Ü., Przybeck, T. R., & Cloninger, C. R. (2004). Mizaç ve Karakter Envanteri (Türkçe TCI): Geçerlik, Güvenirliği ve Faktör Yapısı. *Klinik Psikofarmakoloji Bülteni*, *14*, 107–131.

Kotler, P., Ang, S. H., Leong, S. M., & Tan, C. T. (1999). *Marketing Management: An Asian Perspective*. Prentice Hall Inc.

Kraal, D., & Kasipillai, J. (2015). *Finally, a Goods and Services Tax for Malaysia: A Comparison to Australia's GST Experience*. SSRN Electronic Journal. doi:10.2139srn.2804416

Krippendorff, K. (1980). *Content Analysis: An Introduction to Its Methodology*. Newbury Park, CA: Sage Publications.

Kuisma, T., Laukkanen, T., & Hiltunen, M. (2007). Mapping the reasons for resistance to Internet banking: A means-end approach. *International Journal of Information Management*, *27*(2), 75–85. doi:10.1016/j.ijinfomgt.2006.08.006

Kuran, T. (1995). *Private Truths, Public Lies: The Social Consequences of Preference Falsification*. Cambridge, MA: Harvard University Press.

Kyereboah-Coleman, A., & Agyire-Tettey, K. F. (2008). Impact of macroeconomic indicators on stock market performance: The case of the Ghana Stock Exchange. *The Journal of Risk Finance*, *9*(4), 365–378. doi:10.1108/15265940810895025

Laura, B., & Kate, S. (2002). A Delphi study of the drivers and inhibitors of Internet banking. *International Journal of Bank Marketing*, *20*(6), 250–260. doi:10.1108/02652320210446715

Lawrence, F. K., & Josiah, M. (1939). *Projective Methods for the Study of Personality. The New York Academy of Sciences, 1(8).*

Lawrence, S., & Collins, E. (2004). *Sustainability Practices of New Zealand Business*. Hamilton, New Zealand: Waikato Management School, University of Waikato.

Lease, R. C., Lewellen, W. G., & Schlarbaum, G. G. (1974). The Individual Investor: Attributes and Attitudes. *The Journal of Finance*, *29*(2), 413–433. doi:10.1111/j.1540-6261.1974.tb03055.x

Lee, B. S., & Rui, O. M. (2002). The dynamic relationship between stock returns and trading volume: Domestic and cross – country evidence. *Journal of Banking & Finance*, *26*(1), 51–78. doi:10.1016/S0378-4266(00)00173-4

Leibfritz, W., Thornton, J., & Bibbee, A. (1997). *Taxation and economic performance*. Academic Press.

Leith, K. P., & Baumeister, R. F. (1996). Why do bad moods increase self-defeating behavior? Emotion, risk taking and self-regulation. *Journal of Personality and Social Psychology*, *71*(6), 1250–1267. doi:10.1037/0022-3514.71.6.1250 PMID:8979390

Leonard, F. S., & Sasser, W. E. (1982). The incline of quality. *Harvard Business Review*, *60*(5), 163–171.

Lepori, G. M. (2015). Investor mood and demand for stocks: Evidence from popular TV series finales. *Journal of Economic Psychology*, *48*, 33–47. doi:10.1016/j.joep.2015.02.003

Levy, T., & Yagil, J. (2011). Air pollution and stock returns in the US. *Journal of Economic Psychology*, *32*(3), 374–383. doi:10.1016/j.joep.2011.01.004

Lewin, K. (1952). *Field Theory in Social Science: Selected Theoretical Papers*. London: Tavistock Publications.

Lewis, A. (2002). *Morals, Markets and Money: Ethical, Green and Socially Responsible Investing*. London: Pearson Education.

Lewis, C. A., Francis, L. J., Shevlin, M., & Forrest, S. (2002). Confirmatory factor analysis of the French translation of the abbreviated form of the Revised Eysenck Personality Questionnaire (EPQR-A). *European Journal of Psychological Assessment, 18*(2), 79–85. doi:10.1027//1015-5759.18.2.179

Liaropoulos, L., & Tragakes, E. (1998). Public/private financing in the Greek health care system: Implications for equity. *Health Policy (Amsterdam), 43*(2), 153–169. doi:10.1016/S0168-8510(97)00093-6 PMID:10177616

Lin, C. H., Yen, H. R., & Chuang, S. C. (2007). The effects of emotion and need for cognition on consumer choice involving risk. *Journal of Business and Psychology, 22*(1), 65–78.

Lin, H. F. (2011). An empirical investigation of mobile banking adoption: The effect of innovation attributes and knowledge-based trust. *International Journal of Information Management, 31*(3), 252–260. doi:10.1016/j.ijinfomgt.2010.07.006

Lin, H. W. (2011). Elucidating the Influence of Demographics and Psychological Traits on Investment Biases. *World Academy of Science, Engineering and Technology.*

Lintner, G. (1998). Behavioral finance: Why investors make bad decisions. *The Planner, 13*(1), 7–8.

Lo, A. W., Repin, D. V., & Steenbarger, B. N. (2005). Fear and Geed in Financial Markets: A Clinical Study of Day-Traders. *The American Economic Review, 95*(2), 352–359. doi:10.1257/000282805774670095

Loewenstein, G., Weber, E., Hsee, C., & Welch, N. (2001). Risk As Feelings. *Psychological Bulletin, 127*(2), 267–286. doi:10.1037/0033-2909.127.2.267 PMID:11316014

Louzis, D. P., Vouldis, A. T., & Metaxas, V. L. (2012). Macroeconomic and bank-specific determinants of non- performing loans in Greece: A comparative study of mortgage, business and consumer loan portfolios. *Journal of Banking & Finance, 36*(4), 1012–1027. doi:10.1016/j.jbankfin.2011.10.012

Luarn, P., & Lin, H. H. (2005). Toward an understanding of the behavioral intention to use mobile banking. *Computers in Human Behavior, 21*(6), 873–891. doi:10.1016/j.chb.2004.03.003

Lucey, B. M. (2005). Does volume provide information? Evidence from the Irish stock market. *Applied Financial Economics Letters, 1*(2), 105–109. doi:10.1080/08935690500047205

Luo, J., Gan, C., Hu, B., & Kao, T. K. (2009). An empirical analysis of Chinese stock price anomalies and volatility. *Investment Management and Financial Innovations, 6*(1), 1–18.

Lusardi, A. (2008). *Household saving behavior: The role of financial literacy, information, and financial education programs (No. w13824).* National Bureau of Economic Research. doi:10.3386/w13824

Mackenzie, C., & Lewis, A. (1999). Morals and Markets: The Case of Ethical Investing. *Business Ethics Quarterly, 9*(3), 439–452. doi:10.2307/3857511

Madhavi. (2015). A Study of the CSR Policies and Practices of Indian Companies. *DAWN: Journal for Contemporary Research in Management*, 17-26.

Mallat, N. (2007). Exploring consumer adoption of mobile payments–A qualitative study. *The Journal of Strategic Information Systems, 16*(4), 413–432. doi:10.1016/j.jsis.2007.08.001

Mandelo, M., & Pinho, C. (2012). International stock market indices comovements: A new look. *International Journal of Finance & Economics, 17*(1), 89–102. doi:10.1002/ijfe.448

Mangla, S., Kumar, P., & Barua, M. (2014). Monte Carlo Simulation Based Approach to Manage Risks in Operational Networks in Green Supply Chain. *Procedia Engineering, 97*, 2186–2194. doi:10.1016/j.proeng.2014.12.462

Mankiw, N. G. (2008). *Principles of Macroeconomics* (5th ed.). South-Western: Cengage Learning.

Mann, G. (1994). The origins of double-entry. *Australian Accountant, 64*(6), 17. Retrieved from https://search.proquest.com/docview/211265265?accountid=175698

Mathews. (2005). A situation-based Decision-making process. *The ICFAI Journal of Organisation Behaviour, 4*(3), 19-25.

Matthew, R. (2000). Risk Aversion and Expected-Utility Theory: A Calibration Theorem. *Econometrica, 68*(5), 1281–1292. doi:10.1111/1468-0262.00158

Maurice, A. (1953). Le Comportement de l'Homme Rationnel devant le Risque: Critique des Postulats et Axiomes de l'Ecole Americaine. *Econometrica, 21*(4), 503–546. doi:10.2307/1907921

Mayer, C. (1988). New issues in corporate finance. *European Economic Review, 32*(5), 1167–1183. doi:10.1016/0014-2921(88)90077-3

Mayer, C. (1990). Financial systems, corporate finance and economic development. In R. Glenn Hubbard (Ed.), *Asymmetric Information, Corporate Finance and Investment*. Chicago, IL: The University of Chicago Press.

Mayer, J. D., Gaschke, Y. N., Braverman, D. L., & Evans, T. W. (1992). Mood-congruent judgment is a general effect. *Journal of Personality and Social Psychology, 63*(1), 119–132. doi:10.1037/0022-3514.63.1.119

McCarthy, C. J., Lambert, R. G., & Brack, G. (1997). Structural model of coping, appraisals, and emotions after relationship breakup. *Journal of Counseling and Development, 76*(1), 53–64. doi:10.1002/j.1556-6676.1997.tb02376.x

McKinnon, R. (1973). *Money and Capital in Economic Development*. Washington, DC: Brookings Institution.

Mehwish, Z. (2013). Determinants of Stock Market Performance in Pakistan. *Interdisciplinary Journal of Contemporary Research in Business, 4*(5), 1017–1018.

Mercer, J. J. (2003). *Corporate Social Responsibility and Its Importance to Consumers* (Unpublished doctoral dissertation). Claremont, CA: Claremont Graduate University.

Mick, D. G., & DeMoss, M. (1990). Self-gifts: Phenomenological insights from four contexts. *The Journal of Consumer Research, 17*(3), 322–332. doi:10.1086/208560

Mikesell, J. (2013). *Fiscal administration*. Cengage Learning.

Mirrlees, J., Adam, S., Besley, T., Blundell, R., Bond, S., Chote, R., & Poterba, J. (2011). The Mirrlees Review: Conclusions and recommendations for reform. *Fiscal Studies, 32*(3), 331–359. doi:10.1111/j.1475-5890.2011.00140.x

Mishkin, F. (1999). International experiences with different monetary policy regimes). Any views expressed in this paper are those of the author only and not those of Columbia University or the National Bureau of Economic Research. *Journal of Monetary Economics, 43*(3), 579–605. doi:10.1016/S0304-3932(99)00006-9

Mittal, V., & Ross, W. T. Jr. (1998). The impact of positive and negative affect and issue framing on issue interpretation and risk taking. *Organizational Behavior and Human Decision Processes, 76*(3), 298–324. doi:10.1006/obhd.1998.2808 PMID:9878512

Miyakoshi, T. (2003). Spillovers of stock return volatility to Asian equity markets from Japan and the US. *Journal of International Financial Markets, Institutions and Money, 13*(4), 383–399. doi:10.1016/S1042-4431(03)00015-5

Modigliani, F., & Miller, M. H. (1958). The cost of capital, corporation finance and the theory of investment. *The American Economic Review, 48*(3), 261–297.

Moneybiz. (2008). Available at: www.moneybiz.co.za/personal_finance/jse_6.asp

Moore, G. C., & Benbasat, I. (1991). Development of an instrument to measure the perceptions of adopting an information technology innovation. *Information Systems Research*, *2*(3), 192–222. doi:10.1287/isre.2.3.192

Morse, D. (1981). Price and Trading Volume Reaction Surrounding Earnings Announcements: A Closer Examination. *Journal of Accounting Research*, *19*(2), 374–383. doi:10.2307/2490871

Mowery, D. C. (1998). The Changing Structure of the US National Innovation System: Implications for International Conflict and Cooperation in R&D Policy. *Research Policy*, *27*(6), 639–654. doi:10.1016/S0048-7333(98)00060-2

Mukherjee, A., & Nath, P. (2003). A model of trust in online relationship banking. *International Journal of Bank Marketing*, *21*(1), 5–15. doi:10.1108/02652320310457767

Mukherjee, T. K., & Naka, A. (1995). Dynamic relations between macroeconomic variables and the Japanese stock market: An application of a vector error correction model. *Journal of Financial Research*, *18*(2), 223–237. doi:10.1111/j.1475-6803.1995.tb00563.x

Muller & Kolk. (2009, October). Economic Empowerment Through Microfinance: An Assessment of CSR Activity run by Forbes Marshall Ltd. *International Journal of Business Insights & Transformation*, 64-74.

Muller, D. (2001, August), *Shareholders Project: A Quantitative Study of Shareholder Attitudes to Investment-related Issues*. Available at http://www. ethics.org.au/our_services/ projects/shareholders_project

Mumford, M. D., Connelly, M. S., Helton, W. B., Van Doorn, J. R., & Osburn, H. K. (2002). Alternative Approaches for Measuring Values: Direct and Indirect Assessments in Performance Prediction. *Journal of Vocational Behavior*, *61*(2), 348–373. doi:10.1006/jvbe.2001.1860

Muniappan, G. P. (2002). *Indian Banking: Paradigm Shift – A regulatory point of view*. Address at the Bank Economist Conference, Kolkata, India.

Munnell, A. H., Sunden, A., & Taylor, C. (2001). What determines 401 (k) participation and contributions? *Social Security Bulletin*, *64*(3), 64–75. PMID:12655741

Munson, J. M., & Posner, B. Z. (1980). The Factorial Validity of a Modified Rokeach Value Survey for Four Diverse Samples. *Educational and Psychological Measurement*, *40*(4), 1073–1079. doi:10.1177/001316448004000435

Nair, A. S., & Ladha, N. (2014). Determinants of non-economic investment goals among Indian investors. *Corporate Governance*, *14*(5), 714–727. doi:10.1108/CG-09-2014-0102

Nair, N. K., & Sodhi, J. S. (2012, April). CSR Practices by SMEs in India: Lessons from Five Case Studies. *Indian Journal of Industrial Relations*, *47*(4).

Narasimham Committee on Banking Sector Reforms (Narsimham Committee II). (n.d.). Retrieved from https://www.rbi.org.in/scripts/PublicationReportDetails.aspx?ID=251

Ndubisi, N., & Sinti, Q. (2006). Consumer attitudes, system's characteristics and internet banking adoption in Malaysia. *Management Research News*, *29*(1/2), 16–27. doi:10.1108/01409170610645411

Neri, C. (2005). What is the function of faith and trust in psychoanalysis? *The International Journal of Psycho-Analysis*, *86*(1), 79–97. doi:10.1516/H27X-L81H-PPLM-MNVG PMID:15859223

Ng, S. H. (1982). Choosing Between the Ranking and Rating Procedures for the Comparison of Values Across Cultures. *European Journal of Social Psychology*, *12*(2), 169–172. doi:10.1002/ejsp.2420120204

Nicholas, B., & Richard, T. (2003). *A survey of behavioral finance. Handbook of the Economics of Finance*. Elsevier Science B.V. doi:10.1016/S1574-0102(03)01027-6

Nitsure, R. R. (2007). Corrective Steps towards Sound Banking. *Economic and Political Weekly*, *42*(13).

Nkusu, M. (2011). *Nonperforming loans and macrofinancial vulnerabilities in advanced economies*. St. Louis, MO: Federal Reserve Bank of St Louis. doi:10.5089/9781455297740.001

Nofsinger, J. (2011). The Psychology of Investing (3rd ed.). Pearson.

Nofsinger, J. R. (2001). *Investment madness: how psychology affects your investing – and what to do about it*. Pearson Education.

Oates, W. E. (1969). The effects of property taxes and local public spending on property values: An empirical study of tax capitalization and the Tiebout hypothesis. *Journal of Political Economy*, *77*(6), 957–971. doi:10.1086/259584

Oktay, T. A. Ş., Tokmakçıoğlu, K., & Çevikcan, G. (2016). Borsa İstanbul'da Pay Senedi Getirileri ile İşlem Hacmi arasındaki İlişki. *Dokuz Eylül Üniversitesi Sosyal Bilimler Enstitüsü Dergisi*, *18*(1), 11–30.

Okuyan, H. A., & Erbaykal, E. (2011). İMKB'de yabancı işlemleri ve pay senedi getirileri ilişkisi. *Doğuş Üniversitesi Dergisi*, *12*(2), 256–264. doi:10.31671/dogus.2018.141

Olsen, R. A. (1998). Behavioural Finance and its implications for Stock-Price volatility. *Financial Analysts Journal*, *54*(2), 2, 10–17. doi:10.2469/faj.v54.n2.2161

Omran, M., & Pointon, J. (2004). The determinants of the cost of capital by industry within an emerging economy: Evidence from Egypt. *International Journal of Business*, *9*, 3.

Ondrus, J., & Pigneur, Y. (2006). Towards a holistic analysis of mobile payments: A multiple perspectives approach. *Electronic Commerce Research and Applications*, *5*(3), 246–257. doi:10.1016/j.elerap.2005.09.003

Opler, T. C., & Titman, S. (1994). Financial distress and corporate performance. *The Journal of Finance*, *49*(3), 1015–1040. doi:10.1111/j.1540-6261.1994.tb00086.x

Osborne, J. W. (Ed.). (2008). *Best practices in quantitative methods*. Sage. doi:10.4135/9781412995627

Osborne, M. F. (1959). Brownian motion in the stock market. *Operations Research*, *7*(2), 145–173. doi:10.1287/opre.7.2.145

Özer, Ö., & Çınar, E. (2012). Evaluation of a foundation university academic personal perspective to private pension system. *Mustafa Kemal Üniversitesi Sosyal Bilimler Enstitüsü Dergisi*, *9*(19).

Palil, M. R. (2011). Factors affecting tax compliance behaviour in self assessment system. *African Journal of Business Management*, *5*(33). doi:10.5897/ajbm11.1742

Pal, K., & Mittal, R. (2011). Impact of macroeconomic indicators on Indian capital markets. *The Journal of Risk Finance*, *12*(2), 84–97. doi:10.1108/15265941111112811

Pantula, S. G. (1989). Testing for unit roots in time series data. *Econometric Theory*, *5*(02), 256–271. doi:10.1017/S0266466600012421

Parasuraman, A., Zeithaml, V. A., & Berry, L. L. (1998). SERVQUAL: A Multiple Item Scale for Measuring Consumer Perceptions of Service Quality. *Journal of Retailing*, *64*(1), 12–40.

Pasework, W. R., & Riley, M. E. (2009). It's a Matter of Principle: The Role of Personal Values in Investment. *Journal of Business Ethics*, *93*(2), 237–253. doi:10.100710551-009-0218-6

Patidar, S. (2012). *Analysis of NPA in priority sector lending: A comparative study between public sector banks and Private sector banks of India*. Academic Press.

Patnaik, B., Satpathy, I., & Mohapatra, A. (2011). NPA's side effect and curative mantra. *International Journal of Research in Commerce and Management*, *2*(7), 77–80.

Patton, M. Q. (1990). *Qualitative Evaluation and Research Methods* (2nd ed.). Newbury Park, CA: Sage Publications.

Paull, P., Bose, S. K., & Dhalla, R. S. (2011). Efficiency measurement of Indian public sector banks: Non-performing assets as negative output. *Asia Pacific Journal of Finance and Banking Research*, *5*(5), 38–46.

Peachman, J. B. (1975). *Anatomy of Fiscal Crisis.* University of Michigan.

Peggs, K. (2000). Which pension? Women, risk and pension choice. *The Sociological Review*, *48*(3), 349–364. doi:10.1111/1467-954X.00220

Peng, G., & Nunes, M. (2009). Using PEST Analysis as a Tool for Refining and Focusing Contexts for Information Systems Research. *ECRM 2007: 6Th European Conference On Research Methodology For Business And Management Studies.* Retrieved from http://file:///C:/Users/hp/Downloads/SSRN-id1417274.pdf

Percival, D. B., & Walden, A. T. (2000). *Wavelet Methods for Time Series Analysis.* Cambridge University Press. doi:10.1017/CBO9780511841040

Pesaran, M. H., Shin, Y., & Smith, R. P. (1999). Pooled mean group estimation of dynamic heterogeneous panels. *Journal of the American Statistical Association*, *94*(446), 621–634. doi:10.1080/01621459.1999.10474156

Philippa, W. (2013). Corporate Sustainability/CSR and the Influence of the Independent Director: "100% Pure." *European Conference on Management, Leadership & Governance*, 372-380.

Pinches, G. E., & Mingo, K. A. (1973). A multivariate analysis of industrial bond ratings. *The Journal of Finance*, *28*(1), 1–18. doi:10.1111/j.1540-6261.1973.tb01341.x

Pisedtasalasai, A., & Gunasekarage, A. (2007). Causal and dynamic relationships among stock returns, return volatility, and trading volume: Evidence from emerging markets in South-East Asia. *Asia-Pacific Financial Markets*, *14*(4), 277–297. doi:10.100710690-008-9063-3

Pixley, J. (2004). *Emotions in finance: Distrust and uncertainty in global markets.* Cambridge University Press. doi:10.1017/CBO9781139195041

Pogue, T. F., & Soldofsky, R. M. (1969). What's in a Bond Rating. *Journal of Financial and Quantitative Analysis*, *4*(2), 201–228. doi:10.2307/2329840

Pommerehne, W. W., & Schneider, F. (1978). Fiscal illusion, political institutions, and local public spending. *Kyklos*, *31*(3), 381-408.

Pompian, M. (2012a). *Behavioral Finance and Wealth Management; How to Build Investment Strategies That Account For Investor Bias* (2nd ed.). John Wiley & Sons, Inc. doi:10.1002/9781119202400

Pompian, M. (2012b). *Behavioral Finance And Investor Types: Managing Behavior To Make Better Investment Decisions* (1st ed.). John Wiley & Sons, Inc. doi:10.1002/9781119202417

Pompian, M., & Longo, J. (2004). A New Paradigm For Practical Application of Behavioral Finance: Creating Investment Programs Based On Personality Type And Gender To Produce Better Investment Outcomes. *The Journal of Wealth Management*, *7*(2), 9–15. doi:10.3905/jwm.2004.434561

Poon, J. P. (2003). Hierarchical tendencies of capital markets among international financial centers. *Growth and Change*, *34*(2), 135–156. doi:10.1111/1468-2257.00211

Poon, W. C. (2007). Users' adoption of e-banking services: The Malaysian perspective. *Journal of Business and Industrial Marketing*, *23*(1), 59–69. doi:10.1108/08858620810841498

Poterba, J. M., & Rueben, K. S. (2001). Fiscal news, state budget rules, and tax-exempt bond yields. *Journal of Urban Economics*, *50*(3), 537–562. doi:10.1006/juec.2001.2233

Poudel, R. P. S. (2013). Macroeconomic Determinants of credit risk in Nepalese banking industry. In *Proceedings of 21st International Business Research Conference* (pp. 10-11). Academic Press.

Prasad, B. G., & Veena, V. D. (2011). NPAS in Indian banking sector- trends and issues. *Journal of Banking Financial Services and Insurance Research*, *1*(9), 67–84.

Pratt, J. (1964). Risk aversion in the small and in the large. *Econometrica*, *32*(1/2), 122–136. doi:10.2307/1913738

Prelec, D., & Simester, D. (2001). Always leave home without it: A further investigation of the credit-card effect on willingness to pay. *Marketing Letters*, *12*(1), 5–12. doi:10.1023/A:1008196717017

Prosad, J. M., Kapoor, S., & Sengupta, J. (2015). Theory of Behavioral Finance. In Handbook of Research on Behavioral Finance and Investment Strategies: Decision Making in the Financial Industry. Academic Press. doi:10.4018/978-1-4666-7484-4.ch001

Purohit, H.C., & Pathardikar, A.D. (2007, March). Service Quality Measurement and Consumer Perception about the Services of Banking Institutions. *Indian Journal of Marketing*, 12-18.

Qi, R. (2001). *Return-volume relation in the tail: evidence from six emerging markets.* Columbia Business School Working Paper.

Raghunathan, V., & Varma, J. R. (1993). *When AAA means B: The State of Credit Rating in India.* Working Paper No. 1141, Indian Institute of Management, Ahmedabad. Available at www.rediff.com

Raghunathan, R., & Pham, M. T. (1999). All negative moods are not equal: Motivational influences of anxiety and sadness on decision making. *Organizational Behavior and Human Decision Processes*, *79*(1), 56–77. doi:10.1006/obhd.1999.2838 PMID:10388609

Rakow, T. (2010). Risk, uncertainty and prophet: The psychological insights of Frank H. Knight. *Judgment and Decision Making*, *5*(6), 458–466.

Ram Mohan, T.T. (2002). *Banking Reform in India.* Lecture at the Indian Institute of Management, Ahmedabad, India.

Ramsey, F. P. (1927). A Contribution to the Theory of Taxation. *Economic Journal (London)*, *37*(145), 47–61. doi:10.2307/2222721

RBI. (2001). *Prudential Norms on Income Recognition, Asset Classification and Provisioning Pertaining to Advances.* Reserve Bank of India.

RBI. (2002a). *Selected Ratios of Scheduled Commercial Bankis: 2000 and 2001.* Retrieved from www.rbi.org.in

RBI. (2002b). *Financial Institutions.* Retrieved from www.rbi.org.in

RBI. (2010). *Prudential Norms on Income Recognition, Asset Classification and Provisioning Pertaining to Advances.* Reserve Bank of India.

Reddy, P. K. (2002). A *comparative study of Non Performing Assets in India in the Global context – Similarities and dissimilarities, remedial measures.* The Indian Institute of Management, Ahmedabad, unpublished report.

Reichheld, F. F., & Sasser, E. (1990). Zero Defections: Quality Comes to Services. *Harvard Business Review*, *68*, 105–111. PMID:10107082

Rennings, K. (2000). Redefining innovation— Eco-innovation research and the contribution from ecological economics. *Ecological Economics*, *32*(2), 319–332. doi:10.1016/S0921-8009(99)00112-3

Reserve Bank of India. (2002). *Financial Institutions*. Retrieved from www.rbi.org.in

Revelle, W. (2009). Personality Structure and Measurement: The Contributions of Raymond Cattell. *British Journal of Psychology*, *V*, 100, 253–257. PMID:19351450

Rhoades, G. K., Kamp-Dush, C. M., Atkins, D. C., Stanley, S. M., & Markman, H. J. (2011). Breaking up is hard to do: The impact of unmarried relationship dissolution on mental health and life satisfaction. *Journal of Family Psychology*, *25*(3), 366–374. doi:10.1037/a0023627 PMID:21517174

Ricciardi, V., & Simon, H. K. (2000). What's Behavioral Finance? *Business. Education and Technology Journal*, *2*(2), 1–9.

Richins, M. L., & Rudmin, F. W. (1994). Materialism and economic psychology. *Journal of Economic Psychology*, *15*(2), 217–231. doi:10.1016/0167-4870(94)90001-9

Rieger, H. (1978). *Prinzipien des internationalen Steuerrechts als Problem der Steuerplanung in dr multinationalen Unternehmung* (Vol. 4). Erich Schmidt.

Ritter, J. R. (2003). Behavioral Finance. *Pacific-Basin Finance Journal*, *11*(: 4), 429–437. doi:10.1016/S0927-538X(03)00048-9

Rivoli, P. (1995). Ethical Aspects of Investor Behavior. *Journal of Business Ethics*, *14*(4), 265–277. doi:10.1007/BF00871897

Robinson, J. (1933). A Parable on Savings and Investment. *Economica*, (39), 75–84. doi:10.2307/2548862

Rogers, E. M. (2003). The diffusion of innovation (5th ed.). New York: Free Press.

Rogers, E. M. (1995). Diffusion of Innovations: modifications of a model for telecommunications. In *Die diffusion von innovationen in der telekommunikation* (pp. 25–38). Berlin: Springer. doi:10.1007/978-3-642-79868-9_2

Roig-Alonso, M. (1998). Fiscal visibility in the European Union member countries: New estimates. *International Advances in Economic Research*, *4*(1), 1–15. doi:10.1007/BF02295231

Rokeach, M. (1973). *The Nature of Human Values*. New York: The Free Press.

Rokeach, M., & Regan, J. F. (1980). The Role of Values in the Counseling Situation. *The Personnel and Guidance Journal*, *58*(9), 576–582. doi:10.1002/j.2164-4918.1980.tb00454.x

Romer, C. (2011). What do we know about the effects of fiscal policy? Separating evidence from ideology. Speech at Hamilton College.

Ross, E. B. (1991). *Management control of Aviation Career Incentive Pay for selected reservists of the Naval Reserve* (Doctoral dissertation). Naval Postgraduate School.

Rothbart, M. K., & Derryberry, D. (1981). Development of İndividual Differences İn Temperament. In M. E. Lamb & A. Brown (Eds.), *Advances in developmental psychology* (Vol. 1, pp. 37–86). Hillsdale, NJ: Erlbaum.

Rozeff, M., & Kinney, W. Jr. (1976). Capital market seasonality: The case of stock returns. *Journal of Financial Economics*, *3*(4), 379–402. doi:10.1016/0304-405X(76)90028-3

RTÜK. (2013). *Televizyon İzleme Eğilimleri Araştırması 2012.* Retrieved from http://www.rtuk.org.tr/Icerik/DownloadReport/13

Rubin, R. B., & McHugh, M. P. (1987). Development of Parasocial Relationships. *Journal of Broadcasting & Electronic Media, 31*(3), 279–292. doi:10.1080/08838158709386664

Ryan, L. V. (1994). *Reconcilable Differences: Goals, Values, and Virtues of American Shareholders and Executives* (Unpublished doctoral dissertation). University of Washington.

Ryan, L. V., & Gist, M. E. (1995). *An Innovative Approach to Business-values Measurement.* Paper presented at the Sixth Annual Meeting of the International Association for Business and Society.

Sadi, R., Ghalibaf, H., Asl, R., Mohammad, R., Gholipour, A., & Gholipour, F. (2011). Behavioral Finance: The Explanation of Investor's Personality and Perceptual Biases Effects on Financial Decisions. *International Journal of Economics and Finance, 3*(5).

Sáez, L. (2009). The political economy of financial services reform in india: Explaining variations in political opposition and barriers to entry. *The Journal of Asian Studies, 68*(4), 1137. doi:10.1017/S0021911809990805

Samir & Kamra. (2013). A Comparative Analysis of Non- Performing Assets (NPAs) of Selected Commercial Banks in India. *International Journal of Management, 3*(1), 68–80.

Sammons, A. (n.d.). Eysenck's theory of the criminal personality. In *Eysenck's Personality Theory of Offending. Criminological Psychology.* Available from: http://www.psychlotron.org.uk/newresources/criminological/AZ_AQB.Crim.EysenckTheory.pdf

Sapienza, H., Manigart, S., & Vermeir, W. (1996). Venture capitalist governance and value added in four countries. *Journal of Business Venturing, 11*(6), 439–469. doi:10.1016/S0883-9026(96)00052-3

Sathye, M. (1999). Adoption of Internet banking by Australian consumers: An empirical investigation. *International Journal of Bank Marketing, 17*(7), 324–334. doi:10.1108/02652329910305689

Saunders, E. M. (1993). Stock prices and Wall Street weather. *The American Economic Review*, 1337–1345.

Sayın, A., & Aslan, S. (2005). Duygudurum Bozuklukları ile Huy, Karakter ve Kişilik İlişkisi. *Türk Psikiyatri Dergisi, 16*(4), 276–283. PMID:16362847

Schanz, S. (2008). *Strategien optimaler Repatriierung.* Springer-Verlag.

Scharpf, F. W., & Schmidt, V. A. (Eds.). (2000). Welfare and work in the open economy: volume II: diverse responses to common challenges in twelve countries. OUP Oxford. doi:10.1093/0199240922.001.0001

Schmidt, F. L., & Hunter, J. E. (1998). The Validity and Utility of Selection Methods in Personnel Psychology: Practical and Theoretical Implications of 85 Years of Research Findings. *Psychological Bulletin, 124*(2), 262–274. doi:10.1037/0033-2909.124.2.262

Schubert, R., Brown, M., Gysler, M., & Brachinger, H. W. (1999). Financial decision-making: Are women really more risk-averse? *The American Economic Review, 89*(2), 381–385. doi:10.1257/aer.89.2.381

Schulmerich, M., Leporcher, Y.M., & Eu, C.H. (2015). Modern Portfolio Theory and Its Problems. *Applied Asset and Risk Management*, 101-173.

Schulmerich, M., Leporcher, Y.M., & Eu, C.H. (n.d.). Explaining Stock Market Crashes: A Behavioral Finance Approach. *Applied Asset and Risk Management*, 355-413.

Schumpeter, J. (1912). The Theory of Economic Development. Cambridge, MA: Harvard University Press.

Schwartz, S. H. (1992). Universals in the Content and Structure of Values: Theoretical Advances and Empirical Tests in 20 Countries. *Advances in Experimental Social Psychology, 25*, 1–65. doi:10.1016/S0065-2601(08)60281-6

Schwartz, S. H. (1994). Are There Universal Aspects in the Structure and Contents of Human Values? *The Journal of Social Issues, 50*(4), 19–45. doi:10.1111/j.1540-4560.1994.tb01196.x

Schwartz, S. H., & Bardi, A. (2001). Value Hierarchies Across Cultures: Taking a Similarities Perspective. *Journal of Cross-Cultural Psychology, 32*(3), 268–290. doi:10.1177/0022022101032003002

Schwartz, S. H., & Bilsky, W. (1987). Toward a Universal Psychological Structure of Human Values. *Journal of Personality and Social Psychology, 53*(3), 550–562. doi:10.1037/0022-3514.53.3.550

Schwarz, N., & Clore, G. L. (1983). Mood, misattribution, and judgments of well-being: Informative and directive functions of affective states. *Journal of Personality and Social Psychology, 45*(3), 513–523. doi:10.1037/0022-3514.45.3.513

Schwarz, N., & Clore, G. L. (1988). How do I feel about it? The informative function of affective states. In K. Fiedler & J. Forgas (Eds.), *Affect, cognition, and social behavior* (pp. 44–62). Göttigen, Germany: Hogrefe.

Sehrawat, M., & Dhanda, U. (2015). GST in India: A Key Tax Reform. *International Journal Of Trad-Granthaalayah, 3*(12), 133-141.

Selden, G. C. (1912). *Psychology of the Stock Market: Human Impulses Lead To Speculative Disasters.* New York: Ticker Publishing.

Şenkesen, E. (2009). *Davranışsal Finans ve Yatırımcı Duyarlılığının Tahvil Verimi Üzerindeki Etkisi: İMKB Tahvil ve Bono Piyasasında Bir Uygulama.* Basılmamış Doktora Tezi, İstanbul Üniversitesi Sosyal Bilimler Enstitüsü İşletme Bölümü.

Şenyuva, H. (2007). *Aydın İlinden Alınan Normal Bir Örneklemde Kişilik Bozukluklarının Yaygınlık Çalışması.* Yayınlanmamış Doktora Tezi, Adnan Menderes Üniversitesi Sağlık Bilimleri Enstitüsü Psikiyatri Anabilim Dalı.

Sewell, M. W. (2012). *The Application of Intelligent System Financial Time Series Analysis.* Department of Computer Science University College London.

Sezer, D. (2013). *Yatırımcı Davranışlarının Etkinliği ve Psikolojik Yanılsamalar.* Adnan Menderes Üniversitesi Sosyal Bilimler Enstitüsü İşletme Anabilim Dalı, Doktora Tezi.

Shackelford, D., & Shevlin, T. (2000). *Empirical Tax Research in Accounting.* SSRN Electronic Journal. doi:10.2139srn.235796

Shah, A. (2006). *Fiscal Incentives for Investment and Innovation.* Available at SSRN: https://ssrn.com/abstract=896144

Shah, T. (2006). *Attaining zero Non-Performing Asset (NPA) by Transparency, Trust and & Service* (Unpublished paper). Indian Institute of Planning and Management (IIPM).

Shaik, S., Sameera, S., & Firoz, S. (2015). Does Goods and Services Tax (GST) Leads to Indian Economic Development? *Journal of Business and Management, 17*(12), 1-5.

Shapiro, S. (2012). The grammar of trust. In *New Perspectives on Emotions in Finance* (pp. 115–134). Routledge.

Sharma, D., & George, M. (2017). GST-A Game Changer in Indian Tax Structure. *IOSR Journal Of Business And Management, 19*(04), 55–62. doi:10.9790/487X-1904015562

Sharma, M. (2014). A Study on Goods and services Tax in India. *International Journal's Research Journal Of Social Science And Management, 3*(10), 119–123.

Shefrin, H. (2000). *Beyond Greed and Fear: Understanding Behavioral Finance and the Psychology of Investing*. Boston, MA: Harvard Business School Press.

Shefrin, H. (2000). *Beyond Greed and Fear: understanding behavioural finance and the psychology of investing*. Boston: Harvard Business School Press.

Shefrin, H., & Statman, M. (1985). The disposition to sell winners too early and ride losers too long: Theory and evidence. *The Journal of Finance*, *40*(3), 777–790. doi:10.1111/j.1540-6261.1985.tb05002.x

Shefrin, H., & Statman, M. (1985). The Disposition To Sell Winners Too Early And Ride Losers Too Long: Theory And Evidence. *The Journal of Finance*, *40*(3).

Shefrin, H., & Statman, M. (1994). Behavioral capital asset pricing theory. *Journal of Financial and Quantitative Analysis*, *29*(3), 323–349.

Shefrin, H., & Statman, M. (2000). Behavioral Capital Asset Pricing Model. *Journal of Financial and Quantitative Analysis*, *35*(2), 127–151. doi:10.2307/2676187

Shiffman, L. G., & Kanuk, L. L. (2004). *Consumer Behavior* (8th ed.). Pearson Prentice Hall.

Shiller, R. J. (1981). Do Stock Prices Move Too Much to be Justified by Subsequent Changes in Dividends? *The American Economic Review*, *71*(3), 421–436.

Shiller, R. J. (2000). *Irrational Exuberance*. Princeton, NJ: Princeton University Press.

Shiller, R. J. (2008). *The Subprime Solution: How Today's Global Financial Crisis Happened, and What to Do about It*. Princeton, NJ: Princeton University Press.

Shleifer, A. (2000). *Inefficient Markets: A Introduction to Behavioral Finance*. Oxford, UK: Oxford University Press. doi:10.1093/0198292279.001.0001

Sibanda, K., Hove, P., & Murwirapachena, G. (2015). Oil prices, exchange rates, and inflation expectations in South Africa. *The International Business & Economics Research Journal (Online)*, *14*(4), 587.

Simon, H. A. (1955). A behavioral model of rational choice. *The Quarterly Journal of Economics*, *69*(1), 99–118. doi:10.2307/1884852

Simon, H. A. (1956). Rational choice and the structure of the environment. *Psychological Review*, 63. PMID:13310708

Singh, T., & Singh, S. G. (2015). The Influence of Investor Psychology on Regret Aversion. *Global Journal of Management and Business Research: C Finance, 15*(2), 55-69.

Singh, T. (2010). Does international trade cause economic growth? A survey. *World Economy*, *33*(11), 1517–1564. doi:10.1111/j.1467-9701.2010.01243.x

Skinner, B. F. (1966). *The Behavior of Organisms: An Experimental Analysis*. New York: Appleton-Century -Crofts. (Original work published 1938)

Slotter, E. B., Gaedner, W. L., & Finkel, E. J. (2010). Who am I without you? The influence of romantic breakup on the self-concept. *Personality and Social Psychology Bulletin*, *36*(2), 147–160. doi:10.1177/0146167209352250 PMID:20008964

Slovic, P. (1972). Psychological study of human judgement: Implications for investment decision making. *The Journal of Finance*, *27*(4), 779–801. doi:10.1111/j.1540-6261.1972.tb01311.x

Smith, A. (1759). *The theory of moral sentiments*. London: A. Millar. doi:10.1093/oseo/instance.00042831

Smith, A. (1776). *The Wealth of Nations*. London, W.: Strahan and T. Cadell.

Smith, J. P. (2014). *Taxpayer effects of immigration*. IZA World of Labor. doi:10.15185/izawol.50

Smith, S. (1992). Taxation and the environment: A survey. *Fiscal Studies*, *13*(4), 21–57. doi:10.1111/j.1475-5890.1992.tb00505.x

Solomon, R. C. (1997). *It's Good Business: Ethics and Free Enterprise for the New Millennium*. Lanham, MD: Rowman and Littlefield Publishers.

Songole, R. K. (2012). *The Relationship between Selected Macroeconomic Variables and Stock Return at the Nairobi Securities Exchange*. Nairobi: University of Nairobi.

Spitz, B. (1972). *International tax planning*. Butterworths.

Srinivasan, R. (2009). *Performance measurement of Banks - NPA analysis & credentials of Parameters*. Retrieved from www.articlesbase.com/banking -articles/performance measurement-of-banks-NPA-analysis

Stafford, M. R. (1996). Demographic Disriminations of Service Quality in Banking Industry. *Journal of Services Marketing*, *10*(4), 6–22. doi:10.1108/08876049610124554

Starmer, C. (2000). Developments in Non-Expected Utility Theory: The Hunt for a Descriptive Theory of Choice under Risk. *Journal of Economic Literature*, *38*(2), 332–382. doi:10.1257/jel.38.2.332

Statman, M. (1999). Behavioral Finance: Past Battles and Future Engagements. *Financial Analysts Journal, 55*(6), 18–27.

Statman, M., Thorley, S., & Vorkink, K. (2006). Investor Overconfidence and Trading Volume. *The Review of Financial Studies*, *19*(4), 1531–1565.

Statman, M. (2008). What is behavioral finance? In *Handbook of Finance* (Vol. 2). John Wiley & Sons, Inc. doi:10.1002/9780470404324.hof002009

Statman, M. (2014). Behavioral finance: Finance with normal people. *Borsa Istanbul Review*, *14*(2), 65–73. doi:10.1016/j.bir.2014.03.001

Strahilevitz, M. A., Odean, T., & Barber, B. M. (2011). Once Burned, Twice Shy: How Naive Learning, Counterfactuals and Regret Affect The Repurchase of Stock Previously Sold. *JMR, Journal of Marketing Research*, *48*(SPL), 102–120. doi:10.1509/jmkr.48.SPL.S102

Stuart-Hamilton, I. (2007). *Dictionary of Psychological Testing, Assessment and Treatment 2*. Jessica Kingsley Publishers.

Subash, R. (2012). *Role of Behavioral Finance in Portfolio Investment Decisions: Evidence from India* (Master's thesis). Charles University in Prague, Faculty of Social Sciences Institute of Economic Studies.

Sureshchander, G. S., Rajendran, C., & Ananthraman, R. N. (2002). Determinants of Customer-Perceived Service Quality: A Confirmatory Factor Analysis Approach. *Journal of Services Marketing*, *16*(1), 9–32. doi:10.1108/08876040210419398

Svrakic, D. M., Draganic, S., Hill, K., Bayon, C., Przybeck, T. R., & Cloninger, C. R. (2002). Temperament, Character, and Personality Disorders: Etiologic, Diagnostic, and Treatment İssues. *Acta Psychiatrica Scandinavica*, *106*(3), 189–195. doi:10.1034/j.1600-0447.2002.02196.x PMID:12197856

Sylla, R. (1969). Federal policy, banking market structure and capital mobilization in the United States, 1863-1913. *The Journal of Economic History*, *29*(04), 657–686. doi:10.1017/S002205070007193X

Talwar, S.P. (2001). *Financial Stability and the Role of Banks*. Address at the Ban Economists' Conference, New Delhi, India.

Tambi, M. K. (2005). *An empirical study of return-volume relationship for Indian market*. Retrieved from http://econwpa.repec.org/eps/fin/papers/0504/0504013.pdf

Tan, M., & Teo, T. S. (2000). Factors influencing the adoption of Internet banking. *Journal of the AIS, 1*(5).

Taylor, J. B. (2000). Reassessing discretionary fiscal policy. *The Journal of Economic Perspectives, 14*(3), 21–36. doi:10.1257/jep.14.3.21 PMID:15179965

Taymur, İ., & Türkçapar, M. H. (2012). Kişilik: Tanımı, Sınıflaması ve Değerlendirmesi. *Psikiyatride Güncel Yaklaşımlar-Current Approaches in Psychiatry, 4*(2), 154–177. doi:10.5455/cap.20120410

Tehulu, T.A., & Olana, D.R. (2014). Bank-specific determinants of credit risk: Empirical evidence from Ethiopian banks. *Research Journal of Finance and Accounting, 5*(7), 80-85.

Tekin, B. (2016). Beklenen Fayda ve Beklenti Teorileri Bağlamında Geleneksel Finans - Davranışsal Finans Ayrımı. *Journal of Accounting, Finance and Auditing Studies, 2/4*, 75–107.

Thaler. (1999). Mental Accounting Matters. *Journal of Behavioural Decision Making, 12*, 183-206.

Thaler, R. H. (1985). Mental accounting and consumer choice. *Marketing Science, 4*(3), 199–214. doi:10.1287/mksc.4.3.199

Thaler, R. H. (1999). Mental accounting matters. *Journal of Behavioral Decision Making, 12*(3), 183–206. doi:10.1002/(SICI)1099-0771(199909)12:3<183::AID-BDM318>3.0.CO;2-F

Thaler, R. H. (2015). *Misbehaving: The making of behavioral economics*. New York: W. W. Norton & Company.

Thaler, R. H., & Johnson, E. J. (1990). Gambling with the house money and trying to break even: The effects of prior outcomes on risky choice. *Management Science, 36*(6), 643–660. doi:10.1287/mnsc.36.6.643

Thaler, R., & Shefrin, H. (1981). An economic theory of self control. *Journal of Political Economy, 89*(2), 392–410. doi:10.1086/260971

Tippet, J. (2000). 'Investors' Perceptions of the Relative Importance of Investment Issues'. *Accounting Forum, 24*(3), 278–295. doi:10.1111/1467-6303.00042

Tomer, J. F. (2001). Economic Man vs. Heterodox Men: The Concepts of Human Nature in Schools of Economic Thought. *Journal of Socio-Economics, 30*(4), 281–293. doi:10.1016/S1053-5357(01)00100-7

Torrence, C., & Compo, G. P. (1998). A Practical Guide to Wavelet Analysis. *Bulletin of the American Meteorological Society, 79*(1), 61–78. doi:10.1175/1520-0477(1998)079<0061:APGTWA>2.0.CO;2

Tversky, A., & Kahneman, D. (1974). Judgment Under Uncertainty: Heuristics and Biases. *Science, 185*(4157), 1124–1131. doi:10.1126cience.185.4157.1124 PMID:17835457

Tversky, A., & Kahneman, D. (1981). The framing of decisions and the psychology of choice. *Science, 211*(4481), 453–458. doi:10.1126cience.7455683 PMID:7455683

Tversky, A., & Kahneman, D. (1992). Advances in prospect theory: Cumulative representation of uncertainty. *Journal of Risk and Uncertainty, 5*(4), 297–323. doi:10.1007/BF00122574

Twari, A. K., Mutascu, M. I., & Albulescu, C. T. (2013). The Influence of International Oil Prices on the Real Effective Exchange Rate in Romania in a Wavelet Transform Framework. *Energy Economics, 40*, 714–733. doi:10.1016/j.eneco.2013.08.016

Uddin, G. Z., Arouri, M., & Tiwari, A. K. (2014). *Co-movements Between Germany and International Stocks Markets: Some New Evidence from DCC-GARCH and Wavelet Approaches.* Working Paper Series. Retrieved from https://www.ipag.fr/wp-content/uploads/recherche/WP/IPAG_WP_2014_143.pdf

Valadkhani, A., & Layton, A. (2004). Quantifying the Effect of the GST on Inflation in Australia's Capital Cities: An Intervention Analysis. *The Australian Economic Review*, *37*(2), 125–138. doi:10.1111/j.1467-8462.2004.00314.x

Van Horne James, C. (2002). *Financial Management and Policy* (12th ed.). Pearson Education.

Van Lieshout, C. F. M. (2000). Lifespan Personality Development: Self-Organising Goal-Oriented Agents and Developmental Outcome. *International Journal of Behavioral Development*, *24*(3), 276–288. doi:10.1080/01650250050118259

Vandenberghe, C., Bentein, K., & Michon, R. (2007). An examination of the role of perceived support and employee commitment in employee-customer encounters. *Journal of Applied Psychology, 92*(4), 1177. Retrieved from https://search.proquest.com/docview/213938270?accountid=175698

Vasanthagopal, R. (2011). GST in India: A Big Leap in the Indirect Taxation System. *International Journal of Trade Economics and Finance, 144-146.* doi:10.7763/ijtef.2011.v2.93

Veerakumar, K. (2012). Non-performing assets in priority sector: A threat to Indian scheduled commercial banks. *International Journal of Finance & Economics*, (93): 6–23.

Venkatesh, B. (2002, December 1). What is Loss Aversion? *Business Line.*

Venkatesh, V., & Davis, F. D. (2000). A theoretical extension of the technology acceptance model: Four longitudinal field studies. *Management Science*, *46*(2), 186–204. doi:10.1287/mnsc.46.2.186.11926

Venkatesh, V., Morris, M. G., Davis, G. B., & Davis, F. D. (2003). User acceptance of information technology: Toward a unified view. *Management Information Systems Quarterly*, *27*(3), 425–478. doi:10.2307/30036540

Verick, S., & Islam, I. (2010). The Great Recession of 2008-2009: Causes, Consequences and Policy Responses. Institute for the Study of Labour, (4934), 3–61.

Vickrey, W. (1939). Averaging of income for income-tax purposes. *Journal of Political Economy*, *47*(3), 379–397. doi:10.1086/255390

Virkola, T. (2014). *Exchange Rate Regime, Fiscal Foresight and the Effectiveness of Fiscal Policy in a Small Open Economy (No. 20).* The Research Institute of the Finnish Economy.

Wang, C., & Chin, S. (2004). Profitability of return and volume-based investment strategies in China's stock market. *Pacific-Basin Finance Journal*, *12*(12), 541–564. doi:10.1016/j.pacfin.2003.12.002

Wärneryd, K. E. (2001). *Stock-market Psychology: How People Value and Trade Stocks.* Cheltenham, UK: Edward Elgar Publishing.

Watson, J. B. (1913). Psychology as the behaviorist views it. *Psychological Review*, *20*(2), 158–177. doi:10.1037/h0074428

Weber, J. (1990). Managerial Value Orientations: A Typology and Assessment. *International Journal of Value Based Management*, *3*(2), 37–54. doi:10.1007/BF01732412

Weiner, I. B. (2003). *The Assessment Process.* Handbook of Psychology. doi:10.1002/0471264385.wei1001

Welsch, G. A., & Anthony, R. N. (1974). *Fundamentals of Financial Accounting.* Richard D. Irwin.

Westbrook, R. A. (1980). Intrapersonal affective influences on consumer satisfaction with products. *The Journal of Consumer Research*, *7*(1), 49–54. doi:10.1086/208792

West, R. R. (1970). An alternative approach to predicting corporate bond ratings. *Journal of Accounting Research*, *8*(1), 118–125. doi:10.2307/2674717

Wijayatunga, P., Mase, S., & Nakamura, M. (2006). Appraisal of companies with Bayesian networks. *International Journal of Business Intelligence and Data Mining*, *1*(3), 329–346. doi:10.1504/IJBIDM.2006.009138

Willam, E. C. (1976). *Business Research Methods*. Homewood, IL: Richard D. Irwin.

Williams, R. M. Jr. (1970). *American Society: A Sociological Interpretation* (3rd ed.). New York: Alfred A. Knopf.

Williams, T. G., & Hall, P. (2006). Personal Values and Management Priorities: Marketing Students vs. Top Level Marketing Managers. *Marketing Management Journal*, *16*(1), 104–124.

Wright, W. F., & Bower, G. H. (1992). Mood effects on subjective probability assessment. *Organizational Behavior and Human Decision Processes*, *52*(2), 276–291. doi:10.1016/0749-5978(92)90039-A

Yaari, M. E. (1987). The Dual Theory of Choice under Risk. *Econometrica*, *55*(1), 95–115. doi:10.2307/1911158

Yıldırım, N., & Taştan, H. (2009). *Capital Flows and Economic Growth across Spectral Frequencies: Evidence from Turkey*. Turkish Economic Association Discussion Paper 2009/2.

Yildiz, A. (2014). Corporate ratings based on the corporate governance index and altman z score applying with the logistic regression method. *Suleyman Demirel University The Journal of Faculty of Economics and Administrative Sciences*, *19*(3), 71–89.

Ying, C. C. (1966). Stock market prices and volumes of sales. *Econometrica*, *34*(3), 676–685. doi:10.2307/1909776

Yörükan, T. (2006). *Alfred Adler Sosyal Roller ve Kişilik. Türkiye İş Bankası Yayınları, 2.*

Yuen, K. S., & Lee, T. M. (2003). Could mood state affect risk-taking decisions? *Journal of Affective Disorders*, *75*(1), 11–18. doi:10.1016/S0165-0327(02)00022-8 PMID:12781345

Zahler. (2015). An Analysis of CSR Expenditure by Indian Companies. *Indian Journal of Corporate Governance*, *7*(2), 82-94.

Zaib, A., Farid, F., & Khan, M. K. (2014). Macroeconomic and bank-specific determinants of nonperforming loans in the banking sector in Pakistan. International Journal of Information. *Business and Management*, *6*(2), 53.

Zaidi, F. B., & Tauni, M. Z. (2012). Influence of Investor's Personality Traits and Demographics on Overconfidence Bias. *Interdisciplinary Journal of Contemporary Research in Business*, *4*(6).

Zanghieri, P. (2013). *Participation to Pension Funds in Italy: The Role of Expectations and Financial Literacy*. Academic Press.

Zarowin, P. (1990). Size, seasonality and stock market overreaction. *Journal of Financial and Quantitative Analysis*, *25*(1), 113–125. doi:10.2307/2330891

Zhao. (2012). Efficient Water Management through Public Private Partnership Model: An Experiment in CSR by Coca Cola India. *Vikalpa*, *38*(4), 97.

Zillmann, D. (1988). Mood management through communication choices. *The American Behavioral Scientist*, *31*(3), 327–340. doi:10.1177/000276488031003005

Ziu & Fishta. (2004). Historia e ekonomisw sw Shqipwrisw (1944-1960). *Shtepia botuese Dita.*

About the Contributors

Manoj Kumar Dash earned his M.A. with specialization in Econometrics, M.Phil. with specialization in Econometrics, Ph.D. in Economics on topic 'Econometrics of Complete Demand System' and M.B.A. in Marketing from Berhampur University, Berhampur (Orissa). He had published more than 67 research paper in various journals of International and National repute. He is the author of three books titled 'Managerial Economics', 'Applied Demand Analysis' and "Think New-Think Better: A case study of Entrepreneurship" and edited five books till date. He received several prizes in the Research Paper presentation competitions in both National and International Seminar/Conferences. He was involved as Chair Member in International Conference of Arts and Science held at Harvard University, Boston (USA), Member of Steering Committee in International Conference on ESTD 2014 held at ABV- Indian Institute of Information Technology and Management Gwalior. He had conducted 22 Faculty Development Pogramme sponsored by AICTE, MHRD and IIITM on Multivariate Analysis, Econometrics, Research Methodology, Mulch-Criteria Optimization, Multivariate analysis in Marketing, SPSS software etc. He introduced many courses in Marketing such as Digital Marketing, New Product and Service Development, Multivariate Analysis in Marketing, Established Behavioural Economics and Experimental Laboratory at ABV- IIITM Gwalior. He is now Associate Professor at Khallikote University, India. He visited two countries USA and Cyprus for presenting paper in international conferences. His area of interest are Multi-criteria Optimization, Behavioural Economics, Decision Making Modelling, Econometrics Modelling, and Marketing Research.

* * *

Otuo Serebour Agyemang holds a Ph.D. in Business Economics and Management from the University of Ferrara, Italy. He is currently a Senior Lecturer in the School of Business, University of Cape Coast, Ghana. His research interests largely focus on corporate governance, Corporate Social Responsibility, Business ethics and Healthcare Management. He teaches courses in Corporate Governance and control, International Finance, Governance in Management of SMEs, Managerial Economics, Financial Markets and Institutions and Business Economics. His papers have appeared in international journals such as Corporate Governance, Society and Business Review, Management Research Review, Social Responsibility Journal, Journal of Global Responsibility, International Journal of Law and Management, Corporate Ownership & Control, Population Health Management, International Business Research, IUP Journal of Corporate Governance, Health Economics Review among others. Currently, he serves as an academic advisor to final year undergraduate students in the Department of Finance, University of Cape Coast. He is also an examiner for the Institute of Chartered Accountants, Ghana.

Emine Ebru Aksoy is an Associate Professor of Finance at Ankara Hacı Bayram Veli University Department of Management, Ankara, Turkey. Dr. Aksoy has a BS in Business Administration from Gazi University, an MS from Gazi University, and a PhD in Accounting-Finance from Gazi University. Her research interests are financial management, evolution of project investment, firm valuation. She has taught financial management, international portfolio management, evolution of project investment, firm valuation courses, among others, at both graduate and undergraduate levels. She has been an ad hoc reviewer for journals. She is a member of the Finance Community and Finance Platform.

Reenu Bansal is an Assistant Professor of Finance & Accounting at IILM Graduate School of Management. Prior to this she worked as Program Director with IMS, Noida from June 2009 to Dec 2017. Expertise in the area of Finance & Accounts, she earned her BCCA & MBA degree from Maharshi Dayanand University, Rohtak (Haryana) in the year 2005 and 2007 respectively. She obtained her PhD from University of Rajasthan, Jaipur in the year 2016. Her PhD research work was focused on Role of Credit Ratings Agencies in India- with special reference to Crisil, Icra, Care and Fitch. She stepped into the world of teaching after several years of experience in the industry. She has previously been associated with ICICI Prudential and IndiaBulls before she began her teaching career. She has rich corporate and academic experience of more than 11 years. She is passionate about Accounting & Finance and highly engrossed in research activities. She is instrumental in organizing and conducting FDPs, workshops, symposiums, National & International Conferences.

İbrahim Bozkurt is an Associate Professor of Finance at Karatekin University (Cankırı, Turkey). He received a PhD in Finance (2013) from the Gazi University, Ankara. His BA degree is in Accounting and Finance (2005) from Gazi University. He is working at the Banking and Finance Department as an associate professor of finance since 2017. He teaches finance theory, credit management in banking, technical analysis courses at this faculty. His current research interests lie in the broad area of behavioural finance, valuation and financial inclusion.

Sadullah Çelik is a full time Professor of Economics at the Department of Economics (Eng.), Marmara University Faculty of Economics, Istanbul, Turkey. He received his BA and MA in Economics (Eng.) from Marmara University, Faculty of Economics and Administrative Sciences. He received his Ph.D. in Economics from University of Nebraska-Lincoln, USA. He has published numerous articles on applied economics, financial markets, behavioral economics and consumer sentiment in both Turkish and English in many international and national journals, co-authored three books and authored two book chapters. He has co-organized the 73rd International Atlantic Economic Conference and has been a member of the Board of Editors for the journal International Advances in Economic Research since 2011.

Biswajit Prasad Chhatoi is having 18 years of experience in Post Graduate Teaching and research. To his credit 20 research papers have been published in various national and international journals.

Chandrika Prasad Das is working as Asst. Professor of Dept. of Economics & Management, Khallikote University. He has published 1 international research book and 15 national & international articles. He has presented more than 25 papers in national and international seminars. His area of strength is Cost Accounting, Banking and Finance.

Engin Demirel is Associate Professor of Finance in the Faculty of Economics and Administrative Sciences at Trakya University. He received his master degree (MA) in the field of Finance (Options Pricing) in 2005 from Trakya University and Doctorate (Ph.D.) (Fixed Income Securities Portfolio Optimization) in Accounting and Finance in 2009 from Marmara University. He teaches finance courses at graduate and undergraduate levels. His research interests include financial markets and institutions, portfolio optimizations and international finance. Demirel has published four books, book chapters, and articles in national and international journals.

Sinem Derindere Köseoğlu was born in İstanbul in 1981. She got Associate Professor of Finance title in January, 2014 from Inter-University Council in Turkey. She is a graduate of the Business Administration from Istanbul University with a honors degree and got a scholarship to do an intensive business English course from Institute of Business Economics. Then, Dr. D. Köseoğlu began her master studies in Finance in the Institute of Social Sciences at Istanbul University in 2003 and has held a master degree with a dissertation of 'An Empirical Study on Factors Affecting of Tanker Freight Rates in International Markets' in 2005. While doing her master, Dr. D. Köseoğlu commenced her academic career as a research and teaching assistant for the School of Transport and Logistics at Istanbul University in 2004. Following her master graduation, Dr. D. Köseoğlu began her Ph. D. studies in Finance at the same University in 2006. She has held a Ph.D. with a dissertation of 'Analysis of Risks in International Maritime Transportation Industry and Factors that Affect Cargo Ship Investment Decisions' since 2010. Her Ph.D. dissertation has been published by ERF (Economics Research Foundation) as the best dissertation in 2012. In the same year, her article entitled "Market Risk of Index Futures and Stock Indices: Turkey as a Developing Country vs. Developed Countries" has been selected as the best paper by the World Business Institute. She also holds a certificate of Logistics Management and Transportation Program from Istanbul University Institute of Business Economics. Dr. D. Köseoğlu, now She is an independent finance consultant and trainer. She is married and has two children.

Mercan Hatipoglu is an Assistant Professor of Finance at Karatekin University (Cankırı, Turkey). He received a PhD in Business (2015) from the University of Eskisehir Osmangazi. He obtained a master of science from Karatekin University (2011). His BA degree is in Businesss Management (2008) from Dokuz Eylul University. His current research interests lie in the broad area of financial markets and volatility. Specifically, He has worked on the areas of volatility spillover, finance-growth nexus, firm valuation and published in various academic journals.

Eglantina Hysa is a Lecturer of Economics at the Epoka University where she teaches International Economy, Development and Growth, and Microeconomics courses. Eglantina Hysa's research focuses on International Trade, Development and Econometric Models. She has been part of some training programs related to the Public Interior Auditing and International/National Standards of Accounting. Her recent papers examine characteristics that cover the economical aspects such as the pension system, demographic change, corruption, inequality, human development and the foreign direct investment in Western Balkans and with a particular focus in Albania. She is part of national networks by being either the founder or active member in associations related to economics and sociology. Actually she is head of Economics Department at Epoka University. At the same time, she is engaged as an External Expert on behalf of Public Accreditation Agency for Higher Education, Republic of Albania.

Pooja Jain is a research scholar from Jiwaji University Gwalior. She obtained MBA, M.COM, M.PHIL from Jiwaji University, Gwalior(M.P.). She has more than three years teaching experience. She has 11 National Publications and 1 International Publications on her credit. Her area of interest are Finance and Accounting.

Ayben Koy is an Assistant Professor of Finance at Istanbul Commerce University. She holds a PhD in Finance and a BA in Economics from Istanbul University, an MBA from Yıldız Technical University. Her areas of research interest include financial economics, international financial markets, derivatives, capital markets, economics and nonlinear econometric analysis and modelling in finance. She has published widely in these areas.

Nihan Tomris Kucun graduated from Uludag University, Faculty of Arts and Science in 2008. In 2011 she achieved the Master of Science degree in Marketing at Eskisehir Osmangazi University Institute of SocialSciences and attended to Business Administration PhD Programme of Trakya University. The author focuses on neuromarketing practices on consumer behavior in her academic studies. She has articles in national and international journals in the field of neuromarketing. She has been working as an expert at Eskisehir Osmangazi University since 2015.

Amith Vikram Megaravalli is a PhD in Management (Finance and Economics) from Università degli Studi di Napoli Federico II, Naples Italy and was Visiting Scholar at Indian Institute of Management, Ahmedabad (Sep 2016 – Mar 2017). His area of research is into financial analysis of Family Business firms, Small and Medium scale enterprises and Macro-Economics.

Shraddha Mishra is an Assistant Professor of Finance & Accounting at IILM University. She was also teaching at the Department of Rural Management, School of Management Studies, Babasaheb Bhimrao Ambedkar University, India. She was a Senior Research Fellow at the Institute of Management Studies, Banaras Hindu University, Varanasi, Uttar Pradesh. Her areas of research interests are stock market and international financial management. She is pursuing her research on the topic of capital market and its efficiency. She has contributed many national and international research papers and participated in seminars, conferences, and workshops. She has been invited as a resource person in various conferences, workshops and seminars. Her current research interests includes Corporate Finance, Cost Accounting, Statistical Analysis, Financial Planning and Strategy, Reporting Research Results, Econometrics Analysis, and Financial literacy.

Dorina Plaku is graduated from Master of Sciences in Banking and Finance. She is interested in taxation, taxation policies and market studies. She has completed her studies with very good results. During her studies she has been part of several scientific conferences related to the economy, management and businesses. Dorina Plaku has worked as a "Brand Manager" of some of the most well-known brands which operates in Albania.

Sharada Prasad Sahoo is having 9 years of post graduate teaching and research experience in the areas of behavioral management. To his credit, 4 articles have been published in reputed journals.

Rabindra Kumar Swain is Asst. Professor of P.G. Dept. of Commerce, Utkal University. Presently he is working as OSD finance in Utkal university and placement coordinator of MBA FM Utkal University. He has published 4 international research books, 2 national research books and 30 national & international articles. He has presented more than 80 papers in national and international seminars. He has got 23 years of teaching experience in UG, PG, M.Phil and PhD courses. His area of strength is Accounting and Financial Management.

Deepika Singh Tomar has been awarded with PhD degree in the year 2012 on the topic "Customer Perception towards Service Quality of Public & Private Sector Banks with special reference to SBI and ICICI Bank" from Dr. Bhimrao Ambedker University, Agra. She is an MBA with major specialization in finance and minor in marketing from UP Technical University in the year 2005. She has ten years of academic experience of different institutes and universities including ITM universe, Gwalior (M.P.), GLA University, Mathura (U.P.) and presently she is working as an assistant professor at Amity University, Gwalior (M.P.) Other than the core responsibility of teaching and research her job responsibilities in various organization also includes working as assistant head of the institute, member- NAAC steering committee, member- board of studies, coordinator- entrepreneurship cell, member- departmental research committee, coordinator for few FDPs and workshops. Dr. Tomar has also launched an e- news letter for her department at Amity University, named 'Management Vista'. Her research area includes behavioural finance, banking, service quality in financial institution and macro economics. She has 17 papers to her credit published in various national and international journal of good repute and 8 papers presented in national and international conferences/seminars. She has also attended various programmes like FDPs/Workshops/Conferences/Seminars, etc.

Rohit Singh Tomar is Ph.D in Retail Management from Dr. B.R. Ambedkar University, Agra. He is an MBA from - Institute of Commerce & Management from Jiwaji University and is UGC-NET Qualified. Dr. Tomar has more than Thirteen years of teaching and research experience. He has worked with the reputed national institutes. He has specialized in the field of Microeconomics, Research Methodology, Marketing Research, Consumer Behaviour and Service Marketing. Dr. Tomar has wide experience in the field of research and development with more than Twenty national and international publications to his credit. He is the Managing Editor of Amity Journal of Management, the prestigious bi-annual 'Refereed' Journal of Amity Business School (in UGC list of journal). He is member of the the editorial board of the IJLTEMAS which is an international journal. He edited two books with ISBN and compiled four abstract books. He has worked as a coordinator of foreign collaborative M.B.A - International Business Programme affiliated to the University of Greenwich, London, U.K, Under United Kingdom and India Education and Research Initiative (UKIERI) scheme. He has travelled across the country and has visited U.K and Bhutan for the educational training and counseling. He has organized workshops and seminars at the national level and conducted workshop and training programs for the faculty members of Kendriya Vidhyalay Sangathan and other higher education institutes of national repute.

Index

www.ingramcontent.com/pod-product-compliance
Lightning Source LLC
LaVergne TN
LVHW062137300926
849161LV00010B/2552